MICROSOFT Office 97

Introductory Concepts and Techniques

ESSENTIALS EDITION

Gary B. Shelly
Thomas J. Cashman
Misty E. Vermaat

Contributing Authors
Marvin M. Boetcher
Steven G. Forsythe
Sherry L. Green
Philip J. Pratt
James S. Quasney

SHELLY
CASHMAN
SERIES®

COURSE TECHNOLOGY
ONE MAIN STREET
CAMBRIDGE MA 02142

an International Thomson Publishing company I(T)P°

CAMBRIDGE • ALBANY • BONN • CINCINNATI • LONDON • MADRID • MELBOURNE

MEXICO CITY • NEW YORK • PARIS • SAN FRANCISCO • TOKYO • TORONTO • WASHINGTON

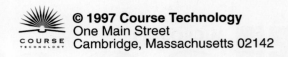

© 1997 Course Technology
One Main Street
Cambridge, Massachusetts 02142

I(T)P® International Thomson Publishing
The ITP logo is a registered trademark
of International Thomson Publishing.

Printed in the United States of America

For more information, contact Course Technology:

Course Technology
One Main Street
Cambridge, Massachusetts 02142, USA

International Thomson Publishing Europe
Berkshire House
168-173 High Holborn
London, WC1V 7AA, United Kingdom

Thomas Nelson Australia
102 Dodds Street
South Melbourne
Victoria 3205 Australia

Nelson Canada
1120 Birchmont Road
Scarborough, Ontario
Canada M1K 5G4

International Thomson Editores
Campos Eliseos 385, Piso 7
Colonia Polanco
11560 Mexico D.F. Mexico

International Thomson Publishing GmbH
Konigswinterer Strasse 418
53227 Bonn, Germany

International Thomson Publishing Asia
Block 211, Henderson Road #08-03
Henderson Industrial Park
Singapore 0315

International Thomson Publishing Japan
Hirakawa-cho Kyowa Building, 3F
2-2-1 Hirakawa-cho, Chiyoda-ku
Tokyo 102, Japan

ISBN 0-7895-4385-0 (perfect bound)
ISBN 0-7895-4387-7 (spiral bound)

PHOTO CREDITS: **Microsoft Windows 95** *Project 1, page WIN 1.4* Bill Gates, © Matthew McVay, Stock Boston; Seattle skyline, © Paul Conklin, PhotoEdit; *page WIN 1.5* International Business Machines Corporation; *Project 2, page WIN 2.3* Quantum Corp; **Microsoft Word 97** *Project 1, pages WD 1.4-5* Pen and ink well, hieroglyphics, deers, hunters, book, mallet, Courtesy of Corel Professional Photos CD-ROM Image usage; Computer, monitor, keyboard, stone background, © Metatools, created by Photospin; Computer with CD-ROM provided by PhotoDisc, Inc. © 1996; *Project 2, pages W 2.2-3;* Globe and street signs, Courtesy of Corel Professional Photos CD-ROM Image usage; **Microsoft Excel 97** *Project 1, pages E 1.4-5* Race car and laptop, Courtesy of Corel Professional Photos CD-ROM Image usage; Hot Lap and scope on tripod, Courtesy of Serena Industries; *Project 2, pages E 2.2-3* Runner, biker, watch, swimmer, soccer ball, skiing, cycling, bowling ball, and pins, Courtesy of Corel Professional Photos CD-ROM Image usage; **Microsoft Access 97** *Project 1, pages A 1.4-5* James Smithson, Courtesy of Smithsonian Institute; American flag, © Metatools, created by PhotoSpin; *Project 2, pages A 2.2-3* Credit card and mail sign, Courtesy of Corel Professional Photos CD-ROM Image usage; David Janssen, provided by Motion Picture & Television Photo Archive; sign post and path, © Metatools, created by PhotoSpin; **Microsoft PowerPoint 97** *Project 1, pages PP 1.4-5* Man, money bag, and movie camera, Courtesy of Corel Professional Photos CD-ROM Image usage; food collage, © Metatools, created by PhotoSpin; *Project 2, pages PP 2.2-3* Iceberg, Courtesy of Corel Professional Photos CD-ROM Image usage; Titanic provided by Brown Brothers; Molly Brown provided by Colorado Historical Society; Euro-poster provided by PhotoDisc, Inc. © 1996.

4 5 6 7 8 9 10 BC 1098

MICROSOFT
Office 97

Introductory Concepts and Techniques

ESSENTIALS EDITION

C O N T E N T S

▶ **PROJECT ONE**

FUNDAMENTALS OF USING WINDOWS 95

Objectives	WIN 1.1
Introduction	WIN 1.4
Microsoft Windows 95	WIN 1.4
What Is a User Interface?	WIN 1.5
Starting Microsoft Windows 95	WIN 1.6
Closing the Welcome Screen	WIN 1.7
The Desktop as a Work Area	WIN 1.7
Communicating with Microsoft Windows 95	WIN 1.8
Mouse Operations	WIN 1.8
Point and Click	WIN 1.8
Right-Click	WIN 1.10
Double-Click	WIN 1.11
My Computer Window	WIN 1.12
Minimize Button	WIN 1.13
Maximize and Restore Buttons	WIN 1.14
Close Button	WIN 1.16
Drag	WIN 1.17
Sizing a Window by Dragging	WIN 1.19
Scrolling in a Window	WIN 1.19
Resizing a Window	WIN 1.21
Closing a Window	WIN 1.21
Right-Drag	WIN 1.21
The Keyboard and Keyboard Shortcuts	WIN 1.23
Creating a Document by Starting an Application Program	WIN 1.23
Creating a Document	WIN 1.26
Saving a Document on Disk	WIN 1.26
Printing a Document	WIN 1.30
Closing a Program	WIN 1.32
Modifying a Document Stored on Disk	WIN 1.32
Closing the Notepad Program	WIN 1.35
Using Windows Help	WIN 1.36
Contents Sheet	WIN 1.36
Index Sheet	WIN 1.40
Shutting Down Windows 95	WIN 1.42
Project Summary	WIN 1.44

What You Should Know	WIN 1.44
Test Your Knowledge	WIN 1.45
Use Help	WIN 1.48
In the Lab	WIN 1.50
Cases and Places	WIN 1.52

▶ **PROJECT TWO**

USING WINDOWS EXPLORER

Objectives	WIN 2.1
Introduction	WIN 2.4
Starting Windows 95	WIN 2.4
Starting Windows Explorer and Maximizing Its Window	WIN 2.5
Windows Explorer	WIN 2.7
Displaying the Contents of a Folder	WIN 2.8
Expanding a Folder	WIN 2.10
Collapsing a Folder	WIN 2.11
Copying Files to a Folder on a Floppy Disk	WIN 2.12
Creating a New Folder	WIN 2.12
Displaying the Destination Folder	WIN 2.15
Displaying the Contents of the Windows Folder	WIN 2.16
Changing the View	WIN 2.18
Selecting a Group of Files	WIN 2.20
Copying a Group of Files	WIN 2.22
Displaying the Contents of the My Files Folder	WIN 2.23
Renaming a File or Folder	WIN 2.24
Deleting a File or Folder	WIN 2.26
Deleting a File by Right-Clicking Its Filename	WIN 2.27
Deleting a File by Right-Dragging Its Filename	WIN 2.28
Deleting a Folder	WIN 2.31
Quitting Windows Explorer and Shutting Down Windows 95	WIN 2.32
Project Summary	WIN 2.33
What You Should Know	WIN 2.33
Test Your Knowledge	WIN 2.34
Use Help	WIN 2.37
In the Lab	WIN 2.
Cases and Places	WIN

Microsoft Office 97 — MO 1.1

▶ **PROJECT ONE**

INTRODUCTION TO MICROSOFT OFFICE 97

Microsoft Office 97	**MO 1.2**
Microsoft Office 97 and the Internet	MO 1.2
Microsoft Word 97	**MO 1.3**
Microsoft Word 97 and the Internet	MO 1.4
Microsoft Excel 97	**MO 1.4**
Microsoft Excel 97 and the Internet	MO 1.5
Microsoft Access 97	**MO 1.6**
Microsoft Access 97 and the Internet	MO 1.6
Microsoft PowerPoint 97	**MO 1.7**
Microsoft PowerPoint 97 and the Internet	MO 1.7
The Web Toolbar	**MO 1.8**
Microsoft Outlook 97	**MO 1.9**
Viewing Electronic Mail (E-Mail)	MO 1.9
Viewing Appointments	MO 1.10
Viewing Contacts	MO 1.11
Viewing Tasks	MO 1.11
Viewing Journal Entries	MO 1.12
Viewing Notes	MO 1.13
The Office Assistant	**MO 1.14**
Hardware Innovations and Microsoft Office 97	**MO 1.14**
Project Summary	**MO 1.15**
In the Lab	**MO 1.16**

Microsoft Word 97 — WD 1.1

▶ **PROJECT ONE**

CREATING AND EDITING A WORD DOCUMENT

Objectives	**WD 1.3**
What Is Microsoft Word?	**WD 1.6**
Project One – Paradise Island Announcement	**WD 1.6**
Document Preparation Steps	WD 1.7
Mouse Usage	WD 1.8
Starting Word	**WD 1.8**
The Word Screen	**WD 1.10**
Word Document Window	WD 1.10
Menu Bar, Toolbars, Rulers, and Status Bar	WD 1.12
Changing the Default Font Size	**WD 1.14**
...ing Text	**WD 1.15**
...Blank Lines into a Document	WD 1.17
...inting Characters	WD 1.18
...ext	WD 1.19
...wrap Feature	WD 1.19
...ling Automatically as You Type	WD 1.20

Entering Documents that Scroll the Document Window	WD 1.21
AutoFormat As You Type	WD 1.23
Saving a Document	**WD 1.25**
Formatting Paragraphs and Characters in a Document	**WD 1.28**
Selecting and Formatting Paragraphs and Characters	WD 1.29
Selecting Multiple Paragraphs	WD 1.29
Centering Selected Paragraphs	WD 1.30
Selecting a Single Line	WD 1.31
Changing the Font Size of Selected Text	WD 1.31
Changing the Font of Selected Text	WD 1.32
Bold Selected Text	WD 1.33
Continuing to Format Text	WD 1.34
Scrolling	WD 1.34
Selecting a Single Word	WD 1.35
Underlining Selected Text	WD 1.36
Selecting a Group of Words and Formatting Them	WD 1.36
Centering a Paragraph	WD 1.38
Inserting a Picture from the Web into a Word Document	**WD 1.39**
Resizing an Imported Graphic	WD 1.44
Restoring a Resized Graphic to Its Original Size	WD 1.46
Saving an Existing Document with the Same File Name	**WD 1.46**
Printing a Document	**WD 1.47**
Quitting Word	**WD 1.49**
Opening a Document	**WD 1.50**
Correcting Errors	**WD 1.51**
Types of Changes Made to Documents	WD 1.51
Inserting Text into an Existing Document	WD 1.52
Deleting Text from an Existing Document	WD 1.53
Undoing Recent Actions	WD 1.53
Closing the Entire Document	WD 1.54
Word Online Help	**WD 1.54**
Using the Office Assistant	WD 1.54
Using the Contents and Index Command to Obtain Help	WD 1.57
Obtaining Web Information	WD 1.59
Using What's This? or the Question Mark Button	WD 1.59
Wizards	WD 1.60
Project Summary	**WD 1.60**
What You Should Know	**WD 1.60**
Test Your Knowledge	**WD 1.61**
Use Help	**WD 1.63**
Apply Your Knowledge	**WD 1.64**
In the Lab	**WD 1.65**
Cases and Places	**WD 1.69**

▶ **PROJECT TWO**

CREATING A RESEARCH PAPER WITH A TABLE

Objectives	**WD 2.1**
Introduction	**WD 2.4**
Project Two – Research Paper with a Table	**WD 2.4**
MLA Documentation Style	WD 2.6
Document Preparation Steps	WD 2.6
Starting Word	WD 2.7
Displaying Nonprinting Characters	WD 2.7
Changing the Margins	**WD 2.7**
Adjusting Line Spacing	**WD 2.9**
Using a Header to Number Pages	**WD 2.12**
Headers and Footers	WD 2.12
Typing the Body of the Research Paper	**WD 2.15**
Changing the Default Font Size	WD 2.15
Entering Name and Course Information	WD 2.16
Centering a Paragraph Before Typing	WD 2.16
Saving the Research Paper	WD 2.18
Indenting Paragraphs	WD 2.18
Zooming Page Width	WD 2.20
Using Word's AutoCorrect Feature	WD 2.21
Adding Footnotes	WD 2.25
Automatic Page Breaks	WD 2.29
Creating a Table with the Insert Table Button	**WD 2.30**
Entering Data into a Word Table	WD 2.32
Formatting a Table	WD 2.34
Changing the Line Spacing of the Table	WD 2.35
Changing Paragraph Formatting	WD 2.36
Creating an Alphabetical Works Cited Page	**WD 2.37**
Manual Page Breaks	WD 2.38
Centering the Title of the Works Cited Page	WD 2.39
Creating a Hanging Indent	WD 2.40
Creating a Hyperlink	WD 2.41
Sorting Paragraphs	WD 2.43
Proofing and Revising the Research Paper	**WD 2.44**
Going to a Specific Location in a Document	WD 2.45
Finding and Replacing Text	WD 2.46
Finding Text	WD 2.48
Using the Thesaurus	WD 2.48
Using Word Count	WD 2.49
Checking Spelling, Saving Again, and Printing the Document	WD 2.50
Navigating to a Hyperlink	**WD 2.51**
Project Summary	**WD 2.52**
What You Should Know	**WD 2.52**
Test Your Knowledge	**WD 2.53**
Use Help	**WD 2.55**
Apply Your Knowledge	**WD 2.56**
In the Lab	**WD 2.57**
Cases and Places	**WD 2.63**

Microsoft Excel 97   **E 1.1**

▶ **PROJECT ONE**

CREATING A WORKSHEET AND EMBEDDED CHART

Objectives	**E 1.3**
What Is Microsoft Excel?	**E 1.6**
Project One – Computer Discount Daily Sales	**E 1.6**
Preparation Steps	E 1.7
Starting Excel	E 1.8
The Excel Window	**E 1.10**
The Workbook	E 1.10
The Worksheet	E 1.10
Cell, Active Cell, Gridlines, and Mouse Pointer	E 1.11
Worksheet Window	**E 1.12**
Menu Bar, Standard Toolbar, Formatting Toolbar, Formula Bar, Sheet and Scroll Tabs, and Status Bar	E 1.12
Selecting a Cell	**E 1.14**
Entering Text	**E 1.14**
Entering the Worksheet Title	E 1.15
Correcting a Mistake While Typing	E 1.16
AutoCorrect	E 1.16
Entering Column Titles	E 1.17
Entering Row Titles	E 1.18
Entering Numbers	**E 1.20**
Calculating a Sum	**E 1.21**
Using the Fill Handle to Copy a Cell to Adjacent Cells	**E 1.23**
Determining Row Totals	E 1.25
Formatting the Worksheet	**E 1.26**
Fonts, Font Size, and Font Style	E 1.27
Bolding a Cell	E 1.28
Increasing the Font Size	E 1.29
Centering the Worksheet Title Across Columns	E 1.30
Using AutoFormat to Format the Body of a Worksheet	**E 1.31**
Using the Name Box to Select a Cell	**E 1.33**
Adding a 3-D Column Chart to the Worksheet	**E 1.35**
Saving a Workbook	**E 1.39**
Printing the Worksheet	**E 1.43**
Quitting Excel	**E 1.44**
Starting Excel and Opening a Workbook	**E 1.45**
AutoCalculate	**E 1.47**
Correcting Errors	**E 1.49**
Correcting Errors Prior to Entering Data into a Cell	E 1.49
In-Cell Editing	E 1.49
Undoing the Last Entry	E 1.50
Clearing a Cell or Range of Cells	E 1.51
Clearing the Entire Worksheet	E 1.51
Quitting Excel	E 1.52

Excel Online Help   E 1.52
Project Summary   E 1.52
What You Should Know   E 1.53
Test Your Knowledge   E 1.54
Use Help   E 1.56
Apply Your Knowledge   E 1.58
In the Lab   E 1.59
Cases and Places   E 1.63

▶ PROJECT TWO
FORMULAS, FORMATTING, CHARTS, AND WEB
QUERIES

Objectives   E 2.1
Introduction   E 2.4
Project Two – High-Tech Stock Club   E 2.4
    Preparation Steps   E 2.5
    Starting Excel   E 2.7
Entering the Titles and Numbers into the Worksheet   E 2.7
Entering Formulas   E 2.9
    Order of Operations   E 2.10
    Entering Formulas Using Point Mode   E 2.11
    Entering Formulas Using Natural Language   E 2.12
    Copying the Formulas Using the Fill Handle   E 2.13
    Determining the Totals Using the AutoSum Button   E 2.14
Using the AVERAGE, MAX, and MIN Functions   E 2.15
    Determining the Average of a Range of Numbers   E 2.15
    Determining the Highest Number in a Range of
        Numbers   E 2.16
    Determining the Lowest Number in a Range of
        Numbers   E 2.17
    Copying the AVERAGE, MAX, and
        MIN Functions   E 2.19
    Entering the Percentage Gain/Loss Formula   E 2.20
Applying Formats to the Text   E 2.21
    Changing the Font and Centering the Worksheet
        Title   E 2.23
    Changing Worksheet Title Background and Font
        Colors and Applying an Outline Border   E 2.25
    Applying Formats to the Column Titles   E 2.27
Applying Formats to the Numbers   E 2.28
    Formatting Numbers Using the Formatting
        Toolbar   E 2.29
    Formatting Numbers Using the Format Cells
        Command on the Shortcut Menu   E 2.31
    Formatting Numbers Using the Percent Style Button
        and Increase Decimal Button   E 2.33
Changing the Widths of Columns and Heights of Rows   E 2.34
    Changing the Widths of Columns   E 2.35
    Changing the Heights of Rows   E 2.37
Checking Spelling   E 2.39

Saving the Workbook a Second Time Using the Same
    File Name   E 2.41
Adding a 3-D Pie Chart to the Workbook   E 2.41
    Drawing the 3-D Pie Chart   E 2.42
    Formatting the Chart Title and Chart Labels   E 2.46
    Changing the Colors of the Slices   E 2.47
    Exploding the 3-D Pie Chart   E 2.49
    Rotating and Tilting the 3-D Pie Chart   E 2.49
Changing the Sheet Names and Rearranging the
    Order of the Sheets   E 2.51
Previewing and Printing Selected Sheets in a
    Workbook   E 2.53
    Printing Selected Sheets in a Workbook   E 2.55
    Printing a Section of the Worksheet   E 2.57
Displaying and Printing the Formulas in the
    Worksheet   E 2.59
    Changing the Print Scaling Option Back to 100%   E 2.61
Getting External Data from a Web Source Using a
    Web Query   E 2.61
Quitting Excel   E 2.65
Project Summary   E 2.65
What You Should Know   E 2.66
Test Your Knowledge   E 2.67
Use Help   E 2.70
Apply Your Knowledge   E 2.71
In the Lab   E 2.72
Cases and Places   E 2.80

Microsoft Access 97   A 1.1

▶ PROJECT ONE
CREATING A DATABASE USING
DESIGN AND DATASHEET
VIEWS

Objectives   A 1.3
Introduction   A 1.6
Project One – Pilotech Services Database   A 1.8
What Is Microsoft Access?   A 1.8
Overview of Project Steps   A 1.9
Starting Access and Creating a New Database   A 1.9
The Access Desktop and the Database Window   A 1.12
Creating a Table   A 1.13
    Defining the Fields   A 1.16
    Correcting Errors in the Structure   A 1.18
Saving a Table   A 1.19
Adding Records to a Table   A 1.20
Closing a Table and a Database and Quitting Access   A 1.24
Opening a Database   A 1.24
Adding Additional Records   A 1.26
    Correcting Errors in the Data   A 1.28

Previewing and Printing the Contents of a Table   **A 1.28**
Creating Additional Tables   **A 1.32**
  Adding Records to the Additional Table   A 1.34
Using a Form to View Data   **A 1.35**
  Creating a Form   A 1.35
  Closing and Saving the Form   A 1.36
  Opening the Saved Form   A 1.37
  Using the Form   A 1.38
  Switching Between Form View and Datasheet View   A 1.39
Creating a Report   **A 1.40**
  Selecting the Fields for the Report   A 1.42
  Completing the Report   A 1.43
  Printing the Report   A 1.45
Closing the Database   **A 1.46**
Designing a Database   **A 1.46**
Access Online Help   **A 1.49**
Project Summary   **A 1.49**
What You Should Know   **A 1.49**
Test Your Knowledge   **A 1.50**
Use Help   **A 1.53**
Apply Your Knowledge   **A 1.54**
In the Lab   **A 1.57**
Cases and Places   **A 1.65**

▶ **PROJECT TWO**
QUERYING A DATABASE USING THE SELECT
QUERY WINDOW

Objectives   **A 2.1**
Introduction   **A 2.4**
Project Two – Querying the Pilotech Services Database   **A 2.4**
  Overview of Project Steps   A 2.6
  Opening the Database   A 2.6
Creating a New Query   **A 2.7**
  Using the Select Query Window   A 2.10
  Displaying Selected Fields in a Query   A 2.10
  Running a Query   A 2.12
  Printing the Results of a Query   A 2.13
  Returning to the Select Query Window   A 2.14
  Closing a Query   A 2.15
Including All Fields in a Query   **A 2.16**
Clearing the Design Grid   **A 2.17**
Entering Criteria   **A 2.18**
  Using Text Data in Criteria   A 2.18
  Using Wildcards   A 2.19
  Criteria for a Field Not in the Result   A 2.20
  Using Numeric Data in Criteria   A 2.22
  Using Comparison Operators   A 2.23
Using Compound Criteria   **A 2.24**
Sorting Data in a Query   **A 2.27**
  Sorting on Multiple Keys   A 2.28
  Omitting Duplicates   A 2.30

Joining Tables   **A 2.32**
  Restricting Records in a Join   A 2.35
Using Computed Fields in a Query   **A 2.36**
Calculating Statistics   **A 2.38**
  Using Criteria in Calculating Statistics   A 2.40
  Grouping   A 2.42
Saving a Query   **A 2.44**
Closing a Database   **A 2.45**
Project Summary   **A 2.46**
What You Should Know   **A 2.46**
Test Your Knowledge   **A 2.47**
Use Help   **A 2.50**
Apply Your Knowledge   **A 2.52**
In the Lab   **A 2.53**
Cases and Places   **A 2.57**

Microsoft PowerPoint 97   **PP 1.1**

▶ **PROJECT ONE**
USING A DESIGN TEMPLATE
AND STYLE CHECKER TO
CREATE A PRESENTATION

Objectives   **PP 1.3**
What Is Microsoft PowerPoint?   **PP 1.6**
Project One – Unlocking the Internet   **PP 1.8**
  Slide Preparation Steps   PP 1.9
Starting a Presentation as a New Office Document   **PP 1.10**
  The PowerPoint Window   PP 1.14
PowerPoint Views   **PP 1.15**
  PowerPoint Window in Slide View   PP 1.15
Creating a Title Slide   **PP 1.18**
  Entering the Presentation Title   PP 1.18
  Correcting a Mistake When Typing   PP 1.19
  Entering the Presentation Subtitle   PP 1.19
Text Attributes   **PP 1.20**
  Changing the Font Size   PP 1.21
  Changing the Style of Text to Italic   PP 1.22
Saving a Presentation on a Floppy Disk   **PP 1.23**
Adding a New Slide to a Presentation   **PP 1.25**
Creating a Bulleted List Slide   **PP 1.27**
  Entering a Slide Title   PP 1.28
  Selecting a Text Placeholder   PP 1.28
  Typing a Multi-level Bulleted List   PP 1.29
Adding a New Slide with the Same AutoLayout   **PP 1.31**
Saving a Presentation with the Same File Name   **PP 1.33**
Moving to Another Slide in Slide View   **PP 1.34**
  Using the Vertical Scroll Bar to Move to
    Another Slide   PP 1.34
Viewing the Presentation Using Slide Show   **PP 1.35**
  Starting Slide Show View   PP 1.35

Advancing through a Slide Show Manually   PP 1.36
Displaying the Popup Menu in Slide Show View   PP 1.37
Using the Popup Menu to End a Slide Show   PP 1.38
Quitting PowerPoint   **PP 1.38**
Opening a Presentation   **PP 1.39**
Opening an Existing Presentation   PP 1.39
Checking a Presentation for Visual Clarity,
Consistency, and Style   **PP 1.41**
Starting Style Checker   PP 1.42
Correcting Errors   **PP 1.44**
Types of Corrections Made to Presentations   PP 1.45
Deleting Text   PP 1.45
Replacing Text into an Existing Slide   PP 1.45
Changing Line Spacing   **PP 1.45**
Displaying the Slide Master   PP 1.46
Changing Line Spacing on the Slide Master   PP 1.47
Displaying a Presentation in Black and White   **PP 1.50**
Printing a Presentation   **PP 1.51**
Saving Before Printing   PP 1.52
Printing the Presentation   PP 1.52
Making a Transparency   **PP 1.54**
Quitting PowerPoint   **PP 1.54**
PowerPoint Online Help   **PP 1.54**
Project Summary   **PP 1.55**
What You Should Know   **PP 1.56**
Test Your Knowledge   **PP 1.58**
Use Help   **PP 1.67**
Apply Your Knowledge   **PP 1.60**
In the Lab   **PP 1.61**
Cases and Places   **PP 1.64**

▶ **PROJECT TWO**

USING OUTLINE VIEW AND CLIP ART
TO CREATE AN ELECTRONIC SLIDE SHOW

Objectives   **PP 2.1**
Creating a Presentation from an Outline   **PP 2.4**
Project Two – Break Away Bargains   **PP 2.5**
Presentation Preparation Steps   PP 2.6
Starting a New Presentation   **PP 2.7**
Using Outline View   **PP 2.7**
The PowerPoint Window in Outline View   PP 2.9
Creating a Presentation in Outline View   **PP 2.10**
Creating a Title Slide in Outline View   PP 2.10
Adding a Slide in Outline View   **PP 2.12**
Creating Multi-level Bulleted List Slides in
Outline View   **PP 2.13**
Creating a Subordinate Slide   PP 2.15
Creating a Second Subordinate Slide   PP 2.16

Creating a Slide with Multiple Text Objects in
Outline View   **PP 2.16**
Creating a Closing Slide in Outline View   **PP 2.17**
Saving a Presentation   **PP 2.18**
Reviewing a Presentation in Slide Sorter View   **PP 2.19**
Adding a Blank Line to a Bulleted List   **PP 2.20**
Adding a Blank Line to Slide 2   PP 2.21
Changing Slide Layout   **PP 2.23**
Moving Text   **PP 2.24**
Adding Clip Art to a Slide   **PP 2.26**
Using AutoLayouts to Add Clip Art   PP 2.26
Changing Slide Layout to Clip Art & Text   PP 2.27
Inserting Clip Art into a Clip Art Placeholder   PP 2.28
Inserting Clip Art on a Slide without a
Clip Art Placeholder   PP 2.32
Moving Clip Art   **PP 2.33**
Changing the Size of Clip Art   **PP 2.33**
Saving the Presentation Again   PP 2.36
Adding a Header and Footer to Outline Pages   **PP 2.36**
Using the Notes and Handouts Sheet to Add
Headers and Footers   PP 2.36
Checking the Presentation for Spelling and Style
Errors   **PP 2.38**
Adding Animation Effects   **PP 2.38**
Adding Slide Transitions to a Slide Show   PP 2.39
Slide Sorter Toolbar   PP 2.42
Applying Animation Effects to Bulleted Slides   **PP 2.42**
Animating Clip Art Objects   **PP 2.47**
Displaying a Slide in Slide View   PP 2.47
Animating Clip Art   PP 2.47
Formatting and Animating a Title Slide   **PP 2.50**
Saving the Presentation Again   PP 2.51
Running an Animated Slide Show   **PP 2.51**
Printing in Outline View   **PP 2.53**
Printing an Outline   PP 2.53
Printing Presentation Slides   PP 2.56
Saving and Quitting PowerPoint   PP 2.58
Project Summary   **PP 2.58**
What You Should Know   **PP 2.58**
Test Your Knowledge   **PP 2.59**
Use Help   **PP 2.62**
Apply Your Knowledge   **PP 2.63**
In the Lab   **PP 2.65**
Cases and Places   **PP 2.72**

Index   **I.1**

Preface

The Shelly Cashman Series® offers the finest textbooks in computer education. The Microsoft Office 97 books continue with the innovation, quality, and reliability that you have come to expect from this series. We are proud that both our Office 95 and Office 4.3 books are best-sellers, and we are confident that our Office 97 books will join their predecessors.

With Office 97, Microsoft has raised the stakes by adding a number of new features, especially the power of the Internet. The Shelly Cashman Series team has responded with Office 97 books that present the core application concepts required in any introductory application software course, as well as new features such as the Office 97 Internet tools.

In our Office 97 books, you will find an educationally sound and easy-to-follow pedagogy that combines a step-by-step approach with corresponding screens. Every project and exercise in the books are new and designed to take full advantage of the Office 97 features. The popular Other Ways and More About features have been amended to offer in-depth knowledge of Office 97. The all-new project openers provide a fascinating perspective on the subject covered in the project. The Shelly Cashman Series Office 97 books will make your computer applications class exciting and dynamic and one that your students will remember as one of their better educational experiences.

Objectives of This Textbook

Microsoft Office 97: Introductory Concepts and Techniques, Essentials Edition is intended for a course that covers Microsoft Word 97, Microsoft Excel 97, Microsoft Access 97, Microsoft PowerPoint 97, and an overview of Microsoft Windows 95 and Microsoft Outlook 97. No experience with a computer is assumed, and no mathematics beyond the high school freshman level is required. The objectives of this book are:

▶ To teach the fundamentals of Microsoft Office 97

▶ To expose students to examples of the computer as a useful tool

▶ To develop an exercise-oriented approach that allows students to learn by example

▶ To encourage independent study and help those who are working alone in a distance education environment

The Shelly Cashman Approach

Features of the Shelly Cashman Series Office 97 books include:

▶ **Project Orientation:** Each project in the book uses the unique Shelly Cashman Series screen-by-screen, step-by-step approach.

▶ **Screen-by-Screen, Step-by-Step Instructions:** Each of the tasks required to complete a project is identified throughout the development of the project. Then, steps to accomplish the task are specified. The steps are accompanied by full-color screens. Hence, students learn from this book the same as if they were using a computer.

Other Ways

1. On Common Tasks toolbar click Slide Layout, double-click desired slide layout
2. On Format menu click Slide Layout, double-click desired slide layout
3. Press ALT+L, press arrow keys to select desired slide layout, press ENTER
4. Press ALT+O, press L, press arrow keys to select desired slide layout, press ENTER

More *About* **Charting**

Line chart, bar chart, pie chart – which chart will best describe my worksheet data? For answers, click Contents and Index on the Help menu. Click the Contents tab. Double-click the Working with Charts book. Double-click the Changing the Type of a Chart book. Double-click the Examples of chart types link and click each chart type.

▶ Thoroughly Tested Projects: The computer screens in the Shelly Cashman Series Office 97 books are captured from the author's computer. The screen is captured immediately after the author performs the step specified in the text. Therefore, every screen in the book is correct because it is produced only after performing a step, resulting in unprecedented quality in a computer textbook.

▶ Multiple Ways to Use the Book: This book can be used in a variety of ways, including: (a) Lecture and textbook approach — The instructor lectures on the material in the book. Students read and study the material and then apply the knowledge to an application on the computer; (b) Tutorial approach — Students perform each specified step on a computer. At the end of the project, students have solved the problem and are ready to solve comparable student assignments; (c) Other approaches — Many instructors lecture on the material and then require their students to perform each step in the project, reinforcing the material lectured. Students then complete one or more of the In the Lab exercises at the end of the project; and (d) Reference — Each task in a project is clearly identified. Therefore, the material serves as a complete reference.

▶ Other Ways Boxes for Reference: Office 97 provides a wide variety of ways to carry out a given task. The Other Ways boxes displayed at the end of most of the step-by-step sequences specify the other ways to do the task completed in the steps. Thus, the steps and the Other Ways box make a comprehensive reference unit. You no longer have to reference tables at the end of a project or the end of a book.

▶ More About Feature: These marginal annotations provide background information that complements the topics covered, adding interest and depth to the learning process.

Organization of This Textbook

Microsoft Office 97: Introductory Concepts and Techniques, Essentials Edition consists of two projects on Microsoft Windows 95, an introduction to Microsoft Office 97, and two projects each on Microsoft Word 97, Microsoft Excel 97, Microsoft Access 97, and Microsoft PowerPoint 97. A short description of each follows.

Microsoft Windows 95

Project 1 – Fundamentals of Using Windows 95   In this project, students learn about user interfaces and Windows 95. Topics include using the Windows 95 desktop as a work area; using the mouse; the keyboard and keyboard shortcuts; using context-sensitive menus; sizing and scrolling windows; creating a document by starting an application program; saving a document on disk; printing a document; closing a program; modifying a document; using Windows 95 Help; and shutting down Windows 95.

Project 2 – Using Windows Explorer   In this project, students are introduced to Windows Explorer. Topics include displaying the contents of a folder; expanding and collapsing a folder; creating a folder; changing the view; selecting and copying a group of files; creating, renaming, and deleting a folder; and renaming and deleting a file.

Microsoft Office 97

Project 1 – Introduction to Microsoft Office 97   In this project, students are introduced to each Office 97 application. A brief explanation of Word 97, Excel 97, Access 97, PowerPoint 97, and examples of how these applications take advantage of the Internet, World Wide Web, and intranets are presented. Outlook 97 and the applications within Outlook (Inbox, Calendar, Contacts, Tasks, Journal, and Notes) also are explained.

Microsoft Word 97

Project 1 – Creating and Editing a Word Document   In this project, students are introduced to Word terminology and the Word window by preparing an announcement. Topics include starting and quitting Word; entering text; adding bullets to paragraphs while typing; checking spelling while typing; saving a document; selecting characters, lines, and paragraphs; centering, bolding, italicizing, and changing the font and font size of selected text; importing a picture from the Web and then resizing the picture; printing a document; opening a document; correcting errors; and using Word Help.

Project 2 – Creating a Research Paper with a Table   In this project 2, students use the MLA style of documentation to create a research paper. Topics include changing margins; adjusting line spacing; using a header to number pages; first-line indenting paragraphs; using Word's AutoCorrect features; creating a Word table, entering data into the table, and formatting the table; adding a footnote; inserting a manual page break; creating a hanging indent; creating a text hyperlink; sorting paragraphs; using the thesaurus; and counting the words in a document.

Microsoft Excel 97

Project 1 – Creating a Worksheet and Embedded Chart   In this project, students are introduced to Excel terminology, the Excel window, and the basic characteristics of a worksheet and workbook. Topics include starting and quitting Excel; entering text and numbers; selecting a range; using the AutoSum button; copying using the fill handle; changing font size; bolding; centering across columns; using the AutoFormat command; charting using the Chart Wizard; saving and opening a workbook; editing a worksheet; and using the AutoCalculate area.

Project 2 – Formulas, Formatting, Charts, and Web Queries   In this project, students use formulas and functions to build a worksheet and learn more about formatting and printing a worksheet. Topics include entering formulas; using functions; formatting text; formatting numbers; drawing borders and adding colors; changing the widths of columns and rows; spell checking; creating a 3-D Pie chart on a separate sheet; previewing a worksheet; printing a section of a worksheet; and displaying and printing the formulas in a worksheet. This project also introduces students to accessing real-time data using Web queries.

Microsoft Access 97

Project 1 – Creating a Database Using Design and Datasheet Views   In this project, students are introduced to the concept of a database and shown how to use Access to create a database. Topics include creating a database; creating a table; defining the fields in a table; opening a table; adding records to a table; closing a table; and previewing and printing the contents of a table. Other topics in this project include using a form to view data; and using the Report Wizard to create a report. Students also learn how to design a database to eliminate redundancy.

Project 2 – Querying a Database Using the Select Query Window   In this project, students learn to use queries to obtain information from the data in their databases. Topics include creating queries, running queries, and printing the results. Specific query topics include displaying only selected fields; using character data in criteria; using wildcards; using numeric data in criteria; using various comparison operators; and creating compound criteria. Other related topics include sorting, joining tables, and restricting records in a join. Students also use computed fields, statistics, and grouping.

Microsoft PowerPoint 97

Project 1 – Using a Design Template and Style Checker to Create a Presentation   In this project, students are introduced to PowerPoint terminology, the PowerPoint window, and the basics of creating a multi-level bulleted list presentation. Topics include selecting a design template; changing font style; decreasing font size; saving a presentation; displaying slides in an electronic slide show; checking a presentation for spelling errors; identifying design inconsistencies using Style Checker; and printing copies of the slides.

Project 2 – Using Outline View and Clip Art to Create an Electronic Slide Show   In this project, students create a presentation in outline view, insert clip art, and add animation effects. Topics include creating a slide presentation by promoting and demoting text in outline view; changing slide layouts; inserting clip art; adding slide transition effects; adding text animation effects; animating clip art; running an animated slide show, and printing audience handouts from an outline.

End-of-Project Student Activities

A notable strength of the Shelly Cashman Series Office 97 books is the extensive student activities at the end of each project. Well-structured student activities can make the difference between students merely participating in a class and students retaining the information they learn. The activities in the Shelly Cashman Series Office 97 books include the following.

▶ What You Should Know   A listing of the tasks completed within a project together with the pages where the step-by-step, screen-by-screen explanations appear. This section provides a perfect study review for students.

▶ Test Your Knowledge   Four pencil-and-paper activities designed to determine students' understanding of the material in the project. Included are true/false questions, multiple-choice questions, and two short-answer activities.

▶ **Use Help**   Any user of Office 97 must know how to use Help. Therefore, this book contains two Help exercises per project. These exercises alone distinguish the Shelly Cashman Series from any other set of Office 97 instructional materials.

▶ **Apply Your Knowledge**   This exercise requires students to open and manipulate a file on the Data Disk that accompanies the Office 97 books.

▶ **In the Lab**   Three in-depth assignments per project require students to apply the knowledge gained in the project to solve problems on a computer.

▶ **Cases and Places**   Seven unique case studies require students to apply their knowledge to real-world situations.

Instructor's Resource Kit

A comprehensive Instructor's Resource Kit (IRK) accompanies this textbook in the form of a CD-ROM. The CD-ROM includes an electronic Instructor's Manual (called *ElecMan*) and teaching and testing aids. The CD-ROM (ISBN 0-7895-1334-X) is available through your Course Technology representative or by calling one of the following telephone numbers: Colleges and Universities, 1-800-648-7450; High Schools, 1-800-824-5179; and Career Colleges, 1-800-477-3692. The contents of the CD-ROM are listed below.

▶ **ElecMan** (*Electronic Instructor's Manual*)   ElecMan is made up of Microsoft Word files. The files include lecture notes, solutions to laboratory assignments, and a large test bank. The files allow you to modify the lecture notes or generate quizzes and exams from the test bank using your own word processor. Where appropriate, solutions to laboratory assignments are embedded as icons in the files. When an icon appears, double-click it and the application will start and the solution will display on the screen.

▶ **Figures on CD-ROM**   Illustrations for every screen in the textbook are available. Use this ancillary to create a slide show from the illustrations for lecture or to print transparencies for use in lecture with an overhead projector.

▶ **Course Test Manager**   This cutting-edge Windows-based testing software helps instructors design and administer tests and pretests. The full-featured online program permits students to take tests at the computer where their grades are computed immediately following completion of the exam. Automatic statistics collection, student guides customized to the student's performance, and printed tests are only a few of the features.

▶ **Lecture Success System**   Lecture Success System files are for use with the application software, a personal computer, and projection device to explain and illustrate the step-by-step, screen-by-screen development of a project in the textbook without entering large amounts of data.

▶ **Instructor's Lab Solutions**   Solutions and required files for all the In the Lab assignments at the end of each project are available.

▶ **Lab Tests/Test Outs**   Tests that parallel the In the Lab assignments are supplied for the purpose of testing students in the laboratory on the material covered in the project or testing students out of the course.

▶ **Student Files**   All the files that are required by students to complete the Apply Your Knowledge exercises are included.

▶ **Interactive Labs** Eighteen hands-on interactive labs that take students from ten to fifteen minutes each to step through help solidify and reinforce mouse and keyboard usage and computer concepts.

Shelly Cashman Online

Shelly Cashman Online is a World Wide Web service available to instructors and students of computer education. Visit Shelly Cashman Online at www.scseries.com. Shelly Cashman Online is divided into four areas:

▶ **Series Information** Information on the Shelly Cashman Series products.

▶ **The Community** Opportunities to discuss your course and your ideas with instructors in your field and with the Shelly Cashman Series team.

▶ **Teaching Resources** This area includes password-protected instructor materials.

▶ **Student Center** Dedicated to students learning about computers with Shelly Cashman Series textbooks and software. This area includes cool links, data from Data Disks that can be downloaded, and much more.

Acknowledgments

The Shelly Cashman Series would not be the leading computer education series without the contributions of outstanding publishing professionals. First, and foremost, among them is Becky Herrington, director of production and designer. She is the heart and soul of the Shelly Cashman Series, and it is only through her leadership, dedication, and tireless efforts that superior products are made possible. Becky created and produced the award-winning Windows 95 series of books.

Under Becky's direction, the following individuals made significant contributions to these books: Peter Schiller, production manager; Ginny Harvey, series specialist and developmental editor; Ken Russo, Mike Bodnar, Stephanie Nance, Greg Herrington, and Dave Bonnewitz, graphic artists; Jeanne Black, Quark expert; Patti Koosed, editorial assistant; Nancy Lamm, Lyn Markowicz, Marilyn Martin, Cherilyn King, and Steve Marconi, proofreaders; Cristina Haley, indexer; Sarah Evertson of Image Quest, photo researcher; and Peggy Wyman and Jerry Orton, Susan Sebok, and Nancy Lamm, contributing writers.

Special thanks go to Jim Quasney, our dedicated series editor; Lisa Strite, senior product manager; Lora Wade, associate product manager; Scott MacDonald and Tonia Grafakos, editorial assistants; and Sarah McLean, product marketing manager. Special mention must go to Suzanne Biron, Becky Herrington, and Michael Gregson for the outstanding book design; and Dennis Tani for the cover design.

Gary B. Shelly
Thomas J. Cashman
Misty E. Vermaat

Shelly Cashman Series – Traditionally Bound Textbooks

The Shelly Cashman Series presents the following computer subjects in a variety of traditionally bound textbooks. For more information, see your Course Technology representative or call one of the following telephone numbers: Colleges and Universities, 1-800-648-7450; High Schools, 1-800-824-5179; and Career Colleges, 1-800-477-3692.

COMPUTERS	
Computers	Discovering Computers: A Link to the Future, World Wide Web Enhanced
	Discovering Computers: A Link to the Future, World Wide Web Enhanced Brief Edition
	Using Computers: A Gateway to Information, World Wide Web Edition
	Using Computers: A Gateway to Information, World Wide Web Brief Edition
	Exploring Computers: A Record of Discovery 2e with CD-ROM
	A Record of Discovery for Exploring Computers 2e
	Study Guide for Discovering Computers: A Link to the Future, World Wide Web Enhanced
	Study Guide for Using Computers: A Gateway to Information, World Wide Web Edition
	Brief Introduction to Computers 2e (32-page)

WINDOWS APPLICATIONS	
Integrated Packages	Microsoft Office 97: Introductory Concepts and Techniques, Brief Edition (6 projects)
	Microsoft Office 97: Introductory Concepts and Techniques, Essentials Edition (10 projects)
	Microsoft Office 97: Introductory Concepts and Techniques (15 projects)
	Microsoft Office 97: Advanced Concepts and Techniques
	Microsoft Office 95: Introductory Concepts and Techniques (15 projects)
	Microsoft Office 95: Advanced Concepts and Techniques
	Microsoft Office 4.3 running under Windows 95: Introductory Concepts and Techniques
	Microsoft Office for Windows 3.1 Introductory Concepts and Techniques Enhanced Edition
	Microsoft Office: Introductory Concepts and Techniques
	Microsoft Office: Advanced Concepts and Techniques
	Microsoft Works 4* • Microsoft Works 3.0*
Windows	Introduction to Microsoft Windows NT Workstation 4
	Microsoft Windows 95: Introductory Concepts and Techniques (96-page)
	Introduction to Microsoft Windows 95 (224-page)
	Microsoft Windows 95: Complete Concepts and Techniques
	Microsoft Windows 3.1 Introductory Concepts and Techniques
	Microsoft Windows 3.1 Complete Concepts and Techniques
Word Processing	Microsoft Word 97* • Microsoft Word 7* • Microsoft Word 6* • Microsoft Word 2.0
	Corel WordPerfect 7 • WordPerfect 6.1* • WordPerfect 6* • WordPerfect 5.2
Spreadsheets	Microsoft Excel 97* • Microsoft Excel 7* • Microsoft Excel 5* • Microsoft Excel 4
	Lotus 1-2-3 97* • Lotus 1-2-3 Release 5* • Lotus 1-2-3 Release 4* • Quattro Pro 6
Database Management	Microsoft Access 97* • Microsoft Access 7* • Microsoft Access 2
	Paradox 5 • Paradox 4.5 • Paradox 1.0 • Visual dBASE 5/5.5
Presentation Graphics	Microsoft PowerPoint 97* • Microsoft PowerPoint 7* • Microsoft PowerPoint 4*

DOS APPLICATIONS	
Operating Systems	DOS 6 Introductory Concepts and Techniques
	DOS 6 and Microsoft Windows 3.1 Introductory Concepts and Techniques
Word Processing	WordPerfect 6.1 • WordPerfect 6.0 • WordPerfect 5.1
Spreadsheets	Lotus 1-2-3 Release 4 • Lotus 1-2-3 Release 2.4 • Lotus 1-2-3 Release 2.3
Database Management	dBASE 5 • dBASE IV Version 1.1 • dBASE III PLUS • Paradox 4.5

PROGRAMMING AND NETWORKING	
Programming	Microsoft Visual Basic 5
	Microsoft Visual Basic 4 for Windows 95* (available with Student version software)
	Microsoft Visual Basic 3.0 for Windows*
	QBasic • QBasic: An Introduction to Programming • Microsoft BASIC
	Structured COBOL Programming (Micro Focus COBOL also available)
Networking	Novell NetWare for Users
	Business Data Communications: Introductory Concepts and Techniques
Internet	The Internet: Introductory Concepts and Techniques (UNIX)
	Netscape Navigator 4: An Introduction
	Netscape Navigator 3: An Introduction • Netscape Navigator 2 running under Windows 3.1
	Netscape Navigator: An Introduction (Version 1.1)
	Netscape Composer
	Microsoft Internet Explorer 3: An Introduction

SYSTEMS ANALYSIS	
Systems Analysis	Systems Analysis and Design, Second Edition

*Also available as a Double Diamond Edition, which is a shortened version of the complete book

Shelly Cashman Series – Custom Edition® Program

If you do not find a Shelly Cashman Series traditionally bound textbook to fit your needs, the Shelly Cashman Series unique **Custom Edition** program allows you to choose from a number of options and create a textbook perfectly suited to your course. Features of the **Custom Edition** program are:

▶ Textbooks that match the content of your course

▶ Windows- and DOS-based materials for the latest versions of personal computer applications software

▶ Shelly Cashman Series quality, with the same full-color materials and Shelly Cashman Series pedagogy found in the traditionally bound books

▶ Affordable pricing so your students receive the **Custom Edition** at a cost similar to that of traditionally bound books

The table on the right summarizes the available materials.

For more information, see your Course Technology representative or call one of the following telephone numbers: Colleges and Universities, 1-800-648-7450; High Schools, 1-800-824-5179; and Career Colleges, 1-800-477-3692.

For Shelly Cashman Series information, visit Shelly Cashman Online at **www.scseries.com**

COMPUTERS	
Computers	Discovering Computers: A Link to the Future, World Wide Web Enhanced
	Discovering Computers: A Link to the Future, World Wide Web Enhanced Brief Edition
	Using Computers: A Gateway to Information, World Wide Web Edition
	Using Computers: A Gateway to Information, World Wide Web Brief Edition
	A Record of Discovery for Exploring Computers 2e (available with CD-ROM)
	Study Guide for Discovering Computers: A Link to the Future, World Wide Web Enhanced
	Study Guide for Using Computers: A Gateway to Information, World Wide Web Edition
	Introduction to Computers (32-page)

OPERATING SYSTEMS	
Windows	Microsoft Windows 95: Introductory Concepts and Techniques (96-page)
	Introduction to Microsoft Windows NT Workstation 4
	Introduction to Microsoft Windows 95 (224-page)
	Microsoft Windows 95: Complete Concepts and Techniques
	Microsoft Windows 3.1 Introductory Concepts and Techniques
	Microsoft Windows 3.1 Complete Concepts and Techniques
DOS	Introduction to DOS 6 (using DOS prompt)
	Introduction to DOS 5.0 or earlier (using DOS prompt)

WINDOWS APPLICATIONS	
Integrated Packages	Microsoft Works 4*
	Microsoft Works 3.0*
Microsoft Office	Using Microsoft Office 97 (16-page)
	Using Microsoft Office 95 (16-page)
	Microsoft Office 97:Introductory Concepts and Techniques, Brief Edition (396-page)
	Microsoft Office 97: Introductory Concepts and Techniques, Essentials Edition (672-page)
	Object Linking and Embedding (OLE) (32-page)
	Microsoft Outlook 97 • Microsoft Schedule+ 7
	Introduction to Integrating Office 97 Applications (48-page)
	Introduction to Integrating Office 95 Applications (80-page)
Word Processing	Microsoft Word 97* • Microsoft Word 7* • Microsoft Word 6* • Microsoft Word 2.0
	Corel WordPerfect 7 • WordPerfect 6.1* • WordPerfect 6* • WordPerfect 5.2
Spreadsheets	Microsoft Excel 97* • Microsoft Excel 7* • Microsoft Excel 5* • Microsoft Excel 4
	Lotus 1-2-3 97* • Lotus 1-2-3 Release 5* • Lotus 1-2-3 Release 4* • Quattro Pro 6
Database Management	Microsoft Access 97* • Microsoft Access 7* • Microsoft Access 2*
	Paradox 5 • Paradox 4.5 • Paradox 1.0 • Visual dBASE 5/5.5
Presentation Graphics	Microsoft PowerPoint 97* • Microsoft PowerPoint 7* • Microsoft PowerPoint 4*

DOS APPLICATIONS	
Word Processing	WordPerfect 6.1 • WordPerfect 6.0 • WordPerfect 5.1
Spreadsheets	Lotus 1-2-3 Release 4 • Lotus 1-2-3 Release 2.4 • Lotus 1-2-3 Release 2.3 • Quattro Pro 3.0 • Quattro with 1-2-3 Menus
Database Management	dBASE 5 • dBASE IV Version 1.1 • dBASE III PLUS • Paradox 4.5 • Paradox 3.5

PROGRAMMING AND NETWORKING	
Programming	Microsoft Visual Basic 5 • Microsoft Visual Basic 4 for Windows 95* (available with Student version software) • Microsoft Visual Basic 3.0 for Windows*
	Microsoft BASIC • QBasic
Networking	Novell NetWare for Users
Internet	The Internet: Introductory Concepts and Techniques (UNIX)
	Netscape Navigator 4: An Introduction
	Netscape Navigator 3: An Introduction
	Netscape Navigator 2 running under Windows 3.1
	Netscape Navigator: An Introduction (Version 1.1)
	Netscape Composer
	Microsoft Internet Explorer 3: An Introduction

*Also available as a mini-module

Windows 95

PROJECT ONE

FUNDAMENTALS OF USING WINDOWS 95

PROJECT ONE

FUNDAMENTALS OF USING WINDOWS 95

Project 1

A $14 Billion Mistake?

Digital Research officials would not yield to IBM's demands

Have you ever missed a meeting you should have attended but something else was more important? Did you lose $14 billion dollars because you were absent? Gary Kildall might have.

In the 1970s, Kildall's company, Digital Research, had developed an operating system called CP/M that was used on most microcomputers except the Apple II. Kildall was a leader in the microcomputer software business. Then, in 1980, IBM came calling.

Having decided to build a personal computer, IBM approached Bill Gates, president of a small company called Microsoft, in Redmond, Washington, to create the operating system. Gates demurred, suggesting IBM contact Kildall.

MICROSOFT

MS-DOS

Bill Gates

SEATTLE COMPUTER PRODUCTS

When IBM arrived for the meeting in Pacific Grove, California, Kildall was off flying his airplane. The reasons are not entirely clear. Some say Kildall was a free spirit and not inclined to do business with the monolithic IBM. Kildall claimed he was flying to another important meeting.

Without Kildall at the meeting, IBM insisted on knowing everything about CP/M while disclosing nothing about its new computer. Fearing IBM would steal their secrets, Digital Research officials would not yield to IBM's demands. Rebuffed, IBM scurried back to Gates.

Sensing an opportunity, Gates agreed to provide an operating system to IBM even though he had no idea how. It just so happened, however, that a small company named Seattle Computer Products, almost next door to Microsoft, was writing an operating system called QDOS v0.110 (QDOS stood for Quick and Dirty Operating System).

Gates learned of QDOS and approached Seattle Computer Products to ask if the operating system was for sale. For a few favors and a little money, Microsoft, in December 1980, acquired non-exclusive rights to QDOS. Later, Microsoft acquired all rights and renamed the operating system MS-DOS. Seattle Computer Products received about $1 million.

Microsoft made substantial changes to MS-DOS and when IBM announced its personal computer in August 1981, MS-DOS was the operating system. The IBM machine was an instant hit. Microsoft sold millions of copies of MS-DOS and grew to be the largest software company in the world. Bill Gates became the world's richest man, with assets in excess of $14 billion dollars.

And Gary Kildall? He continued to develop software at Digital Research. Eventually, Digital Research was sold to Novell, Inc. In the summer of 1994, Kildall died. He left a legacy as an early pioneer who made a significant contribution to microcomputing, but perhaps his most memorable act was missing a meeting.

QDOS

```
Enter today's date (m-d-y): 8-4-1981

The IBM Personal Computer DOS
Version 1.00 (C)Copyright IBM Corp 1981

A>
```

Courtesy of Tim Paterson,
reprinted by permission of Microsoft Corporation.

The Microsoft Disk Operating System, or MS-DOS, was shipped as PC-DOS on the original IBM Personal Computer and later with many IBM compatible machines. Like other operating systems, MS-DOS oversees all the functions of a computer. Various upgrades to MS-DOS and further product refinements led to the release of Windows, an operating system that uses a graphical user interface. Microsoft's current version of Windows, released in August of 1995, is called Windows 95.

CP/M

GARY KILDALL

IBM

DIGITAL RESEARCH

Microsoft sold millions of copies of MS-DOS and grew to be the largest software company in the world

Project 1

Microsoft
Windows 95

Fundamentals of Using Windows 95

Case Perspective

Need: Each day millions of Windows 95 users turn on their computers, whether at home, in the office, at school, on an airplane, or at the beach. When the computer starts, the first image on the monitor is the Windows 95 desktop. If these users did not know how to start application programs from the desktop, manipulate files and images on the desktop, and preserve the work accomplished, their computers would be useless. You have just acquired a computer containing Windows 95. Your task is to learn the basics of Windows 95 so your computer will be useful to you.

Introduction

An **operating system** is the set of computer instructions, called a computer program, that controls the allocation of computer hardware such as memory, disk devices, printers, and CD-ROM drives, and provides the capability for you to communicate with your computer. The most popular and widely used operating system for personal computers is **Microsoft Windows. Microsoft Windows 95** (called Windows 95 for the rest of this book), the newest version of Microsoft Windows, allows you to easily communicate with and control your computer. Windows 95 is easier to use and more efficient than previous versions of Windows and can be customized to fit individual needs. Windows 95 simplifies the process of working with documents and applications, transferring data between documents, and organizing the manner in which you interact with your computer.

In Project 1, you will learn about Windows 95 and how to use the Windows 95 user interface.

Microsoft Windows 95

Microsoft Windows 95 is an operating system that performs every function necessary for you to communicate with and use your computer. Unlike previous versions of Windows, no associated operating system is required. Windows 95 is called a **32-bit operating system** because it uses 32 bits for addressing and other purposes, which means the operating system can address more than four gigabytes of RAM and perform tasks faster than older operating systems.

Windows 95 is designed to be compatible with all existing **application programs**, which are programs that perform an application-related function such as word processing. To use the application programs that can be executed under Windows 95, you must know about the Windows 95 user interface.

What Is a User Interface?

A **user interface** is the combination of hardware and software that you use to communicate with and control your computer. Through the user interface, you are able to make selections on your computer, request information from your computer, and respond to messages displayed by your computer. Thus, a user interface provides the means for dialogue between you and your computer.

Hardware and software together form the user interface. Among the hardware devices associated with a user interface are the monitor, keyboard, and mouse (Figure 1-1). The monitor displays messages and provides information. You respond by entering data in the form of a command or other response using the keyboard or mouse. Among the responses available to you are responses that specify what application program to run, what document to open, when to print, and where to store data for future use.

The computer software associated with the user interface consists of the programs that engage you in dialogue (Figure 1-1). The computer software determines the messages you receive, the manner in which you should respond, and the actions that occur based on your responses.

USER INTERFACE

monitor

Computer Hardware

keyboard   mouse

MAIN MEMORY
Display messages
Accept responses   USER
Determine actions   INTERFACE
                     PROGRAMS

intel pentium

FIGURE 1-1

Computer Software

The goal of an effective user interface is to be **user friendly**, meaning that the software can be used easily by individuals with limited training. Research studies have indicated that the use of graphics can play an important role in aiding users to interact effectively with a computer. A **graphical user interface**, or **GUI** (pronounced gooey), is a user interface that displays graphics in addition to text when it communicates with the user.

The Windows 95 graphical user interface was carefully designed to be easier to set up, simpler to learn, and faster and more powerful than previous versions of Microsoft Windows.

Starting Microsoft Windows 95

When you turn on your computer, an introductory screen consisting of the Windows 95 logo and the Microsoft Windows 95 name displays on a blue sky and clouds background (Figure 1-2).

The screen clears and several items display on a background called the **desktop**. The default color of the desktop background is green, but your computer may display a different color. Your screen might display as shown in Figure 1-3. It also might display without the Welcome screen shown in Figure 1-3.

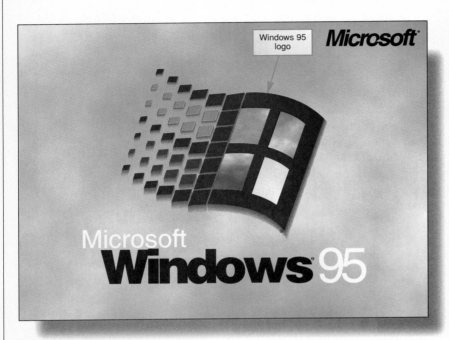

Windows 95 logo

FIGURE 1-2

The items on the desktop in Figure 1-3 include six icons and their names on the left of the desktop, the Welcome screen in the center of the desktop, and the taskbar at the bottom of the desktop. Through the use of the six **icons**, you can view the contents of your computer (**My Computer**), work with other computers connected to your computer (**Network Neighborhood**), receive and send electronic faxes and mail (e-mail) from or to other computers (**Inbox**), discard unneeded objects (**Recycle Bin**), connect to the Microsoft online service (**The Microsoft Network**), and transfer data to and from a portable computer (**My Briefcase**). Your computer's desktop might contain more, fewer, or some different icons because the desktop of your computer can be customized.

The Welcome screen that might display on your desktop is shown in Figure 1-3. The **title bar**, which is dark blue in color at the top of the screen, identifies the name of the screen (Welcome) and contains the Close button, which can be used to close the Welcome screen. In the Welcome screen, a welcome message (Welcome to Windows 95) displays together with a helpful tip for using Windows 95, a check box containing a check mark, and several command buttons. The **check box** represents an option to display the Welcome screen each time Windows 95 starts that you can turn on or turn off. The **command buttons** allow you to perform different operations such as displaying the next tip or closing the screen.

Below the screen is the mouse pointer. On the desktop, the **mouse pointer** is the shape of a block arrow. The mouse pointer allows you to point to items on the desktop.

The **taskbar** at the bottom of the screen in Figure 1-3 contains the Start button, the Welcome button, and the Tray status area. The **Start button** provides an entry point to begin using the features of Windows 95, the Welcome button indicates the Welcome screen is open on the desktop, and the current time (6:06 PM) displays in the Tray status area.

Nearly every item on the Windows 95 desktop is considered an object. Even the desktop itself is an object. Every **object** has properties. The **properties** of an object are unique to that specific object and may affect what can be done to the object or what the object does. For example, the properties of an object may be the color of the object, such as the color of the desktop.

FIGURE 1-3

Closing the Welcome Screen

As noted, the Welcome screen might display when you start Windows 95. If the Welcome screen does display on the desktop, normally you should close it prior to beginning any other operations using Windows 95. To close the Welcome screen, complete the following step.

TO CLOSE THE WELCOME SCREEN

Step 1: Press the ESC key on the keyboard as shown in Figure 1-4.

The Welcome screen closes.

The Desktop as a Work Area

The Windows 95 desktop and the objects on the desktop were designed to emulate a work area in an office or at home. The Windows desktop may be thought of as an electronic version of the top of your desk. You can move objects around on the desktop, look at them and then put them aside, and so on. In Project 1, you will learn how to interact with and communicate with the Windows 95 desktop.

FIGURE 1-4

FIGURE 1-5

FIGURE 1-6

Communicating with Microsoft Windows 95

The Windows 95 interface provides the means for dialogue between you and your computer. Part of this dialogue involves your requesting information from your computer and responding to messages displayed by your computer. You can request information and respond to messages using either a mouse or a keyboard.

Mouse Operations

A **mouse** is a pointing device used with Windows 95 that is attached to the computer by a cable. It contains two buttons — the primary mouse button and the secondary mouse button (Figure 1-5). The **primary mouse button** is typically the left mouse button and the **secondary mouse button** is typically the right mouse button although Windows 95 allows you to switch them. In this book, the left mouse button is the primary mouse button and the right mouse button is the secondary mouse button.

Using the mouse, you can perform the following operations: (1) point; (2) click; (3) right-click; (4) double-click; (5) drag; and (6) right-drag. These operations are demonstrated on the following pages.

Point and Click

Point means you move the mouse across a flat surface until the mouse pointer rests on the item of choice on the desktop. As you move the mouse across a flat surface, the movement of a ball on the underside of the mouse (Figure 1-6) is electronically sensed, and the mouse pointer moves across the desktop in the same direction.

Click means you press and release the primary mouse button, which in this book is the left mouse button. In most cases, you must point to an item before you click. To become acquainted with the use of a mouse, perform the following steps to point to and click various objects on the desktop.

Steps **To Point and Click**

1 **Point to the Start button on the taskbar by moving the mouse across a flat surface until the mouse pointer rests on the Start button.**

The mouse pointer points to the Start button and a **ToolTip** *(Click here to begin) displays (Figure 1-7). The ToolTip, which provides instructions, displays on the desktop for approximately five seconds.*

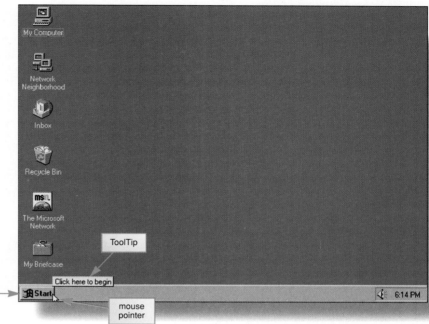

FIGURE 1-7

2 **Click the Start button on the taskbar by pressing and releasing the left mouse button.**

Windows 95 opens the **Start menu** *and indents the Start button (Figure 1-8). A* **menu** *is a list of related commands. Nine commands display on the Start menu. A* **command** *directs Windows 95 to perform a specific action such as opening another menu or shutting down the operating system. Each command consists of an icon and a command name. Some commands (Run and Shut Down) are followed by an* **ellipsis** *(...) to indicate Windows 95 requires more information before executing the command. Other commands (Programs, Documents, Settings, and Find) are followed by a* **right arrow***. A right arrow indicates that pointing to the command will open a submenu containing more commands.*

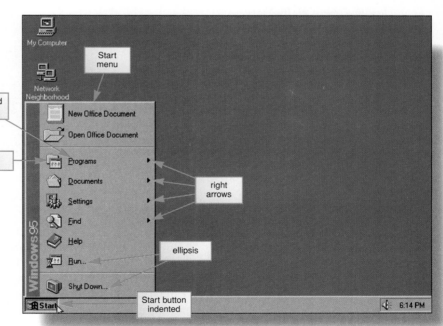

FIGURE 1-8

3 Point to Programs on the Start menu.

*When you point to Programs, Windows 95 highlights the Programs command on the Start menu and opens the **Programs submenu** (Figure 1-9). A **submenu** is a menu that displays when you point to a command that is followed by a right arrow.*

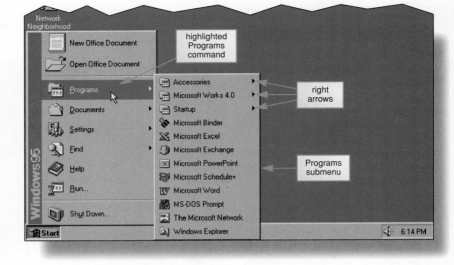

FIGURE 1-9

4 Point to an open area of the desktop and then click the open area of the desktop.

Windows 95 closes the Start menu and the Programs submenu (Figure 1-10). The mouse pointer points to the desktop. To close a menu anytime, click anywhere on the desktop except the menu itself. The Start button is not indented.

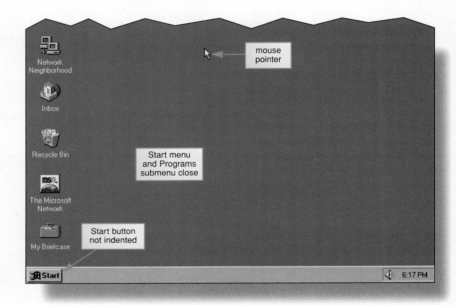

FIGURE 1-10

Notice in Figure 1-9 that whenever you point to a command on a menu, the command is highlighted.

When you click an object such as the Start button in Figure 1-8 on the previous page, you must point to the object before you click. In the steps that follow, the instruction that directs you to point to a particular item and then click is, Click the particular item. For example, Click the Start button, means point to the Start button and then click.

Right-Click

Right-click means you press and release the secondary mouse button, which in this book is the right mouse button. As when you use the primary mouse button, normally you will point to an object on the screen prior to right-clicking. Perform the following steps to right-click the desktop.

Steps **To Right-Click**

1 **Point to an open area on the desktop and press and release the right mouse button.**

Windows 95 displays a context-sensitive menu containing six commands (Figure 1-11). Right-clicking an object, such as the desktop, opens a **context-sensitive menu** *(also referred to as a* **shortcut menu** *or an* **object menu***) that contains a set of commands specifically for use with that object. The Paste command in Figure 1-11 is dimmed, meaning that command cannot be used at the current time.*

FIGURE 1-11

2 **Point to New on the context-sensitive menu.**

When you move the mouse pointer to the New command, Windows 95 highlights the New command and opens the **New submenu** *(Figure 1-12). The New submenu contains a variety of commands. The number of commands and the actual commands that display on your computer might be different.*

3 **Point to an open area of the desktop and click the open area to remove the context-sensitive menu and the New submenu.**

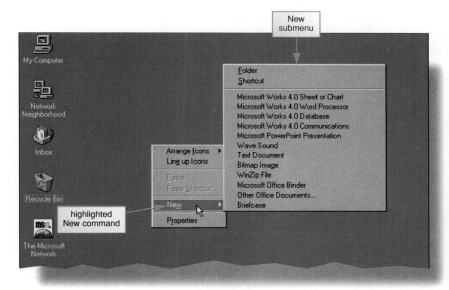

FIGURE 1-12

Whenever you right-click an object, a context-sensitive, or shortcut, menu will display. As you will see, the use of shortcut menus speeds up your work and adds flexibility to your interface with the computer.

Double-Click

Double-click means you quickly press and release the left mouse button twice without moving the mouse. In most cases, you must point to an item before you double-click. Perform the step on the next page to open the My Computer window on the desktop by double-clicking the My Computer icon.

Steps To Open a Window by Double-Clicking

1 **Point to the My Computer icon on the desktop and double-click by quickly pressing and releasing the left mouse button twice without moving the mouse.**

*Windows 95 opens the My Computer window and adds the My Computer button to the taskbar (Figure 1-13). The My Computer window is the active window. The **active window** is the window currently being used. Whenever you double-click an object that can be opened, Windows 95 will open the object; and the open object will be identified by a button on the taskbar. The active window is identified by the indented button.*

FIGURE 1-13

My Computer Window

The thin line, or **window border**, surrounding the My Computer window in Figure 1-13 determines its shape and size. The **title bar** at the top of the window contains a small icon that is the same as the icon on the desktop and the **window title** (My Computer) that identifies the window. The color of the title bar (dark blue) and the indented My Computer button on the taskbar indicate the My Computer window is the active window. The color of the active window on your computer might be different from the dark blue color.

Clicking the icon at the left on the title bar will open the Control menu, which contains commands to carry out actions associated with the My Computer window. At the right on the title bar are three buttons, the Minimize button, the Maximize button, and the Close button, that can be used to specify the size of the window and can close the window.

The **menu bar**, a horizontal bar below the title bar of a window (see Figure 1-13), contains a list of menu names for the My Computer window: File, Edit, View, and Help. One letter in each menu name is underlined. You can open a menu by clicking the menu name on the menu bar.

Six icons display in the My Computer window. A name below each icon identifies the icon. The three icons in the top row represent a 3½ floppy disk drive (3½ Floppy [A:]), a hard disk drive (Hard disk [C:]), and a CD-ROM drive ([D:]). The contents of the My Computer window on your computer might be different than shown in Figure 1-13.

The icons in the second row are folders. A **folder** is an object created to contain related documents, applications, and other folders. A folder in Windows 95 contains items in much the same way a folder on your desk contains items. If you double-click a folder, the items within the folder display in a window. A message at the left of the **status bar** located at the bottom of the window indicates the window contains six objects (see Figure 1-13).

Minimize Button

Two buttons on the title bar of a window, the Minimize button and the Maximize button, allow you to control the way a window displays or does not display on the desktop. When you click the **Minimize button** (see Figure 1-13), the My Computer window no longer displays on the desktop and the indented My Computer button on the taskbar changes to a non-indented button. A minimized window or application program is still open but it does not display on the screen. To minimize and then redisplay the My Computer window, complete the following steps.

More *About*
Minimizing Windows

Window management on the Windows 95 desktop is important in order to keep the desktop uncluttered. You will find yourself frequently minimizing windows, and then later reopening them with a click of a button on the taskbar.

Steps **To Minimize and Redisplay a Window**

1 **Point to the Minimize button on the title bar of the My Computer window.**

The mouse pointer points to the Minimize button on the My Computer window title bar (Figure 1-14). The My Computer button on the taskbar is indented.

FIGURE 1-14

2 **Click the Minimize button.**

The My Computer window disappears from the desktop and the My Computer button on the taskbar changes to a non-indented button (Figure 1-15).

FIGURE 1-15

3 **Click the My Computer button on the taskbar.**

The My Computer window displays on the desktop in the same place and size as before it was minimized (Figure 1-16). In addition, the My Computer window is the active window because it contains the dark blue title bar and the My Computer button on the taskbar is indented.

FIGURE 1-16

Whenever a window is minimized, it does not display on the desktop but a non-indented button for the window does display on the taskbar. Whenever you want a window that has been minimized to display and be the active window, click the window's button on the taskbar.

Maximize and Restore Buttons

The **Maximize button** maximizes a window so the window fills the entire screen, making it easier to see the contents of the window. When a window is maximized, the **Restore button** replaces the Maximize button on the title bar. Clicking the Restore button will return the window to its size before maximizing. To maximize and restore the My Computer window, complete the following steps.

> **More** *About*
> **Maximizing Windows**
>
> Many application programs run in a maximized window by default. Often you will find that you want to work with maximized windows.

Steps **To Maximize and Restore a Window**

1 **Point to the Maximize button on the title bar of the My Computer window.**

The mouse pointer points to the Maximize button on the title bar of the My Computer window (Figure 1-17).

FIGURE 1-17

2 **Click the Maximize button.**

The My Computer window expands so it and the taskbar fill the entire screen (Figure 1-18). The Restore button replaces the Maximize button. The My Computer button on the taskbar does not change. The My Computer window is still the active window.

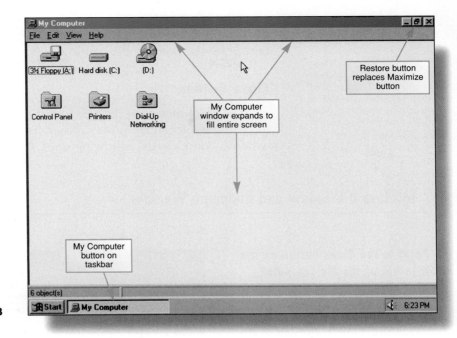

FIGURE 1-18

3 **Point to the Restore button on the title bar of the My Computer window.**

The mouse pointer points to the Restore button on the title bar of the My Computer window (Figure 1-19).

FIGURE 1-19

4 **Click the Restore button.**

The My Computer window returns to the size and position it occupied before being maximized (Figure 1-20). The My Computer button on the taskbar does not change. The Maximize button replaces the Restore button.

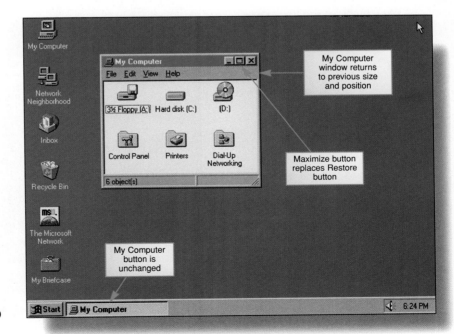

FIGURE 1-20

When a window is maximized, you can also minimize the window by clicking the Minimize button. If, after minimizing the window, you click the window button on the taskbar, the window will return to its maximized size.

Close Button

The **Close button** on the title bar of a window closes the window and removes the window button from the taskbar. To close and then reopen the My Computer window, complete the following steps.

Steps **To Close a Window and Reopen a Window**

1 **Point to the Close button on the title bar of the My Computer window.**

The mouse pointer points to the Close button on the title bar of the My Computer window (Figure 1-21).

FIGURE 1-21

2 **Click the Close button.**

The My Computer window closes and the My Computer button no longer displays on the taskbar (Figure 1-22).

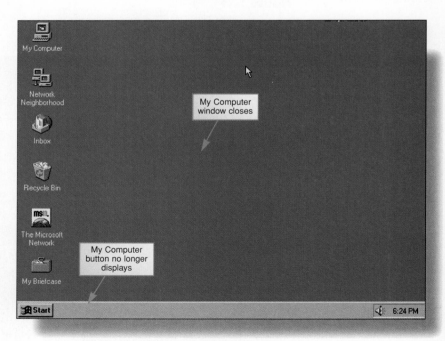

FIGURE 1-22

3 **Point to and double-click the My Computer icon on the desktop.**

The My Computer window opens and displays on the screen (Figure 1-23). The My Computer button displays on the taskbar.

FIGURE 1-23

Drag

Drag means you point to an item, hold down the left mouse button, move the item to the desired location on the screen, and then release the left mouse button. You can move any open window to another location on the desktop by pointing to the title bar of the window and dragging the window. To drag the My Computer window, perform the following steps.

 To Move an Object by Dragging

1 **Point to the My Computer window title bar.**

The mouse pointer points to the My Computer window title bar (Figure 1-24).

FIGURE 1-24

More *About* **Dragging**

Dragging is the second-most difficult skill to learn with a mouse. You may want to practice dragging a few times so you are comfortable with it.

2 Hold down the left mouse button and then move the mouse so the window outline moves to the center of the desktop (do not release the left mouse button).

As you drag the My Computer window, Windows 95 displays an outline of the window (Figure 1-25). The outline, which can be positioned anywhere on the desktop, specifies where the window will display when you release the left mouse button.

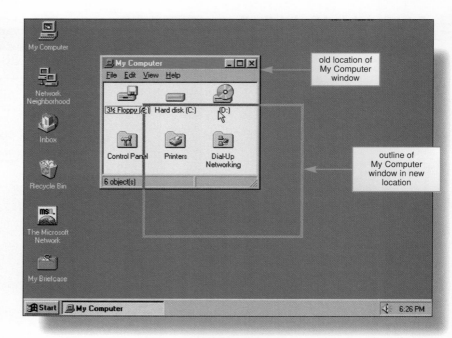

FIGURE 1-25

3 Release the left mouse button.

Windows 95 moves the My Computer window to the location the outline occupied prior to releasing the left mouse button (Figure 1-26).

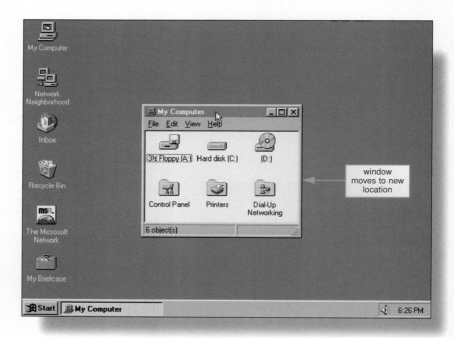

FIGURE 1-26

Sizing a Window by Dragging

You can use dragging for more than just moving an item or object. For example, you can drag the border of a window to change the size of the window. To change the size of the My Computer window, complete the following step.

 Steps **To Size a Window by Dragging**

① **Position the mouse pointer over the lower right corner of the My Computer window until the mouse pointer changes to a two-headed arrow. Drag the lower right corner upward and to the left until the window on your desktop resembles the window in Figure 1-27.**

As you drag the lower right corner, the My Computer window changes size and a vertical scroll bar displays (Figure 1-27). A scroll bar is a bar that displays at the right edge and/or bottom edge of a window when the window contents are not completely visible. A vertical scroll bar contains an up scroll arrow, a down scroll arrow, and a scroll box.

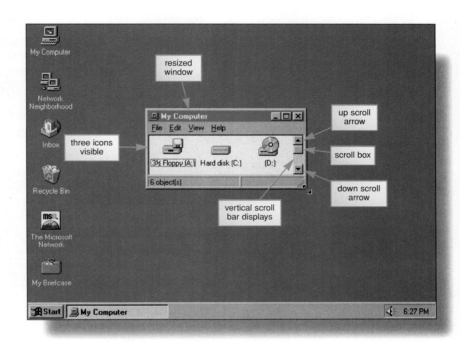

FIGURE 1-27

The size of the scroll box in any window is dependent on the amount of the window that is not visible. The smaller the scroll box, the more of the window that is not visible. In addition to dragging a corner of a window, you can also drag any of the borders of a window.

Scrolling in a Window

You can use the scroll bar to view the contents of a window that are not visible. Scrolling can be accomplished in three ways: click the scroll arrows; click the scroll bar; and drag the scroll box.

To display the contents of the My Computer window by scrolling using scroll arrows, complete the steps on the next page.

Steps To Scroll a Window Using Scroll Arrows

1 **Point to the down scroll arrow on the vertical scroll bar.**

The mouse pointer points to the down scroll arrow on the scroll bar (Figure 1-28).

FIGURE 1-28

2 **Click the down scroll arrow one time.**

The window scrolls down (the icons move up in the window) and displays the tops of icons not previously visible (Figure 1-29). Because the window size does not change when you scroll, the contents of the window will change, as seen in the difference between Figure 1-28 and Figure 1-29.

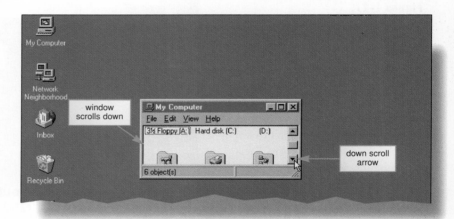

FIGURE 1-29

3 **Click the down scroll arrow two more times.**

The scroll box moves to the bottom of the scroll bar and the icons in the last row of the window display (Figure 1-30).

FIGURE 1-30

You can continuously scroll through a window using scroll arrows by clicking the up or down scroll arrow and holding down the left mouse button. The window continues to scroll until you release the left mouse button or you reach the top or bottom of the window.

You can also scroll by clicking the scroll bar itself. When you click the scroll bar, the window moves up or down a greater distance than when you click the scroll arrows.

A third way in which you can scroll through a window to view the window's contents is by dragging the scroll box. When you drag the scroll box, the window moves up or down as you drag.

Being able to view the contents of a window by scrolling is an important Windows 95 skill because the entire contents of a window may not be visible.

Resizing a Window

You might want to return a window to its original size. To return the My Computer window to about its original size, complete the following steps.

TO RESIZE A WINDOW

Step 1: Position the mouse pointer over the lower right corner of the My Computer window border until the mouse pointer changes to a two-headed arrow.

Step 2: Drag the lower right corner of the My Computer window until the window is the same size as shown in Figure 1-26 on page WIN 1.18, and then release the mouse button.

The My Computer window is about the same size as before you changed it.

Closing a Window

After you have completed your work in a window, normally you will close the window. To close the My Computer window, complete the following steps.

TO CLOSE A WINDOW

Step 1: Point to the Close button on the right of the title bar in the My Computer window.

Step 2: Click the Close button.

The My Computer window closes and the desktop contains no open windows.

Right-Drag

Right-drag means you point to an item, hold down the right mouse button, move the item to the desired location, and then release the right mouse button. When you right-drag an object, a context-sensitive menu displays. The context-sensitive menu contains commands specifically for use with the object being dragged. To right-drag the My Briefcase icon to the center of the desktop, perform the steps on the next page. If the My Briefcase icon does not display on your desktop, you will be unable to perform Step 1 through Step 3 on the next page.

More *About*
the Scroll Bar

In many application programs, clicking the scroll bar will move the window a full screen's worth of information up or down. You can step through a word processing document screen by screen, for example, by clicking the scroll bar.

More *About*
the Scroll Box

Dragging the scroll box is the most efficient technique to scroll long distances. In many application programs, such as Microsoft Word 7, as you scroll using the scroll box, the page number of the document displays next to the scroll box.

More *About*
Scrolling Guidelines

General scrolling guidelines: (1) To scroll short distances (line by line), click the scroll arrows; (2) To scroll one screen at a time, click the scroll bar; (3) To scroll long distances, drag the scroll box.

Steps To Right-Drag

1 **Point to the My Briefcase icon on the desktop, hold down the right mouse button, drag the icon diagonally toward the center of the desktop, and then release the right mouse button.**

The dragged My Briefcase ghosted icon and a context-sensitive menu display in the center of the desktop (Figure 1-31). The My Briefcase icon remains at its original location on the left of the screen. The context-sensitive menu contains four commands: Move Here, Copy Here, Create Shortcut(s) Here, and Cancel. The Move Here command in bold (dark) type identifies what happens if you were to drag the My Briefcase icon with the left mouse button.

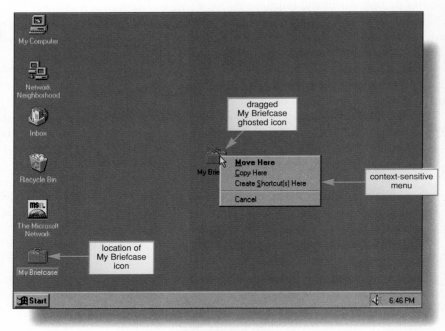

FIGURE 1-31

2 **Point to Cancel on the context-sensitive menu.**

The mouse pointer points to Cancel on the context-sensitive menu (Figure 1-32). The Cancel command is highlighted.

3 **Click Cancel on the context-sensitive menu.**

The context-sensitive menu and the dragged My Briefcase icon disappear from the screen.

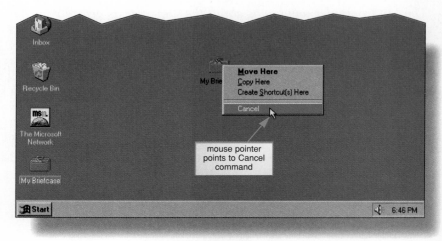

FIGURE 1-32

Whenever you begin an operation but do not want to complete the operation, click Cancel on a context-sensitive menu or click the Cancel button in a dialog box. The Cancel command will reset anything you have done.

If you click Move Here on the context-sensitive menu shown in Figure 1-31, Windows 95 will move the icon from its current location to the new location. If you click the Copy Here command, the icon will be copied to the new location and two icons will display on the desktop. Windows 95 automatically will give the second icon and the associated file a different name. If you click the Create Shortcut(s) Here command, a special object called a shortcut will be created.

Although you can move icons by dragging with the primary (left) mouse button and by right-dragging with the secondary (right) mouse button, it is strongly suggested you right-drag because a menu displays and you can specify the exact operation you want to occur. When you drag using the left mouse button, a default operation takes place and the operation may not do what you want.

The Keyboard and Keyboard Shortcuts

FIGURE 1-33a

The **keyboard** is an input device on which you manually key, or type, data. Figure 1-33a shows the enhanced IBM 101-key keyboard and Figure 1-33b shows a Microsoft keyboard designed specifically for use with Windows 95. Many tasks you accomplish with a mouse also can be accomplished using a keyboard.

To perform tasks using the keyboard, you must understand the notation used to identify which keys to press. This notation is used throughout Windows 95 to identify **keyboard shortcuts**.

Keyboard shortcuts consist of: (1) pressing a single key (example: press F1); or, (2) holding down one key and pressing a second key, as shown by two key names separated with a plus sign (example: press CTRL+ESC). For example, to obtain Help about Windows 95, you can press the F1 key. To open the Start menu, hold down the CTRL key and press the ESC key (press CTRL+ESC).

Often, computer users will use keyboard shortcuts for operations they perform frequently. For example, many users find pressing the F1 key to start Windows 95 Help easier than using the Start menu as shown later in this project. As a user, you will likely find your own combination of keyboard and mouse operations that particularly suit you, but it is strongly recommended that generally you use the mouse.

FIGURE 1-33b

Creating a Document by Starting an Application Program

A **program** is a set of computer instructions that carries out a task on your computer. An **application program** is a program that allows you to accomplish a specific task for which that program is designed. For example, a word processing program is an application program that allows you to create written documents, a spreadsheet program is an application program that allows you to create spreadsheets and charts, and a presentation graphics application program allows you to create graphic presentations for display on a computer or as slides.

More *About*
Application
Programs

Some application programs, such as Notepad, are part of Windows 95. Most application programs, however, such as Microsoft Office 95, Lotus SmartSuite 96, and others must be purchased separately from Windows 95.

The most common activity on a computer is to run an application program to accomplish tasks using the computer. You can start an application program by using the Start button on the taskbar.

To illustrate the use of an application program to create a written document, assume each morning you create a daily reminders list so you will remember the tasks you must accomplish throughout the day. You print the document containing the reminders for your use. On occasion, you must update the daily reminders list as events occur during the day. You have decided to use **Notepad**, a popular application program available with Windows 95, to create your list.

To create the list, one method you can use with Windows 95 is to start the Notepad application program using the Start button on the taskbar. After the Notepad program is started, you can enter your daily reminders.

To start the Notepad program, perform the following steps.

Steps **To Start a Program**

1 **Click the Start button on the taskbar. Point to Programs on the Start menu. Point to Accessories on the Programs submenu. If you happen to point to another command on one of the menus or submenus, a different submenu might display. Merely move the mouse so it points to Programs and then Accessories to display the correct menu and submenus.**

Windows 95 opens the Start menu, the Programs submenu, and the Accessories submenu (Figure 1-34). The mouse pointer points to Accessories on the Programs submenu. The Accessories submenu contains the Notepad command to start the Notepad program. Notice that whenever you point to a menu name that has a right arrow following it, a submenu displays. You might find more, fewer, or different commands on the submenus on your computer.

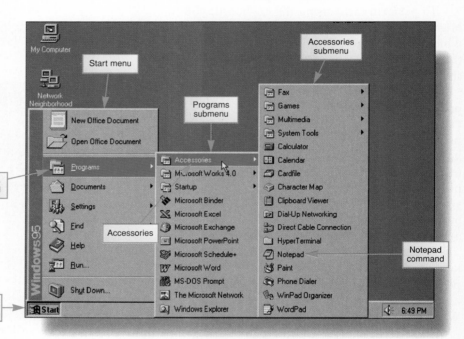

FIGURE 1-34

2 Point to Notepad on the Accessories submenu.

When the mouse pointer points to Notepad on the Accessories submenu, the Notepad command is highlighted (Figure 1-35).

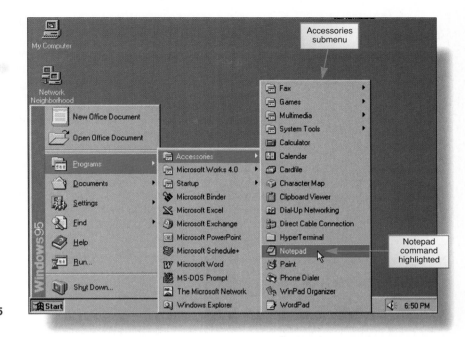

FIGURE 1-35

3 Click Notepad.

Windows 95 starts the Notepad program by opening the Notepad window on the desktop and adding an indented Notepad button to the taskbar (Figure 1-36). Notepad is the active window (dark blue title bar). The word Untitled in the window title (Untitled - Notepad) and on the Notepad button indicates the document has not been saved on disk. The menu bar contains the following menu names: File, Edit, Search, and Help. The area below the menu bar contains an insertion point and two scroll bars. The **insertion point** *is a flashing vertical line that indicates the point at which text typed on the keyboard will be displayed. The scroll bars do not contain scroll boxes, indicating the document is not large enough to allow scrolling.*

FIGURE 1-36

OtherWays

1. Right-click desktop, point to New, click Text Document, double-click the New Text Document icon
2. Click Start button, click Run, type Notepad, click OK button
3. Press CTRL+ESC, press R, type Notepad, press ENTER key

After you have started an application program such as Notepad, you can use the program to prepare your document.

Windows 95 provides a number of ways in which to accomplish a particular task. When a task is illustrated by a series of steps in this book, those steps may not be the only way in which the task can be done. If you can accomplish the same task using other methods, the Other Ways box specifies the other methods. In each case, the method shown in the steps is the preferred method, but it is important you are aware of all the techniques you can use.

Creating a Document

To create a document in Notepad, you must type the text you want in the document. After typing a line of text, press the ENTER key to indicate the end of the line. If you press the ENTER key when the insertion point is on a line by itself, Notepad inserts a blank line in the document. To create the Daily Reminders document, perform the following step.

Steps **To Create a Document**

1 **Type** Daily Reminders - Wednesday **and press the ENTER key twice. Type** 1. Call Tim Hoyle - Photoshop retouch due **and press the ENTER key. Type** 2. Memo to Linda Tomms - Meeting next week **and press the ENTER key. Type** 3. Lunch with Harris - Noon, Remmington's **and press the ENTER key.**

The first five lines of the document are entered (Figure 1-37). A blank line is inserted following the first line. The insertion point is positioned on the sixth line of the document.

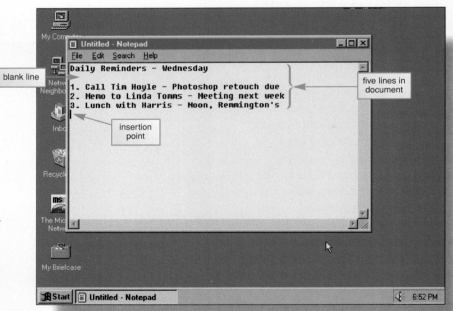

FIGURE 1-37

Saving a Document on Disk

When you create a document using a program such as Notepad, the document is stored in the main memory (RAM) of your computer. If you close the program without saving the document or if your computer accidentally loses electrical power, the document will be lost. To protect against the accidental loss of a document and to allow you to easily modify the document in the future, you can save the document on disk.

When you save a document, you must assign a filename to the document. All documents are identified by a filename. Typical filenames are Daily Reminders - Wednesday, Mileage Log, and Automobile Maintenance. A filename can contain up to 255 characters, including spaces. Any uppercase or lowercase character is valid when creating a filename, except a backslash (\), slash (/), colon (:), asterisk (*), question mark (?), quotation mark ("), less than symbol (<), greater than symbol (>), or vertical bar (|). Filenames cannot be CON, AUX, COM1, COM2, COM3, COM4, LPT1, LPT2, LPT3, PRN, or NUL.

To associate a document with an application, Windows 95 assigns an extension of a period and up to three characters to each document. All documents created using the Notepad program, which are text documents, are saved with the .TXT extension. To save the document you created using Notepad on a floppy disk in drive A of your computer using the filename, Daily Reminders - Wednesday, perform the following steps.

More *About* **Filenames**

Because of restrictions with Microsoft DOS, previous versions of Windows allowed filenames of only eight or fewer characters. F56QPSLA, and similar indecipherable names, were common. Microsoft touts the long filename capability of Windows 95 as a significant breakthrough. Apple Macintosh users, however, shrug and ask what's the big deal. They have used long filenames for years.

 To Save a Document on Disk

1 **Insert a formatted floppy disk into drive A on your computer. Click File on the menu bar.**

Windows 95 highlights the File menu name on the menu bar and opens the File menu in the Notepad window (Figure 1-38). The mouse pointer points to File on the menu bar.

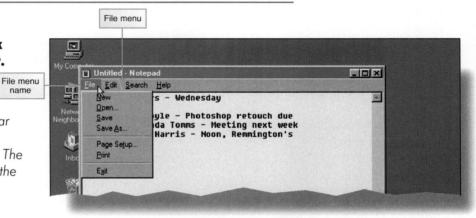

FIGURE 1-38

2 **Point to Save As on the File menu.**

*The mouse pointer points to the Save As command on the File menu (Figure 1-39). The ellipsis (...) following the Save As command indicates Windows 95 requires more information to carry out the Save As command and will open a dialog box when you click Save As. A **dialog box** displays whenever Windows 95 needs to supply information to you or wants you to enter information or select among several options.*

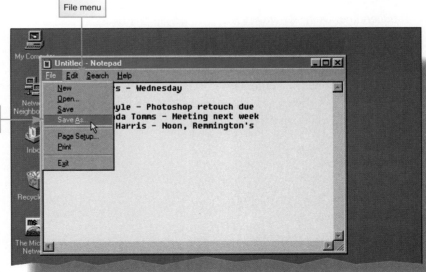

FIGURE 1-39

3 **Click Save As.**

*Windows 95 displays the Save As dialog box (Figure 1-40). The Save As dialog box becomes the active window (dark blue title bar) and the Notepad window becomes the **inactive window** (light blue title bar). The Save As dialog box contains the Save in drop-down list box. A **drop-down list box** is a rectangular box containing text and a down arrow on the right. The Save in drop-down list box displays the Desktop icon and Desktop name. The entry in the Save in drop-down list box indicates where the file will be stored. At the bottom of the dialog box is the File name text box. A **text box** is a rectangular area in which you can enter text. The File name text box contains the highlighted entry, Untitled. When you type the filename from the keyboard, the filename will replace the highlighted entry in the File name text box.*

FIGURE 1-40

4 **Type** Daily Reminders - Wednesday **in the File name text box. Point to the Save in box arrow.**

The filename, Daily Reminders – Wednesday, and an insertion point display in the File name text box (Figure 1-41). When you save this document, Notepad will automatically add the .TXT extension. The mouse pointer points to the Save in box arrow.

FIGURE 1-41

5 **Click the Save in box arrow and then point to the 3½ Floppy [A:] icon.**

Windows 95 displays the Save in drop-down list (Figure 1-42). The list contains various elements of your computer, including the Desktop, My Computer, Network Neighborhood, and My Briefcase. Within My Computer are 3½ Floppy [A:], Hard disk [C:], and [D:]. When you point to the 3½ Floppy [A:] icon, the entry in the list is highlighted.

FIGURE 1-42

6 **Click the 3½ Floppy [A:] icon and then point to the Save button.**

The 3½ Floppy [A:] entry displays in the Save in drop-down list box (Figure 1-43). This specifies that the file will be saved on the floppy disk in drive A using the filename specified in the File name text box. The mouse pointer points to the Save button.

FIGURE 1-43

7 Click the Save button.

*Windows 95 displays an **hourglass icon** while saving the Daily Reminders - Wednesday document on the floppy disk in drive A, closes the Save As dialog box, makes the Notepad window the active window, and inserts the filename on the Notepad window title bar and on the button on the taskbar (Figure 1-44). The filename on the title bar may or may not display the .TXT extension, depending on the setting on your computer. The hourglass icon indicates Windows 95 requires a brief interval of time to save the document. The filename on the button on the taskbar (Daily Reminders - We...) contains an ellipsis to indicate the entire button name does not fit on the button. To display the entire button name for a button on the taskbar, point to the button.*

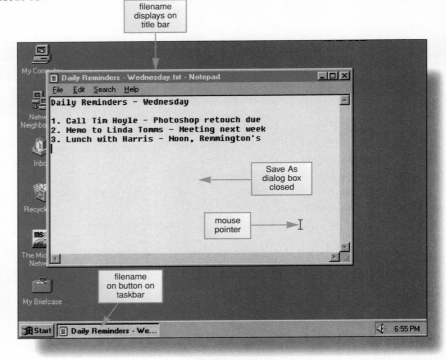

FIGURE 1-44

*Other*Ways

1. On File menu click Save, type filename, select drive and folder, click Save button
2. Press ALT+F, press A, type filename, select drive and folder, press S

More *About* Printing

Printing is and will remain important for documents. Many sophisticated application programs, however, are extending the printing capability to include transmitting faxes, sending e-mail, and even posting documents on Web pages of the World Wide Web.

The method shown in the previous steps for saving a file on a floppy disk can be used to save a file on a hard disk, such as drive C, or even on the desktop.

In Figure 1-38 on page WIN 1.27, the File menu displays. Once you have opened a menu on the menu bar, you need merely point to another menu name on the menu bar to open that menu. Thus, in Figure 1-38, if you point to Edit on the menu bar, the Edit menu will display. If you accidentally move the mouse pointer off the menu you want to display, point back to the menu name to display the desired menu. To close a menu without carrying out a command, click anywhere on the desktop except on the menu.

Printing a Document

Quite often, after creating a document and saving it, you will want to print it. Printing can be accomplished directly from an application program. To print the Daily Reminders – Wednesday document, perform the following steps.

Steps To Print a Document

1 Click File on the menu bar and then point to Print on the File menu.

The File menu displays and the mouse pointer points to the Print command (Figure 1-45). As with all menu commands when you point to them, the Print command is highlighted. **FIGURE 1-45**

2 Click Print.

A Notepad dialog box briefly displays with a message that indicates the Daily Reminders document is being printed (Figure 1-46). The dialog box disappears after the report has been printed. To cancel printing, you can click the Cancel button. The printed report is shown in Figure 1-47. Notepad automatically places the filename at the top of the page and a page number at the bottom of the page.

FIGURE 1-46

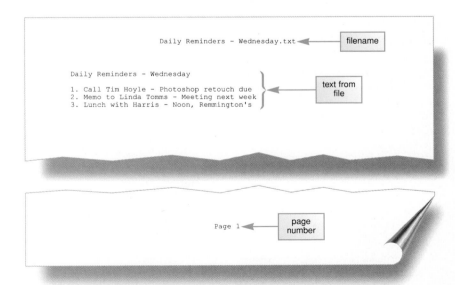

FIGURE 1-47

Closing a Program

After creating the Daily Reminders – Wednesday document, saving the document on the floppy disk in drive A, and printing it, your use of the Notepad program is complete. Therefore, the Notepad program should be closed by performing the following steps.

OtherWays
1. Double-click Notepad logo on title bar
2. On File menu click Exit
3. Press ALT+F4

TO CLOSE A PROGRAM

Step 1: Point to the Close button on the Notepad title bar.
Step 2: Click the Close button.

Windows 95 closes the Daily Reminders – Wednesday.txt – Notepad window and removes the Daily Reminders – Wednesday.txt – Notepad button from the taskbar.

Modifying a Document Stored on Disk

Many documents you create will need to be modified at some point in time after you have created them. For example, the Daily Reminders - Wednesday document should be modified each time you determine another task to be done. To modify an existing document, you can start the application program and open the document. To start the Notepad program and open the Daily Reminders – Wednesday document, complete the following steps.

Steps **To Open a Document Stored on Disk**

1 **Click the Start button on the taskbar. Point to Programs. Point to Accessories. Point to Notepad.**

The Start menu, Programs sub-menu, and Accessories submenu display (Figure 1-48). The mouse pointer points to the Notepad command.

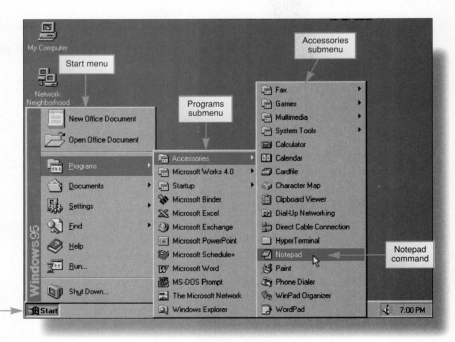

FIGURE 1-48

2 Click Notepad. When the Notepad window opens, click File on the menu bar and then point to Open on the File menu.

Windows 95 starts the Notepad program (Figure 1-49). The Untitled – Notepad button on the taskbar indicates no document has been opened. The File menu displays and the mouse pointer points to the Open command.

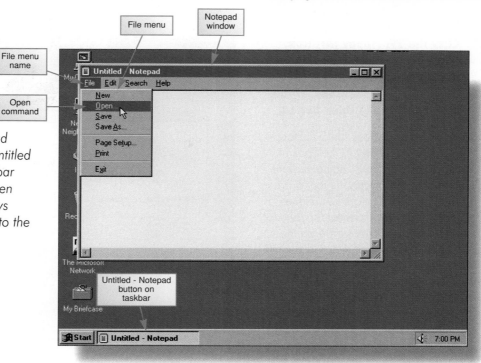

FIGURE 1-49

3 Click Open. Click the Look in box arrow. Point to the 3½ Floppy [A:] icon.

Windows 95 displays the Open dialog box (Figure 1-50). When you click the Look in box arrow, the Look in drop-down list displays. The mouse pointer points to the 3½ Floppy [A:] icon. The 3½ Floppy [A:] entry is highlighted.

FIGURE 1-50

4 Click the 3½ Floppy [A:] icon. When the filenames display in the window, click Daily Reminders — Wednesday.txt and then point to the Open button.

Windows 95 places the 3½ Floppy [A:] icon and entry in the Look in drop-down list box, indicating that the file to be opened is found on the floppy disk in drive A (Figure 1-51). The names of folders and/or text document files stored on the floppy disk in drive A are displayed in the window below the Look in drop-down list box. The Daily Reminders - Wednesday.txt file is selected, as indicated by the highlight, and the mouse pointer points to the Open button. Notice that the Daily Reminders — Wednesday.txt filename displays in the File name text box, indicating this is the file that will be opened.

FIGURE 1-51

5 Click the Open button.

Windows 95 opens the Daily Reminders — Wednesday.txt file and displays it in the Notepad window (Figure 1-52). The filename displays on the title bar of the Notepad window and on the button on the taskbar.

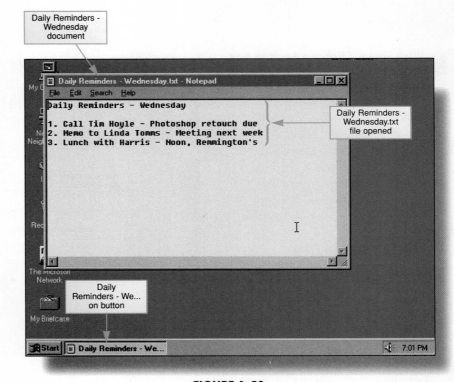

FIGURE 1-52

*Other*Ways

1. Double-click My Computer icon, double-click drive A icon, double-click file icon
2. Press ALT+F, press O, select drive and folder, type filename, press O

After opening the Daily Reminders – Wednesday document, perform the following step to modify the document by adding another line.

TO MODIFY A DOCUMENT

Step 1: Press the DOWN ARROW key five times, type 4. E-Mail Sue Wells - Adobe Illustrator drawing as the new line, and then press the ENTER key.

After modifying the Daily Reminders – Wednesday document, you should save the modified document on the floppy disk in drive A using the same filename. To save the modified document on the disk, complete the following steps.

Steps To Save a Modified Document on Disk

1 **Click File on the menu bar and then point to Save.**

The File menu opens and the mouse pointer points to the Save command (Figure 1-53). The Save command is used to save a file that has already been created.

2 **Click Save.**

The modified document is stored on the floppy disk in drive A and the Notepad window remains open. Whenever you use the Save command, the document is stored using the same filename in the same location from which it was opened.

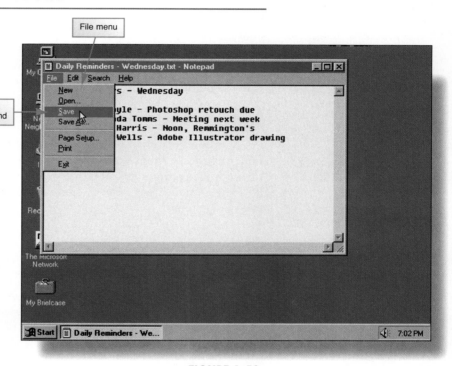

FIGURE 1-53

*Other***Ways**

1. Press ALT+F, press S

If you want to print the modified document, click File on the menu bar and then click Print on the File menu in the same manner as shown in Figure 1-45 and Figure 1-46 on page WIN 1.31.

Closing the Notepad Program

After modifying the document and storing the modified document on the floppy disk in drive A, normally you will close the Notepad program. To close the Notepad program, complete the step on the next page.

<table>
</table>

◆ **More** *About*
Windows 95 Help

If you purchased an operating
system or application program
five years ago, you received at
least one, and more often several, thick and heavy technical
manuals that explained the software. With Windows 95, you
receive a skinny manual less
than 100 pages in length. The
online Help feature of Windows
95 replaces reams and reams
of printed pages in hard-to-
understand technical manuals.

TO CLOSE A PROGRAM

Step 1: Click the Close button on the right of the Notepad title bar.

The Notepad window closes and the Notepad button on the taskbar disappears.

Modifying an existing document is a common occurrence and should be well understood when using Windows 95.

Using Windows Help

One of the more powerful application programs for use in Windows 95 is Windows Help. Windows Help is available when using Windows 95, or when using any application program running under Windows 95, to assist you in using Windows 95 and the various application programs. It contains answers to virtually any question you can ask with respect to Windows 95.

Contents Sheet

Windows 95 Help provides a variety of ways in which to obtain information. One method to find a Help topic involves using the Contents sheet to browse through Help topics by category. To illustrate this method, you will use Windows 95 Help to determine how to find a topic in Help. To start Help, complete the following steps.

Steps **To Start Help**

① **Click the Start button on the taskbar. Point to Help on the Start menu.**

Windows 95 opens the Start menu (Figure 1-54). Because the mouse pointer points to the Help command, the Help command is highlighted.

FIGURE 1-54

2 **Click Help on the Start menu. If the Contents sheet does not display, click the Contents tab.**

Windows 95 opens the Help Topics: Windows Help window (Figure 1-55). The window contains three **tabs** *(Contents, Index, and Find). The* **Contents sheet** *is visible in the window. Clicking either the Index tab or the Find tab opens the Index or Find sheet, respectively. The Contents sheet contains two* **Help topics** *preceded by a question mark icon and five books. Each book consists of a closed book icon followed by a book name. The first Help topic, Tour: Ten minutes to using Windows, is highlighted. Three command buttons (Display, Print, and Cancel) display at the bottom of the window.*

FIGURE 1-55

Other Ways

1. Press F1, press CTRL+TAB or CTRL+SHIFT+TAB to highlight desired sheet

In the Help window shown in Figure 1-55, the closed book icon indicates Help topics or more books are contained within the book. The question mark icon indicates a Help topic without any further subdivisions.

In addition to starting Help by using the Start button, you can also start Help by pressing the F1 key.

After starting Help, the next step is to find the topic in which you are interested. To find the topic that describes how to find a topic in Help, complete the steps on the next two pages.

Steps **To Use Help to Find a Topic in Help**

1 **Double-click How To... in the Help Topics: Windows Help window. Point to the Use Help closed book.**

Windows 95 highlights the How To book and opens the How To book (Figure 1-56). The ellipsis following the How To book indicates additional books will display when you open the book. The list of closed book icons indicates more Help information is available. The mouse pointer points to the Use Help closed book icon. The Close button in Figure 1-56 replaces the Display button in Figure 1-55. If you click the Close button, the How To book will close and the list of books below the How To book disappears.

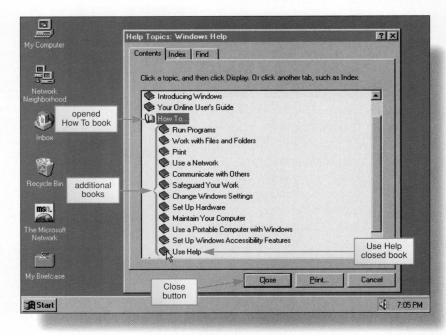

FIGURE 1-56

2 **Double-click the Use Help closed book icon and then point to Finding a topic in Help in the opened Use Help book.**

Windows 95 opens the Use Help book and displays several Help topics in the book (Figure 1-57). The mouse pointer points to Finding a topic in Help.

FIGURE 1-57

3 **Double-click Finding a topic in Help.**

Windows 95 closes the Help Topics: Windows Help window and opens the Windows Help window (Figure 1-58). The window contains three buttons (Help Topics, Back, and Options), steps to find a topic in Help, and a Tip. The Windows Help button displays on the taskbar.

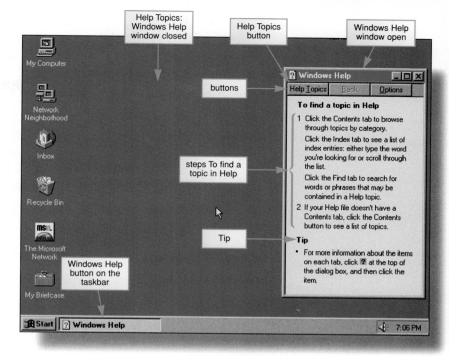

FIGURE 1-58

4 **After reading the information in the Windows Help window, click the Help Topics button in the Windows Help window.**

The Help Topics: Windows Help window displays together with the Windows Help window (Figure 1-59).

FIGURE 1-59

OtherWays

1. Press DOWN ARROW until book or topic highlighted, press ENTER, continue until Help topic displays, read Help topic, press T

Clicking the Help Topics button in the Windows Help window will always display the Help Topics: Windows Help window.

In Figure 1-58 on the previous page, if you click the Back button in the Windows Help window (when the button is not dimmed), Windows 95 will display the previously displayed Help topic. Clicking the Options button in the Windows Help window allows you to annotate a Help topic, copy or print a Help topic, change the font and color scheme of Help windows, and control how Help windows display in relation to other windows on the desktop.

Notice also in Figure 1-58 that the Windows Help title bar contains a Minimize button, a Maximize button, and a Close button. You can minimize and maximize the Windows Help window, and you can also close the Windows Help window without returning to the Help Topics: Windows Help window.

Index Sheet

A second method to find answers to your questions about Windows 95 or application programs is the Index sheet. The **Index sheet** lists a large number of index entries, each of which references one or more Help screens. To learn more about Windows 95 basic skills by using the Index sheet, and to see an example of animation available with Help, complete the following steps.

More *About* the Index Sheet

The Index sheet is probably the best source of information in Windows Help because you can enter the subject you are interested in. Sometimes, however, you will have to be creative to discover the index entry that answers your question because the most obvious entry will not always lead to your answer.

Steps **To Use the Help Index Sheet**

① **Click the Index tab. Type** basic skills **(the flashing insertion point is positioned in the text box). Point to the Display button.**

The Index sheet displays, including a list of entries that can be referenced (Figure 1-60). When you type an entry, the list automatically scrolls and the entry you type, such as basic skills, is highlighted. To see additional entries, use the scroll bar at the right of the list. To highlight an entry in the list, click the entry. On some computers, the basic skills entry may not be present. On those machines, select another topic of interest to you.

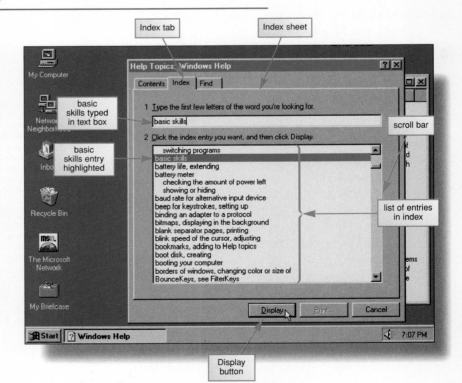

FIGURE 1-60

2 Click the Display button. Click the Maximize button in the Windows Help title bar. Point to the Sizing windows button.

The Windows Help window opens and a screen titled, The Basics, displays (Figure 1-61). The window is maximized and the Restore button displays in place of the Maximize button. The screen includes six buttons to learn Windows essentials and a picture of the Windows 95 desktop. When the mouse pointer is positioned on one of the buttons, it changes to a hand with a pointing finger. The Windows Help button displays on the taskbar.

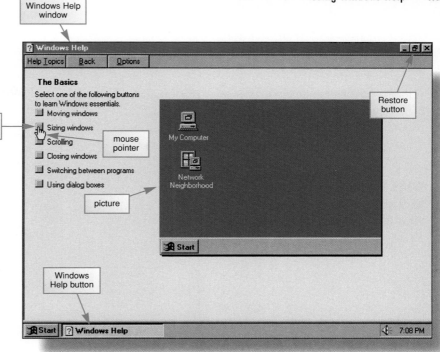

FIGURE 1-61

3 Click the Sizing windows button. Point to the Play button (the button with the right arrow) below the picture on the right.

The words, Sizing windows, display in bold, the My Computer window is added to the picture on the right, and the controls to play the animation display (Figure 1-62). The Play button will play the animation, the Option button displays a series of options regarding the animation, and the slide indicates progress when the animation plays. Text that explains how to accomplish the task, such as sizing windows, displays above the picture. On some computers, the animation might not be available. On those computers, instead of displaying the animation picture, the message, Unable to display graphic, will display on the screen. The text above the picture that explains how to perform the task still displays.

FIGURE 1-62

4 Click the Play button if it displays on the screen.

The Play button changes to a Stop button and the animation plays (Figure 1-63). The slide indicates the progress of the animation.

5 When the animation is complete, click any buttons you wish to view other animations.

FIGURE 1-63

After viewing Help topics, normally you will close Windows Help. To close Windows Help, complete the following step.

TO CLOSE WINDOWS HELP

Step 1: Click the Close button on the title bar of the Windows Help window.

Windows 95 closes the Windows Help window.

Shutting Down Windows 95

After completing your work with Windows 95, you might want to shut down Windows 95 using the **Shut Down command** on the Start menu. If you are sure you want to shut down Windows 95, perform the steps on the next page. If you are not sure about shutting down Windows 95, read the following steps without actually performing them.

Steps **To Shut Down Windows 95**

1 **Click the Start button on the taskbar and then point to Shut Down on the Start menu.**

Windows 95 displays the Start menu (Figure 1-64). The Shut Down command is highlighted because the mouse pointer points to it.

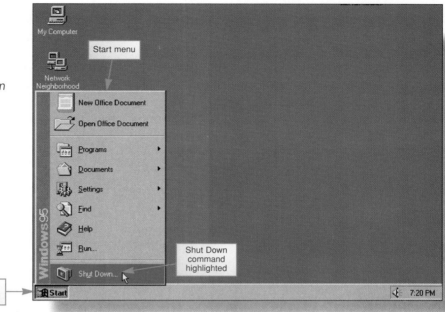

FIGURE 1-64

2 **Click Shut Down. Point to the Yes button in the Shut Down Windows dialog box.**

Windows 95 darkens the entire desktop and opens the Shut Down Windows dialog box (Figure 1-65). The dialog box contains four option buttons. The selected option button, Shut down the computer?, indicates that clicking the Yes button will shut down Windows 95.

3 **Click the Yes button.**

Two screens display while Windows 95 is shutting down. The first screen containing the text, Shutting down Windows, displays momentarily while Windows 95 is being shut down. Then, a second screen containing the text, It is okay to turn off your computer, displays. At this point you can to turn off your computer. When shutting down Windows 95, you should never turn off your computer before this last screen displays.

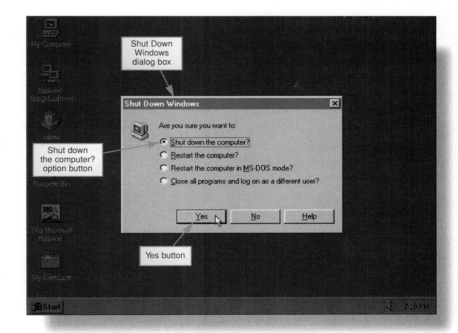

FIGURE 1-65

*Other*Ways

1. Press CTRL+ESC, press U, press UP ARROW or DOWN ARROW until option button selected, press ENTER

2. Press ALT+F4, press UP ARROW or DOWN ARROW until option button selected, press ENTER

If you accidentally click Shut Down on the Start menu and you do not want to shut down Windows 95, click the No button in the Shut Down Windows dialog box to return to normal Windows 95 operation.

Project Summary

Project 1 illustrated the Microsoft Windows 95 graphical user interface. You started Windows 95, learned the parts of the desktop, and learned to point, click, right-click, double-click, drag, and right-drag. You created a document by starting Notepad, entering text, saving the document on a floppy disk, and printing the document. You then modified the Notepad document and saved the modified document. Using both the Help Content and the Help Index sheets you obtained Help about Microsoft Windows 95. You shut down Windows 95 using the Shut Down command on the Start menu.

What You Should Know

Having completed this project, you should now be able to perform the following tasks:

- Close a Program *(WIN 1.32, WIN 1.36)*
- Close the Welcome Screen *(WIN 1.7)*
- Close a Window *(WIN 1.20)*
- Close a Window and Reopen a Window *(WIN 1.16)*
- Close Windows Help *(WIN 1.42)*
- Create a Document *(WIN 1.26)*
- Maximize and Restore a Window *(WIN 1.14)*
- Minimize and Redisplay a Window *(WIN 1.13)*
- Modify a Document *(WIN 1.35)*
- Move an Object by Dragging *(WIN 1.17)*
- Open a Document Stored on Disk *(WIN 1.32)*
- Open a Window by Double-Clicking *(WIN 1.12)*
- Point and Click *(WIN 1.9)*
- Print a Document *(WIN 1.31)*
- Resize a Window *(WIN 1.21)*
- Right-Click *(WIN 1.11)*
- Right-Drag *(WIN 1.22)*
- Save a Document on Disk *(WIN 1.27)*
- Save a Modified Document on Disk *(WIN 1.35)*
- Scroll a Window Using Scroll Arrows *(WIN 1.20)*
- Shut Down Windows 95 *(WIN 1.43)*
- Size a Window by Dragging *(WIN 1.19)*
- Start a Program *(WIN 1.24)*
- Start Help *(WIN 1.36)*
- Use Help to Find a Topic in Help *(WIN 1.38)*
- Use the Help Index Sheet *(WIN 1.40)*

A+ Test Your Knowledge

1 True/False

Instructions: Circle T if the statement is true or F if the statement is false.

(T) F   1. A user interface is a combination of computer hardware and computer software.
T (F)   2. Click means press the right mouse button.
T   F   3. When you drag an object on the desktop, Windows 95 displays a context-sensitive menu.
T   F   4. You can resize a window by dragging the title bar of the window.
T   F   5. Daily Reminders - Friday and Mileage Log are valid filenames.
T   F   6. To save a new document created using Notepad, click Save As on the File menu.
T   F   7. To print a document, click Print on the File menu.
T   F   8. To open a document stored on a floppy disk, click Open on the Start menu.
T   F   9. You can start Help by clicking the Start button and then clicking Help on the Start menu.
T   F   10. To find an item in the Windows Help Index, type the first few characters of the item in the text box on the Contents sheet.

2 Multiple Choice

Instructions: Circle the correct response.

1. Through a user interface, the user is able to _____.
   a. control the computer
   b. request information from the computer
   c. respond to messages displayed by the computer
   d. all of the above
2. A context-sensitive menu opens when you _____ a(n) _____.
   a. right-click, object
   b. click, menu name on the menu bar
   c. click, submenu
   d. double-click, indented button on the taskbar
3. In this book, a dark blue title bar and an indented button on the taskbar indicate a window is _____.
   a. inactive
   b. minimized
   c. closed
   d. active
4. To view contents of a window that are not currently visible in the window, use the _____.
   a. title bar
   b. scroll bar
   c. menu bar
   d. Restore button

(continued)

A+ Test Your Knowledge

Multiple Choice *(continued)*

5. _____ is holding down the right mouse button, moving an item to the desired location, and then releasing the right mouse button.
   a. Double-clicking
   b. Right-clicking
   c. Right-dragging
   d. Pointing

6. The Notepad command used to start the Notepad application program is located on the _____ (sub)menu.
   a. Start
   b. Accessories
   c. Programs
   d. Help

7. To quit the Notepad application and close its window, _____.
   a. click the Close button on the Notepad title bar
   b. click File on the menu bar
   c. double-click the Notepad title bar
   d. click the Minimize button on the Notepad title bar

8. To save a Notepad document after modifying the document, _____.
   a. click the Close button on the Notepad title bar
   b. click the Minimize button on the Notepad title bar
   c. click Save on the File menu
   d. click Exit on the File menu

9. For information about an item on the Index sheet of the Help Topics: Windows Help window, _____.
   a. press the F1 key
   b. click the Question Mark button in the top right corner of the dialog box and then click the item
   c. click the Find tab in the Help Topics: Windows Help window
   d. press CTRL+F3

10. To shut down Windows 95, _____.
   a. click the Start button, click Shut Down on the Start menu, click the Shut down the computer? option button, and then click the Yes button
   b. click the Shut Down button on the Windows 95 File menu
   c. click the taskbar, click Close down Windows 95, and then click the Yes button
   d. press the F10 key and then click the Yes button

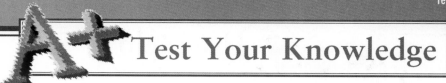

Test Your Knowledge

3 Identifying Objects on the Desktop

Instructions: On the desktop in Figure 1-66, arrows point to several items or objects on the desktop. Identify the items or objects in the spaces provided.

FIGURE 1-66

4 Saving a Document

Instructions: List the steps in the spaces provided to save a new Notepad file on a floppy disk in drive A using the filename, This is my file.

Step 1: _____

Step 2: _____

Step 3: _____

Step 4: _____

Step 5: _____

Step 6: _____

Step 7: _____

Use Help

1 Using Windows Help

Instructions: Use Windows Help and a computer to perform the following tasks.

Part 1: *Using the Question Mark Button*

1. Start Microsoft Windows 95 if necessary.
2. Click the Start button. Click Help on the Start menu to open the Help Topics: Windows Help window. If the Contents tab sheet does not display, click the Contents tab.
3. Click the Question Mark button on the title bar. The mouse pointer changes to a block arrow with question mark pointer. Click the list box containing the Help topics and Help books. A pop-up window explaining the list box displays. Click an open area of the list box to remove the pop-up window.
4. Click the Question Mark button on the title bar and then click the Display button.
5. Click the Question Mark button on the title bar and then click the Print button.
6. Click the Question Mark button on the title bar and then click the Cancel button.
7. Click an open area of the list box to remove the pop-up window.

Part 2: *Finding What's New with Windows 95*

1. Double-click the Introducing Windows book to open the book. Double-click the Welcome book to open the book. Double-click the A List of What's New book to open the book. Double-click the A new look and feel Help topic to open the Windows Help window. Click the first button (Start button and taskbar) and read the contents of the What's New window.
2. Click the Close button in the What's New window.
3. Click the Help Topics button in the Windows Help window to open the Help Topics: Windows Help window. Click the Print button in the Help Topics: Windows Help window. Click the OK button in the Print dialog box to print the Help topic (A new look and feel).
4. Click the Help Topics button in the Windows Help window.
5. Double-click the Welcome book to close the book.

Part 3: *Learning About Getting Your Work Done*

1. Double-click the Getting Your Work Done book to open the book. Double-click the Saving your work Help topic. Click the Save button and read the pop-up window.
2. Click other items in the Save As dialog box and read the pop-up windows.
3. Click the Help Topics button in the Windows Help window to open the Help Topics: Windows Help window. Click the Print button in the Help Topics: Windows Help window. Click the OK button in the Print dialog box to print the Saving your work Help topic.
4. Click the Close buttons in the Windows Help windows to close the windows.

? Use Help

2 Using Windows Help to Obtain Help

Instructions: Use Windows Help and a computer to perform the following tasks.

1. Find Help about viewing the Welcome screen that displays when you start Windows 95 by looking in the Tips of the Day book within the Tips and Tricks book in the Help Topics: Windows Help window. Answer the following questions in the spaces provided.
   a. How can you open the Welcome screen? _____
   b. How can you see the list of tips in the Welcome screen? _____
   c. Open the Welcome screen. Cycle through the tips in the Welcome screen. How can you set your computer's clock? _____
   d. Click the What's New button in the Welcome screen. According to Help, how do you start a program? _____
   e. Close the Welcome screen. Click the Help Topics button in the Windows Help window.

2. Find Help about keyboard shortcuts by looking in the Keyboard Shortcuts book. Answer the following questions in the spaces provided.
   a. What keyboard shortcut is used to quit a program? _____
   b. What keyboard shortcut is used to display the Start menu? _____
   c. What keyboard shortcut is used to view the shortcut menu for a selected item? _____
   d. What keyboard shortcut is used to rename an item? _____
   e. What keyboard shortcut is used to open the Save in list box (drop-down list box)? _____
   f. Click the Help Topics button in the Windows Help window.

3. Find Help about Notepad by looking in the For Writing and Drawing book. Answer the following questions in the spaces provided.
   a. Can you create or edit a text file that requires formatting using Notepad? _____
   b. What size file can you create using Notepad? _____
   c. Which program can you use to create a larger file? _____
   d. What is the only format used by Notepad to store a file? _____

4. Find Help about the Internet by looking in the Welcome to the Information Highway book. Answer the following questions in the spaces provided.
   a. List one source of online information available on the Internet. _____
   b. How do you use The Microsoft Network to sign up for the Internet?
   c. Where else can you find information about connecting to the Internet? _____

5. Find Help about what to do if you have a problem starting Windows 95. The process of solving such a problem is called troubleshooting. Answer the following questions in the spaces provided.
   a. What size floppy disk do you need to create a startup disk? _____
   b. To start Windows in safe mode, what do you do when you see the message "Starting Windows 95?" _____

6. Answer the following questions in the spaces provided.
   a. List two ways you can get Help in a dialog box: _____; _____.
   b. How can you print information displayed in a Help pop-up window?
   _____ *(continued)*

Use Help

Use Help *(continued)*

7. You have been assigned to obtain information on software licensing. Answer the following questions, and find and print information from Windows Help that supports your answers.
   a. How is computer software protected by law?
   b. What is software piracy? Why should you be concerned?
   c. Can you use your own software on both your desktop and your laptop computers?
   d. How can you identify illegal software?
8. Close all open Windows Help windows.

In the Lab

1 Improving Your Mouse Skills

Instructions: Use a computer to perform the following tasks:

1. Start Microsoft Windows 95 if necessary.
2. Click the Start button on the taskbar, point to Programs on the Start menu, point to Accessories on the Programs submenu, point to Games on the Accessories submenu, and click Solitaire on the Games submenu.
3. Click the Maximize button in the Solitaire window.
4. Click Help on the Solitaire menu bar.
5. Click Help Topics on the Help menu.
6. If the Contents sheet does not display, click the Contents tab.
7. Review the How to play Solitaire and Scoring information Help topics on the Contents sheet.
8. After reviewing the topics, close all Help windows.
9. Play the game of Solitaire.
10. Click the Close button on the Solitaire title bar to close the game.

2 Starting an Application, Creating a Document, and Modifying a Document

Instructions: Perform the following steps to start the Notepad application and create and modify a document.

Part 1: *Creating a Document*

1. Start Microsoft Windows 95 if necessary.
2. Click the Start button. Point to Programs on the Start menu. Point to Accessories on the Programs submenu. Click Notepad on the Accessories submenu.

In the Lab

3. Enter the document shown in Figure 1-67 in the Notepad document.

4. Insert a formatted floppy disk in drive A of your computer.

5. Click File on the menu bar. Click Save As on the File menu.

6. Type Office Supplies Shopping List - Tuesday in the File name text box.

```
Office Supplies Shopping List - Tuesday

1. Staples
2. 2 boxes of copier paper
3. Toner for computer printer
4. Box of formatted floppy disks
```

FIGURE 1-67

7. Click the Save in box arrow. Click the 3½ Floppy [A:] icon. Click the Save button.

8. Click File on the menu bar. Click Print on the File menu.

9. Click the Close button on the Notepad title bar.

10. If you are not completing Part 2 of this assignment, remove your floppy disk from drive A.

Part 2: *Modifying a Document*

1. Click the Start button, point to Programs on the Start menu, point to Accessories on the Programs submenu, and then click Notepad on the Accessories submenu.

2. Click File on the menu bar and then click Open on the File menu. Click the Look in box arrow and then click the 3½ Floppy [A:] icon. Click Office Supplies Shopping List - Tuesday. Click the Open button.

3. Press the DOWN ARROW key six times. Type 5. Two boxes of black ink pens and then press the ENTER key.

4. Click File on the menu bar and then click Save on the File menu.

5. Click File on the menu bar and then click Print on the File menu.

6. Click the Close button on the Notepad title bar.

7. Remove the floppy disk from drive A of your computer.

3 Creating a Document

Instructions: As a student, you would like to give a copy of your daily schedule to your parents and friends so you can be contacted in an emergency. To do this, you want to create a document for each weekday (Monday through Friday). Each document will have an appropriate title and contain your daily school and personal schedule. Each course in the document will contain the start and finish time for the course, course number, course title, room number, and instructor name. Other entries for extracurricular activities, sporting events, or personal events also will be included in the documents. Print the five documents on the printer and follow directions from your instructor for turning in this assignment. Store the five documents on a floppy disk.

Cases and Places

The difficulty of these case studies varies:

▶ Case studies preceded by a single half moon are the least difficult. You can complete these case studies using your own computer or a computer in the lab.

▶▶ Case studies preceded by two half moons are more difficult. You must research the topic presented using the Internet, a library, or another resource, and then prepare a brief written report.

▶▶▶ Case studies preceded by three half moons are the most difficult. You must visit a store or business to obtain the necessary information, and then use it to create a brief written report.

1 ▶ Your employer is concerned that some people in the company are not putting enough thought into software purchases. She has prepared a list of steps she would like everyone to follow when acquiring software (Figure 1-68).

You have been asked to use WordPad to prepare a copy of this list that can be posted in every department. Use the concepts and techniques presented in this project to start WordPad and create, save, and print the document. After you have printed one copy of the document, try experimenting with different WordPad features to make the list more eye-catching. If you like your changes, save and print a revised copy of the document. If WordPad is not available on your machine, use Notepad.

Steps in Software Acquisition

1. Summarize your requirements
2. Identify potential vendors
3. Evaluate alternative software packages
4. Make the purchase

FIGURE 1-68

2 ▶ The local community center has asked you to teach an introductory class on Windows 95 to a group of adults with little previous computer experience. The center director has sent you a note about one of his concerns (Figure 1-69).

Think of two topics about which people in the class may have questions.

Is online Help enough for this group?

These people are pretty traditional and are used to having a printed text. Do we need to buy some kind of "help resource book" for everyone? We don't have much money, but on the other hand we don't want people to be disappointed.

Please think about it and get back to me.

FIGURE 1-69

Use online Help to find answers to the questions. Consider how you would find answers to the same questions using a book. Write a response to the center director describing the advantages and disadvantages of using online Help instead of a book. Explain why you feel the class does or does not need a resource book. To make the director aware of online Help's limitations, tell how you think Microsoft could improve Help in Windows 95.

Cases and Places

3 ▶▶ Early personal computer operating systems were adequate, but they were not user-friendly and had few advanced features. Over the past several years, however, personal computer operating systems have become increasingly easy to use, and some now offer features once available only on mainframe computers. Using the Internet, a library, or other research facility, write a brief report on four personal computer operating systems. Describe the systems, pointing out their similarities and differences. Discuss the advantages and disadvantages of each. Finally, tell which operating system you would purchase for your personal computer and explain why.

4 ▶▶ Many feel that Windows 95 was one of the most heavily promoted products ever released. Using the Internet, current computer magazines, or other resources, prepare a brief report on the background of Windows 95. Explain why Windows 95 was two years behind schedule and how it was promoted. Discuss the ways in which Windows 95 is different from earlier versions of Windows (such as Windows 3.1). Based on reviews of the new operating system, describe what people like and do not like about Windows 95. Finally, from what you have learned and your own experience, explain how you think Windows 95 could be improved.

5 ▶▶▶ Software must be compatible with (able to work with) the operating system of the computer on which it will be used. Visit a software vendor and find the five application packages (word processing programs, spreadsheet programs, games, and so on) you would most like to have. List the names of the packages and the operating system used by each. Make a second list of five similar packages that are compatible (meaning they use the same operating system). Using your two lists, write a brief report on how the need to purchase compatible software can affect buying application packages and even the choice of an operating system.

6 ▶▶▶ Because of the many important tasks it performs, most businesses put a great deal of thought into choosing an operating system for their personal computers. Interview people at a local business on the operating system they use with their personal computers. Based on your interviews, write a brief report on why the business chose that operating system, how satisfied they are with it, and under what circumstances they might consider switching to a different operating system.

7 ▶▶▶ In a recent television commercial from Apple Computers, a frustrated father tries to use Windows 95 to display pictures of dinosaurs for his young son. After waiting impatiently, the boy tells his father he is going next door to the neighbor's because they have a Mac. Visit a computer vendor and try an operating system with a graphical user interface other than Windows 95, such as Macintosh System 7.5 or OS/2. Write a brief report comparing the operating system to Windows 95, and explain which operating system you would prefer to have on your personal computer.

Putting the Squeeze on DATA

In 1994, a federal district court ruled that Microsoft violated the rights of Stac Electronics in the data compression software component of MS-DOS 6.2, Microsoft's operating system. In response, Microsoft paid Stac a royalty of $43 million and replaced MS-DOS 6.2 with version 6.21, which did not contain the offending code.

Why the lawsuit? Data compression software, which allows you to store more data on your hard disk, is an important component of your computer's software and is so valuable to its developers that they will sue to protect their rights.

Disk storage capacity has not always been critical. Indeed, the first personal computers did not have disk storage. Instead, they used slow, unreliable tape cassettes. Then, in 1978, Apple demonstrated its first working prototype of the Apple

1978

320K

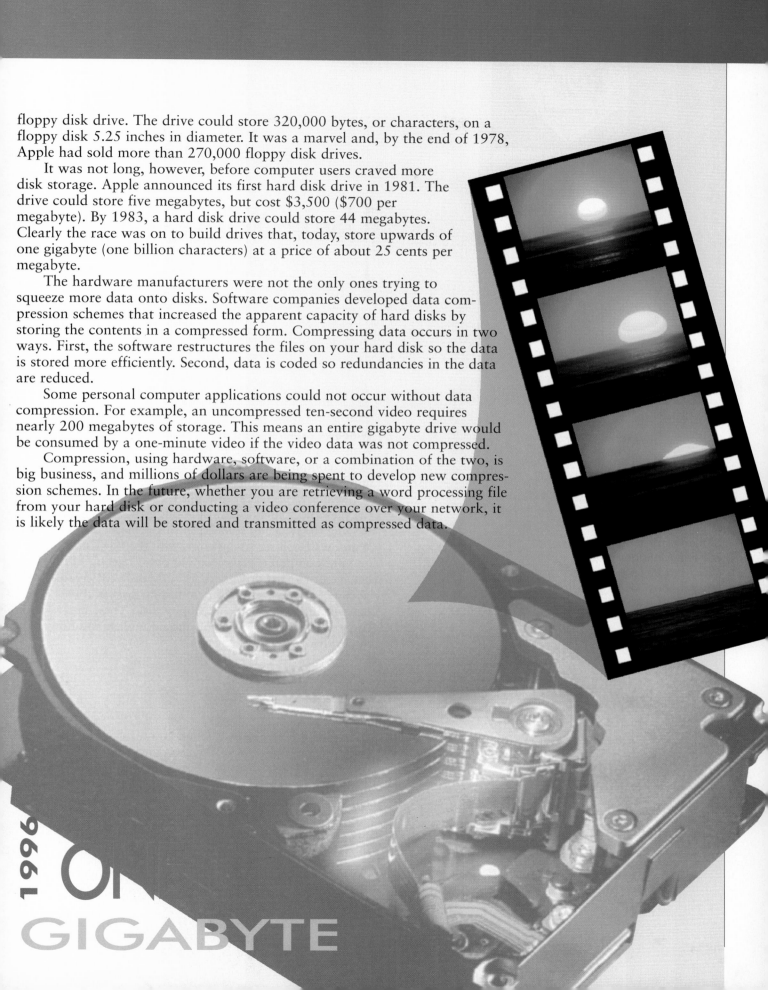

floppy disk drive. The drive could store 320,000 bytes, or characters, on a floppy disk 5.25 inches in diameter. It was a marvel and, by the end of 1978, Apple had sold more than 270,000 floppy disk drives.

It was not long, however, before computer users craved more disk storage. Apple announced its first hard disk drive in 1981. The drive could store five megabytes, but cost $3,500 ($700 per megabyte). By 1983, a hard disk drive could store 44 megabytes. Clearly the race was on to build drives that, today, store upwards of one gigabyte (one billion characters) at a price of about 25 cents per megabyte.

The hardware manufacturers were not the only ones trying to squeeze more data onto disks. Software companies developed data compression schemes that increased the apparent capacity of hard disks by storing the contents in a compressed form. Compressing data occurs in two ways. First, the software restructures the files on your hard disk so the data is stored more efficiently. Second, data is coded so redundancies in the data are reduced.

Some personal computer applications could not occur without data compression. For example, an uncompressed ten-second video requires nearly 200 megabytes of storage. This means an entire gigabyte drive would be consumed by a one-minute video if the video data was not compressed.

Compression, using hardware, software, or a combination of the two, is big business, and millions of dollars are being spent to develop new compression schemes. In the future, whether you are retrieving a word processing file from your hard disk or conducting a video conference over your network, it is likely the data will be stored and transmitted as compressed data.

1996

ONE

GIGABYTE

Microsoft
Windows 95

Using Windows Explorer

Case Perspective

Need: Your organization has finally made the decision to switch to Windows 95 from Windows 3.1. Although most everyone is excited about the change, many are apprehensive about file management. Few of them ever felt comfortable with Windows 3.1 File Manager and, as a result, hardly ever used it. Your boss has read in computer magazines that in order to effectively use Windows 95, people must learn Windows Explorer. She has asked you to teach a class with an emphasis on file management to all employees who will be using Windows 95. Your goal in Project 2 is to become competent using Windows Explorer so you can teach the class.

Introduction

Windows Explorer is an application program included with Windows 95 that allows you to view the contents of the computer, the hierarchy of folders on the computer, and the files and folders in each folder.

Windows Explorer also allows you to organize the files and folders on the computer by copying and moving the files and folders. In this project, you will use Windows Explorer to (1) work with the files and folders on your computer; (2) select and copy a group of files between the hard drive and a floppy disk; (3) create, rename, and delete a folder on floppy disk; and (4) rename and delete a file on floppy disk. These are common operations that you should understand how to perform.

Starting Windows 95

As explained in Project 1, when you turn on the computer, an introductory screen consisting of the Windows 95 logo and the Microsoft Windows 95 name displays on a blue sky and clouds background. The screen clears and Windows 95 displays several items on the desktop.

If the Welcome to Windows screen displays on your desktop, click the Close button on the title bar to close the screen. Six icons (My Computer, Network Neighborhood, Inbox, Recycle Bin, The Microsoft Network, and My Briefcase) display along the left edge of the desktop, the Microsoft Office Manager toolbar displays in the upper right corner of the desktop, and the taskbar displays along the bottom of the desktop (Figure 2-1).

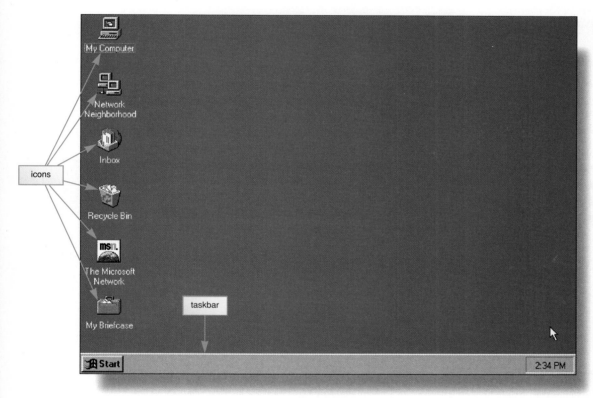

FIGURE 2-1

Starting Windows Explorer and Maximizing Its Window

To start Windows Explorer and explore the files and folders on the computer, right-click the My Computer icon on the desktop, which opens a context-sensitive menu, and then click the Explore command on the menu to open the Exploring – My Computer window. To maximize the Exploring – My Computer window, click the Maximize button on the title bar.

Steps To Start Windows Explorer and Maximize Its Window

1 **Right-click the My Computer icon to open a context-sensitive menu, and then point to the Explore command on the menu.**

Windows 95 highlights the My Computer icon, opens a context-sensitive menu, and highlights the Explore command on the menu (Figure 2-2). The mouse pointer points to the Explore command on the menu.

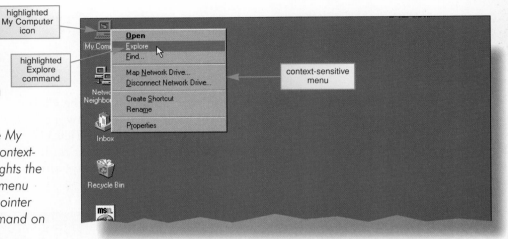

FIGURE 2-2

2 **Click Explore on the context-sensitive menu, and then click the Maximize button on the Exploring – My Computer title bar.**

Windows 95 opens and maximizes the Exploring – My Computer window and adds the indented Exploring – My Compu... button to the taskbar (Figure 2-3).

OtherWays

1. Right-click Start button, click Explore on context-sensitive menu
2. Click Start button, point to Programs, click Windows Explorer on the Programs submenu
3. Right-click Network Neighborhood icon, or Inbox icon, or Recycle Bin icon, or The Microsoft Network icon, or My Briefcase icon, click Explore on context-sensitive menu
4. Right-click Start button or any icons in 3 above, press E

FIGURE 2-3

Windows Explorer

When you start Windows Explorer by right-clicking the My Computer icon, Windows 95 opens the Exploring – My Computer window (Figure 2-4). The menu bar contains the File, Edit, View, Tools, and Help menu names.

These menus contain commands to organize and work with the drives on the computer and the files and folders on those drives.

Below the menu bar is a toolbar. The **toolbar** contains a drop-down list box and thirteen buttons. The drop-down list box contains an icon and the My Computer folder name. The entry in the drop-down list box, called the **current folder**, indicates Windows Explorer was started by right-clicking the My Computer icon. The buttons on the toolbar provide a quick way to perform commonly used tasks in Windows Explorer. Many of the buttons correspond to the commands available from the menu bar. Pointing to a button on the toolbar displays a ToolTip identifying the button. If the toolbar does not display in the Exploring – My Computer window on your computer, click View on the menu bar and then click Toolbar on the View menu.

The window is divided into two areas separated by a bar. The left side of the window, identified by the All Folders title, contains a **hierarchy** of folders on the computer. The right side of the window, identified by the Contents of 'My Computer' title, displays the contents of the current folder (My Computer). In Figure 2-4, the Contents side contains the icons and folder names of six folders (3½ Floppy [A:], Hard drive [C:], and [D:], Control Panel, Printers, and Dial-Up Networking). These folders may be different on your computer. You change the size of the All Folders and Contents sides of the window by dragging the bar that separates the two sides.

Each folder in the All Folders side of the window is represented by an icon and folder name. The first folder, consisting of an icon and the Desktop folder name, represents the desktop of the computer. The four folders indented and aligned below the Desktop folder name (My Computer, Network Neighborhood,

FIGURE 2-4

Recycle Bin, and My Briefcase) are connected to the vertical line below the Desktop icon. These folders correspond to four of the six icons displayed on the left edge of the desktop (see Figure 2-1 on page WIN 2.5). These folders may be different on your computer.

Windows 95 displays a minus sign (–) in a box to the left of any icon in the All Folders side to indicate the corresponding folder contains one or more folders that are visible in the All Folders side. These folders, called **subfolders**, are indented and aligned below the folder name.

In Figure 2-4 on the previous page, a minus sign precedes the My Computer icon, and six subfolders are indented and display below the My Computer folder name. The six subfolders (3½ Floppy [A:], Hard drive [C:], [D:], Control Panel, Printers, and Dial-Up Networking) correspond to the six folders in the Contents side. Clicking the minus sign, referred to as **collapsing the folder**, removes the indented subfolders from the hierarchy of folders in the All Folders side and changes the minus sign to a plus sign.

Windows 95 displays a plus sign (+) in a box to the left of an icon to indicate the corresponding folder consists of one or more subfolders that are not visible in the All Folders side of the window. In Figure 2-4, a plus sign precedes the first three icons indented and aligned below the My Computer name (3½ Floppy [A:], Hard drive [C:], [D:]) and the Network Neighborhood icon. Clicking the plus sign, referred to as **expanding the folders**, displays a list of indented subfolders and changes the plus sign to a minus sign.

If neither a plus sign nor a minus sign displays to the left of an icon, the folder does not contain subfolders. In Figure 2-4, the Control Panel, Printers, Dial-Up Networking, Recycle Bin, and My Briefcase icons are not preceded by a plus or minus sign and do not contain subfolders.

The status bar at the bottom of the Exploring – My Computer window indicates the number of folders, or objects, displayed in the Contents side of the window (6 object(s)). Depending upon the objects displayed in the Contents side, the amount of disk space the objects occupy and the amount of unused disk space may also display on the status bar. If the status bar does not display in the Exploring – My Computer window on your computer, click View on the menu bar and then click Status Bar on the View menu.

In addition to using Windows Explorer to explore your computer by right-clicking the My Computer icon, you can also use Windows Explorer to explore different aspects of your computer by right-clicking the Start button on the taskbar and the Network Neighborhood, Inbox, Recycle Bin, The Microsoft Network, and My Briefcase icons on the desktop.

Displaying the Contents of a Folder

In Figure 2-4 on the previous page, the current folder (My Computer) displays in the drop-down list box on the toolbar and the Contents side of the window contains the subfolders in the My Computer folder. In addition to displaying the contents of the My Computer folder, the contents of any folder in the All Folders side can be displayed in the Contents side. Perform the following steps to display the contents of the Hard drive [C:] folder.

Steps **To Display the Contents of a Folder**

1 **Point to the Hard drive [C:] folder name in the All Folders side of the Exploring – My Computer window (Figure 2-5).**

FIGURE 2-5

2 **Click the Hard drive [C:] folder name.**

Windows 95 highlights the Hard drive [C:] folder name in the All Folders side, changes the current folder in the drop-down list box to the Hard drive [C:] folder, displays the contents of the Hard drive [C:] folder in the Contents side, changes the window title to contain the current folder name (Exploring – Hard drive [C:]), changes the button on the taskbar to contain the current folder name, and changes the messages on the status bar (Figure 2-6). The status bar messages indicate there are 82 objects and 19 hidden objects in the Hard drive [C:] folder, the objects occupy 25.9MB of disk space, and the amount of unused disk space is 12.5MB. The contents of the Hard drive [C:] folder may be different on your computer.

FIGURE 2-6

▶*Other***Ways**

1. Double-click Hard disk [C:] icon in Contents side

2. Press TAB until any icon in All Folders side highlighted, press DOWN ARROW or UP ARROW until Hard disk [C:] highlighted in Contents side

In addition to displaying the contents of the Hard drive [C:] folder, you can display the contents of the other folders by clicking the corresponding icon or folder name in the All Folders side. The contents of the folder you click will then display in the Contents side of the window.

Expanding a Folder

Currently, the Hard drive [C:] folder is highlighted in the All Folders side of the Exploring – Hard drive [C:] window and the contents of the Hard drive [C:] folder display in the Contents side of the window. Windows 95 displays a plus sign (+) to the left of the Hard drive [C:] icon to indicate the folder contains subfolders that are not visible in the hierarchy of folders in the All Folders side of the window. To expand the Hard drive [C:] folder and display its subfolders, click the plus sign to the left of the Hard drive [C:] icon. Perform the following steps to expand the Hard drive [C:] folder.

Steps To Expand a Folder

1 Point to the plus sign to the left of the Hard drive [C:] icon in the All Folders side of the Exploring – Hard drive [C:] window (Figure 2-7).

mouse pointer points to plus sign

FIGURE 2-7

2 **Click the plus sign to display the subfolders in the Hard drive [C:] folder.**

Windows 95 replaces the plus sign preceding the Hard drive [C:] icon with a minus sign, displays a vertical scroll bar, and expands the Hard drive [C:] folder to include its subfolders, indented and aligned below the Hard drive [C:] folder name, (Figure 2-8). Each subfolder in the Hard drive [C:] folder is identified by a closed folder icon and folder name. The window title, current folder in the drop-down list box on the toolbar, and the files and folders in the Contents side of the window remain unchanged.

FIGURE 2-8

Collapsing a Folder

Currently, the subfolders in the Hard drive [C:] folder display indented and aligned below the Hard drive [C:] folder name (see Figure 2-8). Windows 95 displays a minus sign (–) to the left of the Hard drive [C:] icon to indicate the folder is expanded. To collapse the Hard drive [C:] folder and then remove its subfolders from the hierarchy of folders in the All Folders side, click the minus sign preceding the Hard drive [C:] icon. Perform the following steps to collapse the Hard drive [C:] folder.

 Steps **To Collapse a Folder**

1 **Point to the minus sign preceding the Hard drive [C:] icon in the All Folders side of the Exploring – Hard drive [C:] window (Figure 2-9).**

FIGURE 2-9

Other Ways

1. Double-click the folder icon
2. Select folder to expand, press PLUS on numeric keypad
3. Select folder to expand, press RIGHT ARROW

2 Click the minus sign to display the Hard drive [C:] folder without its subfolders.

Windows 95 replaces the minus sign preceding the Hard drive [C:] icon with a plus sign and removes the subfolders in the Hard drive [C:] folder from the hierarchy of folders (Figure 2-10).

plus sign replaces minus sign

subfolders do not display

FIGURE 2-10

Copying Files to a Folder on a Floppy Disk

One common operation that every student should understand how to perform is copying a file or group of files from one disk to another disk or from one folder to another folder. On the following pages, you will create a new folder, named My Files, on the floppy disk in drive A, select a group of files in the Windows folder on drive C, and copy the files from the Windows folder on drive C to the My Files folder on drive A.

When copying files, the drive and folder containing the files to be copied are called the **source drive** and **source folder**, respectively. The drive and folder to which the files are copied are called the **destination drive** and **destination folder**, respectively. Thus, the Windows folder is the source folder, drive C is the source drive, the My Files folder is the destination folder, and drive A is the destination drive.

Creating a New Folder

In preparation for selecting and copying files from a folder on the hard drive to a folder on the floppy disk in drive A, a new folder with the name of My Files will be created on the floppy disk. Perform the following steps to create the new folder.

Steps To Create a New Folder

1 Insert a formatted floppy disk into drive A on your computer.

2 Click the 3½ Floppy [A:] folder name in the All Folders side of the Exploring – Hard drive [C:] window and then point to an open area of the Contents side of the window.

Windows 95 highlights the 3½ Floppy [A:] folder name, changes the current folder to 3½ Floppy [A:], displays the contents of the 3½ Floppy [A:] folder in the Contents side, and changes the messages on the status bar (Figure 2-11). The window title, Contents side title, and button on the taskbar change to include the 3½ Floppy [A:] folder name. Currently, no files or folders display in the Contents side. The files and folders may be different on your computer. The mouse pointer points to an open area of the Contents side.

FIGURE 2-11

3 Right-click the open area of the Contents side of the window to open a context-sensitive menu and then point to New on the menu.

Windows 95 opens a context-sensitive menu and the New sub-menu, highlights the New command in the context-sensitive menu, and displays a message on the status bar (Figure 2-12). The message, Contains commands for creating new items., indicates the New submenu contains commands that allow you to create new items in the Contents side. The mouse pointer points to the New command. Although no subfolders display in the Contents side and no plus sign should precede the 3½ Floppy [A:] icon in the All Folders area, a plus sign precedes the icon.

FIGURE 2-12

4 **Point to Folder on the New submenu.**

Windows 95 highlights the Folder command on the New submenu and displays the message, Creates a new, empty folder., on the status bar (Figure 2-13). The mouse pointer points to the Folder command. Clicking the Folder command will create a folder in the Contents side of the window using the default folder name, New Folder.

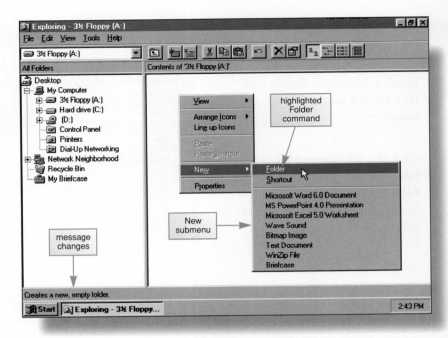

FIGURE 2-13

5 **Click Folder on the New submenu.**

Windows 95 closes the context-sensitive menu and New submenu, displays the highlighted New Folder icon in the Contents side, and changes the message on the status bar (Figure 2-14). The text box below the icon contains the highlighted default folder name, New Folder, followed by the insertion point. A plus sign continues to display to the left of the 3½ Floppy [A:] icon to indicate the 3½ Floppy [A:] folder contains the New Folder subfolder. The message on the status bar indicates one object is selected in the Contents side.

FIGURE 2-14

6 **Type** My Files **in the text box and then press the ENTER key.**

The new folder name, My Files, is entered and Windows 95 removes the text box (Figure 2-15).

plus sign

text box removed

folder name changed

FIGURE 2-15

*Other*Ways

1. Select drive, click File on the menu bar, on File menu click New, click Folder on New submenu

After creating the My Files folder on the floppy disk in drive A, you can save files in the folder or copy files from other folders to the folder. On the following pages, you will copy a group of files consisting of the Black Thatch, Bubbles, and Circles files from the Windows folder on drive C to the My Files folder on drive A.

Displaying the Destination Folder

To copy the three files from the Windows folder on drive C to the My Files folder on drive A, the files to be copied will be selected in the Contents side and right-dragged to the My Files folder in the All Folders side. Prior to selecting or right-dragging the files, the destination folder (My Files folder on drive A) must be visible in the All Folders side and the three files to be copied must be visible in the Contents side.

Currently, the plus sign (+) to the left of the 3½ Floppy [A:] icon indicates the folder contains one or more subfolders that are not visible in the All Folders side (see Figure 2-15). Perform the steps on the next page to expand the 3½ Floppy [A:] folder to display the My Files subfolder.

TO EXPAND THE 3½ FLOPPY [A:] FOLDER

Step 1: Point to the plus sign to the left of the 3½ Floppy [A:] icon in the All Folders side of the Exploring – 3½ Floppy [A:] window.

Step 2: Click the plus sign to display the subfolders in the 3½ Floppy [A:] folder.

Windows 95 replaces the plus sign preceding the 3½ Floppy [A:] folder with a minus sign, highlights the 3½ Floppy [A:] folder name, and displays the subfolders in the 3½ Floppy [A:] folder, indented and aligned below the 3½ Floppy [A:] folder name (Figure 2-16). Currently, only one subfolder (My Files) displays.

FIGURE 2-16

*Other*Ways

1. Right-click 3½ Floppy [A:] icon, click Explore

Displaying the Contents of the Windows Folder

Currently, the My Files folder displays in the Contents side of the Exploring – 3½ Floppy [A:] window. To copy files from the source folder (Windows folder on drive C) to the My Files folder, the Windows folder must be visible in the All Folders side. To make the Windows folder visible, you must expand the Hard drive [C:] folder, scroll the All Folders side to make the Windows folder name visible, and then click the Windows folder name to display the contents of the Windows folder in the Contents side. Perform the following steps to display the contents of the Windows folder.

Steps To Display the Contents of a Folder

1 **Click the plus sign to the left of the Hard drive [C:] icon in the All Folders side of the Exploring – 3½ Floppy [A:] window, scroll the All Folders side to make the Windows folder name visible, and then point to the Windows folder name.**

Windows 95 replaces the plus sign to the left of the Hard drive [C:] icon with a minus sign, displays the subfolders in the Hard drive [C:] folder, and scrolls the hierarchy of folders in the All Folders side to make the Windows folder visible (Figure 2-17). In addition to folders and other files, the Windows folder contains a series of predefined graphics, called **clip art files,** *that can be used with application programs. The mouse pointer points to the Windows folder name. The plus sign to the left of the Hard drive [C:] icon is not visible in Figure 2-17.*

FIGURE 2-17

2 **Click the Windows folder name to display the sub-folders in the Windows folder.**

Windows 95 highlights the Windows folder name in the All Folders side of the window, changes the closed folder icon to the left of the Windows folder name to an open folder icon, and displays the contents of the Windows folder in the Contents side (Figure 2-18).

FIGURE 2-18

3 Scroll the Contents side to make the files in the Windows folder visible.

One folder (Wordview folder) and several files display in the Contents side of the window (Figure 2-19). Each file is identified by a large icon and a filename. The files and folders in the Windows folder may be different and the file extensions may not display on your computer.

FIGURE 2-19

Changing the View

In Figure 2-19, the files and folder in the Contents side of the Exploring – Windows window display in large icons view. In **large icons view**, each file and folder is represented by a large icon and a filename or folder name. Other views include the small icons, list, and details views. The list view is often useful when copying or moving files from one location to another location. In **list view**, each file or folder is represented by a smaller icon and name, and the files and folders are arranged in columns. Perform the following steps to change from large icons view to list view.

Steps **To Change to List View**

1 **Right-click any open area in the Contents side of the Exploring – Windows window to open a context-sensitive menu, point to View on the context-sensitive menu, and then point to List on the View submenu.**

Windows 95 opens a context-sensitive menu, highlights the View command on the context-sensitive menu, opens the View submenu, and highlights the List command on the View submenu (Figure 2-20). A large dot to the left of the Large Icons command on the View submenu indicates files and folders in the Contents side display in large icons view. The mouse pointer points to the List command. Clicking the List command will display the files and folders in the Contents side in list view.

FIGURE 2-20

2 **Click List on the View submenu.**

Windows 95 displays the files and folders in the Contents side of the window in list view, indents the List button on the toolbar, and returns the Large Icons button to normal (Figure 2-21).

FIGURE 2-21

> **Other Ways**
> 1. On View menu click List
> 2. Click List button on toolbar
> 3. Press ALT+V, press L

Selecting a Group of Files

You can easily copy a single file or group of files from one folder to another folder using Windows Explorer. To copy a single file, select the file in the Contents side of the window and right-drag the highlighted file to the folder in the All Folders side where the file is to be copied. Group files are copied in a similar fashion. Select the first file in a group of files by clicking its icon or filename. You select the remaining files in the group by pointing to each file icon or filename, holding down the CTRL key, and clicking the file icon or filename. Perform the following steps to select the group of files consisting of the Black Thatch.bmp, Bubbles.bmp, and Circles.bmp files.

Steps   To Select a Group of Files

1 **Select the Black Thatch.bmp file by clicking the Black Thatch.bmp filename, and then point to the Bubbles.bmp filename.**

Windows highlights the Black Thatch.bmp file in the Contents side and displays two messages on the status bar (Figure 2-22). The messages indicate that one file is selected (1 object(s) selected) and the size of the file (182 bytes). The mouse pointer points to the Bubbles.bmp filename.

FIGURE 2-22

2 Hold down the CTRL key, click the Bubbles.bmp filename, release the CTRL key, and then point to the Circles.bmp filename.

The Black Thatch.bmp and Bubbles.bmp files are highlighted, and the two messages on the status bar change to reflect the additional file selected (Figure 2-23). The messages indicate that two files are selected (2 object(s) selected) and the size of the two files (2.24KB). The mouse pointer points to the Circles.bmp filename.

FIGURE 2-23

3 Hold down the CTRL key, click the Circles.bmp filename, and then release the CTRL key.

The group of files consisting of the Black Thatch.bmp, Bubbles.bmp, and Circles.bmp files is highlighted, and the messages on the status bar change to reflect the selection of a third file (Figure 2-24). The messages indicate that three files are selected (3 object(s) selected) and the size of the three files (2.43KB).

FIGURE 2-24

*Other***Ways**

1. Use arrow keys to select first file, hold down SHIFT key to move to next file, press SPACEBAR
2. To select contiguous files, select first filename, hold down SHIFT key, click last filename
3. To select all files, click Edit on menu bar, click Select All

Copying a Group of Files

After selecting a group of files, copy the files to the My Files folder on drive A by pointing to any highlighted filename in the Contents side, and right-dragging the filename to the My Files folder in the All Folders side. Perform the following steps to copy a group of files.

Steps To Copy a Group of Files

1 Scroll the All Folders side of the Exploring – Windows window to make the My Files folder visible and then point to the highlighted Black Thatch.bmp filename in the Contents side.

Windows 95 scrolls the All Folders side to make the My Files folder visible (Figure 2-25). The mouse pointer points to the high-lighted Black Thatch.bmp filename in the Contents side.

FIGURE 2-25

2 Right-drag the Black Thatch.bmp file over the My Files folder name in the All Folders side of the Exploring – Windows window.

As you drag the file, Windows 95 displays an outline of an icon and a horizontal line of one or more of the three files being copied and highlights the My Files folder name (Figure 2-26). The mouse pointer contains a plus sign to indicate the group of files is being copied, not moved.

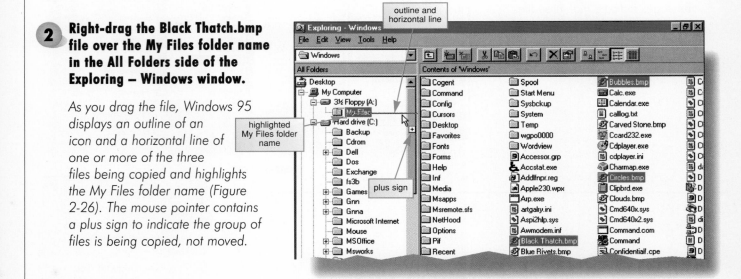

3 **Release the right mouse button to open a context-sensitive menu, and then point to the Copy Here command on the menu.**

Windows 95 opens a context-sensitive menu and highlights the Copy Here command on the menu (Figure 2-27). The mouse pointer points to the Copy Here command. Clicking the Copy Here command will copy the three files to the My Files folder.

FIGURE 2-27

4 **Click Copy Here on the context-sensitive menu.**

Windows 95 opens the Copying dialog box, and the dialog box remains on the screen while Windows 95 copies each file to the My Files folder (Figure 2-28). The Copying dialog box shown in Figure 2-28 indicates the Black Thatch.bmp file is currently being copied.

FIGURE 2-28

*Other*Ways

1. Right-drag file to copy from Contents side to folder icon in All Folders side, click Copy on context-sensitive menu
2. Select file to copy in Contents side, click Edit on menu bar, click Copy on Edit menu, select folder icon to receive copy, click Edit on menu bar, click Paste on Edit menu

Displaying the Contents of the My Files Folder

After copying a group of files, you should verify that the files were copied into the correct folder. To view the files that were copied to the My Files folder, click the My Files folder name in the All Folders side.

More *About* **Copying and Moving**

"Copying, moving, it's all the same to me," you might be tempted to say. They're not the same at all! When you copy a file, it will be located at two different places - the place it was copied to and the place it was copied from. When a file is moved, it will be located at only one place - where it was moved to. Many users have been sorry they did not distinguish the difference when a file they thought they had copied was moved instead.

FIGURE 2-29

TO DISPLAY THE CONTENTS OF A FOLDER

Step 1: Point to the My Files folder name in the All Folders side of the Exploring – Windows window.

Step 2: Click the My Files folder name in the All Folders side.

Windows 95 highlights the My Files folder name in the All Folders side, replaces the closed folder icon to the left of the My Files folder name with an open folder icon, displays the contents of the My Files folder in the Contents side, and changes the message on the status bar (Figure 2-29). The status bar message indicates 1.38MB of free disk space on the disk in drive A.

More *About*
Renaming a File or Folder

A file or folder name can contain up to 255 characters, including spaces. But, they cannot contain any of the following characters: \ / : * ? " < > | .

Renaming a File or Folder

Sometimes, you may want to rename a file or folder on disk. You change the filename by clicking the filename twice, typing the new filename, and pressing the ENTER key. Perform the following steps to change the name of the Circles.bmp file on drive A to Blue Circles.bmp.

Steps **To Rename a File**

1 **Point to the Circles.bmp filename in the Contents side.**

The mouse pointer points to the Circles.bmp filename (Figure 2-30).

FIGURE 2-30

2 **Click the Circles.bmp filename twice (do not double-click the filename).**

Windows 95 displays a text box containing the highlighted Circles.bmp filename and insertion point (Figure 2-31).

FIGURE 2-31

3 **Type** Blue Circles.bmp **and then press the ENTER key.**

Windows 95 changes the filename to Blue Circles.bmp and removes the box surrounding the filename (Figure 2-32).

FIGURE 2-32

To change a folder name, click the folder name twice, type the new folder name, and press the ENTER key. Perform the steps below and on the next page to change the name of the My Files folder to Clip Art Files.

Steps **To Rename a Folder**

1 **Point to the My Files folder name in the All Folders side of the Exploring – My Files window.**

The mouse pointer points to the My Files folder name (Figure 2-33).

FIGURE 2-33

*Other***Ways**

1. Right-click filename in Contents side, click Rename on context-sensitive menu, type name, press ENTER
2. Select filename in Contents side, click File on menu bar, click Rename on File menu, type name, press ENTER

2 **Click the My Files folder name twice (do not double-click the folder name).**

Windows 95 displays a text box containing the highlighted My Files name and insertion point (Figure 2-34).

FIGURE 2-34

3 **Type** Clip Art Files **and then press the ENTER key.**

Windows 95 changes the folder name to Clip Art Files and removes the box surrounding the folder name (Figure 2-35). The new folder name replaces the old folder name in the window title, drop-down list box, Contents side title, and button on the taskbar.

FIGURE 2-35

*Other*Ways

1. Click folder name, press F2, type new name, press ENTER
2. Click folder name, click File on menu bar, click Rename, type new name, press ENTER

Deleting a File or Folder

When you no longer need a file or folder, you can delete it. Two methods are commonly used to delete a file or folder. One method uses the Delete command on the context-sensitive menu that opens when you right-click the filename or folder name. Another method involves right-dragging the unneeded file or folder to the **Recycle Bin**. The Recycle Bin icon is located at the left edge of the desktop (see Figure 2-1 on page WIN 2.5).

When you delete a file or folder on the hard drive using the Recycle Bin, Windows 95 stores the deleted file or folder temporarily in the Recycle Bin until you permanently discard the contents of the Recycle Bin by emptying the Recycle Bin. Until the Recycle Bin is emptied, you can retrieve the files and folders you deleted in error. Unlike deleting files or folders on the hard drive, when you delete a file or folder located on a floppy disk, the file or folder is deleted immediately and not stored in the Recycle Bin.

On the following pages, you will delete the Bubbles.bmp and Black Thatch.bmp files. The Bubbles.bmp file will be deleted by right-clicking the Bubbles.bmp filename and then clicking the Delete command on a context-sensitive menu. Next, the Black Thatch.bmp file will be deleted by dragging the Black Thatch.bmp file to the Recycle Bin.

Deleting a File by Right-Clicking Its Filename

To delete a file using the Delete command on a context-sensitive menu, right-click the filename in the Contents side to open a context-sensitive menu and then click the Delete command on the menu. To illustrate how to delete a file by right-clicking, perform the steps below and on the next page to delete the Bubbles.bmp file.

> **More** *About*
> **Deleting Files**
>
> A few years ago, someone proposed that the Delete command be removed from operating systems. It seems an entire database was deleted by an employee who thought he knew what he was doing, resulting in a company that could not function for more than a week while the database was rebuilt. Millions of dollars in revenue were lost. The Delete command is still around, but it should be considered a dangerous weapon.

 Steps To Delete a File by Right-Clicking

1 Right-click the Bubbles.bmp filename in the Contents side of the Exploring – Clip Art Files window and then point to the Delete command on the context-sensitive menu.

Windows 95 opens a context-sensitive menu and highlights the Bubbles.bmp filename (Figure 2-36). The mouse pointer points to the Delete command on the menu.

FIGURE 2-36

2 Click Delete on the context-sensitive menu. When the Confirm File Delete dialog box opens, point to the Yes button.

Windows 95 opens the Deleting dialog box and then opens a Confirm File Delete dialog box on top of the Deleting dialog box (Figure 2-37). The Confirm File Delete dialog box contains the message, Are you sure you want to delete 'Bubbles.bmp'?, and the Yes and No command buttons. The mouse pointer points to the Yes button. Clicking the Yes button confirms the deletion of the Bubbles.bmp file and causes the file to be deleted.

FIGURE 2-37

3 Click the Yes button in the Confirm File Delete dialog box.

Windows 95 closes the Confirm File Delete dialog box, displays the Deleting dialog box while the file is being deleted, and then removes the Bubbles.bmp file from the Contents side (Figure 2-38).

FIGURE 2-38

OtherWays

1. Click filename, press DELETE

More *About* Deleting Files

Warning! This is your last warning! Be EXTREMELY careful when deleting files. Hours and weeks of hard work can be lost with one click of a button. If you are going to delete files or folders from your hard disk, consider making a backup of those files so that if you inadvertently delete something you need, you will be able to recover.

Deleting a File by Right-Dragging Its Filename

Another method to delete a file is to right-drag the filename from the Contents side of the window to the Recycle Bin icon on the desktop to open a context-sensitive menu, and then click the Move Here command on the context-sensitive menu. Currently, the Exploring – Clip Art Files window is maximized and occupies the entire desktop. With a maximized window, you cannot right-drag a file to the Recycle Bin. To allow you to right-drag a file, restore the Exploring – Clip Art Files window to its original size by clicking the Restore button on the title bar. Perform the following steps to delete the Black Thatch.bmp file by right-dragging its filename.

Steps **To Delete a File by Right-Dragging**

1 **Click the Restore button on the Exploring – Clip Art Files window title bar and then point to the Black Thatch.bmp filename in the Contents side of the window.**

Windows 95 restores the Exploring – Clip Art Files window to its original size before maximizing the window and replaces the Restore button on the title bar with the Maximize button (Figure 2-39). The mouse pointer points to the Black Thatch.bmp filename in the Contents side of the window.

FIGURE 2-39

2 **Right-drag the Black Thatch.bmp filename over the Recycle Bin icon, and then point to the Move Here command on the context-sensitive menu.**

Windows 95 opens a context-sensitive menu and highlights the Move Here command on the menu (Figure 2-40). The Black Thatch.bmp filename displays on top of the Recycle Bin icon on the desktop and the mouse pointer points to the Move Here command on the menu.

FIGURE 2-40

3 **Click Move Here on the context-sensitive menu. When the Confirm File Delete dialog box opens, point to the Yes button.**

Windows 95 opens the Deleting dialog box and then opens the Confirm File Delete dialog box on top of the Deleting dialog box (Figure 2-41). The Confirm File Delete dialog box contains the message, Are you sure you want to delete 'Black Thatch.bmp'?, and the Yes and No command buttons. The mouse pointer points to the Yes button. Clicking the Yes button confirms the deletion of the Black Thatch.bmp file and causes the file to be deleted.

FIGURE 2-41

4 **Click the Yes button in the Confirm File Delete dialog box.**

Windows 95 closes the Confirm File Delete dialog box, displays the Deleting dialog box while the file is being deleted, and then removes the Black Thatch.bmp file from the Contents side (Figure 2-42).

FIGURE 2-42

More *About* **the Recycle Bin**

Once you delete a file or folder, it's gone forever – True or False? Windows stores deleted files and folders in the Recycle Bin. You can recover files or folders you delete in error using the Recycle Bin.

Whether you delete a file by right-clicking or right-dragging, you can use the file selection techniques illustrated earlier in this project to delete a group of files. When deleting a group of files, click the Yes button in the Confirm Multiple File Delete dialog box to confirm the deletion of the group of files.

Deleting a Folder

When you delete a folder, Windows 95 deletes any files or subfolders in the folder. You can delete a folder using the two methods shown earlier to delete files (right-clicking or right-dragging). Perform the steps below and on the next page to delete the Clip Art Files folder on drive A by right-dragging the folder to the Recycle Bin.

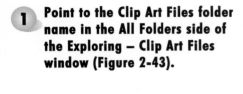

To Delete a Folder

More *About*
Deleting Folders

If you drag a folder to the Recycle Bin, only the files in that folder appear in the Recycle Bin. If you restore a file that was originally located in a deleted folder, Windows recreates the folder, and then restores the file to it.

1 Point to the Clip Art Files folder name in the All Folders side of the Exploring – Clip Art Files window (Figure 2-43).

FIGURE 2-43

2 Right-drag the Clip Art Files icon in the All Folders side to the Recycle Bin icon, and then point to the Move Here command on the context-sensitive menu.

Windows 95 opens a context-sensitive menu (Figure 2-44). The mouse pointer points to the highlighted Move Here command on the menu.

FIGURE 2-44

3 Click Move Here on the context-sensitive menu. When the Confirm Folder Delete dialog box opens, point to the Yes button.

Windows 95 opens the Deleting dialog box and then opens the Confirm Folder Delete dialog box on top of the Deleting dialog box (Figure 2-45). The Confirm Folder Delete dialog box contains the message, Are you sure you want to remove the folder 'Clip Art Files' and all its contents?, and the Yes and No command buttons. The mouse pointer points to the Yes button. Clicking the Yes button confirms the deletion of the Clip Art Files folder and causes the folder and its contents to be deleted.

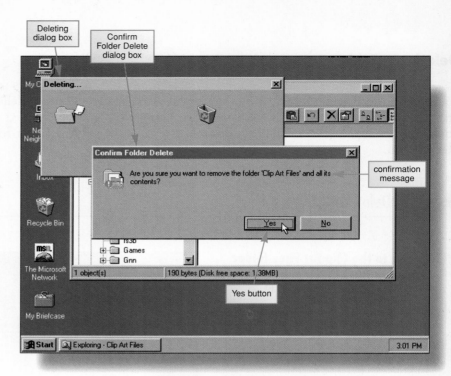

FIGURE 2-45

4 Click the Yes button in the Confirm Folder Delete dialog box.

Windows 95 closes the Confirm Folder Delete dialog box, displays the Deleting dialog box while the folder is being deleted, removes the Clip Art Files folder from the All Folders side, and replaces the minus sign preceding the 3½ Floppy [A:] icon with a plus sign (Figure 2-46).

5 Remove the floppy disk from drive A.

FIGURE 2-46

OtherWays
1. Click folder name, press DELETE

Quitting Windows Explorer and Shutting Down Windows 95

After completing work with Windows Explorer, quit Windows Explorer using the Close button on the Windows Explorer title bar, and then shut down Windows using the Shut Down command on the Start menu.

Perform the following steps to quit Windows Explorer.

TO QUIT AN APPLICATION

Step 1: Point to the Close button in the Exploring window.
Step 2: Click the Close button.

Windows 95 closes the Windows Explorer window and quits Windows Explorer.

Perform the following steps to shut down Windows 95.

TO SHUT DOWN WINDOWS 95

Step 1: Click the Start button on the taskbar.
Step 2: Click Shut Down on the Start menu.
Step 3: Click the Yes button in the Shut Down Windows dialog box.
Step 4: Turn off the computer.

Project Summary

In this project, you used Windows Explorer to select and copy a group of files, change views, display the contents of a folder, create a folder, expand and collapse a folder and rename and delete a file and a folder.

What You Should Know

Having completed this project, you should now be able to perform the following tasks:

- Change to List View *(WIN 2.19)*
- Collapse a Folder *(WIN 2.11)*
- Copy a Group of Files *(WIN 2.22)*
- Create a New Folder *(WIN 2.13)*
- Delete a File by Right-Clicking *(WIN 2.27)*
- Delete a File by Right-Dragging *(WIN 2.29)*
- Delete a Folder *(WIN 2.31)*
- Display the Contents of a Folder *(WIN 2.9, WIN 2.17, WIN 2.24)*
- Expand a Folder *(WIN 2.10)*
- Expand the 3½ Floppy [A:] Folder *(WIN 2.16)*
- Quit an Application *(WIN 2.33)*
- Rename a File *(WIN 2.24)*
- Rename a Folder *(WIN 2.25)*
- Select a Group of Files *(WIN 2.20)*
- Shut Down Windows 95 *(WIN 2.33)*
- Start Windows Explorer and Maximize Its Window *(WIN 2.6)*

Test Your Knowledge

1 True/False

Instructions: Circle T if the statement is true or F if the statement is false.

T F   1. Windows Explorer is an application you can use to organize and work with the files and folders on the computer.

T F   2. Double-clicking the My Computer icon is the best way to open Windows Explorer.

T F   3. The contents of the current folder are displayed in the All Folders side.

T F   4. To display the contents of drive C on your computer in the Contents side, click the plus sign in the small box next to the drive C icon.

T F   5. A folder that is contained within another folder is called a subfolder.

T F   6. To display the contents of a folder, right-click its folder name.

T F   7. Collapsing a folder removes the subfolders from the hierarchy of folders in the All Folders side.

T F   8. After you expand a drive or folder, the information in the Contents side is always the same as the information displayed below the drive or folder icon in the All Folders side.

T F   9. The source folder is the folder containing the files to be copied.

T F 10. You select a group of files in the Contents side by pointing to each icon or filename and clicking the left mouse button.

2 Multiple Choice

Instructions: Circle the correct response.

1. The drop-down list box in the Exploring - My Computer window contains the _____.
   a. hierarchy of folders
   b. source folder
   c. files in the current folder
   d. current folder

2. The _____ contains the hierarchy of folders on the computer.
   a. Contents side
   b. status bar
   c. All Folders side
   d. toolbar

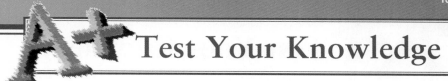

Test Your Knowledge

3. To display the contents of a folder in the Contents side, _____.
   a. double-click the plus sign next to the folder icon
   b. right-click the folder icon in the All Folders side
   c. click the folder icon in the Contents side
   d. click the folder icon in the All Folders side
4. You _____ the minus sign preceding a folder icon to expand a folder.
   a. click
   b. drag
   c. double-click
   d. point to
5. When an expanded file is collapsed in the All Folders side, _____.
   a. the expansion closes and the contents of the folder display in the Contents side
   b. the entire Exploring - My Computer window closes
   c. the computer beeps at you because you cannot perform this activity
   d. the My Computer window opens
6. To select multiple files in the Contents side, _____.
   a. right-click each file icon
   b. hold down the SHIFT key and then click each file icon you want to select
   c. hold down the CTRL key and then click each file icon you want to select
   d. hold down the CTRL key and then double-click each file icon you want to select
7. After selecting a group of files, you _____ the group to copy the files to a new folder.
   a. click
   b. right-drag
   c. double-click
   d. none of the above
8. In _____ view, each file or folder in the Contents side is represented by a smaller icon, and the files or folders are arranged in columns.
   a. large icons
   b. small icons
   c. list
   d. details
9. A file or folder can be renamed by _____.
   a. right-dragging its filename
   b. double-clicking its filename
   c. dragging its filename
   d. clicking its filename twice

(continued)

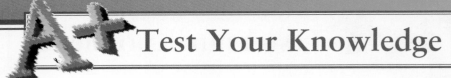

Test Your Knowledge

Multiple Choice *(continued)*

10. A file can be deleted by right-dragging the filename from the Contents side of the window to the
_____ icon on the desktop.
    a. My Computer
    b. Network Neighborhood
    c. Recycle Bin
    d. My Briefcase

3 Understanding the Exploring - My Computer Window

Instructions: In Figure 2-47 arrows point to several items in the Exploring - My Computer window. Identify the items or objects in the spaces provided.

FIGURE 2-47

Use Help

1 Using Windows Help

Instructions: Use Windows Help and a computer to perform the following tasks.

1. Start Microsoft Windows 95 if necessary.
2. Answer the following questions about paths.
   a. What is a path? _____
   b. What does a path include? _____
   c. How do you specify a path? _____
   d. What do you do if your filename contains more than eight characters? _____
3. Open the Help Topics: Windows Help window. Click the Index tab if necessary and then type windows explorer in the text box. Click demo in the Windows Explorer list and then click the Display button. In the Windows Help window, play the demonstration.
   a. How does the demonstration open Windows Explorer? _____
   b. What folders are contained on drive C in the demonstration? _____
4. How can you cause Explorer to start each time you start Windows 95? _____
5. You have recently written a business letter to a manager named Lori Hill. You explained CD-ROM drives to her. You want to see what else you said in the letter, but you can neither remember the name of the file nor where you stored the file on your computer. You read something in your Windows 95 manual that the Find command could be used to find lost files. Using Help, determine what you must do to find your letter. Write those steps in the spaces provided.

   _____
   _____
   _____

6. You and a friend both recently bought computers. She was lucky and received a color printer as her birthday gift. You would like to print some of your more colorful documents on her color printer. You have heard that for not too much money you can buy a network card and some cable and hook up your computers on a network. Then, you can print documents stored on your computer on her color printer. Using Windows Help, determine if you can share her printer. If so, what must you do in Windows 95 to make this become a reality. Print the Help pages that document your answer.
7. You can hardly believe that last week you won a laptop computer at a charity dance. The application programs on the laptop are the same as those on your desktop computer. The only trouble is that when you use your laptop computer to modify a file, you would like the same file on your desktop also to be modified. In that way, you can work on the file either on your desktop computer or on your laptop computer. A friend mentioned that the My Briefcase feature of Windows 95 allows you to do what you want to do. Using Windows Help, find out all you can about My Briefcase. Print the Help pages that specify how to keep files on both your desktop and laptop computers synchronized with each other.

In the Lab

1 File and Program Properties

Instructions: Use a computer to perform the following tasks and answer the questions.

1. Start Microsoft Windows 95 if necessary.
2. Open the My Computer window.
3. Open the drive C window on your computer.
4. Scroll until the Windows icon is visible in the drive C window.
5. Right-click the Windows icon.
6. Click Open on the context-sensitive menu.
7. Scroll until the Black Thatch icon is visible. If the Black Thatch icon does not display on your computer, find another Paint icon.
8. Right-click the Black Thatch icon.
9. Click Properties on the context-sensitive menu.
10. Answer the following questions about the Black Thatch file:
    a. What type of file is Black Thatch? _____
    b. What is the path for the location of the Black Thatch file? (Hint: Point to the location of the file) _____
    c. What is the size (in bytes) of the Black Thatch file? _____
    d. What is the MS-DOS name of the Black Thatch file? _____ The tilde (~) character is placed in the MS-DOS filename when the Windows 95 filename is greater than 8 characters. Windows 95 uses the first six characters of the long filename, the tilde character, and a number to distinguish the file from other files that might have the same first six characters.
    e. When was the file created? _____
    f. When was the file last modified? _____
    g. When was the file last accessed ? _____
11. Click the Cancel button in the Black Thatch Properties dialog box.
12. Scroll in the Windows window until the Notepad icon displays.
13. Right-click the Notepad icon.
14. Click Properties on the context-sensitive menu.
15. Answer the following questions:
    a. What type of file is Notepad? _____
    b. What is the path of the Notepad file? _____
    c. How big is the Notepad file? _____
    d. What is the file extension of the Notepad file? What does it stand for? _____
    e. What is the file version of the Notepad file? _____
    f. What is the file's description? _____
    g. Who is the copyright owner of Notepad? _____
    h. What language is Notepad written for? _____
16. Click the Cancel button in the Notepad Properties dialog box.
17. Close all open windows.

In the Lab

2 Windows Explorer

Instructions: Use a computer to perform the following tasks:

1. Start Microsoft Windows 95.
2. Right-click the My Computer icon.
3. Click Explore on the context-sensitive menu.
4. Maximize the Exploring window.
5. Drag the bar between the All Folders side and the Contents side to the center of the Exploring window. What difference do you see in the Window? _____
   _____
6. Return the bar to its previous location.
7. Click Tools on the menu bar.
8. Click Go to on the Tools menu.
9. Type c:\windows and then click the OK button in the Go To Folder dialog box. What happened in the Exploring window? _____
10. Click View on the menu bar and then click Small Icons on the View menu.
11. Click View on the menu bar and then click Options on the View menu.
12. Drag the Options dialog box so you can see the Contents side of the Exploring window. Click Show all files. Click the Apply button. Do any more folders display? If so, what new folders display? Did more files display?
    _____
    _____
13. Click Hide files of these types. Click Hide MS-DOS file extensions for file types that are registered. Click the Apply button. Did the filenames displayed in the Contents area change? If so, what are the changes? Give three examples of filenames that are different:
    _____
    _____
14. Click Hide MS-DOS file extensions for file types that are registered. Click Hide files of these types. Click the OK button.
15. Click View on the menu bar and then click Details on the View menu.
    a. In the Contents side, scroll until you see only file icons and then click the Name button below the Contents of 'Windows' bar. Did the sequence of file icons change? How?
       _____
    b. Click the Size button. How did the sequence of file icons change? _____
    c. Click the Type button. How did the sequence of file icons change? _____
    d. Click the Modified button. How did the sequence of folder and file icons change?
       _____
    e. Click the Name button.

(continued)

In the Lab

Windows Explorer *(continued)*

16. Click Edit on the menu bar. Click Select All on the Edit menu. If the Select All dialog box displays, click the OK button. What happened? _____

17. Click Edit on the menu bar. Click Invert Selection on the Edit menu. Was there any change?
_____

18. Click File on the menu bar. Point to New on the File menu and then click Bitmap Image on the New submenu. What happened? _____

19. Type In the Lab Image and then press the ENTER key. What is the name of the bitmap image?
_____

20. Right-click the In the Lab Image icon. Click Delete on the context-sensitive menu. Click the Yes button in the Confirm File Delete dialog box.

21. Close the Exploring window.

3 Window Toolbars

Instructions: Use a computer to perform the following tasks:

1. Open the My Computer window.
2. Maximize the My Computer window.
3. Click View on the menu bar. Click Large icons on the View menu.
4. Click View on the menu bar. If a check does not display to the left of the Toolbar command, click Toolbar on the View menu. A toolbar displays in the My Computer window (Figure 2-48).
5. Click the down arrow next to the drop-down list box containing the My Computer icon and name.
6. Click the drive C icon in the drop-down list. How did the window change? _____
_____
7. Double-click the Windows icon. What happened? _____
_____
8. In the Windows window, if the toolbar does not display, click View on the menu bar and then click Toolbar on the View menu.
9. Scroll down if necessary until the Argyle icon displays in the window. If the Argyle icon does not display on your computer, find another Paint icon. Click the Argyle icon and then point to the Copy button on the toolbar (Hint: To determine the function of each button on the toolbar, point to the button).
10. Click the Copy button. Do you see any change? If so, what? _____

In the Lab

11. Insert a formatted floppy disk in drive A of your computer.
12. Click the down arrow next to the drop-down list box containing the Windows icon and name.
13. Click the 3½ Floppy [A:] icon in the drop-down list. What happened? _____
14. If the toolbar does not display in the 3½ Floppy [A:] window, click View on the menu bar and then click Toolbar on the View menu.
15. In the 3½ Floppy [A:] window, click the Paste button on the toolbar. The Argyle icon displays in the 3½ Floppy [A:] window.
16. With the Argyle icon highlighted in the 3½ Floppy [A:] window, click the Delete button on the toolbar and then click the Yes button in the Confirm File Delete dialog box.
17. In the 3½ Floppy [A:] window, return the toolbar status to what it was prior to step 8. Close the 3½ Floppy [A:] window.
18. In the drive C window, click the Small Icons button and then describe the screen. _____
_____
19. Click the List button and then describe the screen. _____
20. Click the Details button and then describe the screen. _____
21. Click the Large Icons button on the toolbar
22. Click the Up One Level button on the toolbar. What is the difference between clicking the Up One Level button and clicking My Computer in the drop-down list box? _____
23. Return the toolbar status to what it was prior to step 4. Close the My Computer and drive C windows.

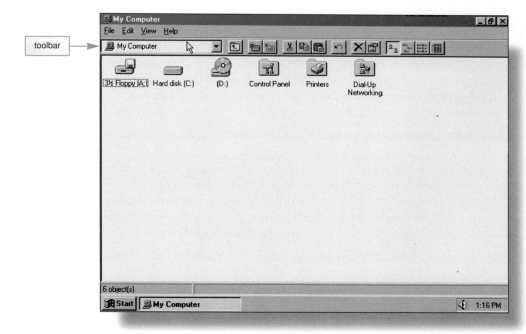

FIGURE 2-48

Cases and Places

The difficulty of these case studies varies:

▶ Case studies preceded by a single half moon are the least difficult. You can complete these case studies using your own computer in the lab.

▶▶ Case studies preceded by two half moons are more difficult. You must research the topic presented using the Internet, a library, or another resource, and then prepare a brief written report.

▶▶▶ Case studies preceded by three half moons are the most difficult. You must visit a store or business to obtain the necessary information, and then use it to create a brief written report.

1 ▶ A key feature of Windows 95 is the capability to modify the view of a window to suit individual preferences and needs. Using Windows Explorer, display the Hard drive [C:] folder in the Contents side and then experiment with the different commands on the View menu. Describe the effects of the Large Icons, Small Icons, List, and Details commands on the icons in the Contents side. When using details view, explain how clicking one of the buttons at the top of the Contents side (such as Name or Type) changes the window. Try out diverse arrangements of icons on the Contents side by pointing to the Arrange Icons command on the View menu and then clicking various commands on the Arrange Icons submenu. Finally, specify situations in which you think some of the views you have seen would be most appropriate.

2 ▶ When the Hard disk [C:] folder is displayed in the Contents side of the Exploring window, it is clear that an enormous number of folders and files are stored on your computer's hard disk. Imagine how hard it would be to manually search through all the folders and files to locate a specific file! Fortunately, Windows 95 provides the Find command to perform the search for you. Click Tools on the Exploring window menu bar, point to Find, and then click Files or Folders on the Find submenu. Learn about each sheet in the Find: All Files dialog box by clicking a tab (Name & Location, Date Modified, or Advanced), clicking the Help menu, clicking What's This? on the Help menu, and then clicking an item on a sheet. Try finding a file using each sheet. Finally, explain how the Find command is used and describe a circumstance in which each sheet would be useful. When you are finished, click the Close button on the window title bar to close the Find: All Files dialog box.

3 ▶▶ Backing up files is an important way to protect data and ensure it is not inadvertently lost or destroyed. File backup on a personal computer can use a variety of devices and techniques. Using the Internet, a library, personal computer magazines, or other resources, determine the types of devices used to store backed up data, the schedules, methods, and techniques for backing up data, and the consequences of not backing up data. Write a brief report of your findings.

Cases and Places

4 ▶▶ A hard disk must be maintained in order to be used most efficiently. This maintenance includes deleting old files, defragmenting a disk so it is not wasteful of space, and from time to time finding and attempting to correct disk failures. Using the Internet, a library, Windows 95 Help, or other research facilities, determine the maintenance that should be performed on hard disks, including the type of maintenance, when it should be performed, how long it takes to perform the maintenance, and the risks, if any, of not performing the maintenance. Write a brief report on the information you obtain.

5 ▶▶▶ The quest for more and faster disk storage continues as application programs grow larger and create sound and graphic files. One technique for increasing the amount of data that can be stored on a disk is disk compression. Disk compression programs, using a variety of mathematical algorithms, store data in less space on a hard disk. Many companies sell software you can load on your computer to perform the task. Windows 95 has disk compression capabilities as part of the operating system. Visit a computer store and find two disk compression programs you can buy. Write a brief report comparing the two packages to the disk compression capabilities of Windows 95. Discuss the similarities and differences between the programs and identify the program that claims to be the most efficient in compressing data.

6 ▶▶▶ Some individuals in the computer industry think both the Windows 3.1 and the Windows 95 operating systems are deficient when it comes to ease of file management. Therefore, they have developed and marketed software that augments the operating systems to provide different and, they claim, improved services for file management. Visit a computer store and inquire about products such as Symantec's Norton Navigator for Windows 95. Write a brief report comparing the products you tested with Windows 95. Explain which you prefer and why.

7 ▶▶▶ Data stored on disk is one of a company's more valuable assets. If that data were to be stolen, lost, or compromised so it could not be accessed, the company could literally go out of business. Therefore, companies go to great lengths to protect their data. Visit a company or business in your area. Find out how it protects its data against viruses, unauthorized access, and even against such natural disasters as fire and tornadoes. Prepare a brief report that describes the procedures. In your report, point out any areas where you see the company has not adequately protected its data.

Index

Accessories submenu, WIN 1.24-25, 1.32
Active window, WIN 1.12, 1.14
Application program, WIN 1.4, 1.5, 1.23-32,

Border, window, WIN 1.12
Button(s)
  command, WIN 1.6
  indented, WIN 1.10
  Windows Explorer toolbar, WIN 2.7
Button name, displaying entire, WIN 1.30

CD-ROM drive, WIN 1.12
Click, WIN 1.8-10, 1.20-21
Close button, WIN 1.16-17, 1.32
  Help and, WIN 1.42
  My Computer window, WIN 1.12
Closing
  application program, WIN 1.32
  menu, WIN 1.10
  My Computer window, WIN 1.16-17
  Notepad program, WIN 1.35-36
  Welcome screen, WIN 1.6, 1.7
  window, WIN 1.21
Collapsing the folder, WIN 2.8, 2.11-12
Command, WIN 1.9, 1.10
Command buttons, WIN 1.6
Context-sensitive menu, WIN 1.11
Control menu, My Computer window, WIN 1.12
Copy Here command, WIN 2.23
Copying
  group of files, WIN 2.22-23
  moving files versus, WIN 2.23
CTRL key, selecting group of files and, WIN 2.20-21
Current folder, WIN 2.7

Data compression, WIN 2.2-3
Deleting, WIN 2.26-32
Desktop, WIN 1.6, 1.7, 1.13
Destination folder, WIN 2.12, 2.15-16
Dialog box, WIN 1.27
Disk
  copying files to folder on, WIN 2.12-26
  modifying document stored on, WIN 1.32-36
  saving document on, WIN 1.26-30
  saving modified document on, WIN 1.35
Disk storage capacity, WIN 2.2-3
Document
  creating by starting application program, WIN 1.23-32
  modifying, WIN 1.32-36
  opening, WIN 1.32-34
  printing, WIN 1.30-31
  saving modified, WIN 1.35
  saving on disk, WIN 1.26-30
Double-click, WIN 1.11-12
Down scroll arrow, WIN 1.20
Drag, WIN 1.17-19
  copying group of files and, WIN 2.22
  scroll box and, WIN 1.21
  sizing window using, WIN 1.19
Drive, WIN 2.12

Edit menu, My Computer window, WIN 1.12
Ellipsis (...), command followed by, WIN 1.9
E-mail, WIN 1.6
ENTER key, blank line and, WIN 1.26
ESC key, closing Welcome screen using, WIN 1.7
Exit command, WIN 1.32
Expanding the folders, WIN 2.8, 2.10-11
Explore command, WIN 2.6
Explorer command, WIN 2.6
Exploring - My Computer window, WIN 2.5-6

F1 key (Help), WIN 1.23, 1.37
Faxes, electronic, WIN 1.6
File(s)
  clip art, WIN 2.17-23
  copying to folder on floppy disk, WIN 2.12-26

deleting, WIN 2.26-30
deleting group of, WIN 2.30
renaming, WIN 2.24-25
selecting group of, WIN 2.20-21
File menu, WIN 1.12
  Exit command, WIN 1.32
  Open command, WIN 1.33
  Print command, WIN 1.31
  Rename command, WIN 2.25
  Save As command, WIN 1.27
  Save command, WIN 1.30, 1.35
Filename
  changing, WIN 2.24-25
  saving document and, WIN 1.27
Floppy disk
  copying files to folder on, WIN 2.12-26
  saving document on, WIN 1.26-30
Floppy disk drive, WIN 1.12
Folder(s), WIN 1.12
  changing view, WIN 2.18-19
  collapsing, WIN 2.8, 2.11-12
  copying files to, on floppy disk, WIN 2.12-26
  creating new, WIN 2.12-15
  current, WIN 2.7
  deleting, WIN 2.31-32
  destination, WIN 2.12, 2.15-16
  displaying contents of, WIN 1.13, 2.8-10, 2.16-18, 2.23-24
  expanding, WIN 2.8, 2.10-11
  names of, WIN 1.34
  renaming, WIN 2.25-26
  saving file and, WIN 1.30
  selecting group of files in, WIN 2.20-21
  source, WIN 2.12

Gates, Bill, WIN 1.2-3
Graphical user interface (GUI), WIN 1.3, 1.6
Group of files, WIN 2.20-23, 2.30

Hard disk drive, WIN 1.12
Hardware, user interface, WIN 1.5
Help, WIN 1.36-42
Help command, WIN 1.36-37
Help menu, My Computer window, WIN 1.12
Help topics, WIN 1.37-40
Help Topics: Windows Help window, WIN 1.37
Hierarchy, WIN 2.7
Hourglass icon, WIN 1.30

IBM, history of operating system and, WIN 1.2-3
IBM 101-key keyboard, WIN 1.23
Icons, WIN 1.6
Inactive window, WIN 1.28
Insertion point, WIN 1.25

Keyboard, WIN 1.5, 1.23
Keyboard shortcuts, WIN 1.23
Kildall, Gary, WIN 1.2-3

Large icons view, WIN 2.18
Left mouse button, WIN 1.8
  continuous scrolling and, WIN 1.21
  dragging and, WIN 1.17-19
Line
  inserting blank, WIN 1.26
  scrolling by, WIN 1.21
List command, WIN 2.19
List view, changing to, WIN 2.18-19

Main memory, WIN 1.5
Maximize button
  My Computer window and, WIN 1.12, 1.14-15
  Windows Explorer window and, WIN 2.5-6
Menu, WIN 1.9, 1.10, 1.11
Menu bar, WIN 1.12
  My Computer window, WIN 1.12
  Windows Explorer, WIN 2.7

Microsoft
  data compression software and, WIN 2.2

history of operating system development, WIN 1.2-3
  usability labs and, WIN 1.6
Microsoft keyboard, WIN 1.23
Microsoft Network, The, WIN 1.6
Minimize button, My Computer window, WIN 1.12, 1.13
Monitor, WIN 1.5
Mouse, WIN 1.5, 1.8-12
Mouse button
  primary, WIN 1.8
  secondary, WIN 1.8, 1.10
Mouse pointer, WIN 1.6, 1.8
Move Here command
  files and, WIN 2.29-30
  window and, WIN 1.22
Moving object, by dragging, WIN 1.17-19
MS-DOS (Microsoft Disk Operating System), history of, WIN 1.3
My Computer icon, WIN 1.6
  double-clicking, WIN 1.12
  opening document from, WIN 1.34
  Windows Explorer and, WIN 2.5-6
My Computer window, WIN 1.12-21

New command, WIN 1.11, 2.13
New submenu, WIN 1.11
  Folder command, WIN 2.14
Notepad, WIN 1.24-32
Notepad command, WIN 1.25, 1.32-33
Notepad window, WIN 1.25, 1.33

Object, WIN 1.7
  folder, WIN 1.12
  moving by dragging, WIN 1.17-19
  opening, WIN 1.12
Object menu, WIN 1.11
Open button, WIN 1.34
Open command, WIN 1.33
Opening
  Notepad document, WIN 1.32-34
  object, WIN 1.12
Operating systems, WIN 1.2-3, 1.4

PC-DOS, WIN 1.3
Point, WIN 1.8-10
  double-click and, WIN 1.11
  right-click and, WIN 1.10-11
Print command, WIN 1.31
Program, WIN 1.23
Programs command, Start menu, WIN 1.10
Programs submenu, WIN 1.10
  Accessories, WIN 1.24, 1.32
  Explorer, WIN 2.6
Properties of an object, WIN 1.7

QDOS (Quick and Dirty Operating System), WIN 1.3
Quitting Windows Explorer, WIN 2.32-33

Recycle Bin, WIN 2.26-31
Rename command, WIN 2.25
Resizing window, WIN 1.21
Restore button, My Computer window, WIN 1.14-15
Right-click, WIN 10-11
  deleting file using, WIN 2.27-28
  deleting folder using, WIN 2.31
Right-drag, WIN 1.21-23
  deleting file using, WIN 2.28-30
  deleting folder using, WIN 2.31
Right mouse button, WIN 1.8, 1.10
Run command, WIN 1.25

Save As command, WIN 1.27
Save As dialog box, WIN 1.27-28
Save button, WIN 1.29-30
Save command, WIN 1.30, 1.35
Saving
  document on disk, WIN 1.26-30
  modified document on disk, WIN 1.35
Screen, scrolling one at a time, WIN 1.21
Scroll arrows, WIN 1.20
Scroll bar, WIN 1.20, 1.21, 1.25
Scroll box, dragging, WIN 1.21
Scrolling in window, WIN 1.19-21

Secondary mouse button, WIN 1.8, 1.10
SHIFT key, selecting group of files and, WIN 2.21
Shortcut menu, WIN 1.11
Shut Down command, WIN 1.42-44, 2.33
Software, user interface and, WIN 1.5
Source drive, WIN 2.12
Source folder, WIN 2.12
SPACEBAR, selecting group of files and, WIN 2.21
Start button, WIN 1.7, 1.9
Starting
  application program, WIN 1.23-25
  Windows 95, WIN 1.6-7, 2.4-5
  Windows Explorer, WIN 2.5-6
Start menu, WIN 1.9
  Help command, WIN 1.36-37
  Programs command, WIN 1.10, 1.24, 1.32, 2.6
  Shut Down command, WIN 1.42-44, 2.33
Status bar, WIN 1.13
  folders and, WIN 2.8, 2.9
Subfolders, WIN 2.8, 2.10, 2.31
Submenu, WIN 1.10

Tabs, WIN 1.37
Taskbar, WIN 1.7, 1.12., 2.5
Text Document, New, WIN 1.25
32-bit operating systems, WIN 1.4
Time, current, WIN 1.7
Title bar, WIN 1.6, 1.12
Toolbar, Windows Explorer, WIN 2.7
Toolbar command, WIN 2.7
ToolTip, WIN 1.9, 1.10
Tray status area, WIN 1.7
.TXT file extension, WIN 1.27, 1.28

User friendly, WIN 1.6
User interface, WIN 1.5-6

Vertical scroll bar, WIN 1.20
View, WIN 2.18-19
View menu, My Computer window, WIN 1.12
View menu (Windows Explorer), Toolbar command, WIN 2.7
View submenu, List command, WIN 2.19

Welcome to Windows screen, WIN 1.6, 1.7, 2.5
Window
  active, WIN 1.12, 1.14
  closing, WIN 1.12, 1.16-17, 1.21
  Help, WIN 1.37, 1.39
  inactive, WIN 1.28
  maximizing, WIN 1.12, 1.14-15
  menu bar, WIN 1.12
  minimizing, WIN 1.12, 13
  moving by dragging, WIN 1.17-18
  My Computer, WIN 1.12-21
  Notepad, WIN 1.25, 1.33
  opening by double-clicking, WIN 1.12
  redisplaying, WIN 1.14
  resizing, WIN 1.19, 1.21
  restoring, WIN 1.14-15
  scrolling in, WIN 1.19-21
  sizing, WIN 1.41
  sizing by dragging, WIN 1.19
  title bar and, WIN 1.12
Windows, WIN 1.3, 1.4
Windows 95, WIN 1.4
  communicating with, WIN 1.8-23
  introduction to, WIN 1.4-7
  introductory screen, WIN 1.6
  shutting down, WIN 1.42-44, 2.33
  starting, WIN 1.6-7, 2.4-5
Windows Explorer, WIN 2.4-2-6
  collapsing and expanding folders, WIN 2.8, 2.10-12
  copying files and folders, WIN 2.12-26
  deleting files and folders, WIN 2.26-32
  maximizing window, WIN 2.5-6
  menu bar, WIN 2.7
  quitting, WIN 2.32-33
  renaming files and folders, WIN 2.24-26
Windows Help window, WIN 1.37, 1.39

▸ PROJECT ONE

INTRODUCTION TO MICROSOFT OFFICE 97

Objectives   MO 1.1
Microsoft Office 97   MO 1.2
Microsoft Word 97   MO 1.3
Microsoft Excel 97   MO 1.4
Microsoft Access 97   MO 1.6
Microsoft PowerPoint 97   MO 1.7
The Web Toolbar   MO 1.8
Microsoft Outlook 97   MO 1.9
The Office Assistant   MO 1.14
Hardware Innovations and Microsoft Office 97   MO 1.14
Project Summary   MO 1.15
In the Lab   MO 1.16

Objectives:

You will have mastered the material in this project when you can:

▸ Identify each application in Microsoft Office 97

▸ Define World Wide Web, intranet, and Internet

▸ Explain how each Microsoft Office 97 application uses the Internet

▸ Identify the purpose of the Web toolbar

▸ View e-mail messages, appointments, contacts, tasks, journal entries, and notes using Microsoft Outlook

▸ Use the Office Assistant

▸ Identify hardware innovations useful with Microsoft Office 97

Microsoft Office 97

Microsoft
Office 97

Introduction to Microsoft Office 97

*C*ase *P*erspective

Your organization recently installed Microsoft Office 97 on all computers. As the computer trainer for an upcoming seminar, you realize you should know more about Microsoft Office 97 but have had little time to learn about it. Since installing Office 97, many employees have come to you with questions about the Office applications and the World Wide Web. You have taken the time to answer their questions by sitting down with them in front of their computers and searching for the answers. From their questions, you have determined that a good starting place to learn about Office 97 would be to learn more about each Office application. Your goal in this project is to become familiar with the Microsoft Office 97 applications so you can teach the seminar.

Microsoft Office 97

Microsoft Office 97, the latest edition of the world's best-selling office suite, is a collection of the more popular Microsoft application software products that work alike and work together as if they were a single program. Microsoft Office 97 Professional Edition includes Microsoft Word 97, Microsoft Excel 97, Microsoft Access 97, Microsoft PowerPoint 97, and Microsoft Outlook 97. Microsoft Office 97 integrates these applications with the power of the Internet so you can move quickly among applications, transfer text and graphics easily among applications, and interact seamlessly with the World Wide Web. An explanation of each of the application software programs in Microsoft Office 97 is given in this project.

Microsoft Office 97 and the Internet

Every application in Microsoft Office 97 allows you to take advantage of the Internet, the World Wide Web, and intranets. The **Internet** is a worldwide network of thousands of computer networks and millions of commercial, educational, government, and personal computers. The **World Wide Web** is an easy-to-use graphical interface for exploring the Internet. The World Wide Web consists of many individual Web sites. A **Web site** can consist of a single **Web page** or multiple Web pages linked together. The first Web page in the Web site is called the **home page**. A unique address, called a **Uniform Resource Locator (URL)**, identifies each Web page.

A software tool, called a **browser**, allows you to locate and view a Web page. One method to view a Web page is to use the browser to enter a URL for the Web page. A widely used browser, called **Microsoft Internet Explorer**, is included with Microsoft Office 97. Another method of viewing Web pages allows you to click a hyperlink. A **hyperlink** is colored or underlined text or a graphic that, when clicked, connects to another Web page.

An **intranet** is a special type of Web that is available only to the users of a particular type of computer network, such as those used within a company or organization for internal communication. Like the Internet, hyperlinks are used within an intranet to access documents, pages, and other destinations on the intranet.

Microsoft Office 97 applications allow you to create hyperlinks to Web sites on the Internet easily, create Web pages for publication on an intranet or the Internet, and retrieve information from the Internet or an intranet into an Office document. Explanations of each of the application software programs in Microsoft Office 97 along with how they are used to access an intranet or the Internet are given on the following pages.

More *About* **Office 97**

For more information about Office 97, click Help on the menu bar on any Office 97 application window, point to Microsoft on the Web, and click Microsoft Office Home Page. Explore a Web page by clicking a hyperlink. After clicking a hyperlink, click the Back button to display the last Web page.

Microsoft Word 97

Microsoft Word 97 is a full-featured word processing program that allows you to create many types of personal and business communications, including announcements, letters, memos, resumes, and business and academic reports, as well as other forms of written documents.

Figure 1-1 illustrates the top portion of the announcement that students create in one of the exercises in Project One of the Microsoft Word section of this book. The steps to create this announcement are shown in Project One of Word.

Microsoft Word AutoCorrect and Spelling and Grammar features allow you to proofread your documents for spelling and grammatical errors, identifying errors and offering corrections as you type. When you are creating specific documents, such as a business letter or resume, Word provides **wizards**, which ask questions and then use your answers to format the document prior to typing information into the document.

announcement displays in Microsoft Word window

FIGURE 1-1

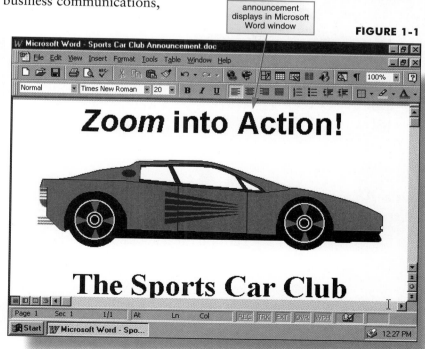

Microsoft Word automates many common tasks and provides you with powerful desktop publishing tools you can use to create professional looking brochures, advertisements, and newsletters. The Office drawing tools allow you to design impressive 3-D effects, shadows, textures, and curves. In addition, the CD-ROM that accompanies Microsoft Office 97 supplies approximately 3,000 clip art images, 150 fonts, and sounds, pictures, and movies that can be used to enhance the appearance of a document.

Microsoft Word 97 and the Internet

Microsoft Word makes it possible to search for information and access Web pages, design and publish Web pages on an intranet or the Internet, and insert a hyperlink to a Web page in a word processing document. Figure 1-2 illustrates a memo that contains a hyperlink to a Web page on Microsoft Corporation's Web site on the Internet.

Clicking the hyperlink starts the Internet Explorer browser and displays the associated Web page in the Microsoft Internet Explorer window (Figure 1-3). The Web page contains tips for using Microsoft Outlook. The URL for the Web page displays in the Address text box.

> **More** *About*
> **Microsoft Word 97**
>
> For more information about Word's tools and features, click Help on the menu bar, point to Microsoft on the Web, click Product News, and click a hyperlink. After clicking a hyperlink, click the Back button to display the last Web page.

FIGURE 1-2

FIGURE 1-3

Microsoft Excel 97

> **More** *About*
> **Microsoft Excel 97**
>
> For more information about Excel's tools and features, click Help on the menu bar, point to Microsoft on the Web, click Product News, and click a hyperlink. After clicking a hyperlink, click the Back button to display the last Web page.

Microsoft Excel 97 is a spreadsheet program that allows you to organize data, perform calculations, make decisions, graphically display data in charts, develop professional looking reports, convert Excel files for use on the Web, and access the Web. Figure 1-4 illustrates the worksheet and 3-D Column chart created in Project One of the Microsoft Excel section of this book as it displays in the Microsoft Excel window. The steps to create the worksheet and 3-D Column chart are shown in Project One of Excel.

Microsoft Excel's natural language formula capability simplifies the process of building formulas by allowing you to enter formulas using the English language and correcting common entry errors automatically. In addition, Microsoft Excel provides a Chart Wizard that allows you to create a variety of charts from the data in a worksheet. Other features allow multiple users to work with the same worksheet simultaneously.

Microsoft Excel 97 and the Internet

Using Microsoft Excel, you can create hyperlinks within a worksheet to other Office 97 documents on your network, your organization's intranet, or the Internet. You can save worksheets and charts in a format that allows you to display them on a Web page. You also can create and run queries to retrieve information from a Web page directly into a worksheet.

Figure 1-5 illustrates a worksheet created by running a Web query to retrieve stock market information for two stocks (Boeing Corporation and Walt Disney Corporation). The two hyperlinks in the first column are created using the Insert HyperLink button on the Standard toolbar. The information in the worksheet was obtained from the PC Quote, Inc. Web site. The External Data toolbar containing the Refresh All button displays on the worksheet.

FIGURE 1-4

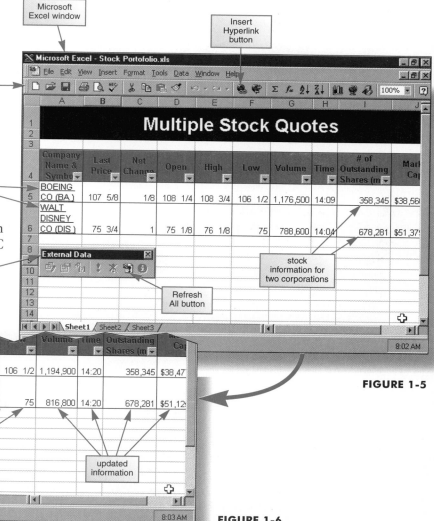

FIGURE 1-5

FIGURE 1-6

Clicking the Refresh All button locates the PC Quote, Inc. Web site, retrieves current information for the stocks in the worksheet using the hyperlinks in the first column, and displays the updated information in the worksheet (see Figure 1-6 on the previous page). Notice that the stock prices and information in this worksheet are different from the worksheet in Figure 1-5 on the previous page.

Microsoft Access 97

Microsoft Access 97 is a comprehensive **database program**. A **database** is a collection of data organized in a manner that allows access, retrieval, and use of that data. Microsoft Access allows you to create a database; add, change, and delete data in the database; sort data in the database; retrieve data from the database; and create forms and reports using the data in the database.

Figure 1-7 illustrates the database created in Project One of the Microsoft Access section of this book as it displays in the Microsoft Access window. The steps to create this database are shown in Project One of Access.

Microsoft Access 97 and the Internet

Databases are used to provide a central location to store related pieces of information. Microsoft Access simplifies the creation of databases with the Database Wizard that can be used to build quickly one of more than twenty types of databases. You also can transform lists or worksheets into databases using Access wizards. As with the other Office applications, Access allows you to share a database with other computer users on your network,

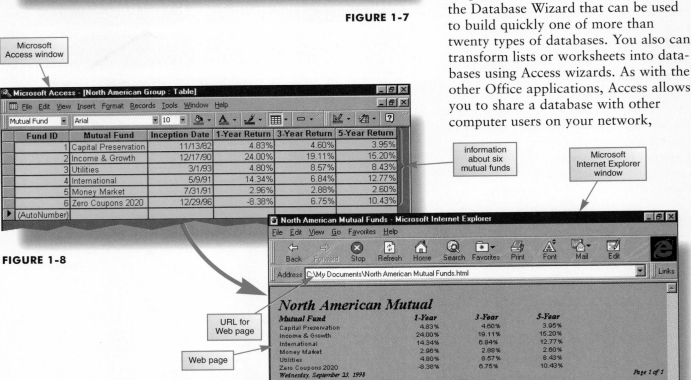

FIGURE 1-7

FIGURE 1-8

FIGURE 1-9

intranet, or over the Internet. The database in Figure 1-8 contains information (fund ID, mutual fund name, inception date, 1-year average return, 3-year average return, and 5-year average return) about six mutual stock funds.

Figure 1-9 illustrates a simple Web page created from information in the database in Figure 1-8. The Web page is displayed using the Microsoft Internet Explorer browser. The URL for the Web page displays in the Address text box in the window.

Microsoft PowerPoint 97

Microsoft PowerPoint 97 is a complete **presentation graphics program** that allows you to produce professional looking presentations. PowerPoint gives you the flexibility to make informal presentations using overhead transparencies, make electronic presentations using a projection device attached to a personal computer, make formal presentations using 35mm slides, or run virtual presentations on the Internet.

Figure 1-10 illustrates the first slide in a presentation created in Project One of the Microsoft PowerPoint section of this book as it displays in the Microsoft PowerPoint window. The steps to create this presentation are shown in Project One of PowerPoint.

Microsoft PowerPoint allows you to create dynamic presentations easily with multimedia features including sounds, movies, and pictures. PowerPoint comes with Design templates and Content templates that assist you in designing a presentation that can be used to create a slide show.

slide displays in Microsoft PowerPoint window

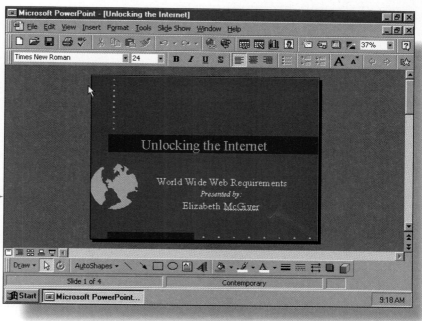

FIGURE 1-10

Microsoft PowerPoint 97 and the Internet

A clip art gallery that contains more than 1,000 clip art images, and sounds, pictures, and movies for use when creating a presentation is located on the Internet and is updated periodically by Microsoft Corporation. In addition, PowerPoint lets you publish your presentations on your intranet or the Internet using the HTML format. **HTML (HyperText Markup Language)** is a system of marking up, or tagging, a document so it can be published on the World Wide Web. Figure 1-11, on the next page, illustrates the first slide in a presentation to be published on the Internet. The slide was created using the Contemporary design, contains a clip art image (blue ribbon), title (Microsoft® Office 97), subtitle (Guide to Office Applications), and creation date (October 1998). Additional slides in this presentation are not visible in Figure 1-11.

FIGURE 1-11

FIGURE 1-12

Figure 1-12 illustrates the first Web page in a series of Web pages created from the presentation in Figure 1-11. The Web page displays in the Microsoft Internet Explorer window. The navigation buttons at the bottom of the page allow you to view additional Web pages in the presentation.

The Web Toolbar

The easiest method to navigate an intranet or the Internet is to use the **Web toolbar**. The Web toolbar allows you to search for and open Microsoft Office 97 documents on your intranet or Web pages on the Internet. The Web toolbar shown in the Microsoft Word window in Figure 1-13 is available in all Microsoft Office 97 applications, except Microsoft Outlook. Currently, a Word document (a memorandum) displays in the window, and the path and file name of the document display in the text box on the Web toolbar.

The buttons and text box on the Web toolbar allow you to jump to Web pages you have previously viewed, cancel a jump to a Web page, update the contents of the current Web page, and replace all other toolbars with the Web toolbar. In addition, you can view the first Web page displayed, search the Web for new Web sites, and add Web pages you select to the Favorites folder so you can return to them quickly in the future.

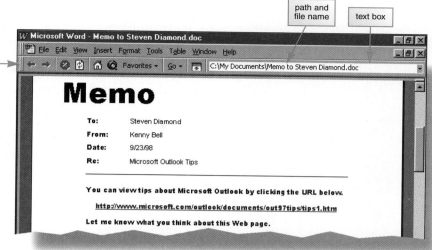

FIGURE 1-13

Microsoft Outlook 97

According to Microsoft Corporation's research, forty percent of the people who use software suites want their suites to include a software application that can manage tasks and appointments, organize and share information with others, and keep track of contacts. In response, Microsoft developed **Microsoft Outlook 97**, an integrated **desktop information management (DIM)** program that helps you organize information on your desktop and share information with others. Microsoft Outlook allows you to manage personal and business information such as e-mail, appointments, contacts, tasks, and documents, and keep a journal of your activities. Outlook organizes and stores this information in folders.

Viewing Electronic Mail (E-Mail)

Electronic mail, or **e-mail**, is the fastest growing desktop application. With this in mind, Microsoft designed Microsoft Outlook to allow you to check for and read e-mail messages easily, compose and send a response to an e-mail message, or compose and send a new e-mail message. When you start Microsoft Outlook, the Inbox – Microsoft Outlook window displays and the contents of the Inbox folder (your e-mail messages) display in the window (Figure 1-14).

The Inbox icon, representing the Inbox folder, displays on the **Outlook Bar** on the left side of the window and the contents of

FIGURE 1-14

More *About*
Inbox

To obtain more information about Inbox, click the Office Assistant button on the toolbar, type inbox in the text box, click the Search button, and click the Inbox option button. Click the hyperlinks on the screen to display Help topics.

the Inbox folder (three e-mail messages) display in the information viewer on the right side of the window. The **information viewer** displays the contents of the active folder (Inbox folder). Also visible on the Outlook Bar are the Calendar, Contacts, and Tasks icons. Clicking an icon on the Outlook Bar displays the contents of the associated folder in the information viewer.

Several Microsoft Outlook features enhance the performance and functionality of the Inbox. The AutoPreview feature displays the first three lines of the body of each e-mail message in the Subject column, allowing you to review the purpose of a message quickly and to read or delete messages without opening them. The AutoName Check feature helps to ensure that an e-mail message is sent to the correct recipient by checking the recipient's name against a list of valid names, quickly identifying invalid names, and resolving ambiguous names. The Voting feature allows you to poll multiple users by sending one or more questions and receiving answers. The Voting feature tallies the votes as they arrive, making individual and group responses available.

Viewing Appointments

Microsoft's research determined that personal and group scheduling is second in popularity only to e-mail. The most common scheduling activity is browsing the schedules of a group of users to find an available time for a group meeting. In response, Microsoft included the Calendar application in Microsoft Outlook. The **Calendar** application allows you to schedule activities (events, appointments, and meetings). An **event** is an activity that lasts 24 hours or longer (seminar, holiday, birthday, and so on), an **appointment** is an activity for which you block time that does not involve other people or resources, and a **meeting** is an appointment requiring resources and to which you invite people.

When you click the Calendar icon on the Outlook Bar, Microsoft Outlook displays the Calendar – Microsoft Outlook window, and the contents of the Calendar folder (today's events, appointments, and meetings) display in the window (Figure 1-15).

The Calendar – Microsoft Outlook window contains a **calendar** that lists the hours from 8:00 a.m. to 2:00 p.m. and the events, appointments, and meetings scheduled for the current day. In Figure 1-15, one event (Allan Preston's birthday), one appointment (Finish Marketing Plan), and one meeting (Weekly Sales Meeting) are scheduled.

To the right of the calendar and at the top of the information viewer is the date navigator. The **date navigator** contains a two-month calendar (September and October) and allows you to navigate through additional months. Bold dates in the date navigator indicate that an activity has been scheduled for that day.

FIGURE 1-15

The **TaskPad**, located below the date navigator, contains a list of tasks to be performed for the current day. A **task** is a personal or business-related activity you want to track from its inception to its completion.

Using Calendar, you can share information with other Office 97 programs, share information with groups of people, connect to and share information across the World Wide Web, and browse and find Office 97 files within your organization or around the world. Other features allow you to use your Outlook information when you leave your computer and use a portable or laptop computer.

Viewing Contacts

The most commonly requested improvement by users of Microsoft Schedule+ (an application included with Office 95 that was enhanced and is included in Microsoft Outlook) is the addition of a contact address book that maintains a list of contacts and e-mail addresses. In response, Microsoft included the **Contacts** application in Microsoft Outlook.

When you click the Contacts icon on the Outlook Bar, the Contacts – Microsoft Outlook window displays and the contents of the Contacts folder (your contacts) display in the window (Figure 1-16).

The Contacts – Microsoft Outlook window contains three contacts (Kenny Bell, Steven Diamond, and Patricia Smith). The contacts display in alphebetical order by last name. Each contact consists of the contact's last name and first name, an address, telephone and fax numbers, and an e-mail address.

Using Contacts, you can maintain an Internet address for each contact for faster access to a contact's home page, store up to 19 different telephone numbers for each contact, automatically dial a telephone number, and send e-mail messages.

FIGURE 1-16

Viewing Tasks

As mentioned above, a task is a personal or business-related activity you want to track from its inception to its completion. A task can occur once or repeat at regular intervals (a recurring task). The TaskPad shown in Figure 1-15 contains a list of the tasks for the current day. When you click the Tasks icon on the Outlook Bar, a detailed list of the tasks in the Tasks folder displays in the Tasks – Microsoft Outlook window (see Figure 1-17 on the next page).

The Tasks – Microsoft Outlook window contains two tasks (Inventory Office Equipment and Hair Cut at Raffi's). The type of task, level of importance, whether or not it contains an attachment, subject, status, due date, percentage complete, and category display for each task.

FIGURE 1-17

FIGURE 1-18

Viewing Journal Entries

The **Journal** application automatically maintains a journal of your activities. A **journal entry** is recorded based upon when an activity occurs. For example, you can tell Office 97 to record a journal entry automatically when you create an Office 97 document, record all e-mail messages for the contacts you specify, or record each telephone number you dial. Journal entries are organized into groups.

When you click the down arrow on the Outlook Bar and then click the Journal icon, Microsoft Outlook displays the Journal – Microsoft Outlook window and the contents of the Journal folder (Figure 1-18).

The Journal – Microsoft Outlook window contains a timeline and six activity groups. The **timeline** consists of a banner containing the current month and year (September 1998) and a banner containing several days in the current month. Below the timeline are six groups (E-mail message, Meeting request, Microsoft Access, Microsoft Excel, Microsoft PowerPoint, and Microsoft Word). The journal entries in two groups (Meeting request and Microsoft PowerPoint) are visible in the information viewer. Thus, a meeting was scheduled for the current day and a PowerPoint document was created, opened, or printed on that day.

Each journal entry is a shortcut to the activity it represents and is identified by the clock in the lower-left corner of the icon that represents the journal entry. Double-clicking the icon for the meeting request entry opens a window containing the details of the meeting. Double-clicking the icon for the PowerPoint document entry opens a window containing the details of the document and another icon. Double-clicking the icon starts Microsoft PowerPoint and displays the document in the PowerPoint window.

The shortcut allows you to find a document easily based on the date you created or worked on the document, without worrying about where you saved the document or what you named the document.

Viewing Notes

Notes are the electronic equivalent of paper *sticky notes*. The **Notes** application provides a location to store bits of information that are important to you that ordinarily would end up on stray scraps of paper. You can use Notes to record questions, lists, ideas, directions, reminders, or anything you would write on paper. When you click the Notes icon on the Outlook Bar, Microsoft Outlook displays the Notes – Microsoft Outlook window and the notes in the Notes folder (Figure 1-19). When you double-click a note, the contents of the note display in the information viewer.

Three notes and the contents of the Weekend Schedule note are visible in the information viewer. The notes contain directions to Anaheim Stadium, a grocery store shopping list, and a weekend schedule. The Weekend Schedule note contains a list of three weekend activities.

The Deleted Items icon on the Outlook Bar in Figure 1-19 represents the Deleted Items folder, which contains all the items (e-mail, appointments, and so on) that were deleted while using Microsoft Outlook.

More *About*
Journal

To obtain more information about Journal, click the Office Assistant button on the toolbar, type `journal` in the text box, click the Search button, and click the Journal option button. Click the hyperlinks on the screen to display Help topics.

More *About*
Notes

To obtain more information about Notes, click the Office Assistant button on the toolbar, type `notes` in the text box, click the Search button, and click the Notes option button. Click the hyperlinks on the screen to display Help topics.

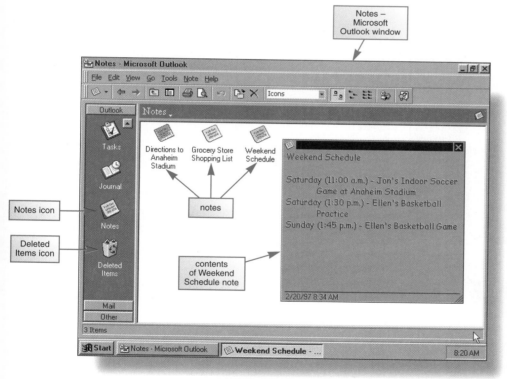

FIGURE 1-19

More *About*
Office Assistant

To change the Office Assistant, right-click the Office Assistant window, click Options on the shortcut menu, if necessary click Gallery tab, click Next button to select Office Assistant, and click the OK button.

The Office Assistant

The **Office Assistant** answers your questions and suggests more efficient ways to complete a task. With the Office Assistant active, for example, you can type a word or phrase in a text box and the Office Assistant provides immediate Help on the subject. As you work with an Office 97 application, the Office Assistant accumulates tips that suggest more effective ways to perform the tasks you completed while using the application. This tip feature is part of the **IntelliSense technology** that is built into Microsoft Office 97. IntelliSense technology allows Office Assistant to understand what you are trying to do and suggest better ways to do it.

The Office Assistant and balloon display whenever you start a Microsoft Office 97 application. The Office Assistant and balloon that display when you start Microsoft Outlook are illustrated in Figure 1-20.

The Office Assistant (a two-dimensional, animated paper clip or other object in a window) is completely customizable so you can select one of nine Office Assistants and the options that best suit the way you work. Detailed instructions about using the Office Assistant will be explained in each section of this book.

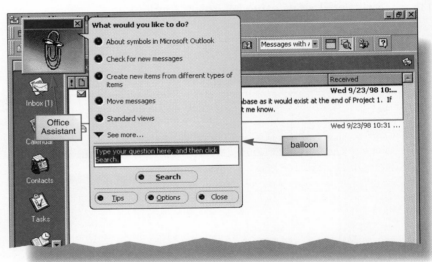

FIGURE 1-20

Hardware Innovations and Microsoft Office 97

Two hardware products from Microsoft Corporation, the Microsoft IntelliMouse and the Microsoft Natural keyboard, make working with Microsoft Office 97 faster and easier (Figure 1-21).

The **Microsoft IntelliMouse** was designed specifically for Office 97 and contains a wheel positioned between the two mouse buttons. The IntelliMouse allows you to scroll, zoom, and navigate through an Office 97 document without taking your hand off the mouse. You can rotate the IntelliMouse wheel to scroll through a document, press the wheel down and move the mouse to quickly scroll vertically or horizontally, or click the wheel once to read a document as it scrolls slowly up the screen.

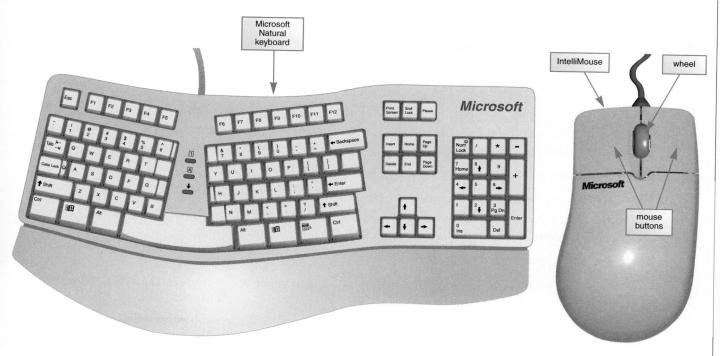

FIGURE 1-21

To zoom, or magnify, a document, hold down the CTRL key as you rotate the wheel to change the magnification within a document. To navigate a document, you can hold down the SHIFT key as you rotate the wheel to jump to a hyperlink, return to a previous Web page, expand or collapse a Microsoft Word document in outline form, or expand or collapse hierarchical structures in Windows Explorer.

Although not designed specifically for Microsoft Office 97, the **Microsoft Natural keyboard** allows you to work more comfortably by helping you place your hands, wrists, and forearms in a relaxed position.

Project Summary

The purpose of this project is to introduce you to the Microsoft Office 97 applications. Brief explanations of the Microsoft Word, Microsoft Excel, Microsoft Access, and Microsoft PowerPoint applications and examples of how these applications interact with the Internet, World Wide Web, and intranets were given. The Microsoft Outlook application and the applications within Outlook (Inbox, Calendar, Contacts, Tasks, Journal, and Notes) also were explained. In addition, the Microsoft IntelliMouse and Microsoft Natural keyboard were illustrated. With this introduction, you are ready to begin the study of each of the Microsoft Office 97 applications explained in this book.

In the Lab

1 Using Office Assistant

Instructions: To better understand Microsoft Outlook, you decide to use Office Assistant to get an overview of Microsoft Outlook. Complete the following steps to get an overview of the Calendar and Contacts applications. Submit your printouts and answers to your instructor.

Part 1:   *Starting Microsoft Outlook and Office Assistant*

1. Click the Start button on the taskbar. Click Microsoft Outlook on the Start menu.
2. If the Office Assistant does not display, click the Office Assistant button on the toolbar at the top of the window. A question mark within a balloon identifies the button.

Part 2:   *Using Office Assistant*

1. When the Office Assistant and balloon display, type `Microsoft Outlook` in the What would you like to do? text box.
2. Click the Search button. Click What is Microsoft Outlook? Click the Basics of Outlook topic to display the Basics of Outlook screen.
3. Click the Outlook Bar link (red and white box) to open a pop-up box containing information about the Outlook Bar. Read the information and then print the information by right-clicking the pop-up box, clicking Print Topic on the shortcut menu, and then clicking the OK button in the Print dialog box.
4. Click the Outlook Bar link again to remove the pop-up box. Click the other links on the screen and read about the other Help topics. Click the Back button in the Microsoft Outlook window.

Part 3:   *Searching for Information about Calendar and Contacts*

1. Click the Calendar topic in the What is Microsoft Outlook? screen. Click the links in the Calendar screen and answer the following questions.
   a. What three activities can you record in the calendar? _____
   b. How can you select nonadjacent days in the date navigator? _____
   c. How do you schedule time to work on a task? _____
2. Click the Back button in the Microsoft Outlook window.
3. Click the Contacts topic in the What is Microsoft Outlook? screen. Read about Contacts by clicking the links in the Contacts screen. Print the Contacts screen by right-clicking the screen, clicking Print Topic on the shortcut menu, and then clicking the OK button in the Print dialog box.
4. Click the Back button in the Microsoft Outlook window.

Part 4:   *Closing Office Assistant and Microsoft Outlook*

1. Click the Close button in the Microsoft Outlook window.
2. Click the Close button in the Office Assistant window.
3. Click the Close button in the Inbox – Microsoft Outlook window.

Microsoft **Word 97**

▶ **PROJECT ONE**

CREATING AND EDITING A WORD DOCUMENT

Objectives WD 1.3
What Is Microsoft Word? WD 1.6
Project One – Paradise Island Announcement WD 1.6
Starting Word WD 1.8
The Word Screen WD 1.10
Changing the Default Font Size WD 1.14
Entering Text WD 1.15
Saving a Document WD 1.25
Formatting Paragraphs and Characters in a Document WD 1.28
Inserting a Picture from the Web into a Word Document WD 1.39
Saving an Existing Document with the Same File Name WD 1.46
Printing a Document WD 1.47
Quitting Word WD 1.49
Opening a Document WD 1.50
Correcting Errors WD 1.51
Word Online Help WD 1.54
Project Summary WD 1.60
What You Should Know WD 1.60
Test Your Knowledge WD 1.61
Use Help WD 1.63
Apply Your Knowledge WD 1.64
In the Lab WD 1.65
Cases and Places WD 1.69

▶ **PROJECT TWO**

CREATING A RESEARCH PAPER WITH A TABLE

Objectives WD 2.1
Introduction WD 2.4
Project Two – Research Paper with a Table WD 2.4
Changing the Margins WD 2.7
Adjusting Line Spacing WD 2.9
Using a Header to Number Pages WD 2.12
Typing the Body of the Research Paper WD 2.15
Creating a Table with the Insert Table Button WD 2.30
Creating an Alphabetical Works Cited Page WD 2.37
Proofing and Revising the Research Paper WD 2.44
Navigating to a Hyperlink WD 2.51
Project Summary WD 2.52
What You Should Know WD 2.52
Test Your Knowledge WD 2.53
Use Help WD 2.55
Apply Your Knowledge WD 2.56
In the Lab WD 2.57
Cases and Places WD 2.63

Microsoft Word 97

Creating and Editing a Word Document

Objectives:

You will have mastered the material in this project when you can:

▶ Start Word
▶ Describe the Word screen
▶ Change the default font size of all text
▶ Enter text into a document
▶ Spell check as you type
▶ Save a document
▶ Select text
▶ Center a paragraph
▶ Change the font size of selected text
▶ Change the font of selected text
▶ Bold selected text
▶ Underline selected text
▶ Italicize selected text
▶ Import a picture from the Web
▶ Resize a picture
▶ Print a document
▶ Correct errors in a document
▶ Use Microsoft Word Help
▶ Quit Word

Letter Perfect

From Carved Tablets to Computerized Font Libraries

Longfellow speaks of the "footprints on the sands of time" left by great ancestors. Indeed, these recordings of events and accomplishments communicate messages of days long gone. In ancient times, thoughts were shared by making symbols in the sand, drawing on cave walls, and etching hieroglyphics and pictoral carvings on tombs. The Egyptians are credited with creating the first alphabet of symbols and pictures, which in approximately 1000 B.C., was modified when the Phoenicians added consonants and the Romans agreed upon 23 unique uppercase letters. The straight shapes of these Roman letters were created out of necessity, as artists had difficulty chiseling curves in stone.

The Roman alphabet influenced early Latin writing, but scribes developed additional lowercase letters. They handwrote on scrolls made from animal skins or on paper made from organic vegetable material. Their Carolingian script was adopted by the Emperor

Charlemagne as an educational standard during the tenth century. These scrolls evolved into folded manuscript books produced by monks in monasteries and lay people in universities.

Several centuries later, the developing European bourgeoisie longed for multiple copies of documents and reading materials. Thus, when Johann Gutenberg developed the printing press in the fifteenth century, he caused a European upheaval. In 1454, he printed Bibles, which were the first mass-produced books printed with moveable type. To make this type, he painstakingly punched a mirror image of a letter in a soft piece of metal, poured molten metal into this hole, and produced a letter. The letters were arranged in a matrix, inked, and pressed onto paper. By the end of the century, more than 1,000 printers worked in 200 European cities.

During the Industrial Revolution in the 1800s, steam presses cut the printing time by 85 percent. A machine eliminated the need to create punched type by hand. In the 1900s, the need for metal type ceased. Letters were created by the photocomposition process, which projects letters on photosensitive paper. In today's digital age, letters are created by the computer, and an abundance of font styles are available.

Microsoft Word 97 provides a font list that allows you to add variety to and enhance the appearance of your documents. Now, thousands of fonts are available from numerous sources including the Internet and for purchase on CD-ROM.

Each font has a unique name. Some are named after the designer. For example, the Baskerville font was developed by John Baskerville, a teacher turned printer in the seventeenth century. Other fonts named for their designers are Giambattista Bodoni, William Caslon, and Claude Garamond. Times New Roman resembles the letters inscribed on the base of Trajan's Column in the Roman Forum in A.D. 114. As you work through the projects in this book, recall that the letters you type are descendants of the footprints left by our printing forefathers.

Microsoft
Word 97

Creating and Editing a Word Document

*C*ase *P*erspective

Tropical Travel, a local travel agency, specializes in customized vacation packages to locations around the world. One popular package is to Paradise Island. Surrounded by crystal-clear waters and lined with white-sand beaches, Paradise Island offers swimming, surfing, SCUBA diving, snorkeling, sailing, and scenic hiking.

Each month, Tropical Travel prepares a flier announcing exciting vacation packages. The announcement is posted in local retail stores, printed in magazines and newspapers, and mailed to the general public. You have been asked the prepare an announcement for the Paradise Island vacation packages. To add appeal to the announcement, you are asked to include a picture of Paradise Island in the announcement. When you are finished creating the announcement, you print it for distribution.

You surf the Internet for a picture of Paradise Island and locate one at the Web site of www.scsite.com/off97e/pr1.htm. Details for the announcement, such as information about Paradise Island, can be obtained from any travel agent at Tropical Travel.

What Is Microsoft Word?

Microsoft Word is a full-featured word processing program that allows you to create professional looking documents such as announcements, letters, resumes, and reports; and revise them easily. You can use Word's desktop publishing features to create high-quality brochures, advertisements, and newsletters. Word has many features designed to simplify the production of documents. For example, you can instruct Word to create a prewritten document for you, and then you can modify the document to meet your needs. Using its expanded **IntelliSense**™ technology, Word can perform tasks such as correcting text, checking spelling and grammar, and formatting text – *all while you are typing*. Using Word's thesaurus, you can add variety and precision to your writing. With Word, you easily can include tables, graphics, pictures, and live hyperlinks in your documents. From within Word, you can search the Web for documents or create your very own Web pages.

Project One – Paradise Island Announcement

To illustrate the features of Word, this book presents a series of projects that use Word to create documents similar to those you will encounter in the academic and business environments. Project 1 uses Word to produce the announcement shown in Figure 1-1. The announcement informs the public about exciting vacation packages at Paradise Island through the Tropical Travel agency. Below the headline, PARADISE ISLAND, is a picture of the breathtaking scenery at Paradise Island, designed to catch the attention of the reader. The picture is located at the Web page www.scsite.com/off97e/pr1.htm. Below the picture is the body title, Ready For A Vacation?, followed by a brief paragraph about Paradise Island. Next, a bulleted list identifies vacation package details. Finally, the last line of the announcement lists the telephone number of Tropical Travel.

Document Preparation Steps

Document preparation steps give you an overview of how the document in Figure 1-1 will be developed. The following tasks will be completed in this project:

1. Start Word.
2. Change the size of the displayed and printed characters.
3. Enter the document text.
4. Spell check as you type.
5. Add bullets as you type.
6. Save the document on a floppy disk.
7. Format the document text (center, enlarge, bold, underline, and italicize).
8. Insert the picture from a Web page.
9. Resize the picture.
10. Save the document again.
11. Print the document.
12. Quit Word.

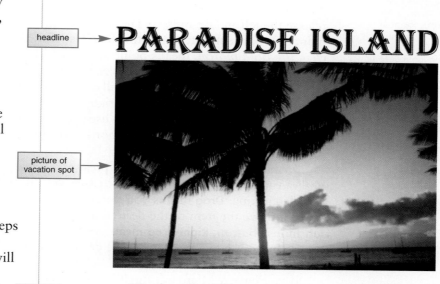

headline

picture of vacation spot

body title

bulleted list

FIGURE 1-1

The following pages contain a detailed explanation of each of these tasks.

Mouse Usage

In this book, the mouse is the primary way to communicate with Word. You can perform six operations with a standard mouse: point, click, right-click, double-click, drag, and right-drag. If you have a **Microsoft IntelliMouse**™, then you also have a wheel between the left and right buttons. This wheel can be used to perform three additional operations: rotate wheel, click wheel, or drag wheel.

Point means you move the mouse across a flat surface until the mouse pointer rests on the item of choice on the screen. As you move the mouse, the mouse pointer moves across the screen in the same direction. **Click** means you press and release the left mouse button. The terminology used in this book to direct you to point to a particular item and then click is, click the particular item. For example, *click the Bold button*, means point to the Bold button and then click.

Right-click means you press and release the right mouse button. As with the left mouse button, you normally will point to an item on the screen prior to right-clicking. In many cases, when you right-click, Word displays a **shortcut menu** that contains the commands most often used for the current activity. Thus, when these projects instruct you to display a shortcut menu, point to the item being discussed and then right-click.

Double-click means you quickly press and release the left mouse button twice without moving the mouse. In most cases, you must point to an item before double-clicking. **Drag** means you point to an item, hold down the left mouse button, move the item to the desired location on the screen, and then release the left mouse button. **Right-drag** means you point to an item, hold down the right mouse button, move the item to the desired location, and then release the right mouse button.

If you have a Microsoft IntelliMouse™, then you can use the **rotate wheel** to view parts of the document that are not visible. The wheel also can serve as a third button. When the wheel is used as a button, it is referred to as the **wheel button**. For example, dragging the wheel button causes Word to scroll in the direction you drag.

The use of the mouse is an important skill when working with Microsoft Word 97.

Starting Word

Follow these steps to start Word, or ask your instructor how to start Word for your system.

More *About* Mouse Usage

Some mouse users bend their wrists frequently while moving the mouse. To help prevent wrist injuries, place the mouse at least six inches from the edge of a workstation. In this location, the wrist is forced to be flat, which causes bending to occur at the elbow when the mouse is moved.

More *About* Microsoft IntelliMouse™

You can use the Microsoft IntelliMouse™ to pan (scroll continuously) through a document or zoom a document. To pan up or down, hold down the wheel button and drag the pointer above or below the origin mark (two triangles separated by a dot). To zoom in or out, hold down the CTRL key while rotating the wheel button forward or back.

Steps To Start Word

1 **Click the Start button on the taskbar and then point to New Office Document.**

The programs in the Start menu display above the Start button (Figure 1-2). The New Office Document command is highlighted on the Start menu.

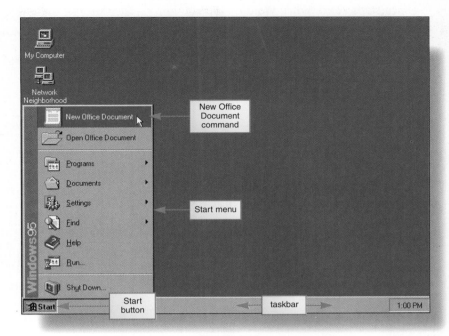

FIGURE 1-2

2 **Click New Office Document. If necessary, click the General tab when the New Office Document dialog box first opens.**

Office displays several icons on the General sheet in the New Office Document dialog box (Figure 1-3). Each icon represents a different type of document you can create in Microsoft Office. In this project, you are to create a new document using Microsoft Word 97.

FIGURE 1-3

3 **Double-click the Blank Document icon.**

Office starts Word. While Word is starting, the mouse pointer changes to an hourglass. After a few moments, an empty document titled Document1 displays on the Word screen (Figure 1-4).

4 **If the Word screen is not maximized, double-click its title bar to maximize it. If the Office Assistant displays, click its Close button.**

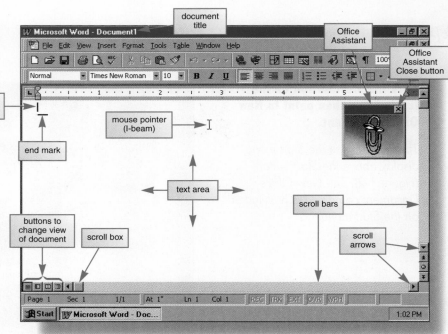

FIGURE 1-4

OtherWays

1. Right-click Start button, click Open, double-click New Office Document, click General tab, double-click Blank Document icon

2. Click Start a New Document button on Microsoft Office Shortcut Bar, click General tab, double-click Blank Document icon

3. On Start menu point to Programs, click Microsoft Word

The Word Screen

The **Word screen** (Figure 1-4) consists of a variety of features to make your work more efficient and the results more professional. If you are following along on a personal computer and your screen differs from Figure 1-4, click View on the menu bar and then click Normal.

Word Document Window

The Word document window contains several elements similar to the document windows in other applications, as well as some elements unique to Word. The main elements of the Word document window are the text area, insertion point, end mark, mouse pointer, and scroll bars (Figure 1-4).

TEXT AREA As you type or insert pictures, your text and graphics display in the **text area**.

INSERTION POINT The **insertion point** is a blinking vertical bar that indicates where text will be inserted as you type. As you type, the insertion point moves to the right and, when you reach the end of a line, it moves downward to the next line. You also insert graphics at the location of the insertion point.

END MARK The **end mark** indicates the end of your document. Each time you begin a new line as you type, the end mark moves downward.

MOUSE POINTER The **mouse pointer** becomes different shapes depending on the task you are performing in Word and the pointer's location on the screen. The mouse pointer in Figure 1-4 has the shape of an I-beam. The mouse pointer displays as an **I-beam** when it is in the text area. Other mouse pointer shapes are described as they appear on the screen during this and subsequent projects.

SCROLL BARS You use the **scroll bars** to display different portions of your document in the document window. At the right edge of the document window is a vertical scroll bar, and at the bottom of the document window is a horizontal scroll bar. On both scroll bars, the **scroll box** indicates your current location in the document. At the left edge of the horizontal scroll bar, Word provides three buttons you use to change the view of your document. These buttons are discussed as they are used in a later project.

Word is preset to use standard 8.5-by-11-inch paper, with 1.25-inch left and right margins and 1-inch top and bottom margins. Only a portion of your document, however, displays on the screen at one time. You view the portion of the document displayed on the screen through the **document window** (Figure 1-5).

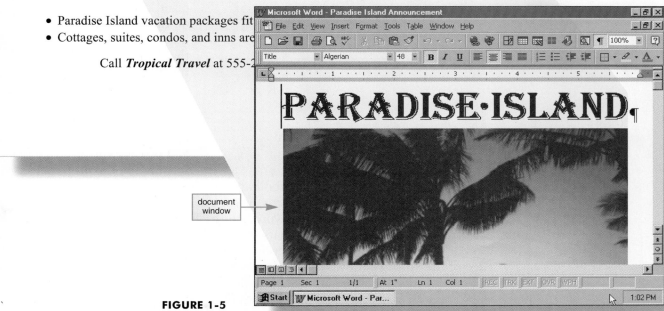

FIGURE 1-5

Menu Bar, Toolbars, Rulers, and Status Bar

The menu bar, toolbars, and horizontal ruler appear at the top of the screen just below the title bar (Figure 1-6). The status bar appears at the bottom of the screen.

FIGURE 1-6

FIGURE 1-7

FIGURE 1-8

MENU BAR The **menu bar** displays the Word menu names. Each menu name contains a list of commands you can use to retrieve, store, print, and format data in your document and perform other tasks. Many of these commands have a picture beside them to help you quickly identify them. For example, the Save command on the File menu has a picture of a floppy disk beside it. To display a menu, such as the File menu, click the menu name on the menu bar.

TOOLBARS The menu bar is actually the first toolbar on the Word screen. Just below the menu bar is the **Standard toolbar**. Immediately below the Standard toolbar is the **Formatting toolbar**.

Toolbars contain buttons, boxes, and menus that allow you to perform tasks more quickly than using the standard menu bar. For example, to print, click the Print button on the Standard toolbar. Each button has a picture on the face that helps you remember its function. Figure 1-7 illustrates the Standard toolbar and identifies its buttons and boxes; Figure 1-8 illustrates the Formatting toolbar. Each button and box is explained in detail as it is used in the projects.

The Standard and Formatting toolbars initially display **docked**, or attached to top edge of the Word window directly below the menu bar. Additional toolbars may display automatically on the Word screen, depending on the task you are performing. These additional toolbars display either stacked below the Formatting toolbar or floating on the Word screen. A floating toolbar is not attached to an edge of the Word window. You can rearrange the order of **docked toolbars** and can move **floating toolbars** anywhere on the Word screen. Later in the book, steps are presented that show you how to float a docked toolbar or dock a floating toolbar.

RULERS   Below the Formatting toolbar is the **horizontal ruler** (Figure 1-9). You use the horizontal ruler, sometimes simply called the **ruler**, to set tab stops, indent paragraphs, adjust column widths, and change page margins. An additional ruler, called the **vertical ruler**, displays at the left edge of the window when you are performing certain tasks.

STATUS BAR   The **status bar** is located at the bottom of the screen. From left to right, the following information displays about the page shown in Figure 1-9: the page number, the section number, the page visible in the document window followed by the total number of pages in the document, the position of the insertion point in inches from the top of the page, the line number and column number of the insertion point, and several **status indicators**. If the insertion point does not display in the document window, then no measurement displays on the status bar for the position of the insertion point, its line, and its column.

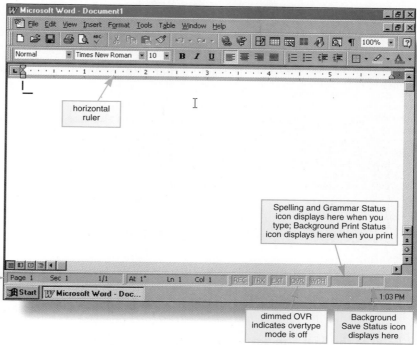

FIGURE 1-9

The right half of the status bar displays several status indicators. Five of these status indicators (REC, TRK, EXT, OVR, and WPH or WPN) appear darkened when on and dimmed when off. For example, the dimmed OVR indicates overtype mode is off. To turn most of these status indicators on or off, double-click the status indicator. These status indicators are discussed as they are used in the project.

Other status indicators appear as you perform certain tasks. When you begin typing in the text area, a Spelling and Grammar Status icon appears at the right edge of the status bar. When Word is saving your document, a Background Save Status icon appears on the status bar. When you print a document, a Background Print Status icon appears. These status icons will be discussed later in this project.

Depending on how you installed Word and the status of certain keys on your keyboard, your status bar may have different status indicators on or off. For example, the dimmed WPH on the status bar indicates WordPerfect Help is off. If your WordPerfect Help status indicator is darkened, WordPerfect Help is active and you need to deactivate it. When WordPerfect Help is on, the keys you press on the keyboard work according to WordPerfect instead of Word. To deactivate the WordPerfect Help, ask for assistance from your instructor or do the following: Click Tools on the menu bar and then click Options; click the General tab; click Help for WordPerfect users and click Navigation keys for WordPerfect users to clear these check boxes; and then click the OK button in the Options dialog box.

If a task you select requires several seconds (such as saving a document), the status bar displays a message informing you of the progress of the task.

More *About*
Horizontal Ruler

If the horizontal ruler does not display on your screen, click View on the menu bar and then click Ruler. This command is a toggle. That is, to hide the ruler, also click View on the menu bar and then click Ruler.

Changing the Default Font Size

Characters that display on the screen are a specific shape, size, and style. The **font**, or typeface, defines the appearance and shape of the letters, numbers, and special characters. The preset, or default, font is Times New Roman (Figure 1-10 below). The **font size** specifies the size of the characters on the screen. Font size is gauged by a measurement system called **points**. A single point is about 1/72 of one inch in height. Thus, a character with a font size of ten is about 10/72 of one inch in height. The default font size in most versions of Word is 10. If more of the characters in your document require a larger font size, you easily can change the default font size before you type. In Project 1, many of the characters in the announcement are a font size of 20. Follow these steps to increase the font size before you begin entering text.

Steps **To Increase the Default Font Size Before Typing**

1 **Point to the Font Size box arrow on the Formatting toolbar.**

The mouse pointer changes to a left-pointing block arrow when positioned on a toolbar (Figure 1-10). When you point to a toolbar button or box, Word displays a **ScreenTip** *immediately below the button or box. The ScreenTip in this figure is Font Size.*

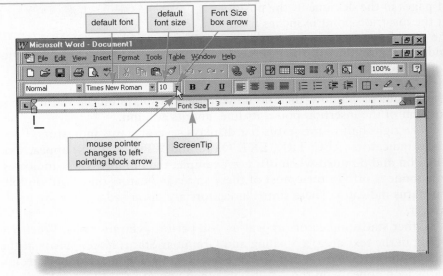

FIGURE 1-10

2 **Click the Font Size box arrow on the Formatting toolbar.**

A list of available font sizes displays in a Font Size list box (Figure 1-11). The font sizes displayed depend on the current font, which is Times New Roman.

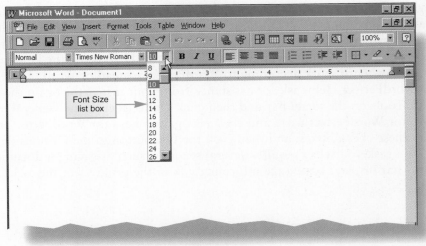

FIGURE 1-11

3 **Point to font size 20.**

Word highlights font size 20 in the list (Figure 1-12).

font size 20 highlighted

FIGURE 1-12

font size changes to 20

4 **Click font size 20.**

The font size for this document changes to 20 (Figure 1-13). The size of the insertion point increases to reflect the current font size of 20.

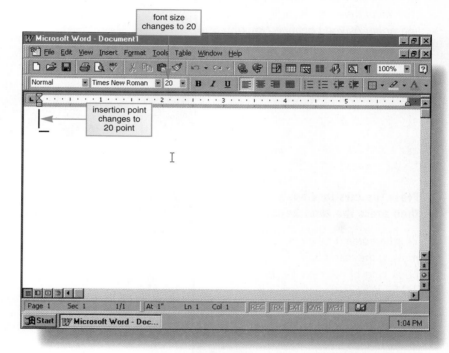

insertion point changes to 20 point

FIGURE 1-13

The new font size takes effect immediately in your document. Word uses this font size for the remainder of this announcement.

Entering Text

To prepare a document in Word, you enter text by typing on the keyboard. In Project 1, the headline (PARADISE ISLAND) is capitalized. The example on the next page explains the steps to enter the headline in all capital letters at the left margin. Later in the project, this headline will be centered across the top of the document, formatted in bold, and enlarged.

▶ *Other* **Ways**

1. Right-click paragraph mark above end mark, click Font on shortcut menu, click Font tab, click desired point size in Size list box, click OK button

2. On Format menu click Font, click Font tab, select desired point size in Size list box, click OK button

3. Press CTRL+SHIFT+P, type desired point size, press ENTER

4. Press CTRL+SHIFT+>

Steps To Enter Text

1 If the CAPS LOCK indicator is not lit on your keyboard, press the CAPS LOCK key. Type PARADISE ISLAND as the headline. If at any time during typing you make an error, press the BACKSPACE key until you have deleted the text in error and then retype the text correctly.

Word places the P in PARADISE ISLAND at the location of the insertion point. As you continue typing this headline, the insertion point moves to the right (Figure 1-14). The insertion point is currently on line 1 in column 16.

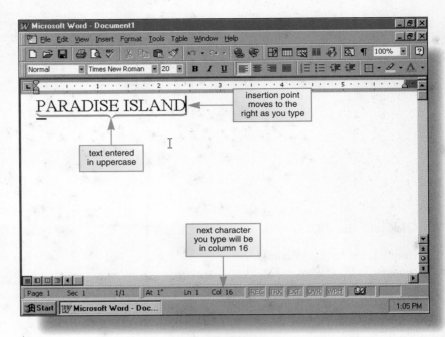

FIGURE 1-14

2 Press the CAPS LOCK key and then press the ENTER key.

Word creates a new paragraph by moving the insertion point to the beginning of the next line (Figure 1-15). Whenever you press the ENTER key, Word considers the previous line and the next line to be different paragraphs. Notice the status bar indicates the current position of the insertion point. That is, the insertion point is currently on line 2 column 1.

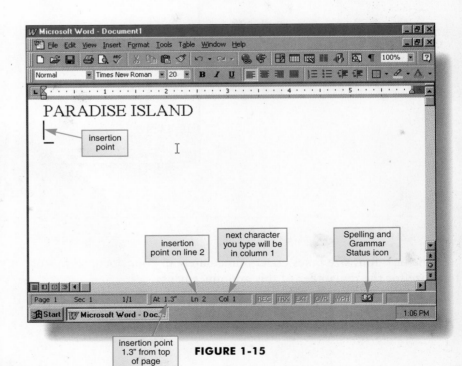

FIGURE 1-15

More *About* Headlines

Because the headline is the first item a reader notices, it should be effective. Headlines of fewer than four words are often typed in all-capital letters.

When you begin entering text into a document, the **Spelling and Grammar Status icon** displays at the right edge of the status bar (Figure 1-15). As you type, the spelling icon shows an animated pencil writing on paper, which indicates Word is checking for possible errors. When you stop typing, the pencil changes to either a red check mark or a red X. In Figure 1-15, the Spelling and Grammar Status icon displays a red check mark. In general, if all of the words you have typed are in Word's dictionary and your grammar is correct, a red check mark appears on the Spelling and Grammar Status icon. If you type a word not in the dictionary (because it is a proper name or misspelled), a red wavy underline appears below the word. If you type text that may be grammatically incorrect, a green wavy underline appears below the text. When Word underlines a possible spelling or grammar error, it also changes the red check mark on the Spelling and Grammar Status icon to a red X. As you enter text into the announcement, your Spelling and Grammar Status icon may show a red X, rather than a red check mark. Later in this project, you check the spelling of these words. At that time, the red X returns to a red check mark.

More *About*
Entering Text

In the days of typewriters, the letter l was used for both the letter l and the number one. Keyboards, however, have both a number one and the letter l. Keyboards also have both a number zero and the letter o. Be careful to press the correct keyboard character when creating a word processing document.

Entering Blank Lines into a Document

To enter a blank line into a document, press the ENTER key without typing anything on the line. The following example explains how to enter two blank lines below the headline, PARADISE ISLAND.

 Steps **To Enter Blank Lines into a Document**

1 **Press the ENTER key two times.**

Word inserts two blank lines into your document below the headline (Figure 1-16).

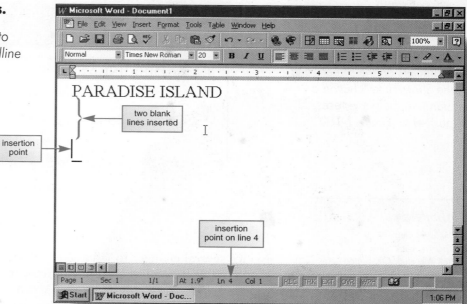

FIGURE 1-16

Displaying Nonprinting Characters

To indicate where in the document you press the ENTER key or SPACEBAR, you may find it helpful to display **nonprinting characters**. The paragraph mark (¶) is a nonprinting character that indicates where you pressed the ENTER key. A raised dot (•) shows where you pressed the SPACEBAR. Nonprinting characters display only on the screen. They do not appear in printed documents. Other nonprinting characters are discussed as they display on the screen in subsequent projects. The following steps illustrate how to display nonprinting characters, if they are not already displaying on your screen.

Steps **To Display Nonprinting Characters**

1 **Point to the Show/Hide ¶ button on the Standard toolbar.**

Word displays the ScreenTip for the button (Figure 1-17).

FIGURE 1-17

2 **If it is not already recessed, click the Show/Hide ¶ button on the Standard toolbar.**

*Word displays nonprinting characters on the screen, and the Show/Hide ¶ button on the Standard toolbar is **recessed**, or pushed in (Figure 1-18).*

FIGURE 1-18

Notice several changes to your screen display (Figure 1-18). A paragraph mark appears at the end of each line to indicate you pressed the ENTER key. Recall that each time you press the ENTER key, Word creates a new paragraph. Because you changed the font size, the paragraph marks are 20 point. Notice the paragraph mark above the end mark – you cannot delete this paragraph mark. Between each word, a raised dot appears, indicating you pressed the SPACEBAR. Finally, the Show/Hide ¶ button is recessed to indicate it is selected.

If you feel the nonprinting characters clutter your screen, you can hide them by clicking the Show/Hide ¶ button again. It is recommended that you display nonprinting characters; therefore, the screens presented in this book show the nonprinting characters.

Entering More Text

The next step is to enter the body title, Ready For A Vacation?, into the document window as explained in the steps below.

TO ENTER MORE TEXT

① Type Ready For A Vacation? to enter the body title.

② Press the ENTER key twice.

The body title displays on line 4 as shown in Figure 1-19.

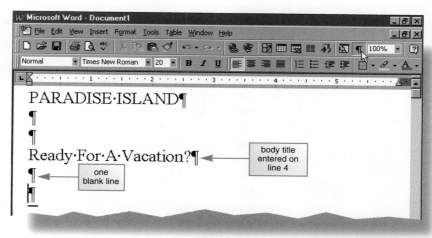

FIGURE 1-19

Using the Wordwrap Feature

Wordwrap allows you to type words in a paragraph continually without pressing the ENTER key at the end of each line. When the insertion point moves beyond the right margin, Word positions it automatically at the beginning of the next line. As you type, if a word extends beyond the right margin, Word also positions the word automatically on the next line with the insertion point. Thus, as you enter text using Word, do not press the ENTER key when the insertion point reaches the right margin. Because Word creates a new paragraph each time you press the ENTER key, press the ENTER key only in these circumstances:

1. To insert blank lines into a document
2. To begin a new paragraph
3. To terminate a short line of text and advance to the next line
4. In response to certain Word commands

Perform the following step to become familiar with the wordwrap feature.

More About Wordwrap

Your printer controls where wordwrap occurs for each line in your document. For this reason, it is possible that the same document could wordwrap on different words if printed on different printers.

 To Wordwrap Text as You Type

① **Type** Paradise Island offers glistening, white-sand beaches and swimming in crystal-clear waters. **to enter the first sentence in the paragraph below the body title of the announcement.**

Word wraps the word, and, to the beginning of line 7 because it is too long to fit on line 6 (Figure 1-20). Your document may wordwrap on a different word depending on the type of printer you are using.

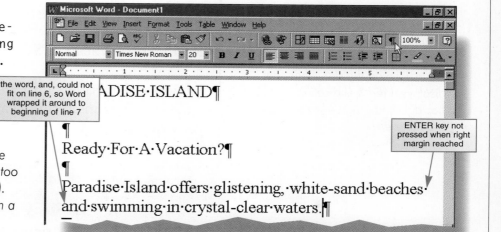

FIGURE 1-20

Checking Spelling Automatically as You Type

As you type text into the document window, Word checks your typing for possible spelling and grammar errors. If a word you type is not in the dictionary, a red wavy underline appears below it. Likewise, if text you type contains possible grammar errors, a green wavy underline appears below the text. In both cases, the Spelling and Grammar Status icon displays a red X, instead of a check mark. Although you can check the entire document for spelling and grammar errors at once, you also can check these errors immediately.

To verify that the spell check as you type feature is enabled, right-click the Spelling and Grammar Status icon on the status bar and then click Options on the shortcut menu. When the Spelling & Grammar dialog box displays, be sure Check spelling as you type is selected and Hide spelling errors in this document is not selected.

When a word is flagged with a red wavy underline, it is not in Word's dictionary. If a word is flagged, it is not necessarily misspelled. For example, many names, abbreviations, and specialized terms are not in the Word's main dictionary. In these cases, you tell Word to ignore the flagged word. As you type, Word also detects duplicate words. For example, if your document contains the phrase, to the the store, Word places a red wavy underline below the second occurrence of the word, the. To display a list of suggested corrections for a flagged word, you right-click it.

In the following example, the word, include, has been misspelled intentionally as incude to illustrate Word's spell check as you type feature. If you are doing this project on a personal computer, your announcement may contain different misspelled words, depending on the accuracy of your typing.

Steps To Spell Check as You Type

1 **Press the SPACEBAR once. Type the beginning of the next sentence:** Recreational activities incude **and then press the SPACEBAR.**

Word flags the misspelled word, incude, by placing a red wavy underline below it (Figure 1-21). Notice the Spelling and Grammar Status icon on the status bar now displays a red X, indicating Word has detected a possible spelling or grammar error.

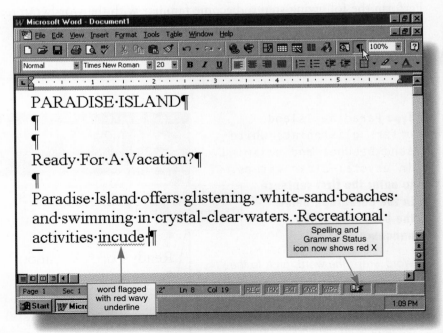

word flagged with red wavy underline

Spelling and Grammar Status icon now shows red X

FIGURE 1-21

2 Position the mouse pointer in the flagged word (incude, in this case).

The mouse pointer's shape is an I-beam when positioned in a word (Figure 1-22).

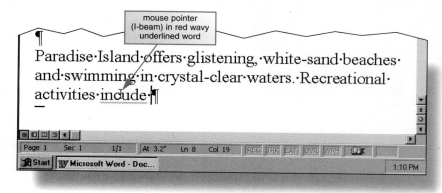

FIGURE 1-22

3 Right-click the flagged word, incude. When the shortcut menu displays, point to include.

Word displays a shortcut menu that lists suggested spelling corrections for the flagged word (Figure 1-23).

4 Click include. Press the END key and then type surfing, SCUBA diving, snorkeling, sailing, and scenic hiking. to enter the remainder of the sentence.

Word replaces the misspelled word with the selected word on the shortcut menu (Figure 1-24 on the next page). The Spelling and Grammar Status icon replaces the red X with a check mark.

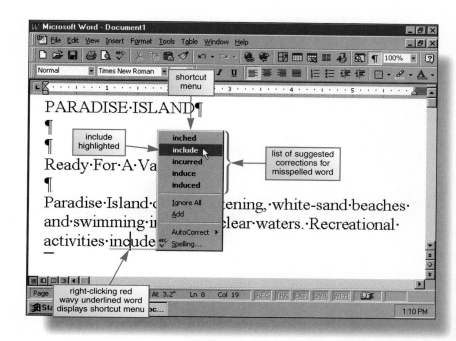

FIGURE 1-23

If your word actually is spelled correctly and, for example, is a proper name, you can right-click it and then click Ignore on the shortcut menu. If, when you right-click the misspelled word, your desired correction is not in the list (Figure 1-23), you can click outside the shortcut menu to make the menu disappear and then retype the correct word.

If you feel the wavy underlines clutter your document window, you can hide them temporarily until you are ready to check for spelling errors. To do this, you right-click the Spelling and Grammar Status icon on the status bar and then click Hide Spelling Errors on the shortcut menu.

Entering Documents that Scroll the Document Window

As you type more lines of text than Word can display in the text area, Word **scrolls** the top portion of the document upward off the screen. Although you cannot see the text once it scrolls off the screen, it remains in the document. Recall that the document window allows you to view only a portion of your document at one time (Figure 1-5 on page WD 1.11).

Follow this step to scroll the document window while entering text.

Steps To Enter a Document that Scrolls the Document Window

 Press the ENTER key twice.

Word scrolls the headline, PARADISE ISLAND, off the top of the screen (Figure 1-24). Your screen may scroll differently depending on the type of monitor you are using.

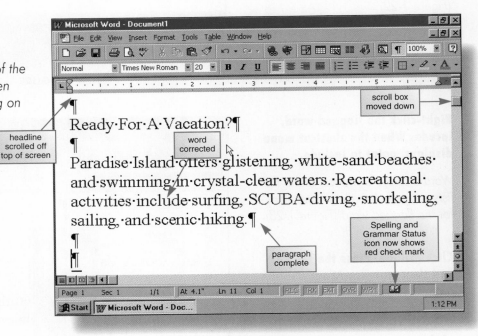

FIGURE 1-24

When Word scrolls text off the top of the screen, the scroll box on the scroll bar at the right edge of the document window moves downward (Figure 1-24). The **scroll box** indicates the current relative location of the insertion point in the document. You may use either the mouse or the keyboard to move the insertion point to a different location in a document.

With the mouse, you use the scroll bars to bring a different portion of the document into the document window, and then click the mouse to move the insertion point to that location. Table 1-1 explains the techniques for scrolling with the mouse.

More *About* **Scrolling**

Computer users frequently switch between the keyboard and the mouse during a word processing session, which places strain on the wrist. To help prevent wrist injury, minimize switching. If your fingers are already on the keyboard, use keyboard keys to scroll; if your hand is already on the mouse, use the mouse to scroll.

TABLE 1-1

SCROLL LOCATION	MOUSE USAGE
Up	Drag the scroll box upward.
Down	Drag the scroll box downward.
Up one screen	Click anywhere above the scroll box.
Down one screen	Click anywhere below the scroll box.
Up one line	Click the scroll arrow at the top of the scroll bar.
Down one line	Click the scroll arrow at the bottom of the scroll bar.

When you use the keyboard, the insertion point moves automatically when you press the appropriate keys. Table 1-2 outlines the various techniques to scroll through a document with the keyboard.

AutoFormat As You Type

The next step is to enter the bulleted list in the announcement. In Word, a **list** is a series of paragraphs. A **bullet** is a small circle positioned at the beginning of a paragraph. Bullets differ from the nonprinting character for the SPACEBAR because bullets print. You can type the list and then place the bullets on the paragraphs at a later time, or you can instruct word to place a bullet character automatically as you type the paragraphs. For example, you can type an asterisk (*) at the beginning of the first paragraph in the list. When you press the ENTER key to add another item to the list, Word automatically changes the asterisk to a bullet character.

This type of automatic change is one of the many **AutoFormat As You Type** features of Word. To be sure this feature is on, click Tools on the menu bar, click AutoCorrect, click the AutoFormat As You Type tab, be sure these two check boxes are selected: Automatic bulleted lists and Format beginning of list item like the one before it, and then click the OK button.

Perform the following steps to add bullets automatically to a list as you type.

TABLE 1-2	
SCROLL LOCATION	*KEY(S) TO PRESS*
Left one character	LEFT ARROW
Right one character	RIGHT ARROW
Left one word	CTRL+LEFT ARROW
Right one word	CTRL+RIGHT ARROW
Up one line	UP ARROW
Down one line	DOWN ARROW
To end of a line	END
To beginning of a line	HOME
Up one paragraph	CTRL+UP ARROW
Down one paragraph	CTRL+DOWN ARROW
Up one screen	PAGE UP
Down one screen	PAGE DOWN
Previous page	CTRL+PAGE UP
Next page	CTRL+PAGE DOWN
To the beginning of a document	CTRL+HOME
To the end of a document	CTRL+END

 Steps To Bullet a List as You Type

1 **Type an asterisk (*) and then press the SPACEBAR. Type** Paradise Island vacation packages fit any budget **as the first item in the list.**

The asterisk character must be followed by pressing the SPACEBAR for the AutoFormat As You Type feature to work properly (Figure 1-25).

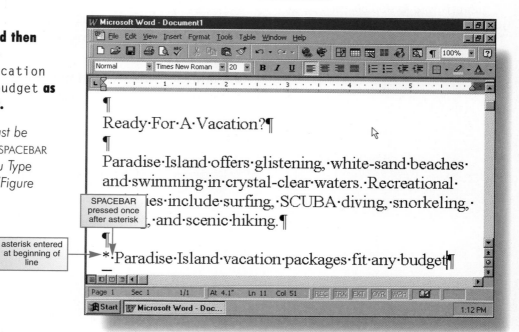

SPACEBAR pressed once after asterisk

asterisk entered at beginning of line

FIGURE 1-25

2 **Press the ENTER key.**

Word converts the asterisk on line 11 to a bullet character and places another bullet character on line 12 (Figure 1-26). Each time you press the ENTER key, Word considers the next line a new paragraph and places a bullet character automatically at the beginning of the line. The Bullets button on the Formatting toolbar is recessed, indicating the current paragraph is bulleted.

asterisk converted to bullet character when ENTER key pressed

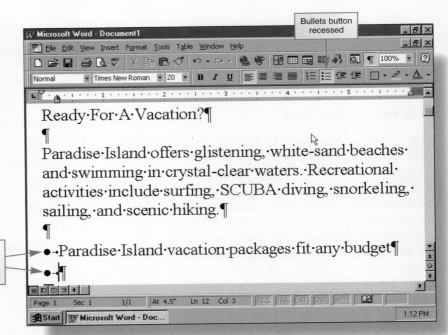

FIGURE 1-26

3 **Type** Cottages, suites, condos, and inns are available **and then press the ENTER key.**

Word places a bullet character on line 13 (Figure 1-27). Because you are finished with the list, you must instruct Word to stop bulleting paragraphs. To stop automatic bulleting, you press the ENTER key again.

bullet character on line below list

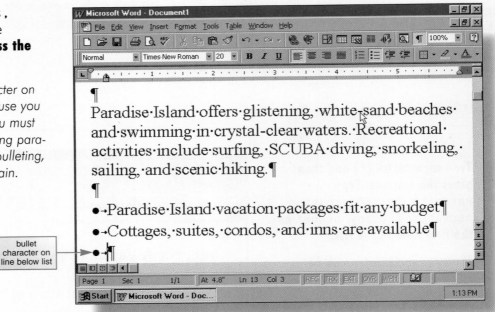

FIGURE 1-27

4 Press the ENTER key. Type Call Tropical Travel at 555-2121 as the last line in the announcement.

Word removes the lone bullet character after the list because you pressed the ENTER key twice (Figure 1-28). The text of the announcement is completely entered.

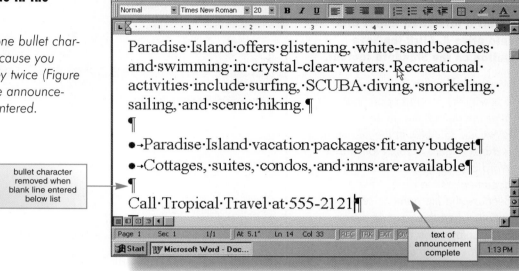

bullet character removed when blank line entered below list

text of announcement complete

FIGURE 1-28

If you know before you type a list that it is to be numbered, you can add numbers as you type, just as you add bullets as you type. To add numbers, type the number one followed by a period and a space (1.) at the beginning of the first item and then type your text. When you press the ENTER key, Word places the number two and a space (2 .) at the beginning of the next line automatically. As with automatic bullets, to stop automatic numbering, press the ENTER key twice at the end of the list.

Saving a Document

When you are creating a document in Word, the computer stores it in memory. If the computer is turned off or if you lose electrical power, the document is lost. Hence, it is mandatory to save on disk any document that you will use later. The steps on the next page illustrate how to save a document on a floppy disk inserted in drive A using the Save button on the Standard toolbar.

Steps To Save a New Document

1 **Insert a formatted floppy disk into drive A. Click the Save button on the Standard toolbar.**

Word displays the Save As dialog box with the insertion point blinking after the default file name, PARADISE ISLAND, in the File name text box (Figure 1-29). Notice that Word chooses the first line of the document as the default file name. Because the file name is selected initially when the Save As dialog box displays, you can change the file name by immediately typing the new name. If you do not enter a new file name, the document will be saved with the default file name, PARADISE ISLAND.

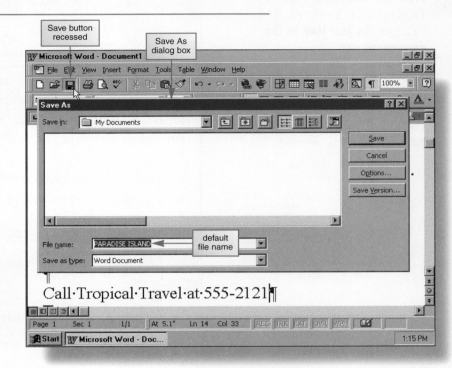

FIGURE 1-29

2 **Type the file name** Paradise Island Announcement **in the File name text box. Do not press the ENTER key after typing the file name.**

*The file name, Paradise Island Announcement, displays in the File name text box (Figure 1-30). When creating file names, you should be as meaningful as possible. Thus, the first words in this file name (Paradise Island) relate to the nature of this document, and the last word (Announcement) relates to the category of this document. Using this technique, all files relating to Paradise Island, whether a letter, a memo, or an announcement, will be grouped together in a folder. A **folder** is a specific location on a disk. Notice that the current folder is My Documents. To change to a different drive or folder, you must use the Save in box.*

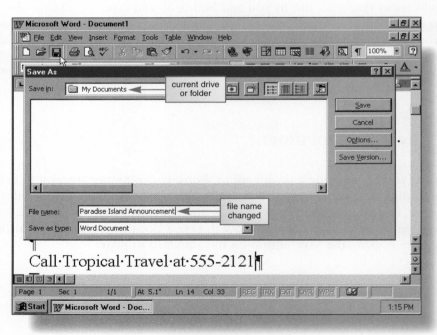

FIGURE 1-30

3 Click the Save in box arrow and then point to 3½ Floppy (A:).

A list of the available drives displays with 3½ Floppy (A:) highlighted (Figure 1-31). Your list may differ depending on your system configuration.

FIGURE 1-31

4 Click 3½ Floppy (A:) and then point to the Save button in the Save As dialog box.

The 3½ Floppy (A:) drive becomes the selected drive (Figure 1-32). The names of existing files stored on the floppy disk in drive A display. In Figure 1-32, no files currently are stored on the floppy disk in drive A.

FIGURE 1-32

5 Click the Save button in the Save As dialog box.

Word saves the document on the floppy disk in drive A with the file name Paradise Island Announcement (Figure 1-33). Although the announcement is saved on a floppy disk, it also remains in main memory and displays on the screen.

*Other***Ways**

1. On File menu click Save, type file name, select location in Save in box, click Save button in dialog box
2. Press CTRL+S, type file name, select location in Save in box, click Save button in dialog box

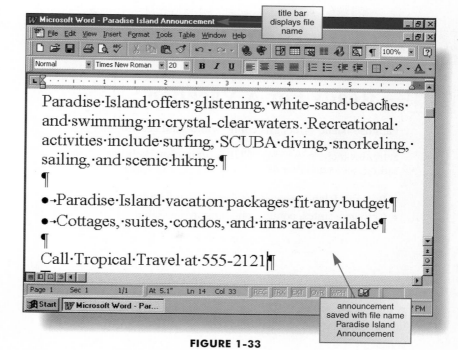

FIGURE 1-33

Formatting Paragraphs and Characters in a Document

The text for Project 1 now is complete. The next step is to format the characters and paragraphs within the announcement. Paragraphs encompass the text up to and including the paragraph mark (¶). **Paragraph formatting** is the process of changing the appearance of a paragraph. For example, you can center or indent a paragraph.

document
before formatting

PARADISE ISLAND

Ready For A Vacation?

Paradise Island offers glistening, white-sand beaches and swimming in crystal-clear waters. Recreational activities include surfing, SCUBA diving, snorkeling, sailing, and scenic hiking.

• Paradise Island vacation packages fit any budget
• Cottages, suites, condos, and inns are available

Call Tropical Travel at 555-2121

FIGURE 1-34

Characters include letters, numbers, punctuation marks, and symbols. **Character formatting** is the process of changing the way characters appear on the screen and in print. You use character formatting to emphasize certain words and improve readability of a document.

With Word, you can format before you type or apply new formats after you type. Earlier, you changed the font size before you typed any text, and then you entered the text. You also used AutoFormat to insert bullets as you typed the list in the announcement. In this section, you format existing text.

Figure 1-34 shows the announcement before formatting the paragraphs and characters in it. Figure 1-35 shows the announcement after formatting it. As you can see from the two figures, a document that is formatted not only is easier to read, but it also looks more professional.

In the pages that follow, you will change the unformatted announcement in Figure 1-34 to the formatted announcement in Figure 1-35 using these steps:

document
after formatting

48-point
Algerian
bold font

PARADISE ISLAND

centered

36-point
bold font

Ready For A Vacation?

Paradise Island offers glistening, white-sand beaches and swimming in crystal-clear waters. Recreational activities include surfing, SCUBA diving, snorkeling, sailing, and scenic hiking.

underlined

• Paradise Island vacation packages fit <u>any</u> budget
• Cottages, suites, condos, and inns are available

Call ***Tropical Travel*** at 555-2121

centered

bold and
italicized

FIGURE 1-35

1. Center the headline and body title across the page.
2. Enlarge the headline.
3. Change the font of the headline.
4. Bold the headline.
5. Bold and enlarge the body title.
6. Underline a word in the bulleted list.
7. Bold and italicize a series of words in the last line of the announcement.
8. Center the last line of the announcement.

The process required to format the announcement is explained on the following pages. The first formatting step is to center the first two lines of text between the margins. Recall that each line is considered a separate paragraph because each line ends with a paragraph mark.

Selecting and Formatting Paragraphs and Characters

To format a single paragraph, move the insertion point into the paragraph and then format it. To format multiple paragraphs in a document, however, the paragraphs you want to format first must be selected and then they can be formatted. In the same manner, to format characters, you first must select the characters to be formatted and then format your selection. Selected text is highlighted. For example, if your screen normally displays dark letters on a light background, then selected text appears as light letters on a dark background.

Selecting Multiple Paragraphs

The headline (PARADISE ISLAND) and the body title (Ready For A Vacation?) are separated by two paragraph marks. Thus, the headline and the body title are actually four separate paragraphs. Recall that each time you press the ENTER key, Word creates a new paragraph.

To center the headline and body title in Project 1, you must first **select** all four paragraphs as shown in the following steps.

More *About* **Formatting**

Character formatting includes changing the font, font style, font size; adding an underline, color, strikethrough, shadow, outline; embossing; engraving; making a superscript or subscript; and changing the case of the letters. Paragraph formatting includes alignment; indentation; and spacing above, below, or in between lines.

 To Select Multiple Paragraphs

1 Press CTRL+HOME to position the insertion point at the top of the document; that is, press and hold the CTRL key, then press the HOME key, and then release both keys. Move the mouse pointer to the left of the first paragraph to be centered (the headline) until the mouse pointer changes to a right-pointing block arrow.

The mouse pointer changes to a right-pointing block arrow when positioned to the left of a paragraph (Figure 1-36).

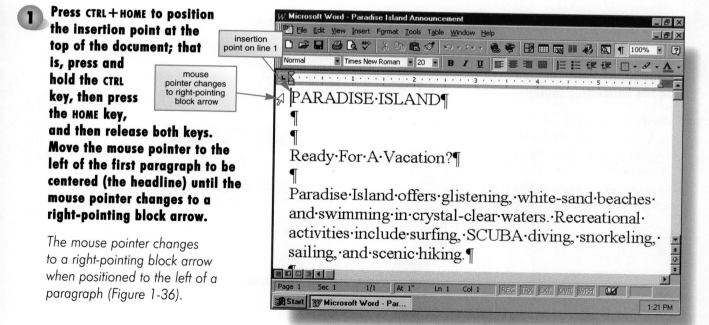

FIGURE 1-36

2 Drag downward to the last line of the last paragraph to be centered (the body title).

All of the paragraphs to be centered are selected; that is, light letters on a dark background (Figure 1-37). Recall that dragging is the process of holding down the mouse button while moving the mouse, and finally releasing the mouse button.

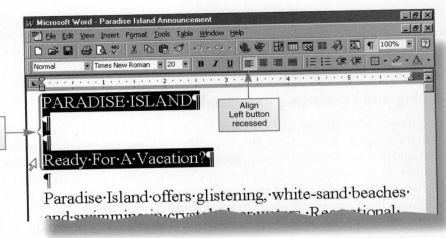

FIGURE 1-37

Centering Selected Paragraphs

The default alignment for paragraphs is **left-aligned**; that is, flush margins at the left edge, and jagged edges at the right edge. In Figure 1-37, the **Align Left button** is recessed to indicate the selected paragraphs currently are left-aligned. To center selected paragraphs, click the Center button as shown in the following step.

Steps **To Center Selected Paragraphs**

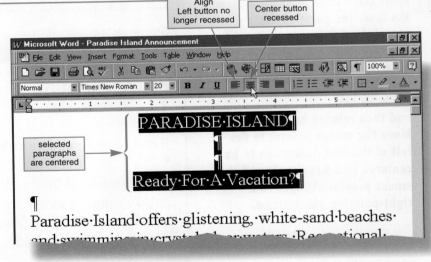

FIGURE 1-38

1 With the paragraphs still selected, click the Center button on the Formatting toolbar.

Word centers the headline and body title between the left and right margins (Figure 1-38). The Center button on the Formatting toolbar is recessed, which indicates the highlighted paragraphs are centered.

When a selected paragraph(s) is centered, the Center button on the Formatting toolbar is recessed. If, for some reason, you wanted to return the selected paragraphs to left-aligned, you would click the Align Left button on the Formatting toolbar.

The next series of steps selects the headline and formats the characters in it. In the pages that follow, you select the headline, increase the font size of the selected characters to 48, change the font of the selected characters to Algerian, and then bold the selected characters.

Selecting a Single Line

To select the headline, the first line of the announcement, perform the following step.

 To Select a Single Line

1 **Move the mouse pointer to the left of the line to be selected (the headline) until it changes to a right-pointing block arrow and then click.**

The entire line to the right of the mouse pointer is selected (Figure 1-39).

FIGURE 1-39

Changing the Font Size of Selected Text

The next step in formatting the headline is to increase its font size. Recall that the font size specifies the size of the characters on the screen. Earlier in this project, you changed the font size for the entire announcement from 10 to 20. The headline, however, requires a larger font size than the rest of the document. Follow these steps to increase the font size of the headline from 20 to 48 points.

 To Change the Font Size of Selected Text

1 **While the text is selected, click the Font Size box arrow on the Formatting toolbar, and then point to the down arrow on the Font Size scroll bar.**

Word displays a list of the available font sizes (Figure 1-40). Available font sizes vary depending on the font and printer driver.

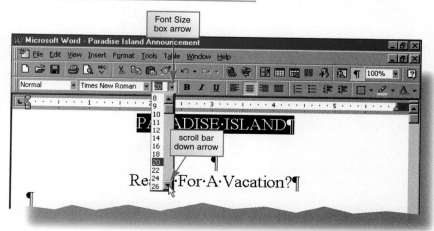

FIGURE 1-40

2 Click the down arrow on the scroll bar until the font size 48 displays in the list and then point to 48.

Font size 48 is highlighted (Figure 1-41).

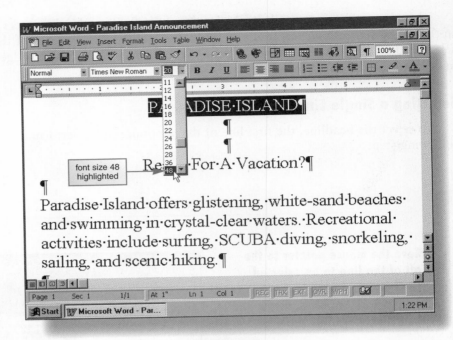

FIGURE 1-41

3 Click font size 48.

Word increases the font size of the headline from 20 to 48 (Figure 1-42). The Font Size box on the Formatting toolbar displays 48, indicating the selected text has a font size of 48.

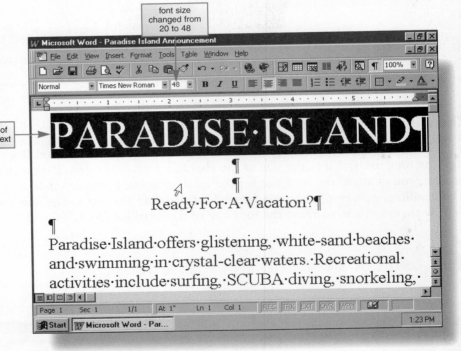

FIGURE 1-42

Changing the Font of Selected Text

Recall that the default font is Times New Roman. Word, however, provides many other fonts to add variety to your documents. Thus, change the font of the headline in the announcement to Algerian as shown in these steps.

Steps **To Change the Font of Selected Text**

1 **While the text is selected, click the Font box arrow on the Formatting toolbar, scroll through the list until Algerian displays, and then point to Algerian.**

Word displays a list of available fonts (Figure 1-43). Your list of available fonts may be different, depending on the type of printer you are using.

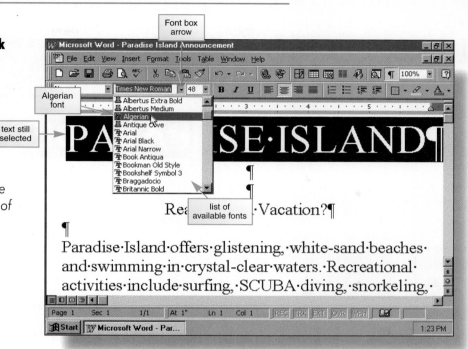

FIGURE 1-43

2 **Click Algerian.**

Word changes the font of the selected text to Algerian (Figure 1-44).

FIGURE 1-44

Bold Selected Text

To further emphasize the headline of the announcement, perform the step on the next page to make it bold.

Other Ways

1. Right-click selected text, click Font on shortcut menu, click Font tab, select desired font in Font list box, click OK button

2. On Format menu click Font, click Font tab, select desired font in Font list box, click OK button

3. Press CTRL+SHIFT+F, press DOWN ARROW key until desired font displays, press ENTER

Steps **To Bold Selected Text**

1 **While the text is selected, click the Bold button on the Formatting toolbar.**

Word formats the headline in bold (Figure 1-45). The Bold button is recessed.

FIGURE 1-45

When the selected text is bold, the Bold button on the Formatting toolbar is recessed. If, for some reason, you wanted to remove the bold format of the selected text, you would click the Bold button a second time.

Continuing to Format Text

The next step is to select the body title (Ready For A Vacation?), increase its font size, and bold it.

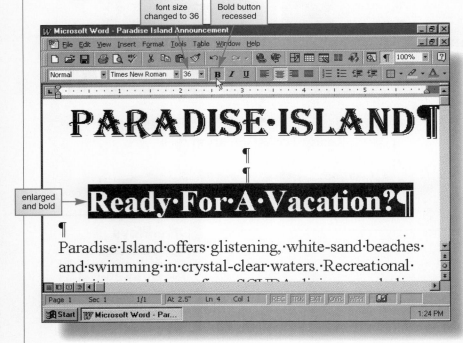

FIGURE 1-46

TO FORMAT A LINE OF TEXT

1 Click to the left of the line to be formatted (the body title).

2 Click the Font Size box arrow on the Formatting toolbar and scroll to the font size 36. Click font size 36.

3 Click the Bold button on the Formatting toolbar.

The body title is enlarged and bold (Figure 1-46).

Scrolling

Continue formatting the document by scrolling down one screen so the bottom portion of the announcement displays in the document window.

Steps **To Scroll Through the Document**

1 **Position the mouse pointer below the scroll box on the vertical scroll bar (Figure 1-47).**

2 **Click below the scroll box on the vertical scroll bar.**

Word scrolls down one screenful in the document (see Figure 1-48 below). Depending on your monitor type, your screen may scroll differently.

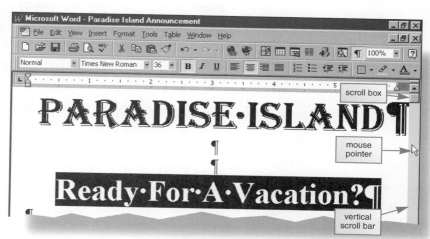

FIGURE 1-47

Selecting a Single Word

Follow these steps to select the word, any, so it can be underlined.

Steps **To Select a Single Word**

1 **Position the mouse pointer somewhere in the word to be formatted (any, in this case).**

The mouse pointer's shape is an I-beam in a word that has not yet been selected (Figure 1-48).

> **Other Ways**
>
> 1. Drag scroll box on vertical scroll bar
> 2. Click scroll arrows on vertical scroll bar
> 3. Press PAGE DOWN or PAGE UP
> 4. See Tables 1-1 and 1-2 on pages WD 1.22 and WD 1.23

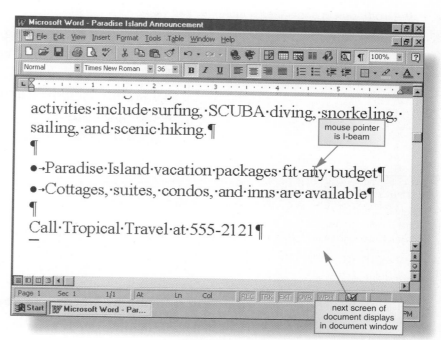

FIGURE 1-48

2 **Double-click the word to be formatted.**

The word, any, is selected (Figure 1-49). Notice that when the mouse pointer is positioned in a selected word, its shape is a left-pointing block arrow.

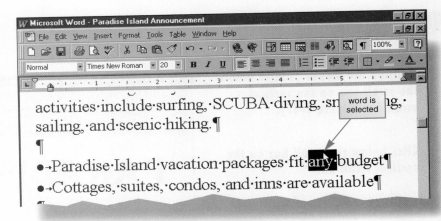

FIGURE 1-49

Underlining Selected Text

The next step is to underline the selected word, any.

 To Underline Selected Text

1 **With the text still selected, click the Underline button on the Formatting toolbar.**

The word, any, is underlined (Figure 1-50). The Underline button is recessed.

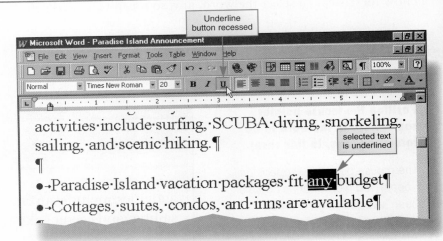

FIGURE 1-50

When the selected text is underlined, the Underline button on the Formatting toolbar is recessed. If, for some reason, you wanted to remove the underline from the selected text, you would click the Underline button a second time.

Selecting a Group of Words and Formatting Them

The next formatting step is to italicize and bold the phrase, Tropical Travel, in the last line of the announcement. The first set of steps selects the text. Then perform the second set of steps to bold and italicize the selected text.

Steps To Select a Group of Words

1 **Position the mouse pointer on the first character of the first word to be selected.**

The mouse pointer, an I-beam, is at the beginning of the word, Tropical (Figure 1-51).

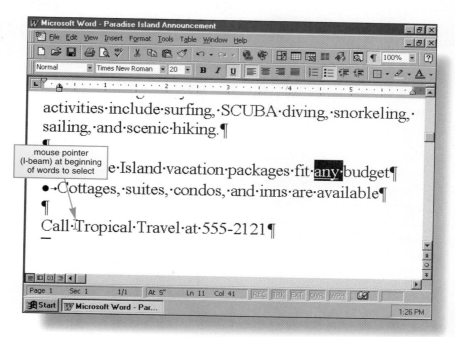

FIGURE 1-51

2 **Drag the mouse pointer through the last character of the last word to be selected.**

The phrase, Tropical Travel, is selected (Figure 1-52).

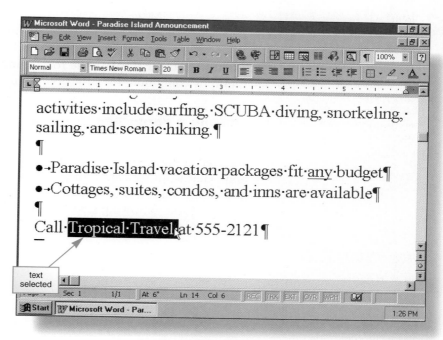

FIGURE 1-52

Other Ways

1. With insertion point at beginning of first word in the group, press CTRL+SHIFT+RIGHT ARROW until words are selected

Steps **To Italicize and Bold Selected Text**

1 **With the text still selected, click the Italic button on the Formatting toolbar. Click the Bold button on the Formatting toolbar. Click inside the selected text to remove the highlight.**

Word italicizes and bolds the text and positions the insertion point inside the bold and italicized text (Figure 1-53). When the insertion point is inside the bold and italicized text, the Bold and Italic buttons on the Formatting toolbar are recessed.

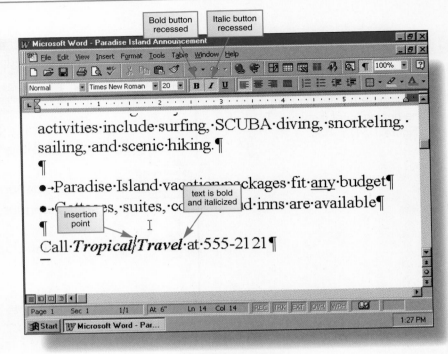

FIGURE 1-53

To remove a highlight, click the mouse. If you click inside the highlight, the Formatting toolbar displays the formatting characteristics of the characters and paragraphs containing the insertion point.

Centering a Paragraph

The last step in formatting Project 1 is to center the last line of the announcement. Recall that paragraph formatting does not require you to select the paragraph. That is, just position the insertion point in the paragraph to be formatted and then format it accordingly.

Perform the following step to center the last line in the announcement.

More *About*
the Formatting
Toolbar

Many of the buttons on the Formatting toolbar are toggles; that is, click them once to format the selected text, and click them again to remove the format from the selected text. For example, clicking the Italic button italicizes selected text; clicking the Italic button again de-italicizes the selected text.

Steps **To Center a Single Paragraph**

1 Be sure the insertion point is still in the last line of the announcement. Click the Center button on the Formatting toolbar.

The last line of the announcement is centered (Figure 1-54). Notice that you did not have to select the paragraph before centering; paragraph formatting requires only that the insertion point be some-where in the paragraph.

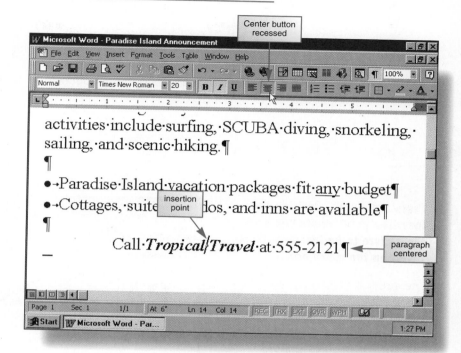

FIGURE 1-54

The formatting for the announcement is now complete. The next step is to import a graphic from the Web and then resize it.

Inserting a Picture from the Web into a Word Document

Graphic files are available from a variety of sources. Word 97 includes a series of predefined graphic files called **clip art** that you can insert into a Word document. These clip art files are located in the Clip Gallery, which contains its own Help system to assist you in locating an image suited to your application. If you have a scanner attached to your system, Word can insert the scanned photograph directly from the scanner; or, you can scan the picture into a file and then insert the scanned file into the Word document at a later time. Instead of scanning your own pictures, you can purchase photographs from a local software retailer, usually on a CD-ROM, or you can locate a picture on the Internet.

Once you have a graphic file, you can then insert, or **import**, it into a Word document. If you locate the picture on the Web, some browsers require you to copy the picture to a file on a local drive and then import the picture from your own disk. Other browsers, such as Microsoft Internet Explorer, allow you to copy the picture to the Clipboard and paste it into your Word document – *without first having to copy the file to a local disk!*

In this project, you locate a picture of Paradise Island at the Web site of www.scsite.com/off97e/pr1.htm that you want to use in the announcement. If you do not have access to the Web, go to the steps on page WD 1.44 to insert the picture from the Data Disk that accompanies this book.

*Other***Ways**

1. With insertion point in desired paragraph, click Paragraph on shortcut menu, click Indents and Spacing tab, click Alignment box arrow, click Centered, click OK button

2. With insertion point in desired paragraph, on For-mat menu click Paragraph, click Indents and Spacing tab, click Alignment box arrow, click Centered, click OK button

3. Press CTRL+E

More *About* **Using Graphics**

Emphasize a graphic in an announcement by placing it at the optical center of the page. To determine optical center, divide the page in half horizon-tally and vertically. The optical center is located one third of the way up the vertical line from the point of intersection of the two lines.

NOTE: The following steps assume you are using Microsoft Internet Explorer as your browser. If you are not using Internet Explorer and your browser does not allow you to copy pictures to the Windows Clipboard, you will need to perform a different set of steps. Your browser's handling of pictures on the Web will be discovered in Step 6 on page WD 1.42. If necessary, you may be directed to follow the steps on page WD 1.44 to save the Paradise Island picture on a disk and then insert the picture into the announcement from the disk.

Steps **To Insert a Picture from the Web**

1 **Press CTRL+HOME. Position the insertion point where you want the picture to be inserted. Click Insert on the menu bar.**

The insertion point is positioned on the paragraph mark immediately below the headline of the announcement (Figure 1-55). The Insert menu and its list of commands display.

FIGURE 1-55

2 **Point to Picture on the Insert menu and then point to From File on the Picture submenu (Figure 1-56).**

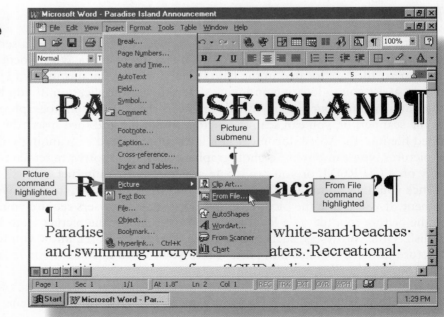

FIGURE 1-56

3 **Click From File. When the Insert Picture dialog box displays, point to the Search the Web button.**

Word displays the Insert Picture dialog box (Figure 1-57). The current folder is Clipart; graphic files supplied with Word are located in this folder. The Paradise Island picture is located on the Web.

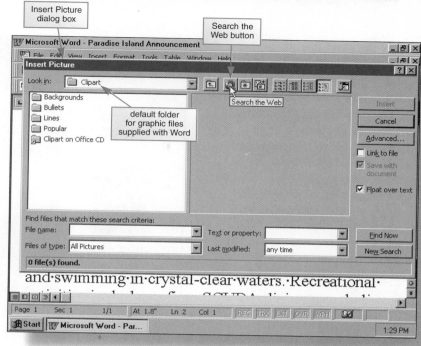

FIGURE 1-57

4 **Click the Search the Web button. When the Find it Fast – Microsoft Internet Explorer window displays, click the Address text box to select its contents and then type** www.scsite.com/off97e/pr1.htm **in the Address text box.**

If you currently are not connected to the Web, Word connects you using your default browser. Word displays the Find it Fast window (Figure 1-58). You can search by words or phrases in the Internet Searches text box; or if you know the exact address of the Web site containing the desired picture, you can enter the address in the Address text box.

FIGURE 1-58

5 Press the ENTER key. If necessary, maximize the Web page window. Right-click the picture of Paradise Island. Point to Copy on the shortcut menu. (If you do not have a Copy command, go to the steps on page WD 1.44.)

The http://www.scsite.com/ off97e/pr1.htm Web page displays (Figure 1-59). This Web page displays several pictures used in this project. This announcement uses the picture of Paradise Island. Your browser displays a shortcut menu. If you do not have a Copy command on your shortcut menu, your browser requires that you save the picture on a disk and then insert the picture from the disk. Thus, if you do not have a Copy command on your shortcut menu, go to the steps on page WD 1.44 to copy the picture onto a disk and then insert the picture into the announcement from your disk.

FIGURE 1-59

6 Click Copy on the shortcut menu. Close the browser window. Be sure the insertion point is still on the paragraph mark below the headline in the announcement. Click Edit on the menu bar and then point to Paste Special (Figure 1-60).

*The picture of Paradise Island is copied to the **Clipboard**, which is a temporary Windows storage area. You will paste the picture into the announcement from the Clipboard.*

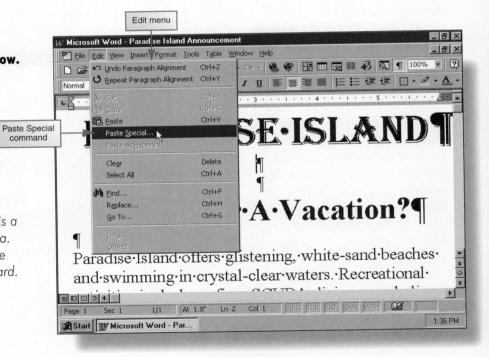

FIGURE 1-60

7 **Click Paste Special. When the Paste Special dialog box displays, click Float over text to clear the check box. Point to the OK button.**

Word displays the Paste Special dialog box (Figure 1-61). You want to clear the Float over text check box so the picture of Paradise Island is inserted as an inline picture, instead of a floating picture. A floating picture is one inserted in a layer over the text; whereas, an inline picture is positioned directly in the text at the location of the insertion point. Floating pictures are discussed in a later project.

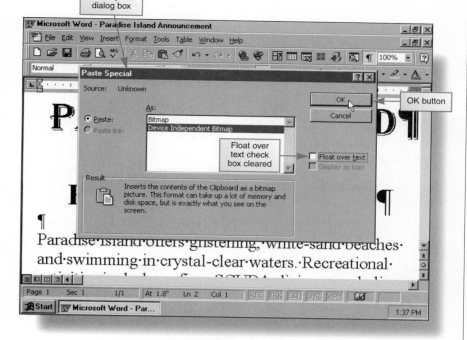

FIGURE 1-61

8 **Click the OK button.**

Word inserts the picture into your document at the location of the insertion point (Figure 1-62).

FIGURE 1-62

Because you inserted the picture as an inline picture, it is part of a paragraph. Therefore, you can use any of the paragraph alignment buttons on the Formatting toolbar to reposition the picture. Recall that earlier you formatted that paragraph mark to centered. Thus, the Paradise Island picture is centered across the page.

◆ **More** *About* **Shortcut Menus**

Right-clicking an object opens a shortcut menu (also called a context-sensitive or object menu). Depending on the object, the commands in the shortcut menu vary. A dimmed command in a shortcut menu means the command cannot be used at the current time.

If, when you right-click the Paradise Island picture on the Web, you did not have a Copy command on the shortcut menu, you have to save the picture on a disk and then insert it from the disk. With the shortcut menu on the screen, proceed with these steps.

TO SAVE A PICTURE ON THE WEB ON A DISK AND THEN INSERT IT IN THE DOCUMENT

① Click Save Image As (or a similar command) on the shortcut menu.

② Insert a formatted floppy disk into drive A.

③ When the Save As dialog box displays, type a:vacation and then click the Save button. Close your browser.

④ Be sure the insertion point is still positioned on the paragraph mark immediately below the headline. Click Insert on the menu bar, point to Picture, and then click From File.

⑤ When the Insert Picture dialog box displays, click Float over text to clear the check box.

⑥ Type a:vacation in the File name text box and then click the Insert button.

⑦ If Word displays a ruler at the left edge of the screen, click View on the menu bar and then click Normal.

Word inserts the picture into your document at the location of the insertion point as shown in Figure 1-62 on the previous page.

If you do not have access to the Web, follow the steps below to insert the picture from the Data Disk that accompanies this book.

TO INSERT A PICTURE FROM THE DATA DISK THAT ACCOMPANIES THIS BOOK

① Press CTRL+HOME. Position the insertion point where you want the picture to be inserted (on the paragraph mark immediately below the headline of the announcement).

② Insert the Data Disk that accompanies this book into drive A.

③ Click Insert on the menu bar, point to Picture, and then click From File.

④ When the Insert Picture dialog box displays, click Float over text to clear the check box.

⑤ Type a:\Word\vacation in the File name text box and then click the Insert button.

⑥ Replace the Data Disk with your floppy disk.

Word inserts the picture into your document at the location of the insertion point as shown in Figure 1-62 on the previous page.

The picture in Figure 1-62 is a little too small for this announcement. The next step is to resize the imported graphic.

Resizing an Imported Graphic

Once a graphic has been imported into a document, you can easily change its size. **Resizing** includes both enlarging and reducing the size of a graphic. To resize a graphic, you first must select it. The following steps show how to select and then resize the picture you just imported from the Web.

To Resize a Graphic

1 Click anywhere in the graphic. If your screen does not display the Picture toolbar, right-click the Paradise Island picture and then click Show Picture Toolbar.

Word selects the graphic (Figure 1-63). The Picture toolbar floats on the Word screen when a graphic is selected. Selected graphics display surrounded by a **selection rectangle** *with small squares, called* **sizing handles,** *at each corner and middle location of the selection rectangle. To resize the graphic, you drag the sizing handles until the graphic is the desired size. Dragging a corner sizing handle maintains the proportions of the graphic; whereas, dragging a middle sizing handle distorts the proportions of the graphic.*

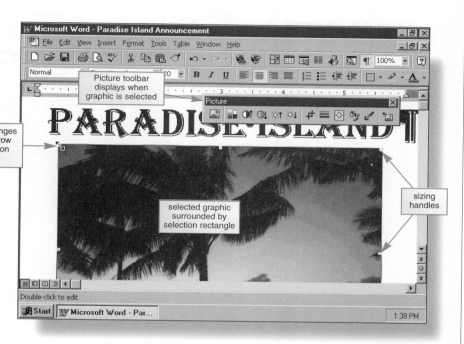

FIGURE 1-63

2 Point to the upper-left corner sizing handle.

The mouse pointer changes to a two-headed arrow when it is on a sizing handle.

3 Drag the sizing handle outward until the selection rectangle is positioned approximately at the position shown in Figure 1-64.

FIGURE 1-64

4 Release the mouse button. Click outside the graphic, above it or below it in the text, or to the right of it to deselect it.

Word resizes the graphic (Figure 1-65). The Picture toolbar disappears from the screen when you deselect the graphic.

FIGURE 1-65

Instead of resizing a selected graphic with the mouse, you also can use the Format Picture dialog box to resize a graphic by clicking the Format Picture button on the Picture toolbar and then clicking the Size tab. Using the Size sheet, you enter exact width and height measurements. If you have a precise measurement for the graphic, use the Format Picture dialog box; otherwise, drag the sizing handles to resize the graphic.

Restoring a Resized Graphic to Its Original Size

Sometimes you may resize a graphic and realize it is the wrong size. In these cases, you may want to return the graphic to its original size and start over. To return a resized graphic to its original size, click the graphic to select it and then click the Format Picture button on the Picture toolbar to display the Format Picture dialog box. Click the Size tab and then click the Reset button. Finally, click the OK button.

Saving an Existing Document with the Same File Name

The announcement for Project 1 is now complete. To transfer the formatting changes and imported graphic to your floppy disk in drive A, you must save the document again. When you saved the document the first time, you assigned a file name to it (Paradise Island Announcement). Word assigns this same file name automatically to the document each time you subsequently save it if you use the following procedure.

Steps **To Save an Existing Document with the Same File Name**

1 **Click the Save button on the Standard toolbar.**

Word saves the document on a floppy disk inserted in drive A using the currently assigned file name, Paradise Island Announcement. When the save is finished, the document remains in memory and displays on the screen (Figure 1-66).

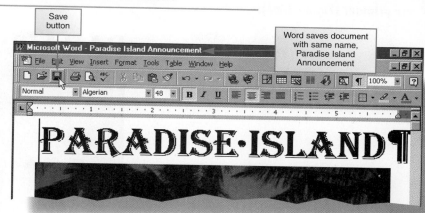

FIGURE 1-66

If, for some reason, you want to save an existing document with a different file name, click Save As on the File menu to display the Save As dialog box. Then, fill in the Save As dialog box as discussed in Steps 2 through 5 on pages WD 1.26 and WD 1.27.

*Other***Ways**
1. On File menu click Save
2. Press CTRL+S

Printing a Document

The next step is to print the document you created. A printed version of the document is called a **hard copy** or **printout**. Perform the following steps to print the announcement created in Project 1.

Steps **To Print a Document**

1 **Ready the printer according to the printer instructions. Click the Print button on the Standard toolbar.**

The mouse pointer briefly changes to an hourglass shape, and then Word quickly displays a message on the status bar, indicating it is preparing to print the document. A few moments later, the document begins printing on the printer. The right edge of the status bar displays a printer icon while the document is printing (Figure 1-67).

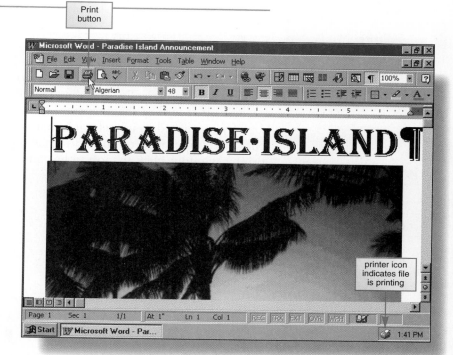

FIGURE 1-67

2 When the printer stops, retrieve the printout (Figure 1-68).

PARADISE ISLAND

Ready For A Vacation?

Paradise Island offers glistening, white-sand beaches and swimming in crystal-clear waters. Recreational activities include surfing, SCUBA diving, snorkeling, sailing, and scenic hiking.

- Paradise Island vacation packages fit <u>any</u> budget
- Cottages, suites, condos, and inns are available

Call ***Tropical Travel*** at 555-2121

FIGURE 1-68

Other Ways
1. On File menu click Print, click OK button
2. Press CTRL+P, press ENTER

More *About* **Printing**

To print multiple copies of the same document, click File on the menu bar and then click Print. When the Print dialog box displays, type the desired number of copies in the Number of copies text box in the Copies area and then click the OK button.

When you use the Print button to print a document, Word prints the entire document automatically. You then may distribute the hard copy or keep it as a permanent record of the document.

If you wanted to cancel a job that is printing or waiting to be printed, double-click the printer icon on the status bar (Figure 1-67 on the previous page). In the printer window, click the job to be canceled and then click Cancel Printing on the Document menu.

Quitting Word

After you create, save, and print the announcement, Project 1 is complete. To quit Word and return control to Windows 95, perform the following steps.

Steps **To Quit Word**

Close button

1 **Point to the Close button in the upper-right corner of the title bar (Figure 1-69).**

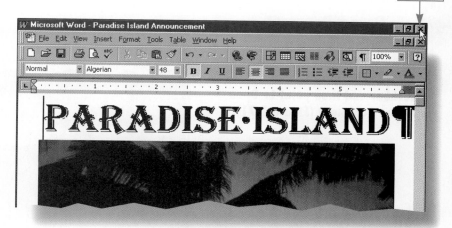

FIGURE 1-69

2 **Click the Close button.**

If you made changes to the document since the last save, Word displays a dialog box asking if you want to save the changes (Figure 1-70). Clicking the Yes button saves changes; clicking the No button ignores the changes; and clicking the Cancel button returns to the document. If you did not make any changes since you saved the document, this dialog box does not display.

FIGURE 1-70

Other Ways
1. On File menu click Exit
2. Press ALT+F4

Project 1 is now complete. You created and formatted the announcement, inserted a picture from the Web on it, printed it, and saved it as both a Word document and a Web document. You might decide, however, to change the announcement at a later date. To do this, you must start Word and then retrieve your document from the floppy disk in drive A.

Opening a Document

Earlier, you saved the Word document built in Project 1 on floppy disk using the file name Paradise Island Announcement. Once you have created and saved a document, you often will have reason to retrieve it from the disk. For example, you might want to revise the document. The following steps illustrate how to open the file Paradise Island Announcement.

Steps   To Open a Document

1 **Click the Start button on the taskbar and then point to Open Office Document (Figure 1-71).**

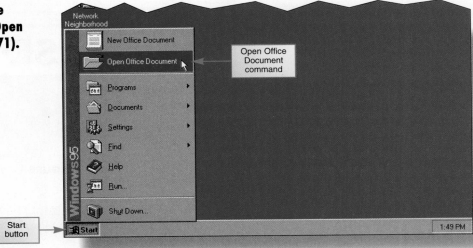

FIGURE 1-71

2 **Click Open Office Document. If necessary, click the Look in box arrow, and then click 3½ Floppy (A:). If it is not already selected, click the file name Paradise Island Announcement. Point to the Open button.**

Office displays the Open Office Document dialog box (Figure 1-72). Office displays the files on the floppy disk in drive A.

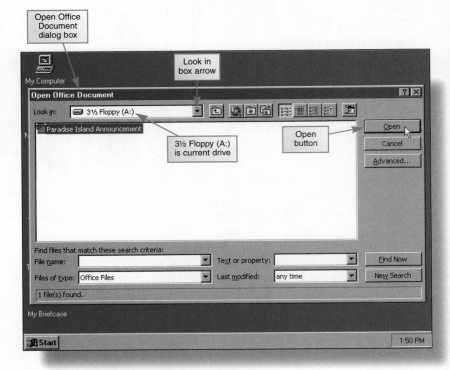

FIGURE 1-72

3 **Click the Open button.**

Office starts Word, and then Word opens the document, Paradise Island Announcement, from the floppy disk in drive A and displays the document on the screen (Figure 1-73).

FIGURE 1-73

Correcting Errors

After creating a document, you often will find you must make changes to the document. Changes can be required because the document contains an error or because of new circumstances.

Types of Changes Made to Documents

The types of changes made to documents normally fall into one of the three following categories: additions, deletions, or modifications.

ADDITIONS Additional words, sentences, or paragraphs may be required in the document. Additions occur when you omit text from a document and are required to add it later. For example, you accidentally may forget to put the telephone number in the last line of Project 1.

DELETIONS Sometimes, text in a document is incorrect or is no longer needed. For example, the agency might remove condos from their package deals. In this case, you would delete the word condos from the bulleted list.

MODIFICATIONS If an error is made in a document, you might have to revise the word(s) in the text. For example, SCUBA diving might be offered to only certified divers.

Word provides several methods for correcting errors in a document. For each of the error correction techniques, you first must move the insertion point to the error.

More *About* Opening Files

In Word, you can open a recently used file by clicking File on the menu bar and then clicking the file name on the File menu. To instruct Word to show the recently used documents on the File menu, click Tools on the menu bar, click Options, click the General tab, click Recently used file list, and then click the OK button.

Inserting Text into an Existing Document

If you leave a word or phrase out of a sentence, you can include it in the sentence by positioning the insertion point where you intend to insert the text. Word always inserts the text to the left of the insertion point. The text to the right of the insertion point moves to the right and downward to accommodate the new text. The following steps illustrate inserting the word, beautiful, before the word, crystal, in the first sentence of the paragraph below the body title in Project 1.

Steps To Insert Text into an Existing Document

1 Scroll through the document and click immediately to the left of the letter c in the word, crystal.

The insertion point displays immediately to the left of the letter c in crystal (Figure 1-74).

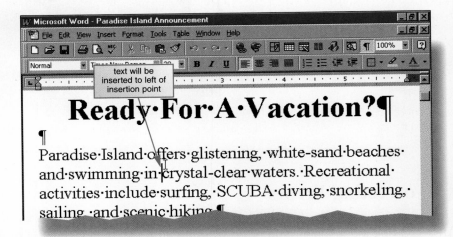

FIGURE 1-74

2 Type beautiful, and then press the SPACEBAR.

The word, beautiful, is inserted between the words, in and crystal, in the announcement for Project 1 (Figure 1-75). Be sure to include the comma after the word, beautiful, as shown in the figure.

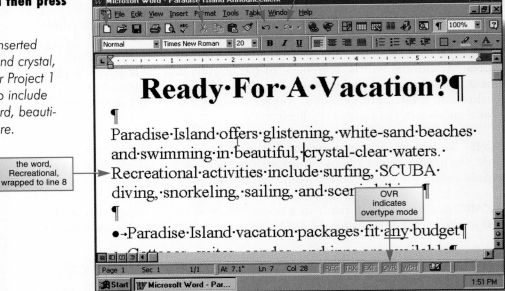

FIGURE 1-75

Notice in Figure 1-75 that the text to the right of the word, crystal, moved to the right and downward to accommodate the insertion of the word, beautiful. That is, the word, Recreational, moved down to line 8.

In Word, the default typing mode is insert mode. In **insert mode**, as you type a character, Word inserts the character and moves all the characters to the right of the typed character one position to the right. In the example just given, you used insert mode to add the word, beautiful. You can change to overtype mode by double-clicking the **OVR status indicator** on the status bar (Figure 1-75). In **overtype mode**, Word replaces characters to the right of the insertion point. Double-clicking the OVR status indicator a second time returns you to insert mode.

Deleting Text from an Existing Document

It is not unusual to type incorrect characters or words in a document. In such a case, to correct the error, you may want to delete certain letters or words.

TO DELETE AN INCORRECT CHARACTER IN A DOCUMENT

1. Click next to the incorrect character.
2. Press the BACKSPACE key to erase to the left of the insertion point; or press the DELETE key to erase to the right of the insertion point.

TO DELETE AN INCORRECT WORD OR PHRASE IN A DOCUMENT

1. Select the word or phrase you want to erase.
2. Right-click the selected word or phrase, and then click Cut on the shortcut menu; or click the Cut button on the Standard toolbar (Figure 1-75); or press the DELETE key.

Undoing Recent Actions

Word provides an **Undo button** on the Standard toolbar that you can use to cancel your recent command(s) or action(s). If you delete some text accidentally, you can bring it back. If you want to cancel your undo, you can use the **Redo button**. Some actions, such as saving or printing a document, cannot be undone or redone.

TO CANCEL YOUR MOST RECENT ACTION

1. Click the Undo button (Figure 1-75) on the Standard toolbar.

TO CANCEL YOUR MOST RECENT UNDO

1. Click the Redo button (Figure 1-75) on the Standard toolbar.

TO CANCEL A SERIES OF PRIOR ACTIONS

1. Click the Undo button arrow to display the undo actions list.
2. Drag through the actions to be undone.

Closing the Entire Document

Sometimes, everything goes wrong. If this happens, you may want to close the document entirely and start over. You also may want to close a document when you are finished with it so you can begin your next document. To close the document, follow these steps.

TO CLOSE THE ENTIRE DOCUMENT AND START OVER

1. Click File on the menu bar and then click Close.
2. If Word displays a dialog box, click the No button to ignore the changes since the last time you saved the document.
3. Click the New button (Figure 1-75 on page WD1.52) on the Standard toolbar.

You also can close the document by clicking the Close button at the right edge of the menu bar.

Word Online Help

At any time while you are working in Word, you can answer your Word questions by using **Help**. Used properly, this form of online assistance can increase your productivity and reduce your frustrations by minimizing the time you spend learning how to use Word. Table 1-3 summarizes the five categories of Word Help available to you.

Table 1-3		
HELP CATEGORY	**DESCRIPTION**	**HOW TO ACTIVATE**
Office Assistant	Answers your questions, offers tips, and provides Help for a variety of Word features.	Click the Office Assistant button on the Standard toolbar.
Contents Sheet	Groups Help topics by general categories. Similar to a table of contents in a book.	Click Contents and Index on the Help menu and then click the Contents tab.
Index Sheet	Accesses Help topics by subject. Similar to an index in a book.	Click Contents and Index on the Help menu and then click the Index tab.
Find Sheet	Searches the index for all phrases that include the term in question.	Click Contents and Index on the Help menu and then click the Find tab.
Question Mark button and What's This? command	Used to identify unfamiliar items on the screen.	In a dialog box, click the Question Mark button and then click an item in a dialog box. Click What's This? on the Help menu and then click an item on the screen.

The following sections show examples of the various types of Help described in Table 1-3.

Using the Office Assistant

The **Office Assistant** answers your questions and suggests more efficient ways to complete a task. With the Office Assistant active, for example, you can type a word or phrase in a text box, and the Office Assistant provides immediate Help on the subject. Also, as you create a document, the Office Assistant accumulates tips that suggest more efficient ways to complete a task you performed while creating the document, such as formatting, printing, or saving. This tip feature is part of the **IntelliSense™ technology** that is built into Word.

The following steps show how to use the Office Assistant to obtain information on saving a Word document as a Web page.

Steps **To Obtain Help Using the Office Assistant**

1 **If the Office Assistant is not on the screen, click the Office Assistant button on the Standard toolbar. If the Office Assistant is on the screen, click it. Type** save Word document as a Web page **in the What would you like to do? text box and then point to the Search button (Figure 1-76).**

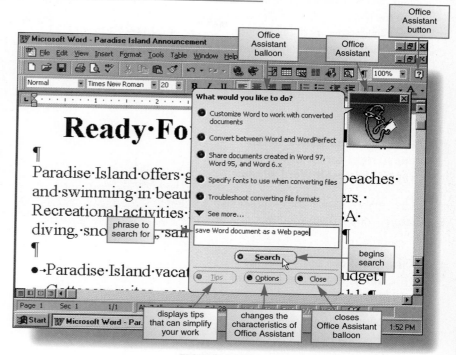

FIGURE 1-76

2 **Click the Search button and then point to the Learn what happens when you save a Word 97 document as a Web page topic.**

The Office Assistant displays a list of topics relating to the phrase, save Word document as a Web page (Figure 1-77).

FIGURE 1-77

3 **Click Learn what happens when you save a Word 97 document as a Web page.**

The Office Assistant displays the Help Topics: Microsoft Word window (Figure 1-78). Word Help windows contain a variety of links, which include buttons and green underlined words. When you point to a link, the mouse pointer shape changes to a pointing hand.

4 **Click the Close button in the upper-right corner of the Help Topics: Microsoft Word window.**

The Help window closes and control returns to the Word window.

5 **Click the Close button on the title bar of the Office Assistant window.**

The Office Assistant disappears from the screen.

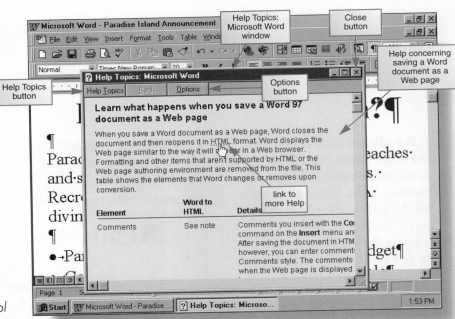

FIGURE 1-78

OtherWays

1. To display Office Assistant, press F1 or on Help menu click Microsoft Word Help
2. To hide Office Assistant, right-click Office Assistant window, click Hide Assistant on shortcut menu

You can use the Office Assistant to search for Help on any topic concerning Word. Once Help displays, you can read it, print it, or click one of its links to display a related Help topic. To print the Help information, click the Print button if one exists. If the window does not contain a Print button, click the Options button or right-click the window and then click Print Topic. The Help Topics button in the Help window allows you to obtain Help through the Contents, Index, and Find sheets.

DISPLAYING TIPS TO IMPROVE YOUR WORK HABITS If you click the Office Assistant Tips button (Figure 1-76 on the previous page), Word displays tips on how to work more efficiently. Once a tip displays (Figure 1-79), you can move backward or forward through the list of accumulated tips. As you work through creating a document, Word adds tips to the list. If the Office Assistant displays on the screen and it has a new tip for you, a light bulb appears in the Office Assistant window. If the Office Assistant does not display on the screen and it has a new tip for you, the light bulb appears on the Office Assistant button on the Standard toolbar.

FIGURE 1-79

OFFICE ASSISTANT SHORTCUT MENU When you right-click the Office Assistant window, a shortcut menu displays, which allows you to change the characteristics of the Office Assistant. For example, you can hide the Office Assistant, display tips, change its appearance, select a different icon for the assistant, or view animation of the Office Assistant. These options also are available by clicking the Options button that displays when you click the Office Assistant.

Using the Contents and Index Command to Obtain Help

The Contents and Index command provides access to the Contents, Index, and Find sheets. The **Contents sheet** in the Help Topics: Microsoft Word dialog box offers you assistance when you know the general category of the topic in question, but not the specifics. Use the Contents sheet in the same manner you would use a table of contents at the front of a textbook. The following steps show how to use the Contents sheet to obtain information on getting assistance while you work.

 Steps To Obtain Help Using the Contents Sheet

1 Click Help on the menu bar and then point to Contents and Index (Figure 1-80).

FIGURE 1-80

2 Click Contents and Index. If necessary, click the Contents tab. Double-click the Getting Help book. Point to the Ways to get assistance while you work topic.

*The Help Topics: Microsoft Word dialog box displays (Figure 1-81). This dialog box contains three tabbed sheets: Contents, Index, and Find. In Figure 1-81, the Getting Help topic is preceded by a book icon. A **book icon** means subtopics exist. To display the subtopics associated with a topic, you double-click its book icon. The subtopics are preceded by a **question mark icon**. To display information on a subtopic, you double-click the subtopic. A book icon opens when you double-click it.*

FIGURE 1-81

3 **Double-click the Ways to get assistance while you work topic.**

Word displays the Microsoft Word window containing tips on Word's Help (Figure 1-82). When you click a link, Word displays additional Help information.

4 **Click the Close button in the upper-right corner of the Microsoft Word Help window.**

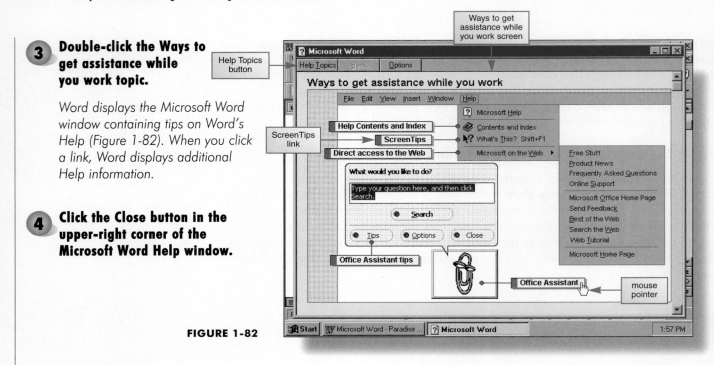

FIGURE 1-82

Instead of closing the Microsoft Word window in Step 3, you could click the Help Topics button in Figure 1-82 to return to the Contents sheet (Figure 1-81 on the previous page).

The Contents sheet in the Help Topics: Microsoft Word dialog box is much like a table of contents in the front of a book. The **Index sheet**, however, is similar to an index in the back of a book. For example, if you wanted help on formatting characters in bold, you would display the Index sheet, type bold (Figure 1-83) and then double-click the bold formatting topic to display Help information on formatting characters in bold. Then, click the Close button.

FIGURE 1-83

The **Find sheet** is used to locate a Help topic on a particular word or phrase. For example, if you wanted help on inserting an inline floating picture, you would display the Find sheet, type insert picture (Figure 1-84) and then double-click the Change a floating picture to an inline picture and vice-versa topic. Then, close the Help window.

Obtaining Web Information

To obtain Web-related information, click Help on the menu bar and then point to Microsoft on the Web to display a submenu of Web-related commands. The Help window in Figure 1-82 shows this submenu. If you click any command on the submenu, your system will launch your browser and connect to a corresponding page on the World Wide Web. Use the commands on the Web submenu to obtain up-to-date information on a variety of topics.

Using What's This? or the Question Mark Button

To obtain Help on an item on the Word screen, click Help on the menu bar and then click What's This? To obtain help on an item in a Word dialog box, click the **Question Mark button** that displays in the upper-right corner of a dialog box. Using either technique, the mouse pointer changes to an arrow and a question mark as shown in Figure 1-85. Move the **question mark pointer** to any item on the Word screen or in a dialog box, and then click to display a **ScreenTip**, which offers an explanation of the item on which you clicked. For example, clicking the Print button on the Standard toolbar displays the Help message shown in Figure 1-86.

FIGURE 1-84

FIGURE 1-85

FIGURE 1-86

If you click text with the question-mark pointer, Word displays the paragraph and character formatting characteristics of the text on which you click.

Word Help has features that make it powerful and easy to use. The best way to familiarize yourself with Word Help is to use it.

Wizards

Word supplies **wizards** to assist you in creating common types of documents, such as letters, memos, resumes, and newsletters. To use a wizard, click File on the menu bar, click New, and then select the wizard you desire from the appropriate tabbed sheet. The wizard asks you a few basic questions, and then displays a formatted document on the screen for you to customize or fill in blanks.

Project Summary

Project 1 introduced you to starting Word and creating a document. Before entering any text in the document, you learned how to change the font size. You also learned how to save and print a document. You used Word's spell check as you type feature and automatically added bullets to paragraphs as you typed them into the document. Once you saved the document, you learned how to format its paragraphs and characters. Then, you imported a graphic file from the Web and resized it. With the technologies presented, you learned to move the insertion point so you could insert, delete, and modify text. Finally, you learned to use Word Help.

What You Should Know

Having completed this project, you now should be able to perform the following tasks:

▶ Bold Selected Text *(WD 1.34)*
▶ Bullet a List as You Type *(WD 1.23)*
▶ Cancel a Series of Prior Actions *(WD 1.53)*
▶ Cancel Your Most Recent Action *(WD 1.53)*
▶ Cancel Your Most Recent Undo *(WD 1.53)*
▶ Center a Single Paragraph *(WD 1.39)*
▶ Center Selected Paragraphs *(WD 1.30)*
▶ Change the Font of Selected Text *(WD 1.33)*
▶ Change the Font Size of Selected Text *(WD 1.31)*
▶ Close the Entire Document and Start Over *(WD 1.54)*
▶ Delete an Incorrect Character in a Document *(WD 1.53)*
▶ Delete an Incorrect Word or Phrase in a Document *(WD 1.53)*
▶ Display Nonprinting Characters *(WD 1.18)*
▶ Enter a Document that Scrolls the Document Window *(WD 1.22)*
▶ Enter Blank Lines into a Document *(WD 1.17)*
▶ Enter More Text *(WD 1.19)*
▶ Enter Text *(WD 1.16)*
▶ Format a Line of Text *(WD 1.34)*
▶ Increase the Default Font Size Before Typing *(WD 1.14)*
▶ Insert a Picture from the Data Disk that Accompanies this Book *(WD 1.44)*

▶ Insert a Picture from the Web *(WD 1.40)*
▶ Insert Text into an Existing Document *(WD 1.52)*
▶ Italicize and Bold Selected Text *(WD 1.38)*
▶ Obtain Help Using the Contents and Index Command *(WD 1.57)*
▶ Obtain Help Using the Office Assistant *(WD 1.55)*
▶ Open a Document *(WD 1.50)*
▶ Print a Document *(WD 1.47)*
▶ Quit Word *(WD 1.49)*
▶ Resize a Graphic *(WD 1.45)*
▶ Save a New Document *(WD 1.26)*
▶ Save a Picture on the Web on a Disk and Insert It in the Document *(WD 1.44)*
▶ Save an Existing Document with the Same File Name *(WD 1.47)*
▶ Scroll Through the Document *(WD 1.35)*
▶ Select a Group of Words *(WD 1.37)*
▶ Select a Single Line *(WD 1.31)*
▶ Select a Single Word *(WD 1.35)*
▶ Select Multiple Paragraphs *(WD 1.29)*
▶ Spell Check as You Type *(WD 1.20)*
▶ Start Word *(WD 1.9)*
▶ Underline Selected Text *(WD 1.36)*
▶ Wordwrap Text as You Type *(WD 1.19)*

Test Your Knowledge

1 True/False

Instructions: Circle T if the statement is true or F if the statement is false.

T   F   1. Microsoft Word 97 is an operating system.
T   F   2. The insertion point indicates where text will be inserted as you type.
T   F   3. The Standard toolbar initially displays floating on the Word screen.
T   F   4. To create a new paragraph, press the ENTER key.
T   F   5. Double-click a red wavy underlined word to display a shortcut menu that lists suggested spelling corrections for the flagged word.
T   F   6. To save a document with the same file name, click the Open button on the taskbar.
T   F   7. Italicizing a word is an example of character formatting.
T   F   8. To center selected paragraphs, click the Center button on the Formatting toolbar.
T   F   9. A floating picture is one positioned directly in the text at the location of the insertion point.
T   F   10. The Office Assistant button is on the Standard toobar.

2 Multiple Choice

Instructions: Circle the correct response.

1. _____ are used to display different portions of your document in the document window.
   a. Status indicators   b. Toolbars   c. Scroll bars   d. Rulers
2. If a word you type is not in Word's dictionary, a _____ wavy underline appears below the word and a red _____ displays on the Spelling and Grammar Status icon.
   a. green, check mark   b. green, X   c. red, check mark   d. red, X
3. To scroll down one entire screenful at a time, _____.
   a. click below the scroll box on the scroll bar   b. click scroll arrow at bottom of the scroll bar
   c. press PAGE DOWN   d. both a and c
4. To place a bullet automatically at the beginning of a paragraph, type a(n) _____ and then press the SPACEBAR.
   a. asterisk (*)   b. plus (+)   c. letter o   d. exclamation point (!)
5. To select a single word, _____ the word.
   a. click   b. right-click   c. double-click   d. drag
6. Selected graphics display _____ handles at the corner and middle locations.
   a. selection   b. sizing   c. picture   d. resizing
7. To erase the character to the right of the insertion point, press the _____ key.
   a. DELETE   b. INSERT   c. BACKSPACE   d. both a and c
8. _____ the OVR status indicator to toggle between overtype and insert mode.
   a. Click   b. Right-click   c. Double-click   d. Drag
9. To close a document and start over, _____.
   a. click Close on File menu   b. click Close button on menu bar
   c. click Close button on Standard toolbar   d. both a and b
10. If Office Assistant has a new tip, a _____ displays in the Office Assistant button or window.
   a. light bulb   b. flashlight   c. paper clip   d. magic wand

A+ Test Your Knowledge

3 Understanding the Word Screen

Instructions: In Figure 1-87, arrows point to major components of the Word screen. Identify the various parts of the screen in the spaces provided.

FIGURE 1-87

4 Understanding the Standard and Formatting Toolbars

Instructions: In Figure 1-88, arrows point to several of the buttons and boxes on the Standard and Formatting toolbars. In the spaces provided, briefly explain the purpose of each button and box.

FIGURE 1-88

Use Help

1 Reviewing Project Activities

Instructions: Perform the following tasks using a computer.

1. Start Word.

2. If the Office Assistant is on your screen, click it to display its balloon. If the Office Assistant is not on your screen, click the Office Assistant button on the Standard toolbar.

3. Click Options in the Office Assistant balloon and then click the Gallery tab. Click the Next button repeatedly to view the various assistants. Display Mother Nature. Click the Options tab and then review the different options for the Office Assistant. Close the Office Assistant dialog box. Change the Office Assistant icon back to the original one.

4. Click the Office Assistant to display its balloon. Type select text in the What would you like to do? text box. Click the Search button. Click the Select text and graphics link.

5. Click Select text and graphics by using the mouse. Read the information. Use the shortcut menu or Options button to print the information. Click the Back button. Click Select text and graphics by using shortcut keys. Read and print the information. Click the Close button in the Help window. Close the Office Assistant window.

6. Click Help on the menu bar and then click Contents and Index. Click the Contents tab. Double-click the Key Information book. Double-click the For Customers Using Word for the First Time book. Double-click the What's new in Word 97 topic. Read and print the following help topics: Automating your tasks and getting assistance, Editing and proofing tools, Working with Web tools. Close any open Help window(s).

2 Expanding on the Basics

Instructions: Use Word Help to better understand the topics listed below. Answer the questions on your own paper or hand in the printed Help topic to your instructor.

1. In this project, you checked spelling as you typed. Use the Office Assistant to answer the following questions about checking spelling all at once.
   a. What button do you click to spell check the document all at once?
   b. If you want to do a grammar check with a spelling check, how do you turn on the grammar check feature?
   c. What are the readability scores? How do you turn them on?

2. In this project, you opened a single file from the Open dialog box. Use the Contents tab in the Help Topics: Microsoft Word dialog box to determine how to select multiple files in the Open dialog box.

3. In this project, you imported a Graphics Interchange Format (GIF) file from the Web into the announcement. Use the Index tab in the Help Topics: Microsoft Word dialog box to determine the complete list of graphic file types that may be inserted into a Word document.

4. In this project, you saved a Word document as a Web page. Use the Find tab in the Help Topics: Microsoft Word dialog box to learn how to use the Web wizard to create a Web page.

5. Use the What's This? command on the Help menu to display ScreenTips for five buttons that you are unfamiliar with on the Standard and Formatting toolbars. Print each ScreenTip by right-clicking it, clicking Print Topic on the shortcut menu, and then clicking the OK button.

Apply Your Knowledge

1 Spell Checking a Document

Instructions: Start Word. Open the document, apply-1, from the Word folder on the Data Disk that accompanies this book. As shown in Figure 1-89, the document is an announcement for Computers Made Easy that contains many spelling and grammar errors. You are to right-click each of the errors and then click the desired correction on the shortcut menu. You may need to refer to your Use Help 2 responses to information on how to verify that the grammar checker is enabled.

spelling and grammar errors are circled to help you identify them

Perform the following tasks:

1. Position the insertion point at the beginning of the document. Scroll down until you encounter the first error.

2. Right-click the flagged phrase, goal at Computers Made Easy are. Change the incorrect verb in the flagged phrase by clicking the phrase, goal at Computers Made Easy is, on the shortcut menu.

FIGURE 1-89

3. Right-click the flagged word, comptuer. Change the incorrect word, comptuer, to computer by clicking computer on the shortcut menu.

4. Right-click the flagged word, three. Click Delete Repeated Word on the shortcut menu to remove the duplicate occurrence of the word, three.

5. Right-click the flagged word, ard. Because the correct word is not on the shortcut menu, click outside the shortcut menu to remove it from the screen. Correct the misspelled word, ard, to the correct word, and, by removing the letter r and replacing it with the letter n.

6. Right-click the flagged phrase, also offering. Change the phrase, also offering, to the correct phrase by clicking the phrase, also offer, on the shortcut menu.

7. Right-click the flagged phrase, these application. Change the word, application, to its plural form by clicking the phrase, these applications, on the shortcut menu.

Apply Your Knowledge

8. Right-click the flagged word, Coarses. Change the incorrect word, Coarses, to Courses by clicking Courses on the shortcut menu.
9. Right-click the incorrect word, eacxh. Change the incorrect word, eacxh, to each by clicking each on the shortcut menu.
10. Right-click the flagged word, to. Capitalize the word, to, by clicking To on the shortcut menu.
11. Click File on the menu bar and then click Save As. Save the document using Corrected apply-1 as the file name.
12. Print the revised document.

In the Lab

1 Creating an Announcement with an Imported Picture from the Web

Problem: You own the cutest golden retriever puppy named Pumpkin. The problem is that you cannot keep Pumpkin because you are moving to a condominium that does not allow pets. You have a picture of Pumpkin in a file called puppy. You decide to prepare an announcement for the sale of Pumpkin. The unformatted announcement is shown in Figure 1-90, and the formatted document is shown in Figure 1-91 on the next page.

> unformatted document
>
> PUPPY FOR SALE!
>
> Pumpkin Needs a Home
>
> Pumpkin is a two-month old, purebred, female golden retriever. A playful puppy with a sweet temperament, Pumpkin is current on all her shots. Owner has a three-generation pedigree.
>
> • Owner is moving and must leave Pumpkin behind
> • Take home this great family companion for $450
>
> Interested? Please call (607) 555-0909

FIGURE 1-90

Instructions:

1. Change the font size from 10 to 20 by clicking the Font Size box arrow and then clicking 20.
2. If necessary, click the Show/Hide ¶ button on the Standard toolbar to display paragraph marks and spaces.
3. Create the unformatted announcement shown in Figure 1-90. Add the bullets to the list as you type by beginning the first item in the list with an asterisk followed by a space.
4. Save the document on a floppy disk with Puppy Announcement as the file name.
5. Select the headline and body title line. Center them.

(continued)

In the Lab

Creating an Announcement with an Imported Picture from the Web *(continued)*

6. Select the headline. Bold it. Change its font size from 20 to 48. Change its font to Comic Sans MS. If the headline wraps to the next line, adjust the font size so it fits on one line.

7. Select the body title line. Increase its font size from 20 to 36. Bold it.

8. Select the words, great family companion, in the bulleted list. Bold them.

9. Select the word, Please, in the last line of the announcement. Italicize it.

10. Click somewhere in the last line of the announcement. Center it.

11. Import the graphic file called Puppy on the paragraph mark below the headline. The picture is located on the Web page www.scsite.com/off97e/pr1.htm and also on the Data Disk that accompanies this book. Enlarge the picture of the puppy about 25%. If the last line of the announcement moves to another page when you resize the picture, make the picture smaller.

12. Check the spelling of the announcement.

13. Save the announcement again with the same file name.

14. Print the announcement (Figure 1-91).

48-point Comic Sans MS bold font →

PUPPY FOR SALE!

36-point bold →

Pumpkin Needs a Home

Pumpkin is a two-month old, purebred, female golden retriever. A playful puppy with a sweet temperament, Pumpkin is current on all her shots. Owner has a three-generation pedigree.

- Owner is moving and must leave Pumpkin behind
- Take home this **great family companion** for $450

Interested? *Please* call (607) 555-0909

FIGURE 1-91

2 Creating an Announcement with Clip Art

Problem: You are the president of The Sports Car Club and you are preparing an announcement inviting new members (Figure 1-92). You decide to use the Sports Car Clip Art from the Clip Gallery supplied with Word.

Instructions:

1. Change the font size from 10 to 20 by clicking the Font Size box arrow and then clicking 20.
2. If it is not already selected, click the Show/Hide ¶ button on the Standard toolbar to display paragraph marks and spaces.
3. Create the announcement shown in Figure 1-92. Enter the document first without the graphic file and unformatted; that is, without any bolding, underlining, italicizing, or centering.
4. Save the document on a floppy disk with Sports Car Club Announcement as the file name.
5. Select the headline and body title line. Center them.
6. Select the headline. Bold it. Change its font size from 20 to 48. Change its font to Arial.
7. Select the body title line. Increase its font size from 20 to 48. Bold it.

48-point Arial bold font → **Zoom** into Action!

48-point bold → **The Sports Car Club**

Do you have a sports car? Do you wish you had a sports car? The Sports Car Club is just for you! At our monthly meetings, members share ideas and learn from knowledgeable guest speakers. Exciting events include an annual **road rally**, **car shows**, **picnics**, **contests**, **fund-raisers**, and a variety of members-only social activities.

- Individual membership dues are $30 per year; family membership dues are $50 per year
- Meetings are the first Saturday of each month from 3:00 p.m. to 6:00 p.m.

Call Dave at 555-4235 for all the details!

FIGURE 1-92

8. Select the word, Zoom, in the headline and italicize it.
9. Select the following words one at a time in the paragraph and bold them: road rally, car shows, picnics, contests, and fund-raisers.
10. Click somewhere in the last line of the announcement. Center it.
11. Import the Sports Car clip art file located in the Transportation category of the Clip Gallery below the headline. That is, click Insert on the menu bar, point to Picture, and then click Clip Art. Scroll through the files, select the sports car, and then click the Insert button.

(continued)

In the Lab

Creating an Announcement with Clip Art *(continued)*

12. Change the clip art from a floating object to an inline object. To do so, click the picture, then click the Format Picture button on the Picture toolbar. Click the Position tab and then clear the Float over text check box. Click the OK button. Click View on the menu bar and then click Normal to return to normal view.
13. Enlarge the graphic if necessary. If the last line of the announcement moves to a second page, then make the graphic smaller.
14. Check the spelling of the announcement. Save the announcement again with the same file name.
15. Print the announcement.

3 Composing an Announcement from a Draft

Problem: You are the marketing director for Water World Park. You want to prepare an announcement of the park and its activities for the public. You have obtained a picture of one of the park's bears to use in the announcement.

Instructions: You are to create the unformatted announcement shown in Figure 1-93. The picture of the bear is located on Web page www.scsite.com/off97e/pr1.htm and also on the Data Disk that accompanies this book. Then, using the techniques presented in this project, format the announcement. Below are some general guidelines:

1. Center the headline and title.
2. Bullet short lists.
3. Use italics, bold, and underlining to emphasize words or phrases.
4. Change font to emphasize text.
5. Increase font size of headline and title.
6. Increase the size of the picture.

unformatted document

Polar Bear Show!

WATER WORLD PARK

Offering fun and entertainment for the whole family, Water World Park is both an amusement park and a water zoo. We have rides for children and adults of all ages. The water zoo has hundreds of aquariums and pools. Our arena has a water show every hour.

Admission is $15 per adult and $8 for children under 10 years
Park is open from 10:00 a.m. to 8:00 p.m. every day between March 1 and October 31

Call 555-0762 for more information

FIGURE 1-93

Cases and Places

The difficulty of these case studies varies: ❱ are the least difficult; ❱❱ are more difficult; and ❱❱❱ are the most difficult.

1 ❱ You have been assigned the task of preparing an announcement for World Wide Communications. The announcement contains a picture to be imported from the Web. Use the following text and picture: headline – Need a Second Phone Line?; picture located on Web site www.scsite.com/off97e/pr1.htm of a girl on the telephone; body title – World Wide Communications; paragraph text – For our current customers, we are offering a special promotion through the month of October. You can have a second telephone line installed into your home without charge. All you pay is $14 per month thereafter for the second telephone line. What a small price to pay for an available telephone line!; first bulleted item – We guarantee installation within four days of your order; second bulleted item – Select a telephone number of your choice; last line – To order, call us at (888) 555-9898. Use the concepts and techniques presented in this project to create and format this announcement.

2 ❱ You have been assigned the task of preparing an announcement for Buckley School of Business. The announcement contains a clip art image from the Clip Gallery. Use the following text and picture: headline – Registration Begins Today!; picture located in Business category of Clip Gallery; body title – Buckley School of Business; paragraph text – Our school offers the finest education in word processing, spreadsheets, databases, presentation graphics, electronic mail, the Internet, computer programming, systems analysis and design, and much more! We have the latest technology and the highest quality instructors, which enables us to provide a job-placement guarantee to all our graduates; first bulleted item – Classes cost $85 per credit hour and parking is $40 per semester; second bulleted item – Fall classes begin Monday, August 31, at 8:00 a.m.; last line – Call 555-8989 to register today. Use the concepts and techniques presented in this project to create and format this announcement.

3 ❱❱ Your Aunt Ruth, a graduate of Green Grove High School, will be celebrating her fortieth high school reunion this year. She has asked you to prepare an announcement that can be sent to each member of the graduating class. The reunion will feature dinner at Broadway Restaurant, live entertainment by The Bakers Band, and a special guest appearance by Joey Williams, a local comedian. The reunion will be held on Saturday, November 14, at 6:00 p.m. Guests will have the opportunity to reminisce about old times, catch up on current projects, and share future plans. Everyone is encouraged to take part in the food and fun. More information can be obtained by calling Mrs. Betty Travis at (576) 555-2223. Use the concepts and techniques presented in this project to create the announcement. Be sure to include at least two bulleted items in a list and insert an appropriate graphic from the Clip Gallery or the Web.

Cases and Places

4 ▶▶ You have just been hired by Nature Valley, a public nature park, as the marketing director. You decide to put together an announcement for the upcoming open house, which has been scheduled for the weekend of September 14 and 15 from 9:00 a.m. to 7:00 p.m. both days. Admission for the open house is $4 per person. Nature Valley offers breathtaking scenery with abundant, lush vegetation and friendly animals. Guests can take nature walks or hikes on trails; swim or boat in crystal-clear lakes; or fish in rippling rivers. More information can be obtained by calling John Gray at 555-9087. Use the concepts and techniques presented in this project to create the announcement. Be sure to include at least two bulleted items in a list and insert an appropriate graphic from the Clip Gallery or the Web.

5 ▶▶▶ Many organizations, such as schools, libraries, grocery stores, child-care centers, and so on, have a place where announcements are posted on a public bulletin board. Often, so many announcements are displayed that some go unnoticed. Find a posted announcement at one of the above mentioned organizations that you think might be overlooked. Copy the text from the announcement. Using this text, together with the techniques presented in this project, create an announcement that would be more likely to catch a reader's eye. Format the announcement effectively and include a bulleted list and suitable graphic from the Clip Gallery or the Web.

6 ▶▶▶ Both small and large companies advertise on the World Wide Web. Some of these advertisements are written as plain text without any formatting or graphics. Surf the Web for an advertisement that you feel lacks luster. Copy the text from the announcement. Using this text, together with the techniques presented in this project, create an announcement that would be more likely to catch a reader's eye. Format the announcement effectively and include a bulleted list and suitable graphic from the Clip Gallery or the Web.

7 ▶▶▶ Many retail stores post announcements throughout the store to promote new or unique products or products on sale. These announcements are designed to encourage consumers to purchase products they were not even considering when they first entered the store. Visit a local electronics store and select an item you believe could have greater sales with increased in-store advertising. Write the text for a promotional announcement and then, using the techniques presented in this project, create an announcement that could be posted around the store to enhance the sales of the item. Format the announcement effectively and include a bulleted list and suitable graphic from the Clip Gallery or the Web.

Creating a Research Paper with a Table

Objectives:

You will have mastered the material in this project when you can:

▶ Describe the MLA documentation style for research papers

▶ Change the margin settings in a document

▶ Adjust line spacing in a document

▶ Use a header to number pages of a document

▶ Indent paragraphs

▶ Use Word's AutoCorrect feature

▶ Add a footnote to a research paper

▶ Insert a Word table into a document

▶ Enter data into a Word table

▶ Format a Word table

▶ Insert a manual page break

▶ Create a hanging indent

▶ Create a text hyperlink

▶ Sort selected paragraphs

▶ Scroll by a page

▶ Find and replace text

▶ Use Word's thesaurus

▶ Display the number of words in a document

▶ Display the Web site associated with a hyperlink

Project

2

Researching, Writing, and Referencing

Citing Sources in Style

Throughout your collegiate career, adhering to one or more styles from a number of established guidelines, you will write research papers and other reports on a diversity of topics covered in your courses of study. After you have researched your subjects, found your reference materials, and written your essays, the crucial step of documenting these resources remains. The citation procedure may seem tedious, but it is the way your readers know how to find additional information on the subjects and the way you ethically give credit to the individuals who have researched these topics before you.

Depending on the course you are taking and the type of document that is assigned, your method of presenting these sources will vary. In academia, three major style systems for writers of research and scientific papers generally are recognized. Your instructors likely will direct you to the required style

Smith 1

Joe Smith

Professor J. Brown

History 421

December 1, 1998

The Copernican Revolution

In the sixteenth century, scientific thought on
ny was dominated by the ideas of the
such as Aristotle and Ptolemy. For
nicus, his ideas on a sun-centered system
challenged the popular belief and brought

Biblio

MLA Handbook
for Writers of
Research Papers

citation

quotes

and appropriate handbooks as assignments are given. The research paper you are to create in this project with Microsoft Word 97 uses the Modern Language Association (MLA) style, which is used by scholars in the humanities fields. Another popular citation style developed by the American Psychological Association (APA) is used by researchers in the social sciences. The third style is the number system used by writers in the applied sciences.

These writers consult standard style manuals that describe, in detail, how to acknowledge reference sources in the body of the paper and in a general list at the end of the report. The MLA style is explained in the *MLA Handbook for Writers of Research Papers*, and the APA style is documented in the *Publication Manual of the American Psychological Association*. The researchers also consult other style guides, such as the University of Chicago's *The Chicago Manual of Style*, the *American Chemical Society Handbook for Authors*, and *The Microsoft Manual of Style for Technical Publications*.

Teams of instructors and scholars develop the style guidelines in each of these publications. The *MLA Handbook,* for example, originated in 1951 for MLA members. In 1977, it was expanded to become a guide for undergraduate students and renamed the *MLA Handbook for Writers of Research Papers*. Subsequent editions were published in 1984, 1988, and 1995. Keeping up with necessary revisions, however, is a never-ending task, especially with the evolution of online references on the Internet. Researchers are challenged continually to keep methods of style and citation accurate and current.

Until scholars agree on a universal style of documentation, you can familiarize yourself with the numerous citation systems and style guides available. Writers of virtually all types of commentary find the guides essential in preparation of essays, research papers, reports, and manuscripts of every kind. Attention to style and detail is evident in the finished product and just may make the difference in an excellent grade.

Raymond Chandler, U.S. author, stated in his 1947 *Letter*, "The most durable thing in writing is style, and style is the most valuable investment a writer can make with his time . . . the writer who puts his individual mark on the way he writes will always pay off."

Project 2

Microsoft
Word 97

Creating a Research Paper with a Table

Case Perspective

Anna L. Porter is a full-time student at Michigan State University, majoring in Information Systems and Computer Programming. The professor in one of her computer classes, CIS 201, has assigned a 500-word research paper. The paper must discuss some aspect of personal computers. Because Anna's computer at home recently was infected with a computer virus, Anna decides to write the research paper on computer viruses. The paper must be written according to the MLA documentation style, which specifies guidelines for report preparation. Professor Brown suggests students use the Internet to obtain the MLA guidelines. The paper also must contain one footnote, a table, and three references – one of which must be from the World Wide Web.

Anna will visit a library, surf the Internet, stop by a computer store, and interview the director of the Information Systems department at her school for information on computer viruses. She also plans to surf the Internet to obtain information and the guidelines for the MLA style of documentation.

Introduction

In both the academic and business environments, you will be asked to write reports. Business reports range from proposals to cost justifications to five-year plans to research findings. Academic reports focus mostly on research findings. Whether you are writing a business report or an academic report, you should follow a standard style when preparing it.

Many different styles of documentation exist for report preparation, depending on the nature of the report. Each style requires the same basic information; the differences among styles appear in the manner of presenting the information. For example, one documentation style may use the term *bibliography*, whereas another uses *references*, and yet a third prefers *works cited*. The **Modern Language Association (MLA)** presents a popular documentation style used today for research papers. Thus, this project uses the **MLA style of documentation**.

Project Two – Research Paper with a Table

Project 2 illustrates the creation of a short research paper describing computer viruses. A table at the end of the research paper outlines techniques for virus protection and system backup. As depicted in Figure 2-1, the paper follows the MLA style of documentation. The first two pages present the research paper and the third page lists the works cited alphabetically.

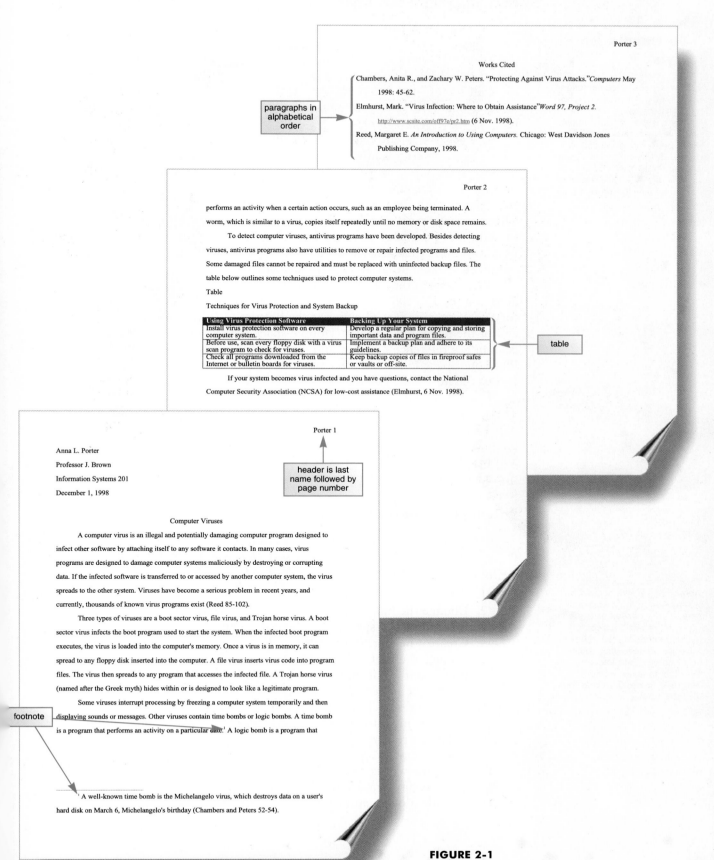

Porter 3

Works Cited

Chambers, Anita R., and Zachary W. Peters. "Protecting Against Virus Attacks."*Computers* May
    1998: 45-62.

Elmhurst, Mark. "Virus Infection: Where to Obtain Assistance"*Word 97, Project 2.*
    http://www.scsite.com/off97e/pr2.htm (6 Nov. 1998).

Reed, Margaret E. *An Introduction to Using Computers.* Chicago: West Davidson Jones
    Publishing Company, 1998.

paragraphs in alphabetical order

Porter 2

performs an activity when a certain action occurs, such as an employee being terminated. A

worm, which is similar to a virus, copies itself repeatedly until no memory or disk space remains.

    To detect computer viruses, antivirus programs have been developed. Besides detecting

viruses, antivirus programs also have utilities to remove or repair infected programs and files.

Some damaged files cannot be repaired and must be replaced with uninfected backup files. The

table below outlines some techniques used to protect computer systems.

Table

Techniques for Virus Protection and System Backup

Using Virus Protection Software	Backing Up Your System
Install virus protection software on every computer system.	Develop a regular plan for copying and storing important data and program files.
Before use, scan every floppy disk with a virus scan program to check for viruses.	Implement a backup plan and adhere to its guidelines.
Check all programs downloaded from the Internet or bulletin boards for viruses.	Keep backup copies of files in fireproof safes or vaults or off-site.

table

    If your system becomes virus infected and you have questions, contact the National

Computer Security Association (NCSA) for low-cost assistance (Elmhurst, 6 Nov. 1998).

Porter 1

Anna L. Porter

Professor J. Brown

Information Systems 201

December 1, 1998

header is last name followed by page number

Computer Viruses

    A computer virus is an illegal and potentially damaging computer program designed to

infect other software by attaching itself to any software it contacts. In many cases, virus

programs are designed to damage computer systems maliciously by destroying or corrupting

data. If the infected software is transferred to or accessed by another computer system, the virus

spreads to the other system. Viruses have become a serious problem in recent years, and

currently, thousands of known virus programs exist (Reed 85-102).

    Three types of viruses are a boot sector virus, file virus, and Trojan horse virus. A boot

sector virus infects the boot program used to start the system. When the infected boot program

executes, the virus is loaded into the computer's memory. Once a virus is in memory, it can

spread to any floppy disk inserted into the computer. A file virus inserts virus code into program

files. The virus then spreads to any program that accesses the infected file. A Trojan horse virus

(named after the Greek myth) hides within or is designed to look like a legitimate program.

    Some viruses interrupt processing by freezing a computer system temporarily and then

displaying sounds or messages. Other viruses contain time bombs or logic bombs. A time bomb

is a program that performs an activity on a particular date.[1] A logic bomb is a program that

footnote

----
[1] A well-known time bomb is the Michelangelo virus, which destroys data on a user's
hard disk on March 6, Michelangelo's birthday (Chambers and Peters 52-54).

FIGURE 2-1

MLA Documentation Style

When writing papers, you must be sure to adhere to some form of documentation style. The research paper in this project follows the guidelines presented by
the MLA. To follow the MLA style, double-space all pages of the paper with one-
inch top, bottom, left, and right margins. Indent the first word of each paragraph
one-half inch from the left margin. At the right margin of each page, place a page
number one-half inch from the top margin. On each page, precede the page
number by your last name.

The MLA style does not require a title page; instead, it requires you to place
your name and course information in a block at the left margin beginning one
inch from the top of the page. Center the title two double-spaces below your
name and course information. In the body of the paper, place author references in
parentheses with the page number(s) where the referenced information is located.
These in-text **parenthetical citations** are used instead of footnoting each source at
the bottom of the page or at the end of the paper. In the MLA style, **footnotes** are
used only for explanatory notes. In the body of the paper, use **superscripts** (raised
numbers) to signal that an explanatory note exists.

According to the MLA style, explanatory notes are optional. **Explanatory
notes** are used to elaborate on points discussed in the body of the paper. Explanatory notes may be placed either at the bottom of the page as footnotes or at the
end of the paper as endnotes. Double-space the explanatory notes. Superscript
each note's reference number, and indent it one-half inch from the left margin.
Place one space following the note number before beginning the note text. At the
end of the note text, you may list bibliographic information for further reference.

The MLA style uses the term **works cited** for the bibliographical references.
The works cited page alphabetically lists works that are directly referenced in the
paper by each author's last name. Place the works cited on a separate numbered
page. Center the title, Works Cited, one inch from the top margin. Double-space
all lines. Begin the first line of each work cited at the left margin; indent subsequent lines of the same work one-half inch from the left margin.

Document Preparation Steps

Document preparation steps give you an overview of how the research paper
in Figure 2-1 on the previous page will be developed. The following tasks will be
completed in this project:

1. Start Word.
2. Change the margin settings for the document.
3. Adjust the line spacing for the document.
4. Create a header to number pages.
5. Change the font size to 12.
6. Enter your name and course information.
7. Center the paper title.
8. Save the research paper.
9. First-line indent paragraphs in the paper.
10. Enter the research paper with footnotes and a table.
11. Insert a manual page break.
12. Enter the works cited page.
13. Sort the paragraphs on the works cited page.
14. Save the document again.

15. Use Word's thesaurus.
16. Check the number of words in the document.
17. Print the research paper.
18. Visit the Web site associated with a hyperlink in the document.
19. Quit Word.

The following pages contain a detailed explanation of each of these tasks.

Starting Word

Follow these steps to start Word or ask your instructor how to start Word for your system.

TO START WORD

① Click the Start button on the taskbar.
② Click New Office Document on the Start menu. If necessary, click the General tab when the New dialog box first opens.
③ Double-click the Blank Document icon on the General sheet.
④ If the Word screen is not maximized, double-click its title bar to maximize it.

Office starts Word. After a few moments, an empty document titled Document1 displays on the Word screen.

Displaying Nonprinting Characters

As discussed in the previous projects, it is helpful to display **nonprinting characters** that indicate where in the document you pressed the ENTER key, SPACEBAR, or TAB key. Follow this step to display nonprinting characters.

TO DISPLAY NONPRINTING CHARACTERS

① If the Show/Hide ¶ button on the Standard toolbar is not already recessed, click it.

Word displays nonprinting characters in the document window, and the Show/Hide ¶ button on the Standard toolbar is recessed (Figure 2-2 on the next page).

Changing the Margins

Word is preset to use standard 8.5-by-11-inch paper, with 1.25-inch left and right margins and 1-inch top and bottom margins. These margin settings affect every paragraph in the document. Often, you may want to change these default margin settings. For example, the MLA documentation style requires one-inch top, bottom, left, and right margins throughout the paper. The steps on the next page illustrate how to change the default margin settings for a document when your screen is in normal view.

More *About* Changing Margins

In page layout view, you can change the margins using the ruler. The current margins are shaded in gray, and the margin boundary is positioned where the gray meets the white. You drag the margin boundary to change the margin. Hold down the ALT key while dragging the margin boundary to display the margin settings.

Steps **To Change the Default Margin Settings**

1 **Click File on the menu bar and then point to Page Setup (Figure 2-2).**

Show/Hide ¶ button recessed

File menu

current right margin setting

Page Setup command

Normal View button recessed

FIGURE 2-2

2 **Click Page Setup. If necessary, click the Margins tab when the Page Setup dialog box first opens.**

Word displays the Page Setup dialog box (Figure 2-3). Word lists the current margin settings in the respective text boxes and displays the settings graphically in the Preview area of the dialog box.

Page Setup dialog box

Margins tab

Left text box

current margin settings display graphically in Preview area

margin settings apply to entire document

FIGURE 2-3

3 Drag through the text in the Left text box to highlight 1.25". Type 1 and then press the TAB key. Type 1 and then point to the OK button.

The new left and right margin settings are 1 inch (Figure 2-4). The Preview area in the Page Setup dialog box adjusts accordingly to reflect the new margin settings.

FIGURE 2-4

4 Click the OK button.

Word changes the left and right margins in the current document window (Figure 2-5).

FIGURE 2-5

*Other***Ways**

1. In page layout view, drag margin boundary(s) on ruler

Compare Figure 2-2 to Figure 2-5. Notice that the right margin does not display in the document window in Figure 2-5, as it did in Figure 2-2, because you increased the width of your typing area when you changed the margins. The new margin settings take effect in the document immediately, and Word uses these margins for the entire document.

Adjusting Line Spacing

Word, by default, single-spaces between lines of text and automatically adjusts line height to accommodate various font sizes and graphics. The MLA documentation style requires that you double-space the entire paper; that is, one blank line should display between each line of text. Thus, you must adjust the line spacing from single to double as described in the steps on the next page.

More *About*
Line Spacing

Sometimes when you increase the font size of characters or import a graphic, the top of the characters or graphic is chopped off. If this happens, someone has set the line spacing in Word to Exactly. To correct it, change the line spacing to At least in the Paragraph dialog box, which accommodates the largest font or graphic.

Steps To Double-Space a Document

1 Right-click the paragraph mark above the end mark in the document window. Point to Paragraph on the shortcut menu.

Word displays a shortcut menu in the document window (Figure 2-6).

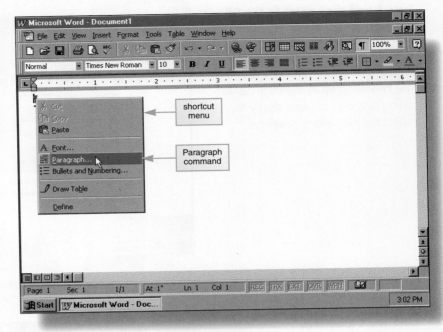

FIGURE 2-6

2 Click Paragraph. If necessary, click the Indents and Spacing tab when the Paragraph dialog box first opens.

Word displays the Paragraph dialog box, which lists the current settings in the text boxes and displays them graphically in the Preview area.

3 Click the Line spacing box arrow and then point to Double.

A list of available line spacing options displays (Figure 2-7).

FIGURE 2-7

4 **Click Double. Point to the OK button.**

Word displays Double in the Line spacing text box and graphically portrays the new line spacing in the Preview area (Figure 2-8).

FIGURE 2-8

5 **Click the OK button.**

Word changes the line spacing to double in the current document (Figure 2-9). Notice that when line spacing is double, the end mark is positioned one blank line below the insertion point.

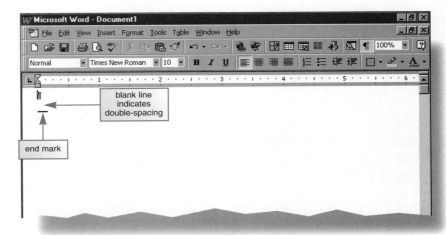

FIGURE 2-9

OtherWays

1. On Format menu click Paragraph, click Indents and Spacing tab, click Line spacing box arrow, click Double, click OK button

2. Press CTRL+2

The Line spacing list box contains a variety of settings for the line spacing (Figure 2-7). The default, Single, and the options 1.5 lines and Double instruct Word to adjust line spacing automatically to accommodate the largest font or graphic on a line. The next two options, At least and Exactly, enable you to specify a line spacing not provided in the first three options. The difference is that the At least option instructs Word to increase the designation if necessary; whereas, the Exactly option does not allow Word to increase the specification. With the last option, Multiple, you enter a multiple numeric value. For example, a multiple of 3 is the same as triple-spacing.

Using a Header to Number Pages

In Word, you can number pages easily by clicking Insert on the menu bar and then clicking Page Numbers. Once you have clicked the Page Numbers command, it places page numbers on every page after the first. You cannot, however, place your name as required by the MLA style in front of the page number with the Page Numbers command. To place your name in front of the page number, you must create a header that contains the page number.

Headers and Footers

A **header** is text you want printed at the top of each page in the document. A **footer** is text you want printed at the bottom of every page. In Word, headers are printed in the top margin one-half inch from the top of every page, and footers are printed in the bottom margin one-half inch from the bottom of each page, which meets the MLA style. Headers and footers can include both text and graphics, as well as the page number, total number of pages, current date, and current time.

In this project, you are to precede the page number with your last name placed one-half inch from the top of each page. Your name and the page number should print **right-aligned**, that is, at the right margin. Use the procedures in the following steps to create the header with page numbers according to the MLA style.

Steps To Create a Header

1 **Click View on the menu bar and then point to Header and Footer (Figure 2-10).**

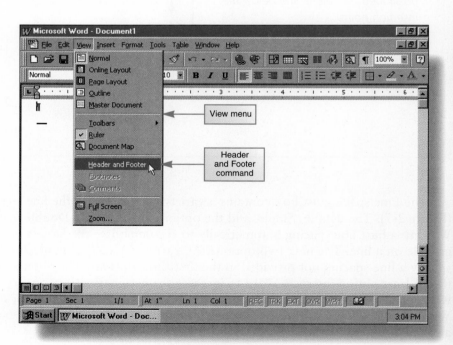

FIGURE 2-10

2 **Click Header and Footer. Point to the Align Right button on the Formatting toolbar.**

*Word switches from normal view to page layout view and displays the **Header and Footer toolbar** (Figure 2-11). The Header and Footer toolbar floats in the middle of the document window. You type header text in the **header area**, which displays enclosed by a nonprinting dashed rectangle above the Header and Footer toolbar. Notice that both the left and right margins display in the document window because Word switched to page layout view. Your zoom percentage may differ from this figure.*

FIGURE 2-11

3 **Click the Align Right button on the Formatting toolbar. Type** Porter **and then press the SPACEBAR. Point to the Insert Page Number button on the Header and Footer toolbar.**

Word displays the last name, Porter, right-aligned in the header area (Figure 2-12). The Align Right button is recessed because the paragraph containing the insertion point is right-aligned.

FIGURE 2-12

4 **Click the Insert Page Number button.**

Word displays the page number 1 in the header area (Figure 2-13). Notice that the header text is 10 point. You want all text in your research paper to be 12 point.

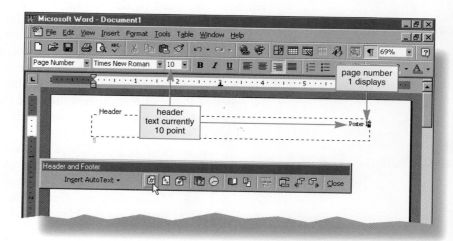

FIGURE 2-13

5 Select the text, Porter 1, by clicking to its left. Click the Font Size box arrow on the Formatting toolbar and then point to 12.

Word highlights the text, Porter 1, in the header area (Figure 2-14).

FIGURE 2-14

6 Click font size 12. Point to the Close Header and Footer button on the Header and Footer toolbar.

Word changes the font size of the selected text from 10 to 12 (Figure 2-15).

7 Click the Close Header and Footer button.

Word closes the Header and Footer toolbar and returns to normal view (Figure 2-16 on the opposite page).

FIGURE 2-15

More *About*
Page Layout View

To see the exact positioning of headers, footers, and notes, switch to page layout view. Headers and footers display dimmed in page layout view. Use the scroll bars to move around the pages of the document. To advance forward or backward an entire page, click the double arrows on the bottom of the vertical scroll bar.

The header does not display on the screen when the document window is in normal view because it tends to clutter the screen. You will, however, want to verify that the header will print correctly. To see the header in the document window, you must switch to page layout view or display the document in print preview. These views display the header on the screen with the rest of the text. You can edit header text in both these views.

Just as the Insert Page Number button on the Header and Footer toolbar inserts the page number into the document, three other buttons on the Header and Footer toolbar (Figure 2-15 above) insert items into the document. The Insert Number of Pages button inserts the total number of pages in the document; the Insert Date button inserts the current date into the document; and the Insert Time button inserts the current time.

To edit an existing header, you can follow the same procedure that you use to create a new header. That is, click View on the menu bar and then click Header and Footer to display the Header and Footer toolbar; or switch to page layout view and then double-click the dimmed header. If you have multiple headers, click the Show Next button on the Header and Footer toolbar (Figure 2-15) until the appropriate header displays in the header area. Edit the header as you would any Word text and then click the Close Header and Footer button on the Header and Footer toolbar.

To create a footer, click View on the menu bar, click Header and Footer, click the Switch Between Header and Footer button on the Header and Footer toolbar, and then follow the same procedure as to create a header.

Notice that the Header and Footer toolbar initially floats in the middle of the document window. You can **dock**, or anchor, the floating toolbar below the Formatting toolbar by double-clicking its title bar. To move a docked toolbar, point between two buttons or boxes or to the edge of the toolbar and then drag it to the desired location. If you drag it to an edge of the window, the toolbar snaps to the edge of the window. If you drag it to the middle of the window, the toolbar floats in the Word window. If you double-click between two buttons or boxes or the edge of the toolbar, it floats in its original floating position.

Typing the Body of the Research Paper

The body of the research paper encompasses the first two pages in Figure 2-1 on page WD 2.5. The steps on the following pages illustrate how to enter the body of the research paper.

Changing the Default Font Size

As discussed in previous projects, a font size of 10 point is difficult for many people to read. In this project, all characters in all paragraphs should be a font size of 12. Perform the following steps to change the font size to 12.

TO CHANGE THE DEFAULT FONT SIZE

1️⃣ Click the Font Size box arrow on the Formatting toolbar.
2️⃣ Click font size 12.

Word changes the font size to 12 (Figure 2-16).

More *About*
Writing Papers

When beginning to write a paper, many students take notes to keep track of information. One method is to summarize, or condense, the information. Another is to paraphrase, or rewrite the information in your own words. And yet a third is to quote, or record the exact words of the original. Be sure to use quotation marks when directly quoting a source.

FIGURE 2-16

Entering Name and Course Information

Recall that the MLA style does not require a separate title page for research papers. Instead, you place your name and course information in a block at the top of the page at the left margin. Thus, follow the step below to begin the body of the research paper.

Steps To Enter Name and Course Information

1 **Type** Anna L. Porter **and then press the ENTER key. Type** Professor J. Brown **and then press the ENTER key. Type** Information Systems 201 **and then press the ENTER key. Type** December 1, 1998 **and then press the ENTER key twice.**

The student name displays on line 1, the professor name on line 2, the course name on line 3, and the paper due date on line 4 (Figure 2-17). Each time you press the ENTER key, Word advances two lines on the screen, but increments the line counter on the status bar by only one because earlier you set line spacing to double.

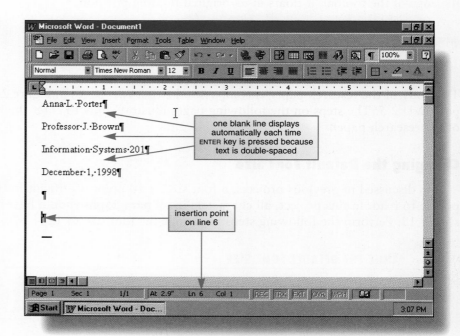

FIGURE 2-17

If you watch the screen as you type, you may have noticed that as you typed the first few characters, Dece, Word displayed the **AutoComplete tip**, December, above the characters. To save typing, you could press the ENTER key while the AutoComplete tip displays, which instructs Word to place the text of the AutoComplete tip at the location of your typing.

Centering a Paragraph Before Typing

In Project 1, you learned how to center a paragraph after you typed it. You also can center a paragraph before you type it. Because your fingers are already on the keyboard, you will use shortcut keys to format the paragraph as shown in the following steps.

More *About*
APA Guidelines

APA guidelines call for a title page as a separate page of a research paper, rather than entering name and course information on the first page of the paper. The running head (the brief summary of the title and the page number) should appear on the title page also, with the page number 1 on the title page.

Steps **To Center a Paragraph Before Typing**

1 **Position the insertion point on the paragraph mark to be centered and then press the CTRL+E keys. Type** Computer Viruses **and then press the ENTER key.**

Word centers the title between the left and right margins and the insertion point advances to line 7 (Figure 2-18). Notice that the paragraph mark and insertion point on line 7 are centered because the formatting specified in the prior paragraph (line 6) is carried forward to the next paragraph (line 7). Thus, the Center button on the Formatting toolbar remains recessed, indicating the next text you type will be centered. You do not, however, want the next line of text to be centered.

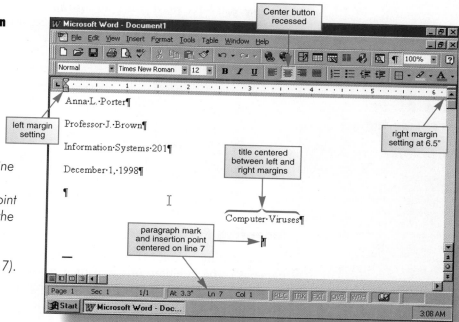

FIGURE 2-18

2 **Press the CTRL+L keys.**

Word positions the paragraph mark and the insertion point at the left margin (Figure 2-19). The next text you type will be left-aligned. CTRL+L is the keyboard shortcut to left-align a paragraph.

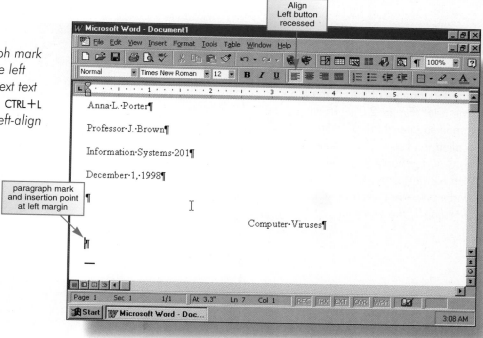

FIGURE 2-19

*Other***Ways**

1. Click Center button
2. Right-click paragraph, click Paragraph on shortcut menu, click Indents and Spacing tab, click Alignment box arrow, click Centered, click OK button
3. On Format menu click Paragraph, click Indents and Spacing tab, click Alignment box arrow, click Centered, click OK button

Saving the Research Paper

Recall that it is prudent to save your work on disk at regular intervals. Because you have performed several tasks thus far, you should save your research paper. For a detailed example of the procedure summarized below, refer to pages WD 1.25 through WD 1.27 in Project 1.

TO SAVE A DOCUMENT

1. Insert your floppy disk into drive A.
2. Click the Save button on the Standard toolbar.
3. Type the file name Virus Research Paper in the File name text box. Do not press the ENTER key after typing the file name.
4. Click the Save in box arrow and then click 3½ Floppy (A:).
5. Click the Save button in the Save As dialog box.

Indenting Paragraphs

According to the MLA style, the first line of each paragraph in the research paper is to be indented one-half inch from the left margin. This procedure, called **first-line indent**, can be accomplished using the horizontal ruler as shown in the following steps.

Steps **To First-Line Indent Paragraphs**

1 **Point to the First Line Indent marker on the ruler.**

The *First Line Indent marker* is the top triangle at the 0" mark on the ruler (Figure 2-20). The small square at the 0" mark, called the **Left Indent marker**, is used to change the entire left margin, whereas the First Line Indent marker affects only the first line of the paragraph.

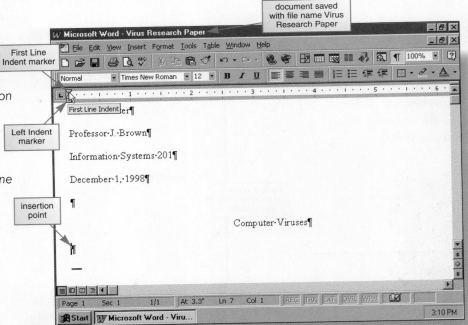

FIGURE 2-20

2 **Drag the First Line Indent marker to the .5" mark on the ruler.**

As you drag the mouse, a vertical dotted line displays in the document window, indicating the proposed location of the First Line Indent marker (Figure 2-21).

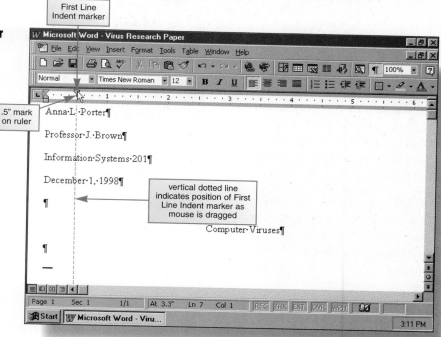

FIGURE 2-21

3 **Release the mouse button.**

The First Line Indent marker displays at the location of the first tab stop, which is one-half inch from the left margin (Figure 2-22). The paragraph mark containing the insertion point in the document window also moves one-half inch to the right.

FIGURE 2-22

4 Type the first paragraph of the research paragraph as shown in Figure 2-24 below. Press the ENTER key. Type the first sentence of the second paragraph: Three types of viruses are a boot sector virus, file virus, and Trojan horse virus.

When you press the ENTER key at the end of the first paragraph of text, the insertion point automatically indents the first line of the second paragraph by one-half inch (Figure 2-23). Recall that each time you press the ENTER key, the paragraph formatting in the prior paragraph is carried forward to the next paragraph.

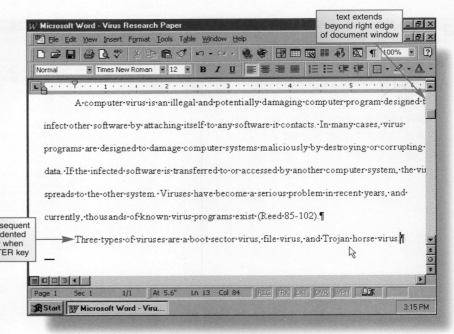

FIGURE 2-23

A computer virus is an illegal and potentially damaging computer program designed to infect other software by attaching itself to any software it contacts. In many cases, virus programs are designed to damage computer systems maliciously by destroying or corrupting data. If the infected software is transferred to or accessed by another computer system, the virus spreads to the other system. Viruses have become a serious problem in recent years, and currently, thousands of known virus programs exist (Reed 85-102).

FIGURE 2-24

By setting the first-line indent with the ruler, the first-line indent format is carried automatically to each subsequent paragraph you type.

Zooming Page Width

When you changed the left and right margin settings earlier in this project, the right margin moved beyond the right edge of the document window. (Depending on your Word settings, your right margin may already display in the document window.) Thus, some of the text at the right edge of the document does not display in the document window (Figure 2-23 above). In this project, you want to make the characters smaller by using the Zoom feature.

Because you often want to see both margins in the document window at the same time, Word provides a **page width zoom**, which brings both the left and right margins into view as shown in the following steps.

Steps To Zoom Page Width

1 Click the Zoom box arrow on the Standard toolbar and then point to Page Width.

Word displays a list of available zoom percentages, as well as the Page Width zoom option (Figure 2-25).

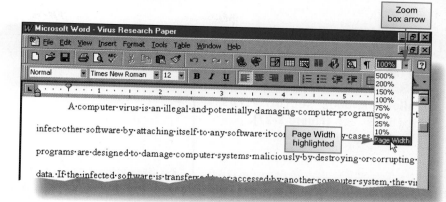

FIGURE 2-25

2 Click Page Width.

Word brings both the left and right margins into view in the document window (Figure 2-26). The Zoom box now displays 92%, which Word computes based on your margin settings. Your percentage may be different depending on your system configuration.

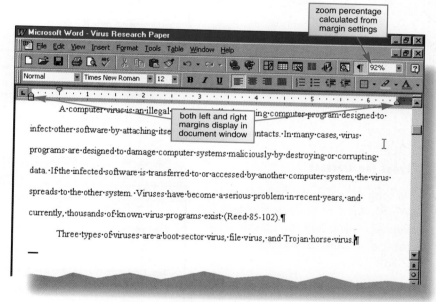

FIGURE 2-26

*Other***Ways**

1. On View menu click Zoom, select desired zoom percentage, click OK button

If you want to zoom to a percentage not displayed in the Zoom list box, you can click View on the menu bar, click Zoom, and then enter any zoom percentage you desire.

Using Word's AutoCorrect Feature

Because you may often misspell words or phrases when you type, Word provides an **AutoCorrect** feature, which automatically corrects your misspelled words as you type them into the document. For example, if you type *adn*, Word automatically changes it to *and* for you. Word has predefined many commonly misspelled words, which it automatically corrects for you as shown on the next page.

◆ **M**ore *About* **AutoCorrect**

In addition to correcting misspelled words, the AutoCorrect feature fixes other mistakes. If you type two capital letters at the beginning of a sentence, Word makes the second letter lower case. If you forget to capitalize the first letter of a sentence, Word capitalizes it for you. Word also capitalizes names of days of the week, if you forget to.

Steps To AutoCorrect As You Type

1 **Press the SPACEBAR. Type the beginning of the second sentence in the second paragraph, and misspell the word, the, as follows:** A boot sector virus infects teh **(Figure 2-27).**

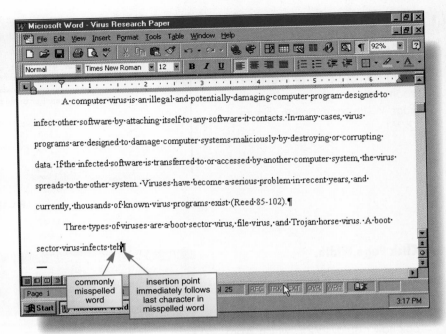

FIGURE 2-27

2 **Press the SPACEBAR.**

As soon as you press the SPACEBAR, Word's AutoCorrect feature detects the misspelling and corrects the misspelled word for you (Figure 2-28).

3 **Type** boot program used to start the system. **and then press the SPACEBAR.**

The second sentence of the second paragraph is complete.

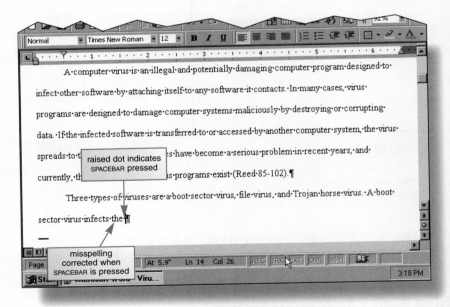

FIGURE 2-28

Word has a list of predefined misspelled words that AutoCorrect can detect and correct. In addition to the predefined list of commonly misspelled words, you can create your own AutoCorrect entries to add to the list. For example, if you often misspell the word *virus* as *vires*, you should make an AutoCorrect entry for it as shown in these steps.

Steps To Create an AutoCorrect Entry

1 **Click Tools on the menu bar and then point to AutoCorrect (Figure 2-29).**

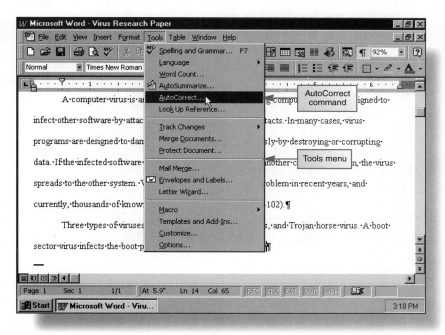

FIGURE 2-29

2 **Click AutoCorrect.**

Word displays the AutoCorrect dialog box (Figure 2-30). The insertion point blinks in the Replace text box, ready for you to create an AutoCorrect entry.

FIGURE 2-30

3 Type vires **in the Replace text box. Press the TAB key to advance to the With text box. Type** virus **in the With text box. Point to the Add button.**

The Replace text box contains the misspelled word, and the With text box contains its correct spelling (Figure 2-31).

4 **Click the Add button. (If your dialog box displays a Replace button instead, click it and then click the Yes button in the Microsoft Word dialog box.) Click the OK button.**

Word adds the entry alphabetically to the list of words to correct automatically as you type.

FIGURE 2-31

In addition to creating AutoCorrect entries for words you commonly misspell, you can create entries for abbreviations, codes, and so on. For example, you could create an AutoCorrect entry for *asap*, indicating that Word should replace this text with the phrase *as soon as possible*.

If you look at the list of AutoCorrect entries in the AutoCorrect dialog box (Figure 2-30 on the previous page), you will notice that Word also predefines commonly used symbols. For example, to insert a smiling face into a document, you type :) and word automatically changes it to ☺. Table 2-1 lists the characters you type to insert arrows, faces, and symbols into a Word document.

If, for some reason, you do not want Word to correct automatically as you type, you can turn off the replace as you type feature by clicking Tools on the menu bar, clicking AutoCorrect, clicking the AutoCorrect tab, clicking the Replace text as you type check box to deselect it, and then clicking the OK button.

The AutoCorrect sheet also contains four other check boxes that correct your typing if selected. If you type two capital letters in a row such as TH, Word will make the second letter lowercase, Th. If you begin a sentence with a lowercase letter, Word will capitalize the first letter of the sentence. If you type the name of a day in lowercase such as tuesday, Word will capitalize the first letter of the day, Tuesday. Finally, if you leave the CAPS LOCK key on and begin a new sentence such as aFTER, Word corrects the typing, After, and turns off the CAPS LOCK key.

Table 2-1	
TYPE	TO DISPLAY
(c)	©
(r)	®
(tm)	™
:)	☺
:|	☺
:(	☹
-->	→
<--	←
<==	←
==>	→
<=>	↔

Adding Footnotes

Recall that **explanatory notes** are optional in the MLA documentation style. They are used primarily to elaborate on points discussed in the body of the paper. The style specifies to use superscripts (raised numbers) to signal that an explanatory note exists either at the bottom of the page as a **footnote** or at the end of the document as an **endnote**.

Word, by default, places notes at the bottom of each page. In Word, **note text** can be any length and format. Word automatically numbers notes sequentially for you by placing a **note reference mark** in the body of the document and in front of the note text. If you rearrange, insert, or remove notes, the remaining note text and reference marks are renumbered according to their new sequence in the document. Perform the following steps to add a footnote to the research paper.

More *About* **Footnotes**

Both the MLA and APA guidelines suggest the use of in-text parenthetical citation, as opposed to footnoting each source of material in a paper. These parenthetical acknowledgments guide the reader to the end of the paper for complete information on the source, if the reader desires it.

teps To Add a Footnote

1 **Type the text shown in Figure 2-33. Click Insert on the menu bar and then point to Footnote.**

The insertion point is positioned immediately after the period following the word, date, in the research paper (Figure 2-32).

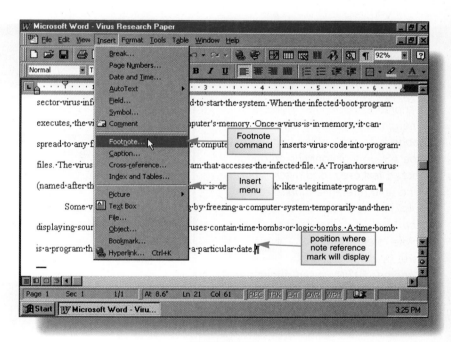

FIGURE 2-32

When the infected boot program executes, the virus is loaded into the computer's memory. Once a virus is in memory, it can spread to any floppy disk inserted into the computer. A file virus inserts virus code into program files. The virus then spreads to any program that accesses the infected file. A Trojan horse virus (named after the Greek myth) hides within or is designed to look like a legitimate program.

Some viruses interrupt processing by freezing a computer system temporarily and then displaying sounds or messages. Other viruses contain time bombs or logic bombs. A time bomb is a program that performs an activity on a particular date.

FIGURE 2-33

2 **Click Footnote. When the Footnote and Endnote dialog box displays, point to the OK button.**

Word displays the Footnote and Endnote dialog box (Figure 2-34). The selected Footnote option button indicates that footnotes are the default placement for notes.

FIGURE 2-34

3 **Click the OK button.**

*Word opens a **note pane** in the lower portion of the window with the note reference mark (a super-scripted 1) positioned at the left margin of the pane (Figure 2-35). A **pane** is an area at the bottom of the screen that contains an **option bar**, a **text area**, and a **scroll bar**. The note reference mark also displays in the document window at the location of the insertion point. Note **reference marks** are, by default, super-scripted; that is, raised above other letters. Notice that the default font size of footnote text is 10 point.*

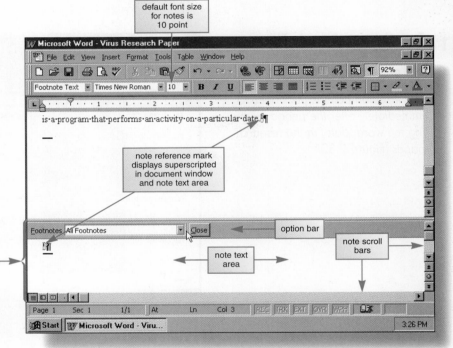

FIGURE 2-35

4 **Right-click to the right of the paragraph mark in the note pane. Point to Paragraph on the shortcut menu.**

Word displays a shortcut menu (Figure 2-36). Because you want to change both first-line indent and line spacing for the notes, you will use the Paragraph dialog box to perform both changes.

FIGURE 2-36

5 Click Paragraph. If necessary, click the Indents and Spacing tab when the Paragraph dialog box first opens. Click the Special box arrow and then point to First line.

Word displays the Paragraph dialog box (Figure 2-37). You can change the first-line indent in the Indents and Spacing sheet in the Paragraph dialog box.

FIGURE 2-37

6 Click First line. Click the Line spacing box arrow and then click Double. Point to the OK button.

Word displays First line in the Special box and Double in the Line spacing box (Figure 2-38). The Preview area reflects the current settings in the Paragraph dialog box.

FIGURE 2-38

7 **Click the OK button.**

Word indents the first line of the note by one-half inch and sets the line spacing for the note to double.

8 **Click the Font Size box arrow and then click 12. Type the note text:**
A well-known time bomb is the Michelangelo virus, which destroys data on a user's hard disk on March 6, Michelangelo's birthday (Chambers and Peters 52-54).

The note text is entered in the note pane in 12-point font (Figure 2-39).

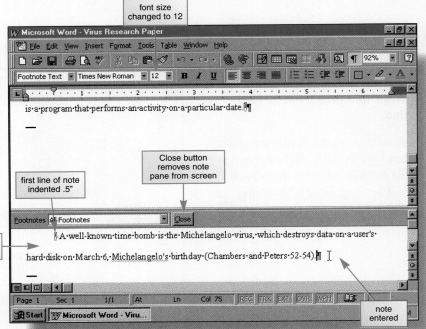

FIGURE 2-39

9 **Click the Close button on the note pane option bar. Point to the note reference mark in the document window.**

Word closes the note pane (Figure 2-40).

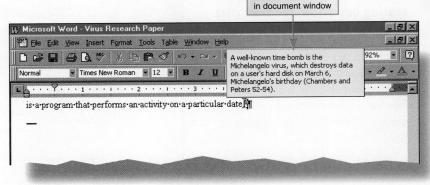

FIGURE 2-40

When Word closes the note pane and returns to the document, the note text disappears from the screen. Although the note text still exists, it is usually not visible as a footnote in normal view. If, however, you point to the note reference mark as shown in Figure 2-40, the note text appears above the note reference mark as a ScreenTip. To display footnotes in a note pane at the bottom of the screen, double-click the note reference mark in the document. If you want to verify that the note text is positioned correctly on the page, you must switch to page layout view or display the document in print preview.

To edit an existing footnote, click View on the menu bar and then click Footnotes or double-click the note reference mark in the document to display the note pane. Edit the footnote as you would any Word text and then click the Close button on the note pane option bar.

Automatic Page Breaks

As you type documents that exceed one page, Word automatically inserts page breaks, called **automatic page breaks** or **soft page breaks**, when it determines the text has filled one page according to paper size, margin settings, line spacing, and other settings. If you add text, delete text, or modify text on a page, Word recomputes the position of automatic page breaks and adjusts them accordingly. Word performs page recomputation between the keystrokes, that is, in between the pauses in your typing. Thus, Word refers to the automatic page break task as **background repagination**. In normal view, automatic page breaks appear on the Word screen as a single dotted horizontal line. Word's automatic page break feature is illustrated below.

More *About*
Background Repagination

If background repagination has been deactivated on your system, Word stops all activities while repaginating the document. You can enable background repagination by clicking Tools on the menu bar, clicking Options, clicking the General tab, clicking the Background Repagination check box, and then clicking the OK button.

 To Page Break Automatically

1 **Press the SPACEBAR and then type** A logic bomb is a program that performs an activity when a certain action occurs, such as an employee being terminated. A worm, which is similar to a virus, copies itself repeatedly until no memory or disk space remains. **Press the ENTER key and then type the next paragraph of the research paper, as shown in Figure 2-42 below.**

As you begin typing the paragraph, Word places an automatic page break above the line containing the note reference mark. When Word detects an additional line at the end of the paragraph, it moves the automatic page break down one line, below the line with the note reference mark (Figure 2-41). The status bar now displays Page 2 as the current page.

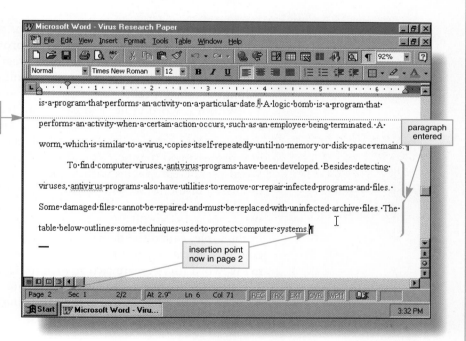

FIGURE 2-41

To find computer viruses, antivirus programs have been developed. Besides detecting viruses, antivirus programs also have utilities to remove or repair infected programs and files. Some damaged files cannot be repaired and must be replaced with uninfected archive files. The table below outlines some techniques used to protect computer systems.

FIGURE 2-42

Word, by default, prevents widows and orphans from occurring in a document. A **widow** is created when the last line of a paragraph displays by itself at the top of a page, and an **orphan** occurs when the first line of a paragraph displays by itself at the bottom of a page. When you typed the end of the third paragraph, Word placed the automatic page break above the line with the note reference mark to ensure that the last two lines of the paragraph would be at the top of the next page (avoiding a widow). When you continued typing the paragraph, however, Word recognized the multiple lines at the end of the paragraph and moved the automatic page break. If, for some reason, you wanted to allow a widow or an orphan in a document, you would right-click the paragraph in question, click Paragraph on the shortcut menu, click the Line and Page Breaks tab in the Paragraph dialog box, click Widow/Orphan control to deselect the check box, and then click the OK button.

Creating a Table with the Insert Table Button

At the end of the fourth paragraph of the research paper, you are to place a table outlining the techniques for virus protection and system archive (Figure 2-1 on page WD 2.5). In this project, you create a table using Word's table feature. A Word **table** is a collection of rows and columns. The intersection of a row and a column is called a **cell**.

Within a Word table, you easily can rearrange rows and columns, change column widths, sort rows and columns, and sum the contents of rows and columns. You can use the Table AutoFormat dialog box to make the table display in a professional manner. You also can chart table data. For these reasons, many Word users create tables with the Insert Table button, rather than using tabs as discussed in the previous project.

The first step in creating a table is to insert an empty table into the document. When inserting a table, you must specify the total number of rows and columns in the table, called the **dimension** of the table. The table in this project has two columns. Because you often do not know the total number of rows in a table, many Word users create two rows initially and then add rows as they need them. The first number in a dimension is the number of rows, and the second is the number of columns. Perform the following steps to insert a 2 x 2 table, that is, a table with two rows and two columns.

More *About*
Word Tables

Although you can use the TAB key to create a table, many Word users prefer to use its table feature. With a Word table, you can arrange numbers in columns. For emphasis, tables can be shaded and have borders. Word tables can be sorted. And you can have Word add the contents of an entire row or column.

Steps To Insert an Empty Table

1 **With the insertion point at the end of the document, press the SHIFT+ENTER keys. Type** Table **and then press the SHIFT+ENTER keys. Type** Techniques for Virus Protection and System Archive **as the table title. Point to the Insert Table button on the Standard toolbar.**

Word places a line break character at the end of each line entered (Figure 2-43). Recall that a line break causes Word to ignore paragraph formatting when advancing the insertion point to the next line. Thus, Word does not first-line indent the table caption or title.

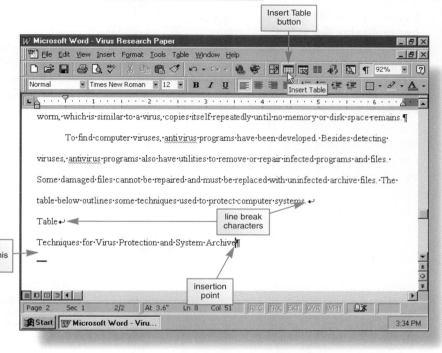

FIGURE 2-43

2 **Click the Insert Table button on the Standard toolbar. Point to the cell in the second row and second column of the grid.**

*Word displays a **grid** to define the dimensions of the desired table (Figure 2-44). The first two columns and first two rows in the grid are selected. The Insert Table button on the Standard toolbar is recessed. Word will insert the 2 × 2 table below the insertion point in the document window.*

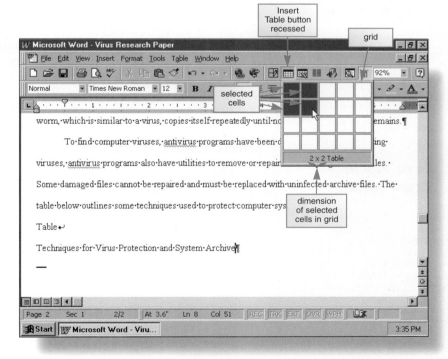

FIGURE 2-44

3 **Click the cell in the second row and second column of the grid. If necessary, use the scroll bar to display the entire table in the document window.**

Word inserts an empty 2 × 2 table into the document (Figure 2-45). The insertion point is in the first cell (row 1 and column 1) of the table.

FIGURE 2-45

Each row has an **end-of-row mark**, which is used to add columns to the right of a table. Each cell has an **end-of-cell mark**, which is used to select a cell. Notice the end-of-cell marks are currently left-aligned within each cell, which indicates the data will be left-aligned within the cells.

For simple tables, such as the one just created, Word users click the Insert Table button to create a table. For more complex tables, such as one with a varying number of columns per row, Word has a new Draw Table feature that allows you to use a pen pointer to draw the table on the screen.

Entering Data into a Word Table

The next step is to enter data into the empty table. Cells are filled with data. The data you enter within a cell wordwraps just as text does between the margins of a document. To place data into a cell, you click the cell and then type. To advance rightward from one cell to the next, press the TAB key. When you are at the rightmost cell in a row, also press the TAB key to move to the first cell in the next row; do not press the ENTER key. The ENTER key is used to begin a new paragraph within a cell. Perform the following steps to enter the data into the table.

Steps **To Enter Data into a Table**

1 **With the insertion point in the upper-left cell of the table, type** Using Virus Protection Software **and then press the TAB key. Type** Backing Up Your System **and then press the TAB key. Type** Install virus protection software on every computer system. **Press the TAB key. Type** Develop a regular plan for copying and storing important data and program files.

*The table data is entered into the header row and the second row of the table (Figure 2-46). When the first row of a table contains column titles, it is called the **header row**.*

FIGURE 2-46

The insertion point currently is positioned at the cell intersecting row 2 and column 2. To create a new row at the bottom of a table, you press the TAB key while the insertion point is in the lower-right cell of the table.

2 **Press the TAB key. Type** Before use, scan every floppy disk with a virus scan program to check for viruses. **Press the TAB key. Type** Implement a backup plan and adhere to its guidelines. **Press the TAB key. Type** Check all programs downloaded from the Internet or bulletin boards for viruses. **Press the TAB key. Type** Keep backup copies of files in fireproof safes or vaults or off-site.

The table data is completely entered (Figure 2-47).

FIGURE 2-47

More *About*
Tables

To select a single cell in a table, click to the left of the cell. To select an entire row, click to the left of the row. To select an entire column, click the column's top border. To add a row or column to the middle of a table, select the row below or column to the right, right-click the selection and then click Insert Row or Insert Column.

You modify the contents of cells just as you modify text in a document. To delete the contents of a cell, select the cell contents by pointing to the left edge of the cell and clicking when the mouse pointer changes direction, and then press the DELETE key. To modify text within a cell, click in the cell, and then correct the entry. You can double-click the OVR indicator on the status bar to toggle between insert and overtype modes. You also may drag and drop or cut and paste the contents of cells.

Because the TAB key advances you from one cell to the next in a table, press the CTRL+TAB keys to insert a tab character into a cell.

Formatting a Table

Although you can format each row, column, and cell of a table individually, Word provides a Table AutoFormat feature that contains predefined formats for tables. Perform the following steps to format the entire table using **Table AutoFormat**.

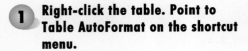

Steps To AutoFormat a Table

1 **Right-click the table. Point to Table AutoFormat on the shortcut menu.**

Word displays a shortcut menu for tables (Figure 2-48).

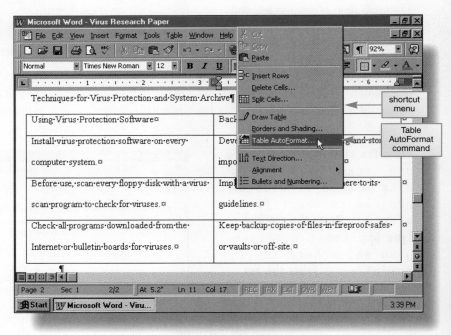

FIGURE 2-48

2 ▶ **Click Table AutoFormat. When the Table AutoFormat dialog box displays, if necessary, click Color in the Formats to apply area to turn color on for the table. Scroll through the Formats list and then click Grid 8. Point to the OK button.**

Word displays the Table AutoFormat dialog box (Figure 2-49). The Preview area shows the Grid 8 format. Because Heading rows is selected in the dialog box, the header row of the table has formatting different from the rest of the rows in the table.

FIGURE 2-49

3 ▶ **Click the OK button.**

Word formats the table according to the Grid 8 format (Figure 2-50).

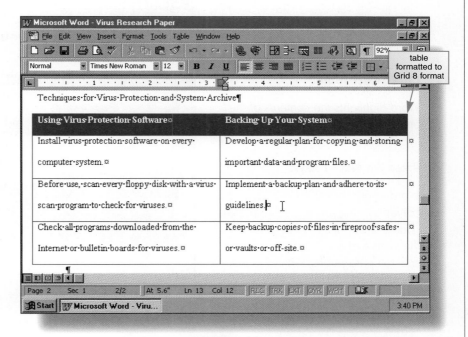

FIGURE 2-50

Changing the Line Spacing of the Table

Notice in Figure 2-50 that the cell contents are double-spaced; you want the paragraphs within the cells to be single-spaced. To change the line spacing of paragraphs in the table, you first must select the entire table and then format as shown in the steps on the next page.

◗Other Ways

1. Click table, on Table menu click Table AutoFormat, click appropriate settings, click OK button

Steps | To Select an Entire Table

1 With the insertion point somewhere in the table, click Table on the menu bar and then point to Select Table (Figure 2-51).

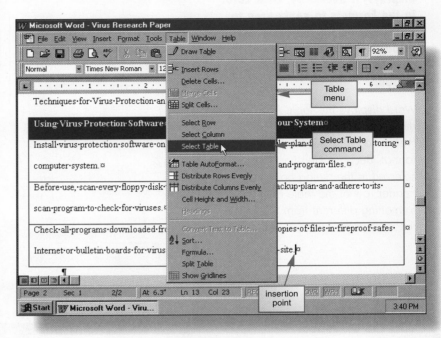

FIGURE 2-51

2 Click Select Table.

Word highlights the contents of the entire table.

3 Press the CTRL+1 keys.

Word single-spaces the contents of the table (Figure 2-52). CTRL+1 is the keyboard shortcut for single-spacing paragraphs; CTRL+2 is the keyboard shortcut for double-spacing paragraphs.

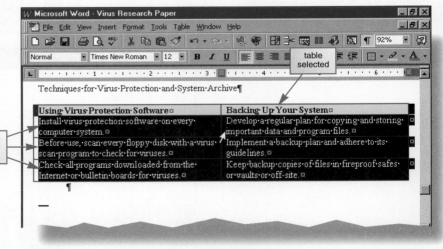

FIGURE 2-52

▶OtherWays

1. With insertion point somewhere in table, press ALT+5 (on numeric keypad with NUM LOCK off)

Changing Paragraph Formatting

When Word placed the table into the research paper, it placed a paragraph mark immediately below the table with no blank line between the paragraph mark and the table. Because the MLA style requires double-spacing of the entire document, you must change the line spacing above the paragraph mark. Perform the following steps to insert a blank line above the paragraph mark below the table.

Steps To Insert a Blank Line above a Paragraph

1 Position the insertion point on the paragraph mark directly below the table (Figure 2-53).

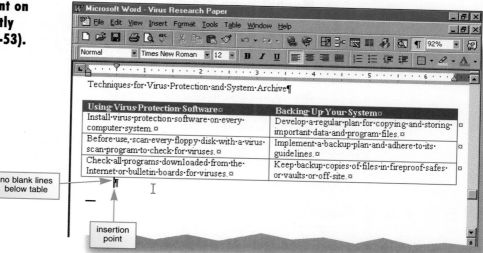

FIGURE 2-53

2 Press the CTRL+0 (zero) keys.

Word inserts a blank line between the paragraph mark and the table.

3 Type the last sentence of the research paper: If your system becomes virus infected and you have questions, contact the National Computer Security Association (NCSA) for low-cost assistance (Elmhurst, 6 Nov. 1998).

The body of the research paper is complete (Figure 2-54).

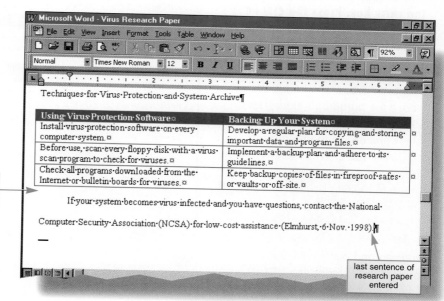

FIGURE 2-54

Creating an Alphabetical Works Cited Page

According to the MLA style, the **works cited page** is a bibliographical list of works you reference directly in your paper. The list is placed on a separate page with the title, Works Cited, centered one inch from the top margin. The works are to be alphabetized by author's last name. The first line of each work begins at the left margin; subsequent lines of the same work are indented one-half inch from the left margin.

OtherWays

1. Right-click paragraph, click Paragraph on shortcut menu, click Indents and Spacing tab, type 12 in Spacing Before text box, click OK button

2. On Format menu click Paragraph, click Indents and Spacing tab, type 12 in Spacing Before text box, click OK button

The first step in creating the works cited page is to force a page break so the works display on a separate page.

Manual Page Breaks

Because the works cited are to display on a separate numbered page, you must insert a manual page break following the body of the research paper. A **manual page break** or **hard page break** is one that you force into the document at a specific location. Manual page breaks display on the screen as a horizontal dotted line, separated by the words, Page Break. Word never moves or adjusts manual page breaks; however, Word does adjust any automatic page breaks that follow in the document. Word inserts manual page breaks just before the location of the insertion point. Perform the following steps to insert a manual page break after the body of the research paper.

Steps To Page Break Manually

1 **With the insertion point at the end of the research paper, press the ENTER key. Press the CTRL+0 (zero) keys. Click Insert on the menu bar and then point to Break.**

Word removes the extra blank line above the paragraph mark (Figure 2-55). Recall that you inserted a blank line above the paragraph below the table. When you pressed the ENTER key, this paragraph formatting carried forward; thus, two blank lines displayed between these paragraphs (one for the double-spacing and one for the extra blank line). Pressing the CTRL+0 keys a second time removes one blank line from above a paragraph. The insertion point now is positioned one blank line below the body of the research paper.

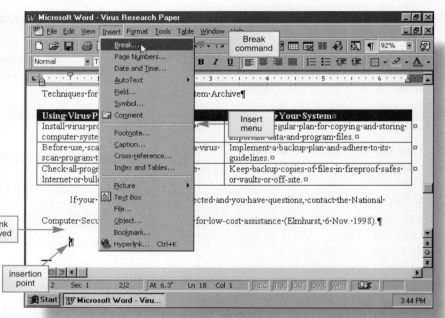

FIGURE 2-55

2 **Click Break.**

Word displays the Break dialog box (Figure 2-56). The default option is Page Break.

FIGURE 2-56

3 **Click the OK button.**

Word inserts a manual page break immediately above the insertion point and positions the insertion point immediately below the manual page break (Figure 2-57). The manual page break displays as a horizontal dotted line with the words, Page Break, in the middle of the line. The status bar indicates the insertion point is located on page 3.

FIGURE 2-57

Other Ways

1. Press CTRL+ENTER

If, for some reason, you wanted to remove a manual page break from your document, you must first select it by double-clicking it. Then, right-click the selection and click Cut on the shortcut menu; or click the Cut button on the Standard toolbar; or press the DELETE key.

Centering the Title of the Works Cited Page

The works cited title is to be centered between the margins. If you simply click the Center button on the Formatting toolbar, the title will not be properly centered; instead, it will be one-half inch to the right of the center point because earlier you set first-line indent at the first tab stop. Thus, the first line of every paragraph is indented one-half inch. To properly center the title of the works cited page, you must move the First Line Indent marker back to the left margin before clicking the Center button as described on the next page.

More *About* **Sources**

When writing a research paper, you must acknowledge sources of information. Citing sources boils down to ethics and honesty. Caution must be used when summarizing or paraphrasing a source. Be sure to avoid plagiarism, which includes using someone else's words and ideas and claiming them as your own.

First Line Indent marker moved to left margin

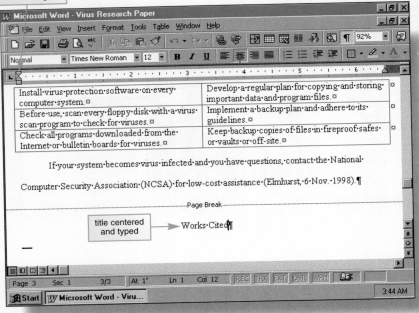

FIGURE 2-58

TO CENTER THE TITLE OF THE WORKS CITED PAGE

1. Drag the First Line Indent marker to the 0" mark on the ruler.
2. Click the Center button on the Formatting toolbar.
3. Type Works Cited as the title.

The title displays centered properly (Figure 2-58).

Creating a Hanging Indent

On the works cited page, the works begin at the left margin. Subsequent lines in the same paragraph are indented one-half inch from the left margin. In essence, the first line *hangs* to the left of the rest of the paragraph; thus, this type of paragraph formatting is called a **hanging indent**. Perform the following steps to create a hanging indent.

Steps **To Create a Hanging Indent**

1. **Press the ENTER key. Click the Align Left button on the Formatting toolbar. Point to the Hanging Indent marker on the ruler (Figure 2-59).**

Recall that the small square at the 0" mark, called the Left Indent marker, is used to change the entire left margin, whereas the Hanging Indent marker affects only the subsequent lines of the same paragraph.

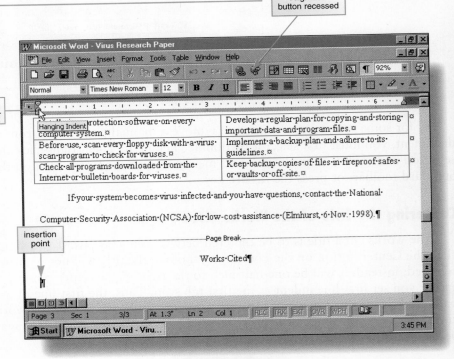

FIGURE 2-59

2 **Drag the Hanging Indent marker to the .5-inch mark on the ruler.**

The Hanging Indent marker and Left Indent marker display at the location of the first tab stop, one-half inch from the left margin (Figure 2-60). When you drag the Hanging Indent marker, the Left Indent marker moves with it. The paragraph containing the insertion point in the document window is positioned at the left margin because only subsequent lines in the paragraph are to be indented.

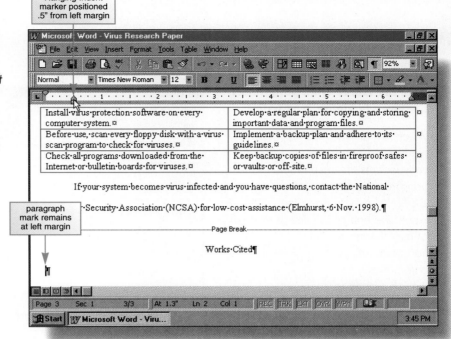

FIGURE 2-60

To drag both the First Line Indent and Hanging Indent markers at the same time, you drag the Left Indent marker on the ruler.

Creating a Hyperlink

A **hyperlink** is a shortcut that allows a user to jump easily and quickly to other documents, objects, or pages. **Jumping** is the process of following a hyperlink to its destination. For example, by clicking hyperlink text on the Word screen, you jump to another document on your computer, on your network, or on the World Wide Web. When you close the hyperlink destination page or document, you return to the original location in your Word document. When the hyperlink text displays initially, it is underlined and colored blue. Once you click a hyperlink, the hyperlink text color changes to purple. When you create a Word document and wish to create a hyperlink to a Web page, you do not have to be connected to the Internet.

Recall from Project 2 that Word has an AutoFormat As You Type feature. Using this feature, you can create a hyperlink simply by typing the address of the file or Web page to which you want to jump. Be sure this feature is enabled by clicking Tools on the menu bar, clicking AutoCorrect, clicking the AutoFormat As You Type tab, clicking the Internet and network paths with hyperlinks, and then clicking the OK button.

In this project, one of the works is from a Web page on the Internet. When someone displays your research paper on the screen, you want him or her to be able to click the Web address in the work and jump to the site for more information. Perform the steps on the next page to create a hyperlink as you type.

*Other*Ways

1. Right-click paragraph, click Paragraph on shortcut menu, click Indents and Spacing tab, click Special box arrow, click Hanging, click OK button

2. On Format menu click Paragraph, click Indents and Spacing tab, click Special box arrow, click Hanging, click OK button

3. Press CTRL+T

More *About* **Citing Sources**

Information that is commonly known or accessible to the audience constitutes common knowledge and does not have to be listed as a parenthetical citation or in the bibliography. If, however, you question whether certain information is common knowledge, you should document it – just to be safe.

Steps   To Create a Hyperlink As You Type

1 Type the Works Cited paragraphs as shown in Figure 2-62 below.

When Word wraps the text in each works cited paragraph, it automatically indents the second line of the paragraph by one-half inch (Figure 2-61). When you press the ENTER key at the end of the first paragraph of text, the insertion point returns automatically to the left margin for the next paragraph. Recall that each time you press the ENTER key, the paragraph formatting in the prior paragraph is carried forward to the next paragraph. The insertion point is positioned to the right of the Web address.

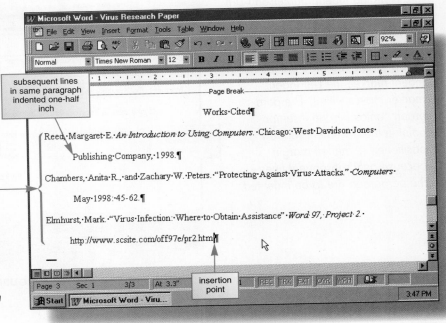

FIGURE 2-61

Reed, Margaret E. *An Introduction to Using Computers*. Chicago: West
Davidson Jones Publishing Company, 1998.
Chambers, Anita R., and Zachary W. Peters. "Protecting Against Virus
Attacks."*Computers* May 1998: 45-62.
Elmhurst, Mark. "Virus Infection: Where to Obtain Assistance" *Word 97,
Project 2*. http://www.scsite.com/off97e/pr2.htm

FIGURE 2-62

2 Press the SPACEBAR and then type (6 Nov. 1998).

As soon as you press the SPACEBAR after typing the Web address, the address formats as a hyperlink (Figure 2-63).

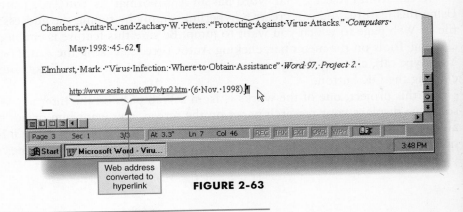

FIGURE 2-63

▶OtherWays

1. Click Insert Hyperlink button on Standard toolbar, type Web address in Link to file or URL text box, click OK button

Later in this project, you will jump to the hyperlink destination.

Sorting Paragraphs

The MLA style requires that the works cited be listed in alphabetical order by author's last name. With Word, you can arrange paragraphs in alphabetic, numeric, or date order based on the first character in each paragraph. Ordering characters in this manner is called **sorting**. Arrange the works cited paragraphs in alphabetical order as illustrated in the following steps.

 Steps **To Sort Paragraphs**

More *About*
Sorting

You can also sort the contents of a table. First, select the rows in the table to be sorted. Click Table on the menu bar, click Sort Text, click Ascending or Descending, and then click the OK button. Once a document has been saved with sorted paragraphs or tables, you cannot return to original order of the paragraphs or table.

1 **Select all the works cited paragraphs by pointing to the left of the first paragraph and dragging down. Click Table on the menu bar and then point to Sort.**

All of the paragraphs to be sorted are selected (Figure 2-64).

FIGURE 2-64

2 **Click Sort.**

Word displays the Sort Text dialog box (Figure 2-65). In the Sort by area, Ascending is selected. Ascending sorts in alphabetic or numeric order.

FIGURE 2-65

3 Click the OK button. Click outside of the selection to remove the highlight.

Word sorts the works cited paragraphs alphabetically (Figure 2-66).

FIGURE 2-66

If you accidentally sort the wrong paragraphs, you can undo a sort by clicking the Undo button on the Standard toolbar.

In the Sort Text dialog box (Figure 2-65 on the previous page), the default sort order is Ascending. If the first character of each paragraph to be sorted is a letter, Word sorts alphabetically on the first letter of the paragraphs. If the first character of each paragraph to be sorted is a number, Word sorts numerically on the first number of the paragraphs. Word by default, orders in **ascending sort order**, which means from the beginning of the alphabet, lowest number, or earliest date. If the first character of the paragraphs to be sorted contains a mixture of letters, numbers, and dates, then the numbers appear first and letters appear last once the paragraphs are sorted. Uppercase letters appear before lowercase letters. In case of ties, Word looks to the first character with a nonidentical character and sorts on that character for the paragraphs where the tie occurs.

You also can sort in descending order by clicking Descending in the Sort Text dialog box. **Descending sort order** begins sorting from the end of the alphabet, the highest number, or the most recent date.

The research paper is now complete and ready for proofing.

Proofing and Revising the Research Paper

As discussed in Project 1, once you complete a document, you might find it necessary to make changes to it. Before submitting a paper to be graded, you should proofread it. While proofreading, you look for grammatical errors and spelling errors. You want to be sure the transitions between sentences flow smoothly and the sentences themselves make sense. Very often, you may count the words in a paper to meet minimum word guidelines specified by an instructor. To assist you in this proofreading effort, Word provides several tools. You already have used the spell checker and grammar checker in previous projects. Other helpful tools are discussed in the following pages.

Going to a Specific Location in a Document

Often, you would like to bring a certain page or footnote into view in the document window. To do this, you could scroll though the document to find the desired page or note. Instead of scrolling though the document, Word provides an easier method of going to a specific location via the **Select Browse Object menu**. Perform the following steps to go to the top of page two in the research paper.

 teps **To Browse by Page**

1 **Click the Select Browse Object button on the vertical scroll bar. When the Select Browse Object menu displays, point to Browse by Page.**

Word displays the Select Browse Object menu (Figure 2-67). As you point to various commands in the Select Browse Object menu, Word displays the command name at the bottom of the menu. For example, you could browse by footnote, endnote, table, and so on.

FIGURE 2-67

2 **Click Browse by Page. Point to the Previous Page button on the vertical scroll bar.**

Word closes the Select Browse Object menu (Figure 2-68). Depending on the command you select in the Select Browse Object menu, the function of the buttons above and below the Select Browse Object button on the vertical scroll bar changes. Because Browse by Page was selected, the buttons move to the previous or next page.

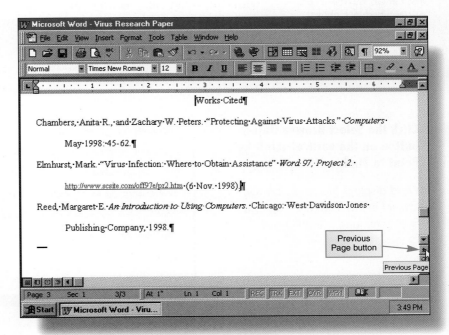

FIGURE 2-68

3 **Click the Previous Page button.**

Word places the top of page 2 (the previous page) at the top of the document window (Figure 2-69).

FIGURE 2-69

Finding and Replacing Text

While proofreading the paper, notice that it contains the word, archive, more than once in the document (see Figure 2-70 below); and you would rather use the word, backup. Therefore, you must change all occurrences of the word, archive, to the word, backup. To do this, you can use Word's find and replace feature, which automatically locates each occurrence of a specified word or phrase and then replaces it with specified text as shown in these steps.

 Steps 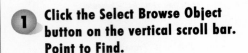 To Find and Replace Text

1 **Click the Select Browse Object button on the vertical scroll bar. Point to Find.**

Word displays the Select Browse Object menu (Figure 2-70). The Find command is highlighted.

FIGURE 2-70

2 Click Find. When the Find and Replace dialog box displays, click the Replace tab. Type archive in the Find what text box. Press the TAB key. Type backup in the Replace with text box. Point to the Replace All button.

Word displays the Find and Replace dialog box (Figure 2-71). Clicking the Replace All button replaces all occurrences of the Find what text with the Replace with text.

FIGURE 2-71

3 Click the Replace All button.

Word replaces all occurrences of the word, archive, with the word, backup, and then displays a Microsoft Word dialog box indicating the total number of replacements made (Figure 2-72).

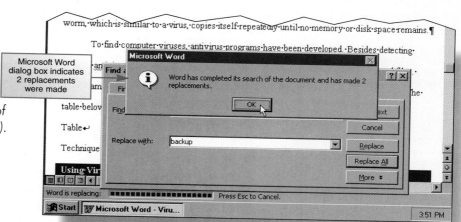

FIGURE 2-72

4 Click the OK button in the Microsoft Word dialog box. Click the Close button in the Find and Replace dialog box.

Word returns to the document window. The word, backup, now displays instead of the word, archive (Figure 2-73).

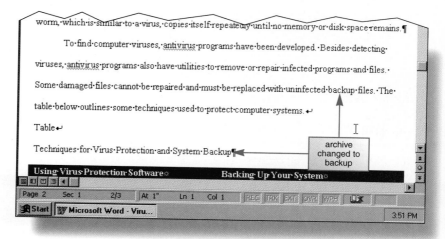

FIGURE 2-73

▶**Other Ways**

1. On Edit menu click Replace, type Find what text, type Replace with text, click Replace All button, click OK button, click Close button

2. Press CTRL+H, and then proceed starting with type Find what text as described in 1 above

In some cases, you may want to replace only certain occurrences of the text, not all of them. To instruct Word to confirm each change, click the Find Next button in the Find and Replace dialog box (Figure 2-71 on the previous page) instead of the Replace All button. When Word locates an occurrence of the text in the Find what text box, it pauses and waits for you to click either the Replace button or the Find Next button. Clicking the Replace button changes the text; clicking the Find Next button instructs Word to disregard the replacement and look for the next occurrence of the Find what text.

If you accidentally replace the wrong text, you can undo a replacement by clicking the Undo button on the Standard toolbar. If you used the Replace All button, Word undoes all replacements. If you used the Replace button, Word only undoes the most recent replacement.

Finding Text

Sometimes, you may want to find only text instead of find and replace text. To search for just an occurrence of text, you follow these steps.

TO FIND TEXT

1. Click the Select Browse Object button on the vertical scroll bar.
2. Click Find on the Select Browse Object menu.
3. Type the text you want to locate in the Find what text box on the Find sheet.
4. Click the Find Next button.
5. To edit the text, click the Close button in the Find and Replace dialog box; to search for the next occurrence of the Find what text, click the Find Next button.

Using the Thesaurus

When writing papers, you may find that you used the same word in multiple locations or that a word you used was not quite appropriate. In these instances, you will want to look up a word similar in meaning to the duplicate or inappropriate word. These similar words are called **synonyms**. A book of synonyms is referred to as a **thesaurus**. Word provides its own thesaurus for your convenience. In this project, you need a synonym for the word, find, at the beginning of the fourth paragraph. Perform the following steps to use Word's thesaurus.

Steps ▸ **To Use Word's Thesaurus**

1. **Click the word for which you want to look up a synonym. Click Tools on the menu bar, point to Language on the Tools menu, and then point to Thesaurus on the Language submenu.**

   The insertion point is positioned in the word, find, at the beginning of the fourth paragraph in the research paper (Figure 2-74).

FIGURE 2-74

2 Click Thesaurus. When the Thesaurus: English (United States) dialog box displays, click detect (verb) in the Meanings list box.

Word displays the Thesaurus: English (United States) dialog box. The Meanings list box displays the different uses of the selected word, and the Replace with Synonym list box displays a variety of words with similar meanings. The Replace with Synonym list changes based on the meaning you select in the Meanings list.

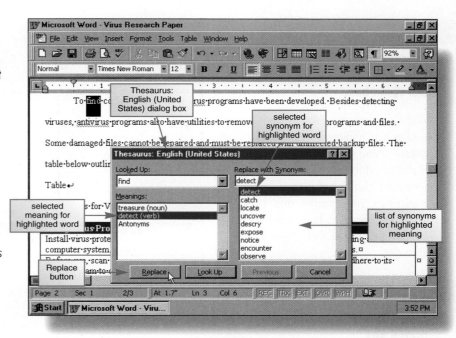

FIGURE 2-75

3 Click the synonym you want (detect) and then point to the Replace button.

The word, detect, is highlighted in the Replace with Synonym list (Figure 2-75).

4 Click the Replace button.

Word replaces the word, find, with detect and returns to the document window (Figure 2-76 below).

> ▶**Other**Ways
> 1. Press SHIFT+F7

Using Word Count

Often when you write papers, you are required to compose a paper with a specified number of words. The requirement for the research paper in this project was 500 words. For this reason, Word provides a command that displays the number of words, as well as the number of pages, characters, paragraphs, and lines in your document. Perform the following steps to use Word Count.

 To Count Words

1 Click Tools on the menu bar and then point to Word Count (Figure 2-76).

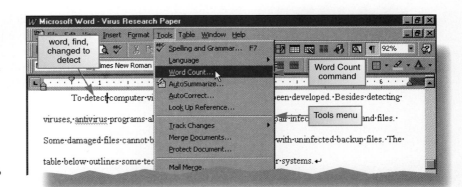

FIGURE 2-76

2 Click Word Count. When the Word Count dialog box displays, if necessary, click Include footnotes and endnotes to select the check box.

Word displays the Word Count dialog box (Figure 2-77). Word presents you with a variety of statistics on the current document, including number of pages, words, characters, paragraphs, and lines. You can choose to have note text included or not included in these statistics.

3 Click Include footnotes and endnotes to deselect it. Click the Close button in the Word Count dialog box.

Word deselects the Include footnotes and endnotes check box and then returns you to the document.

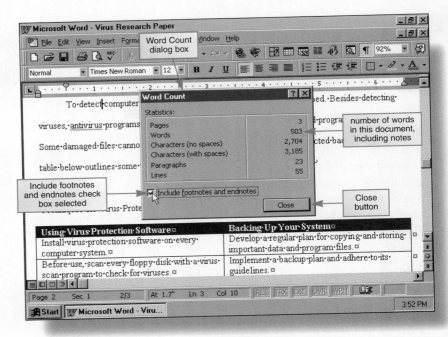

FIGURE 2-77

*Other**Ways***

1. On File menu click Properties, click Statistics tab, click OK button

If you want statistics on only a section of your document, select the section before invoking the Word Count command.

You should change the zoom control back to 100% so the next person that uses Word will not have a reduced display.

TO ZOOM TO 100%

1 Click the Zoom box arrow.

2 Click 100% in the list of zoom percentages.

Word displays 100% in the Zoom box.

Checking Spelling, Saving Again, and Printing the Document

The document is now complete. After completing the document, you should check the spelling of the document by clicking the Spelling and Grammar button on the Standard toolbar. Because you have performed several tasks since the last save, you should save the research paper again by clicking the Save button on the Standard toolbar. Finally, you should print the research paper by clicking the Print button on the Standard toolbar. The completed research paper prints as shown in Figure 2-1 on page WD 2.5.

Navigating to a Hyperlink

Recall that one requirement of this research paper is that one of the works be a site on the Web. Your instructor, Professor J. Brown, has requested that you turn in a floppy disk with this research paper on it so he can verify information at the site. Perform the following steps to check your hyperlink.

Steps To Navigate to a Hyperlink

1 **Display the third page of the research paper in the document window and then point to the hyperlink text.**

When you point to hyperlink text in a Word document, the mouse pointer changes to a pointing hand (Figure 2-78). To follow the link, click it.

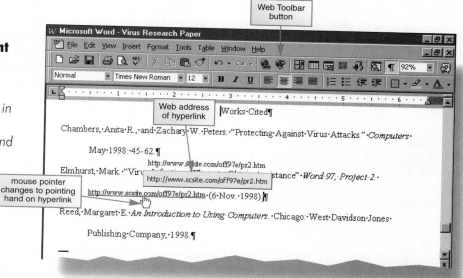

FIGURE 2-78

2 **Click the hyperlink text.**

If you currently are not connected to the Web, Word connects you using your default browser. After a few moments, the http://www.scsite.com/off97e/ pr2.htm Web page displays (Figure 2-79).

3 **Close the browser window.**

The Word screen redisplays.

4 **Click the Web Toolbar button on the Standard toolbar to remove the Web toolbar.**

FIGURE 2-79

The final step in this project is to quit Word.

TO QUIT WORD

> **1** Click the Close button in the Word window.

The Word window closes.

Project Summary

Project 2 introduced you to creating a research paper with a table using the MLA documentation style. You learned how to change margin settings, adjust line spacing, create headers with page numbers, and indent paragraphs. You learned how to use Word's AutoCorrect feature. Then, you added a footnote and created a table in the research paper. You alphabetized the works cited page by sorting its paragraphs and included a hyperlink to a Web page in one of the works. You learned how to browse through a Word document and find and replace text. Finally, you used Word's thesaurus to look up synonyms and saw how to display statistics about your document.

What You Should Know

Having completed this project, you now should be able to perform the following tasks:

- Add a Footnote (*WD 2.25*)
- AutoCorrect As You Type (*WD 2.22*)
- AutoFormat a Table (*WD 2.34*)
- Browse by Page (*WD 2.45*)
- Center a Paragraph before Typing (*WD 2.17*)
- Center the Title of the Works Cited Paragraph (*WD 2.40*)
- Change the Default Font Size (*WD 2.15*)
- Change the Default Margin Settings (*WD 2.8*)
- Count Words (*WD 2.49*)
- Create a Hanging Indent (*WD 2.40*)
- Create a Header (*WD 2.12*)
- Create a Hyperlink As You Type (*WD 2.42*)
- Create an AutoCorrect Entry (*WD 2.23*)
- Display Nonprinting Characters (*WD 2.7*)
- Double-Space a Document (*WD 2.10*)
- Enter Data into a Table (*WD 2.33*)
- Enter Name and Course Information (*WD 2.16*)
- Find and Replace Text (*WD 2.46*)
- Find Text (*WD 2.48*)
- First-Line Indent Paragraphs (*WD 2.18*)
- Insert a Blank Line above a Paragraph (*WD 2.37*)
- Insert an Empty Table (*WD 2.31*)
- Navigate to a Hyperlink (*WD 2.51*)
- Page Break Automatically (*WD 2.29*)
- Page Break Manually (*WD 2.38*)
- Quit Word (*WD 2.52*)
- Save a Document (*WD 2.18*)
- Select an Entire Table (*WD 2.36*)
- Sort Paragraphs (*WD 2.43*)
- Start Word (*WD 2.7*)
- Use Word's Thesaurus (*WD 2.48*)
- Zoom Page Width (*WD 2.21*)
- Zoom to 100% (*WD 2.50*)

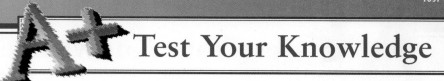

Test Your Knowledge

True/False

Instructions: Circle T if the statement is true or F if the statement is false.

F   1. The MLA presents a popular documentation style used today for research papers.

F   2. The MLA style uses the term works cited rather than bibliography.

F   3. A footer is text you want to print at the bottom of each page in a document.

F   4. Subscripted numbers are those that appear raised above other text in a document.

F   5. An automatic page break displays on the screen as a single dotted horizontal line, separated by the words Page Break.

F   6. A cell is the intersection of a row and a column in a Word table.

F   7. To insert a tab character into a cell, press the TAB key.

F   8. A hanging indent indents subsequent lines in the same paragraph one-half inch from the right margin.

F   9. Word's thesaurus enables you to look up synonyms for a selected word.

F 10. To jump to a hyperlink destination from a Word document, click the hyperlink text.

Multiple Choice

Instructions: Circle the correct response.

MLA stands for _____.

a. Modern Language Abbreviation   c. Modern Lexical Abbreviation

b. Modern Language Association   d. Modern Lexical Association

How can you edit header text?

a. switch to page layout view

b. display the document in print preview

c. click View on the menu bar and then click Header and Footer

d. all of the above

The AutoCorrect feature automatically fixes misspelled words when you _____ after entering the misspelled word.

a. press the ESC key   c. type a period

b. click the AutoCorrect button   d. press the SPACEBAR

If an AutoComplete tip displays on the screen, _____ to instruct Word to place the text of the AutoComplete tip at the location of your typing.

a. press the ENTER key   c. click the AutoComplete button

b. press the SHIFT+ENTER keys   d. either b or c

A(n) _____ occurs when the first line of a paragraph displays by itself at the bottom of a page.

a. twin   b. orphan   c. sibling   d. widow

A table with 7 rows and 4 columns is referred to as a(n) _____ table.

a. 28   b. 11   c. 7 × 4   d. 4 × 7   *(continued)*

Test Your Knowledge

Multiple Choice *(continued)*

7. To insert a blank line above a paragraph, press the _____ keys.
   a. CTRL+0 (zero)   b. CTRL+B   c. ALT+0 (zero)   d. ALT+B

8. To move both the First Line Indent marker and Hanging Indent marker on the ruler at the same time, you _____.
   a. drag the Left Indent marker   c. right-drag the First Line Indent marker
   b. select both markers and then drag   d. none of the above

9. A hyperlink is a shortcut that allows you to jump to _____.
   a. another document on your computer   c. a page on the World Wide Web
   b. another document on your network   d. all of the above

10. The Select Browse Object button is located on the _____.
    a. Standard toolbar   c. vertical scroll bar
    b. Formatting toolbar   d. horizontal scroll bar

3 Understanding the Ruler

FIGURE 2-8

Instructions: Answer the following questions concerning the ruler in Figure 2-80. The numbers in the figure correspond to the numbers of the questions below.

1. What is the name of the top triangle? What is the purpose of dragging this triangle?
2. What is the name of the bottom triangle? What is the purpose of dragging this triangle?
3. What is the name of the small square? What is the purpose of dragging this square?

4 Understanding the Note Pane

FIGURE 2-81

Instructions: In Figure 2-81, arrows point to major components of the note pane. Identify the various parts of the note pane in the spaces provided.

Use Help

1 Reviewing Project Activities

Instructions: Perform the following tasks using a computer.

1. Start Word.
2. If the Office Assistant is on your screen, click it to display its balloon. If the Office Assistant is not on your screen, click the Office Assistant button on the Standard toolbar.
3. Type create a hyperlink in the What would you like to do? text box. Click the Search button. Click the Create hyperlinks link. Read the information. Use the shortcut menu or Options button to print the information.
4. Click the Help Topics button to display the Help Topics: Microsoft Word dialog box. Click the Contents tab. Double-click the Working with Tables and Adding Borders book. Double-click the Parts of a table topic. Read and print the information.
5. Click the Help Topics button. Click the Index tab. Type margins and then double-click the overview topic. Double-click the Paragraph indenting vs. page margins topic. Read and print the information.
6. Click the Help Topics button. Click the Find tab. Type header and then double-click the Add page numbers topic. Read and print the information.
7. Close any open Help window(s) by clicking its Close button. Close the Office Assistant.

2 Expanding on the Basics

Instructions: Use Word Help to better understand the topics listed below. Answer the questions on your own paper or hand in the printed Help topic to your instructor.

1. In this project, you worked with a header. Use the Office Assistant to answer the following questions about headers and footers.
   a. What would cause the correct date, time, or other item to not appear in the header? When you locate the Help window containing this answer, the term, field, is used. What is a field?
   b. How do you create a unique header or footer for the first page of a document? When you locate the Help window containing the answer, the term, section, is used. What is a section?
   c. How do you delete a header or a footer?
2. In this project, you created a Word table. Use the Contents tab in the Help Topics: Microsoft Word dialog box to locate Help windows describing keys used for the following tasks: type and move around in a table and select items in a table. Print each of the two Help topics. Next, obtain answers to the following questions.
   a. How do you add a row to the end of a table? the middle of a table?
   b. How do you add a column to the right edge of a table? the middle of a table?
3. In this project, you inserted a hyperlink. Use the Index tab in the Help Topics: Microsoft Word dialog box to answer the following questions about hyperlinks.
   a. How do you change a hyperlink destination?
   b. How do you change existing hyperlink text?

(continued)

Use Help

Expanding on the Basics *(continued)*

   c. What is a Word publication?

   d. Assume when you click a hyperlink, an error message displays. Identify three reasons the error message might display.

4. In this project, you created an AutoCorrect entry. Use the Find tab in the Help Topics: Microsoft Word dialog box to answer the following questions about AutoCorrect entries.

   a. How do you change the contents of an AutoCorrect entry?

   b. How do you delete an AutoCorrect entry?

   c. How can you prevent AutoCorrect from correcting abbreviations or capitalized text?

   d. How can you add an AutoCorrect entry during a spelling check?

5. Click the Web Toolbar button on the Standard toolbar to display the Web toolbar. Use the What's This? command on the Help menu to display ScreenTips for each button on the Web toolbar. Print each ScreenTip by right-clicking it, clicking Print Topic on the shortcut menu, and then clicking the OK button.

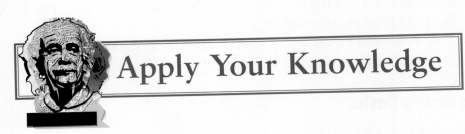

Apply Your Knowledge

1 Working with a Table

Instructions: Start Word. Open the document, apply-3, from the Word folder on the Data Disk that accompanies this book. The document is a Word table that you are to edit and format. You may need to refer to your Use Help 2 responses for information on how to select items in the table and modify them. The revised table is shown in Figure 2-82.

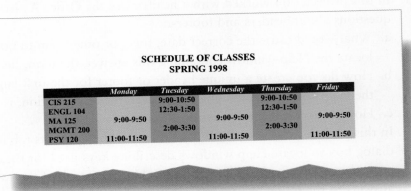

SCHEDULE OF CLASSES
SPRING 1998

	Monday	Tuesday	Wednesday	Thursday	Friday
CIS 215		9:00-10:50		9:00-10:50	
ENGL 104		12:30-1:50		12:30-1:50	
MA 125	9:00-9:50		9:00-9:50		9:00-9:50
MGMT 200		2:00-3:30		2:00-3:30	
PSY 120	11:00-11:50		11:00-11:50		11:00-11:50

FIGURE 2-82

Perform the following tasks:

1. Right-click the table and then click Table AutoFormat on the shortcut menu. Click Column 2 in the Formats area of the Table AutoFormat dialog box. Be sure all of the check boxes in the Formats to apply area are checked. Also, be sure that only the Heading rows check box is checked in the Apply special formats to area; you may need to deselect First column. Click the OK button.

Apply Your Knowledge

2. Add a new row to the table for ENGL 104, which meets on Tuesdays and Thursdays from 12:30-1:50.

3. Delete the Saturday column by selecting it, right-clicking the selection, and then clicking Delete Columns on the shortcut menu. You do not have any Saturday classes scheduled.

4. Click in the table, click Table on the menu bar, and then click Select Table.

5. Click Table on the menu bar and then click Cell Height and Width. If necessary, click the Row tab, click Center in the Alignment area, and then click the OK button to center the table between the left and right margins.

6. With the table still selected, click Table on the menu bar, click Sort, and then click the OK button. Click anywhere to remove the highlight from the table.

7. Select the header row and then click the Italic button on the Formatting toolbar.

8. Select the cells containing the class times and then click the Align Right button on the Formatting toolbar.

9. Click File on the menu bar and then click Save As. Use the file name Revised Class Schedule and then save the document on your floppy disk.

10. Print the revised table.

In the Lab

1 Preparing a Research Paper with a Table

Problem: You are a college student currently enrolled in an introductory computer class. Your assignment is to prepare a short research paper (400-450 words) about Computer Security. The requirements are that the paper be prepared according to the MLA documentation style, contain a table, and have three references — one of which must be from the Internet (Figure 2-83 on the next two pages).

Instructions:

1. If necessary, click the Show/Hide ¶ button on the Standard toolbar. Change all margins to one inch. Adjust line spacing to double. Create a header to number pages. Change the font size of all characters to 12 point. Type the name and course information at the left margin. Center and type the title. First-line indent all paragraphs in the paper.

2. Type the body of the paper as shown in Figure 2-83a and Figure 2-83b on pages WD 2.58 and WD 2.59. The table is formatted in the Grid 8 format with the all check boxes selected except Last row and Last column. At the end of the body of the research paper, press the ENTER key and insert a manual page break.

3. Create the works cited page (Figure 2-83c) on page WD 2.59.

4. Check the spelling of the paper.

(continued)

In the Lab

Preparing a Research Paper with a Table *(continued)*

5. Save the document on a floppy disk with Computer Security Research Paper as the file name.
6. Print the research paper. Above the title of your printed research paper, hand write the number of words in the research paper.

West 1

Jonathan Paul West

Professor M. Carter

Information Systems 200

September 9, 1998

Computer Security

Many commercial software packages are designed with computer security features that control who can access the computer. These types of access controls use a process called identification and authentication. Identification verifies that the user is a valid user, and authentication verifies that the user is who he or she claims to be. Three common methods of authentication are remembered information, possessed objects, and biometric devices.

With remembered information, a user is required to enter a word or series of characters that match an entry in a security file in the computer. Most multiuser operating systems provide for a logon code, a user ID, and a password (all forms of remembered information) that all must be entered correctly before a user is allowed to use an application program. A logon code usually identifies the application, and a user ID identifies the user. A password usually is confidential, often known only by the user and the system administrator (Baker and Danville 29-47).

A possessed object is any item that a user must carry to gain access to the computer facility. Examples of possessed objects are badges, cards, and keys. Possessed objects often are used in conjunction with a personal identification number (PIN), which is a numeric password (Price 40-68).

A biometric device is one that verifies personal characteristics to authenticate a user. Examples of personal characteristics are fingerprints, voice pattern, signature, hand size, and

FIGURE 2-83a

In the Lab

West 2

retinal (eye) patterns. A biometric device usually translates a user's personal characteristics into a digital code that is compared to a digital code stored in the computer (Victors 22-85). If the digital code in the computer does not match the user's code, access is denied.

Each of these authentication techniques has advantages and disadvantages. The table below outlines the major advantage and disadvantage of each technique.

Table

Advantages and Disadvantages of Authentication Techniques

	Remembered Information	Possessed Object	Biometric Device
Advantages	Inexpensive	Relatively inexpensive	Virtually foolproof
Disadvantages	Can be forgotten or guessed by a perpetrator	Can be lost or forgotten	Expensive

A computer system should implement one or more of these authentication techniques to secure it from accidental or intentional misuse. In addition, the organization should review the techniques in place regularly to determine if they are still appropriate.

FIGURE 2-83b

West 3

Works Cited

Baker, Jamie D. and Cynthia I. Danville. "Security, Ethics, and Privacy." <u>Computers and Society Journal</u> Feb. 1998: 29-47.

Price, Karen E. "Identification and Authentication Controls." *Word 97, Project 2.*
http://www.scsite.com/off97e/pr2.htm (31 Aug. 1998).

Victors, Michael R. <u>The Computer Auditor</u>. St. Louis: Green Valley Publishing Company, 1998.

FIGURE 2-83c

2 Preparing a Research Report with a Footnote and a Table

Problem: You are a college student currently enrolled in an English class. Your assignment is to prepare a short research paper in any area of interest to you. The only requirements are that the paper be presented according to the MLA documentation style, contain a table, and have three references, one of which must be from the Internet. You decide to prepare a paper comparing word processing software and desktop publishing software (Figure 2-84 on the next two pages).

(continued)

In the Lab

Preparing a Research Report with a Footnote and a Table *(continued)*

Reed 1

Sally Reed

Professor P. Harmon

English 204

December 9, 1998

Word Processing vs. Desktop Publishing

Many organizations distribute brochures and newsletters to promote their products and/or services. In the past, preparing these desktop publishing documents was best accomplished through outside agencies. In the 1980s, however, word processors began including graphics and different fonts as part of their standard software package (Larkin and Green, 8 Oct. 1998). That is, many word processors were emerging with desktop publishing capabilities.

Desktop publishing software (DTP) allows users to design and produce professional looking documents that contain both text and graphics. Examples of such documents include newsletters, marketing literature, technical manuals, and annual reports. The common thread among these packages is the ability to import graphic images, change fonts, draw lines, and display in WYSIWYG mode (What You See Is What You Get).

Graphic images can be imported from previously created art, called clip art. Clip art may be included with the software package being used or may be purchased.[1] Collections of clip art contain several hundred to several thousand images grouped by type, such as holidays, vehicles, or people. Input devices, called scanners, also can be used to import photographs and art into

---

[1] Winters found that nearly all of today's word processing software includes clip art, which can be enlarged, reduced, moved, and altered in other ways.

FIGURE 2-84a

Reed 2

DTP documents (Brown 14-35). Regardless of how it is accomplished, once the image has been imported into the document, it can be enlarged, reduced, rotated, or moved.

Many word processing software packages today include features that previously were considered to be the domain of desktop publishing software. Conversely, many recent releases of DTP software contain enhanced word processing capabilities. The table below outlines the DTP features in word processing packages and features not yet in most word processing packages.

Table

DTP Features

DTP Features in Word Processing Packages	Additional DTP Features in DTP Software
Alters typefaces, styles, and point sizes	Includes color libraries
Adjusts margins, alignment, and spacing	Creates master pages, larger page sizes, and page grids
Includes columns, tables, graphics, borders, and shading	Stacks and overlaps multiple objects on a page and traps objects

With each release of word processing and DTP software, the differences between the two will decrease and their similarities will increase.

FIGURE 2-84b

Instructions: Perform the following tasks:

1. Change all margin settings to one inch. Adjust line spacing to double. Create a header to number pages. Change the font size of all characters to 12 point. Type the name and course information at the left margin. Center and type the title. First-line indent all paragraphs in the paper.

2. Type the body of the paper as shown in Figure 2-84a and Figure 2-84b. The table is formatted in the Grid 8 format with all check boxes selected except Last row and Last column. At the end of the body of the research paper, press the ENTER key once and insert a manual page break.

3. Create the works cited page. Enter the works cited shown below as separate paragraphs and then alphabetize the paragraphs.

    a. Larkin, Henry P., and Janice A. Green. "Word Processing." *Word 97, Project 2.* http://www.scsite.com/off97e/pr2.htm (8 Oct. 1998).

    b. Winters, Jill. "Word Processing Software Packages Today." *Microcomputer Journal* Nov. 1998: 58-66.

    c. Brown, Robert. *Introductory Computer Concepts and Techniques.* Boston: International Publishing Company, 1998.

4. Check the spelling of the paper. Use Word's thesaurus to change the word, domain, in the last paragraph to a word of your choice.

5. Save the document on a floppy disk with Word Processing Paper as the file name.

6. Print the research paper. Above the title of your printed research paper, hand write the number of words, including the footnote, in the research paper.

In the Lab

3 Composing a Research Report with a Table and Footnotes

Problem: You have drafted the notes shown in Figure 2-85. Your assignment is to prepare a short research paper based on these notes. You are to review the notes and then rearrange and reword. Embellish the paper as you deem necessary. Add a footnote elaborating on a personal experience you have had. Create a table listing examples of peripherals. Present the paper according to the MLA documentation style.

Instructions: Perform the following tasks:

1. If necessary, click the Show/Hide ¶ button on the Standard toolbar. Change all margin settings to one inch. Adjust line spacing to double. Create a header to number pages. Change the font size of all characters to 12 point. Type the name and course information at the left margin. Center and type the title. First-line indent all paragraphs in the paper.

2. Compose the body of the paper from the notes in Figure 2-85. Be sure to include a footnote and a table as specified above. At the end of the body of the research paper, press the ENTER key once and insert a manual page break.

3. Create the works cited page from the listed sources. Be sure to alphabetize the works.

4. Check the spelling and grammar of the paper.

5. Save the document on a floppy disk with YourName Research Paper as the file name (where Your-Name is your last name).

6. Print the research paper. Above the title of your printed research paper, hand write the number of words, including the footnote, in the research paper.

The five major categories of computers are (1) personal computers, (2) servers, (3) minicomputers, (4) mainframe computers, and (5) supercomputers.

Personal computers also are called micros, PCs, or microcomputers. Examples include hand-held, palmtop, notebook, subnotebook, laptop, pen, desktop, tower, and workstation. Hand-held, palmtop, notebook, subnotebook, laptop, and pen computers are considered portable computers. Prices range from several hundred to several thousand dollars. Source: Personal Computers, a book published by Windy City Publishing Company in Chicago, 1998, pages 15-45, author Jane A. Polson.

A server supports a computer network. A network allows multiple users to share files, application software, and hardware. Small servers range from $5,000 to $20,000; larger servers can cost as much as $150,000. Source: "Serving Networks," an article in Network World, September 1998 issue, pages 135-148, author Peter S. Thorn.

Minicomputers are more powerful than PCs and can support multiple users performing different tasks. Originally, they were developed to perform specific tasks such as engineering calculations. Many businesses use them today for information processing requirements. Costs range from $15,000 to several hundred thousand dollars. Source: "Evaluating Computers," an article in Computer Monthly, August 1998 issue, pages 98-105, authors Karen D. Samuels and Benjamin R. Edwards.

A mainframe computer is a large system that can handle hundreds of users, store large amounts of data, and process transactions at a very high rate. They usually require a specialized environment with separate air conditioning and electrical power. Raised flooring often is built to accommodate the many cables connecting the system components. Prices range from several hundred thousand to several million dollars. Source: Web page article "Mainframe Issues" on Web page Word 97, Project 2 at site http://www.scsite.com/off97e/pr2.htm on September 4, 1998.

Supercomputers are the most powerful computers. They process hundreds of millions of instructions per second and are used for applications such as weather forecasting and space exploration. The cost is several million dollars. Same source as for minicomputers.

FIGURE 2-85

Cases and Places

The difficulty of these case studies varies: ❯ are the least difficult; ❯❯ are more difficult; and ❯❯❯ are the most difficult.

Having completed two projects with Word 97, you should be comfortable with its capabilities. To reinforce your knowledge of Word, write a research paper that discusses its components and features (such as spell checking, grammar checking, wizards, AutoCorrect, and so on). Use your textbook, Word Help, and any other resources available. Explain why you think the component or feature is important and then explain exactly how to perform the task in Word. Include at least two references. Use the concepts and techniques presented in this project to format the paper.

Windows is a graphical user interface (GUI), which claims to be a much more user-friendly environment than DOS. Write a brief research paper that discusses the features of Windows. Use your textbook, Windows Help, and any other resources available. For each feature you identify, discuss whether or not you feel this feature is user-friendly and state your reason(s). Include at least two references. Use the concepts and techniques presented in this project to format the paper.

❯ This project required the MLA style of documentation in the preparation of the research paper. Another popular documentation style is by the American Psychological Association (APA). The MLA style generally is used in the humanities, whereas the APA style is preferred in the social sciences. Many differences exist between the two styles. Using the school library or other resources (such as the Internet), research the APA style. Then, prepare a brief research paper that compares and contrasts the two styles. Include at least one explanatory note and three references, one of which must be a Web site on the Internet. Use the concepts and techniques presented in this project to format the paper.

❯ When you install Windows, two accessories are provided: a word processor and a text editor. Although Windows supplies these two programs, most users purchase a separate word processing package, such as Word, for creating documents. Try creating the research paper from this project in the Windows word processor and also the text editor. Use Windows Help or any other resources to assist you with these documents. Then, prepare a brief research paper comparing and contrasting Word 97 to the word processor and text editor supplied with Windows. Include at least one explanatory note and two references. Use the concepts and techniques presented in this project to format the paper.

Cases and Places

5 ▶▶ Microsoft Word was introduced in 1983. Since then, it has experienced many version changes and upgrades. Using a school library or other resources (such as the Internet), learn how Microsoft Word has evolved to the product it is today. Identify when and how the first word processors came to be. Then, prepare a brief research paper on the evolution of Microsoft Word since the beginning of word processors through today. Include at least one explanatory note and three references, one of which must be a Web site on the Internet. Use the concepts and techniques presented in this project to format the paper.

6 ▶▶▶ Many different word processing packages are on the market, e.g., Word, WordPerfect, and so on. Using a school library or other resources (such as the Internet), determine the top three word processing packages and their features. Contact two businesses and ask which word processor they use; find out what they like and dislike about their word processor. Then, prepare a brief research paper comparing and contrasting the three word processing packages. At the end of the paper, identify the one you feel is the best. Include at least two explanatory notes and three references, one of which must be a Web site on the Internet. Use the concepts and techniques presented in this project to format the paper.

7 ▶▶▶ When you purchase a personal computer, the price often includes some installed software. Sometimes, it is more economical to buy the package; however, you may not receive the exact software you desire. Visit or call two computer stores. Obtain package prices for their latest personal computers. Also, obtain prices of the hardware and software individually. Ask why they chose the software they did for the package deals. Then, prepare a brief research paper on computer package deals; discuss whether you would buy a package deal or not at the present time. Include at least two explanatory notes and three references. Use the concepts and techniques presented in this project to format the paper.

Microsoft Excel 97

▶ **PROJECT ONE**

CREATING A WORKSHEET AND EMBEDDED CHART

bjectives   E 1.3
hat Is Microsoft Excel?   E 1.6
ject One – Computer Discount Daily Sales
   E 1.6
e Excel Window   E 1.10
orksheet Window   E 1.12
ecting a Cell   E 1.14
ering Text   E 1.14
ering Numbers   E 1.20
culating a Sum   E 1.21
ng the Fill Handle to Copy a Cell
   to Adjacent Cells   E 1.23
matting the Worksheet   E 1.26
ng AutoFormat to Format the Body of a
   Worksheet   E 1.31
ng the Name Box to Select a Cell   E 1.33
ding a 3-D Column Chart to the Worksheet
   E 1.35
ving a Workbook   E 1.39
nting the Worksheet   E 1.43
itting Excel   E 1.44
rting Excel and Opening a Workbook
   E 1.45
oCalculate   E 1.47
rrecting Errors   E 1.49
cel Online Help   E 1.52
ject Summary   E 1.53
hat You Should Know   E 1.53
t Your Knowledge   E 1.54
e Help   E 1.56
ply Your Knowledge   E 1.58
he Lab   E 1.59
ses and Places   E 1.63

▶ **PROJECT TWO**

FORMULAS, FORMATTING, CHARTS, AND WEB QUERIES

Objectives   E 2.1
Introduction   E 2.4
Project Two – High-Tech Stock Club   E 2.4
Entering the Titles and Numbers
   into the Worksheet   E 2.7
Entering Formulas   E 2.9
Using the AVERAGE, MAX, and MIN Functions
   E 2.15
Applying Formats to the Text   E 2.21
Applying Formats to the Numbers   E 2.28
Changing the Widths of Columns and Heights
   of Rows   E 2.34
Checking Spelling   E 2.39
Saving the Workbook a Second Time Using
   the Same File Name   E 2.41
Adding a 3-D Pie Chart to the Workbook
   E 2.41
Changing the Sheet Names and Rearranging
   the Order of the Sheets   E 2.51
Previewing and Printing Selected Sheets
   in a Workbook   E 2.53
Displaying and Printing the Formulas in the
   Worksheet   E 2.59
Getting External Data from a Web Source Using
   a Web Query   E 2.61
Quitting Excel   E 2.65
Project Summary   E 2.65
What You Should Know   E 2.66
Test Your Knowledge   E 2.67
Use Help   E 2.70
Apply Your Knowledge   E 2.71
In the Lab   E 2.72
Cases and Places   E 2.80

Microsoft Excel 97

Creating a Worksheet and Embedded Chart

Objectives:

You will have mastered the material in this project when you can:

▶ Start Excel
▶ Describe the Excel worksheet
▶ Select a cell or range of cells
▶ Enter text and numbers
▶ Use the AutoSum button to sum a range of cells
▶ Copy a cell to a range of cells using the fill handle
▶ Change the size of the font in a cell
▶ Bold cell entries
▶ Center cell contents over a series of columns
▶ Apply the AutoFormat command to format a range
▶ Use the Name box to select a cell
▶ Create a 3-D Column chart using the Chart Wizard
▶ Save a workbook
▶ Print a worksheet
▶ Quit Excel
▶ Open a workbook
▶ Use the AutoCalculate area to determine totals
▶ Correct errors on a worksheet

It's the Pits

Number-crunching notebooks are race cars' driving force

When six drivers first gathered in Chicago on Thanksgiving Day more than 100 years ago, little did they know they were pioneering the sport of auto racing. Two of them completed the 55-mile jaunt through foot-high snow, and the winner finished in 10 hours with an average speed of 5.5 miles per hour.

Since that first race, the sport has grown to a multibillion-dollar business. Stock car racing is the country's fastest growing professional sport. Drivers at the Indianapolis Motor Speedway, dash in 1,100-horsepower IndyCars at speeds averaging 150 mph and exceeding 235 mph.

To run a top racing team requires at least $10 million, with a crew that includes up to 200 people or more. While spectators may recognize drivers such as Michael Andretti and Jimmy Vasser, they may be less aware of the DAGs (Data Acquisition Geeks) — the engine engineers behind the scenes who gather data and scrutinize the results of calculations to optimize every facet of a race car's performance.

The DAGs perform their jobs with the assistance of notebook computers and data acquisition technology that can cost as much as $37,000. Sensors on various parts of the car collect readings on the suspension, G-force, wheel speed, fuel flow, brakes, tire temperatures, rpm, throttle position, and gear selection and send the data to sophisticated onboard control units, some of which can handle 100 analog and digital channels concurrently and have four megabytes of storage.

These onboard computers put each piece of data in a predefined area, or cell, of an electronic worksheet. This rectangular grid of columns and rows contains formulas that crunch the data. Then, the worksheet immediately displays vital information and graphs on the driver's digital instrument panel. Simultaneously, the processed data from the worksheet is beamed via telemetry to the DAGs' notebooks in the pits. The DAGs analyze the information and use headsets to instruct the driver to make adjustments, such as changing the stiffness of the suspension or modifying braking performance. The pit crew can analyze this output and make other modifications to the car when the driver comes into the pits, such as altering the tire air pressure to adapt to changing track conditions.

Other data acquisition systems use worksheets, such as those you will work with in Microsoft Excel, to perform pivotal functions. For example, one uses an infrared signal beamed at the start/finish line to trigger another onboard computer to perform lap counting and timing calculations. Another system analyzes chassis weights. This worksheet identifies handling problems and performs what-if analysis, such as what would happen if 40 pounds of lead were added in front of the rear axle. Another spreadsheet uses a fuel management strategy to determine when fuel stops should be made. Diagrams produced by the spreadsheet program precisely trace the driver's path on the track and superimpose color-coded parameters such as speed, braking effort, and throttle position.

Now that computer technology has become portable, powerful, and less expensive, the data acquisition systems are considered as much an essential part of a racer's equipment as the helmet and fireproof suit of the driver.

Project 1

Microsoft
Excel 97

Creating a Worksheet and Embedded Chart

Case Perspective

The Computer Discount Company has experienced explosive growth since its inception a year ago. Thanks to the popularity of personal computers and the World Wide Web, the company has grown faster than anyone could have imagined — yet they still have little or no day-to-day accounting. As sales continue to grow, the management at Computer Discount finally has realized they need a better tracking system for daily sales. As a result, they have asked you to begin each day by preparing a worksheet that shows each previous day's sales.

In particular, they want to know the daily sales for the four key product groups (Computers, Monitors, Printers, and Software) by channel (Mail Order, Telephone, and Web). They want the totals by product group and by channel.

Your task is to develop a worksheet to show these daily sales. In addition, Kelly Montgomery, the president, also has asked you to create a graphical representation of the daily sales because she has little tolerance for lists of numbers.

What Is Microsoft Excel?

Microsoft Excel is a spreadsheet program that allows you to organize data, complete calculations, make decisions, graph data, develop professional-looking reports, convert Excel files for use on the Web, and access the Web. The three major parts of Excel are:

- **Worksheets** Worksheets allow you to enter, calculate, manipulate, and analyze data such as numbers and text. The term worksheet means the same as spreadsheet.
- **Charts** Charts pictorially represent data. Excel can draw a variety of two-dimensional and three-dimensional charts.
- **Databases** Databases manage data. For example, once you enter data onto a worksheet, Excel can sort the data, search for specific data, and select data that meets a criteria.

Project One – Computer Discount Daily Sales

From your meeting with Computer Discount's management, you have determined the following needs, source of data, calculations, and graph requirements.

Need: An easy-to-read worksheet (Figure 1-1) that shows Computer Discount's daily sales for each product group (Computers, Monitors, Printers, and Software) by channel (Mail Order, Telephone, and Web). The worksheet also includes total sales for each product group, each channel, and total company sales for the day.

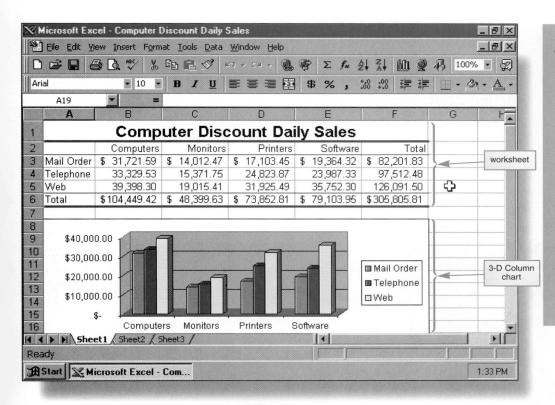

FIGURE 1-1

Source of Data: The data for the worksheet is available each morning from Emma Jo Winslow, Chief Financial Officer (CFO) of Computer Discount.

Calculations: You have determined that the following calculations must be made for the worksheet: (a) total daily sales for each of the four product groups; (b) total daily sales for each of the three sales channels; and (c) total company daily sales.

Graph Requirements: Below the worksheet, construct a 3-D Column chart that compares the three sales channels for each product group.

Preparation Steps

The preparation steps below and on the next page summarize how the worksheet and chart shown in Figure 1-1 will be developed in Project 1.

1. Start the Excel program.
2. Enter the worksheet title (Computer Discount Daily Sales), the column titles (Computers, Monitors, Printers, Software, and Total), and the row titles (Mail Order, Telephone, Web, and Total).
3. Enter the daily sales for each product group by sales channel.

4. Calculate the daily sales for each product group, for each sales channel, and the total company daily sales.
5. Format the worksheet title (center it across the six columns, enlarge it, and make it bold).
6. Format the body of the worksheet (add underlines, display the numbers in dollars and cents).
7. Direct Excel to create the 3-D Column chart.
8. Save the workbook on a floppy disk.
9. Print the worksheet and 3-D Column chart.
10. Quit Excel.

The following pages contain a detailed explanation of these tasks.

Starting Excel

To start Excel, Windows 95 must be running. Perform the following steps to start Excel

 Steps To Start Excel

1 Click the Start button on the taskbar and then point to New Office Document (Figure 1-2).

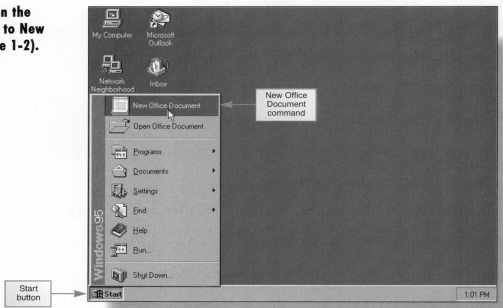

FIGURE 1-2

2 Click New Office Document. If necessary, click the General tab in the New Office Document dialog box, and then point to the Blank Work-book icon (Figure 1-3).

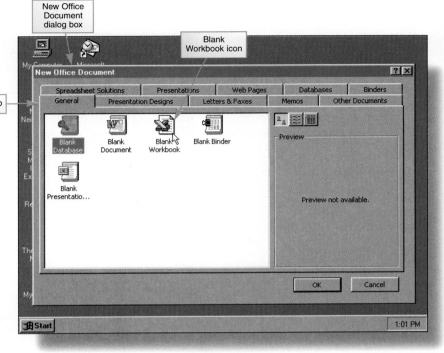

FIGURE 1-3

3 Double-click the Blank Workbook icon. If necessary, enlarge the Excel window by double-clicking its title bar.

Excel displays an empty workbook titled Book1 (Figure 1-4).

FIGURE 1-4

4 **If the Office Assistant displays (Figure 1-4 on the previous page), click its Close button.**

Excel closes the Office Assistant (Figure 1-5). The purpose of the Office Assistant will be discussed later in this project.

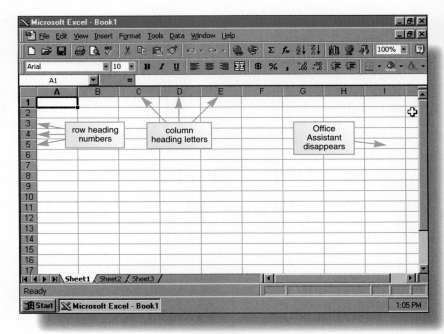

FIGURE 1-5

The Excel Window

The **Excel window** consists of a variety of features to help you work more efficiently. It contains a title bar, menu bar, toolbars, formula bar, the worksheet window, sheet tabs, scroll bars, and the status bar. Each of these Excel window features and their components are described in this section.

The Workbook

When Excel starts, it creates a new empty workbook, called Book1. The **workbook** (Figure 1-6) is like a notebook. Inside the workbook are sheets, called **worksheets**. Each sheet name appears on a **sheet tab** at the bottom of the workbook. For example, Sheet1 is the name of the active worksheet displayed in the workbook called Book1. If you click on the tab labeled Sheet2, Excel displays the Sheet2 worksheet. A new workbook opens with three worksheets. If necessary, you can add additional worksheets to a maximum of 255. This project will use only the Sheet1 worksheet.

The Worksheet

The worksheet is organized into a rectangular grid containing columns (vertical) and rows (horizontal). A column letter above the grid, also called the column heading, identifies each **column**. A row number on the left side of the grid, also called the row heading, identifies each **row**. Nine complete columns (A through I) and seventeen complete rows (1 through 17) of the worksheet appear on the screen when the worksheet is maximized as shown in Figure 1-5.

FIGURE 1-6

Cell, Active Cell, Gridlines, and Mouse Pointer

The intersection of each column and row is a **cell**. A cell is the basic unit of a worksheet into which you enter data. A cell is referred to by its unique address, or **cell reference**, which is the coordinates of the intersection of a column and a row. To identify a cell, specify the column letter first, followed by the row number. For example, cell reference C5 refers to the cell located at the intersection of column C and row 5 (Figure 1-6).

One cell on the worksheet, designated the **active cell**, is the one in which you can enter data. The active cell in Figure 1-6 is A1. Cell A1 is identified in three ways. First, a heavy border surrounds the cell; second, the **active cell reference** displays immediately above column A in the **Name box**; and third, the column heading A and row heading 1 "light up" so it is easy to see which cell is active (Figure 1-6).

The horizontal and vertical lines on the worksheet itself are called **gridlines**. Gridlines make it easier to see and identify each cell in the worksheet. If desired, you can turn the gridlines off so they do not display on the worksheet, but it is recommended that you leave them on.

> **More** *About*
> **the Mouse Pointer**
>
> The mouse pointer can change to one of more than 15 different shapes, such as an arrow, cross hair, or chart symbol, depending on the task you are performing in Excel and the mouse pointer's location on the screen.

The mouse pointer in Figure 1-6 on the previous page has the shape of a block plus sign. The mouse pointer displays as a **block plus sign** whenever it is located in a cell in the worksheet. Another common shape of the mouse pointer is the block arrow. The mouse pointer turns into the **block arrow** whenever you move it outside the worksheet or when you drag cell contents between rows or columns. The other mouse pointer shapes are described when they appear on the screen during this and subsequent projects.

Worksheet Window

Each worksheet in a workbook has 256 columns and 65,536 rows for a total of 16,777,216 cells. The column headings begin with A and end with IV. The row headings begin with 1 and end with 65,536. Only a small fraction of the active worksheet displays on the screen at one time. You view the portion of the work-sheet displayed on the screen through a **worksheet window** (Figure 1-6 on the pre-vious page). Below and to the right of the worksheet window are **scroll bars**, **scroll arrows**, and **scroll boxes,** which you can use to move the window around to view different parts of the active worksheet. To the right of the sheet tabs at the bot-tom of the screen is the **tab split box**. You can drag the tab split box (Figure 1-6) to increase or decrease the view of the sheet tabs. When you decrease the view of the sheet tabs, you increase the length of the horizontal scroll bar; and vice versa.

Menu Bar, Standard Toolbar, Formatting Toolbar, Formula Bar, Sheet and Scroll Tabs, and Status Bar

The menu bar, Standard toolbar, Formatting toolbar, and formula bar appear at the top of the screen just below the title bar (Figure 1-7). The sheet tabs, tab scrolling buttons, and the status bar appear at the bottom of the screen, above the Windows 95 taskbar.

FIGURE 1-7

MENU BAR The **menu bar** is a special toolbar that includes the Excel menu names (Figure 1-7). The menu bar that displays when you start Excel is the **Worksheet menu bar.** Each menu name represents a menu of commands that you can use to retrieve, store, print, and manipulate data on the worksheet. When you point to a menu name on the menu bar, the area of the menu bar containing the name changes to a button. To display a menu, such as the **File menu,** click the menu name File on the menu bar. Once a menu displays, you can point to any command and its submenu displays.

The menu bar can change to include other menu names depending on the type of work you are doing in Excel. For example, if you are working with a chart sheet rather than a worksheet, the **Chart menu bar** will display with menu names that reflect charting command options.

STANDARD TOOLBAR AND FORMATTING TOOLBAR The Standard toolbar and Formatting toolbar (Figure 1-7) contain buttons and list boxes that allow you to perform frequent tasks more quickly than when using the menu bar. For example, to print a worksheet, you click the Print button. Each button has a picture on the button face that helps you remember the button's function. Also, when you move the mouse pointer over a button or box, the name of the button or box appears below it. This is called a **ScreenTip.**

Figure 1-8 illustrates the Standard and Formatting toolbars and describes the functions of the buttons. Each of the buttons and list boxes will be explained in detail when they are used in the projects.

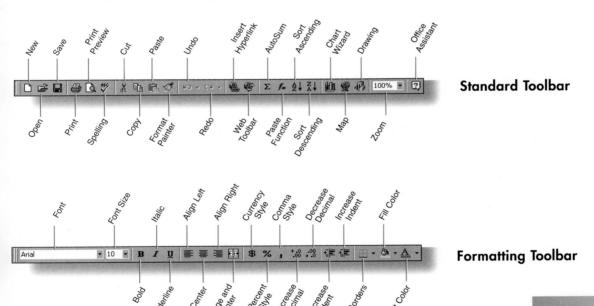

FIGURE 1-8

Excel has several additional toolbars you can activate by clicking View on the menu bar. You also can point to a toolbar, such as the Formatting toolbar, and then right-click to display a shortcut menu, which lists the toolbars available (Figure 1-7). A **shortcut menu** contains a list of commands or items to choose from that relate to the item you are pointing to when you right-click. Once a shortcut menu displays, you can click or right-click a command or item. The recessed check mark to the left of Standard and Formatting in the shortcut menu in Figure 1-7 indicates those toolbars are displaying on the screen.

FORMULA BAR Below the Formatting toolbar is the **formula bar** (Figure 1-7 on page E 1.12). As you type, the data appears in the formula bar. Excel also displays the active cell reference on the left side of the formula bar in the Name box.

STATUS BAR Immediately above the Windows 95 taskbar at the bottom of the screen is the status bar. The **status bar** displays a brief description of the command selected (highlighted) in a menu, the function of the button the mouse pointer is pointing to, or the current activity (mode) in progress (Figure 1-7). **Mode indicators**, such as Enter and Ready, display on the status bar and specify the current mode of Excel. When the mode is Ready, Excel is ready to accept the next command or data entry. When the mode indicator reads Enter, Excel is in the process of accepting data through the keyboard into the active cell.

In the middle of the status bar is the AutoCalculate area. The **AutoCalculate area** can be used in place of a calculator to view the sum, average, or other types of totals of a group of numbers on the worksheet.

Keyboard indicators, such as NUM (Num Lock), show which keys are engaged. Keyboard indicators display on the right side of the status bar within the small rectangular boxes (Figure 1-7).

Selecting a Cell

To enter data into a cell, you first must select it. The easiest way to **select a cell** (make it active) is to use the mouse to move the block plus sign to the cell and click.

An alternative method is to use the **arrow keys** that are located just to the right of the typewriter keys on the keyboard. An arrow key selects the cell adjacent to the active cell in the direction of the arrow on the key.

You know a cell is selected (active) when a heavy border surrounds the cell and the active cell reference displays in the Name box on the left side of the formula bar.

Entering Text

In Excel, any set of characters containing a letter, hyphen (as in a telephone number), or space is considered **text**. Text is used to place titles on the worksheet, such as worksheet titles, column titles, and row titles. In Project 1 (Figure 1-9), the worksheet title centered in row 1, Computer Discount Daily Sales, identifies the worksheet. The column titles in row 2 (Computers, Monitors, Printers, Software, and Total) identify the data in each column. The row titles in column A (Mail Order, Telephone, Web, and Total) identify the data in each row.

FIGURE 1-9

Entering the Worksheet Title

The following steps show how to enter the worksheet title (Computer Discount Daily Sales) in cell A1. Later in this project, the worksheet title will be centered over the column titles as shown in Figure 1-9.

 Steps **To Enter the Worksheet Title**

1 Click cell A1.

Cell A1 becomes the active cell and a heavy border surrounds it (Figure 1-10).

FIGURE 1-10

2 Type Computer Discount Daily Sales **in cell A1.**

*When you type the first character, the mode indicator in the status bar changes from Ready to Enter and Excel displays three boxes in the formula bar: the **Cancel box**, the **Enter box**, and the **Edit Formula box** (Figure 1-11). The entire title displays in the formula bar and the text also displays in cell A1 followed immediately by the insertion point. The **insertion point** is a blinking vertical line that indicates where the next character typed will appear.*

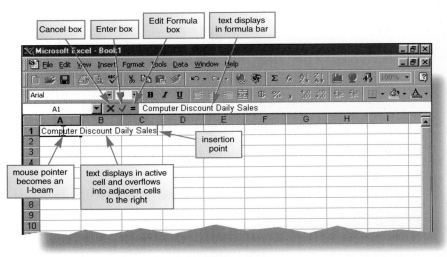

FIGURE 1-11

3 Point to the Enter box (Figure 1-12).

FIGURE 1-12

4 **Click the Enter box to complete the entry.**

Excel enters the worksheet title in cell A1 (Figure 1-13).

FIGURE 1-13

When you complete a text entry into a cell, a series of events occurs. First, Excel positions the text left-aligned in the cell. **Left-aligned** means the cell entry is to the far left in the cell. Therefore, the C in the worksheet title, Computer Discount Daily Sales, begins in the leftmost position of cell A1.

Second, when the text is longer than the width of a column, Excel displays the overflow characters in adjacent cells to the right as long as these adjacent cells contain no data. In Figure 1-13, the width of cell A1 is approximately nine characters. The text entered consists of 26 characters. Therefore, Excel displays the overflow characters from cell A1 in cells B1 and C1, because these cells are empty. If cell B1 contained data, only the first nine characters in cell A1 would display on the worksheet. Excel would hide the overflow characters, but they still would remain stored in cell A1 and display in the formula bar whenever cell A1 was the active cell.

Third, when you complete an entry by clicking the Enter box, the cell in which the text is entered remains the active cell.

Correcting a Mistake While Typing

If you type the wrong letter and notice the error before clicking the Enter box or pressing the **ENTER key**, use the **BACKSPACE key** to erase all the characters back to and including the one that is wrong. To cancel the entire entry before entering it into the cell, click the Cancel box in the formula bar or press the **ESC key**. If you see an error in a cell, select the cell and retype the entry. Later in this project, additional error-correction techniques are covered.

AutoCorrect

The **AutoCorrect feature** of Excel works behind the scenes, correcting common mistakes when you complete a text entry in a cell. AutoCorrect makes three types of corrections for you:

1. Corrects two initial capital letters by changing the second letter to lowercase.
2. Capitalizes the first letter in the names of days.

3. Replaces commonly misspelled words with their correct spelling. For example, it will change the misspelled word *recieve* to *receive* when you press the ENTER key, click the Enter box, or press an arrow key to complete an entry. AutoCorrect will correct automatically the spelling of more than 400 words.

You can add misspelled words and their corresponding corrections to the AutoCorrect list and turn off any of the AutoCorrect features by clicking **AutoCorrect** on the **Tools menu.**

Entering Column Titles

To enter the column titles, select the appropriate cell and then enter the text, as described in the following steps.

More *About*
the AutoCorrect Feature

AutoCorrect is part of the IntelliSense™ technology that is built into Excel, which understands what you are trying to do and helps you do it. For example, Excel can correct common misspellings automatically. When you press the ENTER key, the corrected text is entered in the cell.

Steps **To Enter Column Titles**

1 **Click cell B2.**

Cell B2 becomes the active cell. The active cell reference in the Name box changes from A1 to B2 (Figure 1-14).

active cell reference in Name box changes to B2

B2 is active cell

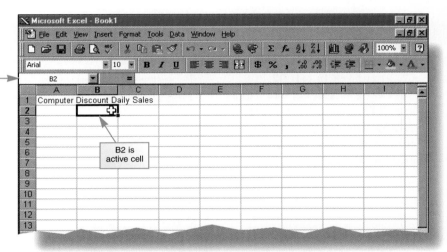

FIGURE 1-14

2 **Type** Computers **in cell B2.**

Excel displays Computers in the formula bar and in cell B2 (Figure 1-15).

Computers displays in the formula bar and cell B2

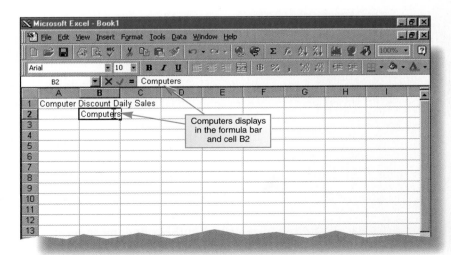

FIGURE 1-15

3 **Press the RIGHT ARROW key.**

Excel enters the column title, Computers, in cell B2 and makes cell C2 the active cell (Figure 1-16). When you press an arrow key to complete an entry, the adjacent cell in the direction of the arrow (up, down, left, or right) becomes the active cell.

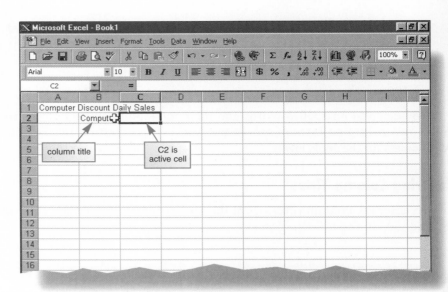

FIGURE 1-16

4 **Repeat Steps 2 and 3 for the remaining column titles in row 2. That is, enter** Monitors **in cell C2,** Printers **in cell D2,** Software **in cell E2, and** Total **in cell F2. Complete the last column title entry in cell F2 by clicking the Enter box or by pressing the ENTER key.**

The column titles display left-aligned as shown in Figure 1-17.

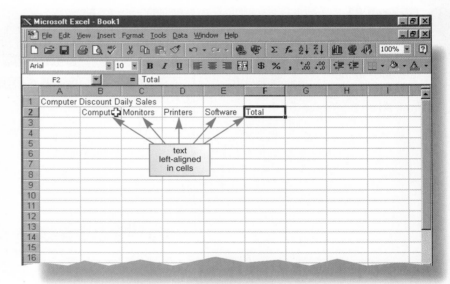

FIGURE 1-17

If the next entry is in an adjacent cell, use the arrow keys to complete the entry in a cell. If the next entry is in a non-adjacent cell, click the next cell in which you plan to enter data, or click the Enter box, or press the ENTER key and then click the appropriate cell for the next entry.

Entering Row Titles

The next step in developing the worksheet in Project 1 is to enter the row titles in column A. This process is similar to entering the column titles and is described in the following steps.

Steps **To Enter Row Titles**

---

1 **Click cell A3.**

Cell A3 becomes the active cell (Figure 1-18). The active cell reference in the Name box changes from F2 to A3.

FIGURE 1-18

---

2 **Type** `Mail Order` **and then press the DOWN ARROW key.**

Excel enters the row title Mail Order in cell A3 and cell A4 becomes the active cell (Figure 1-19).

FIGURE 1-19

---

3 **Repeat Step 2 for the remaining row titles in column A. Enter** `Telephone` **in cell A4,** `Web` **in cell A5, and** `Total` **in cell A6. Complete the last row title in cell A6 by clicking the Enter box or by pressing the ENTER key.**

The row titles display as shown in Figure 1-20.

FIGURE 1-20

Entering Numbers

In Excel, you can enter numbers into cells to represent amounts. **Numbers** can include the digits zero through nine and any one of the following special characters:

$$+ - ( ) , / . \$ \% \ E \ e$$

If a cell entry contains any other keyboard character (including spaces), Excel interprets the entry as text and treats it accordingly.

In Project 1, the daily sales numbers obtained from Emma Jo Winslow, Chief Financial Officer (CFO) of Computer Discount, are summarized in Table 1-1.

These numbers, which represent daily sales for each of the channels and product groups, must be entered in rows 3, 4, and 5. The following steps illustrate how to enter these values one row at a time.

Table 1-1

	COMPUTERS	MONITORS	PRINTERS	SOFTWARE
MAIL ORDER	31,721.59	14,012.47	17,103.45	19,364.32
TELEPHONE	33,329.53	15,371.75	24,823.87	23,987.33
WEB	39,398.30	19,015.41	31,925.49	35,752.30

Steps **To Enter Numeric Data**

1 **Click cell B3. Type** 31721.59 **and then press the RIGHT ARROW key.**

Excel enters the number 31721.59 in cell B3 and changes the active cell to cell C3 (Figure 1-21). The numbers are formatted with dollar signs and commas later in this project.

FIGURE 1-21

2 **Enter** 14012.47 **in cell C3,** 17103.45 **in cell D3, and** 19364.32 **in cell E3.**

Row 3 now contains the daily sales by mail order for the four product groups. The numbers in row 3 are right-aligned (Figure 1-22). **Right-aligned** *means Excel displays the cell entry to the far right in the cell.*

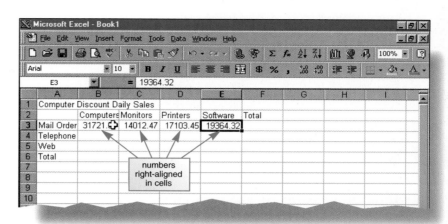

FIGURE 1-22

3 **Click cell B4. Enter the daily sales by Telephone for the four product groups (**33329.53 **for Computers,** 15371.75 **for Monitors,** 24823.87 **for Printers, and** 23987.33 **for Software) in row 4. Enter the daily sales by Web for the four product groups (**39398.30 **for Computers,** 19015.41 **for Monitors,** 31925.49 **for Printers, and** 35752.30 **for Software) in row 5.**

The daily sales by Telephone and Web display in rows 4 and 5 (Figure 1-23).

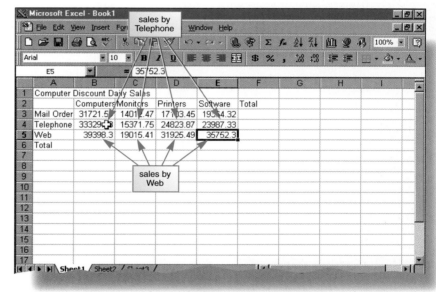

FIGURE 1-23

Steps 1 through 3 complete the numeric entries. You are not required to type dollar signs, commas, or trailing zeros. When you enter a number that has cents, however, you must add the decimal point and the numbers representing the cents when you enter the number. Later in this project, dollar signs, commas, and trailing zeros will be added to improve the appearance of the numbers.

The next section instructs Excel to calculate the totals in row 6 and in column F. Indeed, the capability of Excel to perform calculations is one of its major features.

Calculating a Sum

The next step in creating the daily sales worksheet is to determine the total daily sales for the Computers product group in column B. To calculate this value in cell B6, Excel must add the numbers in cells B3, B4, and B5. Excel's **SUM function** provides a convenient means to accomplish this task.

More *About* **Numbers**

In Excel, a number can be between approximately -1×10^{308} and 1×10^{308}. To enter a number such as 93,000,000,000, you can type 93,000,000,000 or you can type 9.3E10, which stands for 9.3×10^{10}. If the cell is not wide enough to display a number, Excel displays it in Scientific format. If you enter a large number in a cell with an assigned format, Excel automatically increases the column width so the number displays properly.

To use the SUM function, first you must identify the cell in which the sum will be stored after it is calculated. Then, you can use the **AutoSum button** on the Standard toolbar to enter the SUM function.

Although you can enter the SUM function in cell B6 through the keyboard as =SUM(B3:B5), the following steps illustrate how to use the AutoSum button to accomplish the same task.

Steps To Sum a Column of Numbers

1 **Click cell B6 and then point to the AutoSum button on the Standard toolbar.**

Cell B6 becomes the active cell (Figure 1-24).

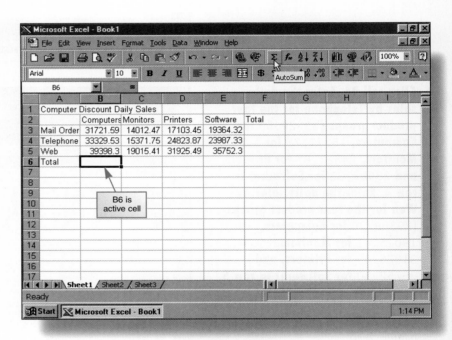

FIGURE 1-24

2 **Click the AutoSum button.**

*Excel responds by displaying =SUM(B3:B5) in the formula bar and in the active cell B6 (Figure 1-25). The =SUM entry identifies the SUM function. The B3:B5 within parentheses following the function name SUM is Excel's way of identifying the cells B3, B4, and B5. Excel also surrounds the proposed cells to sum with a moving border, called a **marquee**.*

FIGURE 1-25

3 **Click the AutoSum button a second time.**

Excel enters the sum of the daily sales for Computers (104449.4 = 31721.59 + 33329.53 + 39398.3) in cell B6 (Figure 1-26). The SUM function assigned to cell B6 displays in the formula bar when B6 is the active cell.

FIGURE 1-26

When you enter the SUM function using the AutoSum button, Excel automatically selects what it considers to be your choice of the group of cells to sum. The group of cells B3, B4, and B5 is called a range. A **range** is a series of two or more adjacent cells in a column or row or a rectangular group of cells. Many Excel operations, such as summing numbers, take place on a range of cells.

When proposing the range to sum, Excel first looks for a range of cells with numbers above the active cell and then to the left. If Excel proposes the wrong range, you can drag through the correct range anytime prior to clicking the AutoSum button a second time. You also can enter the correct range by typing the beginning cell reference, a colon (:), and the ending cell reference.

When using the AutoSum button, you can click it once and then click the Enter box or press the ENTER key to complete the entry. Clicking the AutoSum button twice in succession, however, is the quickest way to enter the SUM function into a single cell.

Using the Fill Handle to Copy a Cell to Adjacent Cells

On the daily sales worksheet, Excel also must calculate the totals for Monitors in cell C6, Printers in cell D6, and for Software in cell E6. Table 1-2 illustrates the similarities between the entry in cell B6 and the entries required for the totals in cells C6, D6, and E6.

To place the SUM functions in cells C6, D6, and E6, you can follow the same steps shown in Figures 1-24 through 1-26. A second, more efficient method is to copy the SUM function from cell B6 to the range C6:E6. The cell being copied is called the **copy area**. The range of cells receiving the copy is called the **paste area**.

Table 1-2

CELL	SUM FUNCTION ENTRIES	REMARK
B6	=SUM(B3:B5)	Sums cells B3, B4, and B5
C6	=SUM(C3:C5)	Sums cells C3, C4, and C5
D6	=SUM(D3:D5)	Sums cells D3, D4, and D5
E6	=SUM(E3:E5)	Sums cells E3, E4, and E5

Notice from Table 1-2 on the previous page that although the SUM function entries are similar, they are not exact copies. The range in each SUM function entry to the right of cell B6 uses cell references that are one column to the right of the previous column. When you copy cell references, Excel adjusts them for each new position, resulting in the SUM function entries illustrated in Table 1-2 on the previous page. Each adjusted cell reference is called a **relative reference**.

The easiest way to copy the SUM formula from cell B6 to cells C6, D6, and E6 is to use the fill handle. The **fill handle** is the small black square located in the lower-right corner of the heavy border around the active cell (Figure 1-26 on the previous page). Perform the following steps to use the fill handle to copy cell B6 to the adjacent cells C6:E6.

Steps To Copy a Cell to Adjacent Cells in a Row

1 **With cell B6 active, point to the fill handle.**

The mouse pointer changes to a cross hair (Figure 1-27).

FIGURE 1-27

2 **Drag the fill handle to select the paste area C6:E6.**

Excel displays a shaded border around the paste area C6:E6 and the copy area B6 (Figure 1-28).

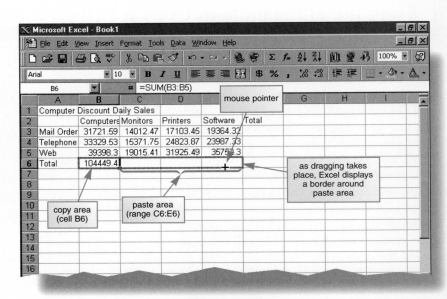

FIGURE 1-28

3 **Release the left mouse button.**

Excel copies the SUM function in cell B6 to the range C6:E6 (Figure 1-29). In addition, Excel calculates the sums and enters the results in cells C6, D6, and E6.

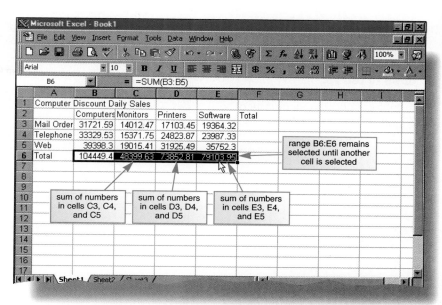

FIGURE 1-29

Determining Row Totals

The next step in building the daily sales worksheet is to determine totals for each sales channel and company total sales in column F. Use the SUM function in the same manner as you did when the daily sales by product group were totaled in row 6. In this example, however, all the rows will be totaled at the same time. The following steps illustrate this process.

  To Determine Multiple Totals at the Same Time

1 **Click cell F3.**

Cell F3 becomes the active cell (Figure 1-30).

FIGURE 1-30

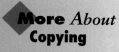

More *About* **Copying**

Another way to copy a cell or range of cells is to select the copy area, point to the border of the copy area, and then, while holding down the CTRL key, drag the copy area to the paste area. If you drag without holding down the CTRL key, Excel moves the data, rather than copying it.

2 With the mouse pointer in cell F3 and in the shape of a block plus sign, drag the mouse pointer down to cell F6.

Excel highlights the range F3:F6 (Figure 1-31).

FIGURE 1-31

3 Click the AutoSum button on the Standard toolbar.

Excel assigns the functions =SUM(B3:E3) to cell F3, =SUM(B4:E4) to cell F4, =SUM(B5:E5) to cell F5, and =SUM(B6:E6) to cell F6, and then calculates and displays the sums in the respective cells (Figure 1-32).

FIGURE 1-32

More About the AutoSum Button

A quick way to determine all the totals in row 6 and column F in Figure 1-32 at once is to select the range (B3:F6) and then click the AutoSum button. The range B3:F6 includes the numbers to sum plus an additional row (row 6) and an additional column (column F), in which the totals will display.

If each cell in the selected range is next to a row of numbers, Excel assigns the SUM function to each cell in the selected range when the AutoSum button is clicked. Thus, four SUM functions with different ranges were assigned to the selected range, one for each row. This same procedure could have been used earlier to sum the columns. That is, rather than selecting cell B6, clicking the AutoSum button twice, and then copying the SUM function to the range C6:E6, you could have selected the range B6:E6 and then clicked the AutoSum button once.

Formatting the Worksheet

The text, numeric entries, and functions for the worksheet now are complete. The next step is to format the worksheet. You **format** a worksheet to emphasize certain entries and make the worksheet easier to read and understand.

Figure 1-33a shows the worksheet before formatting. Figure 1-33b shows the worksheet after formatting. As you can see from the two figures, a worksheet that is formatted not only is easier to read, but also looks more professional.

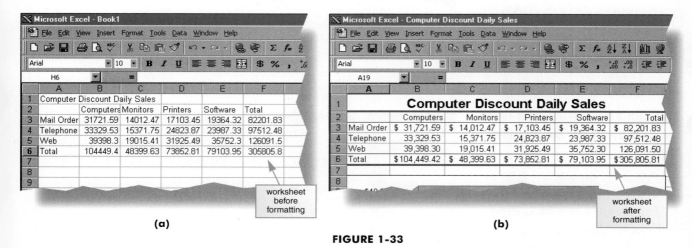

(a)   (b)

FIGURE 1-33

To change the unformatted worksheet in Figure 1-33a to the formatted worksheet in Figure 1-33b, the following tasks must be completed:

1. Bold the worksheet title in cell A1.
2. Enlarge the worksheet title in cell A1.
3. Center the worksheet title in cell A1 across columns A through F.
4. Format the body of the worksheet. The body of the worksheet, range A2:F6, includes the column titles, row titles, and numbers. Formatting the body of the worksheet results in numbers represented in a dollars-and-cents format, dollar signs in the first row of numbers and the total row, underlines that emphasize portions of the worksheet, and modified column widths.

The process required to format the daily sales worksheet is explained in the remainder of this section. Although the format procedures will be carried out in the order described above, you should be aware that you can make these format changes in any order.

Fonts, Font Size, and Font Style

Characters that display on the screen are a specific shape, size, and style. The **font type** defines the appearance and shape of the letters, numbers, and special characters. The **font size** specifies the size of the characters on the screen. Font size is gauged by a measurement system called points. A single **point** is about 1/72 of one inch in height. Thus, a character with a **point size** of 10 is about 10/72 of one inch in height.

Font style indicates how the characters are formatted. Common font styles include regular, bold, underlined, or italicized.

When Excel begins, the default font type for the entire workbook is Arial with a size and style of 10-point regular. Excel allows you to change the font characteristics in a single cell, a range of cells, the entire worksheet, or the entire workbook.

Bolding a Cell

You **bold** an entry in a cell to emphasize it or make it stand out from the rest of the worksheet. Perform the following steps to bold the worksheet title in cell A1.

 Steps To Bold a Cell

1 Click cell A1 and then point to the Bold button on the Standard toolbar.

The ScreenTip displays immediately below the Bold button to identify the function of the button (Figure 1-34).

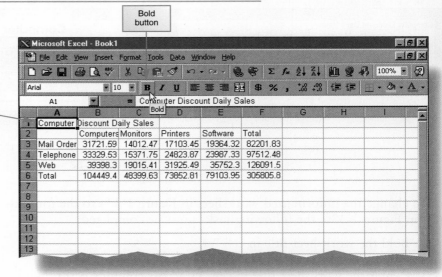

FIGURE 1-34

2 Click the Bold button.

Excel applies a bold format to the worksheet title Computer Discount Daily Sales (Figure 1-35).

FIGURE 1-35

 OtherWays

1. Press CTRL+B
2. Right-click cell, click Format Cells on shortcut menu, click Font tab, click Bold, click OK button
3. On Format menu click Cells, click Font tab, click Bold, click OK button

When the active cell is bold, the Bold button on the Standard toolbar is recessed (Figure 1-35). Clicking the Bold button a second time removes the bold format.

Increasing the Font Size

Increasing the font size is the next step in formatting the worksheet title. You increase the font size of a cell so that the entry stands out and is easier to read.

Steps To Increase the Font Size of a Cell Entry

1 **With cell A1 selected, click the Font Size box arrow on the Formatting toolbar and then point to 16 in the Font Size list box (Figure 1-36).**

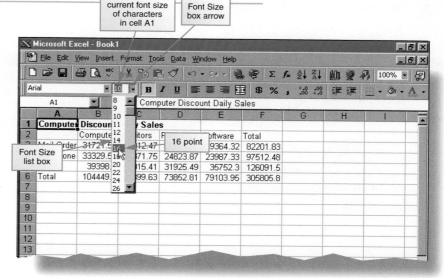

FIGURE 1-36

2 **Click 16.**

The characters in the worksheet title in cell A1 increase from 10 point to 16 point (Figure 1-37).

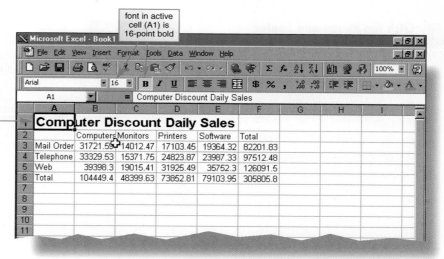

FIGURE 1-37

An alternative to clicking a font size in the Font Size list box is to type the font size in the Font Size box and press the ENTER key. With cell A1 selected (Figure 1-37), the Font Size box shows the new font size 16 and the recessed Bold button shows the active cell is bold.

OtherWays

1. Press CTRL+1, click Font tab, select font size, click OK button

2. Right-click cell, click Format Cells on shortcut menu, click Font tab, select font size, click OK button

3. On Format menu click Cells, click Font tab, select font size, click OK button

Centering the Worksheet Title Across Columns

The final step in formatting the worksheet title is to center it over columns A through F. Centering a worksheet title over the columns used in the body of the worksheet improves the worksheet's appearance.

Steps   To Center a Cell's Contents Across Columns

1 **With cell A1 selected, drag the block plus sign to the rightmost cell (F1) of the range through which to center (A1:F1).**

When you drag the mouse pointer through the range A1:F1, Excel highlights the cells (Figure 1-38).

FIGURE 1-38

2 **Click the Merge and Center button on the Formatting toolbar.**

Excel merges the cells A1 through F1 to create a new cell A1 and centers the contents of cell A1 across columns A through F (Figure 1-39).

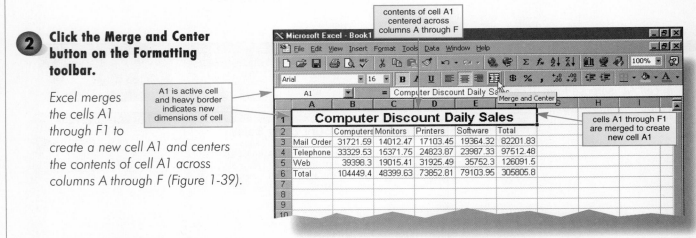

FIGURE 1-39

OtherWays

1. Right-click cell, click Format Cells on shortcut menu, click Alignment tab, click Center Across Selection in Horizontal list box, click OK button
2. On Format menu click Cells, click Alignment tab, click Center Across Selection in Horizontal list box, click OK button

Excel not only centers the worksheet title, but also merges cells A1 through F1 into one cell, cell A1. Thus, the heavy border that defines the active cell in Figure 1-39 covers what was originally cells A1 through F1. For the Merge and Center button to work properly, all the cells except the leftmost cell in the range of cells must be empty.

Most formats assigned to a cell will display on the Formatting toolbar when the cell is selected. For example, the font type and font size display in their appropriate boxes. Recessed buttons indicate an assigned format. To determine if less frequently used formats are assigned to a cell, point to the cell and right-click. Next, click **Format Cells**, and then click each of the tabs in the **Format Cells dialog box**.

Using AutoFormat to Format the Body of a Worksheet

Excel has several customized format styles called table formats that allow you to format the body of the worksheet. The table formats can be used to give your worksheet a professional appearance. Follow these steps to format automatically the range A2:F6 in the daily sales worksheet using **AutoFormat** on the **Format menu**.

Steps To Use AutoFormat to Format the Body of a Worksheet

1 Select cell A2, the upper-left corner cell of the rectangular range to format (Figure 1-40).

FIGURE 1-40

2 Drag the mouse pointer to cell F6, the lower-right corner cell of the range to format.

Excel highlights the range to format (Figure 1-41).

FIGURE 1-41

3 **Click Format on the Worksheet menu bar and then point to AutoFormat.**

The Format menu displays (Figure 1-42).

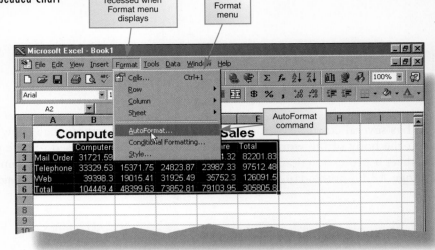

FIGURE 1-42

4 **Click AutoFormat. Click Accounting 2 in the Table format list box. Point to the OK button.**

Excel displays the AutoFormat dialog box (Figure 1-43). On the left side of the dialog box is the Table format list box with the Table format name, Accounting 2, highlighted. In the Sample area of the dialog box is a sample of the format that corresponds to the highlighted Table format name, Accounting 2.

FIGURE 1-43

5 **Click the OK button. Select cell A8 to deselect the range A2:F6.**

Excel displays the worksheet with the range A2:F6 using the customized format, Accounting 2 (Figure 1-44).

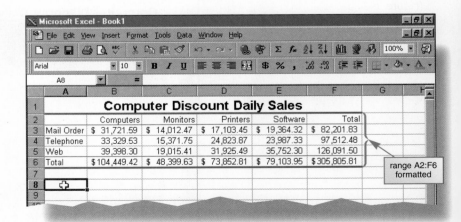

FIGURE 1-44

Excel provides 17 customized format styles from which to choose. Each format style has different characteristics. The format characteristics associated with the customized format, Accounting 2 (Figure 1-44), include right-alignment of column titles, numbers displayed as dollars and cents with comma separators, numbers aligned on the decimal point, dollar signs in the first row of numbers and in the total row, and top and bottom rows assigned borders. The width of column A also has been decreased so that the longest row title, Mail Order, just fits in the column.

The AutoFormat dialog box in Figure 1-43 includes five buttons. On the rightmost side of the title bar is the Close button. Use the **Close button** to terminate current activity without making changes. You also can use the **Cancel button**, immediately below the **OK button**, for this purpose. Use the **Question Mark button**, to obtain Help on any box or button located in the dialog box. The **Options button** allows you to select specific formats to assign as part of the customized format.

The worksheet now is complete. The next step is to chart the daily sales for the four product groups. To create the chart, you must select the cell in the upper-left corner of the range to chart. In this case, you must select cell A2 to make it the active cell. To select cell A2, you can move the mouse pointer to it and click. This is the procedure used in previous examples. You also can use the Name box to select a cell as described in the next section.

▶ **M**ore *About*
**Customizing the
AutoFormat**

The Options button on the right side of the AutoFormat dialog box in Figure 1-43 allows you to modify any of the formats associated with a customized format. If you assign two different customized formats to a range, Excel does not remove the assigned format from the range; it simply adds the second customized format to the first. Thus, if you decide to change a customized format, first select the range, click Clear on the Edit menu, and then click Formats on the submenu.

Using the Name Box to Select a Cell

The **Name box** is located on the left side of the formula bar. To select any cell, click the Name box and enter the cell reference of the cell you want to select. The following steps show how to select cell A2.

 Steps To Use the Name Box to Select a Cell

1 **Click the Name box in the
formula bar. Type** a2 **in
the Name box.**

Even though cell A8 is the active cell, the Name box displays the typed cell reference a2 (Figure 1-45).

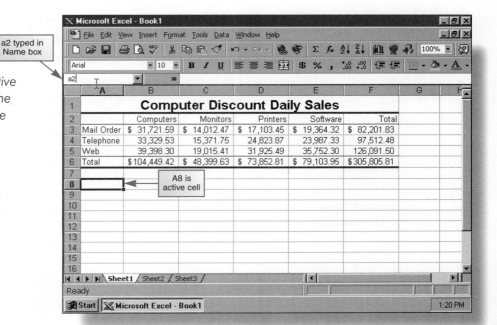

FIGURE 1-45

2 **Press the ENTER key.**

Excel changes the active cell from cell A8 to cell A2 (Figure 1-46).

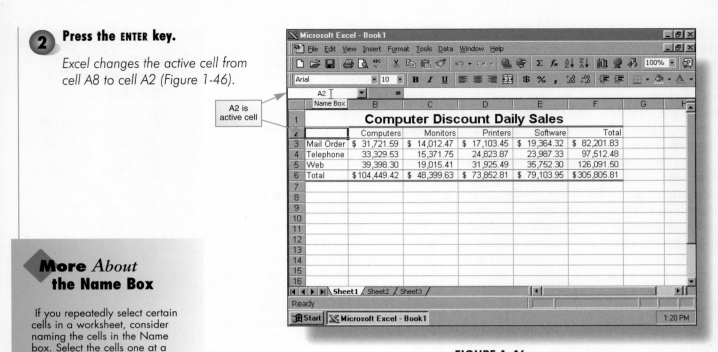

FIGURE 1-46

More *About* the Name Box

If you repeatedly select certain cells in a worksheet, consider naming the cells in the Name box. Select the cells one at a time and then type a name in the Name box for each, such as Company Total for cell F6 in Figure 1-45. Then, when you want to select one of the named cells, click the Name box arrow and then click the cell name in the Name box list box.

As you will see in later projects, besides using the Name box to select any cell in a worksheet, you also can use it to assign names to a cell or range of cells.

Excel supports several additional ways to select a cell, as summarized in Table 1-3.

Table 1-3

KEY, BOX, OR COMMAND	FUNCTION
ALT+PAGE DOWN	Selects the cell one window to the right and moves the window accordingly
ALT+PAGE UP	Selects the cell one window to the left and moves the window accordingly
ARROW	Selects the adjacent cell in the direction of the arrow on the key
CTRL+ARROW	Selects the border cell of the worksheet in combination with the arrow keys and moves the window accordingly. For example, to select the rightmost cell in the row that contains the active cell, press CTRL+RIGHT ARROW. You also can press the END key, release it, and then press the arrow key to accomplish the same task.
CTRL+HOME	Selects cell A1 or the cell one column and one row below and to the right of frozen titles and moves the window accordingly
Find command on Edit menu	Finds and selects a cell that contains specific contents that you enter in the Find dialog box. If necessary, Excel moves the window to display the cell. You can press SHIFT+F5 or CTRL+F to display the Find dialog box.
F5 or GoTo command on Edit menu	Selects the cell that corresponds to the cell reference you enter in the Go To dialog box and moves the window accordingly. You can press CTRL+G to display the Find dialog box.
HOME	Selects the cell at the beginning of the row that contains the active cell and moves the window accordingly
Name box	Selects the cell in the workbook that corresponds to the cell reference you enter in the Name box
PAGE DOWN	Selects the cell down one window from the active cell and moves the window accordingly
PAGE UP	Selects the cell up one window from the active cell and moves the window accordingly

Adding a 3-D Column Chart to the Worksheet

The 3-D Column chart drawn by Excel in this project is based on the data in the daily sales worksheet (Figure 1-47). It is called an **embedded chart** because it is drawn on the same worksheet as the data.

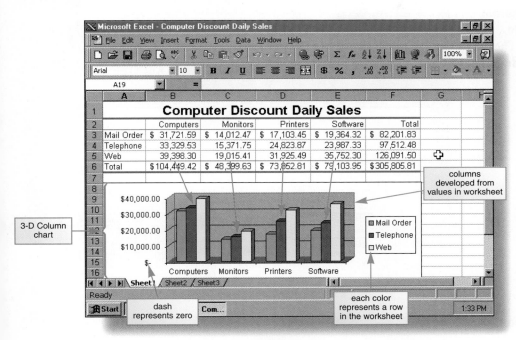

FIGURE 1-47

For the product Computers, the light blue column represents the sales by mail order ($31,721.59), the purple column represents the sales by Telephone ($33,329.53), and the light yellow column represents the sales by Web ($39,398.30). For the products Monitors, Printers, and Software, the columns follow the same color scheme to represent the comparable daily sales. The totals from the worksheet are not represented because the totals were not in the range specified for charting.

Excel derives the scale along the vertical axis (also called the **y-axis** or **value axis**) of the chart on the basis of the values in the worksheet. For example, no value in the range A2:E5 is less than zero or greater than $40,000.00. Excel also determines the $10,000.00 increments along the y-axis automatically. The format used by Excel for the numbers along the y-axis includes representing zero (0) with a dash (Figure 1-47).

To draw a chart like the one in Figure 1-47, select the range to chart, click the **Chart Wizard button** on the Standard toolbar, and select the type of chart. The area on the worksheet where the chart is drawn is called the **chart location**. In Figure 1-47, the chart is located immediately below the worksheet data.

Follow the detailed steps on the next page to draw a 3-D Column chart that compares the daily sales by channel for the four product groups.

Steps To Add a 3-D Column Chart to the Worksheet

1 With cell A2 selected, position the block plus sign within the cell's border and drag the mouse pointer to the lower-right corner cell (cell E5) of the range to chart (A2:E5). Point to the Chart Wizard button on the Standard toolbar.

Excel highlights the range to chart (Figure 1-48).

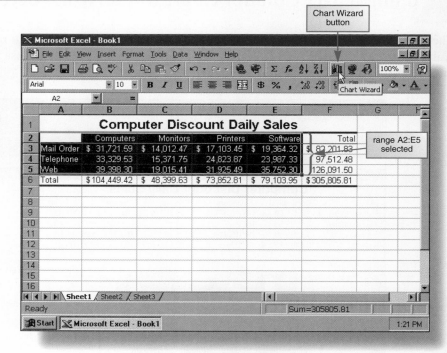

FIGURE 1-48

2 Click the Chart Wizard button.

The Chart Wizard – Step 1 of 4 – Chart Type dialog box displays.

3 With Column selected in the Chart type list, click the 3-D Column chart sub-type (column 1, row 2) in the Chart sub-type area. Point to the Finish button.

Column is highlighted in the Chart type list and 3-D Column is highlighted in the Chart sub-type area (Figure 1-49).

FIGURE 1-49

4 **Click the Finish button.**

*Excel draws a 3-D Column chart comparing the daily sales of the four product groups by channel (Figure 1-50) and the Chart menu bar displays. The chart displays in the middle of the window in a **selection rectangle**. The small **sizing handles** at the corners and along the sides of the selection rectangle indicate the chart is selected. When the chart is selected, you can drag the chart to any location on the worksheet. You also can resize the chart by dragging the sizing handles.*

FIGURE 1-50

5 **Point to an open area in the lower-right section of the chart area so the ScreenTip, Chart Area, displays (Figure 1-50). Drag the chart down and to the left to position the upper-left corner of the dotted line rectangle over the upper-left corner of cell A8.**

Excel displays a dotted line rectangle showing the new chart location (Figure 1-51). As you drag the selected chart, the mouse pointer changes to a cross hair with four arrowheads.

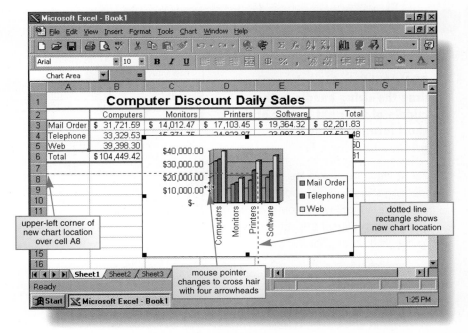

FIGURE 1-51

6 Release the left mouse button. Point to the sizing handle in the middle of the lower border of the chart.

The chart displays in a new location (Figure 1-52). The mouse pointer changes to a vertical line with two arrowheads.

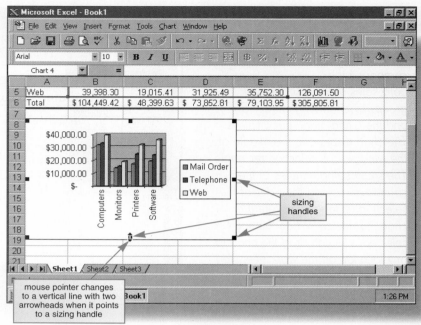

FIGURE 1-52

7 While holding down the ALT key, drag the sizing handle to the bottom gridline of row 17. Release the left mouse button. While holding down the ALT key, drag the sizing handle in the middle of the right border of the chart location to the right gridline of column F.

The dotted line shows the new chart location (Figure 1-53). Holding down the ALT key while you drag a chart snaps (aligns) the new border to the worksheet gridlines.

FIGURE 1-53

8 Release the left mouse button and then the ALT key. Select any cell outside the Chart Area to deselect the chart. Use the vertical scroll bar to scroll to the top of the worksheet.

The new chart location extends from the top of cell A8 to the bottom of cell F17 (Figure 1-54).

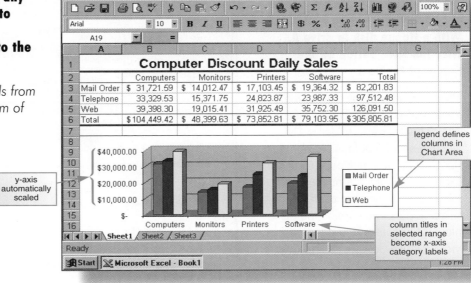

y-axis automatically scaled

legend defines columns in Chart Area

column titles in selected range become x-axis category labels

FIGURE 1-54

Other Ways

1. Select range, press F11
2. Select range, on Insert menu click Chart

The embedded 3-D Column chart in Figure 1-54 compares the three sales channels for each of the four product groups. It also allows you to compare daily sales between the product groups. Excel automatically selects the entries in the topmost row of the range (row 2) as the titles for the horizontal axis (also called the **x-axis** or **category axis**) and draws a column for each of the 12 cells in the range containing numbers. The small box to the right of the column chart in Figure 1-54 contains the legend. The **legend** identifies each bar in the chart. Excel automatically selects the leftmost column of the range (column A) as titles within the legend. As indicated earlier, it also automatically scales the y-axis on the basis of the magnitude of the numbers in the chart range.

Excel offers 14 different chart types (Figure 1-49 on page E 1.36). The **default chart type** is the chart Excel draws if you click the Finish button in the first Chart Wizard dialog box. When you install Excel on a computer, the default chart type is the 2-D (two-dimensional) Column chart.

Saving a Workbook

While you are building a workbook, the computer stores it in memory. If the computer is turned off or if you lose electrical power, the workbook is lost. Hence, you must save on a floppy disk any workbook that you will use later. A saved workbook is referred to as a **file** or **workbook**. The steps on the next page illustrate how to save a workbook on a floppy disk in drive A using the Save button on the Standard toolbar.

More *About*
Changing the Chart Type

Excel has 14 chart types from which to choose. You can change the embedded 3-D Column chart to another type by double-clicking the chart location. When a heavy gray border surrounds the chart location, right-click the chart and then click Chart Type on the shortcut menu. You also can use the shortcut menu to format the chart to make it look more professional. Subsequent projects will discuss changing charts, sizing charts, adding text to charts, and drawing a chart on a chart sheet.

Steps **To Save a Workbook**

1 **With a floppy disk in drive A, click the Save button on the Standard toolbar.**

Excel responds by displaying the Save As dialog box (Figure 1-55). The default Save in folder is My Documents, the default file name is Book1, and the file type is Microsoft Excel Workbook. The buttons next to the Save in box are used to select folders and change the display of file names and other information in the Save As dialog box.

FIGURE 1-55

2 **Type** Computer Discount Daily Sales **in the File name text box.**

*The file name Computer Discount Daily Sales replaces Book1 in the File name text box (Figure 1-56). A **file name** can be up to 255 characters and can include spaces.*

FIGURE 1-56

3 Click the Save in box arrow and then point to 3½ Floppy (A:).

A list of available drives and folders displays (Figure 1-57).

FIGURE 1-57

4 Click 3½ Floppy (A:) and then point to the Save button.

Drive A becomes the selected drive (Figure 1-58).

FIGURE 1-58

5 **Click the Save button.**

Excel saves the workbook on the floppy disk in drive A using the file name Computer Discount Daily Sales.xls. Excel automatically appends the extension .xls to the file name you entered in Step 2, which stands for Excel workbook. Although the Computer Discount Daily Sales workbook is saved on a floppy disk, it also remains in memory and displays on the screen (Figure 1-59). Notice the file name in the title bar.

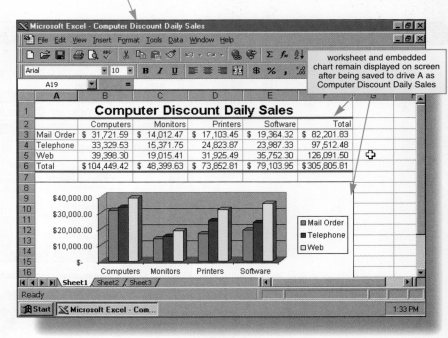

FIGURE 1-59

More *About*
**Saving a
Worksheet as a
Web Page**

Excel allows you to save a worksheet in HTML format so you can post it on the World Wide Web. Click Save as HTML on the File menu and follow the instructions in the Internet Assistant Wizard dialog box.

While Excel is saving the workbook, it momentarily changes the word Ready on the status bar to Saving. It also displays a horizontal bar on the status bar indicating the amount of the workbook saved. After the save operation is complete, Excel changes the name of the workbook in the title bar from Book1 to Computer Discount Daily Sales (Figure 1-59).

The **Options button** in the Save As dialog box (Figure 1-58 on the previous page), allows you to save a backup copy of the workbook or create a password to limit access to the workbook. Saving a **backup workbook** means that each time you save a workbook, Excel copies the current version of the workbook on disk to a file with the same name, but with a **.bak** extension. Thus, the second time you save a workbook, and each time thereafter, you will have two workbooks on disk with the same name, one with an extension of .xls and the other with an extension of .bak. In the case of a power failure or some other problem, use the backup version (.bak) to restore your work.

You also can use the Options button to assign a **password** to your workbook so others cannot open it. A password is case sensitive and can be up to 15 characters long. **Case sensitive** means Excel can differentiate between uppercase and lowercase letters. If you assign a password and forget the password, you cannot access the workbook.

The seven buttons at the top and to the right in the Save As dialog box (Figure 1-58) and their functions are summarized in Table 1-4.

Table 1-4

BUTTON	BUTTON NAME	FUNCTION
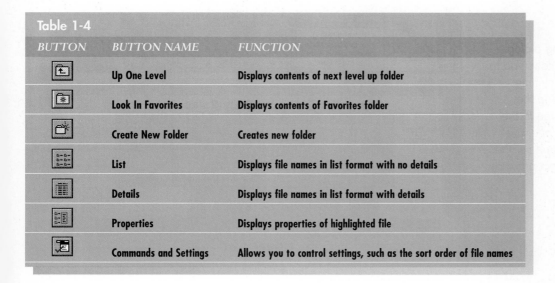	Up One Level	Displays contents of next level up folder
	Look In Favorites	Displays contents of Favorites folder
	Create New Folder	Creates new folder
	List	Displays file names in list format with no details
	Details	Displays file names in list format with details
	Properties	Displays properties of highlighted file
	Commands and Settings	Allows you to control settings, such as the sort order of file names

Printing the Worksheet

Once you have created the worksheet and saved it on disk, you might want to print it. A printed version of the worksheet is called a **hard copy** or **printout**.

You might want a printout for several reasons. First, to present the worksheet and chart to someone who does not have access to a computer, it must be in printed form. A printout, for example, can be handed out in a management meeting about daily sales. In addition, worksheets and charts often are kept for reference by persons other than those who prepare them. In many cases, worksheets and charts are printed and kept in binders for use by others. This section describes how to print a worksheet and an embedded chart.

 Steps To Print a Worksheet

1 Ready the printer according to the printer instructions. Point to the Print button on the Standard toolbar (Figure 1-60).

More *About* Printing

Interested in saving trees? Rather than printing a worksheet over and over until it's right, you can preview the printout on your screen, make adjustments to the worksheet, and then print it only when it appears exactly as you want. The Print Preview button is immediately to the right of the Print button on the Standard toolbar. Clicking it displays an onscreen image of how the printout will appear. Each time you preview rather than print, you save paper destined for the wastepaper basket, which, in turn, saves trees.

FIGURE 1-60

Click the Print button.

Excel displays the Printing dialog box (Figure 1-61) that allows you to cancel the print job at any time while the system is sending the worksheet and chart image to the printer. Several seconds after the Printing dialog box disappears, the worksheet and chart begin printing on the printer.

FIGURE 1-61

 When the printer stops printing the worksheet and the chart, retrieve the printout (Figure 1-62).

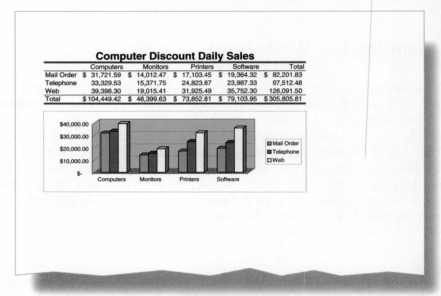

FIGURE 1-62

Prior to clicking the Print button, you can select which columns and rows in the worksheet to print. The range of cells you choose to print is called the **print area**. If you do not select a print area, as was the case in the previous set of steps, Excel automatically selects a print area on the basis of used cells. As you shall see in future projects, Excel has many different print options, such as allowing you to preview the printout on the screen to see if the printout is satisfactory prior to sending it to the printer.

Quitting Excel

After you build, save, and print the worksheet and chart, Project 1 is complete. To quit Excel, complete the following steps.

Steps **To Quit Excel**

① **Point to the Close button on the right side of the title bar (Figure 1-63).**

FIGURE 1-63

② **Click the Close button.**

If you made changes to the work-book, Microsoft Excel dialog box displays the question, Do you want to save the changes you made to 'Computer Discount Daily Sales.xls'? (Figure 1-64). Click the Yes button to save the changes before quitting Excel. Click the No button to quit Excel without saving the changes. Click the Cancel but-ton to stop the Exit command and return to the worksheet.

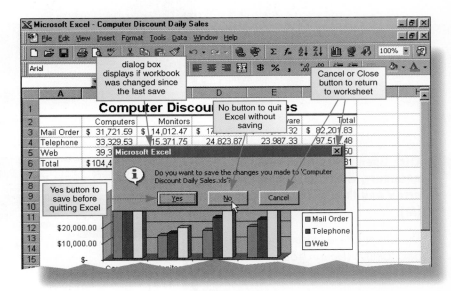

FIGURE 1-64

OtherWays

1. Double-click Control-menu icon
2. Right-click Microsoft Excel button on taskbar, click Close
3. On File menu click Exit

In Figure 1-63, you can see that two Close buttons and two Control-menu icons display. The Close button and Control-menu icon on the title bar close Excel. The Close button and Control-menu icon on the menu bar close the workbook.

Starting Excel and Opening a Workbook

Once you have created and saved a workbook, you often will have reason to retrieve it from a floppy disk. For example, you may want to review the calcula-tions on the worksheet and enter additional or revised data to it. The steps on the next page assume Excel is not running.

Steps To Start Excel and Open a Workbook

1 **With your floppy disk in drive A, click the Start button and then point to Open Office Document (Figure 1-65).**

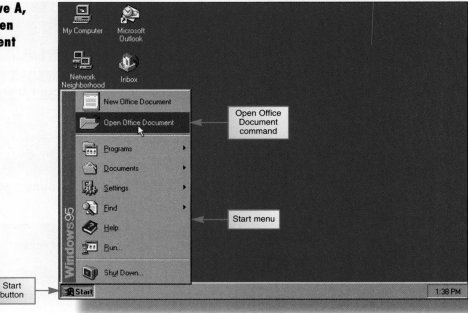

FIGURE 1-65

2 **Click Open Office Document. If necessary, click the Look in box arrow and then click 3½ Floppy (A:).**

The Open Office Document dialog box displays (Figure 1-66).

FIGURE 1-66

③ **Double-click the file name Computer Discount Daily Sales.**

Excel starts, opens the workbook Computer Discount Daily Sales.xls from drive A, and displays it on the screen (Figure 1-67). An alternative to double-clicking the file name is to click it and then click the Open button.

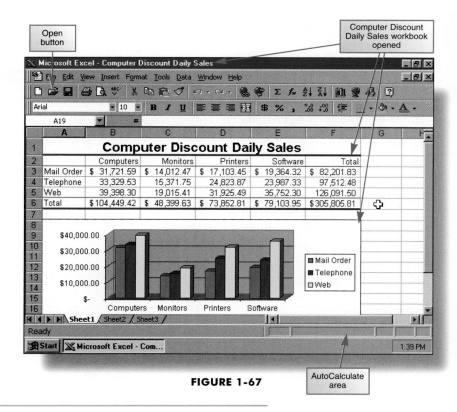

FIGURE 1-67

AutoCalculate

You easily can obtain a total, an average, or other information about the numbers in a range by using the AutoCalculate area on the status bar (Figure 1-67). All you need do is select the range of cells containing the numbers you want to check. Next, right-click the AutoCalculate area to display the shortcut menu (Figure 1-68 on the next page). The recessed check mark to the left of the active function (Sum) indicates that the sum of the selected range displays. The six function commands on the AutoCalculate shortcut menu are described in Table 1-5.

Table 1-5	
COMMAND	FUNCTION
Average	Displays the average of the numbers in the selected range
Count	Displays the number of nonblank cells in the selected range
Count Nums	Displays the number of cells containing numbers in the selected range
Max	Displays the greatest value in the selected range
Min	Displays the least value in the selected range
Sum	Displays the sum of the numbers in the selected range

▶ **More** *About* **Excel's Compatibility with Other Software Products**

Do you have files that were created using another software package? Excel has the capability to save or open Lotus 1-2-3, Quattro Pro, or Microsoft Works files. It's easy. All you have to do is select the file type on the Save As or Open dialog boxes.

The steps on the next page show how to display the average daily sales by mail order.

Steps: To Use the AutoCalculate Area to Determine an Average

1 **Select the range B3:E3. Point to the AutoCalculate area on the status bar and then right-click.**

As shown in Figure 1-68, the sum of the numbers in the range B3:E3 displays ($82,201.83) because Sum is active in the AutoCalculate area (you may see a total other than the Sum in your AutoCalculate area). The shortcut menu listing the various types of functions displays over the AutoCalculate area.

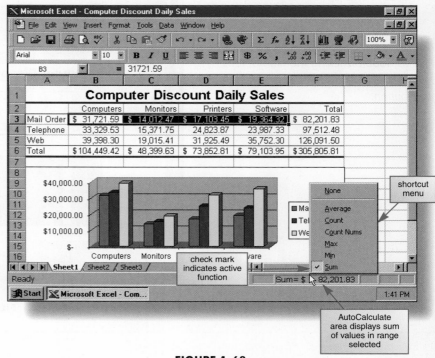

FIGURE 1-68

2 **Click Average on the shortcut menu.**

The average of the numbers in the range B3:E3 displays in the Auto-Calculate area (Figure 1-69).

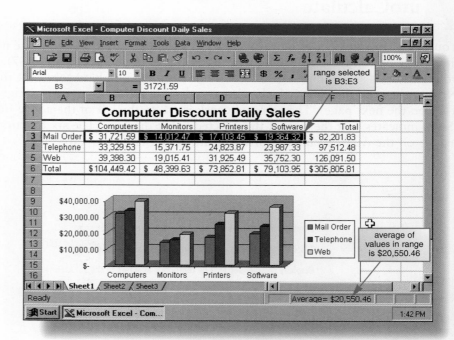

FIGURE 1-69

To change to any one of the other five functions for the range B3:E3, right-click the AutoCalculate area. Then click the desired function. Before continuing, change the total in the AutoCalculate area to Sum by pointing to the AutoCalculate area, right-clicking, and then clicking Sum on the shortcut menu.

Correcting Errors

You can correct errors on a worksheet using one of several methods. The one you choose will depend on the extent of the error and whether you notice it while typing the data or after you have entered the incorrect data into the cell.

Correcting Errors Prior to Entering Data into a Cell

If you notice an error prior to entering data into a cell, use one of the following methods:

1. Press the BACKSPACE key to erase the portion in error and then type the correct characters; or
2. If the error is a major one, click the Cancel box or press the ESC key to erase the entire entry and then reenter the data from the beginning.

In-Cell Editing

If you find an error in the worksheet after entering the data, you can correct the error in one of two ways:

1. If the entry is short, select the cell, retype the entry correctly, and click the Enter box or press the ENTER key. The new entry will replace the old entry.
2. If the entry in the cell is long and the errors are minor, the **Edit mode** may be a better choice. Use the Edit mode as described below.
   a. Double-click the cell containing the error. Excel switches to Edit mode, the active cell contents display in the formula bar, and a flashing insertion point displays in the active cell (Figure 1-70). This editing procedure is called **in-cell editing** because you can edit the contents directly in the cell. The active cell contents also display in the formula bar.
   b. Make your changes, as specified below.
      (1) To insert between two characters, place the insertion point between the two characters and begin typing. Excel inserts the new characters at the location of the insertion point.
      (2) To delete a character in the cell, move the insertion point to the left of the character you want to delete and press the DELETE key, or place the insertion point to the right of the character you want to delete and press the BACKSPACE key. You also can use the mouse to drag over the character or adjacent characters you want to delete and then press the DELETE key or click the **Cut button** on the Standard toolbar.

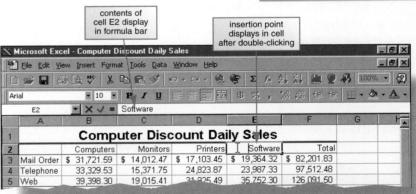

contents of cell E2 display in formula bar

insertion point displays in cell after double-clicking

FIGURE 1-70

> **More** *About*
> **Correcting Errors**
>
> Learning how to correct errors in a worksheet is critical to becoming proficient in Excel. Thus, carefully review this section on how to correct errors prior to entering data in a cell, how to perform in-cell editing, how to undo the last entry, and how to clear cells.

> **More** *About*
> **In-Cell Editing**
>
> An alternative to double-clicking the cell to edit is to select the cell and press F2.

When you are finished editing an entry, click the Enter box or press the ENTER key.

When Excel enters the Edit mode, the keyboard is usually in Insert mode. In **Insert mode**, as you type a character, Excel inserts the character and moves all characters to the right of the typed character one position to the right. You can change to Overtype mode by pressing the INSERT key. In **Overtype mode**, Excel overtypes the character to the right of the insertion point. The INSERT **key** toggles the keyboard between Insert mode and Overtype mode.

While in Edit mode, you may have reason to move the insertion point to various points in the cell, select portions of the data in the cell, or switch from inserting characters to overtyping characters. Table 1-6 summarizes the most common tasks used during in-cell editing.

Table 1-6

TASK	MOUSE	KEYBOARD
Move the insertion point to the beginning of data in a cell	Point to the left of the first character and click	Press HOME
Move the insertion point to the end of data in a cell	Point to the right of the last character and click	Press END
Move the insertion point anywhere in a cell	Point to the appropriate position and click the character	Press RIGHT ARROW or LEFT ARROW
Highlight one or more adjacent characters	Drag the mouse pointer through adjacent characters	Press SHIFT+RIGHT ARROW or SHIFT+LEFT ARROW
Select all data in a cell	Double-click the cell with the insertion point in the cell	
Delete selected characters	Click the Cut button on the Standard toolbar	Press DELETE
Toggle between Insert and Overtype modes		Press INSERT

Undoing the Last Entry

Excel provides the **Undo command** on the **Edit menu** and the **Undo button** on the Standard toolbar (Figure 1-71) that you can use to erase the most recent cell entry. Thus, if you enter incorrect data in a cell, click the Undo command or Undo button and Excel changes the cell contents to what they were prior to entering the incorrect data.

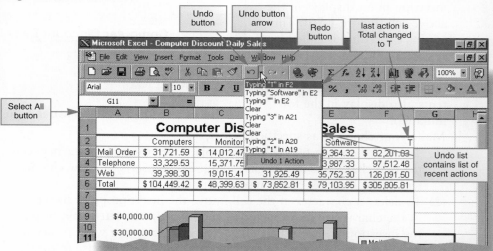

FIGURE 1-71

If Excel cannot undo an action, then the Undo button is inoperative. Excel remembers the last 16 actions you have completed. Thus, you can undo up to 16 previous actions by clicking the Undo box arrow to display the Undo list and clicking the action to be undone (Figure 1-71). You also can click Undo on the Edit menu rather than using the Undo button. If Excel cannot undo an action, then the words Can't Undo appear on the Edit menu in place of Undo.

Next to the Undo button on the Standard toolbar is the Redo button. The **Redo button** allows you to repeat previous actions. You also can click Redo on the Edit menu rather than using the Redo button.

Clearing a Cell or Range of Cells

If you enter data into the wrong cell or range of cells, you can erase or clear the data using one of several methods. **Never press the SPACEBAR to clear a cell.** Pressing the SPACEBAR enters a blank character. A blank character is text and is different from an empty cell, even though the cell may appear empty.

Excel provides three methods to clear the contents of a cell or a range of cells.

TO CLEAR CELL CONTENTS USING THE FILL HANDLE

1 Select the cell or range of cells and point to the fill handle so the mouse pointer changes to a cross hair.
2 Drag the fill handle back into the selected cell or range until a shadow covers the cell or cells you want to erase. Release the left mouse button.

TO CLEAR CELL CONTENTS USING THE SHORTCUT MENU

1 Select the cell or range of cells to be cleared.
2 Right-click the selection.
3 Click Clear Contents.

TO CLEAR CELL CONTENTS USING THE DELETE KEY

1 Select the cell or range of cells to be cleared.
2 Press the DELETE key.

TO CLEAR CELL CONTENTS USING THE CLEAR COMMAND

1 Select the cell or range of cells to be cleared.
2 On the Edit menu, click Clear.
3 Click All on the submenu.

You also can select a range of cells and click the Cut button on the Standard toolbar or click **Cut** on the Edit menu. Be aware, however, that the Cut button or Cut command not only deletes the contents from the range, but also copies the contents of the range to the Clipboard, thus erasing what was previously on the Clipboard.

Clearing the Entire Worksheet

Sometimes, everything goes wrong. If this happens, you may want to clear the worksheet entirely and start over. To clear the worksheet, follow the steps on the next page.

More *About*
Clearing Formats

If you accidentally assign unwanted formats to a range of cells, you can use the Clear command on the Edit menu to delete the formats of a selected range. Doing so changes the format to normal. To view the characteristics of the normal format, click Style on the Format menu or press ALT+' (APOSTROPHE).

More *About* Global Activities

Lotus 1-2-3 users may wonder how to carry out global activities in Excel, because there are no specific global commands. It's easy: simply click the Select All button or press CTRL+A before you issue a command, and the command will affect the entire worksheet.

More *About* Quitting Excel

Do not forget to remove your floppy disk from drive A after quitting Excel, especially if you are working in a laboratory environment. It's frustrating to leave your hard work behind for another user.

TO CLEAR THE ENTIRE WORKSHEET

① Click the Select All button (Figure 1-71 on page E 1.50).

② Press the DELETE key or click Clear on the Edit menu and then click All on the submenu.

The **Select All button** selects the entire worksheet. Instead of clicking the Select All button, you also can press CTRL+A. You also can clear an entire worksheet by clicking the worksheet's Close button or by clicking **Close** on the File menu. If you close the workbook, click the New button on the Standard toolbar or click **New** on the File menu to begin working on the next workbook.

TO DELETE AN EMBEDDED CHART

① Click the chart to select it.

② Press the DELETE key.

Quitting Excel

To quit Excel, complete the following steps.

TO QUIT EXCEL

① Click the Close button on the right side of the title bar.

② If the Microsoft Excel dialog box displays, click the No button.

Excel Online Help

At any time while you are using Excel, you can answer your Excel questions by using **online Help**. Used properly, this form of online assistance can increase your productivity and reduce your frustrations by minimizing the time you spend learning how to use Excel. Table 1-7 summarizes the five categories of online Help available to you. For more information on using online Help, see pages WD 1.54 through WD 1.59 in Project 1 of Microsoft Word 97.

Table 1-7

TYPE	DESCRIPTION	ACTIVATE BY CLICKING
Office Assistant	Answers your questions, offers tips, and provides Help for a variety of Excel features.	Click the Office Assistant button on the Standard toolbar.
Contents sheet	Groups Help topics by general categories. Use when you know only the general category of the topic in question.	Click Contents and Index on the Help menu, and then click the Contents tab.
Index sheet	Similar to an index in a book; use when you know exactly what you want	Click Contents and Index on the Help menu, and then click the Index tab.
Find sheet	Searches the index for all phrases that include the term in question	Click Contents and Index on the Help menu, and then click the Find tab.
Question Mark button and What's This? command	Used to identify unfamiliar items on the screen	In a dialog box, click the Question Mark button and then click an item in the dialog box. Click What's This? on the Help menu, and then click an item on the screen.

Project Summary

The worksheet created in this project (Figure 1-1 on page E 1.7) allows the management of the Computer Discount Company to examine the daily sales for the four main product groups. Furthermore, the 3-D Column chart should meet the needs of the president, Kelly Montgomery, who as you recall from the Case Perspective, has little tolerance for lists of numbers.

In creating the Computer Discount Daily Sales worksheet and chart in this project, you gained a broad knowledge about Excel. First, you were introduced to starting Excel. You learned about the Excel window and how to enter text and numbers to create a worksheet. You learned how to select a range and how to use the AutoSum button to sum numbers in a column or row. Using the fill handle, you learned how to copy a cell to adjacent cells.

Once the worksheet was built, you learned how to change the font size of the title, bold the title, and center the title over a range using buttons on the Formatting toolbar. Using the steps and techniques presented in the project, you formatted the body of the worksheet using the AutoFormat command, and you used the Chart Wizard to add a 3-D Column chart. After completing the worksheet, you saved the workbook on disk and printed the worksheet and chart. Finally, you learned how to edit data in cells.

What You Should Know

Having completed this project, you should be able to perform the following tasks:

- Add a 3-D Column Chart to the Worksheet *(E 1.36)*
- Bold a Cell *(E 1.28)*
- Center a Cell's Contents Across Columns *(E 1.30)*
- Clear Cell Contents Using the Clear Command *(E 1.51)*
- Clear Cell Contents Using the DELETE Key *(E 1.51)*
- Clear Cell Contents Using the Fill Handle *(E 1.51)*
- Clear Cell Contents Using the Shortcut Menu *(E 1.51)*
- Clear the Entire Worksheet *(E 1.52)*
- Copy a Cell to Adjacent Cells in a Row *(E 1.24)*
- Delete an Embedded Chart *(E 1.52)*
- Determine Multiple Totals at the Same Time *(E 1.25)*
- Enter Numeric Data *(E 1.20)*
- Enter Row Titles *(E 1.19)*
- Enter Column Titles *(E 1.17)*
- Enter the Worksheet Title *(E 1.15)*
- Increase the Font Size of a Cell Entry *(E 1.29)*
- Print a Worksheet *(E 1.43)*
- Quit Excel *(E 1.45, E 1.52)*
- Save a Workbook *(E 1.40)*
- Start Excel *(E 1.9)*
- Start Excel and Open a Workbook *(E 1.46)*
- Sum a Column of Numbers *(E 1.22)*
- Use the AutoCalculate Area to Determine an Average *(E 1.48)*
- Use AutoFormat to Format the Body of a Worksheet *(E 1.31)*
- Use the Name Box to Select a Cell *(E 1.33)*

Test Your Knowledge

1 True/False

Instructions: Circle T if the statement is true or F is the statement is false.

T F   1. The column headings in an Excel worksheet begin with A and end with IV.

T F   2. You can use the AutoCalculate area to assign the SUM function to a cell.

T F   3. Press the ESC key to cancel a cell entry.

T F   4. To calculate the totals for multiple rows at the same time, highlight a range of cells with numbers, including a blank row below the range, and then click the AutoSum button.

T F   5. Hold down the CTRL key and drag the sizing handle to snap a chart border to the gridlines.

T F   6. Display the Office Assistant by clicking the What's This? command on the Help menu.

T F   7. The closed book icon on the Help window Contents sheet means subtopics are available.

T F   8. Double-click a toolbar to show its shortcut menu.

T F   9. Click the Question Mark button on a dialog box to display the Office Assistant.

T F   10. To clear the entire worksheet, click the Select All button and press the DELETE key.

2 Multiple Choice

Instructions: Circle the correct response.

1. You can edit text in a cell by _____.
   a. double-clicking the cell
   b. clicking the cell and pressing F2
   c. clicking the entry in the formula bar
   d. all of the above

2. Which button do you click to display ScreenTips in a dialog box?
   a. Office Assistant button
   b. Question Mark button
   c. Tips button
   d. none of the above

3. To display the _____ for a cell, right-click the cell.
   a. shortcut menu
   b. ScreenTip
   c. Office Assistant
   d. AutoCalculate function

4. The fill handle is located on the active _____ border.
   a. cell
   b. chart
   c. form
   d. dialog box

5. The _____ accumulates tips to suggest more efficient ways of completing a task.
   a. Help button
   b. Office Assistant
   c. Tip Wizard
   d. What's This? command

6. You can change the Office Assistant options by _____.
   a. double-clicking Office Assistant
   b. clicking Office Assistant
   c. right-clicking Office Assistant
   d. clicking Options on the Help menu

7. To quickly view the average of a range of cells, use the _____ feature.
   a. Formula
   b. AutoSum
   c. Function Wizard
   d. AutoCalculate

Test Your Knowledge

8. When you create a chart using the Chart Wizard, Excel draws the chart _____.
   a. in the middle of the window
   b. below the selected chart range
   c. on a new sheet
   d. to the right of the selected chart range

9. Hold down the _____ key and drag the sizing handle to snap a chart border to a gridline.
   a. SHIFT
   b. ALT
   c. CTRL
   d. none of the above

10. To quit Excel, click the _____.
   a. Close button on the title bar
   b. Control-menu icon on the menu bar
   c. Close command on the File menu
   d. all of the above

3 Understanding the Excel Worksheet

Instructions: In Figure 1-72, arrows point to components of the Excel window. Identify the various parts of the window in the spaces provided.

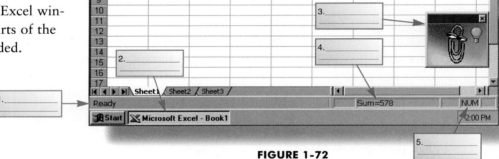

FIGURE 1-72

4 Understanding the Excel Toolbars and the AutoFormat Dialog Box

Instructions: In Figure 1-73, arrows point to buttons on the Standard and Formatting toolbars and in the Auto-Format dialog box. Identify the various buttons in the spaces provided.

FIGURE 1-73

Use Help

1 Reviewing Project Activities

Instructions: Perform the following tasks using a computer.

1. Start Excel.
2. If the Office Assistant is on your screen, click it to display the Office Assistant balloon. If the Office Assistant is not on your screen, then click the Office Assistant button on the Standard toolbar.
3. Click the Options button in the Office Assistant balloon. Click the Gallery tab and then click the Next button to view all the Office Assistants. Choose the Genius Assistant by clicking the OK button and then click the Options tab. Review the different options for the Office Assistant. Close the Office Assistant dialog box.
4. Click the Office Assistant and type ranges in the What would you like to do? text box. Click the Search button or press the ENTER key.
5. Click the See More link and then click the link About cell and range references.
6. Read the information. Use the shortcut menu or Options button to print the information. One at a time, click each of the three underlined green words (Figure 1-74) to display their ScreenTips. Print each definition that displays by right-clicking the ScreenTip and clicking Print Topic. Hand the printouts in to your instructor.
7. Click the Close button in the Microsoft Excel Help window.
8. Click the Office Assistant. Use the Options button and Gallery sheet to change the Office Assistant icon to Clippit.
9. Click Contents and Index on the Help menu. Click the Contents tab. Double-click the Entering Data and Selecting Cells book. Double-click the Selecting and Moving Around in a Workbook book. One at a time, double-click the first two topics under the Selecting and Moving Around in a Workbook book. Read and print the information. Click any underlined green words or other links and read the ScreenTips. Click the Help Topics button to return to the Contents sheet. Hand the printouts in to your instructor.

FIGURE 1-74

Use Help

2 Expanding on the Basics

Instructions: Use Excel online Help to better understand the topics and answer the questions listed below. Answer the questions on your own paper, or hand in the printed Help information to your instructor.

1. Click the Office Assistant if it is on the screen or the Office Assistant button on the Standard toolbar to display the Office Assistant balloon. Search for the topic formatting a chart. Click the link About formatting charts. When the Microsoft Excel Help window displays (Figure 1-75), answer the following questions by clicking the links. Once you have answered the questions, close the Microsoft Excel Help window.
   a. What are three special options for different chart types?   b. How do you apply number formats to an axis as you would on a worksheet?   c. How do you format and rotate text on a chart?
2. Click Contents and Index on the Help menu. Click the Index tab. Type `align` in the top text box labeled 1. Double-click text in cells under aligning in the lower list box labeled 2. One at a time, double-click the four topics in the Topics Found dialog box. Read and print the information. Click the Help Topics button to return to the Contents sheet. Close the Microsoft Excel Help window. Hand the printouts in to your instructor.
3. Click Contents and Index on the Help menu. Click the Find tab. Type `help` in the top text box labeled 1. Double-click Help in the middle list box labeled 2. In the lower list box labeled 3, scroll down to and double-click Connect to Microsoft technical resources. Read through the information that displays. Use the links under Where do you want to go for technical information? to answer the following:

   FIGURE 1-75

   a. What is the Microsoft Knowledge Base (KB)? Can you access the KB on the World Wide Web from the Help menu? If so, how?
   b. What is the Microsoft Software Library (MSL)? Can you access the MSL on the World Wide Web from the Help menu? If so, how?
   c. How can you get answers to your technical questions 24 hours a day from a touch tone phone? Give an example of what kind of information you can receive from this service.
4. Use the What's This? command on the Help menu to display ScreenTips for five of the buttons on the Standard and Formatting toolbars. Read and print the information. Hand the printouts in to your instructor.

Apply Your Knowledge

> **CAUTION:** To ensure you have enough disk space to save your files, it is recommended that you create a copy of the Data Disk that accompanies this book. Then, delete folders from the copy of the Data Disk that are not needed for the application you are working on. Do the following: (1) Insert the Data Disk in drive A; (2) start Explorer; (3) right-click the 3½ Floppy (A:) folder in the All Folders side of the window; (4) click Copy Disk; (5) click Start and OK as required; (6) insert a floppy disk when requested; (7) delete all folders on the floppy disk you created except the Excel folder; (8) remove the floppy disk from drive A and label it Excel Data Disk.

1 Changing Data in a Worksheet

Instructions: Start Excel. Open the workbook, Webmaster Software School, from the Excel folder on the Data Disk that accompanies this book. This worksheet is set up as an annual income statement (Figure 1-76).

1. Change the worksheet data as indicated in Table 1-8. As you edit the values in the cells, watch as Excel automatically updates the total incomes (B7, D7, and F7) and total expenses (B13, D13, and F13) to reflect the new amounts. Each of the values in these cells is based on the SUM function. As you enter a new value, Excel automatically recalculates the SUM function and updates the value displayed in the cell. After you successfully have made the changes listed in the table, the total incomes in cells B7, D7, and F7 should equal $6,359.00, $55,400.00, and $67,500.00, respectively. The total expenses in cells B13, D13, and F13 should equal $67,832.00, $50,369.00, and $48,369.00, respectively.

2. Save the workbook using the file name Web Page Design School.

3. Print the revised worksheet.

FIGURE 1-76

Income Statement for 1998			
Webmaster Software School			
INCOME:	Jan-April	May-Aug	Sept-Dec
Individual Tuition Revenue	$159.00	$5,400.00	$7,500.00
Corporate Tuition Revenue	5,000.00	30,000.00	30,000.00
Community College Revenue	1,000.00	25,000.00	30,000.00
TOTAL INCOME:	$6,159.00	$60,400.00	$67,500.00
EXPENSES:	Jan-April	May-Aug	Sept-Dec
Salaries	$32,400.00	$43,369.00	$43,369.00
Software	5,000.00	2,000.00	2,000.00
Classroom Rental	0.00	2,000.00	2,000.00
Hardware	24,999.00	1,000.00	1,000.00
TOTAL EXPENSES:	$62,399.00	$48,369.00	$48,369.00
NET PROFIT (OR LOSS)	($56,240.00)	$12,031.00	$19,131.00

Table 1-8

CELL	CURRENT CELL CONTENTS	CHANGE CELL CONTENTS TO
A2	Webmaster Software School	Web Page Design School
B4	159.00	359.00
D5	30,000.00	25,000.00
D10	2,000.00	4,000.00
B11	0.00	1,000.00
B12	24,999.00	29,432.00

In the Lab

1 Creating and Modifying a Sales Analysis Worksheet

Problem: As the manager for Gulliver's Travel Bookstore, you want to analyze total sales for the different travel books by bookstore section. The sales figures are shown in Table 1-9.

Instructions: Perform the following tasks.

1. Create the worksheet shown in Figure 1-77 using the title, sales amounts, and categories in Table 1-9.

2. Determine the totals for the types of travel, geographic locations, and store totals.

3. Format the worksheet title, Gulliver's Travel Bookstore, as 16-point Times New Roman, bold, centered over columns A through F.

4. Format the range A2:F7 using the AutoFormat command on the Format menu. Use the table format Colorful 2.

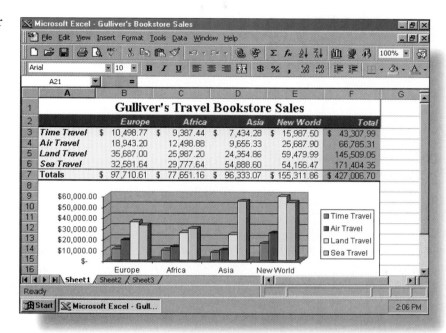

FIGURE 1-77

Table 1-9				
	EUROPE	*AFRICA*	*ASIA*	*NEW WORLD*
TIME TRAVEL	10,498.77	9,387.44	7,434.28	15,987.50
AIR TRAVEL	18,943.20	12,498.88	9,655.33	25,687.90
LAND TRAVEL	35,687.00	25,987.20	24,354.86	59,479.99
SEA TRAVEL	32,581.64	29,777.64	54,888.60	54,156.47

5. Select the range A2:E6 and use the Chart Wizard button on the Standard toolbar to draw a 3-D Column chart (Figure 1-77) and then press the ALT key. Move the chart to the upper-left corner of cell A8 and then, while holding down the ALT key, drag the lower-right corner of the chart location to cell F17. Release the mouse button and then the ALT key.

6. Enter your name, course, laboratory assignment number, date, and instructor name in cells A19 through A23.

7. Save the worksheet using the file name Gulliver's Bookstore Sales.

8. Print the worksheet.

(continued)

In the Lab

Creating and Modifying a Sales Analysis Worksheet *(continued)*

9. Two corrections to the sales amounts need to be made. The corrected sales amounts are: $45,987.99 for Air Travel in Asia and $95,498.33 for Sea Travel in the New World. After you enter the corrections, the company totals should equal $132,665.73 in cell D7 and $196,653.72 in cell E7.

10. Print the modified worksheet. Close the workbook without saving the changes.

2 Creating a Quarterly Personal Budget

Problem: To estimate the funds you need to make it through the upcoming year, you decide to create a personal budget itemizing your quarterly expenses for the past year. The expenses you incurred are listed in Table 1-10.

Instructions: Perform the following tasks.

1. Create the worksheet shown in Figure 1-78 by entering the worksheet title, Quarterly Personal Budget, in cell B1 and using the expenses and category names in Table 1-10.

2. Use the AutoSum button and fill handle to determine the totals in row 9 and column F.

3. Change the worksheet title in cell B1 to 18-point bold. Center the worksheet title over columns B1 through F1.

Table 1-10

	JAN-MAR	APRIL-JUNE	JULY-SEPT	OCT-DEC
MORTGAGE	1500	1500	1500	1500
FOOD	900	950	950	1000
CAR & INS.	600	600	600	600
CLOTHES	567	433	200	459
UTILITIES	600	400	400	550
MISCELLANEOUS	149	121	159	349

FIGURE 1-78

In the Lab

4. Use the AutoFormat command on the Format menu to format the range A2:F9. Use the table format List 1.

5. Use the Chart Wizard button to draw the 3-D Stacked Pyramid chart, as shown in Figure 1-78. Use the chart range A2:E8. Move the chart to the upper-left corner of cell A11. Hold down the ALT key and then drag the lower-right corner of the chart location to to cell H25.

6. Enter your name, course, laboratory assignment number, date, and instructor name in cells A27 through A32.

7. Save the workbook using the file name Quarterly Personal Budget.

8. Print the worksheet.

9. After talking with your banker, you decide to budget more for your last two mortgage payments. Make the following changes: Mortgage, July-Sept – 1700 and Mortgage, Oct-Dec – 1700. The new quarterly totals should now be 4009, and 4658, respectively. Print the worksheet with the revised data.

10. Close the workbook without saving the changes.

3 Analyzing College Expenses and Financial Resources

Problem: College expenses are skyrocketing and your resources are limited. To plan for the upcoming year, you have decided to organize your anticipated expenses and resources in a worksheet. The data required to prepare your worksheet is shown in Table 1-11.

Table 1-11			
COLLEGE EXPENSES	*SEMESTER 1*	*SEMESTER 2*	*SUMMER*
ROOM & BOARD	2150	2150	950
TUITION & BOOKS	2125	2255	805
CLOTHES	250	210	190
ENTERTAINMENT	325	280	225
MISCELLANEOUS	200	200	375
FINANCIAL RESOURCES	*SEMESTER 1*	*SEMESTER 2*	*SUMMER*
SAVINGS	800	600	295
PARENTS	1750	1320	150
JOB	1000	1800	2000
FINANCIAL AID	1500	1375	100

Instructions: Using the numbers in Table 1-11, create the worksheet shown in Figure 1-79 on the next page. Enter the section titles, College Expenses and Financial Resources, in cells B1 and B10 respectively. Use the AutoSum button to calculate the totals in rows 8 and 16 and column E.

(continued)

Analyzing College Expenses and Financial Resources *(continued)*

To format the worksheet, use the table format Accounting 3 for the range A2:E8 and again for the range A11:E16. Center the section titles over columns B through E. Enter your name in cell A19 and your course, laboratory assignment number, date, and instructor name in cells A20 through A23.

Save the workbook using the file name College Expenses and Resources. Print the worksheet. Use the Office Assistant to learn how to print only a specific area of a worksheet and then print the selection A1:E8 of the worksheet.

Increment all summer expenses in column D by $100. Increment the financial aid for summer by $500. The totals in cells E8 and E16 should equal $13,190.00. Print the worksheet. Close the workbook without saving changes.

FIGURE 1-79

Cases and Places

The difficulty of these case studies varies: ▶ are the least difficult; ▶▶ are more difficult; and ▶▶▶ are the most difficult.

▶ You just started as an assistant in an optometrist's office. Your employer, Dr. Mair, has asked you to prepare a worksheet to help him determine what age groups of patients are more likely to wear contacts than glasses. He has compiled some of the data, as shown in Table 1-12.

With this data, along with your employer's additional needs, design a worksheet to present the data in an easy-to-understand format. Use the concepts and techniques presented in this project to create the worksheet.

Table 1-12

AGES	21-30	31-40	41-50	51-60	61+	TOTALS
Glasses	44	51	56	62	65	278
Contacts	73	63	50	35	12	233
Totals	117	114	106	97	77	511

▶ You are a teaching assistant for Professor Firewall. She is known around campus as the *gatekeeper of diplomas*, because her courses are so rigorous. Professor Firewall has asked you to take her grade ledger (Table 1-13), which shows her grade distributions for all her spring classes, and separate them into categories based on the class and the grade. She wants a worksheet and 3-D Column chart to make it easier to view the grades at a glance. Use the concepts and techniques presented in this project to create the worksheet and chart.

Table 1-13 Professor Firewall's Summary of Grades for the Spring Semester

GRADE	CS 210	CS 340	CS 360	CS 431
A	10	3	4	2
B	12	8	2	6
C	25	12	10	3
D	30	6	13	9
F	21	9	18	4

▶▶ The Main Street Rib House restaurant is trying to decide whether it is feasible to open another restaurant in a neighboring community. The owner has asked you to develop a worksheet totaling all the revenue received in a week. The revenue by day is: Monday, $1,500.80; Tuesday, $1,220.09; Wednesday, $1,435.50; Thursday, $1,565.29; Friday, $2,556.32; and Saturday, $3,102.12. On Sunday the restaurant is closed. Create a 3-D Pie chart to illustrate revenue by day and total weekly revenue. Use the AutoCalculate area to find the average daily sales.

Cases and Places

4 ▶▶ The senior accountant at Great Expectations, a local cable company where you are a student consultant, has asked you to prepare a worksheet that can be used at the next annual stockholders' meeting. The worksheet is to compare the company's expenditures last year to its anticipated expenditures this year. Last year, the company spent $1,230,000 on staff salaries and benefits, $3,015,000 on equipment, $2,550,000 on programming, and $121,000 on building and grounds maintenance. This year, the company expects to spend $1,402,000 on staff salaries and benefits, $3,275,000 on equipment, $2,525,000 on programming, and $143,000 on building and grounds maintenance. Use the concepts and techniques presented in this project to prepare the worksheet. Include total expenditures for each category and for each year, and a column chart illustrating yearly expenditures. After completing the worksheet, prepare a second worksheet showing how this year's expenditures would be affected if the amount spent on staff salaries and benefits was changed to $1,504,000 (after hiring two new technicians) and the amount spent on equipment was changed to $3,550,000 (after purchasing four new utility trucks).

5 ▶▶▶ Each year, universities report an increase in the enrollment of undergraduate students 25 years or older, who often are referred to as non-traditional students. Visit your school's Office of the Registrar to determine the number of male and number of female undergraduate students under 25 years old, and the number of male and number of female undergraduate students 25 years or older for each of the last five years. From the data, create a worksheet and a 3-D Column chart to track the data obtained.

6 ▶▶▶ Athletic footwear stores must track carefully the sales of their different shoe brands so they can restock their inventory promptly. Visit an athletic shoe store and make a list of the different brands of running shoes. Find out how many of each brand was sold over the last three months. Using this information, create a worksheet showing the number of each brand sold each month, the total number of each brand sold over three months, and the total number of running shoes sold each month. Include a 3-D Column chart to illustrate your data.

7 ▶▶▶ Drugstores often advertise that they have the lowest prices. Make a list of seven items that can be purchased from any drugstore. Visit at least three drugstores and obtain a price for each of the items listed. Make sure your prices are for similar items. Using this data, together with the techniques presented in this project, create a worksheet showing the price of each individual item in the drugstore and the total price for all seven items in a particular drugstore. Include a 3-D Column chart to illustrate your data.

Microsoft Excel 97

Formulas, Formatting, Charts, and Web Queries

Objectives:

You will have mastered the material in this project when you can:

▸ Enter multiple lines of text in the same cell
▸ Enter a formula using the keyboard
▸ Enter formulas using Point mode
▸ Identify the arithmetic operators +, -, *, /, %, and ^
▸ Apply the AVERAGE, MAX, and MIN functions
▸ Determine a percentage
▸ Change the font of a cell
▸ Vary the font size of characters within a cell
▸ Color the characters and background of a cell
▸ Add borders to a range
▸ Format numbers using the Format Cells dialog box
▸ Align text in cells
▸ Change the width of a column and height of a row
▸ Check the spelling of a worksheet
▸ Create a 3-D Pie chart on a separate sheet
▸ Format chart items
▸ Rename sheets
▸ Preview how a printed copy of the worksheet will look
▸ Print multiple sheets
▸ Print a partial or complete worksheet
▸ Display and print the formulas version of a worksheet
▸ Print to fit
▸ Distinguish between portrait and landscape orientation
▸ Use a Web query to get real-time data from a Web site

Project 2

Cyber Workout...

Takes Fitness to a Higher Level

Dust off that old rowing machine hidden in the back of your closet, and oil that bike hanging from the rafters of your garage. It's time to shape up — with the help of your cybertrainer.

Athletes and rising athletes alike can benefit from software designed to optimize a workout. These programs function by performing calculations on data you input, similarly to the way Excel performs calculations on formulas you enter, as you will learn in this project.

Most individuals exercise to lose weight, remain fit, and prevent heart disease. Few, however, can afford personal trainers or coaches to help develop workout plans or provide guidelines to prevent exhaustion or injury. Fitness and training software available commercially has bridged this gap by creating *virtual workouts*, allowing individuals to achieve maximum fitness through steady, regulated progress while increasing strength and endurance at a fixed pace.

Although the athletic community generally did not recognize computer-based training even 10 years ago, the notion of using a scientific approach in workouts is

Computer-Based Exercise Analysis
Track Your Training Efforts...
PROJECT FUTURE PERFORMANCE!

not new. Eastern bloc Olympic coaches used computers and sophisticated software prior to the Cold War to track their athletes' performances, particularly in the sports of swimming and running. By monitoring the athletes' training times, distances, and efforts, they could show trends mathematically and then use the results of these computations to help achieve amazing athletic successes.

Laboratories now use sophisticated, expensive athletic hardware and software to research specific medical topics, such as extensively analyzing the heart's performance during training with an electrocardiogram. Meanwhile, other less expensive and more generally useful software is available for the serious and occasional athlete. The spreadsheet programs insert data entered by the athlete into worksheets, perform calculations, and produce reports and graphs that track training efforts and project future performance.

One of the first programs, UltraCoach, was developed by a computer programmer for fellow triathletes. It was enhanced by a sports medicine physician who used his iron man triathlete experiences to input data and program actual swimming, biking, and running workouts based on training data. Today, this program has evolved into a sophisticated program using artificial intelligence that uses data downloaded from recordable heart rate monitors.

One of the newer heart rate monitors is the Polar XTrainer Plus. It consists of a one-piece chest transmitter that sends the direct electrical impulses of the heart wirelessly to the wrist receiver, which also functions as a sportswatch. The receiver can perform a myriad of functions, including calculating time spent at, below, and above the target heart rate zone. The target zone is how quickly that heart should beat when exercising based on individual fitness goals and the maximum and average heart rates during the entire workout. The receiver can store up to 67 hours of training performance data in an unlimited number of files that can be downloaded to a personal computer for advanced analysis by the Polar Training Advisor Software, UltraCoach, or other programs on the market.

These effective training tools suit the needs of most athletes at every fitness level. With a customized workout plan generated from calculations in your cybertraining software, you should be well on your way to pumping it up in style.

Project 2

Microsoft
Excel 97

Case Perspective

While in a high-school Economics class, Alex Hansen and four of his friends started *High-Tech Stock Club*, a stock club geared toward researching and investing in technology stocks. Every month, they invested $15 each, researched an assigned company, and came to the meetings with their buy and sell recommendations.

All are out of college, married, and have jobs around the country. They still invest as a group using e-mail and chat rooms on the Internet to conduct their meetings. They have increased their monthly contribution to $50.

Each month, Alex summarizes the month end financial status. The value of the club's portfolio, or group of investments, is almost $150,000. As a result, the members voted to buy trading software and Microsoft Office 97 for Alex. He plans to use the trading software to invest online to reduce the club's broker costs. With Office 97, he plans to create a worksheet summarizing the club's stock activities that he can e-mail to the members. He wants to use its Web query capabilities to access real-time stock quotes. Alex has asked you to show him how to create the workbook and access real-time stock quotes over the Internet using Office 97.

Formulas, Formatting, Charts, and Web Queries

Introduction

In Project 1, you learned about entering data, summing values, how to make the worksheet easier to read, and how to draw a chart. You also learned about online Help and saving, printing, and loading a workbook from floppy disk into memory. This project continues to emphasize these topics and presents some new ones.

The new topics include formulas, changing fonts, adding color to both the characters in and the background of a cell, adding borders, formatting numbers, changing the widths of columns and heights of rows, spell checking, additional charting techniques, and alternative types of worksheet displays and printouts. One alternative display and printout shows the formulas rather than the values in the worksheet. When you display the formulas in the worksheet, you see exactly what text, data, formulas, and functions you have entered into it. Finally, this project covers Web queries to obtain real-time data from a Web site.

Project Two – High-Tech Stock Club

The summary notes from your meeting with Alex include the following: need, source of data, calculations, graph requirements, and Web requirements.

Need: An easy-to-read worksheet that summarizes the club's investments for each stock owned (Figure 2-1a on page E 2.6) is needed. For each stock, the worksheet is to include the name, symbol, date acquired, number of shares, initial price, initial cost, current price, current value, and gain/loss. Alex also has requested that the worksheet include totals and an average, maximum, and minimum for each of the calculations, and a total percentage gain/loss.

Source of Data: The data supplied by Alex includes the stock names, symbols, date acquired, number of shares, the initial price, and the current price. This data is shown in Table 2-1 on page E 2.8.

Calculations: The following calculations must be made for each of the stocks as shown in Figure 2-1a on the next page.

1. Initial Cost = Shares × Initial Price
2. Current Value = Shares × Current Price
3. Gain/Loss = Current Value – Initial Cost
4. Compute the totals for initial cost, current value, gain/loss.
5. Use the AVERAGE, MAX, and MIN functions to determine the average, highest, and lowest values for the number of shares, initial price per share, initial stock cost, current stock price, current stock value, and gain/loss for each stock.
6. Percentage Gain/Loss = $\dfrac{\text{Total Gain/Loss}}{\text{Total Initial Cost}}$

Graph Requirements: Draw a 3-D Pie chart (Figure 2-1b on the next page) that shows the contribution of each of the stocks to the total current value of the portfolio. Highlight the stock that makes the greatest contribution.

Web Requirements: Use the Web query feature of Excel to get real-time stock quotes for the stocks owned by the High-Tech Stock Club (Figure 2-1c on the next page).

Preparation Steps

The preparation steps summarize how the worksheet, chart, and Web query shown in Figure 2-1 will be developed in Project 2. The following tasks will be completed in this project.

1. Start the Excel program.
2. Enter the worksheet title, column titles, row titles, and stock data.
3. Compute the initial cost, current value, and gain/loss for the first stock, Compaq.
4. Copy the formulas for the remaining stocks.
5. Use the AutoSum button to display the totals for initial cost, current value, and gain/loss.
6. Determine the average, highest, and lowest values for the shares, initial price, initial cost, current price, current value, and gain/loss.
7. Compute the percentage gain/loss.
8. Save an intermediate copy of the workbook.
9. Format the worksheet so it has a professional appearance and is easy to read.

More *About* **Order of Operations**

To make full use of Excel, it is important that you understand the order in which multiple operations in a formula are executed. Excel uses the same order as in algebra. That is, first all negations (-), then all percents (%), then all exponentiations (^), then all multiplications (*) and divisions (/) from left to right, and finally all additions (+) and subtractions (-) from left to right. Parentheses can be used to override the order of operations.

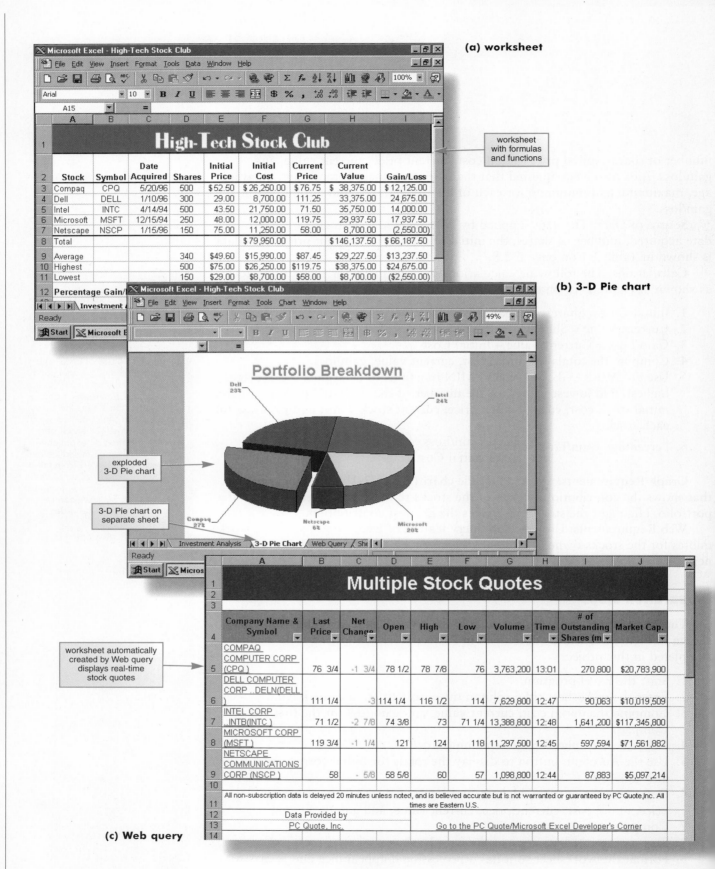

(a) worksheet

(b) 3-D Pie chart

(c) Web query

FIGURE 2-1

10. Draw the 3-D Pie chart on a separate sheet (Figure 2-1b). Highlight the largest slice. Improve the readability of the pie chart by using colors to emphasize the chart title and pie slice labels.
11. Rename the sheets.
12. Save the workbook.
13. Preview and print the worksheet and 3-D Pie chart.
14. Print the formulas version of the worksheet so the formulas can be verified.
15. Use the Run Web Query command to display a worksheet with real-time stock quotes (Figure 2-1c).

The following pages contain a detailed explanation of these tasks.

Starting Excel

To start Excel, Windows 95 must be running. Perform the following steps to start Excel.

TO START EXCEL

1. Click the Start button on the taskbar.
2. Click New Office Document. If necessary, click the General tab in the New dialog box.
3. Double-click the Blank Workbook icon.

An alternative to Steps 1 and 2 is to click the Start button, point to Programs, and click Microsoft Excel on the Programs submenu.

Entering the Titles and Numbers into the Worksheet

The worksheet title in Figure 2-1a is centered over columns A through I in row 1. Because the centered text first must be entered into the leftmost column of the area over which it is centered, it will be entered into cell A1.

TO ENTER THE WORKSHEET TITLE

1. Select cell A1. Type High-Tech Stock Club in the cell.
2. Press the DOWN ARROW key.

The worksheet title displays as shown in cell A1 of Figure 2-2 on page E 2.9.

The column headings in row 2 begin in cell A2 and extend through cell I2. As shown in Figure 2-1a, the column titles in row 2 include multiple lines of text. To start a new line in a cell, press ALT+ENTER after each line, except for the last line, which is completed by clicking the Enter box, pressing the ENTER key, or pressing one of the arrow keys. When you see ALT+ENTER in a step, while holding down the ALT key, press the ENTER key and then release both keys.

More *About*
Starting Excel

An alternative way to start Excel when you want to open a workbook is to start Explorer, display the contents of the folder containing the workbook, and then double-click the workbook name.

More *About*
Formatting a Worksheet

With early spreadsheet packages, users often skipped rows to improve the appearance of the worksheet. With Excel it is not necessary to skip rows because you can increase the height of rows to add white space between information.

Table 2-1

STOCK	SYMBOL	DATE ACQUIRED	SHARES	INITIAL PRICE	CURRENT PRICE
Compaq	CPQ	5/20/96	500	$52.50	$76.75
Dell	DELL	1/10/96	300	29.00	111.25
Intel	INTC	4/14/94	500	43.50	71.50
Microsoft	MSFT	12/15/94	250	48.00	119.75
Netscape	NSCP	1/15/96	150	75.00	58.00

The stock names and total row titles in column A begin in cell A3 and continue down to cell A12. The stock club's investments, as submitted by Alex, are summarized in Table 2-1. These numbers are entered into rows 3 through 7. The steps required to enter the column titles, stock names and symbols, total row titles, and numbers as shown in Figure 2-2 are outlined in the remainder of this section.

More *About* Wrapping Text

If you have a long text entry, such as a paragraph, you can instruct Excel to wrap the text in a cell, rather than pressing ALT+ENTER to end a line. To wrap text, click Format Cells on the shortcut menu, click the Alignment tab, and click the Wrap Text check box. Excel will automatically increase the height of the cell so the additional lines will fit. However, if you want to control the contents of a line in a cell, rather than letting Excel wrap based on the width of a cell, then you must end a line with ALT+ENTER.

TO ENTER THE COLUMN TITLES

1. With cell A2 active, type Stock and then press the RIGHT ARROW key.
2. Type Symbol and then press the RIGHT ARROW key.
3. Type Date and then press ALT+ENTER. Type Acquired and then press the RIGHT ARROW key.
4. Type Shares and then press the RIGHT ARROW key.
5. Type Initial and then press ALT+ENTER. Type Price and then press the RIGHT ARROW key.
6. Type Initial and then press ALT+ENTER. Type Cost and then press the RIGHT ARROW key.
7. Type Current and then press ALT+ENTER. Type Price and then press the RIGHT ARROW key.
8. Type Current and then press ALT+ENTER. Type Value and then press the RIGHT ARROW key.
9. Type Gain/Loss and then click cell A3.

The column titles display as shown in row 2 of Figure 2-2. When you press ALT+ENTER to add more lines to a cell, Excel automatically increases the height of the entire row.

The stock data in Table 2-1 includes a date on which each stock was acquired. Excel considers a date to be a number and, therefore, displays it right-aligned in the cell. When you enter a date, Excel automatically formats the date so it resembles the way you entered it. For example, if you enter May 20, 1996, Excel displays it as 20-May-96. If you enter the same date in the format 5/20/96, then Excel displays it as 5/20/96. The following steps describe how to enter the stock data shown in Table 2-1.

More *About* Entering Numbers into a Range

An efficient way to enter a set of numbers into a range of cells, such as B3:C6 in Figure 2-2, is to select the range by dragging from cell B3 to cell C6 prior to entering the numbers. After initially selecting the range, cell B3 remains the active cell. Thus, type the value for cell B3 and press the ENTER key. Excel responds by entering the number and moving the active cell selection down one cell. When you enter the last value in the first column, Excel will move the active cell selection to the top of the next column and then proceed downward.

TO ENTER THE STOCK DATA

1. With cell A3 selected, type Compaq and then press the RIGHT ARROW key. Type CPQ and then press the RIGHT ARROW key.
2. With cell C3 selected, type 5/20/96 and then press the RIGHT ARROW key. Type 500 and then press the RIGHT ARROW key.
3. With cell E3 selected, type 52.5 and then press the RIGHT ARROW key twice. Type 76.75 and then press the ENTER key.
4. Click cell A4. Enter the data for the four remaining stocks in rows 4 through 7.

The stock data displays in rows 3 through 7 as shown in Figure 2-2.

TO ENTER THE TOTAL ROW TITLES

① Click cell A8. Type `Total` and then press the DOWN ARROW key. Type `Average` and then press the DOWN ARROW key.

② With cell A10 selected, type `Highest` and then press the DOWN ARROW key. Type `Lowest` and then press the DOWN ARROW key.

③ With cell A12 selected, type `Percentage Gain/Loss ====>` and then click cell F3.

The total row titles display as shown in Figure 2-2.

FIGURE 2-2

Entering Formulas

The initial cost for each stock, which displays in column F, is equal to the number of shares in column D times the initial price in column E. Thus, the initial cost for Compaq in row 3 is obtained by multiplying 500 (cell D3) by 52.5 (cell E3).

One of the reasons Excel is such a valuable tool is that you can assign a **formula** to a cell and Excel will calculate the result. Consider, for example, what would happen if you had to multiply 500 × 52.5 and then enter the result, 26250, in cell F3 manually. Every time the values in cells D3 and E3 changed, you would have to recalculate the product and enter the new value in cell F3. By contrast, if you enter a formula in cell F3 to multiply the values in cells D3 and E3, Excel recalculates the product whenever new values are entered into those cells and displays the result in cell F3. Complete the following steps to enter the formula using the keyboard.

More *About* Recalculation of Formulas

Every time you enter a value into a cell in the worksheet, Excel recalculates all formulas. It makes no difference if there is one formula or hundreds of formulas in the worksheet. Excel recalculates the formulas instantaneously. This is one of the reasons why a spreadsheet package, such as Excel, is so powerful.

Steps To Enter a Formula Using the Keyboard

① **With cell F3 selected, type** `=d3*e3` **in the cell.**

The formula displays in the formula bar and in cell F3 (Figure 2-3).

FIGURE 2-3

2 **Press the RIGHT ARROW key twice to select cell H3.**

Instead of displaying the formula in cell F3, Excel completes the arithmetic operation indicated by the formula and displays the result, 26250 (Figure 2-4).

FIGURE 2-4

More *About* Entering Formulas

Besides the equal sign (=), you can start a formula with a plus sign (+) or a minus sign (-). However, do not forget to start with one of these three characters or the formula will be interpreted by Excel as text.

More *About* Troubling Formulas

If Excel will not accept a formula, remove the equal sign from the left side and complete the entry as text. Later, after entering additional data or after you have determined the error, reinsert the equal sign.

The equal sign (=) preceding d3*e3 is an important part of the formula: it alerts Excel that you are entering a formula or function and not text. The asterisk (*) following d3 is the arithmetic operator, which directs Excel to perform the **multiplication operation**. Other valid Excel arithmetic operators include + (**addition**), − (**subtraction** or **negation**), / (**division**), % (**percentage**), and ^ (**exponentiation**).

You can enter the cell references in formulas in uppercase or lowercase, and you can add spaces before and after arithmetic operators to make the formulas easier to read. That is, =d3*e3 is the same as =d3 * e3, =D3 * e3, or =D3 * E3.

Order of Operations

When more than one operator is involved in a formula, Excel follows the same basic order of operations that you use in algebra. Moving from left to right in a formula, the **order of operations** is as follows: first negation (−), then all percentages (%), then all exponentiations (^), then all multiplications (*) and divisions (/), and, finally all additions (+) and subtractions (−). You can use **parentheses** to override the order of operations. For example, if Excel follows the order of operations, 10 * 6 − 3 equals 57. If you use parentheses, however, to change the formula to 10 * (6 − 3), the result is 30 because the parentheses instruct Excel to subtract 3 from 6 before multiplying by 10. Table 2-2 illustrates several examples of valid formulas and explains the order of operations.

Table 2-2	
FORMULA	**REMARK**
=G6	Assigns the value in cell G6 to the active cell.
=4 + -5^2	Assigns the sum of 4 + 25 (or 29) to the active cell.
=3 * J4 or =J4 * 3 or =(3 * J4)	Assigns three times the contents of cell J4 to the active cell.
=25% * 12	Assigns the product of 0.25 times 12 (or 3) to the active cell.
=-J12 * S23	Assigns the negative value of the product of the values contained in cells J12 and S23 to the active cell.
=5 * (L14 − H3)	Assigns the product of five times the difference between the values contained in cells H3 and L14 to the active cell.
=D1 / X6 - A3 * A4 + A5 ^ A6	From left to right: first exponentiation (A5 ^ A6), then division (D1 / X6), then multiplication (A3 * A4), then subtraction (D1 / X6) - (A3 * A4), and finally addition (D1 / X6 - A3 * A4) + (A5 ^ A6). If cells D1 = 10, A3 = 6, A4 = 2, A5 = 5, A6 = 2, and X6 = 2, then Excel assigns the active cell the value 18 (10 / 2 - 6 * 2 + 5 ^ 2 = 18).

The first formula (=d3*e3) in the worksheet was entered into cell F3 using the keyboard. The next section shows you how to enter the formulas in cells H3 and I3 using the mouse to select cell references in a formula.

Entering Formulas Using Point Mode

In the worksheet shown in Figure 2-1a on page E 2.6, the current value of each stock displays in column H. The current value for Compaq in cell H3 is equal to the number of shares in cell D3 times the current price in cell G3. The gain/loss for Compaq in cell I3 is equal to the current value in cell H3 minus the initial cost in cell F3.

Instead of using the keyboard to enter the formulas =d3*g3 in cell H3 and =h3 – f3 in cell I3, you can use the mouse and Point mode to enter these last two formulas. **Point mode** allows you to select cells for use in a formula by using the mouse.

> **More** *About*
> **Using Point Mode**
>
> Point mode allows you to create formulas using the mouse. Rather than typing a cell reference in a formula, simply click a cell and Excel will append the corresponding cell reference at the location of the insertion point. You can also use the Customize command on the shortcut menu that displays when you right-click a toolbar to create a new toolbar made up of buttons that represent the operators. Thus, with Excel you can enter entire formulas without ever touching the keyboard.

 Steps To Enter Formulas Using Point Mode

---

1 **With cell H3 selected, type = (an equal sign) to begin the formula and then click cell D3.**

Excel surrounds cell D3 with a marquee and appends D3 to the equal sign (=) in cell H3 (Figure 2-5).

FIGURE 2-5

---

2 **Type * (an asterisk) and then click cell G3.**

Excel surrounds cell G3 with a marquee and appends G3 to the asterisk (*) in cell H3 (Figure 2-6).

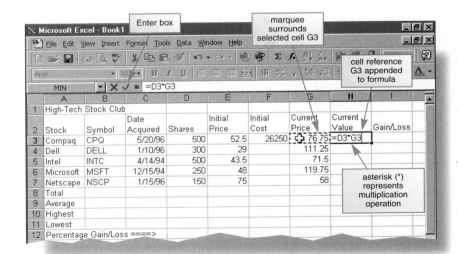

FIGURE 2-6

3 **Click the Enter box or press the ENTER key. Click cell I3.**

Excel determines the product of =D3*G3 and displays the result, 38375, in cell H3 (Figure 2-7).

4 **With cell I3 selected, type = (equal sign) and then click cell H3. Type – (minus sign) and then click cell F3.**

The formula =H3 – F3 displays in cell I3 and in the formula bar (Figure 2-7).

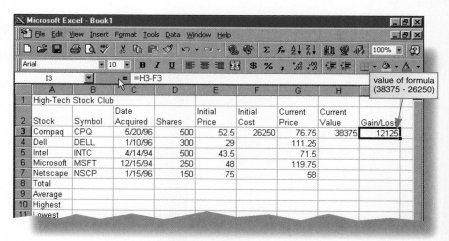

FIGURE 2-7

5 **Click the Enter box or press the ENTER key.**

The gain/loss for Compaq, 12125, displays in cell I3 (Figure 2-8).

FIGURE 2-8

Depending on the length and complexity of the formula, using Point mode to enter formulas often is faster than using the keyboard. As shown later in the project, in some instances, you may want to combine the keyboard and mouse when entering a formula in a cell. You can use the keyboard to begin the formula, for example, and then use the mouse to select a range of cells.

Entering Formulas Using Natural Language

If the column titles in a worksheet are simple (no spaces and no multiple lines), then you can use them, rather than cell references, in formulas. For example, suppose you are creating a payroll worksheet in which the hours and rate columns are titled Hours and Rate, respectively. To determine the corresponding gross pay, you then could enter the formula, =hours*rate. When you enter a formula using the column or row titles, it is referred to as a **natural language formula**. See Test Your Knowledge Exercise 3 on page E 2.68 for additional examples.

◆More *About* Range Finder

Range Finder allows you to check to be sure a formula or chart is referencing the correct cell or range of cells. If you double-click a cell containing a formula or a chart, Excel will use colored frames to indicate the cells that are referenced in the formula. For example, if you double-click H3, Excel will draw colored frames around cells H3 and F3 because they are referenced in the formula. You can then point to the colored frame and move it to adjust the makeup of the formula or chart.

Copying the Formulas Using the Fill Handle

The three formulas for Compaq in cells F3, H3, and I3 now are complete. You could enter the same three formulas one at a time for the four remaining stocks, Dell, Intel, Microsoft, and Netscape. An easier method of entering the formulas, however, is to select the formulas in row 3 and then use the fill handle to copy them through row 7. Perform the following steps to copy the formulas.

 Steps **To Copy Formulas Using the Fill Handle**

1 **Click cell F3 and then point to the fill handle. Drag the fill handle through cell F7 and hold down the left mouse button.**

A border surrounds the copy and paste areas (F3:F7) and the mouse pointer changes to a cross hair (Figure 2-9).

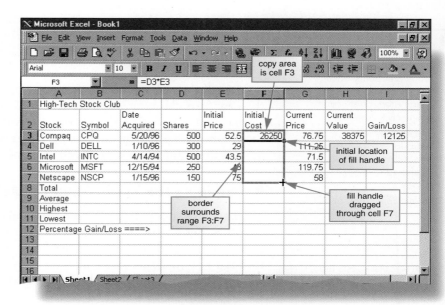

FIGURE 2-9

2 **Release the left mouse button.**

*Excel copies the formula =D3*E3 to the range F4:F7 and displays the initial costs for the remaining four stocks (Figure 2-10).*

3 **Select the range H3:I3 and then point to the fill handle.**

The range H3:I3 is highlighted (Figure 2-10).

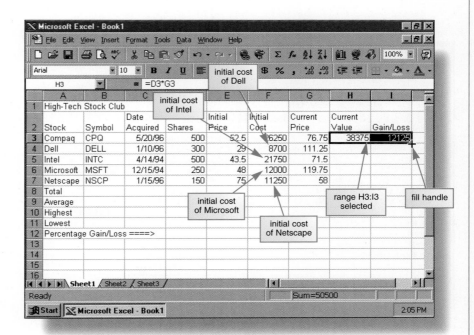

FIGURE 2-10

4 **Drag the fill handle down through H7:I7.**

Excel copies the two formulas =D3*G3 in cell H3 and =H3-F3 in cell I3 to the range H4:I7 and displays the current value and gain/loss for the remaining four stocks (Figure 2-11).

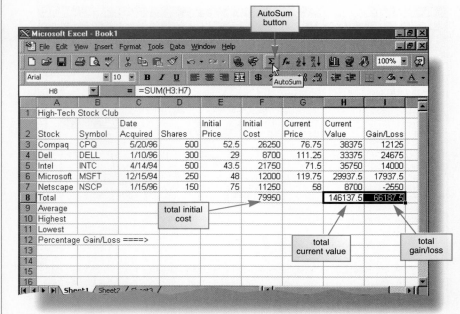

FIGURE 2-11

Recall that when you copy a formula, Excel adjusts the cell references so that the new formulas contain references corresponding to the new location and perform calculations using the appropriate values. Thus, if you copy downward, Excel adjusts the row portion of cell references. If you copy across, then Excel adjusts the column portion of cell references.

Determining the Totals Using the AutoSum Button

The next step is to determine the totals in row 8 for the following three columns: initial cost in column F, current value in column H, and gain/loss in column I. To determine the total initial cost in column F, you must sum cells F3 through F7. To do so, you can enter the function =sum(f3:f7) in cell F8, or you can select cell F8 and then click the AutoSum button on the Standard toolbar twice. Similar SUM functions or the AutoSum button can be used in cells H8 and I8 to determine total current value and total gain/loss, respectively.

FIGURE 2-12

TO DETERMINE TOTALS USING THE AUTOSUM BUTTON

1 Select cell F8. Click the AutoSum button twice. (Do not double-click.)

2 Select the range H8:I8. Click the AutoSum button.

The three totals display in row 8 as shown in Figure 2-12.

Rather than using the AutoSum function to calculate column totals individually, you can select all three cells before clicking the AutoSum button to calculate all three column totals at one time. To select the nonadjacent range F8, H8, and I8, select cell F8, and then, while holding down the CTRL key, drag through the range H8:I8. Next, click the AutoSum button.

Using the AVERAGE, MAX, and MIN Functions

The next step in creating the High-Tech Stock Club worksheet is to compute the average, maximum value, and minimum value for the number of shares in column D. Once the values are determined, the entries can be copied across to the other columns. Excel includes prewritten formulas called **functions** to help you compute these statistics. A function takes a value or values, performs an operation, and returns a value or values. The values that you use with a function are called **arguments**. All functions begin with an equal sign and include the arguments in parentheses after the function name. For example, in the function =AVERAGE(D3:D7), the function name is AVERAGE and the argument is the range D3:D7.

With Excel, you can enter functions using one of three methods: (1) the keyboard or mouse; (2) the Edit Formula box and Function box; and (3) the Paste Function button. The method you choose will depend on whether you can recall the function name and required arguments. In the following pages, each of the three methods is used to calculate a different statistic: the keyboard and mouse are used to determine the average number of shares (cell D9); the Edit Formula box and Function box are used to determine the maximum number of shares (cell D10); and the Paste Function button is used to determine the minimum number of shares (cell D11).

Determining the Average of a Range of Numbers

To determine the average of the numbers in the range D3:D7, use the **AVERAGE function** as shown in the following steps.

Steps To Determine the Average of a Range of Numbers Using the Keyboard and Mouse

1 **Select cell D9. Type** =average(**in the cell.**

Excel displays the beginning of the AVERAGE function in the formula bar and in cell D9.

2 **Click cell D3, the first endpoint of the range to average. Drag through cell D7, the second endpoint of the range to average.**

A marquee surrounds the range D3:D7. When you click cell D3, Excel appends cell D3 to the left parenthesis in the formula bar and surrounds cell D3 with a marquee. When you begin dragging, Excel appends a colon (:) and the cell reference of the cell where the mouse pointer is located to the function (Figure 2-13).

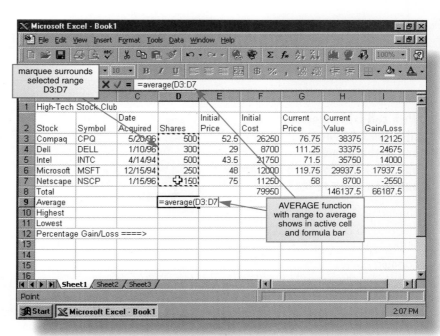

FIGURE 2-13

3 **Click the Enter box or press the ENTER key.**

Excel computes the average of the five numbers in the range D3:D7 and displays the result, 340, in cell D9 (Figure 2-14).

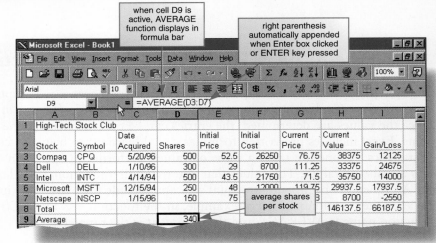

FIGURE 2-14

Other Ways

1. In formula bar click Edit Formula box, in Function box click AVERAGE
2. On Standard toolbar click Paste Function button, click AVERAGE function

The AVERAGE function requires that the range (the argument) be included within parentheses following the function name. Excel thus automatically appends the right parenthesis to complete the AVERAGE function when you click the Enter box or press the ENTER key. When you use the Point mode, as in the previous steps, you cannot use the arrow keys to complete the entry. While in Point mode, the arrow keys change the selected cell reference in the formula being created.

Determining the Highest Number in a Range of Numbers

The next step is to select cell D10 and determine the highest (maximum) number in the range D3:D7. Excel has a function called the **MAX function** that displays the highest value in a range. Although you could enter the MAX function using the keyboard and Point mode as you did in the previous steps, an alternative method to entering the function is to use the Edit Formula box and Function box.

Steps **To Determine the Highest Number in a Range of Numbers Using the Edit Formula Box and Function Box**

1 **With cell D10 selected, click the Edit Formula box in the formula bar. Click the Function box arrow and then point to MAX.**

*The Name box in the formula bar changes to the **Function box**. The **Formula palette** displays immediately below the formula bar (Figure 2-15). An equal sign displays in the formula bar and active cell, D10.*

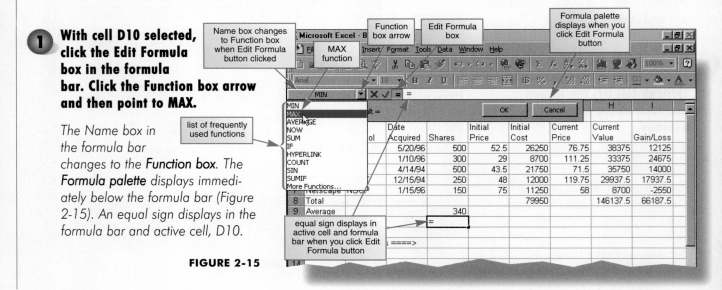

FIGURE 2-15

2 **Click MAX. When the Formula palette displays, type** d3:d7 **in the Number 1 text box. Point to the OK button.**

The MAX Formula palette displays with the range d3:d7 entered in the Number 1 text box (Figure 2-16). The completed MAX function displays in the formula bar and the end of the function displays in the active cell, D10.

FIGURE 2-16

3 **Click the OK button.**

Excel determines that the highest value in the range D3:D7 is 500 (cell D3 and D5) and displays it in cell D10 (Figure 2-17).

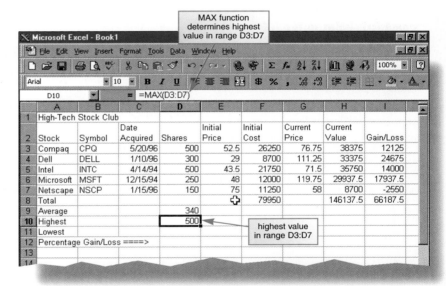

FIGURE 2-17

As shown in Figure 2-16, the Formula palette displays the value the MAX function will return to cell D10. It also lists the first few numbers in the selected range, next to the Number 1 text box.

In this example, rather than entering the MAX function, you easily could scan the range D3:D7, determine that the highest number of shares is 500, and enter the number as a constant in cell B10. The display would be the same as Figure 2-17. Because it contains a constant, cell B10 will continue to display 500, even if the values in the range D3:D7 change. If you use the MAX function, however, Excel will recalculate the highest value in the range D3:D7 each time a new value is entered into the worksheet. Manually determining the highest value in the range also would be more difficult if the club owned more stocks.

Determining the Lowest Number in a Range of Numbers

The next step is to enter the **MIN function** in cell D11 to determine the lowest (minimum) number in the range D3:D7. Although you could enter the MIN

> **Other Ways**
> 1. On Standard toolbar click Paste Function button, click MAX function
> 2. Type MAX function in cell

function using either of the methods used to enter the AVERAGE and MAX functions, the following steps show an alternative using Excel's **Paste Function** button on the Standard toolbar.

Steps — To Determine the Lowest Number in a Range of Numbers Using the Paste Function Button

1 **Click cell D11. Click the Paste Function button on the Standard toolbar. When the Paste Function dialog box displays, click Statistical in the Function category list. Scroll down and click MIN in the Function name list. Point to the OK button.**

Excel displays the Paste Function dialog box (Figure 2-18). Statistical and MIN are selected. An equal sign displays in the formula bar and in the active cell, D11.

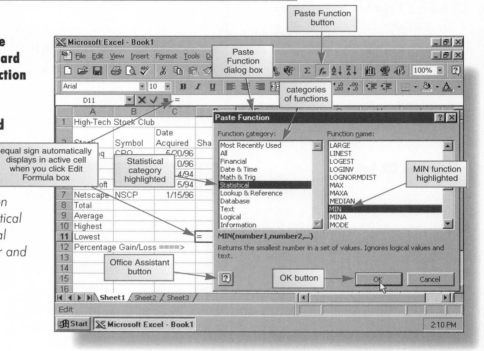

FIGURE 2-18

2 **Click the OK button. When the MIN Formula palette displays, drag it to the bottom of the screen. Click cell D3 and then drag through cell D7.**

The MIN Formula palette displays at the bottom of the screen (Figure 2-19). The range D3:D7 displays in the Number 1 text box. The desired MIN function displays in the formula bar and the end of it displays in the active cell, D11.

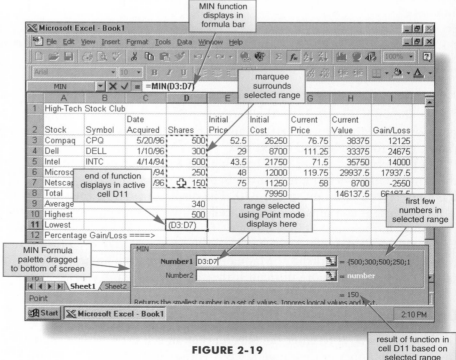

FIGURE 2-19

3 **Click the Enter box or press the ENTER key.**

Excel determines that the lowest value in the range D3:D7 is 150 and displays it in cell D11 (Figure 2-20).

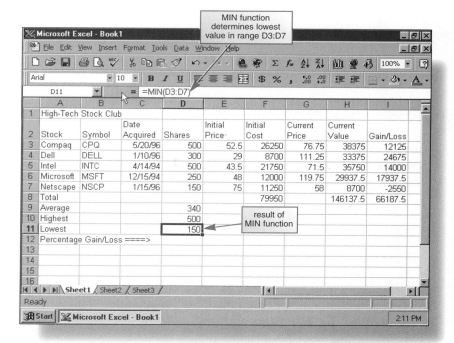

FIGURE 2-20

You can see from the previous example that using the Paste Function button on the Standard toolbar allows you to enter a function into a cell easily without requiring you to memorize its name or the required arguments. Anytime you desire to enter a function, but cannot remember these, simply click the Paste Function button on the Standard toolbar, select the desired function, and enter the arguments in the Formula palette.

Thus far, you have learned to use the SUM, AVERAGE, MAX, and MIN functions. In addition to these four functions, Excel has more than 400 other functions that perform just about every type of calculation you can imagine. These functions are categorized as shown in the Function Category box in Figure 2-18.

To obtain a list and description of the available functions, click Contents and Index on the Help menu. When Excel displays the Help Topics: Microsoft Excel dialog box, click the Index tab and then type functions in the top text box labeled 1. Under functions in the lower list box labeled 2, double-click overview. One at a time, double-click each category. To obtain a printout of any topic, right-click the Help window and then click Print Topic on the shortcut menu. Click the Help Topics button to return to the Index sheet.

Copying the AVERAGE, MAX, and MIN Functions

The next step is to copy the AVERAGE, MAX, and MIN functions in the range D9:D11 to the range E9:I11. The fill handle again will be used to complete the copy.

More About Excel's Add-Ins

Excel comes with add-ins that can simplify your work. Add-ins are installed during the installation process and activated through the Add-Ins command on the Tools menu. Some add-ins add commands to menus or controls to dialog boxes. Some of the more popular add-ins are View Manager (name and save frequently used worksheet locations), Analysis ToolPak (new function category), Engineering (engineering functions), Report Manager (additional printing capabilities), and Solver (linear and nonlinear optimization).

Steps To Copy a Range of Cells Across Columns to an Adjacent Range
Using the Fill Handle

1 Select the range D9:D11. Drag
the fill handle in the lower-right
corner of the selected range
through cell I11 and hold down
the left mouse button.

*Excel highlights the copy area
(range D9:D11) and displays a border around the copy and paste
areas (range D9:I11) (Figure 2-21).*

	Stock	Symbol	Date Acquired	Shares	Initial Price	Cost	Current Price	Current Value	Gain/Loss
2	Stock	Symbol	Acquired	Shares	Price	Cost	Price	Value	Gain/Loss
3	Compaq	CPQ	5/20/96	500	52.		.75	38375	12125
4	Dell	DELL	1/10/96	300	2		25	33375	24675
5	Intel	INTC	4/14/94	500	43.		1.5	35750	1400
6	Microsoft	MSFT	12/15/94	250	48	12000	119.75	29937.5	17937.
7	Netscape	NSCP	1/15/96	150	75	11250	58	8700	-255
8	Total					79950		146137.5	66187.5
9	Average			340					
10	Highest			500					
11	Lowest			150					
12	Percentage Gain/Loss ====>								
13									
14									
15									
16									

border surrounds copy and paste area

mouse pointer

copy range D9:D11 selected

fill handle dragged to select paste area E9:I11

Sheet1 / Sheet2 / Sheet3 /

Drag outside selection to extend series or fill; drag inside

Start | Microsoft Excel - Book1   2:11 PM

FIGURE 2-21

2 Release the left mouse button.

*Excel copies the three functions to
the range E9:I11 (Figure 2-22).*

Microsoft Excel - Book1

File Edit View Insert Format Tools Data Window Help

Arial   10   B I U $ % ,   100%

D9   =   =AVERAGE(D3:D7)

	A	B	C	D	E	F	G	H	I
1	High-Tech Stock Club								
2	Stock	Symbol	Date Acquired	Shares	Initial Price	Initial Cost	Current Price	Current Value	
3	Compaq	CPQ	5/20/96	500	52.5	26250	76.75	38	
4	Dell	DELL	1/10/96	300	29	8700	111.25	33	
5	Intel	INTC	4/14/94	500	43.5	21750	71.5	35	
6	Microsoft	MSFT	12/15/94	250	48	12000	119.75	29937.5	17937.5
7	Netscape	NSCP	1/15/96	150	75	11250	58	8700	-2550
8	Total					79950		146137.5	66187.5
9	Average			340	49.6	15990	87.45	29227.5	13237.5
10	Highest			500	75	26250	119.75	38375	24675
11	Lowest			150	29	8700	58	8700	-2550
12	Percentage Gain/Loss ====>								

AVERAGE, MAX, and MIN functions in range D9:D11 copied to range E9:I11

FIGURE 2-22

Again, remember that Excel adjusts the ranges in the copied functions so that
each function refers to the column of numbers above it. Review the numbers in
rows 9 through 11 in Figure 2-22. You should see that the functions in each column return the appropriate values, based on the the numbers in rows 3 through 7
of that column.

Entering the Percentage Gain/Loss Formula

The last required entry is the formula that displays the percentage gain/loss in
cell D12. The formula determines the percentage gain/loss by dividing the total
gain/loss in cell I8 by the total initial cost in cell F8. After you enter the last entry
in the worksheet, you also will want to save the worksheet on a floppy disk.

Steps To Enter a Percentage Formula

1 **Click cell D12. Type = and then click cell I8. Type / and then click cell F8.**

The formula displays in the formula bar and in cell D12 (Figure 2-23). A marquee surrounds cell F8.

6	Microsoft	MSFT	12/15/94	250	48	12000	119.75	29937.5	17937.5
7	Netscape	NSCP	1/15/96	150	75	11250	58	8700	-2550
8	Total					79950		146137.5	66187.5
9	Average			340	49.6	15990	87.45	29227.5	13237.5
10	Highest			500	75	26250	119.75	38375	24675
11	Lowest			150	29	8700	58	8700	-2550
12	Percentage Gain/Loss ====>			=I8/F8					

marquee surrounds cell F8

formula entered into cell D12 using Point mode

Point

Start | Microsoft Excel - Book1 | 2:12 PM

FIGURE 2-23

2 **Click the Enter box or press the ENTER key.**

Excel assigns the formula to cell D12 and displays the result of the formula (0.827861) in cell D12.

3 **Click the Save button on the Standard toolbar. Type** High-Tech Stock Club **in the File name text box. If necessary, change to 3½ Floppy (A:) in the Save in box. Click the Save button in the Save As dialog box.**

The file name in the title bar changes to High-Tech Stock Club (Figure 2-24).

file name after saving workbook

Microsoft Excel - High-Tech Stock Club

File Edit View Insert Format Tools Data Window Help

Arial 10 B I U $ %

A14

	A	B	C	D	E	F	G	H	I
1	High-Tech Stock Club								
2	Stock	Symbol	Date Acquired	Shares	Initial Price	Initial Cost	Current Price	Current Value	Gain/Loss
3	Compaq	CPQ	5/20/96	500	52.5	26250	76.75	38375	12125
4	Dell	DELL	1/10/96	300	29	8700	111.25	33375	24675
5	Intel	INTC	4/14/94	500	43.5	21750	71.5	35750	14000
6	Microsoft	MSFT	12/15/94	250	48	12000	119.75	29937.5	17937.5
7	Netscape	NSCP	1/15/96	150	75	11250	58	8700	-2550
8	Total					79950		146137.5	66187.5
9	Average			340	49.6	15990	87.45	29227.5	13237.5
10	Highest			500	75	26250	119.75	38375	24675
11	Lowest			150	29	8700	58	8700	-2550
12	Percentage Gain/Loss ====>			0.827861					

data and formulas are complete

percentage gain/loss equals 82.7861%

Sheet1 Sheet2 Sheet3

FIGURE 2-24

This concludes entering the data and formulas into the worksheet. After Excel saves the file, the worksheet remains on the screen with the file name, High-Tech Stock Club, in the title bar. You immediately can continue with the next activity, which is applying formats to the worksheet to make it is easier to read.

Applying Formats to the Text

Although the worksheet contains the appropriate data, formulas, and functions, the text and numbers need to be formatted to improve their appearance and readability.

More *About*
Saving a Workbook

You should save your workbooks every 5 to 10 minutes so that if the system fails you can retrieve a copy without a major loss of work.

In Project 1, you used the AutoFormat command to format the majority of the worksheet. This section describes how to change the unformatted worksheet in Figure 2-25a to the formatted worksheet in Figure 2-25b using the Formatting toolbar and Format Cells command.

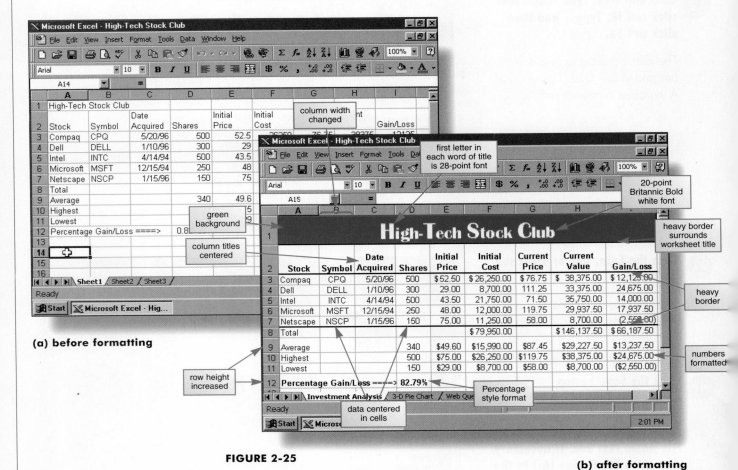

(a) before formatting

(b) after formatting

FIGURE 2-25

The following outlines the type of formatting that is required in Project 2:

1. Worksheet title
   a. Font type — True Type (TT) Britannic Bold (or Impact if your system does not have TT Britannic Bold)
   b. Font size — 28 for first character in each word; 20 for subsequent characters
   c. Alignment — center across columns A through I
   d. Background color (range A1:I1) — green
   e. Font color — white
   f. Border — heavy border outline around A1:I1
2. Column titles
   a. Font style — bold
   b. Alignment — center
   c. Border — heavy bottom border
3. Data
   a. Alignment — center data in columns B and D
   b. Numbers in top row (row 3) — Currency style
   c. Numbers below top row (rows 4 through 7) — Comma style
   d. Border — heavy bottom border on row 7

4. Total line
    a. Numbers — Currency style
5. Function lines
    a. Numbers — Currency style in columns E through I
6. Percentage
    a. Numbers — Percentage style in cell D12
    b. Font style — bold
7. Column widths
    a. Columns B and G — 7.14 characters
    b. Columns D and E — 7.00 characters
    c. Remaining columns — best fit or default
8. Row heights
    a. Row 2 — 36.00 points
    b. Rows 9 and 12 — 18.00 points
    c. Remaining rows — best fit or default

Except for the Currency style assigned to the functions in rows 9 through 12, all of the above formats can be assigned to cells using buttons or boxes on the Formatting toolbar.

Changing the Font and Centering the Worksheet Title

When developing presentation-quality worksheets, different fonts often are used in the same worksheet. Excel allows you to change the font of individual characters in a cell or all the characters in a cell, in a range of cells, or in the entire worksheet. To emphasize the worksheet title in cell A1, the font type, size, and style are changed and the worksheet title is centered as described in the following steps.

 Steps **To Change Font and Center the Worksheet Title**

1 **Click cell A1. Click the Font box arrow on the Formatting toolbar and then point to TT Britannic Bold (or TT Courier New if your system does not have TT Britannic Bold).**

The Font list box displays with TT Britannic Bold highlighted (Figure 2-26).

FIGURE 2-26

2 Click TT Britannic Bold (or Impact). Click the Font Size box arrow on the Formatting toolbar and then point to 20.

The characters in cell A1 display using TT Britannic Bold (or Impact). The font size 20 is highlighted in the Font Size list box (Figure 2-27).

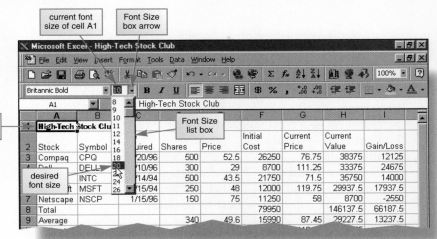

FIGURE 2-27

3 Click 20. Double-click cell A1 to edit the cell contents. Drag through the first character H in the word, High, and then point to the Font Size box arrow.

The text in cell A1 displays in 20-point Britannic Bold font. Excel automatically increases the height of row 1 so that the larger characters fit in the cells. This is called **best fit.** *Excel enters the Edit mode and the letter H in High is selected (Figure 2-28).*

FIGURE 2-28

4 Click the Font Size box arrow and then point to 28 (Figure 2-29).

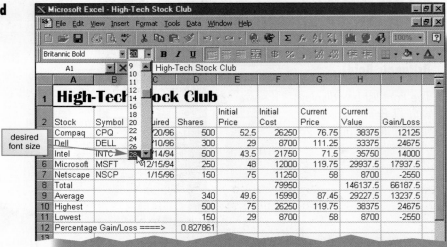

FIGURE 2-29

5 Click 28. While in Edit mode, drag through the first letter of the remaining words in the worksheet title and then change their font size to 28.

The first letter of each word in the worksheet title displays larger than the other characters (Figure 2-30).

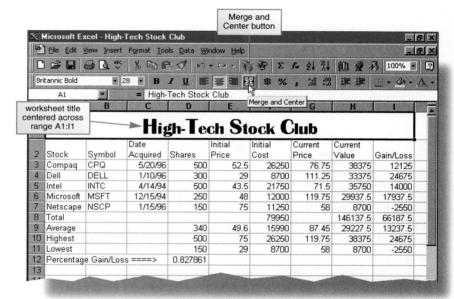

FIGURE 2-30

6 Click the Enter box or press the ENTER key to complete editing the contents of cell A1. Select the range A1:I1. Click the Merge and Center button on the Formatting toolbar.

Excel merges the cells A1 through I1 to create a new cell A1 and centers the worksheet title across columns A through I (Figure 2-31).

FIGURE 2-31

You also can change a font type, size, or style at any time while the worksheet is active. Some Excel users prefer to change fonts before they enter any data. Others change the font while they are building the worksheet or after they have entered all the data.

Changing Worksheet Title Background and Font Colors and Applying an Outline Border

The final formats to be assigned to the worksheet title are the green background color, white font color, and heavy outline border (Figure 2-25b on page E 2.22). Perform the steps on the next page to complete the formatting of the worksheet title.

> **Other Ways**
>
> 1. Right-click cell, click Format Cells, click Font tab, select font formats, click OK button
> 2. On Format menu click Cells, click Font tab, select font formats, click OK button
> 3. Press CTRL+1, click Font tab, select font formats, click OK button

Steps: To Change the Background and Font Colors and Apply an Outline Border

1 With cell A1 selected, click the Fill Color button arrow on the Formatting toolbar and then point to the color green (column 4, row 2 on the Fill Color palette).

The Fill Color palette displays (Figure 2-32).

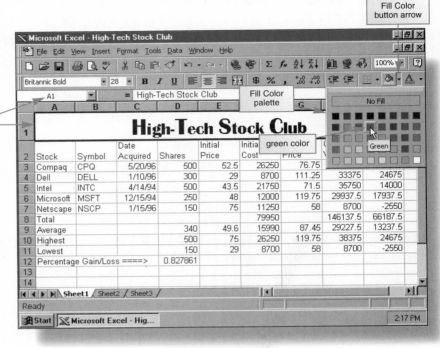

FIGURE 2-32

2 Click the color green. Click the Font Color button arrow on the Formatting toolbar. Point to the color white (column 8, row 5 on the Font Color palette).

The background color of cell A1 changes from white to green (Figure 2-33). The Font Color palette displays.

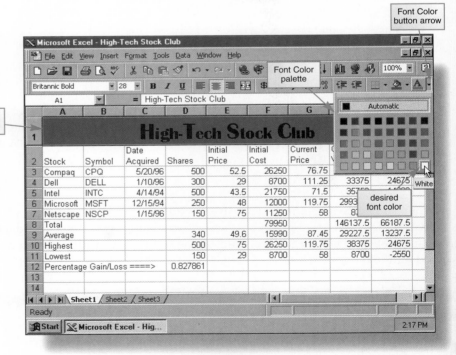

FIGURE 2-33

3 Click the color white. Click the Borders button arrow on the Formatting toolbar and then point to the heavy outline border (column 4, row 3 on the Borders palette).

The font in the worksheet title changes from black to white. The Borders palette displays (Figure 2-34).

FIGURE 2-34

4 Click the heavy outline border. Click cell A2.

Excel displays a heavy outline border around cell A1 (Figure 2-35).

FIGURE 2-35

You can remove borders, such as the outline around the range A1:I1, by selecting the range and then pressing CTRL+SHIFT+_. You can remove a background color by selecting the range, clicking the Fill Color button arrow on the Formatting toolbar, and clicking No Fill on the Fill Color palette. The same technique allows you to change the font color back to Excel's default, except you use the Font Color button arrow and click Automatic.

Applying Formats to the Column Titles

According to Figure 2-25b on page E 2.22, the column titles are bold, centered, and have a heavy underline. The steps on the next page assign these formats to the column titles.

OtherWays

1. Right-click range, on short-cut menu click Format Cells, click Patterns tab, click desired background color, click OK button

2. On Format menu click Cells, click Patterns tab, click desired background color, click OK button

3. Right-click range, on short-cut menu click Format Cells, click Border tab, click desired style, click desired border, click OK button

4. On Format menu click Cells, click Border tab, click desired style, click desired border, click OK button

Steps **To Bold, Center, and Underline the Column Titles**

1 **Select the range A2:I2. Click the Bold button on the Formatting toolbar. Click the Center button on the Formatting toolbar.**

The column titles in row 2 are bold and centered.

2 **Click the Borders button arrow on the Formatting toolbar and then point to the heavy bottom border (column 2, row 2) on the Borders palette.**

The Borders palette displays (Figure 2-36).

3 **Click the heavy bottom border. Select cell B3.**

Excel adds a heavy bottom border to the range A2:I2.

FIGURE 2-36

You can align the contents of cells in several different ways. Left alignment, center alignment, and right alignment are the more frequently used alignments. In fact, these three alignments are used so often that Excel has Left Align, Center, and Right Align buttons on the Formatting toolbar. In addition to aligning the contents of a cell horizontally, you also can align the contents of a cell vertically. You even can rotate the contents of a cell to various angles.

You also can align text as you initially enter it in a cell, by including a special character at the beginning of the entry. An apostrophe (') instructs Excel to left-align the text. A caret (^) centers the text and a quotation mark (") right-aligns the text.

For more information on alignment, click Cells on the Format menu and then click the Alignment tab.

Applying Formats to the Numbers

With the column titles formatted, the next step is to format the data and total lines. If a cell entry is short, such as the stock symbols in column B or the number of shares in column D, centering the entries within their respective columns improves the appearance of the worksheet. The following steps center the data in columns B and D.

TO CENTER DATA IN CELLS

① Select the range B3:B7. Click the Center button on the Formatting toolbar.

② Select the range D3:D12. Click the Center button on the Formatting toolbar.

The stock symbols in column B and the shares in column D are centered (Figure 2-37).

An alternative to centering the data one column at a time is to select the first range and then, while holding down the CTRL key, dragging through the second range. Once the nonadjacent ranges are selected, you can apply the format.

When using Excel, you can use the buttons on the Formatting toolbar to format numbers as dollar amounts, whole numbers with comma placement, and percentages. Customized formats can be assigned using the **Cells command** on the Format menu or the **Format Cells command** on the shortcut menu.

As shown in Figure 2-25b on page E 2.22, the worksheet is formatted to resemble an accounting report. For example, the first row of numbers (row 3) and the monetary totals (rows 8 through 12) display with dollar signs, while the remaining numbers (rows 4 through 7) do not. To display a dollar sign with a number, you should use the Currency style format.

The **Currency style format** displays a dollar sign to the left of the number, inserts a comma every three positions to the left of the decimal point, and displays numbers to the nearest cent (hundredths place). The **Currency Style button** on the Formatting toolbar will assign the desired Currency style format. When you use the Currency Style button, Excel displays a **fixed dollar sign** to the far left in the cell, often with spaces between it and the first digit. To assign a **floating dollar sign** that displays immediately to the left of the first digit with no spaces, you must use the Cells command on the Format menu or the Format Cells command on the shortcut menu. The project specifications call for a fixed dollar sign to be assigned to the numbers in rows 3 and 8, and a floating dollar sign to be assigned to the monetary totals in rows 9 through 11.

To display monetary amounts with commas and no dollar signs, you will want to use the Comma style format. The **Comma style format** inserts a comma every three positions to the left of the decimal point and displays numbers to the nearest hundredths (cents).

The remainder of this section describes how to format the numbers as shown in Figure 2-25b.

Formatting Numbers Using the Formatting Toolbar

The steps on the next page show how to assign formats using the Currency style button and Comma Style button on the Formatting toolbar.

FIGURE 2-37

Steps **To Apply a Currency Style Format and Comma Style Format Using the Formatting Toolbar**

① Select the range E3:I3. While holding down the CTRL key, select the nonadjacent range F8:I8. Point to the Currency Style button on the Formatting toolbar.

The nonadjacent ranges display as shown in Figure 2-38.

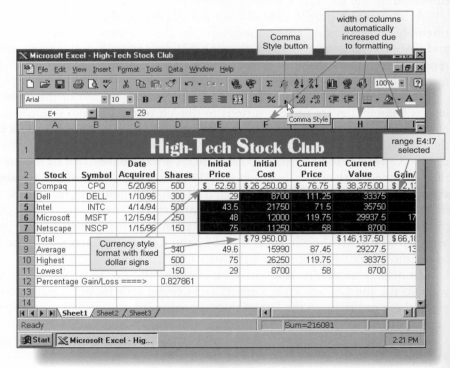

FIGURE 2-38

② Click the Currency Style button. Select the range E4:I7 and then point to the Comma Style button on the Formatting toolbar.

Excel automatically increases the width of columns F, H, and I to best fit, so that the numbers assigned the Currency style format will fit in the cells (Figure 2-39). The right side of column I moves off the screen. The range E4:I7 is highlighted.

FIGURE 2-39

3 **Click the Comma Style button. Select the range A7:I7 and then click the Borders button on the Formatting toolbar. Click cell E9.**

Excel assigns the Comma style format to the range E4:I7 and a heavy bottom border to row 7 (Figure 2-40). The Borders button remains set to the heavy bottom border assigned to row 2. Thus, to assign the heavy bottom border to the range A7:I7, you simply click the Borders button.

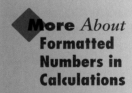

FIGURE 2-40

The Currency Style button assigns a fixed dollar sign to the numbers in the ranges E3:I3 and F8:I8. In each cell in these ranges, the dollar sign displays to the far left with spaces between it and the first digit in the cell. Excel automatically rounds a number to fit the selected format.

Formatting Numbers Using the Format Cells Command on the Shortcut Menu

Thus far, you have been introduced to two ways of formatting numbers in a worksheet. In Project 1, you formatted the numbers using the AutoFormat command on the Format menu. In the previous section, you were introduced to using the Formatting toolbar as a means of applying a format style. A third way to format numbers is to use the Cells command on the Format menu or the Format Cells command on the shortcut menu. Using either command allows you to display numbers in almost any format you want. The steps on the next page show you how to use the Format Cells command to apply the Currency style with a floating dollar sign to the totals in the range E9:I11.

More *About* **Formatted Numbers in Calculations**

The numbers you see on your screen may not be the same ones used in calculations. When a number has more decimal places than are showing on the screen because you formatted it, the actual number and not the displayed number is used in the computation.

Steps **To Apply a Currency Style with a Floating Dollar Sign Using the Format Cells Command**

---

1 **Select the range E9:I11. Right-click the selected range. Point to Format Cells on the shortcut menu.**

The shortcut menu displays (Figure 2-41).

FIGURE 2-41

2 **Click Format Cells. Click the Number tab in the Format Cells dialog box. Click Currency in the Category list, click the third style ($1,234.10) in the Negative numbers list, and then point to the OK button.**

The Format Cells dialog box displays (Figure 2-42).

FIGURE 2-42

3 Click the OK button. Click cell D12 to deselect the range E9:I11.

The worksheet displays with the totals in rows 9 through 11 assigned the Currency style format with a floating dollar sign (Figure 2-43).

4 Click the Save button on the Standard toolbar.

formatting of cells causes Excel to increase column widths to best fit, which increases width of worksheet

	D12		=	=I8/F8				
	A	B	C	D	E	F	G	H	I

	A	B	C	D	E	F	G	H	I
1					High-Tech Stock Club				
2	Stock	Symbol	Date Acquired	Shares	Initial Price	Initial Cost	Current Price	Current Value	Gain/
3	Compaq	CPQ	5/20/96	500	$ 52.50	$ 26,250.00	$ 76.75	$ 38,375.00	$ 12,12
4	Dell	DELL	1/10/96	300	29.00	8,700.00	111.25	33,375.00	24,67
5	Intel	INTC	4/14/94	500	43.50	21,750.00	71.50	35,750.00	14,00
6	Microsoft	MSFT	12/15/94	250	48.00	12,000.00	119.75	29,937.50	17,93
7	Netscape	NSCP	1/15/96	150	75.00	11,250.00	58.00	8,700.00	(2,55
8	Total					$ 79,950.00		$ 146,137.50	66,18
9	Average			340	$49.60	$15,990.00	$87.45	$29,227.50	$13,23
10	Highest			500	$75.00	$26,250.00	$119.75	$38,375.00	$24,67
11	Lowest			150	$29.00	$8,700.00	$58.00	$8,700.00	($2,55
12	Percentage Gain/Loss ====>			0.827861					
13									
14									

Sheet1

Currency style format with a floating dollar sign

negative numbers display surrounded by parentheses

Ready

Start Microsoft Excel - Hig... 2:26 PM

FIGURE 2-43

Other Ways

1. On Format menu click Cells, click Number tab, in Category list click Currency, select desired formats, click OK button

2. Press CTRL+SHIFT+$

Recall that a floating dollar sign always displays immediately to the left of the first digit and the fixed dollar sign always displays on the left side of the cell. Cell E3, for example, has a fixed dollar sign, while cell E9 has a floating dollar sign. Also recall that, while cells E3 and E9 both were assigned a Currency style format, the Currency style was assigned to cell E3 using the Currency Style button on the Formatting toolbar. The result is a fixed dollar sign. The Currency style was assigned to cell E9 using the Format Cells dialog box and the result is a floating dollar sign.

As shown in Figure 2-42, there are 12 categories of formats from which you can choose. Once you select a category, you can select the number of decimal places, whether or not a dollar sign should display, and how negative numbers should display.

Selecting the appropriate negative numbers format in Step 2 is important, because doing so adds a space to the right of the number (as do the Currency Style and Comma Style buttons). Some of the available negative numbers formats do not align the numbers in the worksheet on the decimal points. To verify this, click one of the formatted cells and then assign the Currency category with the negative numbers format (–$1,234.10) instead of ($1,234.10).

The negative number format selected in the previous set of steps displays in cell I11, which has a negative entry. The third selection in the Negative numbers list box (Figure 2-42) purposely was chosen to agree with the negative number format assigned to cell I7 using the Comma Style button.

Formatting Numbers Using the Percent Style Button and Increase Decimal Button

The last entry in the worksheet that needs to be formatted is the percentage gain/loss in cell D12. Currently, the number displays as a decimal fraction (0.827861). Follow the steps on the next page to change the format to the Percentage style with two decimal places. The last step bolds the percentage row title and number to make them stand out.

More *About* Painting Formats

Painting is not an enviable chore. But in Excel, if you know how to paint you can save yourself time and effort when formatting a worksheet. For example, if you see a cell that has the format you want to assign to another cell or range of cells, click the cell with the desired format, click the Format Painter button on the Standard toolbar, and then click the cell or drag through the cells you want to paint.

Steps **To Apply a Percentage Format**

1 **With cell D12 selected, click the Percent Style button on the Formatting toolbar.**

The number in cell D12 (0.827861) displays as a whole percent (83%).

2 **Click the Increase Decimal button on the Formatting toolbar twice.**

The number in cell D12 (83%) displays with two decimal places (82.79%).

3 **Select the range A12:D12. Click the Bold button on the Formatting toolbar. Click cell D12.**

The entries in the range A12:D12 display in bold (Figure 2-44).

FIGURE 2-44

OtherWays

1. Right-click range, on shortcut menu click Format Cells, click Number tab, in Category list click Percentage, select desired formats, click OK button

2. On Format menu click Cells, click Number tab, in Category list box click Percentage, select formats, click OK button

3. Press CTRL+SHIFT+%

The **Percent Style button** on the Formatting toolbar is used to display a value determined by multiplying the cell entry by 100, rounding the result to the nearest percent, and adding a percent sign. For example, when cell D12 is formatted using the Increase Decimal button, the value 0.827861 displays as 83%. While they do not display, Excel does maintain all the decimal places for computational purposes. Thus, if cell D12 is used in a formula, the value used for computational purposes is 0.827861.

The **Increase Decimal button** on the Formatting toolbar is used to display additional decimal places in a cell. Each time you click the Increase Decimal button, Excel adds a decimal place to the selected cell. The **Decrease Decimal button** removes a decimal place from the selected cell each time it is clicked.

With the number formatting complete, the next step is to change the column widths so the entire worksheet displays on the screen.

Changing the Widths of Columns and Heights of Rows

When Excel starts and the blank worksheet displays on the screen, all of the columns have a default width of 8.43 characters. A **character** is defined as a letter, number, symbol, or punctuation mark in 10-point TT Arial font, the default font used by Excel. An average of 8.43 characters in this font will fit in a cell. The default row height in a blank worksheet is 12.75 points. Recall from Project 1 that a point is equal to 1/72 of an inch. Thus, 12.75 points is equal to about one-sixth of an inch. You can change the width of the columns or height of the rows at any time to make the worksheet easier to read or to ensure that an entry displays properly in a cell.

Changing the Widths of Columns

When changing the column width, you can set the width manually or you can instruct Excel to size the column to best fit. Best fit means that the width of the column will be increased or decreased so the widest entry will fit in the column. When the format you assign to a cell causes the entry to exceed the width of a column, Excel automatically changes the column width to best fit. This happened earlier when the Currency style format was used (Figure 2-39 on page E 2.30). To set a column width to best fit, double-click the right boundary of the column heading.

Sometimes, you may prefer more or less white space in a column than best fit provides. Excel thus allows you to manually change column widths. In the case of Project 2, for example, sizing every column to best fit will not allow the entire worksheet to display on the screen at one time. To ensure the entire High-Tech Stock Club worksheet displays at one time, the following changes will be made to the column widths: column B from 8.43 to 7.14; columns D and E from 8.43 to 7.00; and column G from best fit to 7.14. Complete the following steps to change the widths of columns B, D, E, and G.

> ### More *About* Best Fit
>
> Although Excel automatically increases the width of a column or the height of a row when you assign a format to a cell, it will not increase the column width or row height when a cell contains a formula and you change the value of a cell that is referenced in the formula. For example, if you change the number of shares in cell D3 from 500 to 10,0000, Excel will recalculate the formulas and display number signs (#) for the initial cost and gain/loss because the results of the formulas have more digits than can fit in the cell. You can fix the problem by double-clicking the right boundary of the column heading to change to best fit.

 Steps To Change the Width of a Column by Dragging

1 Point to the boundary on the right side of the column B heading above row 1. Drag to the left until the ScreenTip, Width: 7.14, displays.

The mouse pointer becomes a split double arrow. A dotted line shows the proposed right border of column B and the ScreenTip, Width: 7.14, displays (Figure 2-45).

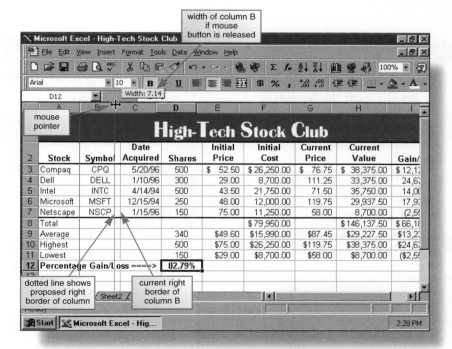

FIGURE 2-45

2 Release the mouse button. Point to the boundary on the right side of the column D heading. Drag to the left until the ScreenTip, Width: 7.00, displays.

A dotted line shows the proposed right border of column D and the ScreenTip, Width: 7.00, displays (Figure 2-46).

FIGURE 2-46

3 Release the mouse button. Point to the boundary on the right side of the column E heading. Drag to the left until the ScreenTip, Width: 7.00, displays.

A dotted line shows the proposed right border of column E and the ScreenTip, Width: 7.00 displays (Figure 2-47).

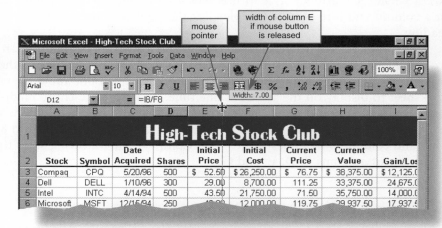

FIGURE 2-47

4 Release the mouse button. Point to the boundary on the right side of the column G heading. Drag to the left until the ScreenTip, Width: 7.14, displays.

A dotted line shows the proposed right border of column G and the ScreenTip, Width: 7.14, displays (Figure 2-48).

5 Release the mouse button.

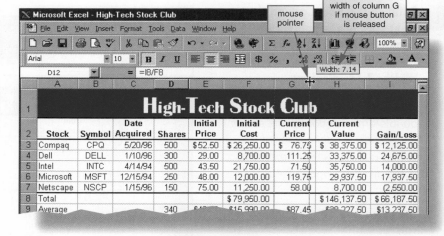

FIGURE 2-48

OtherWays

1. Right-click column heading, click Column Width, enter desired column width, click OK button
2. Select cell or range of cells, on Format menu click Column, click Width, enter desired column width, click OK button

Slightly decreasing the width of the four columns by dragging allows the entire worksheet to display on the screen (Figure 2-49).

If you want to increase or decrease the column width significantly, you can use the Column Width command on the shortcut menu to change a column's width. To use this command, however, you must select one or more entire columns. You select entire columns by dragging through the column headings. If the worksheet title had not been centered across columns A through I earlier, then in Steps 2 and 3 you could have selected columns D and E by dragging through their column headings and changed their width to 7.00 in one step. Excel, however, does not allow you to select columns that contain a merged cell.

A column width can vary from zero (0) to 255 characters. If you decrease the column width to zero, the column is hidden. **Hiding** is a technique you can use to hide data that might not be relevant to a particular report or sensitive data that you do not want others to see. When you print a worksheet, hidden columns do not print. To display a hidden column, position the mouse pointer to the left of the column heading boundary where the hidden column is located and then drag to the right.

Changing the Heights of Rows

When you increase the font size of a cell entry, such as the title in cell A1, Excel automatically increases the row height to best fit so the characters display properly. Recall that Excel also did this when you entered multiple lines in a cell in row 2.

You also can manually increase or decrease the height of a row to improve the appearance of the worksheet. Recall that the height of row 2 was increased automatically from the default row height of 12.75 points to 26.25 points when multiple lines were entered into cells in row 2. The following steps show how to increase the height of row 2 from 26.25 points to 36.00 points and to manually increase the heights of row 8 and 11 from the default 12.75 points to 18.00 points using the mouse. Perform the following steps to change the heights of rows by dragging.

Steps To Change the Height of a Row by Dragging

1 **Point to the boundary below row heading 2. Drag down until the ScreenTip, Height: 36.00, displays.**

The mouse pointer changes to a split double arrow (Figure 2-49). The distance between the dotted line and the top of row 2 indicates the proposed row height for row 2.

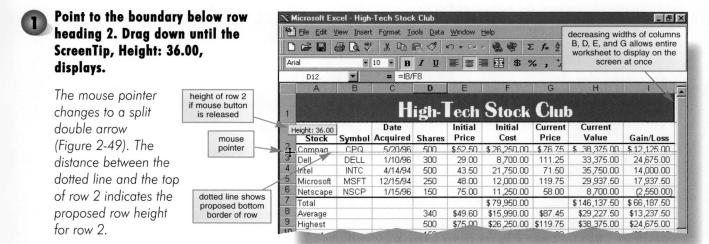

FIGURE 2-49

2 Release the mouse button. Click row heading 9 to select row 9. While holding down the CTRL key, click the row heading 12 to select row 12. With both rows selected, point to the boundary below row heading 12. Drag down until the ScreenTip, Height: 18.00, displays.

Excel displays a horizontal dotted line (Figure 2-50). The distance between the dotted line and the top of row 12 indicates the proposed row height for rows 9 and 12.

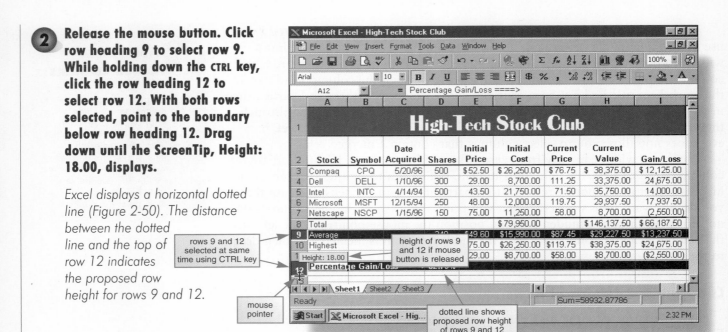

FIGURE 2-50

3 Release the mouse button. Click cell A15.

The High-Tech Stock Club worksheet displays with the new row heights (Figure 2-51).

4 Click the Save button on the Standard toolbar.

FIGURE 2-51

OtherWays

1. Right-click row heading or drag through multiple row headings and right-click, click Row Height, enter desired row height, click OK button

2. Select cell or range of cells in column, on Format menu click Row, click Height, enter desired row height, click OK button

The row height can vary between zero (0) and 409 points. As with column widths, when you decrease the row height to zero, the row is hidden. To display a hidden row, position the mouse pointer just below the row heading boundary where the row is hidden and then drag down. To set a row height to best fit, double-click the bottom boundary of the row heading.

The task of formatting the spreadsheet is complete. The next step is to check the spelling of the worksheet.

Checking Spelling

Excel has a spell checker you can use to check the worksheet for spelling errors. The spell checker looks for spelling errors by comparing words on the worksheet against words contained in its standard dictionary. If you often use specialized terms that are not in the standard dictionary, you may want to add them to a custom dictionary using the Spelling dialog box.

When the spell checker finds a word that is not in either dictionary, it displays the word in the Spelling dialog box. You then can correct it if it is misspelled.

You start the spell checker by clicking the Spelling button on the Standard toolbar. To illustrate how Excel responds to a misspelled word, the word, Stock, in cell A2 is purposely misspelled as the word, Stpck, as shown in Figure 2-52.

More *About*
Hidden Rows

You can use the keyboard to unhide a range of rows. First select the rows immediately above and below the hidden ones and press CTRL+SHIFT+(. To use the keyboard to hide a range of rows, press CTRL+9.

 Steps **To Check Spelling in the Worksheet**

1 **Select cell A2 and enter** Stpck **to misspell the word Stock. Select cell A1. Click the Spelling button on the Standard toolbar. When the spell checker stops on High-Tech, click the Ignore button. When the spell checker stops on cell A2, click the word Stock in the Suggestions list.**

The spell checker starts checking the spelling of the text in the worksheet, beginning with the active cell (cell A1). It continues checking to the right and down row by row. When the spell checker comes across the misspelled word, Stpck, the Spelling dialog box displays (Figure 2-52).

FIGURE 2-52

Click the Change button. As the spell checker checks the remainder of the worksheet, click the Ignore and Change buttons as needed.

The spell checker changes the misspelled word, Stpck, to the correct word, Stock, and continues spell checking the worksheet. When the spell checker is finished, it displays the Microsoft Excel dialog box with a message indicating that the spell check is complete for the entire sheet (Figure 2-53).

FIGURE 2-53

 Click the OK button.

*Other*Ways

1. On Tools menu click Spelling
2. Press F7

More *About*
Checking Spelling

Always take the time to check the spelling of a worksheet before submitting it to your supervisor. Nothing deflates an impression more than a professional-looking report with misspelled words.

When the spell checker identifies that a cell contains a word not in its standard or custom dictionary, it selects that cell as the active cell and displays the Spelling dialog box. The Spelling dialog box (Figure 2-52 on the previous page) lists the word not in the dictionary, a suggested correction, and a list of alternative suggestions. If you agree with the suggested correction in the **Change To box**, click the **Change button**. To change the word throughout the worksheet, click the **Change All button.**

If one of the words in the **Suggestions list** is correct, click the correct word in the Suggestions list and then click the Change button, or double-click the word in the Suggestions list. If none of the suggestions is correct, type the correct word in the Change to box and then click the Change button. To skip correcting the word, click the **Ignore button.** To have Excel ignore the word for the remainder of the worksheet, click the **Ignore All button.**

Consider these additional points regarding the spell checker:

▸ To check the spelling of the text in a single cell, double-click the cell to make the formula bar active and then click the Spelling button on the Standard toolbar.

▸ If you select a single cell so that the formula bar is not active and then start the spell checker, Excel checks the entire worksheet, including notes and embedded charts.

▸ If you select a range of cells before starting the spell checker, Excel checks only the spelling of the words in the selected range.

▸ To check the spelling of a chart, select the chart and then start the spell checker.

▸ To check the spelling of all the sheets in a workbook, click Select All Sheets on the sheet tab shortcut menu and then start the spell checker. To display the sheet tab shortcut menu, right-click the sheet tab.

▸ If you select a cell other than cell A1 before you start the spell checker, a dialog box will display when the spell checker reaches the end of the worksheet, asking if you want to continue checking at the beginning.

▶ To add words to the dictionary, click the **Add button** in the Spelling dialog box (Figure 2-52 on page E 2.39) when Excel identifies the word as not in the dictionary.

▶ Click the **AutoCorrect button** (Figure 2-52) to add the misspelled word and the correct version of the word to the AutoCorrect list. For example, suppose you misspell the word, do, as the word, dox. When the Spelling dialog box displays the correct word, do, in the Change to box, click the Auto-Correct button. Then, anytime in the future that you type the word dox, Excel will change it to the word do.

Saving the Workbook a Second Time Using the Same File Name

Earlier in this project, you saved an intermediate version of the workbook using the file name, High-Tech Stock Club. To save the workbook a second time using the same file name, click the Save button on the Standard toolbar. Excel automatically stores the latest version of the workbook using the same file name, High-Tech Stock Club. When you save a workbook a second time using the same file name, Excel will not display the Save As dialog box as it does the first time you save the workbook. You also can click **Save** on the File menu or press SHIFT+F12 or CTRL+S to save a workbook a second time using the same file name.

If you want to save the workbook using a new name or save it on a different drive, click **Save As** on the File menu. Some Excel users, for example, use the Save button to save the latest version of the workbook on the default drive. Then, they use the Save As command to save a copy on another drive.

Adding a 3-D Pie Chart to the Workbook

The next step in the project is to draw the 3-D Pie chart on a separate sheet, as shown in Figure 2-54. A **pie chart** is used to show the relationship or proportion of parts to a whole. Each slice (or wedge) of the pie shows what percent that slice contributes to the total (100%). The 3-D Pie chart in Figure 2-54 shows the contribution of each stock to the total value of the club's portfolio. The pie chart makes it easy to see that Compaq represents the largest part of the total value.

Unlike the 3-D Column chart in Project 1, the 3-D Pie chart in Figure 2-54 is not embedded in the work-sheet. This pie chart was created on a separate sheet called a **chart sheet**.

FIGURE 2-54

More *About* **Charting**

Line chart, bar chart, pie chart – which chart will best describe my worksheet data? For answers, click Contents and Index on the Help menu. Click the Contents tab. Double-click the Working with Charts book. Double-click the Changing the Type of a Chart book. Double-click the Examples of chart types link and click each chart type.

The ranges in the worksheet to chart are the nonadjacent ranges A3:A7 and H3:H7 (Figure 2-55). The stock names in the range A3:A7 will identify the slices; these entries are called **category names**. The range H3:H7 contains the data that determines the size of the slices in the pie; these entries are called the **data series**. Because there are five stocks, the 3-D Pie chart contains five slices.

This project also calls for emphasizing the stock with the greatest contribution to the total value (Compaq) by offsetting its slice from the main portion. A pie chart with one or more slices offset is called an **exploded pie chart**.

As shown in Figure 2-54 on the previous page, the default 3-D Pie chart also has been enhanced by rotating and tilting the pie forward, changing the colors of the slices, and modifying the chart title and labels that identify the slices.

Drawing the 3-D Pie Chart

To draw the 3-D Pie chart on a separate chart sheet, select the nonadjacent ranges and then click the Chart Wizard button. Once the chart is created, you can format it as shown in Figure 2-54 by completing the following steps:

1. Chart title — change to 36-point Arial, red underlined font.
2. Slice labels — change to 12-point Arial, red font and drag them away from the slices they represent.
3. Slices – change the colors of the slices.
4. Explode the Compaq slice.
5. Rotate and tilt the pie chart to display the Compaq slice more prominently.

Steps To Draw a 3-D Pie Chart

1 Select the range A3:A7. While holding down the CTRL key, select the range H3:H7. Point to the Chart Wizard button on the Standard toolbar.

The nonadjacent ranges are selected (Figure 2-55).

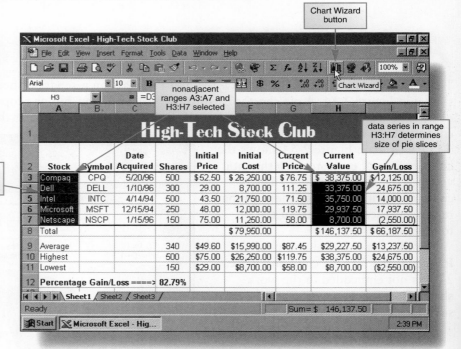

FIGURE 2-55

2 Click the Chart Wizard button. When the Chart Wizard – Step 1 of 4 – Chart Type dialog box displays, click Pie in the Chart type list and then click the 3-D Pie chart (column 2, row 1) in the Chart sub-type box. Point to the Next button.

Excel displays the Chart Wizard – Step 1 of 4 – Chart Type dialog box, which allows you to select one of the fourteen types of charts available in Excel (Figure 2-56).

FIGURE 2-56

3 Click the Next button.

The Chart Wizard – Step 2 of 4 – Chart Source Data dialog box displays, showing a sample of the 3-D Pie chart and the chart data range (Figure 2-57).

FIGURE 2-57

4 **Click the Next button. When the Chart Wizard – Step 3 of 4 – Chart Options dialog box displays, type** Portfolio Breakdown **in the Chart title box. Point to the Legend tab.**

Excel redraws the sample 3-D Pie chart with the chart title, Portfolio Breakdown (Figure 2-58).

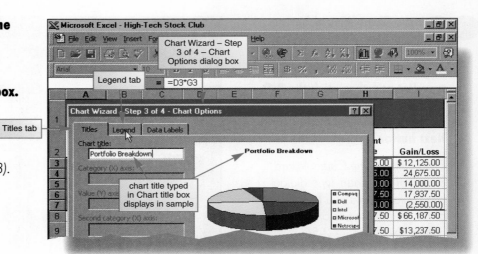

FIGURE 2-58

5 **Click the Legend tab and then click the Show legend check box to remove the check mark. Point to the Data Labels tab.**

The Legend tab displays. Excel redraws the sample 3-D Pie chart without the legend. (Figure 2-59).

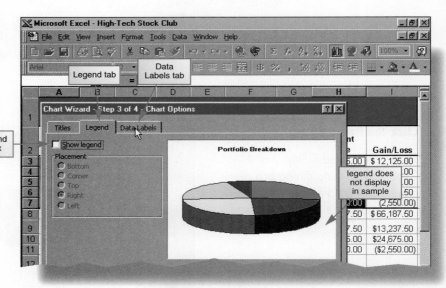

FIGURE 2-59

6 **Click the Data Labels tab. Click the Show label and percent option button in the Data labels area. Point to the Next button.**

The Data Labels sheet displays. Excel redraws the sample 3-D Pie chart with data labels and percents (Figure 2-60).

FIGURE 2-60

7 **Click the Next button. When the Chart Wizard – Step 4 of 4 – Chart Location dialog box displays, click the As new sheet option button. Point to the Finish button.**

The Chart Wizard – Step 4 of 4 – Chart Location dialog box gives you two chart location options: to draw the chart on a new sheet in the workbook or to draw it as an object in a worksheet as you did in Project 1 (Figure 2-61). You also can change the name of the chart sheet in this dialog box.

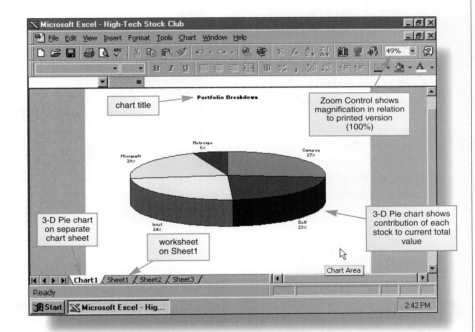

FIGURE 2-61

8 **Click the Finish button.**

Excel draws the 3-D Pie chart on a separate chart sheet in the High-Tech Stock Club workbook (Figure 2-62).

9 **Click the Save button on the Standard toolbar.**

FIGURE 2-62

Each slice of the 3-D Pie chart in Figure 2-62 represents one of the five stocks – Compaq, Dell, Intel, Microsoft, and Netscape. The names of the stocks and the percent contribution to the total value display outside the slices. The chart title, Portfolio Breakdown, displays immediately above the 3-D Pie chart.

Excel determines the direction of the data series range (down a column or across a row) on the basis of the selected range. Because the selection for the 3-D Pie chart is down the worksheet (ranges A3:A7 and H3:H7), Excel automatically selects the Series in Columns option button as shown in Figure 2-57 on page E 2.43.

In any of the four Chart Wizard dialog boxes (Figure 2-56 through Figure 2-61 on pages E 2.43 through E 2.45), you can click the Back button to return to the previous Chart Wizard dialog box. You also can click the Finish button in any of the dialog boxes to create the chart with the options selected thus far.

Formatting the Chart Title and Chart Labels

The next step is to format the chart title and labels that identify the slices. Before you can format a **chart item**, such as the chart title or labels, you must select it. Once a chart item is selected, you can format it using the Formatting toolbar, shortcut menu, special keys, or the Format menu. In the following sections, you will use the Formatting toolbar to format chart items much like you formatted the cell entries earlier in this project. Complete the following steps to format the chart title and labels.

Steps To Format the Chart Title and Labels

1 Click the chart title. Click the Font Size box arrow on the Formatting toolbar and then click 36. Click the Underline button on the Formatting toolbar. Click the Font Color button arrow on the Formatting toolbar and then point to red (column 1, row 3 on the Font Color palette).

Excel displays a box with handles around the chart title, increases the font size of the chart title, and underlines the chart title (Figure 2-63). The Font Color palette displays.

FIGURE 2-63

2 Click the color red. Right-click one of the five data labels that identify the slices. Click the Font Size box arrow on the Formatting toolbar and then click 12. Click the Bold button on the Formatting toolbar. Click the Font Color button on the Formatting toolbar.

The chart title and data labels display in red as shown in Figure 2-64. The data labels are selected.

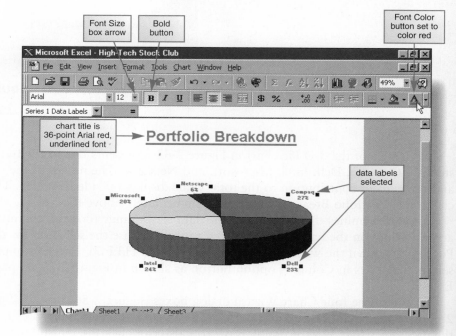

FIGURE 2-64

③ **One at a time, drag each data label away from the slice it represents so the data labels appear as shown in Figure 2-65.**

*The data labels are moved away from each slice. Excel draws thin **leader lines** that connect each data label to its corresponding slice. If the leader lines do not display, click Chart Options on the Chart menu and click the Show leader line option button.*

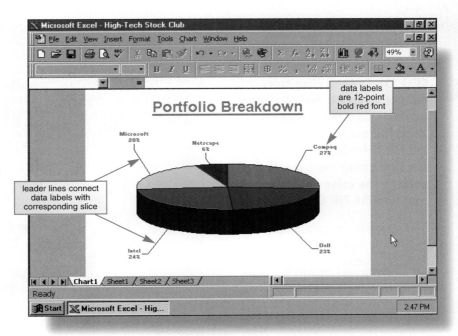

FIGURE 2-65

If you compare Figure 2-65 to Figure 2-62 on page E 2.45, you can see that the labels and chart title are easier to read and make the chart sheet look more professional.

As shown in Figure 2-65, when you drag a data label away from the 3-D Pie chart, Excel draws thin lines, called leader lines, to connect the labels to the corresponding slices. You also can select and format individual labels by clicking a specific data label after all the data labels have been selected. Making an individual data label larger or a different color, for example, helps you emphasize a small or large slice in a pie chart.

Changing the Colors of the Slices

The next step is to change the colors of the slices of the pie. The colors shown in Figure 2-66 on the next page are the default colors Excel uses when you first create a pie chart. Project 2 requires that the colors be changed to those shown in Figure 2-54 on page E 2.41. To change the colors of the slices, select them one at a time and use the Fill Color button on the Formatting toolbar as shown in the steps on the next page.

Steps To Change the Colors of the Pie Slices

1 Click the Compaq slice twice, once to select all the slices and once to select the individual slice. (Do not double-click.) Click the Fill Color button arrow on the Formatting toolbar and then point to the color red (column 1, row 3 on the Fill Color palette).

Excel displays resizing handles around the Compaq slice and the Fill Color palette displays (Figure 2-66).

FIGURE 2-66

2 Click the color red.

Excel changes the Compaq slice to the color red.

3 One at a time, click the remaining slices and then use the Fill Color palette to change each slice to the following colors: Netscape – blue (column 6, row 2); Microsoft – yellow (column 3, row 4); Intel – green (column 4, row 2); Dell – plum (column 7, row 4). Click outside the chart area.

The pie chart displays as shown in Figure 2-67.

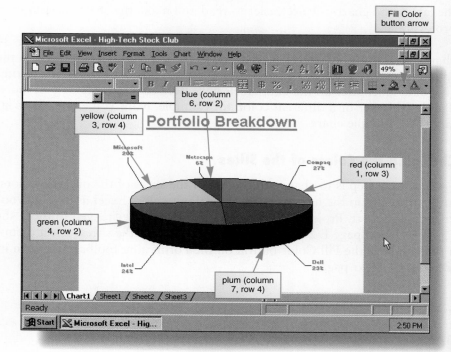

FIGURE 2-67

OtherWays

1. Right-click selected slice, on shortcut menu click Format Data Point, click Patterns tab, click color, click OK button

2. On Format menu click Selected Data Point, click Patterns tab, click color, click OK button

Exploding the 3-D Pie Chart

The next step is to emphasize the slice representing Compaq by offsetting, or **exploding**, it from the rest of the slices. Of the five stocks, Compaq represents the greatest profit contributor in the portfolio; by exploding it, you can make this slice stand out from the rest. Perform the following steps to explode a slice of the 3-D Pie chart.

 Steps To Explode the 3-D Pie Chart

1 **Click the slice labeled Compaq twice. (Do not double-click.)**

Excel displays resizing handles around the Compaq slice.

2 **Drag the slice to the desired position and then release the left mouse button.**

Excel redraws the 3-D Pie chart with the Compaq slice offset from the rest of the slices (Figure 2-68).

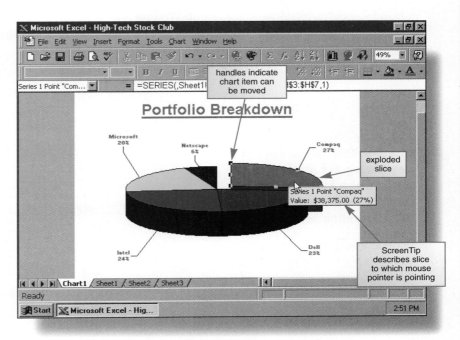

FIGURE 2-68

You can offset as many slices as you want, but remember that the reason for offsetting a slice is to emphasize it. Offsetting multiple slices tends to reduce the impact on the reader.

Rotating and Tilting the 3-D Pie Chart

With a three-dimensional chart, you can change the view to better display the section of the chart you are trying to emphasize. Excel allows you to control the rotation angle, elevation, perspective, height, and angle of the axes by using the **3-D View command** on the Chart menu.

To obtain a better view of the offset Compaq slice, you can rotate the 3-D Pie chart 190⁰ to the left. The rotation angle of the 3-D Pie chart is defined by the line that divides the Compaq and Netscape slices. When Excel initially draws a pie chart, it always points one of the dividing lines between two slices to twelve o'clock (or zero degrees). Besides rotating the 3-D Pie chart, the steps on the next page also change, or tilt, the elevation so the 3-D Pie chart is at less of an angle to the viewer.

More *About*
Exploding a 3-D Pie Chart

If you click the 3-D Pie Chart so that all the slices are selected, you can drag one of the slices to explode all of the slices.

Steps **To Rotate and Tilt the 3-D Pie Chart**

1 **With the Compaq slice selected, click Chart on the menu bar and point to 3-D View.**

The Chart menu displays as shown in Figure 2-69.

FIGURE 2-69

2 **Click 3-D View. When the 3-D View dialog box displays, click the Up Arrow button in the 3-D View dialog box until 25 displays in the Elevation box.**

The 3-D View dialog box displays (Figure 2-70). A sample of the 3-D Pie chart displays in the dialog box. The result of increasing the elevation of the 3-D Pie chart is to tilt it forward.

FIGURE 2-70

3 **Rotate the pie chart by clicking the Right Rotation button until the Rotation box displays 190.**

The new rotation setting (190) displays in the Rotation box as shown in Figure 2-71. A sample of the rotated pie chart displays in the dialog box.

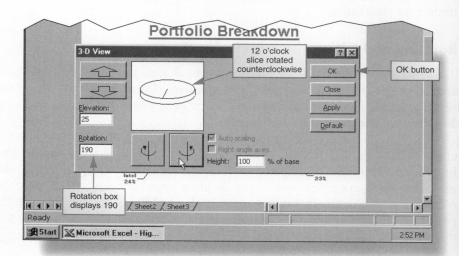

FIGURE 2-71

4 Click the OK button.

Excel displays the 3-D Pie chart tilted forward and rotated to the left, which makes the space between the Compaq slice and the main portion of the pie more prominent (Figure 2-72).

5 Click the Save button on the Standard toolbar.

FIGURE 2-72

Compare Figure 2-72 to Figure 2-68 on page E 2.49. The offset of the Compaq slice is more noticeable in Figure 2-72 because the pie chart has been tilted and rotated to expose the white space between the Compaq slice and the main portion of the 3-D Pie chart.

In addition to controlling the rotation angle and elevation, you also can control the thickness of the 3-D Pie chart by entering a percent smaller or larger than the default 100% in the Height box (Figure 2-70).

The 3-D Pie chart is complete. The next step is to change the names of the sheets and reorder the sheets so the worksheet is first, followed by the chart. If you look at the sheet tabs below the pie chart in Figure 2-72, you will see that Sheet1, which contains the worksheet, follows the sheet labeled Chart1.

Changing the Sheet Names and Rearranging the Order of the Sheets

At the bottom of the screen (Figure 2-72) are the tabs that allow you to display any sheet in the workbook. Excel assigns the default names to the worksheets, such as Sheet1, Sheet2, and so on. When you draw a chart on a separate sheet, Excel assigns the default name Chart1 to the chart sheet, unless you change the sheet name in the last dialog box displayed by the Chart Wizard (Figure 2-61 on page E 2.45). To change the name of a sheet, double-click the sheet tab and then enter the new name. The steps on the next page show you how to rename sheets by double-clicking the sheet tabs and how to reorder the sheets so the worksheet comes before the chart sheet.

> ◆ **More** *About*
> ## Changing a Pie Chart's Perspective
>
> You can increase or decrease the base height (thickness) of the pie chart by changing the height to base ratio in the Format 3-D View dialog box.

> ◆ **More** *About*
> ## Sheet Tabs
>
> To move from sheet to sheet in a workbook, you click the sheet tabs at the bottom of the window. The name of the active sheet is always bold on a white background. Through the shortcut menu, you can rename the sheets, reorder the sheets, add and delete sheets, and move or copy sheets within a workbook or to another workbook.

Steps **To Rename the Sheets and Rearrange the Order of the Sheets**

1 **Double-click the tab labeled Chart1 in the lower-left corner of the window. Type** 3-D Pie Chart **as the new tab label and then press the ENTER key.**

The tab label changes from Chart1 to 3-D Pie Chart (Figure 2-73).

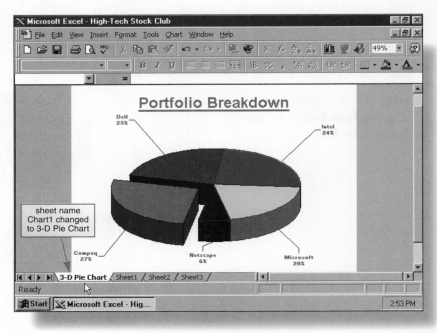

FIGURE 2-73

2 **Double-click the tab labeled Sheet1 in the lower-left corner of the window. Type** Investment Analysis **as the tab label and then press the ENTER key. Drag the Investment Analysis tab to the left and hold.**

The tab label changes from Sheet1 to Investment Analysis (Figure 2-74). The mouse pointer changes to an arrow with a document icon as you drag the tab.

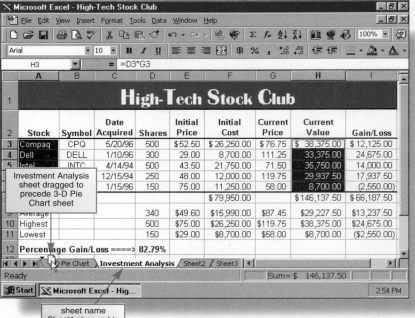

FIGURE 2-74

3 Release the left mouse button. Click any cell.

Excel reorders the sheets so the Investment Analysis worksheet is the first sheet in the workbook (Figure 2-75).

4 Click the Save button on the Standard toolbar.

FIGURE 2-75

Other Ways

1. To rename, right-click sheet tab, click Rename
2. To move, right-click sheet tab, click Move or Copy
3. To move, on the Edit menu click Move or Copy
4. Right-click tab scrolling buttons, on shortcut menu click desired sheet

Sheet names can be up to 31 characters (including spaces) in length. Longer sheet names, however, mean that fewer tabs will display. To display more sheet tabs, you can drag the **tab split box** (Figure 2-75) to the right. This will reduce the size of the scroll bar at the bottom of the screen. Double-click the tab split box to reset it to its normal position.

You also can use the **tab scrolling buttons** to the left of the sheet tabs (Figure 2-75) to move between sheets. The leftmost and rightmost scroll buttons move to the first or last sheet in the workbook. The two middle scroll buttons move one sheet to the left or right.

Previewing and Printing Selected Sheets in a Workbook

In Project 1, you printed the worksheet without previewing it on the screen. By previewing the worksheet, you see exactly how it will look without generating a printout, or hard copy. Previewing a worksheet using the **Print Preview command** or **Print Preview button** on the Standard toolbar can save time, paper, and the frustration of waiting for a printout only to discover it is not what you want.

The Print Preview command, as well as the Print command, will preview or print only selected sheets. You know a sheet is selected when the sheet tab at the bottom of the screen is white. Thus, in Figure 2-75, the Investment Analysis sheet is selected, but the 3-D Pie Chart sheet is not. To select additional adjacent sheets, hold down the SHIFT key and then click the sheet tab of the last sheet you wish to select. This will select all sheets between the active sheet and the one clicked. To select a nonadjacent sheet, hold down the CTRL key and then select the desired sheet tab.

More *About* **Sheets**

You can use the keyboard to move from sheet to sheet in a workbook. Press CRTL+PGUP to move to the next sheet. Press CRTL+PGDN to move to the previous sheet.

Steps: To Preview Selected Sheets in a Workbook

1 While holding down the SHIFT key, click the 3-D Pie Chart sheet tab. Point to the Print Preview button on the Standard toolbar.

Both the worksheet and the chart sheet are selected (Figure 2-76).

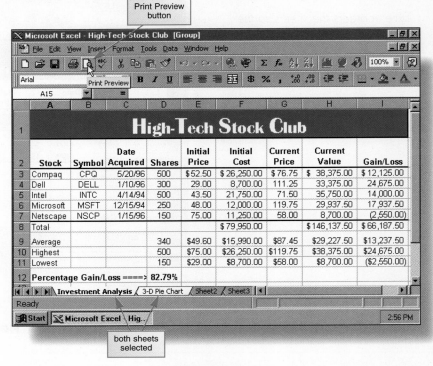

FIGURE 2-76

2 Click the Print Preview button on the Standard toolbar.

Excel displays a preview of the worksheet in the preview window and the mouse pointer changes to a magnifying glass (Figure 2-77). The word [Group] in the title bar indicates that multiple sheets are selected.

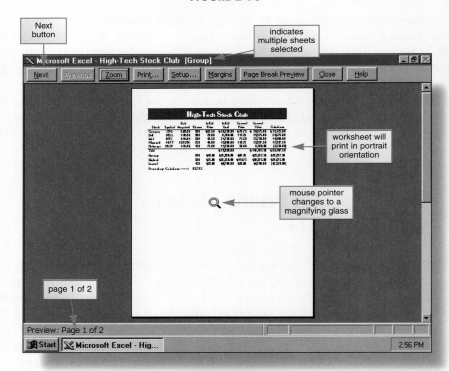

FIGURE 2-77

(3) **Click the Next button to display a preview of the chart.**

A preview of the 3-D Pie chart displays (Figure 2-78).

(4) **Click the Close button in the Preview window to return to the workbook.**

FIGURE 2-78

Excel displays several buttons at the top of the Preview window (Figure 2-78). The functions of these buttons are summarized in Table 2-3.

Rather than click the Next and Previous buttons to move from page to page as described in Table 2-3, you also can press the PAGE UP and PAGE DOWN keys. You also can click the page in the Preview window when the mouse pointer is a magnifying glass to carry out the function of the Zoom button.

Printing Selected Sheets in a Workbook

Although you could have printed the two selected sheets from the Preview window, the steps on the next page show how to print them using the Print button on the Standard toolbar.

Table 2-3

BUTTON	FUNCTION
Next	Previews the next page
Previous	Previews the previous page
Zoom	Magnifies or reduces the print preview
Print...	Prints previewed sheets
Setup...	Displays Print Setup dialog box
Margins	Changes print margins
Page Break Preview	Previews page breaks
Close	Closes the preview window
Help	Displays help on the Preview window

▶*Other*Ways
1. Right-click menu, click Page Setup, click Print Preview button
2. On File menu click Print Preview
3. On File menu click Page Setup, click Print Preview button
4. On File menu click Print, click Entire Workbook, click Preview button

More *About*
Print Preview

A popular button in the Preview window (Figure 2-78) is the Margins button. The Margins button allows you to drag the top, bottom, left, and right margins to center a worksheet or add room to fit a wide or long worksheet on a page. You can even change the column widths.

Steps To Print Selected Sheets in a Workbook

1 **Click the Investment Analysis sheet tab. If both sheets are not selected, while holding down the SHIFT key, click the inactive sheet tab.**

2 **Point to the Print button on the Standard toolbar (Figure 2-79).**

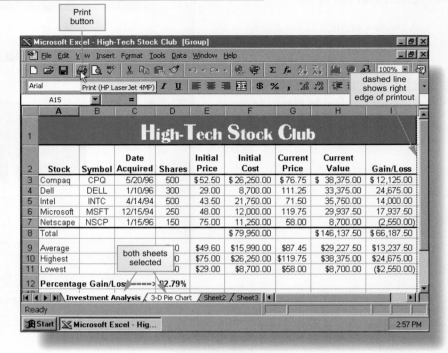

FIGURE 2-79

3 **Click the Print button.**

Excel prints the worksheet (Figure 2-80a) and the 3-D Pie chart on the printer (Figure 2-80b).

4 **While holding down the SHIFT key, click the Investment Analysis tab to deselect the 3-D Pie chart sheet.**

FIGURE 2-80a

FIGURE 2-80b

Other Ways

1. Right-click tab, click Select All Sheets, click Print button

2. On File menu click Print, click Entire workbook option, click OK button

In Step 4, you also could have right-clicked the Investment Analysis tab and then clicked Ungroup Sheets to deselect the 3-D Pie Chart sheet.

As shown in Figures 2-80a and 2-80b, the worksheet is printed in portrait orientation and the chart is printed in landscape orientation. **Portrait orientation** means the printout is printed across the width of the page. **Landscape orientation** means the printout is printed across the length of the page. For any chart created on a separate sheet, Excel automatically sets it to print in landscape orientation.

Printing a Section of the Worksheet

You might not always want to print the entire worksheet. You can print portions of the worksheet by selecting the range of cells to print and then click the **Selection option button** in the **Print what area** on the Print dialog box. The steps on the next page show how to print the range A2:F7.

More *About* Printing

A dark font on a dark background, such as a red font on a blue background, will not print properly on a black and white printer. For black and white printing, use a light colored font on a dark background and a dark font on a light colored background.

Steps To Print a Section of the Worksheet

1 Select the range A2:F7. Click Print on the File menu. Click the Selection option button in the Print what area in the Print dialog box. Point to the OK button.

Excel displays the Print dialog box (Figure 2-81). Because the Selection option button is selected, Excel will print only the selected range.

FIGURE 2-81

2 Click the OK button.

Excel prints the selected range of the worksheet on the printer (Figure 2-82).

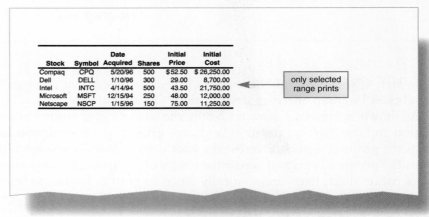

FIGURE 2-82

There are three option buttons in the Print what area in the Print dialog box (Figure 2-81). As shown in the previous steps, the Selection option button instructs Excel to print the selected range. The **Active sheet(s) option button** instructs Excel to print the active sheet (the one displaying on the screen) or the selected sheets. Finally, the **Entire workbook option button** instructs Excel to print all the sheets in the workbook. Selecting the Entire workbook option button is an alternative to selecting tabs by holding down the SHIFT or CTRL keys and then clicking tabs to make the sheets active. The Active sheets option is the default.

Displaying and Printing the Formulas in the Worksheet

Thus far, you have been working with the **values version** of the worksheet, which shows the results of the formulas you have entered, rather than the actual formulas. Excel also allows you to display and print the **formulas version** of the worksheet, which displays the actual formulas you have entered, rather than the resulting values. You can toggle between the values version and formulas version by pressing CTRL+` (left single quotation mark to the left of the number 1 key).

The formulas version is useful for debugging a worksheet. **Debugging** is the process of finding and correcting errors in the worksheet. Because the formula version displays and prints formulas and functions, rather than the results, it makes it easier to see if any mistakes were made in the formulas.

When you change from the values version to the formulas version, Excel increases the width of the columns so the formulas and text do not overflow into adjacent cells on the right. The formulas version of the worksheet thus is usually significantly wider than the values version. To fit the wide printout on one page, you can use landscape orientation and the **Fit to option** on the Page tab in the Page Setup dialog box. To change from the values version to the formulas version of the worksheet and print the formulas on one page, perform the following steps.

Steps To Display the Formulas in the Worksheet and Fit the Printout on One Page

 Press CTRL + ` (left single quotation mark to the left of the number 1 key). Scroll to the right so column I displays.

Excel changes the display of the worksheet from values to formulas (Figure 2-83). The formulas in the worksheet display showing unformatted numbers, formulas, and functions that were assigned to the cells. Excel automatically increases the column widths.

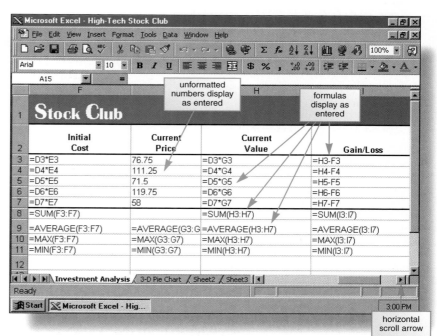

FIGURE 2-83

2 Click Page Setup on the File menu. When the Page Setup dialog box displays, click the Page tab, click the Landscape option, and click the Fit to option button so the wide worksheet prints on one page in landscape orientation. Point to the Print button.

Excel displays the Page Setup dialog box with the Landscape and Fit to option buttons selected (Figure 2-84).

FIGURE 2-84

3 Click the Print button in the Page Setup dialog box. When the Print dialog box displays, click the OK button. When you are done viewing and printing the formulas version, press CTRL+` to display the values version.

Excel prints the formulas in the worksheet on one page in landscape orientation (Figure 2-85).

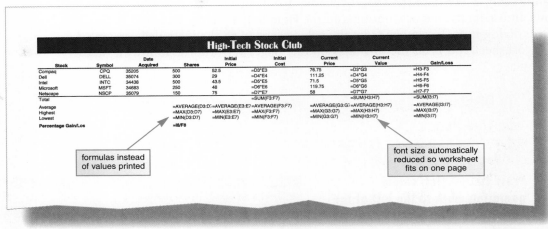

FIGURE 2-85

Although the formulas version of the worksheet was printed in the previous example, you can see from Figure 2-83 on the previous page that the display on the screen also can be used for debugging the worksheet.

As shown in Figure 2-79 on page E 2.56, a dashed line displays on the screen to represent the right edge of the printed worksheet. If the entries in a worksheet extend past this dashed line, the printout will be made up of multiple pages. If you prefer to print the worksheet on one page, click the Fit to option button in the Page Setup dialog box (Figure 2-84) before you print. The Fit to option was used to print the formulas version of the Investment Analysis worksheet, for example, so it would fit on one page.

Changing the Print Scaling Option Back to 100%

Depending on your printer driver, you may have to change the Print Scaling option back to 100% after using the Fit to option. Complete the following steps to reset the Print Scaling option so future worksheets print at 100%, instead of being squeezed on one page.

TO CHANGE THE PRINT SCALING OPTION BACK TO 100%

1. Click Page Setup on the File menu.
2. Click the Page tab in the Page Setup dialog box. Click the Adjust to option in the Scaling area.
3. If necessary, type 100 in the Adjust to box.
4. Click the OK button.

The Adjust to box allows you to specify the percentage of reduction or enlargement in the printout of a worksheet. The default percentage is 100%. When you click the Fit to option, this percentage automatically changes to the percentage required to fit the printout on one page.

Getting External Data from a Web Source Using a Web Query

One of the major features of Excel 97 is its capability to obtain external data from sites on the World Wide Web. To get external data from a World Wide Web site, you must have access to the Internet. You then can run a **Web query** to retrieve data stored on the World Wide Web site. When you run a Web query, Excel returns the external data in the form of a worksheet. As described in Table 2-4, there are four Web queries available when you first install Excel. Three of the four Web queries available relate to investment and stock market activities.

Table 2-4	
QUERY	EXTERNAL DATA RETURNED
Detailed Stock Quote by PC Quote, Inc	Data for a specific stock of your choice
Dow Jones Stocks by PC Quote, Inc	Data for the 30 stocks that make up the Dow Jones Industrial Average
Get More Web Queries	Download additional Web queries
Multiple Stock Quotes by PC Quote, Inc	Data for up to 20 stocks of your choice

The data returned by the stock-related Web queries is real-time in the sense that it is no more than 20 minutes old during the business day. The steps on the next page show how to get the most recent stock quotes for the five stocks owned by the High-Tech Stock Club — Compaq, Dell, Intel, Microsoft, and Netscape. Although you can have a Web query return data to a blank workbook, the following steps have the data returned to a blank worksheet in the High-Tech Stock Club workbook.

Steps To Get External Data from a Web Source Using a Web Query

1 With the High-Tech Stock Club workbook open, click the Sheet2 tab at the bottom of the screen. Click cell A1.

2 On the Data menu, point to Get External Data and then point to Run Web Query on the Get External Data submenu.

The Get External Data submenu displays as shown in Figure 2-86.

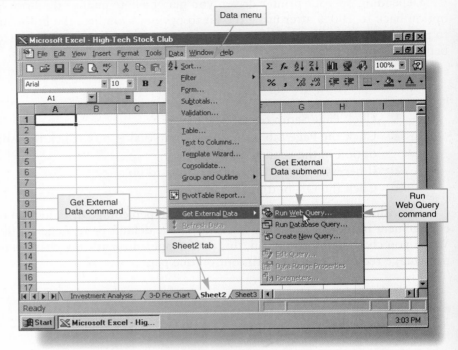

FIGURE 2-86

3 Click Run Web Query. When the Run Query dialog box displays, click Multiple Stock Quotes by PC Quote, Inc. Point to the Get Data button.

The Run Query dialog box displays (Figure 2-87). If your display is different, ask your instructor for the folder location of the Web queries.

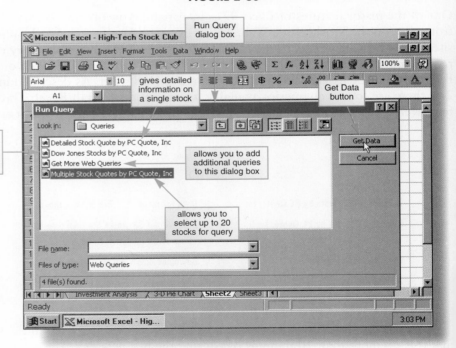

FIGURE 2-87

4 Click the Get Data button. When the Returning External Data to Microsoft Excel dialog box displays, click the Existing worksheet option button, if necessary, to select it. Point to the OK button.

The *Returning External Data to Microsoft Excel dialog box* displays (Figure 2-88). The Existing worksheet option button is selected and the active cell A1 displays in the Existing worksheet box, meaning that the external data will be returned to a range starting with cell A1.

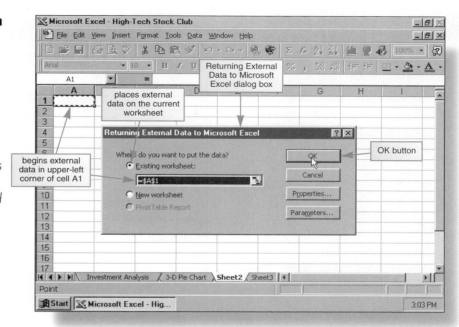

FIGURE 2-88

5 Click the OK button. When the Enter Parameter Value dialog box displays, type the stock symbols cpq dell intc msft nscp in the box. Click the Use this value/reference for future refreshes check box to select it. Point to the OK button.

The *Enter Parameter Value dialog box* displays (Figure 2-89). You can enter up to 20 stock symbols separated by spaces.

FIGURE 2-89

6 **Click the OK button. Double-click the Sheet2 tab and then type** Web Query **as the sheet name. Press the ENTER key.**

If you are using a modem, Excel will display a dialog box that connects you to the Internet via your provider. If you are directly connected to the Internet through a network, the dialog box does not display. Once your computer connects to the Internet, a message displays to inform you that Excel is getting external data. A small spinning globe displays on the status bar to indicate that the query is running. After a short period, Excel displays a new worksheet with the desired data (Figure 2-90).

FIGURE 2-90

7 **Click the Save button on the Standard toolbar.**

As shown in Figure 2-90, Excel displays the data returned from the Web query in an organized, formatted worksheet, which has a worksheet title, column titles, and a row of data for each stock symbol entered. Other than the first column, which contains the stock name and stock symbol, you have no control over the remaining columns of data returned. The latest price of each stock displays in column B.

Once the worksheet displays, you can refresh the data as often as you want. To refresh the data for all the stocks, click the **Refresh All button** on the **External Data toolbar** (Figure 2-91). Because the Use this value/reference for future refreshes check box was clicked (Figure 2-89 on the previous page), Excel will continue to use the same stock symbols each time it refreshes. You can change the symbols by clicking the **Query Parameters button** on the External Data toolbar. You also can refresh one stock at a time by clicking the cell with the company name and symbol in column A and then clicking the **Refresh Data button** on the External Data toolbar.

FIGURE 2-91

If the External Data toolbar does not display, right-click any toolbar and then click External Data. You also can invoke any Web query command by right-clicking the worksheet to display a shortcut menu.

The down arrows that display in the lower-right corner of the cells containing the column titles (row 4) are called **AutoFilter arrows**; they allow you to display only those stocks that meet the selected criteria. For example, if you click the AutoFilter arrow in cell A4 and then click INTEL CORP in the list box, Excel will hide all the stocks except for Intel.

This section gives you an idea of the potential of Web queries by having you use just one of Excel's many available Web queries. To reinforce the topics covered here, work through In the Lab 3 at the end of this project.

Quitting Excel

After completing the worksheet, 3-D Pie chart, and Web query, you can quit Excel by performing the following steps.

TO QUIT EXCEL

① Click the Investment Analysis tab.
② Click the Close button on the upper-right corner of the title bar.
③ When the Microsoft Excel dialog box displays, click the Yes button.

Project Summary

The worksheet, 3-D Pie chart, and Web query (Figure 2-1 on page E 2.6) you created for Alex Hansen will serve his purpose well. The worksheet, which he plans to e-mail to the club members, contains valuable information in an easy to read format. The 3-D Pie chart dramatically shows the contribution of each stock to the current value of the club's portfolio. Finally, the Web query allows Alex to obtain the latest stock prices to keep the workbook as up-to-date as possible.

In creating the High-Tech Stock Club workbook, you learned how to enter formulas, calculate an average, find the highest and lowest numbers in a range, change fonts, draw borders, format numbers, and change column widths and row heights. You learned how to create a 3-D Pie chart on a separate chart sheet, format the pie chart, rename sheet tabs, preview a worksheet, print a workbook, print a section of a worksheet and display and print the formulas in the worksheet using the Fit to option. You also learned how to complete a Web query and generate a worksheet using external data obtained from the World Wide Web.

What You Should Know

Having completed this project, you now should be able to perform the following tasks:

- Apply a Currency Style Format and Comma Style Format Using the Formatting Toolbar (E 2.30)
- Apply a Currency Style with a Floating Dollar Sign Using the Format Cells Command (E 2.32)
- Apply a Percentage Format (E 2.34)
- Bold, Center, and Underline the Column Titles (E 2.28)
- Center Data in Cells (E 2.29)
- Change the Background and Font Colors and Apply an Outline Border (E 2.26)
- Change the Colors of the Pie Slices (E 2.48)
- Change the Font and Center the Worksheet Title (E 2.23)
- Change the Height of a Row by Dragging (E 2.37)
- Change the Print Scaling Option Back to 100% (E 2.61)
- Change the Width of a Column by Dragging (E 2.35)
- Check Spelling in the Worksheet (E 2.39)
- Copy a Range of Cells Across Columns to an Adjacent Range Using the Fill Handle (E 2.20)
- Copy Formulas Using the Fill Handle (E 2.13)
- Determine the Average of a Range of Numbers Using the Keyboard and Mouse (E 2.15)
- Determine the Highest Number in a Range of Numbers Using the Edit Formula Box and Function Box (E 2.16)
- Determine the Lowest Number in a Range of Numbers Using the Paste Function Button (E 2.18)
- Determine Totals Using the AutoSum Button (E 2.14)
- Display the Formulas in the Worksheet and Fit the Printout on One Page (E 2.59)
- Draw a 3-D Pie Chart (E 2.42)
- Enter a Formula Using the Keyboard (E 2.9)
- Enter a Percentage Formula (E 2.21)
- Enter Formulas Using Point Mode (E 2.11)
- Enter the Column Titles (E 2.8)
- Enter the Stock Data (E 2.8)
- Enter the Total Row Titles (E 2.9)
- Enter the Worksheet Title (E 2.7)
- Explode the 3-D Pie Chart (E 2.49)
- Format the Chart Title and Labels (E 2.46)
- Get External Data from a Web Source Using a Web Query (E 2.62)
- Preview Selected Sheets in a Workbook (E 2.54)
- Print a Section of the Worksheet (E 2.58)
- Print Selected Sheets in a Workbook (E 2.56)
- Quit Excel (E 2.65)
- Rename the Sheets and Rearrange the Order of the Sheets (E 2.52)
- Rotate and Tilt the 3-D Pie Chart (E 2.50)
- Start Excel (E 2.7)

Test Your Knowledge

1 True/False

Instructions: Circle T if the statement is true or F if the statement is false.

T F 1. To assign a Currency style format with a floating dollar sign to the selected range, click the Currency Style button on the Formatting toolbar.

T F 2. The minimum row height is zero.

T F 3. If you enter the formula =10 * 3 into a cell, the number 30 displays in the cell.

T F 4. In the formula =4 * 6 – 8, the subtraction operation (–) is completed before the multiplication operation (*).

T F 5. The formulas =A4 * d3, =a4 * d3, and =A4*D3 result in the same value being assigned to the active cell.

T F 6. You can assign a function to a cell by typing it in the formula bar, clicking the Edit Formula box in the formula bar, and selecting a function from the Function box, or by clicking the Paste Function button on the Standard toolbar.

T F 7. If you use Point mode to enter a formula or select a range, you must press the ENTER key to complete the entry.

T F 8. If the function =MAX(A5:A8) assigns a value of 32 to cell H10, and cell H10 then is copied to cell I10, cell I10 may or may not equal 32.

T F 9. To run a Web query, click Consolidate on the Data menu.

T F 10. The Formula palette displays when you click the Edit Formula box in the formula bar.

2 Multiple Choice

Instructions: Circle the correct response.

1. If the following arithmetic operations all are found in a formula with no parentheses, which one is completed last?
   a. +   c. /
   b. *   d. ^

2. To alert Excel that you are entering a formula and not text, type a(n) _____ preceding the formula.
   a. ampersand (&)   c. number sign (#)
   b. equal sign (=)   d. asterisk (*)

3. When you copy a formula with relative cell references down a row, _____.
   a. the row references change in the formula
   b. the column references change in the formula
   c. no references are changed in the formula
   d. the cell reference of the formula remains the same

(continued)

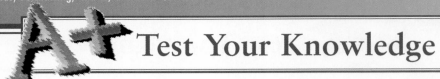

Test Your Knowledge

Multiple Choice *(continued)*

4. The mouse pointer changes to a(n) _____ when you point to the boundary of a column heading or row heading.
    a. magnifying glass   c. cross hair
    b. arrow   d. plus sign with two arrowheads

5. The maximum height of a row is _____ points.
    a. 356   c. 255
    b. 409   d. 31

6. When Excel starts and a blank worksheet displays, the columns have a default width of _____ and the rows have a default height of _____.
    a. 8.43 characters, 12.75 points
    b. 12.75 characters, 8.43 points
    c. 9.43 characters, 15.00 points
    d. 15.00 characters, 9.43 points

7. When Excel automatically sets the width of a column based on the widest entry in the column, it is called _____.
    a. custom fit   c. best fit
    b. choice fit   d. close fit

8. The _____ version of the worksheet displays the results of the formulas entered into its cells.
    a. formulas   c. formatted
    b. displayed   d. values

9. A sheet tab name can be up to _____ characters in length.
    a. 31   c. 12
    b. 255   d. 48

10. To change the elevation of a selected pie chart, click _____ on the Chart menu.
    a. Format Data Series   c. Format 3-D Pie Group
    b. 3-D View   d. Chart Type

3 Entering Formulas

Instructions: Using the values in the worksheet in Figure 2-92, write the formula that accomplishes the task for each of the following items and then compute the value assigned to the specified cell.

	A	B	C	D	E
3	Base	12	0	9	1
4	Height	1	6	1	15
5	Length	3	10	7	8
6	Width	5	2	13	11
7	Volume	4	21	6	2

FIGURE 2-92

Test Your Knowledge

1. Use the natural language method of entering a formula as described on page E 2.12 to assign cell B8 the product of cells B3, B4, and B5.

   Formula: _____   Result: _____

2. Assign cell C8 the result of adding cells C3 and C5 and then dividing the sum by cell C6.

   Formula: _____   Result: _____

3. Assign cell C9 the sum of the range D3:E4 minus the value in cell E6.

   Formula: _____   Result: _____

4. Assign cell E8 three times the product of cells E6 and cell E7.

   Formula: _____   Result: _____

5. Assign cell F3 the sum of the range of cells B3:E3 minus the product of cells B6 and B7.

   Formula: _____   Result: _____

6. Assign cell B9 the result of cell B7 minus cell D4 raised to cell B5.

   Formula: _____   Result: _____

7. Assign cell E9 the expression (A ^ 3 - 4 * B * C) / (2 * B) where the value of A is in cell D7, the value of B is in cell D6, and the value of C is in cell D3. Show the result to four decimal places.

   Formula: _____   Result: _____

4 Understanding Formulas

Instructions: Figure 2-93 displays the formulas version of a worksheet. In the spaces provided, indicate the numeric value assigned to the cells if the numbers display instead of the formulas.

1. D1 _____

2. D2 _____

3. D3 _____

4. A4 _____

5. B4 _____

6. C4 _____

	A	B	C	D
1	12	5	9	=C1+A1*B1
2	2	3	4	=(A3-A1)^A2
3	32	15	11	=A1+C1*A2/B2-B3
4	=C2	=SUM(B1:B3)	=(10+B3)*50%	

FIGURE 2-93

Use Help

1 Reviewing Project Activities

Instructions: Perform the following tasks using a computer.

1. Start Excel. Click Contents and Index on the Help menu. Click the Contents tab. Double-click the Creating Formulas and Auditing Workbooks book.
2. Double-click the Entering Formulas book. One at a time, double-click each of the ten links in the Entering Formulas book. Read and print the information for each link. To print the information, click the Print Topic command on the shortcut menu. To return to the previous dialog box, click the Help Topics button. Hand in the printouts to your instructor.
3. Repeat Step 2 for the Using Functions book. Print six of the thirteen links.
4. If the Help Topics: Microsoft Excel dialog box is not on the screen, click Contents and Index on the Help menu. Click the Find tab. Type row height in the top text box labeled 1. Double-click Change row height in the lower list box labeled 3. Read and print the information. Click the Close button to close the Microsoft Excel Help window. Hand in the printout to your instructor.
5. Click the Office Assistant button on the Standard toolbar. Type how do i format numbers in the Office Assistant balloon. Click the Search button. Click the button labeled Number formatting. One at a time, click the three links. Print the information for each link by using the Print Topic command on the shortcut menu. Hand in the printouts to your instructor.

2 Expanding on the Basics

Instructions: Use Excel online Help and the Office Assistant to better understand the topics listed below. Begin numbers 1 and 2 by clicking Contents and Index on the Help menu. If you are unable to print the Help information, then answer the questions on your own paper.

1. Click the Contents tab. Double-click the book titled, Using Microsoft Excel with the Internet, Your Intranet, or a Local Web. Double-click the book titled, Working with Files on the Web. Double-click the link titled, Get data from a Web source. Read the information and then click the button in step 4 for more information. Print the linked topic, click the Back button, and then print the topic, Get data from a Web source. Click the Close button. Hand in the printouts to your instructor.
2. Click the Find tab and then type web in the text box labeled 1. In the lower list box labeled 3, scroll down and double-click the topic, What's new with Microsoft Excel on the Web? Read and print the information. Hand in the printout to your instructor.
3. Use the Office Assistant to answer the question, How do I use Web queries? Click the button labeled, About creating a PivotTable from an external data source. Read and print the information and then click the Help Topics button. Click the Index tab and then type web in the text box labeled 1. Double-click queries in the list box labeled 2 and then double-click the topic, Create a Web query, in the Topics Found dialog box. Read the information and then print it. Hand in the printouts to your instructor.

Apply Your Knowledge

1 Changing the Appearance of a Pie Chart

Instructions: Start Excel. Open the workbook, Featherbed Factory Cost Analysis, from the Excel folder on the Data Disk that accompanies this book. Perform the following tasks to change the appearance of the 3-D Pie chart that accompanies the worksheet to make it look like Figure 2-94.

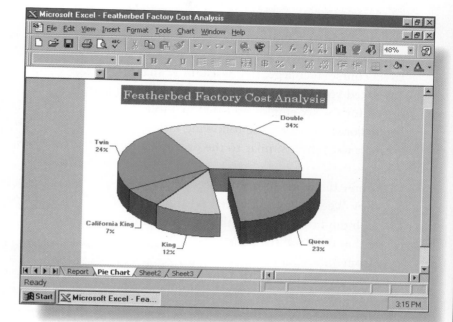

FIGURE 2-94

1. Double-click the Chart1 tab in the lower-left corner of the window. Change the sheet name to Pie Chart. Drag the sheet named Report to the left of the sheet named Pie Chart. Click the Pie Chart tab to display the 3-D Pie chart.

2. Click the 3-D Pie chart title and then change the font to 28 point, silver (column 2, row 5 on the Font Color palette). Change the chart title background to blue-gray (column 7, row 2 on the Fill Color palette).

3. Click one of the data labels that identify the slices. Change the font to 14 point blue-gray, bold.

4. With the Queen slice selected, click 3-D View on the Chart menu. Change the elevation to 30° and the rotation to 240°.

5. Click the Queen slice twice. (Do not double-click.) Drag it away from the other slices. One at a time, drag the data labels away from their slices so the 3-D Pie chart displays as shown in Figure 2-94.

6. If the Queen slice is not selected, click it twice. (Do not double-click.) Change the color of the slice to coral (column 6, row 6 on the Fill Color palette).

7. Print the 3-D Pie chart. Save the workbook using the file name Featherbed Factory Cost Analysis 2.

8. Click the Report tab. Change the Quantity On Hand (column F) for Twin to 19, Double to 27, and Queen to 26. After the changes, the total cost in cell G9 should be $9,734.81. Click the Pie Chart tab. Notice how the size of the slices changed to reflect the new entries. While holding down the CTRL key, click the Report tab. Preview and print the selected sheets. Close the workbook without saving the changes.

In the Lab

1 Security Lock & Key Weekly Payroll Worksheet

Problem: The Security Lock & Key Company has hired you as a work-study student in its software applications area. Because you took an Excel course in college, the Assistant Manager has asked you to prepare a weekly payroll report for the six employees listed in Table 2-5.

Instructions: Perform the following tasks to create a worksheet similar to the one in Figure 2-95.

1. Enter the worksheet title, Security Lock & Key Weekly Payroll, in cell A1. Enter the column titles in row 2, the row titles in column A, and the data from Table 2-5 in columns B through D as shown in Figure 2-95.

2. Use the following formulas to determine the gross pay, federal tax, state tax, and net pay:
   a. Gross Pay = Rate*Hours (*Hint:* Assign cell E3 the formula =B3*C3 for the first employee and then copy the formula in cell E3 to the range E4:E8 for the remaining employees.)
   b. Federal Tax = 20% * (Gross Pay – Dependents * 38.46)
   c. State Tax = 3.2% * Gross Pay
   d. Net Pay = Gross Pay – (Federal Tax + State Tax)

3. Calculate totals for hours, gross pay, federal tax, state tax, and net pay in row 9.

4. Use the appropriate functions to determine the average, highest, and lowest values of each column in rows 10 through 12.

5. Bold the worksheet title.

6. Use buttons on the Formatting toolbar to assign the Comma style with two decimal places to the range B3:H12.

Table 2-5

EMPLOYEE	RATE	HOURS	DEPENDENTS
Scotch, Ben	25.00	40.25	3
Collings, Demi	17.50	53	2
Locken, Viola	27.75	36	4
Carr, Wessley	19.50	43.5	1
Bolte, Ernst	21.50	15	3
Christy, Rupert	15.65	25	4

FIGURE 2-95

Employee	Rate	Hours	Dep.	Gross Pay	Fed. Tax	State Tax	Net Pay
Scotch, Ben	25.00	40.25	3.00	1,006.25	178.17	32.20	795.88
Collings, Demi	17.50	53.00	2.00	927.50	170.12	29.68	727.70
Locken, Viola	27.75	36.00	4.00	999.00	169.03	31.97	798.00
Carr, Wessley	19.50	43.50	1.00	848.25	161.96	27.14	659.15
Bolte, Ernst	21.50	15.00	3.00	322.50	41.42	10.32	270.76
Christy, Rupert	15.65	25.00	4.00	391.25	47.48	12.52	331.25
Totals		212.75		4,494.75	768.19	143.83	3,582.73
Average	21.15	35.46	2.83	749.13	128.03	23.97	597.12
Highest	27.75	53.00	4.00	1,006.25	178.17	32.20	798.00
Lowest	15.65	15.00	1.00	322.50	41.42	10.32	270.76

In the Lab

7. Bold, italicize, and assign a heavy bottom border to the range A2:H2. Right-align the column titles in the range B2:H2.

8. Italicize the range A9:A12. Assign a top border and double line bottom border to the range A9:H9.

9. Change the width of column A to 15.00 characters. If necessary, change the widths of columns B through H to best fit. Change the height of rows 2 and 10 to 24.00 points.

10. Enter your name, course, laboratory assignment number (Lab 2-1), date, and instructor name in the range A14:A18.

11. Save the workbook using the file name Security Lock & Key.

12. Preview and then print the worksheet.

13. Press CTRL+` to change the display from the values version to the formulas version. Print the formulas version of the worksheet using the Fit to option on the Page tab in the Page Setup dialog box. After the printer is finished, press CTRL+` to reset the worksheet to display the values version. Reset the Scaling option to 100% by clicking Adjust to option button on the Page tab in the Page Setup dialog box and then setting the percent value to 100%.

14. Increase the number of hours worked for each employee by 10.25 hours. The total net pay in cell H9 should equal $4,581.69. If necessary, increase the width of column F to best fit to view the new federal tax total. Preview and print the worksheet with the new values. Close the workbook without saving the changes.

2 Esther's Music Emporium Monthly Accounts Receivable Balance Sheet

Problem: You were recently hired as a part-time assistant in the Accounting department of Esther's Music Emporium, a popular music store that sells new and used compact discs. You have been asked to use Excel to generate a report that summarizes the monthly accounts receivable balance. A graphic breakdown of the data also is desired. The customer accounts receivable data in Table 2-6 is available for test purposes.

Table 2-6					
CUSTOMER NUMBER	NAME	BEGINNING BALANCE	PURCHASES	PAYMENTS	CREDITS
2325	Jordan, Van	325.51	83.50	250.00	0.00
5521	Crite, Deyna	56.02	122.85	10.00	25.75
1011	Simp, Bart	225.32	27.15	15.00	12.63
6528	Rose, Mel	455.25	210.66	100.00	175.22
3496	Benz, Bill	62.50	45.31	00.00	33.74

Instructions Part 1: Create a worksheet similar to the one shown in Figure 2-96 on the next page. Include all six items in Table 2-6 in the report, plus a service charge and a new balance for each customer. (Assume no negative unpaid monthly balances.)

(continued)

In the Lab

Esther's Music Emporium Monthly Accounts Receivable Balance Sheet (continued)

Perform the following tasks.

1. Click the Select All button (to the right of column heading A) and then click the Bold button to bold the entire worksheet.

2. Assign the worksheet title, Esther's Music Emporium, to cell A1. Assign the worksheet subtitle, Monthly Accounts Receivable, to cell A2.

3. Enter the column titles in the range A3:H3 as shown in Figure 2-96. Change the width of column A to 9.57. Change the widths of columns B through H to best fit.

FIGURE 2-96

4. Enter the customer numbers and row titles in column A. Enter the customer numbers as text, rather than numbers. To enter the customer numbers as text, begin each entry with an apostrophe ('). Enter the remaining data in Table 2-6.

5. Use the following formulas to determine the monthly service charge in column G and the new balance in column H for each account:
   a. Service Charge = 2.25% * (Beginning Balance − Payments − Credits)
   b. New Balance = Beginning Balance + Purchases − Payments − Credits + Service Charge

6. Calculate totals for beginning balance, purchases, payments, credits, service charge, and new balance in row 9.

7. Assign cell C10 the appropriate function to calculate the maximum value in the range C4:C8. Copy cell C10 to the range D10:H10.

8. Assign cell C11 the appropriate function to calculate the minimum value in the range C4:C8. Copy cell C11 to the range D11:H11.

9. Change the worksheet title in cell A1 to 28-point CG Times font. Format the worksheet subtitle in cell A2 to 16-point CG Times font. Change the first letter of each word in the subtitle to 24-point font. Center the worksheet titles in cells A1 and A2 across the range A1:H2. Change the heights of rows 1 through 3 and row 10 to 27.75. Add a heavy outline to the range A1:H2 using the Borders button on the Formatting toolbar.

In the Lab

10. Select the range A1:H2 and then change the background color to violet (column 7, row 3 of the Fill Color palette). Change the font color in the range A1:H2 to light yellow (column 3, row 5 of the Font Color palette).
11. Italicize the column titles in row 3. Use the Borders button to add a heavy bottom border to the column titles in row 3. Center the column titles in row 3. Italicize the titles in rows 9, 10, and 11. Use the Borders button to add a single top border and double line bottom border to the range A9:H9 (column 4, row 2 on the Borders palette).
12. Use the Format Cells command on the shortcut menu to assign the Currency style with a floating dollar sign to row 4 and rows 9 through 11. Use the same command to assign the Comma style (currency with no dollar sign) to the range C5:H8. The Format Cells command is preferred over the Comma Style button because the worksheet specifications call for displaying zero as 0.00 rather than as a dash (-), as shown in Figure 2-96.
13. Change the widths of columns B through H again to best fit, if necessary.
14. Rename the sheet Accounts Receivable.
15. Enter your name, course, laboratory assignment number (LAB2-2), date, and instructor name in the range A13:A17.
16. Save the workbook using the file name Esther's Music.
17. Preview and then print the worksheet. Print the range A3:C9.
18. Press CTRL+` to change the display from the values version to the formulas version and then print the worksheet to fit on one page in landscape orientation. After the printer is finished, press CTRL+` to reset the worksheet to display the values version. Reset the Scaling option to 100% by clicking the Adjust to option button on the Page tab in the Page Setup dialog box and then setting the percent value to 100%.

Instructions Part 2: Draw the 3-D Pie chart showing the contribution of each customer to the total new balance as shown in Figure 2-97. Select the nonadjacent chart ranges B4:B8 and H4:H8. The category names in the range B4:B8 will identify the slices, while the data series in the range H4:H8 will determine the size of the slices. Click the Chart Wizard button on the Standard toolbar. Draw the 3-D Pie chart on a new chart sheet. Use the 3-D Pie chart sub-type (column 2, row 1). Add the chart title Contributions to Accounts Receivable. Remove the legend. Add data labels with percents to represent the slices.

FIGURE 2-97

(continued)

In the Lab

Esther's Music Emporium Monthly Accounts Receivable Balance Sheet *(continued)*

Once the 3-D Pie chart displays, format the chart title to have a violet background and 28-point Arial, light yellow, bold font. Change the font of the data labels to 16-point Arial, violet, bold font. Drag the data labels away from the slices they represent. Change the colors of the slices to those shown in Figure 2-97. Explode the slice representing the greatest contribution. Select a slice and then use the 3-D View command on the Chart menu to change the chart rotation to 290° and elevation to 40°. Rename the Chart1 sheet 3-D Pie Chart. Rearrange the order of the sheets so the worksheet appears before the chart. Save the workbook using the same file name as in Part 1. Preview and print the chart.

Instructions Part 3: Change the following purchases: account number 2325 to $735.21; account number 6528 to $25.00. The total new balance in cell H9 should equal $1,469.08. Select both sheets. Preview and print the selected sheets. Close the workbook without saving the changes.

3 Online Web Queries

Problem: Nora Dame, president of Quasimodo, Inc., recently attended a Microsoft seminar and learned that Microsoft Excel can connect to the World Wide Web, download real-time stock data into a worksheet, and then refresh the data as often as needed. Because you have had courses in Excel and the Internet, she has hired you as a consultant to develop a stock analysis workbook. Her portfolio is listed in Table 2-7.

Table 2-7	
COMPANY	STOCK SYMBOL
Corel Corp.	COSFF
Microsoft Corp.	MSFT
Netscape Corp.	NSCP
Yahoo Inc.	YHOO

Instructions Part 1: Open a new Excel workbook and then select cell A1. Perform the following steps to run a Web query to obtain multiple stock quotes using the stock symbols in Table 2-7.

1. Point to Get External Data on the Data menu and then click Run Web Query.
2. Double-click Multiple Stock Quotes by PC Quote, Inc in the Run Query dialog box. If the Queries folder does not display, see your instructor for its location.
3. Click the OK button in the Returning External Data to Microsoft Excel dialog box.
4. When the Enter Parameter Value dialog box displays, enter the stock symbols in Table 2-7 into the text box, being sure to separate them by a space. Click the Use this value/reference for future refreshes check box and then click the OK button. The stock data returned by the Web query displays in a worksheet as shown in Figure 2-98. Because the stock data returned is real-time, the numbers on your worksheet may be different.
5. Enter your name, course, laboratory assignment number (Lab 2-3a), date, and instructor name in the range A15:A19.
6. Rename the sheet Multiple Stocks. Save the workbook using the file name Stocks Online. Preview and then print the worksheet in landscape orientation.

Instructions Part 2: Create a detailed stock quote for AT&T as shown in Figure 2-99.

1. With the workbook created in Part 1 open, click the Sheet2 tab. Point to Get External Data on the Data menu and then click Run Web Query.

In the Lab

	Company Name & Symbol	Last Price	Net Change	Open	High	Low	Volume	Time	# of Outstanding Shares (m	Market Cap.
5	COREL CORPORATION (COSFF)	7 3/8	0	7 3/8	7 3/8	7 3/16	53,300	15:53		$
6	MICROSOFT CORP (MSFT)	81 5/8	-1	83 1/8	83 1/8	80 3/4	6,802,400	16:01	1,195,188	$97,557,221
7	NETSCAPE COMMUNICATIONS CORP (NSCP)	55 1/2	-1 3/8	56 3/4	57 1/2	54 3/4	1,197,800	16:00	87,883	$4,877,507
8	YAHOO INC (YHOO)	17 1/2	1/2	17	17 1/2	16 3/4	107,500	16:00	26,504	$463,820

Multiple Stock Quotes

All non-subscription data is delayed 20 minutes unless noted, and is believed accurate but is not warranted or guaranteed by PC Quote,Inc. All times are Eastern U.S.

Data Provided by
PC Quote, Inc.

Go to the PC Quote/Microsoft Excel Developer's Corner

FIGURE 2-98

2. Double-click Detailed Stock Quote by PC Quote, Inc in the Run Query dialog box.
3. Click the OK button in the Returning External Data to Microsoft Excel dialog box, starting the data in cell A1 of the existing worksheet.
4. When the Enter Parameter Value dialog box displays, enter the symbol T (for the company AT&T) in the list box. Do not click the Use this value/reference for future refreshes check box. Click the OK button.
5. The Web query returns the worksheet shown in Figure 2-99. The worksheet contains data that stock experts use to determine if they should buy or sell this company's stock.

FIGURE 2-99

(continued)

In the Lab

Online Web Queries (*continued*)

6. Enter your name, course, laboratory assignment number (Lab 2-3b), date, and instructor name in the range A24:A28.

7. Rename the sheet Detailed Stock. Save the workbook. Preview and then print the worksheet.

Instructions Part 3: Create a worksheet showing the latest currency exchange rates. The Web query for exchange rates is not one of the four queries available in the Queries folder by default. Thus, you must download it from the World Wide Web to your computer system before you can use it. Because the downloading process creates a table of Web queries on the active worksheet, a new workbook will be opened to accept the table. Once you select a Web query from the table and save it on disk, you can delete the workbook with the table and return to the Stocks Online workbook to complete the query. You will need a floppy disk for this exercise.

Perform the following.

1. With the workbook created in Parts 1 and 2 open, open a new workbook using the New command on the File menu.

2. Point to Get External Data on the Data menu, and then click Run Web Query. Double-click Get More Web Queries in the Run Query dialog box.

3. Click the OK button in the Returning External Data to Microsoft Excel dialog box, starting the data in cell A1 of the existing worksheet.

4. When the Get More Web Queries worksheet appears, scroll down and click the link CNN Currencies under Currencies and Exchange Rates. Your Web browser displays. When prompted, select the Save it to disk option. When the Save As dialog box displays, save the Web query, CNNfn_Currencies, to your floppy disk.

5. Close your Web browser. Use the Exit command on the File menu to close the new workbook without saving.

6. With the Stocks Online workbook active, click the Sheet3 tab. Click cell A1. Point to Get External Data on the Data menu and then click Run Web Query.

7. When the Run Web Query dialog box displays, click the Look in box arrow and then click 3½ Floppy (A:). Double-click CNNfn_Currencies.

8. Click the OK button in the Returning External Data to Microsoft Excel dialog box, starting the data in cell A1 of the existing worksheet. The Web query returns the worksheet shown in Figure 2-100 (scroll down so row 13 is at the top of your screen). The data may be different on your worksheet.

9. Double-click the Sheet3 tab in the Stocks Online workbook and then rename the sheet Currencies.

10 Enter your name, course, laboratory assignment number (Lab 2-3c), date, and instructor name below the entries in column A, in separate but adjacent cells.

11. After viewing the Currencies worksheet, preview and print it. Click the Multiple Stocks tab and then save the workbook.

In the Lab

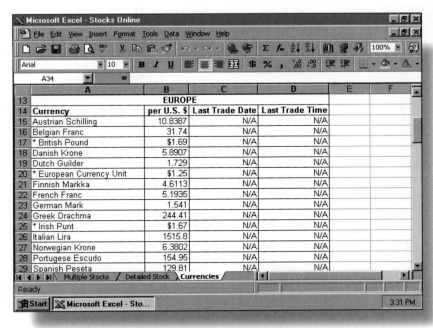

FIGURE 2-100

Instructions Part 4: Refresh the data. To update the sheets, make sure the Stocks Online workbook is open and then do the following.

1. If the External Data toolbar is not showing, right-click any toolbar and then click External Data. Click the Refresh All button on the External Data toolbar. When the Enter Parameter Value dialog box displays, type T for AT&T and then click the OK button. Select all three sheets. Preview and print the updated selected worksheets.

2. Click the Detailed Stock sheet and then click the Refresh Data button. When the Enter Parameter Value dialog box displays, type HDI (for the company Harley Davidson Inc.) in the text box and then click the OK button. Print the Detailed Stock sheet with the new values. Save the workbook and then quit Excel.

Cases and Places

The difficulty of these case studies varies: ❿ are the least difficult; ❿❿ are more difficult; and ❿❿❿ are the most difficult.

1 ❿ Homes4U Realty has hired you to work with their prospective clients. Your job is to help prequalify the clients and determine a proposed monthly mortgage payment. Homes4U has a standard questionnaire clients fill out, but you discovered a mortgage calculator query that looks much more professional and requires less time.

Start Excel and open a new workbook. Type Prequalifying Worksheet in cell A1 and type for Mr. & Mrs. Aarvis Bendix in cell A2. Open a new workbook and then run a Web query to return the Get More Web Queries worksheet. Retrieve and save the CNNfn_Mortgage_Calculator Web query on a floppy disk. Close the workbook without saving your changes. Click cell A4 and then run the CNNfn_Mortgage_Calculator Web query. Use the information in Table 2-8 to fill in the value boxes, clicking the Use this value/reference for future refreshes check box where indicated. Mr. and Mrs. Bendix want their After-tax PITI (Payment, Interest, Taxes, Insurance) payment to be around $750.00. Use the Refresh Data button to input the following data: Price – $110,000; Percent to Borrow – 60%; Interest Rate – 10%. Use the concepts and techniques presented in this project to create and format the worksheet titles and borders in rows 1 and 2.

Table 2-8		
ITEM	USE FOR FUTURE VALUE	REFRESHES
Price	$120,000	no
Closing Costs	3%	yes
Percent to Borrow	75%	no
Days to End of Month	0	yes
Interest Rate	10.75%	no
Real Estate Tax Rate	1.5%	yes
Discount Points	1%	yes
Homeowner's Dues	0	yes
Amortization	30 yrs.	yes
Months to Escrow	6	yes
Seller's Contribution	0	yes
Federal Tax Bracket	28%	yes
Monthly Income	$3500	yes
Monthly Debt	$1100	yes
Earnest Money Deposit	$500	yes
Prepaid Closing Costs	$250	yes

Cases and Places

2 ▶ In order to determine the effectiveness of their endangered species recovery plan, the Fish and Wildlife Department traps and releases red wolves in selected areas and records how many are pregnant. To obtain a representative sample, the department tries to trap approximately 20% of the population. Use the following formula to determine the total red wolf population if the state is divided into 1,000 sections. The following data was collected from five sections:

Section 1: 35 wolves caught, 15 pregnant, one out of every six dies annually (17%);
Section 2: 22 wolves caught, 5 pregnant, one out of every five dies annually (20%);
Section 3: 45 wolves caught, 12 pregnant, one out of every four dies annually (25%);
Section 4: 28 wolves caught, 16 pregnant, one out of every ten dies annually (10%);
Section 5: 59 wolves caught, 22 pregnant, one out of every three dies annually (33%).

Use the following formula to determine the number of red wolves in a section:

Wolves in a Section = 5 * (Total Catch + Pregnant Wolves) – 5 * Annual Deaths * (Total Catch + Pregnant Wolves)

You have been asked to create a worksheet and pie chart using the data provided to determine an estimated red wolf population for the state. Use the concepts and techniques presented in this project to create and format the worksheet and chart.

3 ▶ You are shopping for a vehicle to get you to and from school. After a long search, you finally have it narrowed down to two vehicles. One is a $4,000 truck, the other is a $3,700 two-door coupe. The trade-in value of your car is $850.00. The car dealership is offering a three-year payment plan at 11% interest on the balance. You want to know the total amount you will owe for each vehicle, which can be determined with the following formula:

Amount = (Cost of Vehicle – Trade-in) x (1 + Interest Rate / 12) ^ (Years x 12)

Create a worksheet with the information about each vehicle and then use the formula to calculate the total amount of each. Use the concepts and techniques used in this project to format the worksheet.

▶▶ Frugal Fleet Rental is a company that rents prop planes and Lear jets for commercial use. The rental charge is based on the formula f = 1000d + 8.5m, where f is the rental fee, d is the number of days the airplane is rented, and m is the flight miles. Over the last two weeks three prop planes and one Lear jet were rented. The prop planes rented were as follows: Lazy Sue, rented for three days with a total of 648 flight miles; Top Hat, rented one day with a total of 1280 flight miles; and Hawkeye, rented for four days with a total of 3267 flight miles. The Lear jet, named Fast One, was rented for two days with a total of 900 flight miles. Use the formula and these figures to develop a worksheet showing the number of days each airplane was rented, the flight miles for each airplane, the revenue generated by each airplane, and the percentage of the company's total revenue for these three rentals. Include totals, averages, maximum, and minimum where appropriate. Create a suitable chart on a different sheet to compare the income from each plane.

Cases and Places

5 ▶▶▶ Mortgage companies often use a formula to determine the highest selling price prospective customers can afford when purchasing a house. Visit a local mortgage company to discover how it analyzes the financial status of its clients. Use the company's formulas to create a worksheet based on estimates of your future income to determine the most expensive house you could afford now, and in five, ten, fifteen, twenty, and twenty-five years. Assuming you can make a 10% down payment, calculate the amount of money you would have to put down on each house and the amount you would need to borrow. Use the Run Web Query command and compare the figures obtained by the mortgage company's formula with the query results.

6 ▶▶▶ Pharmacists sometimes use a formula when mixing a prescription for a customer. Visit a local pharmacy and obtain the formulas for two different preparations. Use the formulas to create a worksheet showing the medication quantities for a child who is around 40 pounds, a child who is around 70 pounds, and an adult. Include a chart illustrating how the amount of medication varies based on weight factors.

7 ▶▶▶ Store owners occasionally use formulas to determine the selling price of an item based on that item's wholesale cost. Visit a store and obtain the formulas that are used to price items. Ask to see a list of the wholesale costs and then determine the cost of at least six individual items that are priced on the basis of the formula you are given. With this information, prepare a worksheet showing each item's wholesale cost, retail price, and the retailer's profit. Find the retail price and retailer's profit if the items were put on sale at a 10% discount. Show totals, averages, maximums, and minimums. Include a chart illustrating what part of the profit is represented by each item when all six items are sold.

> ### PROJECT ONE

CREATING A DATABASE
USING DESIGN AND DATASHEET VIEWS

Objectives   A 1.3
Introduction   A 1.6
Project One – Pilotech Services Database
   A 1.8
What Is Microsoft Access?   A 1.8
Overview of Project Steps   A 1.9
Starting Access and Creating a New Database
   A 1.9
The Access Desktop and the Database Window
   A 1.12
Creating a Table   A 1.13
Saving a Table   A 1.19
Adding Records to a Table   A 1.20
Closing a Table and a Database and Quitting
   Access   A 1.24
Opening a Database   A 1.24
Adding Additional Records   A 1.26
Previewing and Printing the Contents of a Table
   A 1.28
Creating Additional Tables   A 1.32
Using a Form to View Data   A 1.35
Creating a Report   A 1.40
Closing the Database   A 1.46
Designing a Database   A 1.46
Access Online Help   A 1.49
Project Summary   A 1.49
What You Should Know   A 1.49
Test Your Knowledge   A 1.50
Use Help   A 1.53
Apply Your Knowledge   A 1.54
In the Lab   A 1.57
Cases and Places   A 1.65

> ### PROJECT TWO

QUERYING A DATABASE
USING THE SELECT QUERY WINDOW

Objectives   A 2.1
Introduction   A 2.4
Project Two – Querying the Pilotech Services
   Database   A 2.4
Creating a New Query   A 2.7
Including All Fields in a Query   A 2.16
Clearing the Design Grid   A 2.17
Entering Criteria   A 2.18
Using Compound Criteria   A 2.24
Sorting Data in a Query   A 2.27
Joining Tables   A 2.32
Using Computed Fields in a Query   A 2.36
Calculating Statistics   A 2.38
Saving a Query   A 2.44
Closing a Database   A 2.45
Project Summary   A 2.46
Test Your Knowledge   A 2.47
Use Help   A 2.50
Apply Your Knowledge   A 2.52
In the Lab   A 2.53
Cases and Places   A 2.57

Microsoft

Access 97

Creating a Database Using Design and Datasheet Views

Objectives:

You will have mastered the material in this project when you can:

▶ Describe databases and database management systems
▶ Start Access
▶ Describe the features of the Access screen
▶ Create a database
▶ Create a table
▶ Define the fields in a table
▶ Open a table
▶ Add records to an empty table
▶ Close a table
▶ Close a database and quit Access
▶ Open a database
▶ Add records to a nonempty table
▶ Print the contents of a table
▶ Use a form to view data
▶ Create a custom report
▶ Design a database to eliminate redundancy

Project 1

Selections
Collections
One of a Kind

Anthology of Data and Other Priceless Keepsakes

Seventy-four years after his death, the skeleton of an obscure, but wealthy English scientist was disinterred and taken across the Atlantic to lie with honor in the institution his money had founded — in a nation he had never seen! His final resting place, known as the "nation's attic," is now home to a fabulous array of artifacts that number in excess of 140 million. When James Smithson left his fortune to the United States to found the Smithsonian Institution, he doubtless never imagined how successful his eccentric bequest would become.

Among its incredible collections, the Smithsonian displays such rarities as the 45.5-karat Hope Diamond, Judy Garland's ruby slippers from *The Wizard of Oz*, Charles Lindbergh's *Spirit of Saint Louis*, the original Star-Spangled Banner, and the wood-encased prototype of the first Apple

DATABASE

ITEM	LOCATION
Ruby slippers	1st floor/rm.5
Spirit of St.	hanging
Apple comp.	2nd. floor/rm.3
Star banner	2nd. floor/rm.2

computer. Managing so many objects is no easy matter for the Smithsonian, which relies on computer databases to inventory and categorize its priceless collections and track the constant stream of donated articles.

Millions flock to see this eclectic display every year, partly from curiosity but also because collecting seems to be a common human fascination. Bootjacks, tintypes, inkwells, Elvis memorabilia, snuffboxes, ceramic dragons, tea cozies, and meerschaum pipes are among the thousands of articles that people collect. At the Southern California Exposition in Del Mar, California, even a collection of "Shoes without Mates — Found Beside the Freeway" was exhibited one year.

Compared to the Smithsonian's needs, most private collections do not require extensive databases. Yet, even in a modest book or music library, databases are convenient for locating an item or providing backup for tax purposes. As a collection expands, however, the need for a sophisticated database management system (DBMS), such as Microsoft Access 97, becomes increasingly important.

One of the more extensive applications of databases in today's world is that of gathering collections of names, addresses, and individual data, that then are used for such purposes as companies selling to or servicing clients, charities soliciting donations, politicians seeking support, or the U.S. government keeping tabs on Medicare benefits.

Whether you collect Pickard China or priceless paintings or just need to keep track of your friends and clients, Microsoft Access 97 provides the means to create your own information collection that can organize data on any subject quickly and easily. The Access Table Wizard helps you choose fields from a variety of predefined tables such as business contacts, household inventory, or medical records. If you want to create your own table, Access guides you each step of the process. With its graphical user interface (GUI), you will find it easy to store, retrieve, and change data.

How favorable for the world that James Smithson did not squander his fortune collecting echoes like the hapless millionaire in Mark Twain's story, "The Canvasser's Tale." Even Access 97, with all its power, might have trouble managing echoes that talk back for fifteen minutes or others that speak only German.

Project
1

Microsoft
Access 97

Creating a Database Using Design and Datasheet Views

Case Perspective

Pilotech Services is a new company offering a variety of technical services to its clients. Such services can include assistance with hardware and software problems, special backup services, archiving services, and so on. Each client is assigned to a specific technician at Pilotech. Services are billed at the technician's hourly billing rate. The management of Pilotech Services needs to maintain data on its technicians as well as its clients. By placing the data in a database, managed by a database management system such as Access, Pilotech ensures that its data is current and accurate. Using Access, managers are able to produce a variety of useful reports. In addition, they need to be able to ask questions concerning the data in the database and obtain answers to these questions easily and rapidly.

Introduction

Creating, storing, sorting, and retrieving data are important tasks. In their personal lives, many people keep a variety of records such as names, addresses, and telephone numbers of friends and business associates, records of investments, records of expenses for tax purposes, and so on. These records must be arranged for quick access. Businesses also must be able to store and access information quickly and easily. Personnel and inventory records, payroll information, client records, order data, and accounts receivable information all are crucial and must be available readily.

The term **database** describes a collection of data organized in a manner that allows access, retrieval, and use of that data. A database management system, such as Access, allows you to use a computer to create a database; add, change, and delete data in the database; sort the data in the database; retrieve data in the database; and create forms and reports using the data in the database.

In Access, a database consists of a collection of tables. Figure 1-1 shows a sample database for Pilotech Services. It consists of two tables. The Client table contains information about Pilotech's clients. The Technician table contains information about the technicians to whom these clients are assigned.

The rows in the tables are called **records**. A record contains information about a given person, product, or event. A row in the Client table, for example, contains information about a specific client.

fields

clients of technician Joanna Levin

Client table

CLIENT NUMBER	NAME	ADDRESS	CITY	STATE	ZIP CODE	BILLED	PAID	TECH NUMBER
AM53	Ashton-Mills	216 Rivard	Grattan	MA	58120	$215.50	$155.00	11
AS62	Alton-Scripps	722 Fisher	Empire	MA	58216	$425.00	$435.00	12
BL26	Blake Suppliers	5752 Maumee	Grattan	MA	58120	$129.50	$0.00	12
DE76	D & E Grocery	464 Linnell	Marshall	VT	52018	$385.75	$300.00	17
GR56	Grant Cleaners	737 Allard	Portage	NH	59130	$215.00	$165.00	11
GU21	Grand Union	247 Fuller	Grattan	MA	58120	$128.50	$0.00	12
JE77	Jones Electric	57 Giddings	Marshall	VT	52018	$0.00	$0.00	12
MI26	Morland Int.	665 Whittier	Frankfort	MA	56152	$212.50	$223.25	11
SA56	Sawyer Inc.	31 Lafayette	Empire	MA	58216	$352.50	$250.00	17
SI82	Simpson Ind.	752 Cadieux	Fernwood	MA	57412	$154.00	$0.00	12

records

Technician table

TECH NUMBER	LAST NAME	FIRST NAME	ADDRESS	CITY	STATE	ZIP CODE	HOURLY RATE	YTD EARNINGS
11	Levin	Joanna	26 Cottonwood	Carlton	MA	59712	$25.00	$6,245.00
12	Rogers	Brad	7972 Marsden	Kaleva	VT	57253	$30.00	$7,143.30
17	Rodriguez	Maria	263 Topsfield	Hudson	MA	57240	$35.00	$7,745.50

technician na Levin

FIGURE 1-1

The columns in the tables are called fields. A **field** contains a specific piece of information within a record. In the Client table, for example, the fourth field, City, contains the city where the client is located.

The first field in the Client table is the Client Number. This is a code assigned by Pilotech to each client. Like many organizations, Pilotech calls it a *number* although it actually contains letters. The client numbers have a special format. They consist of two uppercase letters followed by a two-digit number.

These numbers are unique; that is, no two clients will be assigned the same number. Such a field can be used as a **unique identifier**. This simply means that a given client number will appear only in a single record in the table. Only one record exists, for example, in which the client number is BL26. A unique identifier also is called a **primary key**. Thus, the Client Number field is the primary key for the Client table.

The next eight fields in the Client table include the Name, Address, City, State, Zip Code, Billed, Paid, and Tech Number. The Billed field contains the amount billed to the client. The Paid field contains the amount the client already as paid.

For example, Client AM53 is Ashton-Mills. It is located at 216 Rivard in Grattan, Massachusetts. The zip code is 58120. The client has been billed $215.50 and already has paid $155.00 of this amount.

Each client is assigned to a single technician. The last field in the Client table, Tech Number, gives the number of the client's technician.

The first field in the Technician table, Tech Number, is the number assigned by Pilotech to each technician. These numbers are unique, so Tech Number is the primary key of the Technician table.

The other fields in the Technician table are Last Name, First Name, Address, City, State, Zip Code, Hourly Rate, and YTD Earnings. The Hourly Rate field gives the technician's hourly billing rate, and the YTD Earnings field contains the total amount that has been billed by the technician for the technician's services so far this year.

For example, Technician 11 is Joanna Levin. She lives at 26 Cottonwood in Carlton, Massachusetts. Her zip code is 59712. Her hourly billing rate is $25.00 and her YTD earnings are $6,245.00.

The tech number appears in both the Client table and the Technician table. It is used to relate clients and technicians. For example, in the Client table, you see that the tech number for client AM53 is 11. To find the name of this technician, look for the row in the Technician table that contains 11 in the Tech Number field. Once you have found it, you know the client is assigned to Joanna Levin. To find all the clients assigned to Joanna Levin, look through the Client table for all the clients that contain 11 in the Tech Number field. Her clients are AM53 (Ashton-Mills), GR56 (Grant Cleaners), and MI26 (Morland, Int.).

Project One — Pilotech Services Database

Together with the management of Pilotech Services, you have determined that the data that must be maintained in the database is the data shown in Figure 1-1 on page A 1.7. You first must create the database and the tables it contains. In the process, you must define the fields included in the two tables, as well as the type of data each field will contain. You then must add the appropriate records to the tables. You also must print the contents of the tables. Finally, you must create a report with the Client Number, Name, Billed, and Paid fields for each client of Pilotech Services. Other reports and requirements for the database at Pilotech Services will be addressed with the Pilotech Services management in the future.

What Is Microsoft Access?

Microsoft Access is a powerful database management system (DBMS) that functions in the Windows environment and allows you to create and process data in a database. To illustrate the use of Access, this book presents a series of projects.

The projects use the Client and Technician tables. In Project 1, the two tables that comprise the database are created and the appropriate records are added to them. The project also uses a form to display the data in the tables. In addition, the project presents steps and techniques to prepare and print a custom report that represents the data in the database.

Overview of Project Steps

The database preparation steps give you an overview of how the database consisting of the Client table and the Technician table shown in Figure 1-1 on page A 1.7 will be constructed. The following tasks will be completed in this project.

1. Start Access.
2. Create a database called Pilotech Services.
3. Create the Client table by defining its fields.
4. Save the Client table in the database called Pilotech Services.
5. Add data records to the Client table.
6. Print the contents of the Client table.
7. Create the Technician table, save it, and add data records to it.
8. Create a form to display data in the Client table.
9. Create and print a report that presents the data in the Client table.

The following pages contain a detailed explanation of each of these steps.

> **More** *About*
> **Creating a Database**
>
> In some DBMSs, every table, query, form, or report is stored in a separate file. This is not the case in Access, in which a database is stored in a single file on disk. The file contains all the tables, queries, forms, reports, and programs that you create for this database.

Starting Access and Creating a New Database

To start Access, Windows 95 must be running. Perform the following steps to start Access and create a new database.

Steps To Start Access

1 **Place a formatted floppy disk in drive A, click the Start button, and point to New Office Document near the top of the Start menu.**

The Start menu displays (Figure 1-2).

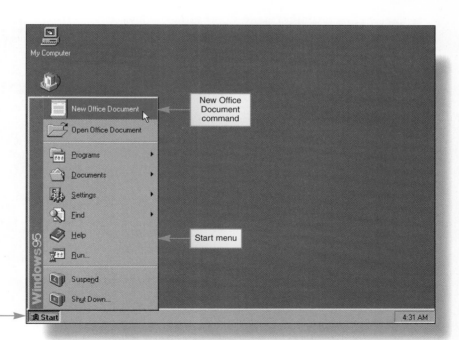

FIGURE 1-2

2 **Click New Office Document. If the General tab is not selected, that is, if it does not display in front of the other tabs, click the General tab. Make sure the Blank Database icon is selected and then point to the OK button.**

The New Office Document dialog box displays (Figure 1-3). The Blank Database icon is selected.

FIGURE 1-3

3 **Click the OK button and then point to the Save in box arrow.**

The File New Database dialog box displays (Figure 1-4).

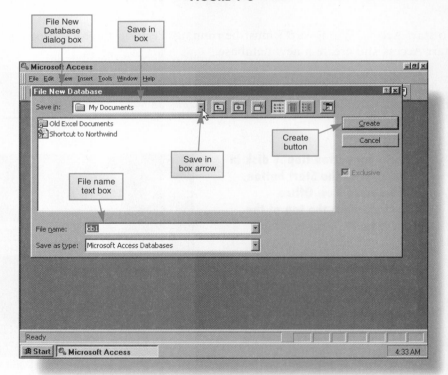

FIGURE 1-4

4 **Click the Save in box arrow and then point to 3½ Floppy (A:).**

The Save in list box displays (Figure 1-5).

FIGURE 1-5

5 **Click 3½ Floppy (A:).**

The Save in box contains 3½ Floppy (A:) (Figure 1-6).

FIGURE 1-6

6 Click in the File name text box. Repeatedly press the BACKSPACE key to delete db1 and then type Pilotech Services as the file name. Point to the Create button.

The file name is changed to Pilotech Services (Figure 1-7).

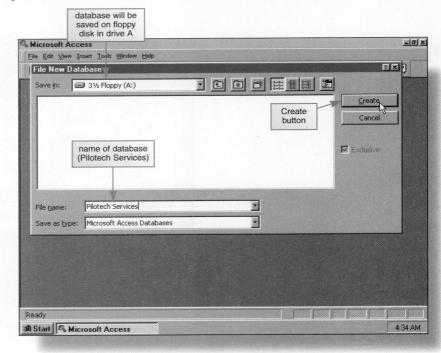

FIGURE 1-7

7 Click the Create button to create the database.

*The Pilotech Services database is created. The Pilotech Services : Database window displays on the desktop (Figure 1-8). The **Office Assistant**, a tool you can use to obtain help while working with Microsoft Access may display. (You will see how to use the Office Assistant later in this project.)*

8 If the Office Assistant displays, click the Close button for the Office Assistant.

The Office Assistant no longer displays.

FIGURE 1-8

Other Ways

1. Right-click Start button, click Open, double-click New Office Document
2. On Office shortcut bar click Start a New Document button
3. On the Start menu click Programs, click Microsoft Access

The Access Desktop and the Database Window

The first bar on the desktop (Figure 1-8) is the **title bar**. It displays the title of the product, Microsoft Access. The button on the right is the **Close button**. Clicking the Close button closes the window.

The second bar is the **menu bar**. It contains a list of menus. You select a menu from the menu bar by clicking the menu name.

The third bar is the **toolbar**. The toolbar contains buttons that allow you to perform certain tasks more quickly than using the menu bar. Each button contains a picture, or **icon**, depicting its function. The specific buttons on the toolbar will vary, depending on the task on which you are working.

The **taskbar** at the bottom of the screen displays the Start button, any active windows, and the current time.

Immediately above the Windows 95 taskbar is the **status bar** (Figure 1-8). It contains special information that is appropriate for the task on which you are working. Currently, it contains the word, Ready, which means Access is ready to accept commands.

The **Database window**, referred to in Figure 1-8 as the Pilotech Services : Database window, is a special window that allows you to access easily and rapidly a variety of objects such as tables, queries, forms, and reports. To do so, you will use the various components of the window.

Creating a Table

An Access database consists of a collection of tables. Once you have created the database, you must create each of the tables within it. In this project, for example, you must create both the Client and Technician tables shown in Figure 1-1 on page A 1.7.

To create a table, you describe the **structure** of the table to Access by describing the fields within the table. For each field, you indicate the following:

1. **Field name** — Each field in the table must have a unique name. In the Client table (Figure 1-9 on page A 1.14), for example, the field names are Client Number, Name, Address, City, State, Zip Code, Billed, Paid, and Tech Number.
2. **Data type** — Data type indicates to Access the type of data the field will contain. Some fields can contain only numbers. Others, such as Billed and Paid, can contain numbers and dollar signs. Still others, such as Name, and Address, can contain letters.
3. **Description** — Access allows you to enter a detailed description of the field.

You also can assign field widths to text fields (fields whose data type is Text). This indicates the maximum number of characters that can be stored in the field. If you do not assign a width to such a field, Access assumes the width is 50.

You also must indicate which field or fields make up the **primary key**; that is, the unique identifier, for the table. In the sample database, the Client Number field is the primary key of the Client table and the Tech Number field is the primary key of the Technician table.

The rules for field names are:

1. Names can be up to 64 characters in length.
2. Names can contain letters, digits, and spaces, as well as most of the punctuation symbols.
3. Names cannot contain periods, exclamation points (!), or square brackets ([ ]).
4. The same name cannot be used for two different fields in the same table.

More *About*
Toolbars

Normally, the correct Access toolbar automatically will display. If it does not, click View on the menu bar, and then click Toolbars. Select the toolbar for the activity in which you are engaged and then click the Close button.

More *About*
Creating a Table

Access includes **Table Wizards** that can guide you through the table-creation process by suggesting some commonly used tables and fields. If you already know the fields you need, however, it usually is easier to simply create the table yourself.

Structure of Client table

FIELD NAME	DATA TYPE	FIELD SIZE	PRIMARY KEY?	DESCRIPTION
Client Number	Text	4	Yes	Client Number (Primary Key)
Name	Text	20		Client Name
Address	Text	15		Street Address
City	Text	15		City
State	Text	2		State (Two-Character Abbreviation)
Zip Code	Text	5		Zip Code (Five-Character Version)
Billed	Currency			Current Billed Amount
Paid	Currency			Current Paid Amount
Tech Number	Text	2		Number of Client's Technician

Data for Client table

CLIENT NUMBER	NAME	ADDRESS	CITY	STATE	ZIP CODE	BILLED	PAID	TECH NUMBER
AM53	Ashton-Mills	216 Rivard	Grattan	MA	58120	$215.50	$155.00	11
AS62	Alton-Scripps	722 Fisher	Empire	MA	58216	$425.00	$435.00	12
BL26	Blake Suppliers	5752 Maumee	Grattan	MA	58120	$129.50	$0.00	12
DE76	D & E Grocery	464 Linnell	Marshall	VT	52018	$385.75	$300.00	17
GR56	Grant Cleaners	737 Allard	Portage	NH	59130	$215.00	$165.00	11
GU21	Grand Union	247 Fuller	Grattan	MA	58120	$128.50	$0.00	12
JE77	Jones Electric	57 Giddings	Marshall	VT	52018	$0.00	$0.00	12
MI26	Morland Int.	665 Whittier	Frankfort	MA	56152	$212.50	$223.25	11
SA56	Sawyer Inc.	31 Lafayette	Empire	MA	58216	$352.50	$250.00	17
SI82	Simpson Ind.	752 Cadieux	Fernwood	MA	57412	$154.00	$0.00	12

FIGURE 1-9

More About Data Types

Different database management systems have different available data types. Even data types that are essentially the same can have different names. The Access Text data type, for example, is referred to as Character in some systems and Alpha in others.

Each field has a **data type**. This indicates the type of data that can be stored in the field. The data types you will use in this project are:

1. **Text** — The field can contain any characters.
2. **Number** — The field can contain only numbers. The numbers can be either positive or negative. Fields are assigned this type so they can be used in arithmetic operations. Fields that contain numbers but will not be used for arithmetic operations usually are assigned a data type of Text. The Tech Number field, for example, is a text field because the Tech Numbers will not be involved in any arithmetic.
3. **Currency** — The field can contain only dollar amounts. The values will be displayed with dollar signs, commas, decimal points, and with two digits following the decimal point. Like numeric fields, you can use currency fields in arithmetic operations. Access assigns a size to currency fields automatically.

The field names, data types, field widths, primary key information, and descriptions for the Client table are shown in Figure 1-9. With this information, you are ready to begin creating the table. To create the table, use the following steps.

Steps To Create a Table

1 **Click the New button in the Pilotech Services : Database window (see Figure 1-8 on page A 1.12). Point to Design View.**

The New Table dialog box displays (Figure 1-10).

FIGURE 1-10

2 **Click Design View and then click the OK button.**

The Table1 : Table window displays (Figure 1-11).

3 **Click the Maximize button for the Table1 : Table window.**

A maximized Table1 : Table window displays.

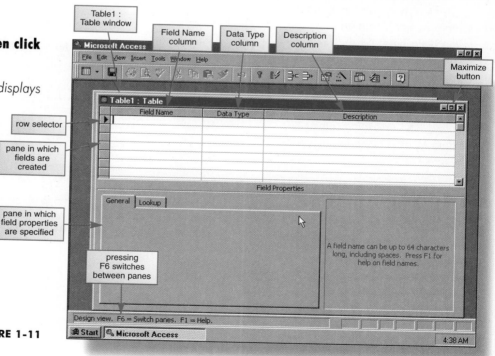

FIGURE 1-11

*Other*Ways

1. Click New Object button arrow on toolbar, click New Table
2. On Insert menu click Table
3. Press ALT+N

Defining the Fields

The next step in creating the table is to define the fields by specifying the required details in the Table window. To do so, make entries in the Field Name, Data Type, and Description columns. Enter additional information in the Field Properties box in the lower portion of the Table window. To do so, press the F6 key to move from the upper **pane** (portion of the screen), the one where you define the fields, to the lower pane, the one where you define field properties. Enter the appropriate field size and then press the F6 key to return to the upper pane. As you define the fields, the **row selector** (Figure 1-11 on page A 1.15) indicates the field you currently are describing. It is positioned on the first field, indicating Access is ready for you to enter the name of the first field in the Field Name column.

Perform the following steps to define the fields in the table.

To Define the Fields in a Table

1 **Type** Client Number **(the name of the first field) in the Field Name column and press the TAB key.**

The words, Client Number, display in the Field Name column and the insertion point advances to the Data Type column, indicating you can enter the data type (Figure 1-12). The word, Text, one of the possible data types, currently displays. The arrow indicates a list of data types is available by clicking the arrow.

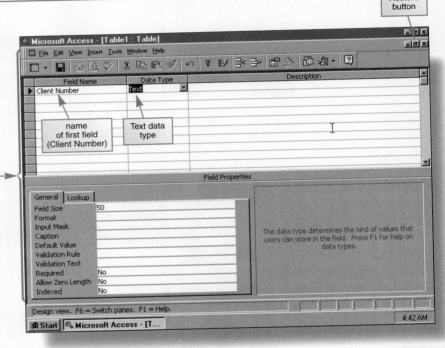

FIGURE 1-12

2 **Because Text is the correct data type, press the TAB key to move the insertion point to the Description column, type** Client Number (Primary Key) **as the description and then point to the Primary Key button on the toolbar.**

A ScreenTip, which is a description of the button, displays partially obscuring the description of the first field (Figure 1-13).

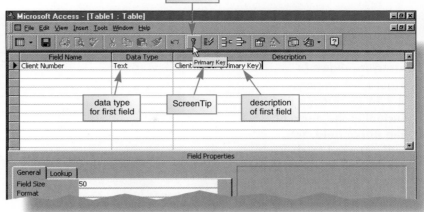

FIGURE 1-13

3 **Click the Primary Key button to make Client Number the primary key and then press the F6 key to move the insertion point to the Field Size text box.**

*The Client Number field is the primary key as indicated by the key symbol that displays in the row selector (Figure 1-14). The **row selector** is a small box or bar that, when clicked, selects the entire row. The current entry in the Field Size text box (50) is selected.*

FIGURE 1-14

4 **Type** 4 **as the size of the Client Number field. Press the F6 key to return to the Description column for the Client Number field and then press the TAB key to move to the Field Name column in the second row.**

The row selector moves to the second row just below the field name Client Number (Figure 1-15).

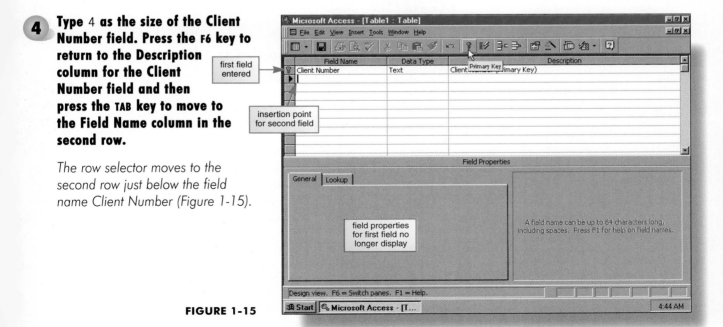

FIGURE 1-15

5 Use the techniques illustrated in Steps 1 through 4 to make the entries from the Client table structure shown in Figure 1-9 on page A 1.14 up through and including the name of the Billed field. You will not need to click the Primary Key button for any of these fields. Click the Data Type column arrow and then point to the Currency data type.

The additional fields are entered (Figure 1-16). A list of available data types displays in the Data Type column for the Billed field.

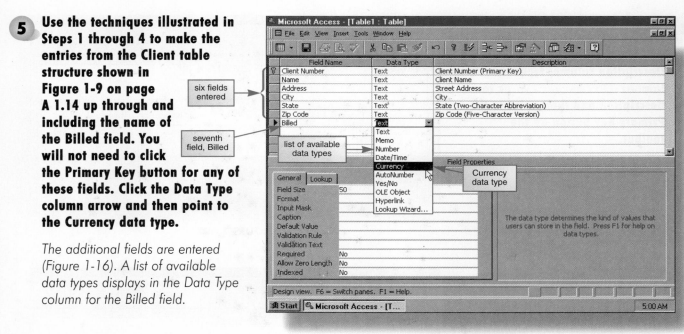

FIGURE 1-16

6 Click the Currency data type and then press the TAB key. Make the remaining entries from the Client table structure shown in Figure 1-9.

The fields are all entered (Figure 1-17).

FIGURE 1-17

Correcting Errors in the Structure

When creating a table, check the entries carefully to ensure they are correct. If you make a mistake and discover it before you press the TAB key, you can correct the error by repeatedly pressing the BACKSPACE key until the incorrect characters are removed. Then, type the correct characters. If you do not discover a mistake until later, you can click the entry, type the correct value and then press the ENTER key.

If you accidentally add an extra field to the structure, select the field, by clicking the leftmost column on the row that contains the field to be deleted. Once you have selected the field, press the DELETE key. This will remove the field from the structure.

If you forget a field, select the field that will follow the field you wish to add, click Insert on the menu bar and then click Rows. The remaining fields move down one row, making room for the missing field. Make the entries for the new field in the usual manner.

If you made the wrong field a primary key field, click the correct primary key entry for the field and then click the Primary Key button on the toolbar.

As an alternative to these steps, you may want to start over. To do so, click the Close button for the Table1 : Table window and then click No. The original desktop displays and you can repeat the process you used earlier.

More *About*
Correcting Errors

Even after you have entered data, it still is possible to correct errors in the structure. Access will make all the necessary adjustments to the structure of the table as well as to the data within it. (It is simplest to make the correction, however, before any data is entered.)

Saving a Table

The Client table structure now is complete. The final step is to **save the table** within the database. At this time, you should give the table a name.

Table names are from one to 64 characters in length and can contain letters, numbers, and spaces. The two table names in this project are Client and Technician.

To save the table, complete the following steps.

Steps **To Save a Table**

1 **Click the Save button on the toolbar (see Figure 1-17). Type** Client **as the name of the table in the Table Name text box and then point to the OK button.**

The Save As dialog box displays (Figure 1-18). The name of the table displays in the Table Name text box.

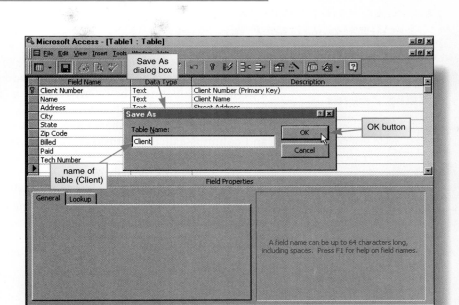

FIGURE 1-18

2 Click the OK button and then point to the Close button for the Client : Table window.

The Table is saved on the floppy disk in drive A. The name of the table is now Client as indicated in the title bar (Figure 1-19).

3 Click the Close button for the Client : Table window. (Be sure not to click the Close button on the first line, because this would close Microsoft Access.)

The Client : Table window no longer displays.

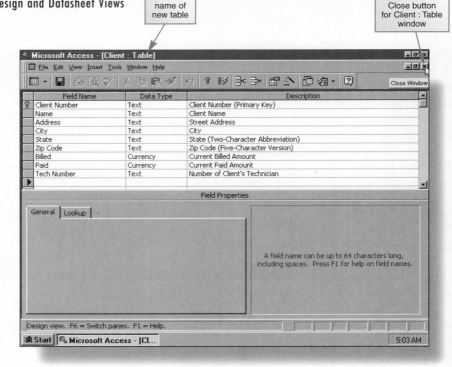

name of new table

Close button for Client : Table window

FIGURE 1-19

More *About* **Adding Records**

As soon as you have entered or modified a record and moved to another record, the original record is saved. This is different from other tools. The rows entered in a spreadsheet, for example, are not saved until the entire spreadsheet is saved.

Adding Records to a Table

Creating a table by building the structure and saving the table is the first step in a two-step process. The second step is to **add records** to the table. To add records to a table, the table must be open. To **open a table**, right-click the table in the Database window and then click Open on the shortcut menu. The table displays in Datasheet view. In **Datasheet view**, the table is represented as a collection of rows and columns called a **datasheet**. It looks very much like the tables shown in Figure 1-1 on page A 1.7.

You often add records in phases. You may, for example, not have enough time to add all the records in one session. To illustrate this process, this project begins by adding the first two records in the Client table (Figure 1-20). The remaining records are added later.

Client table (first 2 records)

CLIENT NUMBER	NAME	ADDRESS	CITY	STATE	ZIP CODE	BILLED	PAID	TECH NUMBER
AM53	Ashton-Mills	216 Rivard	Grattan	MA	58120	$215.50	$155.00	11
AS62	Alton-Scripps	722 Fisher	Empire	MA	58216	$425.00	$435.00	12

FIGURE 1-20

To open the Client table and then add records, use the following steps.

Steps **To Add Records to a Table**

1 **Right-click the Client table in the Pilotech Services : Database window and then point to Open on the shortcut menu.**

The shortcut menu for the Client table displays (Figure 1-21). The Pilotech Services : Database window is maximized because the previous window, the Client : Table window, was maximized. (If you wanted to restore the Database window to its original size, you would click the window's Restore button.)

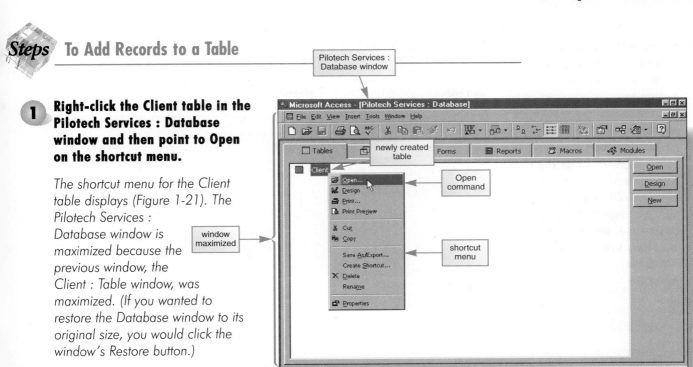

FIGURE 1-21

2 **Click Open on the shortcut menu.**

*The Client : Table window displays (Figure 1-22). The window contains the Datasheet view for the Client table. The **record selector** is positioned on the first record. The status bar at the bottom of the window also indicates that the record selector is positioned on record 1.*

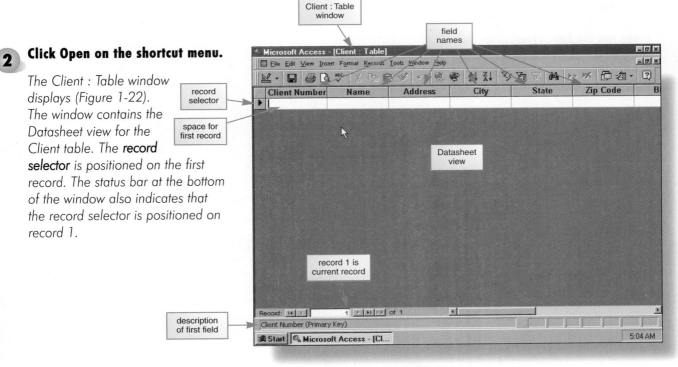

FIGURE 1-22

3 **If your window is not already maximized, click the Maximize button to maximize the window containing the table. Type AM53 as the first Client Number, as shown in Figure 1-20 on page A 1.20. Be sure you type the letters in uppercase, because that is the way they are to be entered in the database.**

The Client Number is entered, but the insertion point is still in the Client Number field (Figure 1-23).

FIGURE 1-23

4 **Press the TAB key to complete the entry for the Client Number field. Type Ashton-Mills as the name and then press the TAB key. Type 216 Rivard as the address and then press the TAB key. Type Grattan as the city and then press the TAB key. Type MA as the state name and then press the TAB key. Type 58120 as the zip code.**

The Name, Address, City, and State fields are entered. The data for the Zip Code field displays on the screen (Figure 1-24), but the entry is not complete because you have not yet pressed the TAB key.

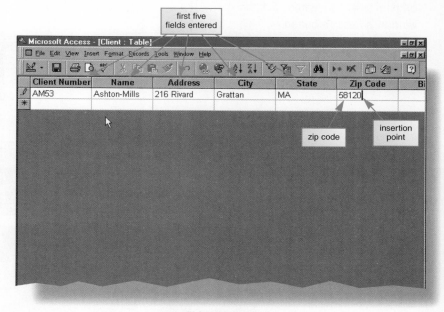

FIGURE 1-24

5 **Press the TAB key.**

The fields shift to the left (Figure 1-25). The Billed field displays.

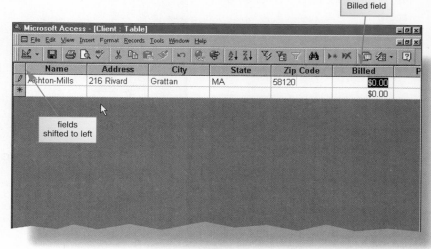

FIGURE 1-25

6 **Type** 215.50 **as the billed amount and then press the TAB key. (You do not need to type dollar signs or commas. In addition, if the digits to the right of the decimal point were both zeros, you would not need to type the decimal point.) Type** 155 **as the paid amount and then press the TAB key. Type** 11 **as the Tech Number to complete the record.**

The fields have shifted to the left (Figure 1-26). The Billed and Paid values display with dollar signs and decimal points. The value for the Tech Number has been entered, but the insertion point still is positioned on the field.

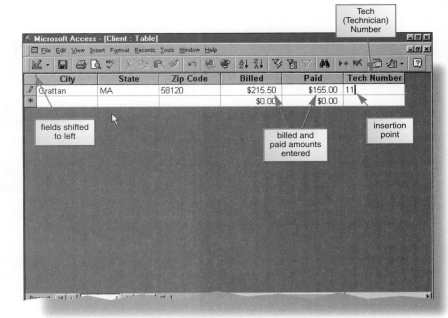

FIGURE 1-26

7 **Press the TAB key.**

The fields shift back to the right, the record is saved, and the insertion point moves to the Client Number on the second row (Figure 1-27).

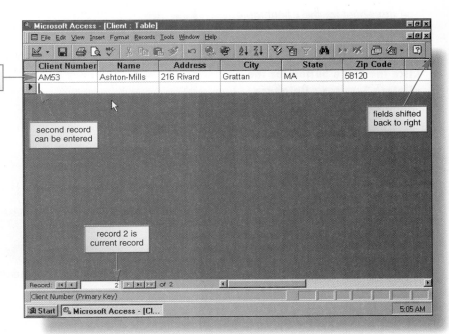

FIGURE 1-27

8 **Use the techniques shown in Steps 3 through 7 to add the data for the second record in Figure 1-20 on page A 1.20.**

The second record is added and the insertion point moves to the Client Number on the third row (Figure 1-28).

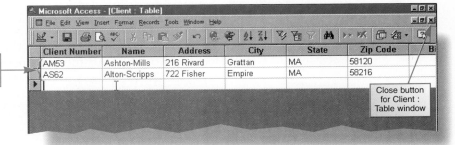

FIGURE 1-28

Closing a Table and a Database and Quitting Access

It is a good idea to close a table as soon as you have finished working with it. It keeps the screen from getting cluttered and prevents you from making accidental changes to the data in the table. If you no longer will work with the database, you should close the database as well. With the creation of the Client table complete, you can quit Access at this point.

Perform the following steps to close the table and the database and then quit Access.

Steps To Close a Table and Database and Quit Access

1 Click the Close button for the Client : Table window (see Figure 1-28 on page A 1.23).

The datasheet for the Client table no longer displays (Figure 1-29).

2 Click the Close button for the Pilotech Services : Database window (see Figure 1-29).

The Pilotech Services : Database window no longer displays.

3 Click the Close button for the Microsoft Access window.

The Microsoft Access window no longer displays.

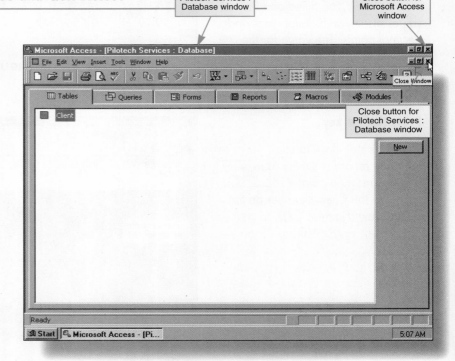

FIGURE 1-29

OtherWays

1. Double-click Control-menu icon on title bar for window
2. On File menu click Close

Opening a Database

To work with any of the tables, reports, or forms in a database, the database must be open. To open a database from the Windows 95 desktop, click Open Office Document on the Start menu by performing the following steps. (The Other Ways box indicates ways to open a database from within Access.)

Steps **To Open a Database**

1 Click the Start button and then point to Open Office Document on the Start menu (Figure 1-30).

FIGURE 1-30

2 Click Open Office Document. If necessary, click the Look in box arrow and then click 3½ Floppy (A:) in the Look in list box. If it is not already selected, click the Pilotech Services database name. Point to the Open button.

The Open Office Document dialog box displays (Figure 1-31). The 3½ Floppy (A:) folder displays in the Look in box and the files on the floppy disk in drive A display. Your list may be different.

3 Click the Open button.

The database opens and the Pilotech Services : Database window displays.

FIGURE 1-31

OtherWays

1. Click Open Database button on toolbar
2. On File menu click Open Database
3. Press CTRL+O

Adding Additional Records

You can add records to a table that already contains data using a process almost identical to that used to add records to an empty table. The only difference is that you place the insertion point after the last data record before you enter the additional data. To do so, use the **Navigation buttons** found near the lower-left corner of the screen. The purpose of each of the Navigation buttons is described in Table 1-1.

Table 1-1	
BUTTON	*PURPOSE*
First Record	Moves to the first record in the table
Previous Record	Moves to the previous record
Next Record	Moves to the next record
Last Record	Moves to the last record in the table
New Record	Moves past the last record in the table to a position for a new record

Complete the following steps to add the remaining records (Figure 1-32) to the Client table.

Client table (last 8 records)								
CLIENT NUMBER	*NAME*	*ADDRESS*	*CITY*	*STATE*	*ZIP CODE*	*BILLED*	*PAID*	*TECH NUMBER*
BL26	Blake Suppliers	5752 Maumee	Grattan	MA	58120	$129.50	$0.00	12
DE76	D & E Grocery	464 Linnell	Marshall	VT	52018	$385.75	$300.00	17
GR56	Grant Cleaners	737 Allard	Portage	NH	59130	$215.00	$165.00	11
GU21	Grand Union	247 Fuller	Grattan	MA	58120	$128.50	$0.00	12
JE77	Jones Electric	57 Giddings	Marshall	VT	52018	$0.00	$0.00	12
MI26	Morland Int.	665 Whittier	Frankfort	MA	56152	$212.50	$223.25	11
SA56	Sawyer Inc.	31 Lafayette	Empire	MA	58216	$352.50	$250.00	17
SI82	Simpson Ind.	752 Cadieux	Fernwood	MA	57412	$154.00	$0.00	12

FIGURE 1-32

Steps **To Add Additional Records to a Table**

1 **Right-click the Client table selected in the Pilotech Services : Database window and then click Open on the shortcut menu.**

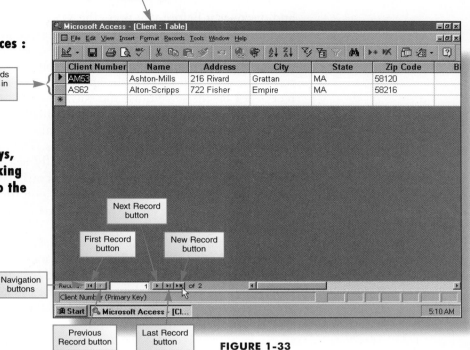

FIGURE 1-33

2 **When the Client table displays, maximize the window by clicking the Maximize button. Point to the New Record button.**

The datasheet displays (Figure 1-33).

3 **Click the New Record button.**

Access places the insertion point in position to enter a new record (Figure 1-34).

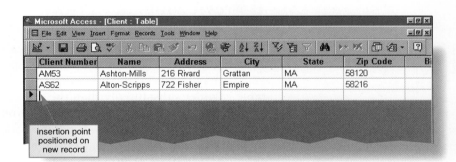

FIGURE 1-34

4 **Add the remaining records from Figure 1-32 using the same techniques you used to add the first two records. Point to the Close button.**

The additional records are added (Figure 1-35).

FIGURE 1-35

5 **Close the window containing the table by clicking its Close button.**

Correcting Errors in the Data

Check your entries carefully to ensure they are correct. If you make a mistake and discover it before you press the TAB key, correct it by pressing the BACKSPACE key until the incorrect characters are removed and then typing the correct characters.

If you discover an incorrect entry later, correct the error by clicking the incorrect entry and then making the appropriate correction. If the record you must correct is not on the screen, use the Navigation buttons (Next Record, Previous Record, and so on) to move to it. If the field you want to correct is not visible on the screen, use the horizontal scroll bar along the bottom of the screen to shift all the fields until the one you want displays. Then make the correction.

If you add an extra record accidentally, select the record by clicking the **record selector** that immediately precedes the record. Then, press the DELETE key. This will remove the record from the table. If you forget a record, add it using the same procedure as for all the other records. Access will place it in the correct location in the table automatically.

If you cannot determine how to correct the data, you are, in effect, stuck on the record. Access neither allows you to move to any other record until you have made the correction, nor allows you to close the table. If you encounter this situation, simply press the ESC key. Pressing the ESC key will remove from the screen the record you are trying to add. You then can move to any other record, close the table, or take any other action you desire.

Previewing and Printing the Contents of a Table

More *About*
Printing the
Contents of a Table

You can change the paper size, paper source, or the printer that will be used to print the report. To change any of these, select the Page sheet of the Page Setup dialog box, click the appropriate down arrow, and then select the desired option.

When working with a database, you often will need to **print** a copy of the table contents. Figure 1-36 shows a printed copy of the contents of the Client table. (Yours may look slightly different, depending on your printer.) Because the Client table is wider substantially than the screen, it also will be wider than the normal printed page in portrait orientation. **Portrait orientation** means the printout is across the width of the page. **Landscape orientation** means the printout is across the length of the page. Thus, to print the wide database table, use landscape orientation. If you are printing the contents of a table that fits on the screen, you will not need landscape orientation. A convenient way to change to landscape orientation is to **preview** what the printed copy will look like by using Print Preview. This allows you to determine whether landscape orientation is necessary and, if it is, to change easily the orientation to landscape. In addition, you also can use Print Preview to determine whether any adjustments are necessary to the page margins.

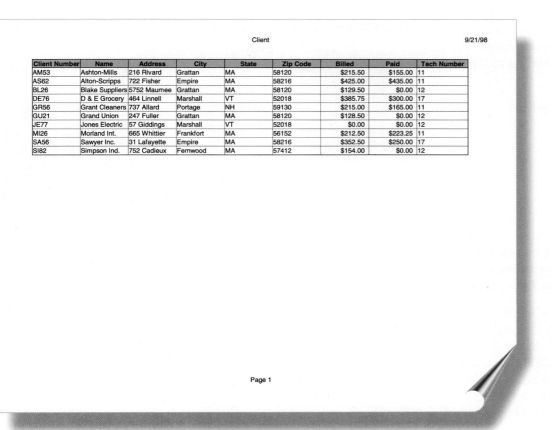

	Client							9/21/98
Client Number	Name	Address	City	State	Zip Code	Billed	Paid	Tech Number
AM53	Ashton-Mills	216 Rivard	Grattan	MA	58120	$215.50	$155.00	11
AS62	Alton-Scripps	722 Fisher	Empire	MA	58216	$425.00	$435.00	11
BL26	Blake Suppliers	5752 Maumee	Grattan	MA	58120	$129.50	$0.00	12
DE76	D & E Grocery	464 Linnell	Marshall	VT	52018	$385.75	$300.00	17
GR56	Grant Cleaners	737 Allard	Portage	NH	59130	$215.00	$165.00	11
GU21	Grand Union	247 Fuller	Grattan	MA	58120	$128.50	$0.00	12
JE77	Jones Electric	57 Giddings	Marshall	VT	52018	$0.00	$0.00	12
MI26	Morland Int.	665 Whittier	Frankfort	MA	56152	$212.50	$223.25	11
SA56	Sawyer Inc.	31 Lafayette	Empire	MA	58216	$352.50	$250.00	17
SI82	Simpson Ind.	752 Cadieux	Fernwood	MA	57412	$154.00	$0.00	12

Page 1

FIGURE 1-36

Perform the following steps to use Print Preview to preview and then print the Client table.

To Preview and Print the Contents of a Table

1 **Right-click the Client table and then point to Print Preview on the shortcut menu.**

The shortcut menu for the Client table displays (Figure 1-37).

FIGURE 1-37

2 Click Print Preview on the shortcut menu. Point anywhere in the upper-right portion of the report.

The preview of the report displays (Figure 1-38).

FIGURE 1-38

3 Click the magnifying glass mouse pointer in the approximate position shown in Figure 1-38.

The portion surrounding the mouse pointer is magnified (Figure 1-39). The last field that displays is the Zip Code field. The Billed, Paid, and Tech Number fields do not display. To display the additional fields, you will need to switch to landscape orientation.

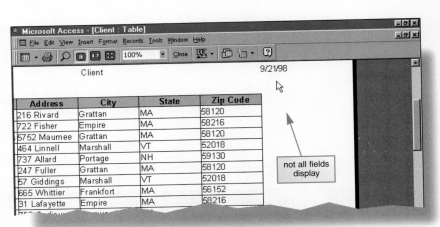

FIGURE 1-39

4 Click File on the menu bar and then point to Page Setup.

The File menu displays (Figure 1-40).

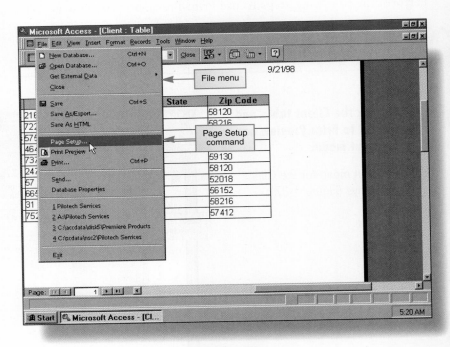

FIGURE 1-40

5 **Click Page Setup and then point to the Page tab.**

The Page Setup dialog box displays (Figure 1-41).

FIGURE 1-41

6 **Click the Page tab and then point to Landscape.**

*The Page sheet displays (Figure 1-42). The Portrait option button currently is selected. (**Option button** refers to the round button that indicates choices in a dialog box. When the corresponding option is selected, the button contains within it a solid circle. Clicking an option button selects it, and deselects all others.)*

FIGURE 1-42

7 Click Landscape and then click the OK button. Click the mouse pointer to view the entire report.

The orientation is changed to landscape as shown by the report that displays on the screen (Figure 1-43). The characters in the report are so small that it is difficult to determine whether all fields currently display. To zoom in on a portion of the report, click the desired portion of the report.

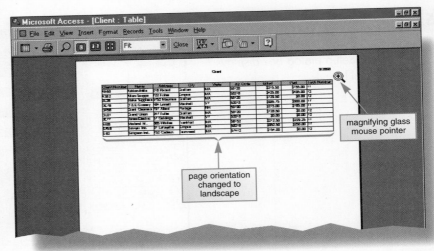

FIGURE 1-43

8 Click the magnifying glass mouse pointer in the approximate position shown in Figure 1-43.

The portion surrounding the mouse pointer is magnified (Figure 1-44). The last field that displays is the Tech Number field, so all fields currently display. If they did not, you could decrease the left and right margins, the amount of space left by Access on the left and right edges of the report.

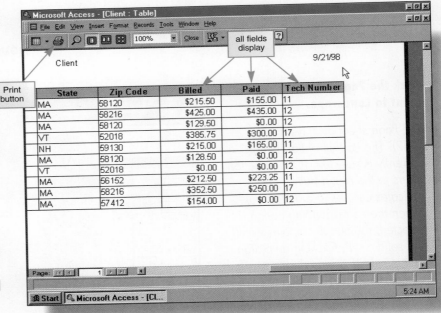

FIGURE 1-44

9 Click the Print button to print the report. Click the Close button when the report has been printed to close the Print Preview window.

The Preview window no longer displays.

OtherWays
1. On File menu click Print Preview to preview
2. On File menu click Print to print
3. Press CTRL+P to print

Creating Additional Tables

A database typically consists of more than one table. The sample database contains two, the Client table and the Technician table. You need to repeat the process of creating a table and adding records for each table in the database. In the sample database, you need to create and add records to the Technician table. The structure and data for the table are given in Figure 1-45. The steps to create the table follow.

ructure of Technician table

ELD NAME	DATA TYPE	FIELD SIZE	PRIMARY KEY?	DESCRIPTION
h Number	Text	2	Yes	Technician Number (Primary Key)
st Name	Text	10		Last Name of Technician
st Name	Text	8		First Name of Technician
dress	Text	15		Street Address
y	Text	15		City
te	Text	2		State (Two-Character Abbreviation)
Code	Text	5		Zip Code (Five-Character Version)
urly Rate	Currency			Hourly Rate of Technician
0 Earnings	Currency			YTD Earnings of Technician

ata for Technician table

CH MBER	LAST NAME	FIRST NAME	ADDRESS	CITY	STATE	ZIP CODE	HOURLY RATE	YTD EARNINGS
	Levin	Joanna	26 Cottonwood	Carlton	MA	59712	$25.00	$6,245.00
	Rogers	Brad	7972 Marsden	Kaleva	VT	57253	$30.00	$7,143.30
	Rodriguez	Maria	263 Topsfield	Hudson	MA	57240	$35.00	$7,745.50

FIGURE 1-45

 To Create an Additional Table

Make sure the Pilotech Services database is open. Point to the New button.

The Pilotech Services : Database window displays (Figure 1-46). If you recently maximized another window, this window also will be maximized as shown in the figure. If not, it will appear in its normal size.

FIGURE 1-46

2 Click the New button, click Design View in the New Table dialog box, click the OK button and then enter the data for the fields for the Technician table from Figure 1-45 on page A 1.33. Be sure to click the Primary Key button when you enter the Tech Number field. Point to the Save button on the toolbar.

The entries display (Figure 1-47).

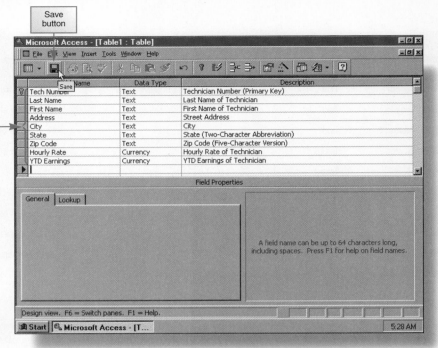

FIGURE 1-47

3 Click the Save button, type `Technician` as the name of the table, and click the OK button. Click the Close button to close the Table window.

The table is saved in the Pilotech Services database. The Table window no longer displays.

Adding Records to the Additional Table

Now that you have created the Technician table, use the following steps to add records to it.

 To Add Records to an Additional Table

1 Right-click the Technician table and point to Open on the shortcut menu.

The shortcut menu for the Technician table displays (Figure 1-48).

FIGURE 1-48

2 Click Open on the shortcut menu and then enter the Technician data from Figure 1-45 into the Technician table.

The datasheet displays with three records entered (Figure 1-49).

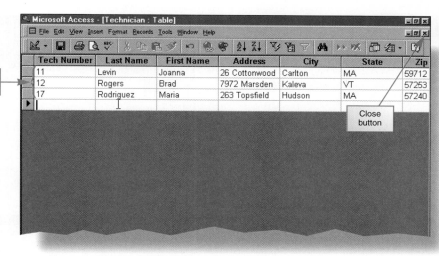

FIGURE 1-49

3 Click the Close button for the Technician : Table window to close the table.

Access closes the table and removes the datasheet from the screen.

Using a Form to View Data

In creating tables, you have used Datasheet view; that is, the data on the screen displayed as a table. You also can use **Form view**, in which you see a single record at a time.

The advantage with Datasheet view is you can see multiple records at once. It has the disadvantage that, unless you have few fields in the table, you cannot see all the fields at the same time. With Form view, you see only a single record, but you can see all the fields in the record. The view you choose is a matter of personal preference.

Creating a Form

To use Form view, you first must **create a form**. The simplest way to create a form is to use the **New Object: AutoForm button** on the toolbar. To do so, first select the table for which the form is to be created in the Database window and then click the New Object: AutoForm button. A list of available objects displays. Select AutoForm from the list by clicking it in the list.

Perform the following steps using the New Object: AutoForm button to create a form for the Client table.

◆ More *About* **Forms**

Attractive and functional forms can improve greatly the data entry process. Forms are not restricted to data from a single table, but can incorporate data from multiple tables as well as special types of data like pictures and sounds. A good DBMS like Access furnishes an easy way to create sophisticated forms.

 teps To Use the New Object: AutoForm Button to Create a Form

1 Make sure the Pilotech Services database is open, the Database window displays, and the Client table is selected. Point to the New Object: AutoForm button arrow on the toolbar (Figure 1-50).

FIGURE 1-50

2 **Click the New Object: AutoForm button arrow and then point to AutoForm.**

A list of objects that can be created displays (Figure 1-51).

FIGURE 1-51

3 **Click AutoForm in the New Object: AutoForm list.**

The form displays (Figure 1-52).

FIGURE 1-52

Closing and Saving the Form

Closing a form is similar to closing a table. The only difference is that you will be asked if you want to **save the form** unless you have previously saved it. Perform the following steps to close the form and save it as Client.

 To Close and Save a Form

1 **Click the Close button for the Client window (see Figure 1-52). Point to the Yes button.**

The Microsoft Access dialog box displays (Figure 1-53).

FIGURE 1-53

2 **Click the Yes button and then point to the OK button.**

The Save As dialog box displays (Figure 1-54). The name of the table (Client) becomes the name of the form automatically. This name can be replaced with any name.

3 **Click the OK button in the Save As dialog box.**

The form is saved as part of the database and is removed from the screen. The Pilotech Services : Database window again displays.

FIGURE 1-54

> **OtherWays**
> 1. Double-click Control-menu icon on title bar for window
> 2. On File menu click Close

Opening the Saved Form

Once you have saved a form, you can use it at any time in the future by opening it. **Opening a form** is similar to opening a table; that is, make sure the form to be opened is selected and then click the Open button. Before opening the form, however, the Forms tab, rather than the Tables tab, must be selected.

Perform the following steps to open the Client form.

Steps **To Open a Form**

1 **With the Pilotech Services database open and the Database window on the screen, point to the Forms tab (Figure 1-55).**

FIGURE 1-55

2 Click the Forms tab, right-click the Client form and then point to Open on the shortcut menu.

The Forms sheet is selected and the list of available forms displays (Figure 1-56). Currently, the Client form is the only form. The shortcut menu for the Client form displays.

FIGURE 1-56

3 Click Open on the shortcut menu.

The Client form displays (Figure 1-57).

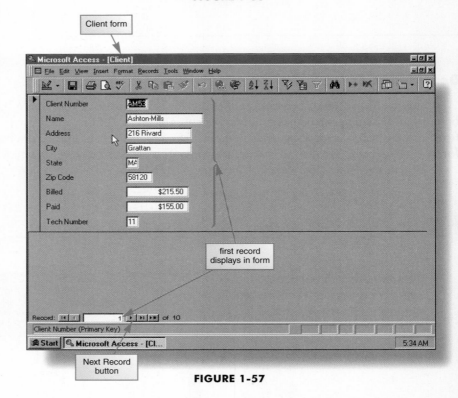

FIGURE 1-57

*Other*Ways

1. Click Forms tab, double-click desired Form
2. Click desired form, click Open button
3. Press ALT+O

Using the Form

You can **use the form** just as you used Datasheet view. You use the Navigation buttons to move between records. You can add new records or change existing ones. To delete the record displayed on the screen, after selecting the record by clicking its record selector, press the DELETE key. Thus, you can perform database operations using either Form view or Datasheet view.

Because you can see only one record at a time in Form view, to see a different record, such as the fifth record, use the Navigation buttons to move to it. To move from record to record in Form view, perform the following step.

To Use a Form

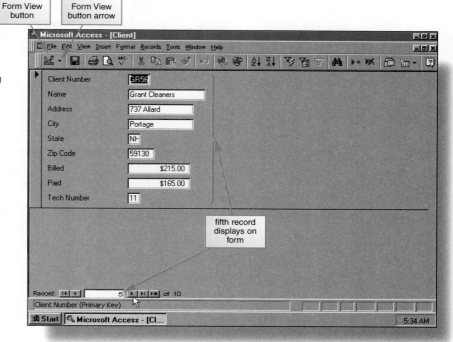

1 **Click the Next Record button four times.**

The fifth record displays on the form (Figure 1-58).

FIGURE 1-58

witching Between Form View and Datasheet View

In some cases, once you have seen a record in Form view, you will want to move to Datasheet view to again see a collection of records. To do so, click the orm View button arrow on the toolbar and then click Datasheet View in the list hat displays.

Perform the following steps to switch from Form view to Datasheet view.

eps **To Switch from Form View to Datasheet View**

1 **Click the Form View button arrow on the toolbar (see Figure 1-58) and then point to Datasheet View.**

The list of available views displays (Figure 1-59).

FIGURE 1-59

2 **Click Datasheet View.**

The table displays in Datasheet view (Figure 1-60). The record selector is positioned on the fifth record.

3 **Close the Client window by clicking its Close button.**

The datasheet no longer displays.

Close button

Microsoft Access - [Client]

File Edit View Insert Format Records Tools Window Help

Client Number	Name	Address	City	State	Zip Code	B
AM53	Ashton-Mills	216 Rivard	Grattan	MA	58120	
AS62	Alton-Scripps	722 Fisher	Empire	MA	58216	
BL26	Blake Suppliers	5752 Maumee	Grattan	MA	58120	
DE76	D & E Grocery	464 Linnell	Marshall	VT	52018	
GR56	Grant Cleaners	737 Allard	Portage	NH	59130	
GU21	Grand Union	247 Fuller	Grattan	MA	58120	
JE77	Jones Electric	57 Giddings	Marshall	VT	52018	
MI26	Morland Int.	665 Whittier	Frankfort	MA	56152	
SA56	Sawyer Inc.	31 Lafayette	Empire	MA	58216	
SI82	Simpson Ind.	752 Cadieux	Fernwood	MA	57412	

fifth record is current record

Datasheet view

Record: ◄◄ ◄ 5 ► ►I ►* of 10

Client Number (Primary Key)

Start | Microsoft Access - [Cl...

5:35 AM

FIGURE 1-60

OtherWays

1. On View menu click Datasheet View

Creating a Report

Earlier in this project, you printed a table using the Print button. The report you produced was shown in Figure 1-36 on page A 1.29. While this type of report presented the data in an organized manner, it was not very flexible. It included all the fields, but in precisely the same order in which they occurred in the table. A way to change the title was not presented; it remained Client.

In this section, you will **create the report** shown in Figure 1-61. This report features significant differences from the one in Figure 1-36. The portion at the top of the report in Figure 1-61, called a **page header**, contains a custom title. The contents of this page header appear at the top of each page. The **detail lines**, which are the lines that are printed for each record, contain only those fields you specify.

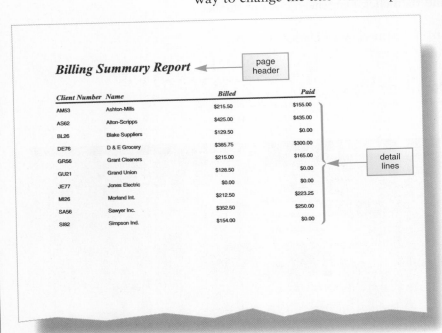

Billing Summary Report

page header

Client Number	Name	Billed	Paid
AM53	Ashton-Mills	$215.50	$155.00
AS62	Alton-Scripps	$425.00	$435.00
BL26	Blake Suppliers	$129.50	$0.00
DE76	D & E Grocery	$385.75	$300.00
GR56	Grant Cleaners	$215.00	$165.00
GU21	Grand Union	$128.50	$0.00
JE77	Jones Electric	$0.00	$0.00
MI26	Morland Int.	$212.50	$223.25
SA56	Sawyer Inc.	$352.50	$250.00
SI82	Simpson Ind.	$154.00	$0.00

detail lines

FIGURE 1-61

Perform the following steps to create the report in Figure 1-61.

Steps **To Create a Report**

1 **Click the Tables tab. Make sure the Client table is selected. Click the New Object: AutoForm button arrow on the toolbar.**

The list of available objects displays (Figure 1-62).

FIGURE 1-62

2 **Click Report and then point to Report Wizard.**

The New Report dialog box displays (Figure 1-63).

FIGURE 1-63

Report Wizard dialog box

3 Click Report Wizard and then click the OK button. Point to the Add Field button.

The Report Wizard dialog box displays (Figure 1-64).

FIGURE 1-64

OtherWays
1. On Insert menu click Report
2. Click Reports tab, click New

Selecting the Fields for the Report

To select a field for the report; that is, to indicate the field that is to be included in the report, click the field in the Available Fields list box. Next, click the Add Field button. This will move the field from the Available Fields list box to the Selected Fields list box, thus including the field in the report. If you wanted to select all fields, a shortcut is available simply by clicking the Add All Fields button.

To select the Client Number, Name, Billed, and Paid fields for the report, perform the following steps.

Steps **To Select the Fields for a Report**

1 Click the Add Field button to add the Client Number field. Add the Name field by clicking it and then clicking the Add Field button. Add the Billed and Paid fields just as you added the Client Number and Name fields.

The fields for the report display in the Selected Fields list box (Figure 1-65).

FIGURE 1-65

2 **Click the Next button.**

The Report Wizard dialog box displays (Figure 1-66).

FIGURE 1-66

Completing the Report

Several additional steps are involved in completing the report. With the exception of changing the title, the Access selections are acceptable, so you simply will click the Next button.

Perform the following steps to complete the report.

To Complete a Report

1 **Because you will not specify any grouping, click the Next button in the Report Wizard dialog box (see Figure 1-66). Click the Next button a second time because you will not need to make changes on the screen that follows.**

The Report Wizard dialog box displays (Figure 1-67). In this dialog box, you can change the layout or orientation of the report.

FIGURE 1-67

2 Make sure that Tabular is selected as the layout and Portrait is selected as the orientation and then click the Next button.

The Report Wizard dialog box displays (Figure 1-68). In this dialog box, you can select a style for the report.

FIGURE 1-68

3 Be sure that the Corporate style is selected and then click the Next button.

The Report Wizard dialog box displays (Figure 1-69). In this dialog box, you can specify a title for the report.

FIGURE 1-69

Type Billing Summary
Report **as the new title and then
click the Finish button.**

*A preview of the report displays
(Figure 1-70). Yours may look
slightly different, depending on your
printer.*

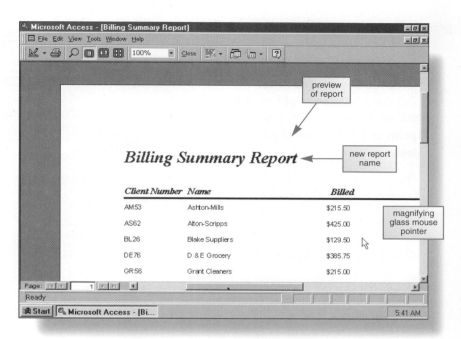

FIGURE 1-70

**Click anywhere within the report
to see the entire report.**

*The entire report displays (Figure
1-71).*

**Close the report by clicking the
Close button for the Billing
Summary Report window.**

*The report no longer displays. It has
been saved automatically using the
name Billing Summary Report.*

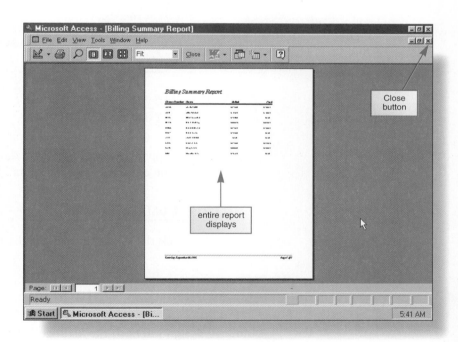

FIGURE 1-71

...ting the Report

To print a report from the Database window, first make sure the report
...lays. Then, you can click Print on the shortcut menu to print the report or
...t Preview on the shortcut menu to see a preview of the report on the screen.
...Perform the following steps to print the report.

More *About*
Reports

Custom reports represent one of
the most important ways of presenting the data in a database.
Reports can incorporate data
from multiple tables and can be
formatted in a wide variety of
ways. The ability to create
sophisticated custom reports is
one of the major benefits of a
DBMS like Access.

Steps To Print a Report

1 **Click the Reports tab in the Database window, right-click the Billing Summary Report and then point to Print on the shortcut menu.**

The shortcut menu for the Billing Summary Report displays (Figure 1-72).

2 **Click Print on the shortcut menu.**

The report prints. It should look similar to the one shown in Figure 1-61 on page A 1.40.

FIGURE 1-72

Closing the Database

Once you have finished working with a database, you should close it. The following step closes the database by closing its Database window.

TO CLOSE A DATABASE

1 Click the Close button for the Pilotech Services : Database window.

Designing a Database

Database design refers to the arrangement of data into tables and fields. In the example in this project, the design is specified, but in many cases, you will have to determine the design based on what you want the system to accomplish.

With large, complex databases, the database design process can be extensive. Major sections of advanced database textbooks are devoted to this topic. Often, however, you should be able to design a database effectively by keeping one simple principle in mind: Design to remove redundancy. **Redundancy** means storing the same fact in more than one place.

To illustrate, you need to maintain the following information shown in Figure [1-7]3. In the figure, all the data is contained in a single table. Notice that the data [for] a given Technician (number, name, address, and so on) occurs on more than [one] record.

[Cl]ient table

CLIENT NUMBER	NAME	ADDRESS	CITY	STATE	ZIP CODE	BILLED	PAID	TECH NUMBER	LAST NAME	FIRST NAME	ADDRESS	CITY	STATE	ZIP CODE	HOURLY RATE	YTD EARNINGS
[53]	Ashton-Mills	216 Rivard	Grattan	MA	58120	$215.50	$155.00	11	Levin	Joanna	26 Cottonwood	Carlton	MA	59712	$25.00	$6,245.00
[62]	Alton-Scripps	722 Fisher	Empire	MA	58216	$425.00	$435.00	12	Rogers	Brad	7972 Marsden	Kaleva	VT	57253	$30.00	$7,143.30
[26]	Blake Suppliers	5752 Maumee	Grattan	MA	58120	$129.50	$5,000.00	12	Rogers	Brad	7972 Marsden	Kaleva	VT	57253	$30.00	$7,143.30
[76]	D & E Grocery	464 Linnell	Marshall	VT	52018	$385.75	$300.00	17	Rodriguez	Maria	263 Topsfield	Hudson	MA	57240	$35.00	$7,745.50
[56]	Grant Cleaners	737 Allard	Portage	NH	59130	$215.00	$165.00	11	Levin	Joanna	26 Cottonwood	Carlton	MA	59712	$25.00	$6,245.00
[21]	Grand Union	247 Fuller	Grattan	MA	58120	$128.50	$0.00	12	Rogers	Brad	7972 Marsden	Kaleva	VT	57253	$30.00	$7,143.30
[7]	Jones Electric	57 Giddings	Marshall	VT	52018	$0.00	$0.00	12	Rogers	Brad	7972 Marsden	Kaleva	VT	57253	$30.00	$7,143.30
[26]	Morland Int.	665 Whittier	Frankfort	MA	56152	$212.50	$223.25	11	Levin	Joanna	26 Cottonwood	Carlton	MA	59712	$25.00	$6,245.00
[56]	Sawyer Inc.	31 Lafayette	Empire	MA	58216	$352.50	$250.00	17	Rodriguez	Maria	263 Topsfield	Hudson	MA	57240	$35.00	$7,745.50
[2]	Simpson Ind.	752 Cadieux	Fernwood	MA	57412	$154.00	$0.00	12	Rogers	Brad	7972 Marsden	Kaleva	VT	57253	$30.00	$7,143.30

duplicate technician names

FIGURE 1-73

Storing this data on multiple records is an example of redundancy, which [cau]ses several problems:

1. Redundancy wastes space on the disk. The address of Technician 11 (Joanna Levin), for example, should be stored only once. Storing this fact several times is wasteful.
2. Redundancy makes updating the database more difficult. If, for example, Joanna Levin moves, her address would need to be changed in several different places.
3. A possibility of inconsistent data exists. Suppose, for example, that you change the address of Joanna Levin on client GR56's record to 146 Valley, but do not change it on client AM53's record. In both cases, the Tech Number is 11, but the addresses are different. In other words, the data is inconsistent.

The solution to the problem is to place the redundant data in a separate tabl one in which the data will no longer be redundant. If, for example, you place t data for technicians in a separate table (Figure 1-74), the data for each technici will appear only once.

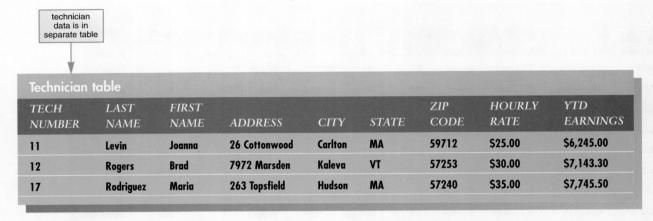

technician data is in separate table

Technician table

TECH NUMBER	LAST NAME	FIRST NAME	ADDRESS	CITY	STATE	ZIP CODE	HOURLY RATE	YTD EARNINGS
11	Levin	Joanna	26 Cottonwood	Carlton	MA	59712	$25.00	$6,245.00
12	Rogers	Brad	7972 Marsden	Kaleva	VT	57253	$30.00	$7,143.30
17	Rodriguez	Maria	263 Topsfield	Hudson	MA	57240	$35.00	$7,745.50

Client table

CLIENT NUMBER	NAME	ADDRESS	CITY	STATE	ZIP CODE	BILLED	PAID	TECH NUMBER
AM53	Ashton-Mills	216 Rivard	Grattan	MA	58120	$215.50	$155.00	11
AS62	Alton-Scripps	722 Fisher	Empire	MA	58216	$425.00	$435.00	12
BL26	Blake Suppliers	5752 Maumee	Grattan	MA	58120	$129.50	$0.00	12
DE76	D & E Grocery	464 Linnell	Marshall	VT	52018	$385.75	$300.00	17
GR56	Grant Cleaners	737 Allard	Portage	NH	59130	$215.00	$165.00	11
GU21	Grand Union	247 Fuller	Grattan	MA	58120	$128.50	$0.00	12
JE77	Jones Electric	57 Giddings	Marshall	VT	52018	$0.00	$0.00	12
MI26	Morland Int.	665 Whittier	Frankfort	MA	56152	$212.50	$223.25	11
SA56	Sawyer Inc.	31 Lafayette	Empire	MA	58216	$352.50	$250.00	17
SI82	Simpson Ind.	752 Cadieux	Fernwood	MA	57412	$154.00	$0.00	12

FIGURE 1-74

Notice that you need to have the Tech Number in both tables. Without it, way exists to tell which technician is associated with which client. All the othe technician data, however, was removed from the Client table and placed in the Technician table. This new arrangement corrects the problems of redundancy i the following ways:

1. Because the data for each technician is stored only once, space is not wasted.
2. Changing the address of a technician is easy. You have only to change o row in the Technician table.
3. Because the data for a technician is stored only once, inconsistent data cannot occur.

Designing to omit redundancy will help you to produce good and valid database designs.

Access Online Help

At any time while you are working with Microsoft Access, you can answer your questions by using Access Help. Used properly, this form of online assistance can increase your productivity and reduce your frustrations by minimizing the time you spend learning how to use Access. Table 1-2 summarizes the categories of Access Help available to you. For more information on using online Help, see pages WD 1.54 through WD 1.59 in Project 1 of Microsoft Word 97.

Table 1-2		
TYPE	DESCRIPTION	ACTIVATE BY
Office Assistant	Answers your questions, offers tips, and provides Help for a variety of Access features	Clicking Office Assistant button on the toolbar
Contents sheet	Groups Help topics by general categories; use when you know only the general category of the topic in question	Clicking Contents and Index on the Help menu, then clicking the Contents tab
Index sheet	Similar to an index in a book; use when you know exactly what you want	Clicking Contents and Index on the Help menu, then clicking the Index tab
Find sheet	Searches the index for all phrases that include the term in question	Clicking Contents and Index on the Help menu, then clicking the Find tab
Question Mark button and What's This? command	Identify unfamiliar items on the screen	Clicking the Question Mark button, then clicking an item in a dialog box; clicking What's This? on the Help menu, then clicking an item on the screen

Project Summary

Project 1 introduced you to starting Access and creating a database. You created the database that will be used by Pilotech Services. Within the Pilotech Services database, you created the Client and Technician tables by defining the fields within them. You then added records to these tables. Once you created the tables, you printed the contents of the tables. You also used a form to view the data in the table. Finally, you used the Report Wizard to create a report containing the Client Number, Name, Billed, and Paid fields for each client of Pilotech Services.

What You Should Know

Having completed this project, you now should be able to perform the following tasks:

- Add Additional Records to a Table *(A 1.27)*
- Add Records to a Table *(A 1.21)*
- Add Records to an Additional Table *(A 1.34)*
- Close a Database *(A 1.46)*
- Close a Table and Database and Quit Access *(A 1.24)*
- Close and Save a Form *(A 1.36)*
- Complete a Report *(A 1.43)*
- Create a Report *(A 1.41)*
- Create a Table *(A 1.15)*
- Create an Additional Table *(A 1.33)*
- Define the Fields in a Table *(A 1.16)*
- Open a Database *(A 1.25)*
- Open a Form *(A 1.37)*
- Preview and Print the Contents of a Table *(A 1.29)*
- Print a Report *(A 1.45)*
- Save a Table *(A 1.19)*
- Select the Fields for a Report *(A 1.42)*
- Start Access *(A 1.10)*
- Switch from Form View to Datasheet View *(A 1.39)*
- Use a Form *(A 1.39)*
- Use the New Object: AutoForm Button to Create a Form *(A 1.35)*

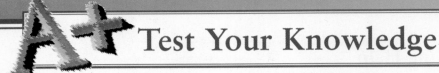

1 True/False

Instructions: Circle T if the statement is true or F if the statement is false.

T F   1. A field contains information about a given person, product, or event.

T F   2. An Access database consists of a collection of tables.

T F   3. If you do not assign a width to a text field, Access assumes the width is 25.

T F   4. You can use the TAB key to move to the next field in a record in Datasheet view.

T F   5. Field names can be no more than 64 characters in length and can include numeric digits.

T F   6. The only field type available for fields that must be used in arithmetic operations is number.

T F   7. To delete a record from a table, select the record and then press the DELETE key.

T F   8. To add a field to a table structure, select the field that will follow the field you want to add, click Edit on the menu bar and then click Insert Row.

T F   9. To add records to a table that already contains data, open the table and then click the Append Record button.

T F   10. Controlling redundancy results in an increase in consistency.

2 Multiple Choice

Instructions: Circle the correct response.

1. A database is _____.
   a. the same as a file
   b. a collection of data organized in a manner that allows access, retrieval, and use of that data
   c. a software product
   d. none of the above

2. Which of the following is not a benefit of controlling redundancy?
   a. greater consistency is maintained
   b. less space is occupied
   c. update is easier
   d. all of the above are benefits

3. A field that uniquely identifies a particular record in a table is called a _____.
   a. secondary key
   b. foreign key
   c. principal key
   d. primary key

4. Access is a(n) _____.
   a. application software package
   b. DBMS
   c. database
   d. both a and b

Test Your Knowledge

5. To add a record to a table that already contains data, open the table and click the _____ button.
   a. Add Record
   b. New Record
   c. Append Record
   d. Insert Record

6. A record in Access is composed of a _____.
   a. series of databases
   b. series of files
   c. series of records
   d. series of fields

7. To make a field the primary key for a table, select the field and then click the _____ button on the toolbar.
   a. Unique Key
   b. Single Key
   c. First Key
   d. Primary Key

8. To remove a field from a table structure, select the field and then press the _____ key(s).
   a. DELETE
   b. CTRL+D
   c. CTRL+DELETE
   d. CTRL+Y

9. To change to landscape orientation to print a table, on the File menu, click _____.
   a. Print Preview
   b. Page Setup
   c. Print
   d. Print Settings

10. To move from the upper pane, the one where you define fields, in the Table window to the lower pane, the one where you define field properties, press the _____ key.
   a. F3
   b. F4
   c. F6
   d. F7

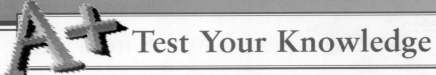

Test Your Knowledge

3 Understanding Access Windows

Instructions: In Figure 1-75, arrows point to the major components of an Access window. In the spaces provided, indicate the purpose of each of these components.

FIGURE 1-75

4 Understanding the Table Window in Datasheet View

Instructions: On the form in Figure 1-76, arrows point to the major components of a Table window in Datasheet view. In the spaces provided, indicate the purpose of each of these components.

FIGURE 1-76

? Use Help

1 Reviewing Project Activities

Instructions: Perform the following tasks using a computer.

1. Start Access.
2. If the Office Assistant is on your screen, then click it to display its balloon. If the Office Assistant is not on your screen, then click the Office Assistant button on the toolbar.
3. Click the Office Assistant and type `data types` in the What would you like to do? text box. Click the Search button.
4. Click What data type should I use for a field in my table?. Read the Help information. Use the shortcut menu or Options button to print the information. Hand in the printout to your instructor.
5. Click the Help Topics button. Click the Index tab. Type `Datasheet` in the top text box labeled 1 and then double-click entering and editing data under Datasheet view in the list box labeled 2. Double-click Delete a record in Datasheet or Form view in the Topics Found dialog box. When the Help information displays, read it. Use the shortcut menu or Options button to print the information. Hand in the printout to your instructor. Click the Help Topics button to return to the Help Topics: Microsoft Access 97 dialog box.
6. Click the Find tab. Type `preview` in the top text box labeled 1. Click Previewing in the list box labeled 2. Double-click Preview a report in the list box labeled 3. When the Microsoft Access 97 window displays, read it and use the shortcut menu or Options button to print the information. Click the Preview all the data in the report page by page button in the Help window. Print the Help information. Hand in the printouts to your instructor. Click the Close button.

2 Expanding on the Basics

Instructions: Use Access Help to better understand the topics listed below. If you are unable to print the Help information, then answer the questions on your own paper.

1. Using the Working with Data book on the Contents sheet in the Help Topics: Microsoft Access 97 dialog box, answer the following questions:
   a. When does Access save the data in a record?
   b. How can you save the data in a record while you are editing it?
2. Using the words, shortcut keys, and the Index tab in the Help Topics: Microsoft Access 97 dialog box, display and print the shortcut keys to use in Datasheet view and Form view. Then, answer the following questions:
   a. Which key or combination of keys add a new record?
   b. Which key or combination of keys delete the current record?
   c. Which key or combination of keys save changes to the current record?

(continued)

Use Help

Expanding on the Basics (continued)

    d. Which key or combination of keys undo changes in the current field?

    e. Which key or combination of keys insert the value from the same field in the previous record?

3. Use the Find sheet in the Help Topics: Microsoft Access 97 dialog box to display and print information about automatically correcting two capital letters in a row.

4. Use the Office Assistant to display and print information about backing up a database.

Apply Your Knowledge

CAUTION: To ensure you have enough disk space to save your files, it is recommended that you create a copy of the Data Disk that accompanies this book. Then, delete folders from the copy of the Data Disk that are not needed for the application you are working on. Do the following: (1) Insert the Data Disk in drive A; (2) start Explorer; (3) right-click the 3½ Floppy (A:) folder in the All Folders side of the window; (4) click Copy Disk; (5) click Start and OK as required; (6) insert a floppy disk when requested; (7) delete all folders on the floppy disk you created except the Access folder; (8) remove the floppy disk from drive A and label it Access Data Disk.

1 Changing Data and Creating Reports

Instructions: Start Access and open the Green Thumb document from the Access folder on the Data Disk that accompanies this book. Green Thumb is a small company that was started by two graduates of the horticulture program at the local college. It provides plants and plant care to local businesses. Green Thumb designs indoor landscapes and does regular maintenance, for example, watering, fertilizing, and pruning. The company employs horticulture students who do internships with the company. Green Thumb has a database that keeps track of its interns and customers. The database has two tables. The Customer table contains data on the customers who use Green Thumb's services. The Intern table contains data on the students employed by Green Thumb. The structure and data are shown for the Customer table in Figure 1-77 below and at the top of the next page and for the Intern table in Figure 1-78.

Structure of Customer table				
FIELD NAME	DATA TYPE	FIELD SIZE	PRIMARY KEY?	DESCRIPTION
Customer Number	Text	4	Yes	Customer Number (Primary Key)
Name	Text	20		Customer Name
Address	Text	15		Street Address
City	Text	15		City
State	Text	2		State (Two-Character Abbreviation)
Zip Code	Text	5		Zip Code (Five-Character Version)
Balance	Currency			Amount Owed by Customer
Intern Id	Text	3		Id of Customer's Intern

FIGURE 1-77

Apply Your Knowledge

Data for Customer table

CUSTOMER NUMBER	NAME	ADDRESS	CITY	STATE	ZIP CODE	BALANCE	INTERN ID
AS36	Asterman Ind.	200 Bard	Howden	MO	59444	$85.00	102
AU54	Author Books	142 Birchwood	Howden	MO	59445	$50.00	109
BI92	Bike Shop	433 Chester	Howden	MO	59441	$40.00	109
CI76	Cinderton Co.	73 Fleming	Dorchester	IL	57342	$0.00	113
CJ16	CJ's Music	277 Fordham	Dorchester	IL	57342	$105.00	102
JO62	Jordan Diner	250 Bard	Howden	MO	59444	$74.00	109
KL55	Klingon Toys	215 Scott	Evansville	MO	59335	$115.00	109
ME71	Meat & Cleaver	543 Fleming	Dorchester	IL	57342	$138.00	102
MO13	Moore Foods	876 Grove	Evansville	MO	59335	$0.00	113
RO32	Royal Mfg Co.	954 Cline	Evansville	MO	59331	$93.00	109

FIGURE 1-77 (continued)

Structure of Intern table

FIELD NAME	DATA TYPE	FIELD SIZE	PRIMARY KEY?	DESCRIPTION
Intern Id	Text	3	Yes	Intern Identification Number (Primary Key)
Last Name	Text	10		Last Name of Intern
First Name	Text	8		First Name of Intern
Address	Text	15		Street Address
City	Text	15		City
State	Text	2		State (Two-Character Abbreviation)
Zip Code	Text	5		Zip Code (Five-Character Version)
Pay Rate	Currency			Hourly Pay Rate

Data for Intern table

INTERN ID	LAST NAME	FIRST NAME	ADDRESS	CITY	STATE	ZIP CODE	PAY RATE
102	Dang	Chou	764 Clay	Howden	MO	59444	$7.50
109	Hyde	Michelle	65 Parkwood	Dorchester	IL	57342	$7.75
113	Lopez	Javier	345 Norton	Howden	MO	59444	$7.65

FIGURE 1-78

(continued)

Apply Your Knowledge

Changing Data and Creating Reports *(continued)*

Perform the following tasks.

1. Open the Intern table in Datasheet view and add the following record to the table:

| 105 | Eckels | Lois | 24 Riley | Evansville | MO | 59335 | 7.40 |

   Close the Intern table.

2. Open the Intern table again. Notice that the record you just added has been moved. It is no longer at the end of the table. The records are in order by the primary key, Intern ID.

3. Print the Intern table.

4. Open the Customer table.

5. Change the Intern ID for customer KL55 to 105.

6. Print the Customer table.

7. Create the report shown in Figure 1-79 for the Customer table.

Balance Due Report

Customer Number	Name	Balance
AS36	Asterman Ind.	$85.00
AU54	Author Books	$50.00
BI92	Bike Shop	$40.00
CI76	Cinderton Co.	$0.00
CJ16	CJ's Music	$105.00
JO62	Jordan Diner	$74.00
KL55	Klingon Toys	$115.00
ME71	Meat & Cleaver	$138.00
MO13	Moore Foods	$0.00
RO32	Royal Mfg Co.	$93.00

FIGURE 1-79

8. Print the report.

In the Lab

1 Creating the Museum Mercantile Database

Problem: The County Museum runs a small gift shop, Museum Mercantile, that is staffed by volunteers. The museum purchases products from vendors that specialize in handcrafted products and vintage merchandise. The director of the museum has asked you to create and update a database that volunteers can use. The database consists of two tables. The Product table contains information on items available for sale. The Vendor table contains information on the vendors.

Instructions: Perform the following tasks.

1. Create a new database in which to store all the objects related to the gift shop data. Call the database Museum Mercantile.

2. Create the Product table using the structure shown in Figure 1-95. Use the name Product for the table.

Structure of Product table

FIELD NAME	DATA TYPE	FIELD SIZE	PRIMARY KEY?	DESCRIPTION
Product Id	Text	4	Yes	Product Id Number (Primary Key)
Description	Text	25		Description of Product
On Hand	Number	Long Integer		Number of Units On Hand
Cost	Currency			Cost of Product
Selling Price	Currency			Selling Price of Product
Vendor Code	Text	2		Code of Product Vendor

Data for Product table

PRODUCT ID	DESCRIPTION	ON HAND	COST	SELLING PRICE	VENDOR CODE
CH04	Chess Set	11	$26.75	$28.90	WW
DI24	Dinosaurs	14	$3.75	$4.95	MS
GL18	Globe	2	$27.50	$29.95	MS
JG01	Jigsaw Puzzle	3	$5.40	$6.95	MS
PC03	Pick Up Sticks	5	$8.50	$10.95	WW
ST23	Stationery	8	$3.95	$5.00	AR
TD05	Tiddly Winks	6	$13.75	$15.95	WW
WI10	Wizard Cards	10	$7.50	$9.95	MS
WL34	Wildlife Posters	15	$2.50	$2.95	AR
YO12	Wooden YoYo	9	$1.60	$1.95	WW

FIGURE 1-95

(continued)

In the Lab

Creating the Museum Mercantile Database *(continued)*

3. Add the data shown in Figure 1-80 on the previous page to the Product table.
4. Print the Product table.
5. Create the Vendor table using the structure shown in Figure 1-81. Use the name Vendor for the table.

Structure of Vendor table				
FIELD NAME	DATA TYPE	FIELD SIZE	PRIMARY KEY?	DESCRIPTION
Vendor Code	Text	2	Yes	Vendor Code (Primary Key)
Name	Text	20		Name of Vendor
Address	Text	15		Street Address
City	Text	15		City
State	Text	2		State (Two-Character Abbreviation)
Zip Code	Text	5		Zip Code (Five-Character Version)
Telephone Number	Text	12		Telephone Number (999-999-9999 Version)

Data for Vendor table						
VENDOR CODE	NAME	ADDRESS	CITY	STATE	ZIP CODE	TELEPHONE NUMBER
AR	Artisan's Co-op	3540 Grand	Hancock	WI	69780	414-555-7865
MS	Museum Stores	134 Union	Delana	SD	41345	605-555-3498
WW	Woodworkers	655 Clive	Great Falls	WV	34567	304-555-4532

FIGURE 1-81

6. Add the data shown in Figure 1-81 to the Vendor table.
7. Print the Vendor table.
8. Create a form for the Product table. Use the name Product for the form.
9. Create and print the report shown in Figure 1-82 for the Product table.

Inventory Report

Product Id	Description	On Hand	Cost
WI10	Wizard Cards	10	$7.50
PC03	Pick Up Sticks	5	$8.50
WL34	Wildlife Posters	15	$2.50
TD05	Tiddly Winks	6	$13.75
ST23	Stationery	8	$3.95
JG01	Jigsaw Puzzle	3	$5.40
YO12	Wooden YoYo	9	$1.60
DI24	Dinosaurs	14	$3.75
GL18	Globe	2	$27.50
CH04	Chess Set	11	$26.75

FIGURE 1-82

In the Lab

2 Creating the City Telephone System Database

Problem: The city government maintains its own internal telephone system. Each user is billed separately for monthly charges and all the bills for a department are sent to the department manager. The telephone manager has asked you to create and update a database that the city government can use as a telephone tracking system. The database consists of two tables. The User table contains information on the individuals with telephone accounts. The Department table contains information on the department in which the individual works.

Instructions: Perform the following tasks.

1. Create a new database in which to store all the objects related to the telephone system data. Call the database City Telephone System.
2. Create the User table using the structure shown in Figure 1-83. Use the name User for the table.

Structure of User table

FIELD NAME	DATA TYPE	FIELD SIZE	PRIMARY KEY?	DESCRIPTION
User Id	Text	4	Yes	User Id Number (Primary Key)
Last Name	Text	14		Last Name of User
First Name	Text	10		First Name of User
Phone Ext	Text	4		Telephone Extension (9999 Version)
Office	Text	3		Office Location (Room Number)
Basic Charge	Currency			Basic Service Charge (per Month)
Extra Charges	Currency			Extra Charges for Special Services and Long Distance Calls (per Month)
Dept Code	Text	3		Code of User's Department

Data for User table

USER ID	LAST NAME	FIRST NAME	PHONE EXT	OFFICE	BASIC CHARGE	EXTRA CHARGES	DEPT CODE
T129	Bishop	Fred	3383	212	$10.00	$22.00	ITD
T238	Chan	Rose	3495	220	$13.00	$29.95	ITD
T347	Febo	Javier	4267	323	$10.00	$7.75	HRS
T451	Ginras	Mary	3156	444	$17.00	$52.85	APV
T536	Hanneman	William	3578	317	$13.00	$18.75	HRS
T645	Johnsen	Paul	4445	234	$21.00	$7.75	ITD
T759	Kim	Lei	3068	310	$10.00	$13.55	ENG
T780	Mentor	Melissa	3418	525	$17.00	$73.95	PLN
T851	Sanchez	Alfredo	3134	438	$11.00	$6.25	APV
T888	TenClink	Brian	3414	521	$10.00	$37.45	PLN

FIGURE 1-83

(continued)

In the Lab

Creating the City Telephone System Database (continued)

3. Add the data shown in Figure 1-83 on the previous page to the User table.
4. Print the User table.
5. Create the Department table using the structure shown in Figure 1-84. Use the name Department for the table.

Structure of Department table

FIELD NAME	DATA TYPE	FIELD SIZE	PRIMARY KEY?	DESCRIPTION
Dept Code	Text	3	Yes	Department Code (Primary Key)
Dept Name	Text	14		Name of Department
First Name	Text	8		First Name of Department Manager
Last Name	Text	12		Last Name of Department Manager

Data for Department table

DEPT CODE	DEPT NAME	FIRST NAME	LAST NAME
APV	Assessment	Joyce	Murphy
ENG	Engineering	Darnell	James
HRS	Housing	Billie	Buchanan
ITD	Income Tax	Maria	Fuentes
PLN	Planning	Joseph	Lippman

FIGURE 1-84

6. Add the data shown in Figure 1-84 to the Department table.
7. Print the Department table.
8. Create a form for the User table. Use the name User for the form.
9. Use the form you created to add the following two new city employees to the User table.

T087	Anders	Jane	3923	531	$10.00	$0.00	PLN
T832	Reison	Jason	3803	312	$13.00	$0.00	ENG

10. Create and print the report shown in Figure 1-85 for the User table. When the Report Wizard asks, What Sort Order do you want for your records?, click the Last Name field.

In the Lab

Telephone List

Last Name	First Name	Phone Ext	Office	Dept Code
Anders	Jane	3923	531	PLN
Bishop	Fred	3383	212	ITD
Chan	Rose	3495	220	ITD
Febo	Javier	4267	323	HRS
Ginras	Mary	3156	444	APV
Hanneman	William	3578	317	HRS
Johnsen	Paul	4445	234	ITD
Kim	Lei	3068	310	ENG
Mentor	Melissa	3418	525	PLN
Reison	Jason	3803	312	ENG
Sanchez	Alfredo	3134	438	APV
TenClink	Brian	3414	521	PLN

FIGURE 1-85

3 Creating the City Scene Database

Problem: The *City Scene* is a local arts magazine that relies on advertising to help finance its operations. Local firms buy advertising from ad representatives who work for the magazine. Ad representatives receive a commission based on the advertising revenues they generate. The managing editor of the magazine has asked you to create and update a database that will keep track of the advertising accounts and ad representatives. The database consists of two tables. The Advertiser table contains information on the organizations that advertise in the magazine. The Ad Rep table contains information on the representative assigned to the advertising account.

Instructions: Perform the following tasks.

1. Create a new database in which to store all the objects related to the advertising data. Call the database City Scene.
2. Create the Advertiser table using the structure shown in Figure 1-86 on the next page. Use the name Advertiser for the table.
3. Add the data shown in Figure 1-86 to the Advertiser table.

(continued)

In the Lab

Creating the City Scene Database (continued)

Structure of Advertiser table

FIELD NAME	DATA TYPE	FIELD SIZE	PRIMARY KEY?	DESCRIPTION
Advertiser Number	Text	4	Yes	Advertiser Number (Primary Key)
Name	Text	20		Name of Advertiser
Address	Text	15		Street Address
City	Text	15		City
State	Text	2		State (Two-Character Abbreviation)
Zip Code	Text	5		Zip Code (Five-Character Version)
Balance	Currency			Amount Currently Owed
Amount Paid	Currency			Amount Paid Year-to-Date
Ad Rep Number	Text	2		Number of Advertising Representative

Data for Advertiser table

ADVERTISER NUMBER	NAME	ADDRESS	CITY	STATE	ZIP CODE	BALANCE	AMOUNT PAID	AD REP NUMBER
A226	Alden Books	74 Benton	Fernwood	WA	91191	$60.00	$535.00	16
B101	Bud's Diner	384 Carter	Crestview	OR	92332	$155.00	$795.00	19
C047	Chip and Putt	1 Golfview	Crestview	OR	92330	$0.00	$345.00	19
C134	Clover Clothes	62 Adams	New Castle	WA	91234	$100.00	$835.00	22
D216	Dogs 'n Draft	3 Riverview	Crestview	OR	92330	$260.00	$485.00	16
F345	Fast Freddie's	507 Oakley	Fernwood	WA	91191	$0.00	$775.00	19
G080	Green Thumb	619 Lincoln	New Castle	WA	91234	$185.00	$825.00	19
L189	Lighthouse Inc.	1 Riverview	Crestview	OR	92330	$35.00	$150.00	16
N034	New Releases	107 Main	Fernwood	WA	91191	$435.00	$500.00	22
S010	Skates R You	67 Adams	New Castle	WA	91234	$85.00	$235.00	16

FIGURE 1-86

4. Print the Advertiser table.
5. Create the Ad Rep table using the structure shown in Figure 1-87. Use the name Ad Rep for the table. Be sure to change the field size for the Comm Rate field to Double.
6. Add the data shown in Figure 1-87 to the Ad Rep table.

In the Lab

Structure of Ad Rep table

FIELD NAME	DATA TYPE	FIELD SIZE	PRIMARY KEY?	DESCRIPTION
Ad Rep Number	Text	2	Yes	Advertising Rep Number (Primary Key)
Last Name	Text	10		Last Name of Advertising Rep
First Name	Text	8		First Name of Advertising Rep
Address	Text	15		Street Address
City	Text	15		City
State	Text	2		State (Two-Character Abbreviation)
Zip Code	Text	5		Zip Code (Five-Character Version)
Comm Rate	Number	Double		Commision Rate on Advertising Sales
Commission	Currency			Year-to-Date Total Commissions

Data for Ad Rep table

AD REP NUMBER	LAST NAME	FIRST NAME	ADDRESS	CITY	STATE	ZIP CODE	COMM RATE	COMMISSION
16	Hammond	Anne	75 Bartow	New Castle	WA	91234	0.08	$6,000.00
19	Morales	Louis	67 Shawmont	Fernwood	WA	91191	0.07	$5,750.00
22	Rodgers	Elaine	43 Manderly	Crestview	OR	92332	0.08	$6,500.00

FIGURE 1-87

7. Print the Ad Rep table.
8. Create a form for the Advertiser table. Use the name Advertiser for the form.
9. Open the form you created and change the address for Advertiser Number B101 to 384 Gartern.
10. Change to Datasheet view and delete the record for Advertiser Number F345.
11. Print the Advertiser table.
12. Create and print the report shown in Figure 1-88 on the next page for the Advertiser table.

(continued)

In the Lab

Creating the City Scene Database *(continued)*

Status Report

Advertiser Number	Name	Balance	Amount Paid
A226	Alden Books	$60.00	$535.00
B101	Bud's Diner	$155.00	$795.00
C047	Chip and Putt	$0.00	$345.00
C134	Clover Clothes	$100.00	$835.00
D216	Dogs 'n Draft	$260.00	$485.00
G080	Green Thumb	$185.00	$825.00
L189	Lighthouse Inc.	$35.00	$150.00
N034	New Releases	$435.00	$500.00
S010	Skates R You	$85.00	$235.00

Monday, September 21, 1998   *Page 1 of 1*

FIGURE 1-88

Cases and Places

For years, the students at your school have complained about the inequities of the book buy-back licy. Student government finally has decided to do something about it by organizing a used textbook operative. As a member of student government, you create a system whereby students can locate her students who have used a particular book in a previous semester and want to sell it to another ident. Student government advertises the plan on its Web page and receives the responses shown in gure 1-89.

Create a database to store the file related to the textbooks. Then create a table, enter the data from gure 1-89, and print the table.

OOK TLE	AUTHOR	COURSE USED	PRICE	SELLER'S NAME	TELEPHONE	CONDITION (E=EXCELLENT, G=GOOD, P=POOR)
ciology Today	Munroe	Soc 101	$14	Joe Van	555-7632	G
eative Writing	Swan & Shell	Eng 150	$18	Mary Nordman	555-9421	E
ach for the Stars	Alvarez	Ast 210	$23	John Mott	555-9981	E
eative Writing	Swan & Shell	Eng 150	$15	Peter Rudd	555-9156	E
s for Today's Society	Garrison & Pierce	Phi 310	$20	Sandi Radle	555-7636	P
ciology Today	Munroe	Soc 101	$17	Daniel Lewis	555-0873	E
derstanding Psychology	Navarone	Psy 101	$22	Karen Sing	555-9802	P
ctronic Circuitry	Carlson	Egr 255	$37	Karen Sing	555-9802	G
trition for Our Souls	Francis	Nrs 330	$18	Dave Corsi	555-2384	E
riatric Nursing	Dyer	Nrs 265	$36	Mary Healy	555-9932	E

FIGURE 1-89

Cases and Places

2 ▶ You have decided to start a meal delivery service. As a first step, you consult the telephone directory for the numbers of local restaurants to make reservations and to order food for carry out and delivery. You have decided to create a database to store these numbers along with other pertinent data about the establishment, such as address, hours of operation, type of food, and days when specials are offered. You gather the information shown in Figure 1-90.

  Create a database to store the file related to the restaurants. Then create a table, enter the data from Figure 1-90, and print the table.

NAME	TELEPHONE	ADDRESS	OPEN	CLOSE	FOOD TYPE	SPECIALS	CARRYOUT	DELIVERY
Noto's	(714) 555-2339	223 N. Jackson	11:00 a.m.	11:00 p.m.	Japanese	Wednesday	Yes	No
Ole Taco	(714) 555-5444	3294 E. Devon	4:00 p.m.	10:00 p.m.	Mexican	Monday	Yes	No
Red Rose	(714) 555-8001	1632 W. Clark	3:00 p.m.	1:00 a.m.	Indian	Friday	No	No
Pan Pacific	(714) 555-2470	3140 W. Halsted	11:00 a.m.	4:00 a.m.	Korean	Thursday	Yes	No
New Crete	(714) 555-9337	1805 W. Broadway	3:30 p.m.	10:00 p.m.	Greek	Monday	Yes	No
Texas Diner	(714) 555-1673	2200 E. Lawrence	4:30 p.m.	1:00 a.m.	American	Thursday	Yes	Yes
Little Venice	(714) 555-8632	13 N. Devon	11:30 a.m.	2:00 a.m.	Italian	Wednesday	Yes	No
Curry and More	(714) 555-3377	1027 E. Wells	5:00 p.m.	2:00 a.m.	Indian	Thursday	Yes	No
Napoli's Pizza	(714) 555-6168	787 N. Monroe	10:30 a.m.	3:00 a.m.	Italian	Tuesday	Yes	Yes
House of China	(714) 555-7373	1939 W. Michigan	11:00 a.m.	11:00 p.m.	Chinese	Wednesday	Yes	No

FIGURE 1-90

3 ▶▶ A local nursing home has a variety of classic movies on videocassette. You are a volunteer at the home and the director of volunteers has asked you to create an inventory of the movies. One afternoon, you sort through the boxes and list each movie's name, leading actors, year produced, and original running time. You also assign a rating system of one to four stars. You create the following list: *The Little Princess*, starring Shirley Temple and Richard Greene, 1939, 94 minutes, three stars; *North by Northwest*, Cary Grant and Eva Marie Saint, 1959, 136 minutes, four stars; *Of Mice and Men*, Burgess Meredith and Lon Chaney Jr., 1939, 107 minutes, four stars; *The Quiet Man*, John Wayne and Maureen O'Hara, 1952, 129 minutes, four stars; *On the Waterfront*, Marlon Brando and Eva Marie Saint, 1954, 108 minutes, four stars; *Pardon My Sarong*, Bud Abbott and Lou Costello, 1942, 84 minutes, three stars; *Ride 'em Cowboy*, Bud Abbott and Lou Costello, 1942, 82 minutes, two stars; *You Can't Take It With You*, Jean Arthur and Lionel Barrymore, 1938, 127 minutes, three stars; *The Undefeated*, John Wayne and Rock Hudson, 1969, 119 minutes, two stars; and *Operation Pacific*, John Wayne and Patricia Neal, 1951, 109 minutes, three stars. Using this information, create a database to store the file related to these movies. Then create a table, enter the data, and print the table.

Cases and Places

4 ▶▶ You are taking a nutrition class this semester, and your instructor has assigned you a research project on the relationship between heart disease and meat. Heart disease is one of the leading killers of adults in this country. With this knowledge, the meat industry has aggressively tried to deliver products that are low in fat and yet high in nutrients. The American Heart Association states that lean meat can be part of a healthy diet, as long as the meat is served in moderation. Three cooked ounces of lean cuts of beef have various nutritional contents. Eye of round has 140 calories, top round steak has 150 calories, tip round roast has 160 calories, sirloin steak has 170 calories, and top loin and tenderloin steaks both have 180 calories. Regarding fat content, eye of round and top round steak have four fat grams in three ounces, tip round roast and sirloin both have six grams, top loin steak has eight grams, and tenderloin steak has the most with nine grams. Cholesterol also varies, with eye of round the lowest at 60 milligrams in three ounces, top loin with 65 mg, top round, tip round, and tenderloin with 70 mg, and sirloin the highest with 75 mg. Create a database to store the file related to the nutritional content of meat. Then create a table, enter the data, and print the table.

5 ▶▶▶ As any comparison shopper knows, food and drug store prices can vary dramatically from one store to another. Make a list of six specific items you purchase frequently from area stores in the four categories of dairy (for example, milk, yogurt, butter, sour cream, cottage cheese), snacks (for example, pretzels, soda, granola bars, raisins, rice cakes), cosmetics/toiletries (for example, deodorant, bath soap, toothpaste, shampoo, contact lens solution), and kitchen supplies (for example, paper towels, dish washing detergent, scouring pads, trash bags, sandwich bags). List the size or weight of each item. Then, visit a local convenience store, grocery store, and discount store to compare prices. Be certain you obtain prices on identical products. Then create a table, enter the data you obtained in each category, and print the table.

6 ▶▶▶ Because you do not live on campus, you do not have easy access to a campus directory. When you do locate the book, usually you cannot find the information you need. Consequently, you have decided to create your own database containing the pertinent information. Obtain important names, telephone numbers, and room numbers of campus offices that you frequent. Start by organizing the data in the categories of faculty, administration, and services. In the faculty category, list your adviser and your instructors from this semester. In the administration category, list the registrar, the dean of your area, and the financial aid director. In the services category, list the bookstore, campus police station, daycare services, and library reference desk. Add other pertinent data to any of the categories. Then create a table, enter the data you obtained, and print the table.

Cases and Places

7 ▶▶▶ Your accounting professor has given every student in the class a hypothetical $1,000. Your assignment is to research Individual Retirement Accounts (IRAs). Visit or call a total of five local banks, credit unions, or savings and loan associations. Make a list of the current interest rates for an IRA opened with $1,000, minimum investment amount, total amount earned by the time you turn age 65, annual fees, and amount you would be penalized if you withdrew the money in two years. Using this information, create a database and enter the data showing the types of financial institutions (bank, savings and loan, or credit union), names of the financial institutions, their addresses and telephone numbers, interest rates, annual fees, total values of the IRAs by age 65, amount of interest earned in this time, and amount you would be penalized if you withdrew the money in two years. Print this table, and then create and print a bar graph indicating the amount of interest you would earn and the total value of your IRA at age 65 for each financial institution.

Microsoft *Access 97*

Project

2

Querying a Database Using the Select Query Window

Objectives:

You will have mastered the material in this project when you can:

▶ State the purpose of queries
▶ Create a new query
▶ Use a query to display all records and all fields
▶ Run a query
▶ Print the answer to a query
▶ Close a query
▶ Clear a query
▶ Use a query to display selected fields
▶ Use character data in criteria in a query
▶ Use wildcards in criteria
▶ Use numeric data in criteria
▶ Use comparison operators
▶ Use compound criteria involving AND
▶ Use compound criteria involving OR
▶ Sort the answer to a query
▶ Join tables in a query
▶ Restrict the records in a join
▶ Use computed fields in a query
▶ Calculate statistics in a query
▶ Use grouping with statistics
▶ Save a query
▶ Use a saved query

Project 2

In Pursuit of the Money Trail

At a bullfight in Madrid during the 1960s, thousands of Spaniards rose from their seats cheering, "El Fugitivo," when they spotted David Janssen in the crowd. Star of the world-popular television series, *The Fugitive*, Janssen portrayed Dr. Richard Kimble, a man unjustly accused of murdering his wife, a crime actually committed by Fred Johnson — a one-armed man. The series aired from 1963 to 1967. Each episode featured Dr. Richard Kimble with his feigned, humble smile and moody, sideways leer engaged in a weekly search to clear his name and escape the clutches of determined, but technologically challenged, Inspector Gerard. In those days before massive worldwide databases shared by law enforcement officials everywhere, the doctor had a much better chance of eluding capture.

Such evasion still is possible in the 1990s, but much more difficult, owing to the fact that virtually all human activity in the modern world creates an economic event of some kind. When a retail clerk swipes your credit card through a reader, not only is the purchase approved according to your credit availability, but the information is recorded and classified for billing purposes and for future research analysis. Similar actions occur when your check shoots around the track of a check verifier.

Credit card and checking account activity have become the two primary sources of information about people. Using these sources to trap tax evaders, the Internal Revenue Service monitors spending activity in order to calculate *imputed income*, and likewise, private and law enforcement investigators routinely use such data to construct personality profiles. Social Security numbers and Driver License numbers, originally based on the economics of pensions and automobile ownership, also aid in collecting data. As we move to so-called *cyberdollars* — money on a debit card — *all* transactions made in the new cash will be recorded.

Usually, if a person tries to disappear it's because of some illegal activity, but occasionally, the law itself needs to hide people, as in the Federal Witness Protection Program. Ironically, this is becoming more difficult because the very tools developed by law enforcement also can be used by the bad guys!

These same databases are used to research new consumer products, streamline mail delivery, supply better foods and medicines, and improve education, among the dozens of beneficial uses. Without databases, activities that we take for granted — utilities, insurance, airline reservations, food services — and a host of other vital functions would be impossible.

Microsoft Access 97 gives you the power to build your own personal or business databases that are every bit as effective as the gigantic repositories maintained by governments and larger companies. Using Access query capabilities and an extensive set of statistical functions, the tasks of retrieving and analyzing data are simplified substantially.

You may not be an aspiring Charlie Chan or Sherlock Holmes, but when it comes to tracking down answers, Access can be the perfect detective.

Microsoft
Access 97

Querying a Database Using the Select Query Window

Case Perspective

Now that Pilotech Services has created a database with client and technician data, the management and staff of the organization hope to gain the benefits they expected when they set up the database. One of the more important benefits is the capability of easily asking questions concerning the data in the database and rapidly obtaining the answers. Among the questions they want answered are the following:

1. What are the billed and paid amounts for client DE76?

2. Which clients' names begin with Gr?

3. Which clients are located in Grattan?

4. What is the outstanding amount (amount billed minus amount paid) for each client?

5. Which clients of technician 12 have been billed more than $300?

Introduction

A database management system such as Access offers many useful features, among them the capability of answering questions such as those posed by the management of Pilotech Services (Figure 2-1). The answers to these questions, and many more, are found in the database, and Access can find the answers quickly. When you pose a question to Access, or any other database management system, the question is called a query. A **query** is simply a question represented in a way that Access can understand.

Thus, to find the answer to a question, you first create a corresponding query using the techniques illustrated in this project. Once you have created the query, you instruct Access to **run the query**; that is, to perform the steps necessary to obtain the answer. When finished, Access will display the answer to your question in the format shown at the bottom of Figure 2-1.

Project Two — Querying the Pilotech Services Database

You must obtain answers to the questions posed by the management of Pilotech Services. These include the questions shown in Figure 2-1, as well as any other questions that management deems important.

What are the billed and paid amounts of client DE76?

Which clients' names begin with Gr?

Which clients are located in Grattan?

What is the outstanding amount (billed - paid) of each client?

Which clients of technician 12 have been billed more than $300.00?

Client table

CLIENT NUMBER	NAME	ADDRESS	CITY	STATE	ZIP CODE	BILLED	PAID	TECH NUMBER
AM53	Ashton-Mills	216 Rivard	Grattan	MA	58120	$215.50	$155.00	11
AS62	Alton-Scripps	722 Fisher	Empire	MA	58216	$425.00	$435.00	12
BL26	Blake Suppliers	5752 Maumee	Grattan	MA	58120	$129.50	$0.00	12
DE76	D & E Grocery	464 Linnell	Marshall	VT	52018	$385.75	$300.00	17
GR56	Grant Cleaners	737 Allard	Portage	NH	59130	$215.00	$165.00	11
GU21	Grand Union	247 Fuller	Grattan	MA	58120	$128.50	$0.00	12
JE77	Jones Electric	57 Giddings	Marshall	VT	52018	$0.00	$0.00	12
MI26	Morland Int.	665 Whittier	Frankfort	MA	56152	$212.50	$223.25	11
SA56	Sawyer Inc.	31 Lafayette	Empire	MA	58216	$352.50	$250.00	17
SI82	Simpson Ind.	752 Cadieux	Fernwood	MA	57412	$154.00	$0.00	12

CLIENT NUMBER	NAME
GR56	Grant Cleaners
GU21	Grand Union

CLIENT NUMBER	NAME
AS62	Alton-Scripps

CLIENT NUMBER	NAME	ADDRESS
AM53	Ashton-Mills	216 Rivard
BL26	Blake Suppliers	5752 Maumee
GU21	Grand Union	247 Fuller

CLIENT NUMBER	NAME	OUTSTANDING AMOUNT
AM53	Ashton-Mills	$60.50
AS62	Alton-Scripps	($10.00)
BL26	Blake Suppliers	$129.50
DE76	D & E Grocery	$85.75
GR56	Grant Cleaners	$50.00
GU21	Grand Union	$128.50
JE77	Jones Electric	$0.00
MI26	Morland Int.	$10.75
SA56	Sawyer Inc.	$102.50
SI82	Simpson Ind.	$154.00

CLIENT NUMBER	NAME	BILLED	PAID
DE76	D & E Grocery	$385.75	$300.00

FIGURE 2-1

Overview of Project Steps

The project steps give you an overview of how the Pilotech Services database will be queried. The following tasks will be completed in this project.

1. Start Access and open the Pilotech Services database.
2. Create a new query
3. Create and run a query to display the client number, name, and technician number for all clients.
4. Print the results of a query; that is, print the answer to the question.
5. Create and run a query to display all fields.
6. Create and run a query to display the client number, name, billed amount, and paid amount of client DE76.
7. Create and run a query to display the number, name, and address of those clients with names that begin with the letters Gr.
8. Create and run a query to display the number, name, and billed amounts for clients located in Grattan.
9. Create and run a query to display all clients whose paid amount is $0.00.
10. Create and run a query to display all clients whose billed amount is more than $300.
11. Create and run a query to display all clients whose billed amount is greater than $300 and whose technician is technician 12.
12. Create and run a query to display all clients whose billed amount is more than $300 or whose technician is technician 12.
13. Create and run a query to display the cities in which the clients are located in alphabetical order.
14. Create and run a query to display the number, name, technician number, and billed amount for all clients sorted by descending billed amount within technician number.
15. Create and run a query to display the client number, name, technician number, technician's last name, and technician's first name for all clients.
16. Create and run a query to display the client number, name, technician number, technician's last name, and technician's first name for all clients whose billed amount is more than $300.
17. Create and run a query to display the number, name, and outstanding amount (billed amount minus paid amount) for all clients.
18. Create and run a query to calculate the average billed amount for all clients.
19. Create and run a query to calculate the average billed amount for clients of technician 12.
20. Create and run a query to calculate the average billed amount for clients of each technician.
21. Save a query for future use.

The following pages contain a detailed explanation of each of these steps.

Opening the Database

Before creating queries, first you must open the database. The following steps summarize the procedure to complete this task.

TO OPEN A DATABASE

1 Click the Start button.

2 Click Open Office Document and then click 3½ Floppy (A:) in the Look in list box. Make sure the database called Pilotech Services is selected.

3 Click the Open button. If the Tables tab is not already selected, click the Tables tab.

The database is open and the Pilotech Services : Database window displays.

Creating a New Query

You **create a query** by making entries in a special window called a **Select Query window**. Once the database is open, the first step in creating a query is to select the table for which you are creating a query in the Database window. Next, using the New Object: AutoForm button, you will design the new query. The Select Query window will display. It typically is easier to work with the Select Query window if it is maximized. Thus, as a standard practice, maximize the Select Query window as soon as you have created it.

Perform the following steps to begin the creation of a query.

More *About*
Queries: Query Languages

Prior to the advent of query languages in the mid 1970s, obtaining answers to questions concerning data in a database was very difficult, requiring that someone write lengthy (several hundred line) programs in languages like COBOL. Query languages made it easy to obtain answers to such questions.

 To Create a Query

1 With the Pilotech Services database open, the Tables tab selected, and the Client table selected, click the New Object: AutoForm button arrow on the toolbar.

The list of available objects displays (Figure 2-2).

FIGURE 2-2

2 Click Query.

The New Query dialog box displays (Figure 2-3).

FIGURE 2-3

3 With Design View selected, click the OK button.

The Query1 : Select Query window displays (Figure 2-4).

FIGURE 2-4

4 Maximize the Query1 : Select Query window by clicking its Maximize button, and then point to the dividing line that separates the upper and lower panes of the window. The mouse pointer will change to a two-headed arrow with a horizontal bar.

The Query1 : Select Query window is maximized (Figure 2-5). The upper pane of the window contains a field list for the Client table. The lower pane contains the design grid, which is the area where you specify fields to be included, sort order, and the criteria the records you are looking for must satisfy.

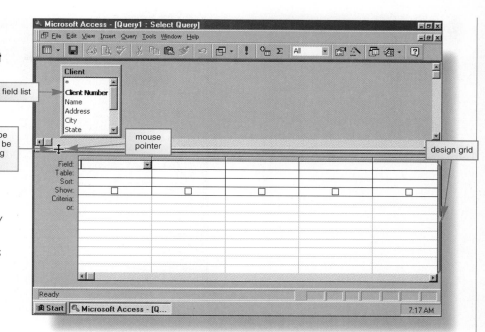

FIGURE 2-5

5 Drag the line down to the approximate position shown in Figure 2-6 and then move the mouse pointer to the lower edge of the field list box so it changes to a two-headed arrow as shown in the figure.

FIGURE 2-6

6 Drag the lower edge of the box down far enough so that all fields in the Client table are visible.

All fields in the Client table display (Figure 2-7).

FIGURE 2-7

Using the Select Query Window

Once you have created a new Select Query window, you are ready to create the actual query by making entries in the design grid in the lower pane of the window. You enter the names of the fields you want included in the Field row in the grid. You also can enter criteria, such as client number must be DE76, in the Criteria row of the grid. When you do so, only the record or records that match the criterion will be included in the answer.

Displaying Selected Fields in a Query

Only the fields that appear in the design grid will be included in the results of the query. Thus, to display only certain fields, place these fields in the grid, and no others. If you place the wrong field in the grid inadvertently, click Edit on the menu bar and then click Delete to remove it. Alternatively, you could click Clear Grid to clear the entire design grid and then start over.

The following steps create a query to show the client number, name, and technician number for all clients by including only those fields in the design grid.

Steps To Include Fields in the Design Grid

1 Make sure you have a maximized Query1 : Select Query window containing a field list for the Client table in the upper pane of the window and an empty design grid in the lower pane (see Figure 2-7).

2 Double-click the Client Number field to include the Client Number field in the query.

The Client Number is included as the first field in the design grid (Figure 2-8).

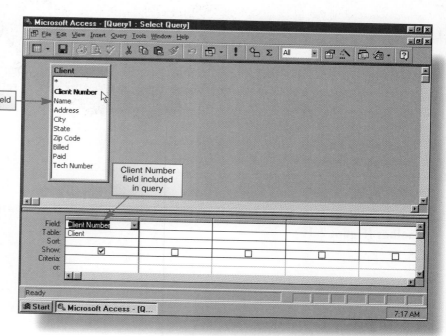

FIGURE 2-8

3 Double-click the Name field to include it in the query. Include the Tech Number field using the same technique.

The Client Number, Name, and Tech Number fields are included in the query (Figure 2-9).

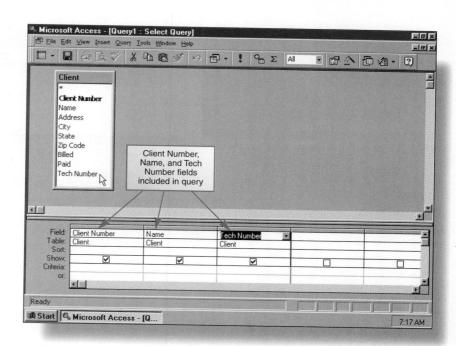

FIGURE 2-9

▶Other Ways
1. Drag field from list box to grid
2. Click column in grid, click arrow, click field

More *About*
Queries: SQL

The most widespread of all the query languages is a language called SQL. In SQL, users type commands like SELECT BILLED FROM CLIENT WHERE CITY = "Marshall" to find the billed amounts of all clients who live in Marshall.

Running a Query

Once you have created the query, you need to **run the query** to produce the results. To do so, click the Run button. Access then will perform the steps necessary to obtain and display the answer. The set of records that makes up the answer will be displayed in Datasheet view. Although it looks like a table that is stored on your disk, it really is not. The records are constructed from data in the existing Client table. If you were to change the data in the Client table and then rerun this same query, the results would reflect the changes. Perform the follwoing steps to run a query.

Steps **To Run the Query**

1 **Point to the Run button on the toolbar (Figure 2-10).**

FIGURE 2-10

2 **Click the Run button.**

The query is executed and the results display (Figure 2-11). If you do not move the mouse pointer at all after clicking the Run button, the ScreenTip for the Sort Ascending button will display as shown in the figure. This ScreenTip may obscure a portion of the first record. (Because only three fields exist in this query, the first record is not obscured by a button's ScreenTip.) As a general practice, it is a good idea to move the mouse pointer as soon as you have run a query, so it no longer points to the toolbar.

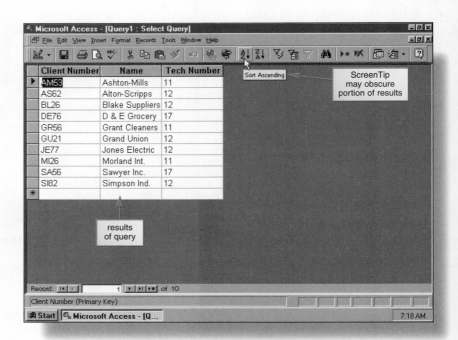

FIGURE 2-11

3 Move the mouse pointer to a position that is outside of the data and is not on the toolbar.

The data displays without obstruction (Figure 2-12). Notice that an extra blank row, marking the end of the table, displays at the end of the results.

FIGURE 2-12

In all future examples, after running a query, move the mouse pointer so the table displays without obstruction.

Printing the Results of a Query

To print the results of a query, use the same techniques you learned in Project 1 to print the data in the table. Complete the following steps to print the query results that currently display on the screen.

TO PRINT THE RESULTS OF A QUERY

1 Ready the printer and then point to the Print button onthe toolbar (Figure 2-13).

2 Click the Print button.

The results print.

FIGURE 2-13

If the results of a query require landscape orientation, switch to landscape orientation before you click the Print button as indicated in Project 1 on page A 1.29.

Returning to the Select Query Window

You can examine the results of a query on your screen to see the answer to your question. You can scroll through the records, if necessary, just as you scroll through the records of any other table. You also can print a copy of the table. In any case, once you are finished working with the results, you can return to the Select Query window to ask another question. To do so, click the View button arrow on the toolbar as shown in the following steps.

Steps To Return to the Select Query Window

1 Point to the View button arrow on the toolbar (Figure 2-14).

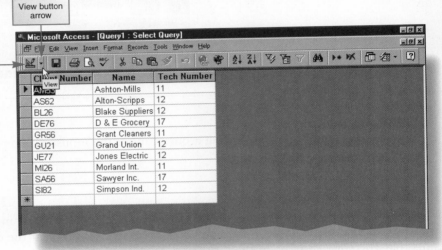

FIGURE 2-14

2 Click the View button arrow. Point to Design View.

The Query View list displays (Figure 2-15).

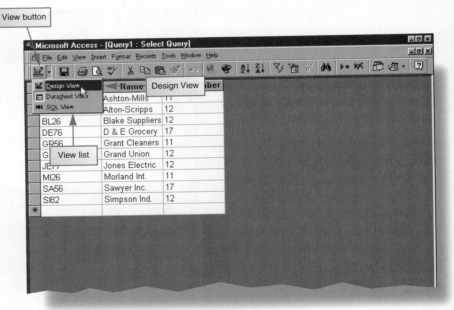

FIGURE 2-15

3 **Click Design View.**

The Query1 : Select Query window displays (Figure 2-16).

FIGURE 2-16

Closing a Query

To **close a query**, close the Select Query window. When you do so, Access displays the Microsoft dialog box asking if you want to save your query for future use. If you think you will need to create the same query often, you should save the query. For now, you will not save any queries. You will see how to save them later in the project. The following steps close a query without saving it.

To Close the Query

1 **Click the Close button for the Query1 : Select Query window (Figure 2-16).**

The Microsoft Access dialog box displays (Figure 2-17). Clicking the Yes button saves the query and clicking the No button closes the query without saving.

2 **Click the No button in the Microsoft Access dialog box.**

The Query1 : Select Query window is removed from the desktop.

FIGURE 2-17

Including All Fields in a Query

If you want to **include all fields** in a query, you could select each field individually. A more simplified way exists to include fields, however. By selecting the **asterisk (*)** that appears in the field list, you are indicating that all fields are to be included. Complete the following steps to use the asterisk to include all fields.

 Steps To Include All Fields in a Query

1 **Be sure you have a maximized Query1 : Select Query window containing a field list for the Client table in the upper pane of the window and an empty design grid in the lower pane. (See Steps 1 through 6 on pages A 2.7 through A 2.10 to create the query and resize the window.) Point to the asterisk at the top of the field list box.**

A maximized Query1 : Select Query window displays (Figure 2-18). The two panes of the window have been resized.

FIGURE 2-18

2 **Double-click the asterisk in the field list box and then point to the Run button on the toolbar.**

The table name, Client, followed by an asterisk is added to the design grid (Figure 2-19), indicating all fields are included.

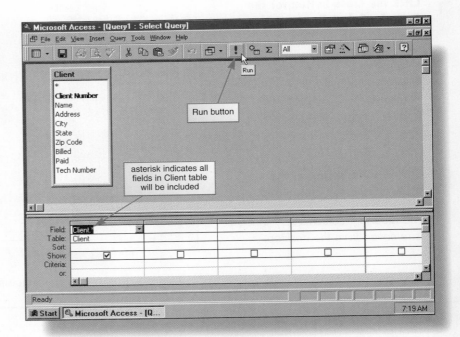

FIGURE 2-19

3 Click the Run button.

The results display and all fields in the Client table are included (Figure 2-20).

4 Click the View button arrow on the toolbar. Click Design View to return to the Query1 : Select Query window.

The datasheet is replaced by the Query1 : Select Query window.

all fields included

View button

Client Number	Name	Address	City	State	Zip Code
AM53	Ashton-Mills	216 Rivard	Grattan	MA	58120
AS62	Alton-Scripps	722 Fisher	Empire	MA	58216
BL26	Blake Suppliers	5752 Maumee	Grattan	MA	58120
DE76	D & E Grocery	464 Linnell	Marshall	VT	52018
GR56	Grant Cleaners	737 Allard	Portage	NH	59130
GU21	Grand Union	247 Fuller	Grattan	MA	58120
JE77	Jones Electric	57 Giddings	Marshall	VT	52018
MI26	Morland Int.	665 Whittier	Frankfort	MA	56152
SA56	Sawyer Inc.	31 Lafayette	Empire	MA	58216
SI82	Simpson Ind.	752 Cadieux	Fernwood	MA	57412

FIGURE 2-20

*Other***Ways**

1. Drag asterisk from list box to grid
2. Click column in grid, click arrow, click asterisk

Clearing the Design Grid

If you make mistakes as you are creating a query, you can fix each one individually. Alternatively, you simply may want to **clear the query**; that is, clear out the entries in the design grid and start over. One way to clear out the entries is to close the Select Query window and then start a new query just as you did earlier. The following steps present a simpler approach to clearing the query by clicking Clear Grid on the Edit menu.

Steps **To Clear a Query**

1 Click Edit on the menu bar.

The Edit menu displays (Figure 2-21).

2 Click Clear Grid.

Access clears the design grid so you can enter your next query.

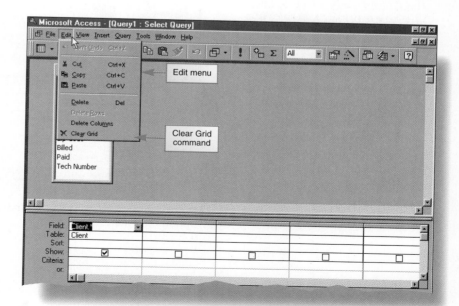

Edit menu

Clear Grid command

FIGURE 2-21

Entering Criteria

When you use queries, usually you are looking for those records that satisfy some criterion. You may want the name, billed, and paid amounts of the client whose number is DE76, for example, or of those clients whose names start with the letters, Gr. To **enter criteria**, enter them on the Criteria row in the design grid below the field name to which the criterion applies. For example, to indicate that the client number must be DE76, type DE76 in the Criteria row below the Client Number field. You first must add the Client Number field to the design grid before you can enter the criterion.

The next examples illustrate the types of criteria that are available.

Using Text Data in Criteria

To use **text data** (data in a field whose type is text) in criteria, simply type the text in the Criteria row below the corresponding field name. The following steps query the Client table and display the client number, name, billed amount, and paid amount of client DE76.

More *About*
Using Text Data in Criteria

Some database systems require that text data must be enclosed in quotation marks. For example, to find customers in Michigan, "MI" would be entered as the criterion for the State field. In Access this is not necessary, because Access will insert the quotation marks automatically.

Steps **To Use Text Data in a Criterion**

1 One by one, double-click the Client Number, Name, Billed, and Paid fields to add them to the query. Point to the Criteria entry for the first field in the design grid.

The Client Number, Name, Billed, and Paid fields are added to the design grid (Figure 2-22). The mouse pointer on the Criteria entry for the first field (Client Number) has changed to an I-beam.

FIGURE 2-22

2 Click the criteria entry, type DE76 **as the criteria for the Client Number field.**

The criteria is entered (Figure 2-23).

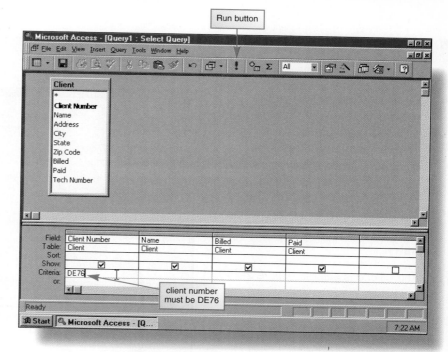

FIGURE 2-23

3 **Run the query by clicking the Run button.**

The results display (Figure 2-24). Only client DE76 is included. (The extra blank row contains $0.00 in the Billed and Paid fields. Unlike text fields, which are left blank, number and currency fields in the extra row contain 0. Because the Billed and Paid fields are currency fields, the values display as $0.00.)

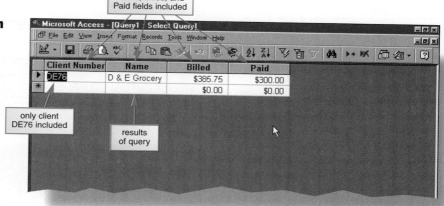

FIGURE 2-24

Using Wildcards

Two special wildcards are available in Microsoft Access. **Wildcards** are symbols that represent any character or combination of characters. The first of the two wildcards, the **asterisk (*)**, represents any collection of characters. Thus Gr* represents the letters, Gr, followed by any collection of characters. The other wildcard symbol is the **question mark (?)**, which represents any individual character. Thus t?m represents the letter, T, followed by any single character followed by the letter, m, such as Tim or Tom.

The steps on the next page use a wildcard to find the number, name, and address of those clients whose names begin with Gr. Because you do not know how many characters will follow the Gr, the asterisk is appropriate.

Steps: To Use a Wildcard

1 Click the View button on the toolbar to return to the Query1 : Select Query window. Click the Criteria row under the Client Number field and then use the DELETE or BACKSPACE key to delete the current entry (DE76). Click the Criteria row under the Name field. Type LIKE Gr* as the entry.

The criteria is entered (Figure 2-25).

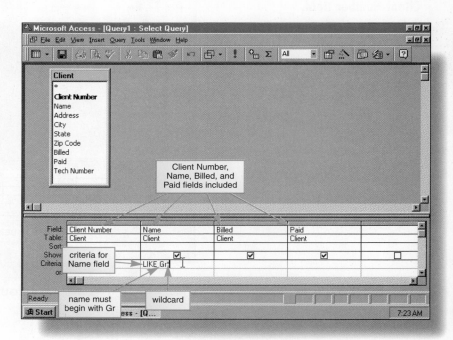

FIGURE 2-25

2 Click the Run button on the toolbar.

The results display (Figure 2-26). Only the clients whose names start with Gr are included.

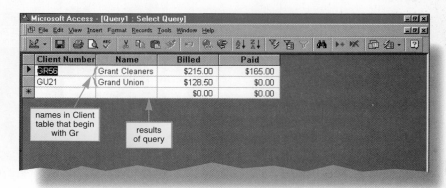

FIGURE 2-26

Criteria for a Field Not in the Result

In some cases, you may have criteria for a particular field that should not appear in the results of the query. For example, you may wish to see the client number, name, address, and billed amounts for all clients located in Grattan. The criteria involves the City field, which is not one of the fields to be included in the results.

To enter a criterion for the City field, it must be included in the design grid. Normally, this also would mean it would appear in the results. To prevent this from happening, remove the check mark from its **Show check box** in the Show row of the grid. The following steps illustrate the process by displaying the client number, name, and billed amounts for clients located in Grattan.

Steps To Use Criteria for a Field Not Included in the Results

1 **Click the View button on the toolbar to return to the Query1 : Select Query window. On the Edit menu, click Clear Grid.**

Access clears the design grid so you can enter the next query.

2 **Include the Client Number, Name, Address, Billed, and City fields in the query. Type** Grattan **as the criteria for the City field and then point to the City field's Show check box.**

The fields are included in the grid, and the criteria for the City field is entered (Figure 2-27). The space between the left scroll arrow and the scroll box indicates that fields are off the leftmost edge of the grid. In this case, the first field, Client Number, currently does not display. Clicking the left scroll arrow would move the scroll box to the left, shift the fields currently in the grid to the right, and cause the Client Number field to display.

FIGURE 2-27

3 **Click the Show check box to remove the check mark.**

The check mark is removed from the Show check box for the City field (Figure 2-28), indicating it will not show in the result. Access has added quotation marks before and after Grattan automatically.

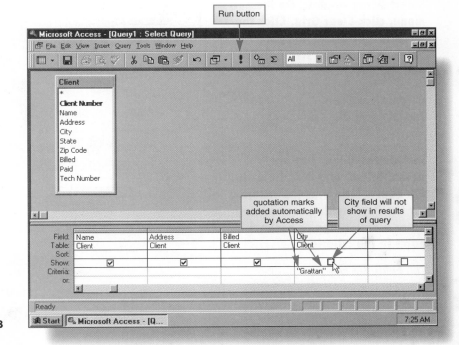

FIGURE 2-28

4 **Click the Run button on the toolbar.**

The results display (Figure 2-29). The City field does not appear. The only clients included are those located in Grattan.

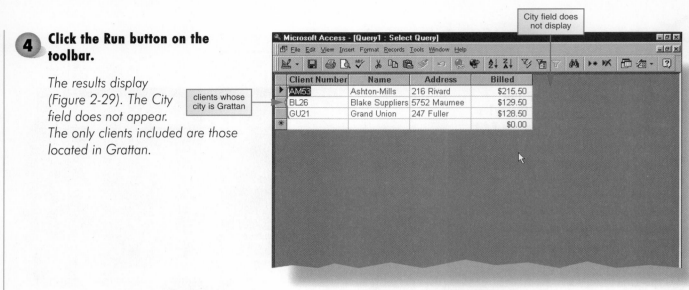

FIGURE 2-29

Using Numeric Data in Criteria

To enter a number in a criterion, type the number without any dollar signs or commas. Complete the following steps to display all clients whose paid amount is $0.00. To do so, you will need to type a zero as the criterion for the Paid field.

Steps **To Use a Number in a Criterion**

1 **Click the View button on the toolbar to return to the Query1 : Select Query window. On the Edit menu, click Clear Grid. Click the left scroll arrow so no space exists between the scroll arrow and the scroll box.**

Access clears the design grid so you can enter the next query.

2 **Include the Client Number, Name, Billed, and Paid fields in the query. Type 0 as the criterion for the Paid field. You need not enter a dollar sign or decimal point in the criterion.**

The fields are selected and the criterion is entered (Figure 2-30).

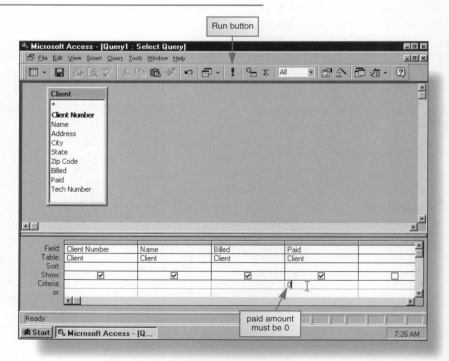

FIGURE 2-30

③ Click the Run button on the toolbar.

The results display (Figure 2-31). Only those clients that have a paid amount of $0.00 are included.

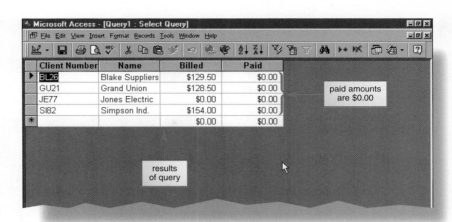

FIGURE 2-31

Using Comparison Operators

Unless you specify otherwise, Access assumes that the criteria you enter involve equality (exact matches). In the last query, for example, you were requesting those clients whose paid amount is equal to 0. If you want something other than an exact match, you must enter the appropriate **comparison operator**. The comparison operators are > (greater than), < (less than), >= (greater than or equal to), <= (less than or equal to), and NOT (not equal to).

Perform the following steps to use the > operator to find all clients whose billed amount is greater than $300.

 To Use a Comparison Operator in a Criterion

① Click the View button on the toolbar to return to the Query1 : Select Query window. On the Edit menu, click Clear Grid.

Access clears the design grid so you can enter the next query.

② Include the Client Number, Name, Billed, and Paid fields in the query. Type >300 as the criterion for the Billed field.

The fields are selected and the criterion is entered (Figure 2-32).

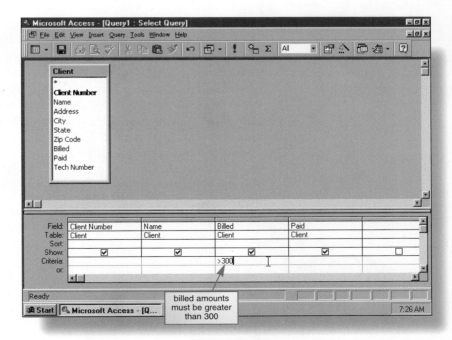

FIGURE 2-32

3 **Click the Run button on the toolbar.**

The results display (Figure 2-33). Only those clients that have a billed amount more than $300 are included.

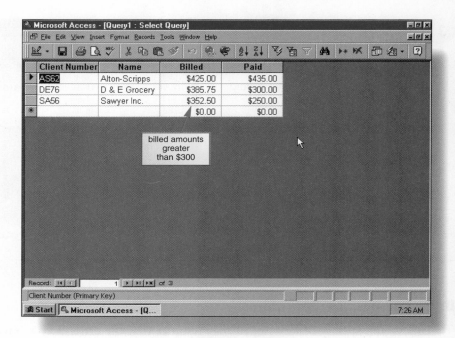

FIGURE 2-33

More *About*
Compound Criteria

Access to compound criteria is precisely the approach that was proposed for Query-by-Example. (Placing criteria on the same lines indicates they are connected by the word AND. Placing criteria on separate lines indicates they are connected by the word OR.)

Using Compound Criteria

Often you will have more than one criterion that the data for which you are searching must satisfy. This type of criterion is called a **compound criterion**. Two types of compound criteria exist.

In **AND criterion**, each individual criterion must be true in order for the compound criterion to be true. For example, an AND criterion would allow you to find those clients that have a billed amount greater than $300 and whose technician is technician 12.

Conversely, **OR criterion** is true provided either individual criterion is true. An OR criterion would allow you to find those clients that have a billed amount greater than $300 or whose technician is technician 12. In this case, any client whose billed amount is greater than $300 would be included in the answer whether or not the client's technician is technician 12. Likewise, any client whose technician is technician 12 would be included whether or not the client had a billed amount greater than $300.

To combine criteria with AND, place the criteria on the same line. Perform the following steps to use an AND criterion to find those clients whose billed amount is greater than $300 and whose technician is technician 12.

Steps To Use a Compound Criterion Involving AND

① Click the View button on the toolbar to return to the Query1 : Select Query window. On the Edit menu, click Clear Grid.

Access clears the design grid so you can enter the next query.

② Include the Client Number, Name, Billed, Paid, and Tech Number fields in the query.

③ Click the Criteria entry for the Billed field, and then type >300 as a criterion for the Billed field. Click the Criteria entry for the Tech Number field and then type 12 as the criterion for the Tech Number field.

The fields shift to the left (Figure 2-34). Criteria have been entered for the Billed and Tech Number fields.

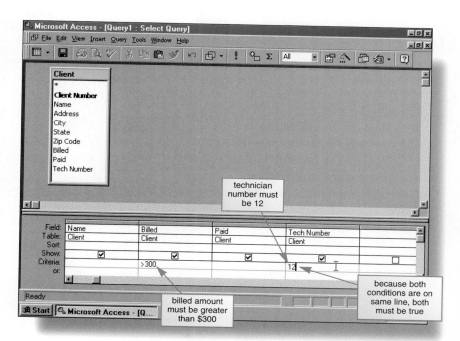

FIGURE 2-34

④ Click the Run button on the toolbar.

The results display (Figure 2-35). Only the single client whose billed amount is greater than $300.00 and whose technician number is 12 is included.

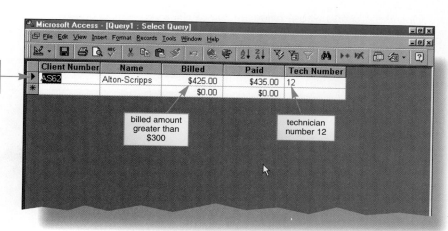

FIGURE 2-35

To combine criteria with OR, the criteria must go on separate lines in the Criteria area of the grid. The steps on the next page use an OR criterion to find those clients whose billed amount is more than $300.00 or whose technician is technician 12 (or both).

Steps To Use a Compound Criterion Involving OR

1 **Click the View button on the toolbar to return to the Query1 : Select Query window.**

2 **Click the Criteria entry for the Tech Number field. Use the BACKSPACE key to delete the entry ("12"). Click the or entry (below Criteria) for the Tech Number field and then type 12 as the entry.**

The criteria are entered for the Billed and Tech Number fields on different lines (Figure 2-36).

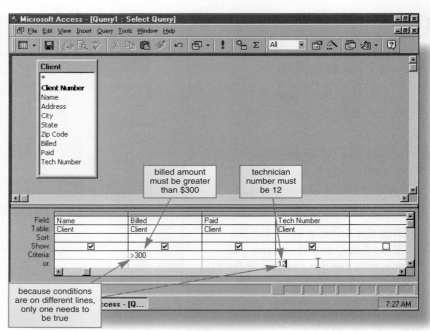

FIGURE 2-36

3 **Click the Run button on the toolbar.**

The results display (Figure 2-37). Only those clients whose billed amount is more than $300.00 or whose technician number is 12 are included.

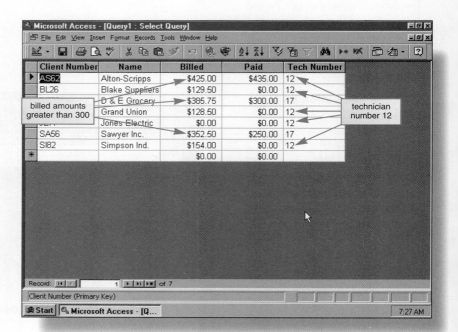

FIGURE 2-37

Sorting Data in a Query

In some queries, the order in which the records are displayed really does not matter. All you need be concerned about are the records that appear in the results. It does not matter which one is first or which one is last.

In other queries, however, the order can be very important. You may want to see the cities in which clients are located and would like them arranged alphabetically. Perhaps you want to see the clients listed by technician number. Further, within all the clients of any given technician, you would like them to be listed by billed amount.

To order the records in the answer to a query in a particular way, you **sort** the records. The field or fields on which the records are sorted is called the **sort key**. If you are sorting on more than one field (such as sorting by billed amount within technician number), the more important field (Tech Number) is called the **major key** (also called the **primary sort key**) and the less important field (Billed) is called the **minor key** (also called the **secondary sort key**).

To sort in Microsoft Access, specify the sort order in the Sort line of the design grid below the field that is the sort key. If you specify more than one sort key, the sort key on the left will be the major sort key and the one on the right will be the minor key.

The following steps sort the cities in the Client table.

More *About*
Sorting Data in a Query

When sorting data in a query, the records in the underlying tables (the tables on which the query is based) are not actually rearranged. Instead, the DBMS will determine the most efficient method of simply displaying the records in the requested order. The records in the underlying tables remain in their original order.

Steps **To Sort Data in a Query**

1 Click the View button on the toolbar to return to the Query1 : Select Query window. On the Edit menu, click Clear Grid. Click the left scroll arrow so no space exists between the scroll arrow and the scroll box.

2 Include the City field in the design grid. Click the Sort row below the City field, and then click the down arrow that appears.

The City field is included (Figure 2-38). A list of available sort orders displays.

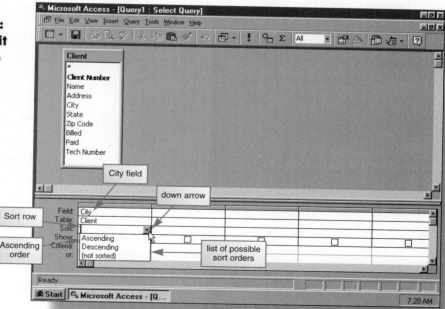

FIGURE 2-38

3 Click Ascending.

Ascending is selected as the order (Figure 2-39).

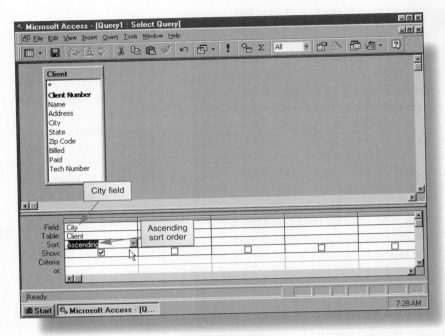

City field

Ascending sort order

FIGURE 2-39

4 Run the query by clicking the Run button on the toolbar.

The results contain the cities from the Client table (Figure 2-40). The cities display in alphabetical order. Duplicates, that is, identical rows, are included.

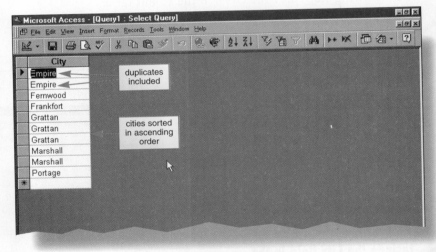

duplicates included

cities sorted in ascending order

FIGURE 2-40

Sorting on Multiple Keys

The next example lists the number, name, technician number, and billed amount for all clients. The data is to be sorted by descending billed amount (high to low) within technician number, which means that the Tech Number field is the major key and the Billed field is the minor key. It also means that the Billed field should be sorted in descending order.

The following steps accomplish this sorting by specifying the Tech Number and Billed fields as sort keys and by selecting Descending as the sort order for the Billed field.

To Sort on Multiple Keys

1 Click the View button on the toolbar to return to the Query1 : Select Query window. On the Edit menu, click Clear Grid.

2 Include the Client Number, Name, Tech Number, and Billed fields in the query in this order. Select Ascending as the sort order for the Tech Number field and Descending as the sort order for the Billed field (Figure 2-41).

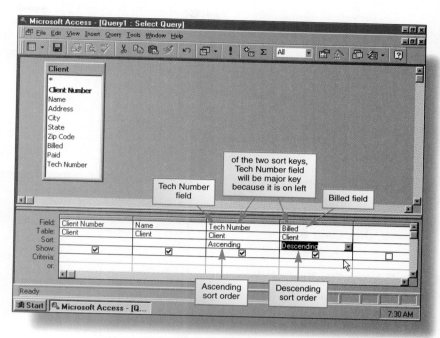

FIGURE 2-41

3 Run the query.

The results display (Figure 2-42). The clients are sorted by technician number. Within the collection of clients having the same technician, the clients are sorted by descending billed amount.

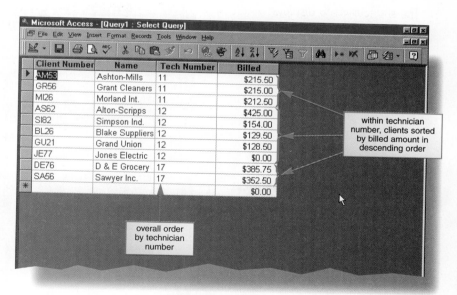

FIGURE 2-42

It is important to remember that the major sort key must appear to the left of the minor sort key in the design grid. If you attempted to sort by billed amount within technician number, but placed the Billed field to the left of the Tech Number field, your results would be incorrect.

Omitting Duplicates

As you saw earlier, when you sort data, duplicates are included. In Figure 2-40 on page A 2.28, for example, Empire appeared twice, Grattan appeared three times, and Marshall appeared twice. If you do not want duplicates included, use the Properties command and specify Unique Values Only. Perform the following steps to produce a sorted list of the cities in the Client table in which each city is listed only once.

Steps **To Omit Duplicates**

1 **Click the View button on the toolbar to return to the Query1 : Select Query window. On the Edit menu, click Clear Grid.**

2 **Include the City field, click Ascending as the sort order, and right-click the second field in the design grid (the empty field following City).**

The shortcut menu displays (Figure 2-43).

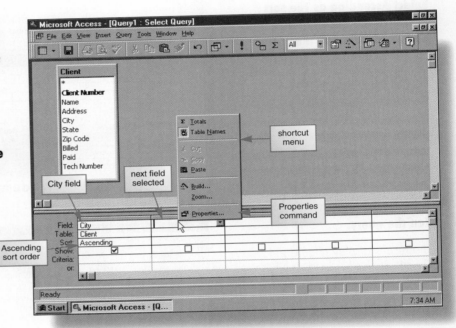

FIGURE 2-43

3 **Click Properties on the shortcut menu.**

The Query Properties sheet displays (Figure 2-44).

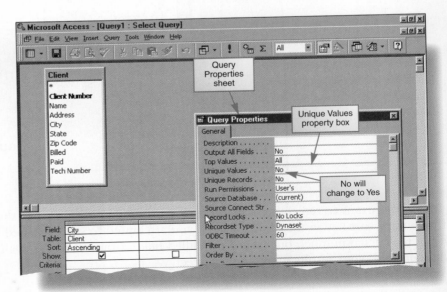

FIGURE 2-44

4 Click the Unique Values property box, and then click the down arrow that displays to produce a list of available choices for Unique Values (Figure 2-45).

FIGURE 2-45

5 Click Yes, and then close the Query Properties sheet by clicking its Close button. Run the query.

The results display (Figure 2-46). The cities are sorted alphabetically. Each city is included only once.

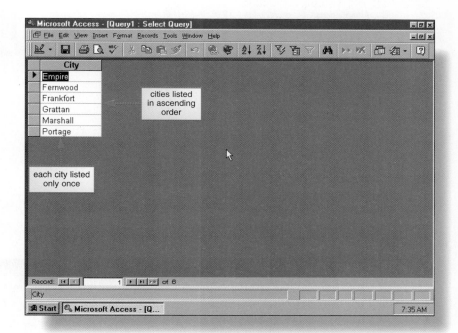

FIGURE 2-46

Other Ways

1. Click Properties button on toolbar

2. On View menu click Properties

More *About*
Joining Tables

One of the key features that distinguishes database management systems from file systems is the ability to join tables; that is, to create queries that draw data from two or more tables. Several types of joins are available. The most common type, the one illustrated in the text, formally is called the natural join.

Joining Tables

Pilotech Services needs to list the number and name of each client along with the number and name of the client's technician. The client's name is in the Client table, whereas the technician's name is in the Technician table. Thus, this query cannot be satisfied using a single table. You need to **join** the tables; that is, to find records in the two tables that have identical values in matching fields (Figure 2-47). In this example, you need to find records in the Client table and the Technician table that have the same value in the Tech Number fields.

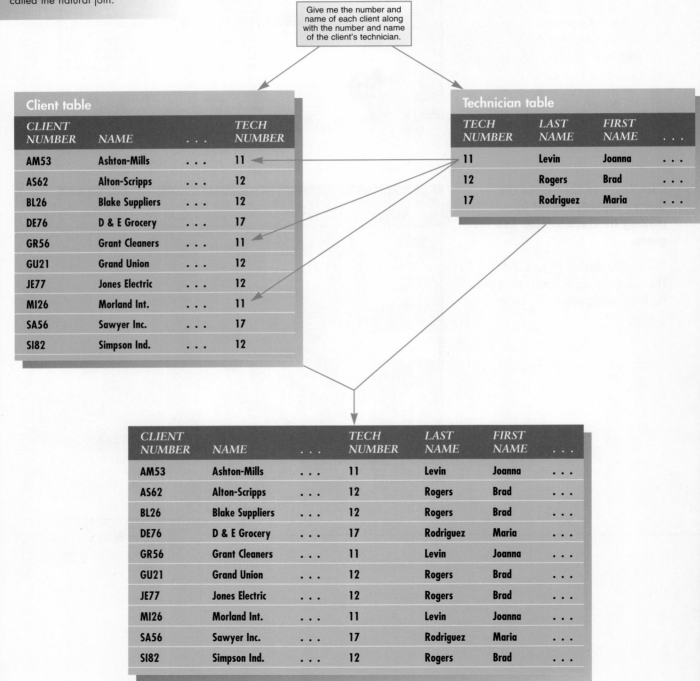

FIGURE 2-47

To join tables in Access, first you bring field lists for both tables to the upper pane of the Select Query window. Access will draw a line, called a **join line**, between matching fields in the two tables indicating that the tables are related. You then can select fields from either table. Access will join the tables automatically.

The first step is to add an additional table to the query as illustrated in the following steps, which add the Technician table.

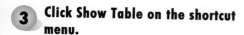

To Join Tables

1 **Click the View button on the toolbar to return to the Query1 : Select Query window. On the Edit menu, click Clear Grid.**

2 **Right-click any open area in the upper pane of the Query1 : Select Query window.**

The shortcut menu displays (Figure 2-48).

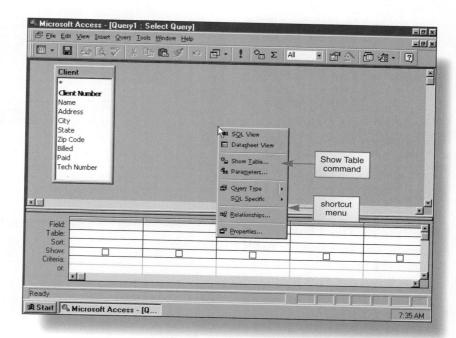

FIGURE 2-48

3 **Click Show Table on the shortcut menu.**

The Show Table dialog box displays (Figure 2-49).

FIGURE 2-49

4 **Click Technician to select the Technician table, and then click the Add button. Close the Show Table dialog box by clicking the Close button. Expand the size of the field list so all the fields in the Technician table display.**

A field list for the Technician table displays (Figure 2-50). It has been enlarged so all the technician fields are visible. A join line appears joining the Tech Number fields in the two field lists. The join line indicates how the tables are related; that is, linked through the matching fields. (If you fail to give the matching fields the same name, Access will not insert the line. You can insert it manually, however, by clicking one of the two matching fields and dragging the mouse pointer to the other matching field.)

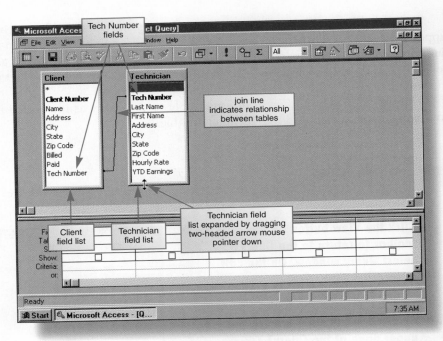

FIGURE 2-50

5 **Include the Client Number, Name, and Tech Number fields from the Client table and the Last Name and First Name fields from the Technician table.**

The fields from both tables are selected (Figure 2-51).

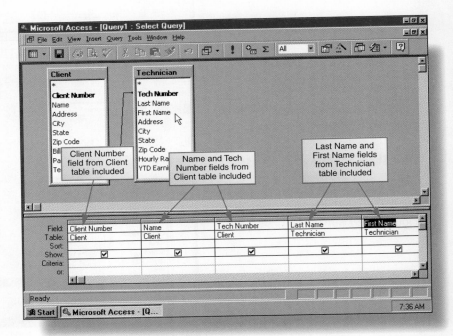

FIGURE 2-51

6 **Run the query.**

The results display (Figure 2-52). They contain data from the Client table as well as data from the Technician table.

FIGURE 2-52

Restricting Records in a Join

Sometimes you will want to join tables, but you will not want to include all possible records. In such cases, you will relate the tables and include fields just as you did before. You also will include criteria. For example, to include the same fields as in the previous query, but only those clients whose billed amount is more than $300, you will make the same entries as before and then also type >300 as a criterion for the Billed field.

The following steps modify the query from the previous example to restrict the records that will be included in the join.

Steps To Restrict the Records in a Join

1 **Click the View button on the toolbar to return to the Query1 : Select Query window. Add the Billed field to the query. If necessary, scroll the fields to the left so the Billed field displays in the design grid. Type >300 as the criterion for the Billed field and then click the Show check box for the Billed field to remove the check mark.**

The Billed field displays in the design grid (Figure 2-53). A criterion is entered for the Billed field and the Show check box is empty, indicating that the field will not display in the results of the query.

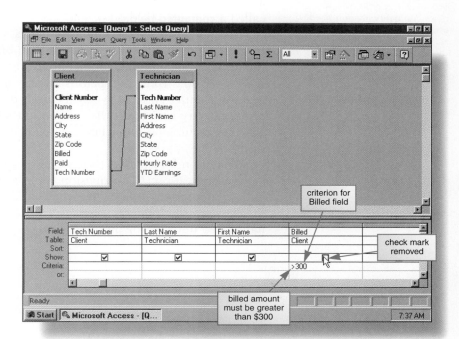

FIGURE 2-53

2 Run the query.

*The results display (Figure 2-54).
Only those clients
with a billed amount
greater than $300
appear in the result.
The Billed field does not display.*

clients with billed
amount greater
than $300

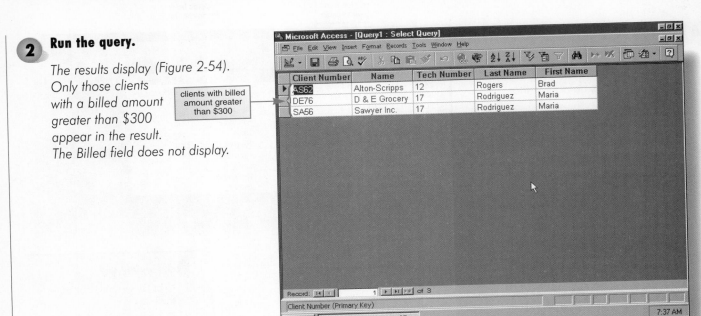

FIGURE 2-54

Using Computed Fields in a Query

It is important to Pilotech Services to know the outstanding amount for each client; that is, the amount billed to the client minus the amount the client already has paid. This poses a problem because the Client table does not include a field for outstanding amount. You can compute it, however, because the outstanding amount is equal to the billed amount minus the paid amount. Such a field is called a **computed field**.

To include computed fields in queries, you enter a name for the computed field, a colon, and then the expression in one of the columns in the Field row. For the outstanding amount, for example, you will type Outstanding Amount: [Billed]–[Paid]. You can type this directly into the Field row. You will not be able to see the entire entry, however, because the Field row is not large enough. The preferred way is to select the column in the Field row, right-click to display the shortcut menu, and then click Zoom. The Zoom dialog box displays where you can type the expression.

You are not restricted to subtraction in computations. You can use addition (+), multiplication (*), or division (/). In addition, you can include parentheses in your computations to indicate which computations should be done first.

Perform the following steps to use a computed field to display the number, name, and outstanding amount of all clients.

Steps To Use a Computed Field in a Query

1 Click the View button on the toolbar to return to the Query1 : Select Query window. Right-click any field in the Technician table field list.

The shortcut menu displays (Figure 2-55).

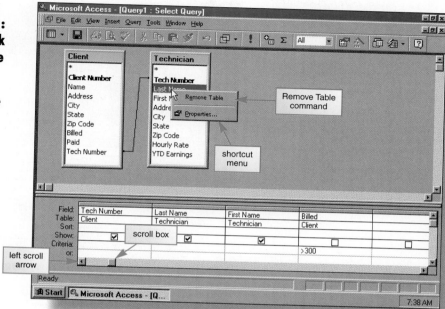

FIGURE 2-55

2 Click Remove Table to remove the Technician table from the Query1 : Select Query window. On the Edit menu, click Clear Grid. Click the left scroll arrow so no space exists between the scroll arrow and the scroll box.

3 Include the Client Number and Name fields. Right-click the Field row in the third column in the design grid and then click Zoom on the shortcut menu. Type Outstanding Amount:[Billed]-[Paid] in the Zoom dialog box that displays.

The Zoom dialog box displays (Figure 2-56). The expression you typed displays within the dialog box.

FIGURE 2-56

4 **Click the OK button.**

The Zoom dialog box no longer displays (Figure 2-57). A portion of the expression you entered displays in the third field within the design grid.

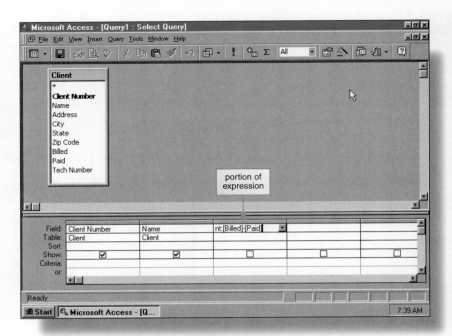

FIGURE 2-57

5 **Run the query.**

The results display (Figure 2-58). Microsoft Access has calculated and displayed the client amounts. The parentheses around $10.00 and $10.75 indicate they are negative numbers; that is, the clients possibly paid more than the amount that was billed.

FIGURE 2-58

1. Press SHIFT+F2

Calculating Statistics

Microsoft Access supports the built-in **statistics**: COUNT, SUM, AVG (average), MAX (largest value), MIN (smallest value), STD (standard deviation), VAR (variance), FIRST, and LAST. To use any of these in a query, you include it in the Total row in the design grid. The Total row routinely does not appear in the grid. To include it, right-click the grid, and then click Totals on the shortcut menu.

The following example illustrates how you use these functions by calculating the average billed amount for all clients.

More *About*
Calculating Statistics

Virtually all database management systems support the basic set of statistical calculations: sum, average, count, maximum, and minimum as part of their query feature. Some systems, including Access, add several more, such as standard deviation, variance, first, and last.

Steps **To Calculate Statistics**

1 Click the View button on the toolbar to return to the Query1 : Select Query window. On the Edit menu, click Clear Grid.

2 Right-click the grid.

The shortcut menu displays (Figure 2-59).

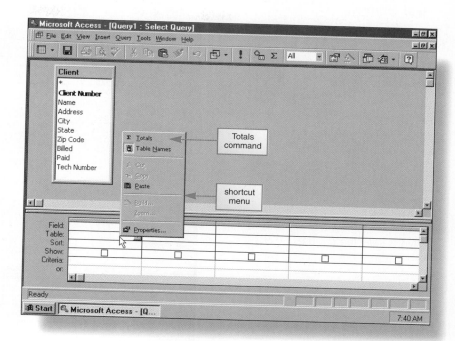

FIGURE 2-59

3 Click Totals on the shortcut menu and then include the Billed field. Point to the Total row in the Billed column.

The Total row now is included in the design grid (Figure 2-60). The Billed field is included, and the entry in the Total row is Group By. The mouse pointer, which has changed shape to an I-beam, is positioned on the Total row under the Billed field.

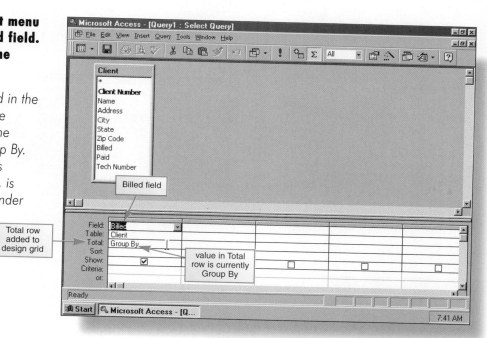

FIGURE 2-60

4 **Click the Total row in the Billed column, and then click the arrow that displays.**

The list of available selections displays (Figure 2-61).

FIGURE 2-61

5 **Click Avg.**

Avg is selected (Figure 2-62).

FIGURE 2-62

6 **Run the query.**

The result displays (Figure 2-63), showing the average billed amount for all clients.

FIGURE 2-63

Using Criteria in Calculating Statistics

Sometimes calculating statistics for all the records in the table is appropriate. In other cases, however, you will need to calculate the statistics for only those records that satisfy certain criteria. To enter a criterion in a field, first you select Where as the entry in the Total row for the field and then enter the criterion in the Criteria row. The following steps use this technique to calculate the average billed amount for clients of technician 12.

Steps **To Use Criteria in Calculating Statistics**

1 Click the View button on the toolbar to return to the Query1 : Select Query window.

2 Include the Tech Number field in the design grid. Next, produce the list of available options for the Total entry just as you did when you selected Avg for the Billed field. Use the vertical scroll bar to move through the options until the word, Where, displays.

The list of available selections displays (Figure 2-64). The Group By entry in the Tech Number field may not be highlighted on your screen, depending on where you clicked in the Total row.

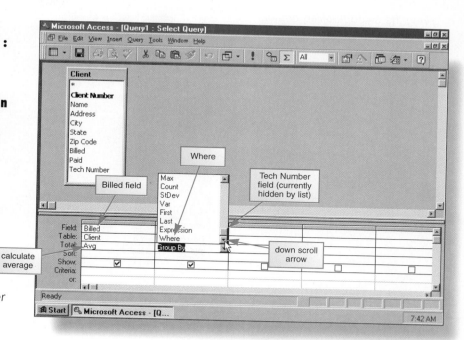

FIGURE 2-64

3 Click Where. Then, type 12 as criterion for the Tech Number field.

Where is selected as the entry in the Total row for the Tech Number field (Figure 2-65) and 12 is entered as the Criteria.

FIGURE 2-65

4 **Run the query.**

The result displays (Figure 2-66), giving the average billed amount for clients of technician 12.

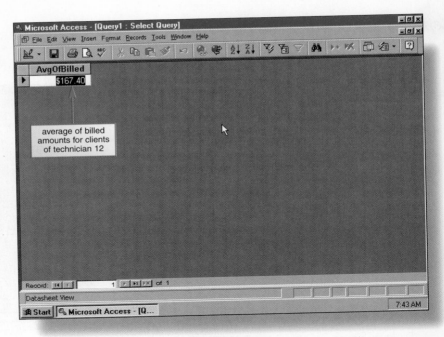

FIGURE 2-66

Grouping

Another way statistics often are used is in combination with grouping, in which statistics are calculated for groups of records. You may, for example, need to calculate the average billed amount for the clients of each technician. You will want the average for the clients of technician 11, the average for clients of technician 12, and so on.

Grouping means creating groups of records that share some common characteristic. In grouping by Tech Number, for example, the clients of technician 11 would form one group, the clients of technician 12 would be a second, and the clients of technician 17 would form a third. The calculations then are made for each group. To indicate grouping in Access, select Group By as the entry in the Total row for the field to be used for grouping.

Perform the following steps to calculate the average billed amount for clients of each technician.

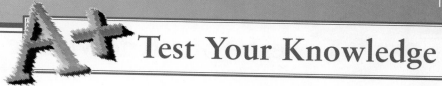

Test Your Knowledge

1 True/False

Instructions: Circle T if the statement is true or F if the statement is false.

T F   1. To include all the fields in a record in a query, click the word ALL that appears at the top of the field list.

T F   2. To create a compound criterion using OR, enter each criterion on a separate line.

T F   3. To create a compound criterion using AND, type the word, INTERSECT, before the second criterion.

T F   4. To create a criterion involving Equals, you do not need to type the equal sign (=).

T F   5. When you enter a criteria for a particular field, that field must appear in the results of the query.

T F   6. To find all clients whose billed amount is $100 or more, type >=100 as the criterion for the Billed field.

T F   7. To clear all the entries in a design grid, on the Query menu, click Clear Grid.

T F   8. When you sort a query on more than one key, the major sort key must appear to the right of the minor sort key.

T F   9. To omit duplicates from a query, use the Properties command and specify Unique Values Only.

T F   10. The wildcard symbols available for use in a query are ? and *.

2 Multiple Choice

Instructions: Circle the correct response.

1. To list only certain records in a table, use a(n) _____.
   a. list
   b. answer
   c. question
   d. query

2. To find all clients whose billed amount is $100 or more, type _____ as the criteria for the Billed field.
   a. >= $100.00
   b. >=100
   c. =>$100.00
   d. =>100

3. To clear all the entries in a design grid, on the _____ menu, click Clear Grid.
   a. Edit
   b. File
   c. Query
   d. View

(continued)

A+ Test Your Knowledge

Multiple Choice *(continued)*

4. The wildcard symbols available for use in a query are the _____ and the _____.
   a. double period (..), asterisk (*)
   b. question mark (?), asterisk (*)
   c. double period (..), at symbol (@)
   d. question mark (?), ampersand (&)

5. Equal to (=), less than (<), and greater than (>) are examples of _____.
   a. criteria
   b. values
   c. comparison operators
   d. compound criteria

6. When two or more criteria are connected with AND or OR, the result is called a _____.
   a. simple criterion
   b. pattern criterion
   c. character criterion
   d. compound criterion

7. To add an additional table to a query, click _____ on the shortcut menu for the Select Query window.
   a. Join Table
   b. Show Table
   c. Add Table
   d. Include Table

8. Use a query to _____ tables; that is, find records in two tables that have identical values in matching fields.
   a. merge
   b. match
   c. combine
   d. join

9. To remove a table from a query, right-click any field in the field list for the table and then click _____ on the shortcut menu.
   a. Remove Table
   b. Delete Table
   c. Clear Table
   d. Erase Table

10. To add a Total row to a design grid, click _____ on the shortcut menu for the Select Query window.
    a. Aggregates
    b. Functions
    c. Statistics
    d. Totals

Test Your Knowledge

3 Understanding the Select Query Window

Instructions: In Figure 2-72, arrows point to the major components of the Select Query window. Identify the various parts of the Query window in the spaces provided.

FIGURE 2-72

4 Understanding Statistics

Instructions: Figure 2-73 shows a created query using statistics for the Customer table and Figure 2-74 on the next page lists the contents of the Customer table. List the answer to this query in the spaces provided.

FIGURE 2-73

(continued)

Test Your Knowledge

Understanding Statistics (continued)

Data for Customer table							
CUSTOMER NUMBER	NAME	ADDRESS	CITY	STATE	ZIP CODE	BALANCE	INTERN ID
AS36	Asterman Ind.	200 Bard	Howden	MO	59444	$85.00	102
AU54	Author Books	142 Birchwood	Howden	MO	59445	$50.00	109
BI92	Bike Shop	433 Chester	Howden	MO	59441	$40.00	109
CI76	Cinderton Co.	73 Fleming	Dorchester	IL	57342	$0.00	113
CJ16	CJ's Music	277 Fordham	Dorchester	IL	57342	$105.00	102
JO62	Jordan Diner	250 Bard	Howden	MO	59444	$74.00	109
KL55	Klingon Toys	215 Scott	Evansville	MO	59335	$115.00	105
ME71	Meat & Cleaver	543 Fleming	Dorchester	IL	57342	$138.00	102
MO13	Moore Foods	876 Grove	Evansville	MO	59335	$0.00	113
RO32	Royal Mfg Co.	954 Cline	Evansville	MO	59331	$93.00	109

FIGURE 2-74

 Use Help

1 Reviewing Project Activities

Instructions: Perform the following tasks using a computer.

1. Start Access.
2. If the Office Assistant is on your screen, then click it to display its balloon. If the Office Assistant is not on your screen, click the Office Assistant button on the toolbar.
3. Type working with queries in the What would you like to do? text box. Click the Search button. Click Queries: What they are and how they work.
4. Read the Help information. Use the page number links in the upper-left corner of the screen to move to the next Help windows. A total of three Help windows will display. When you finish reading the Help information, click the Close button.

Use Help

5. Click the Office Assistant. Type `perform calculations in a query` in the What would you like to do? text box. Click the Search button. Click Ways to perform calculations in queries. Read and print the Help information. Hand in the printout to your instructor. Click the Help Topics button.

6. If necessary, click the Index tab. Type `wildcard` in the top text box labeled 1, and then double-click wildcard characters in the list box labeled 2. Double-click the Search for partial or matching values using wildcard characters topics. When the Help information displays, read it. Next, right-click within the box, and then click Print Topic. Hand in the printout to your instructor. Click the Help Topics button to return to the Help Topics: Microsoft Access 97 dialog box.

7. Click the Find tab. Type `sorting` in the top text box labeled 1. Double-click The records the query retrieves are in the wrong order in the bottom box labeled 3. When the Help information displays, read it, ready the printer, right-click, and click Print Topic. Hand in the printout to your instructor. Click the Close button.

2 Expanding on the Basics

Instructions: Use Access Help to learn about the topics listed below. If you cannot print the Help information, then answer the question on your own paper.

1. Using the Office Assistant, answer the following questions:
   a. How do you insert a field between other fields in the design grid of a query?
   b. How do you remove a field from the design grid?
   c. How do you change a field name in a query?
   d. When you use the asterisk (*) to select all fields, how do you specify criteria for fields?
   e. How do you insert a Criteria row in the design grid?

2. Using the word, format, and the Find sheet in the Help Topics: Microsoft Access 97 dialog box, display and print the information on defining the data display format for a field in query Design view. Then, answer the following questions:
   a. How can you display a field's property sheet using the menu bar?
   b. How do the Regional Settings on the Windows Control Panel affect the formats in a query?

3. Using the word, OR, and the Index sheet in the Help Topics: Microsoft Access 97 dialog box, display and then print the information about ways to use multiple criteria in a query. Then answer the following questions:
   a. How do you enter criteria to OR two values in one field?
   b. How do you enter criteria to AND two values in one field?
   c. How do you enter criteria to OR and AND in three fields?

4. Use the Office Assistant to display and print the information on searching for a range of values.

Apply Your Knowledge

1 Querying the Green Thumb Database

Instructions: Start Access. Open the Green Thumb database from the Access folder on the Data Disk that accompanies this book. Perform the following tasks.

1. Create a new query for the Customer table.
2. Add the Customer Number, Name, and Balance fields to the design grid as shown in Figure 2-75.
3. Restrict retrieval to only those records where the balance is greater than $100.
4. Run the query and print the results.
5. Return to the Select Query window and clear the grid.
6. Add the Customer Number, Name, City, Balance, and Intern Id fields to the design grid.
7. Restrict retrieval to only those records where the Intern Id is either 109 or 113.
8. Sort the records in order by Balance (descending) within City (ascending).
9. Run the query and print the results.
10. Return to the Select Query window and clear the grid.
11. Join the Customer and Intern tables. Add the Customer Number, Name, and Intern Id fields from the Customer table and the Last Name and First Name fields from the Intern table.
12. Sort the records in ascending order by Intern Id.
13. Run the query and print the results.

FIGURE 2-75

In the Lab

1 Querying the Museum Mercantile Database

Problem: The volunteers who staff Museum Mercantile have determined a number of questions they want the database management system to answer. You must obtain answers to the questions posed by the volunteers.

Instructions: Use the database created in the In the Lab 1 of Project 1 for this assignment. Perform the following tasks.

1. Open the Museum Mercantile database and create a new query for the Product table.
2. Display and print the Product Id, Description, and Selling Price for all records in the table as shown in Figure 2-76.
3. Display all fields and print all the records in the table.
4. Display and print the Product Id, Description, Cost, and Vendor Code for all products where the Vendor Code is MS.
5. Display and print the Product Id and Description for all products where the Description begins with the letters, Wi.
6. Display and print the Product Id, Description, and Vendor Code for all products that cost more than $20.
7. Display and print the Product Id and Description for all products that have a Selling Price of $5 or less.
8. Display and print all fields for those products that cost more than $10 and where the number of units on hand is less than 10.
9. Display and print all fields for those products that have a Vendor Code of WW or have a Selling Price less than $10.
10. Join the Product table and the Vendor table. Display the Product Id, Description, Cost, Name, and Telephone Number fields. Run the query and print the results.
11. Restrict the records retrieved in task 10 above to only those products where the number of units on hand is less than 10. Display and print the results.
12. Remove the Vendor table and clear the design grid.
13. Include the Product Id and Description in the design grid. Compute the on-hand value (on hand * cost) for all records in the table. Display and print the results.
14. Display and print the average selling price of all products.

FIGURE 2-76

(continued)

In the Lab

Querying the Museum Mercantile Database *(continued)*

15. Display and print the average selling price of products grouped by Vendor Code.
16. Join the Product and Vendor tables. Include the Vendor Code and Name fields from the Vendor table. Include the Product Id, Description, Cost, and On Hand fields from the Product table. Save the query as Vendors and Products. Run the query and print the results.

2 Querying the City Telephone System Database

Problem: The telephone manager has determined a number of questions that she wants the database management system to answer. You must obtain answers to the questions posed by the telephone manager.

Instructions: Use the database created in the In the Lab 2 of Project 1 for this assignment. Perform the following tasks.

1. Open the City Telephone System database and create a new query for the User table.
2. Display and print the User Id, Last Name, First Name, Phone Ext, and Office for all the records in the table as shown in Figure 2-77 on the next page.
3. Display all fields and print all the records in the table.
4. Display and print the User Id, First Name, Last Name, Basic Charge, and Extra Charges for all users in the department with the code of PLN.
5. Display and print the User Id, First Name, Last Name, and Phone Ext for all users whose basic charge is $13 per month.
6. Display and print the User Id, First Name, Last Name, and Extra Charges for all users in the department with a code ITD who have Extra Charges greater than $20. List the records in descending order by Extra Charges.
7. Display and print the User Id, First Name, Last Name, and Extra Charges for all users who have extra charges greater than $25 and are in either the Assessment (APV) or Planning (PLN) department. (*Hint*: Use information from Use Help 2 on page A 2.52 to solve this problem.)
8. Display and print the Basic Charge in ascending order. List each Basic Charge only once.
9. Join the User table and the Department table. Display and print the User Id, Last Name, First Name, Basic Charge, Extra Charges, and Name of the department.

Microsoft Access - [Query1 : Select Query]

File Edit View Insert Format Records Tools Window Help

User Id	Last Name	First Name	Phone Ext	Office
T087	Anders	Jane	3923	531
T129	Bishop	Fred	3383	212
T238	Chan	Rose	3495	220
T347	Febo	Javier	4267	323
T451	Ginras	Mary	3156	444
T536	Hanneman	William	3578	317
T645	Johnsen	Paul	4445	234
T759	Kim	Lei	3068	310
T780	Mentor	Melissa	3418	525
T832	Reison	Jason	3803	312
T851	Sanchez	Alfredo	3134	438
T888	TenClink	Brian	3414	521

FIGURE 2-77

In the Lab

10. Restrict the records retrieved in task 10 above to only those users who have extra charges greater than $20.
11. Remove the Department table and clear the design grid.
12. Include the User Id, First Name, Last Name, Basic Charge, and Extra Charges fields in the design grid. Compute the total bill for each user (Basic Charge + Extra Charges). Display and print the results.
13. Display and print the average extra charges.
14. Display and print the highest extra charge.
15. Display and print the total extra charges for each department.
16. Join the User and Department tables. Include the Department Name, User Id, Last Name, First Name, Phone Ext, Basic Charge, and Extra Charges fields. Save the query as Departments and Users. Run the query and print the results.

3 Querying the City Scene Database

Problem: The managing editor of the *City Scene* magazine has determined a number of questions that he wants the database management system to answer. You must obtain answers to the questions posed by the managing editor.

Instructions: Use the database created in the In the Lab 3 of Project 1 for this assignment. Perform the following tasks.

1. Open the City Scene database and create a new query for the Advertiser table.
2. Display and print the Advertiser Number, Name, Balance, and Amount Paid for all the records in the table as shown in Figure 2-78 on the next page.
3. Display and print the Advertiser Number, Name, and Balance for all advertisers where the Ad Rep Number is 19.
4. Display and print the Advertiser Number, Name, and Balance for all advertisers where the Balance is greater than $100.
5. Display and print the Advertiser Number, Name, and Amount Paid for all advertisers where the Ad Rep Number is 16 and the Amount Paid is greater than $250.
6. Display and print the Advertiser Number and Name of all advertisers where the Name begins with C.
7. Display and print the Advertiser Number, Name, and Balance for all advertisers where the Ad Rep Number is 19 or the Balance is less than $100.
8. Include the Advertiser Number, Name, City, and State in the design grid. Sort the records in ascending order by City within State. Display and print the results. The City field should display in the result to the left of the State field. (*Hint*: Use information from Use Help 1 on page A 2.51.)
9. Display and print the cities in ascending order. Each city should display only once.
10. Display and print the Advertiser Number, Name, Balance, and Amount Paid fields from the Adver-

(continued)

In the Lab

Querying the City Scene Database *(continued)*

tiser table and the First Name, Last Name, and Comm Rate fields from the Ad Rep table.

11. Restrict the records retrieved in task 10 above to only those advertisers that are in WA. Display and print the results.

12. Clear the design grid and add the Last Name, First Name, and Comm Rate fields from the Ad Rep table to the grid. Add the Amount Paid field from the Advertiser table. Compute the Commission (Amount Paid * Comm Rate) for the Ad Rep table. Sort the records in ascending order by Last Name and format Commission as currency. (*Hint*: Use information from Use Help 2 on page A 2.52 to solve this problem.) Run the query and print the results.

13. Display and print the following statistics: the total balance and amount paid for all advertisers; the total balance for advertisers of ad rep 16; and the total amount paid for each ad rep.

14. Display and print the Ad Rep Number, Last Name, First Name, Advertiser Number, Name, Balance, and Amount Paid. Save the query as Ad Reps and Advertisers.

FIGURE 2-78

Cases and Places

The difficulty of these case studies varies: ◗ are the least difficult; ◗◗ are more difficult; and ◗◗◗ are the most difficult.

1 ◗ Use the textbook database created in Case Study 1 of Project 1 for this assignment. Perform the following: (a) The textbook cooperative receives a call asking if anyone is selling a book for Eng 150. Display and print the sellers' names and telephone numbers and their asking prices for books available for that course. (b) Karen Sing asks which books she has submitted. Display and print the titles, authors, and courses of her books. (c) Several nursing students call to ask which textbooks from that department are available. Display and print the titles, authors, and courses of the nursing books. (d) Display and print the titles, authors, and prices of books listed for less than $20. (e) Display and print the titles and course numbers for books in excellent condition.

2 ◗ Use the restaurant database created in Case Study 2 of Project 1 for this assignment. You decide to survey the campus community to get some marketing ideas for your meal delivery service. You want to know the students' restaurant habits. Perform the following: (a) It is 10:30 p.m. and a student has a craving for pizza. Display and print the names and telephone numbers of all Italian restaurants open that will deliver the order. (b) Students are cramming for an exam at 2:00 a.m. and would settle for any type of food. Display and print the names, telephone numbers, addresses, and closing times of all restaurants that are open. (c) A student's last class on Wednesday ends at 3:50 p.m., and he wants to pick up some food to take home to eat before he leaves for work. Display and print the names, addresses, and opening times of all restaurants that open before 5:00 p.m. (d) Payday for student employees is Friday, and they are short on cash at midweek. Display and print the names, addresses, telephone numbers, and food types of all restaurants that have specials on Wednesday or Thursday. (e) A group of students decides to meet for lunch. Display and print the names, addresses, telephone numbers, and opening times of all restaurants that open before noon.

3 ◗◗ Use the movie collection database created in Case Study 3 of Project 1 for this assignment. Perform the following: (a) Display and print the movie titles in ascending order, along with the two actors and year produced. (b) You have less than two hours to show a movie to the nursing home residents. Display and print the movie titles and running times that would fit this time constraint. (c) Display and print the movie titles starring John Wayne. (d) Display and print the movie titles starring Jean Arthur. (e) The nursing home is having a comedy night. Display and print the movies starring Abbott and Costello. (f) Display and print the movie titles and leading actors of films rated more than two stars. (g) It's Grandparents' Weekend at the nursing home. Display and print the movies produced in the 1930s and 1940s.

Cases and Places

4 ▶▶ The American Heart Association recommends a maximum of two, three-ounce cooked servings of lean meat, or six ounces total daily. A three-ounce serving is the size of a woman's palm. Use the nutritional content database created in Case Study 4 of Project 1 for this assignment. Perform the following: (a) Display and print the cuts of beef with less than 70 milligrams of cholesterol in one, three-ounce serving. (b) Display and print the cuts of beef with more than 160 calories in a three-ounce serving. (c) For your research project, you are to consume less than 20 grams of fat daily. During the day, you have eaten food with a total fat gram content of 15. Display and print the cuts of beef that would be within the project's requirements.

5 ▶▶▶ Use the product comparison database created in Case Study 5 of Project 1 for this assignment. Display and print the following: (a) The six specific items in ascending order, along with sizes and prices for the dairy items at the convenience, grocery, and discount stores; (b) The six specific items in ascending order, along with sizes and prices for the snack items at the convenience, grocery, and discount stores; (c) The six specific items in ascending order, along with sizes and prices for the cosmetics/toiletries items at the convenience, grocery, and discount stores; (d) The six specific items in ascending order, along with sizes and prices for the kitchen supplies items at the convenience, grocery, and discount stores.

6 ▶▶▶ Use the campus directory database created in Case Study 6 of Project 1 for this assignment. Display and print the following: (a) The names of your instructors in ascending order, along with their telephone numbers and room numbers; (b) The names of the administrators in ascending order, along with their telephone numbers and room numbers; (c) The services in ascending order, including telephone numbers and room numbers.

7 ▶▶▶ Use the financial institutions database created in Case Study 7 of Project 1 for this assignment. Display and print the following: (a) The names of the financial institutions and total values of the IRAs at age 65 in descending order; (b) The names and telephone numbers of the financial institutions and total amounts of interest earned at age 65 in descending order; (c) The average value of the IRAs at age 65; (d) The average interest rates for the banks, savings and loans, and credit unions; (e) The name, address, and interest rate of the financial institution with the highest interest rate; (f) The name, telephone number, and interest rate of the financial institution with the lowest interest rate; (g) The names of the financial institutions and penalties for early withdrawal in two years in ascending order; and (h) The names of the financial institutions and annual fees in descending order.

Microsoft PowerPoint 97

▶ PROJECT ONE

USING A DESIGN TEMPLATE AND STYLE CHECKER TO CREATE A PRESENTATION

Objectives   PP 1.3
What Is Microsoft PowerPoint?   PP 1.6
Project One – Unlocking the Internet   PP 1.8
Starting a Presentation as a New Office Document
     PP 1.10
PowerPoint Views   PP 1.15
Creating a Title Slide   PP 1.18
Text Attributes   PP 1.20
Saving a Presentation on a Floppy Disk   PP 1.23
Adding a New Slide to a Presentation   PP 1.25
Creating a Bulleted List Slide   PP 1.27
Adding a New Slide with the Same AutoLayout
     PP 1.31
Saving a Presentation with the Same File Name
     PP 1.33
Moving to Another Slide in Slide View   PP 1.34
Viewing the Presentation Using Slide Show
     PP 1.35
Quitting PowerPoint   PP 1.38
Opening a Presentation   PP 1.39
Checking a Presentation for Visual Clarity,
     Consistency, and Style   PP 1.41
Correcting Errors   PP 1.44
Changing Line Spacing   PP 1.45
Displaying a Presentation in Black and White
     PP 1.50
Printing a Presentation   PP 1.51
Making a Transparency   PP 1.54
Quitting PowerPoint   PP 1.54
PowerPoint Online Help   PP 1.54
Project Summary   PP 1.55
What You Should Know   PP 1.55
Test Your Knowledge   PP 1.56
Use Help   PP 1.58
Apply Your Knowledge   PP 1.60
In the Lab   PP 1.61
Cases and Places   PP 1.64

▶ PROJECT TWO

USING OUTLINE VIEW AND CLIP ART TO CREATE AN ELECTRONIC SLIDE SHOW

Objectives   PP 2.3
Creating a Presentation from an Outline   PP 2.4
Project Two – Break Away Bargains   PP 2.5
Starting a New Presentation   PP 2.7
Using Outline View   PP 2.7
Creating a Presentation in Outline View   PP 2.10
Adding a Slide in Outline View   PP 2.12
Creating Multi-level Bulleted List Slides in Outline
     View   PP 2.13
Creating a Slide with Multiple Text Objects in
     Outline View   PP 2.16
Creating a Closing Slide in Outline View   PP 2.17
Saving a Presentation   PP 2.18
Reviewing a Presentation in Slide Sorter View
     PP 2.19
Adding a Blank Line to a Bulleted List   PP 2.20
Changing Slide Layout   PP 2.23
Moving Text   PP 2.24
Adding Clip Art to a Slide   PP 2.26
Moving Clip Art   PP 2.33
Changing the Size of Clip Art   PP 2.33
Adding a Header and Footer to Outline Pages
     PP 2.36
Checking the Presentation for Spelling and Style
     Errors   PP 2.38
Adding Animation Effects   PP 2.38
Applying Animation Effects to Bulleted Slides
     PP 2.42
Animating Clip Art Objects   PP 2.47
Formatting and Animating a Title Slide   PP 2.50
Running an Animated Slide Show   PP 2.51
Printing in Outline View   PP 2.53
Project Summary   PP 2.58
What You Should Know   PP 2.58
Test Your Knowledge   PP 2.59
Use Help   PP 2.62
Apply Your Knowledge   PP 2.63
In the Lab   PP 2.65
Cases and Places   PP 2.72

Using a Design Template and Style Checker to Create a Presentation

Objectives:

You will have mastered the material in this project when you can:

◗ Start a new PowerPoint document
◗ Describe the PowerPoint window
◗ Select a design template
◗ Create a title slide
◗ Change the font size of selected text
◗ Italicize selected text
◗ Save a presentation
◗ Add a new slide
◗ Demote a bulleted paragraph
◗ Promote a bulleted paragraph
◗ View a presentation in slide show view
◗ Quit PowerPoint
◗ Open a presentation
◗ Use Style Checker to identify spelling, visual clarity, case, and end punctuation inconsistencies
◗ Edit a presentation
◗ Change line spacing on the slide master
◗ Display a presentation in black and white
◗ Print a presentation in black and white

A THoUsaNd aND OnE WaYs tO MaKE a HiT

What if your very life depended on your ability to make a captivating presentation? This was the predicament faced by Princess Scheherazade, the fabled storyteller to whom we owe the tales of the *Arabian Nights*. Married to King Schahriar, who beheaded each new bride after the wedding night, she beguiled him with a continuing story so fabulous and intriguing, that each night he spared her life, so she might relate the next installment. Thus, she successfully staved off the king's sword for a thousand and one nights, when at last, he granted her a permanent stay of execution, a tribute to her powers of presentation.

Fortunately, in today's world, the stakes usually are not that high. Yet, the skill to present an argument or a concept in the most dynamic and pleasing way possible may spell the difference between huge success or severe failure. Salespeople the world over know the truth in this, as do politicians seeking election, scientists pursuing funding for a project, or any of countless situations where the ability to persuade is the key to victory.

In some ways, modern requirements are more demanding than in Scheherazade's time. Today, mere words are not enough. Because audiences have developed a taste for multimedia, they demand both aural and graphical ingredients in presentations. This means that appearance is just as important as the words — you not only have to "talk the talk," you have to "walk the walk." The presentation of food in commercials is an excellent example. Food stylists, who are a special breed of presenters, prepare food especially for displays, photographs, or films, *styling* the product to fit the message. And for many people, the presentation of food in restaurants — from the chef's artistic arrangement of food on a plate to the waiter's proud delivery to the table — is just as important as the cuisine.

Conversely, the wrong image can confuse or distort one's message. Many familiar instances exist in literature and movies: *The Hunchback of Notre Dame*, Yoda in *Star Wars*, *Rain Man*, *Powder*, *Mask*, *Forrest Gump*, and *The Elephant Man*, where appearances obscure the understanding of true worth.

Now, Microsoft's PowerPoint 97 makes it easier than ever to deliver your presentation with panache while ensuring your audience understands the true value of your message. Whether you are a new user or just in a hurry, templates give you ready-made patterns, and the AutoLayout feature provides shortcuts for maintaining your design. With PowerPoints's Style Checker, you analyze visual clarity and consistency, and then you can make your presentation sizzle with clip art and multimedia effects.

So, before you plunge into that next persuasive effort, take a cue from the Princess Scheherazade. Leave them thirsting for more — with help from PowerPoint.

the ability to persuade

Project

1

Microsoft
PowerPoint 97

Using a Design Template and Style Checker to Create a Presentation

Case Perspective

Everyday, more and more people are connecting to the Internet via the World Wide Web. The World Wide Web, often called the Web, is a collection of hypertext links that creates an interconnected network of links within the Internet. The most popular method of accessing the World Wide Web is a graphical software program called a browser. A person having a browser, and the proper hardware and communications requirements, easily can explore a wealth of information on the Internet. But what exactly are those requirements?

Elizabeth McGiver is a World Wide Web expert. She has prepared a short presentation to explain the requirements for connecting to the World Wide Web. Her presentation identifies the minimum hardware and software requirements for connecting to the World Wide Web as well as options for Internet service providers. Ms. McGiver selected a design template to create a consistent look throughout the presentation. To make the presentation more appealing, she adjusted paragraph spacing. In the event that the location in which she speaks does not have the equipment necessary to conduct an electronic presentation, she prepared a copy of the presentation on transparency film to use with an overhead projector.

What Is Microsoft PowerPoint?

Microsoft PowerPoint is a complete presentation graphics program that allows you to produce professional-looking presentations. PowerPoint gives you the flexibility to make informal presentations using overhead transparencies (Figure 1-1a), make electronic presentations using a projection device attached to a personal computer (Figure 1-1b), make formal presentations using 35mm slides (Figure 1-1c), or take advantage of the World Wide Web and run virtual presentations on the Internet (Figure 1-1d). Additionally, PowerPoint can create paper printouts, outlines, speaker notes, and audience handouts.

PowerPoint contains several features to simplify creating a presentation. For example, you can instruct PowerPoint to create a predesigned presentation, and then you can modify the presentation to fulfill your requirements. You quickly can format a presentation using one of the professionally designed presentation design templates. To make your presentation more impressive, you can add tables, graphs, pictures, video, sound, and animation effects. You can be certain your presentation meets specific design criteria by using Style Checker to locate inconsistencies in spelling, visual clarity, uppercase and lowercase usage, and end punctuation.

(a) Overhead Transparencies

(b) Projection Device Connected to a Personal Computer

(c) 35mm Slides

(d) PowerPoint Presentation Over the World Wide Web

FIGURE 1-1

For example, you can instruct PowerPoint to restrict the number of bulleted items on a slide or limit the number of words in each paragraph. Additional PowerPoint features include the following:

▶ **Word processing** — allows you to create bulleted lists, combine words and images, find and replace text, and use multiple fonts and type sizes. Using its IntelliSense™ features, PowerPoint can perform tasks such as checking spelling and formatting text – *all while you are typing.*

▶ **Outlining** — allows you quickly to create your presentation using an outline format. You also can import outlines from Microsoft Word or other word processing programs.

▶ **Graphing** — allows you to create and insert charts into your presentations. Graph formats include two-dimensional (2-D) graphs: area, bar, column, combination, line, pie, xy (scatter); and three-dimensional (3-D) graphs: area, bar, column, line, and pie.

▶ **Drawing** — allows you to create diagrams using shapes such as arcs, arrows, cubes, rectangles, stars, and triangles. Drawing also allows you to modify shapes without redrawing.

▶ **Clip art** — allows you to insert artwork into your presentation without creating it yourself. You can find hundreds of graphic images in the Microsoft Clip Gallery, or you can import art from other applications. With the **AutoClipArt feature**, PowerPoint can suggest a clip art image appropriate for your presentation.

▶ **Multimedia effects** — adds interest and keeps your audience attentive by adding effects, such as sound and video, to your presentations. PowerPoint 97 allows you to create interactive multimedia presentations that can be placed on the World Wide Web.

▶ **Wizards** — a tutorial approach for quickly and efficiently creating a presentation. PowerPoint wizards make it easy to create quality presentations by prompting you for specific content criteria. For example, the **AutoContent Wizard** prompts you for what are you going to talk about and the type of presentation you are going to give, such as recommending a strategy or selling a product. When giving a presentation away from the computer, on which it was created, it is important you take all the necessary files. The **Pack and Go Wizard** helps you bundle everything you need, including any objects associated with that presentation. If you cannot confirm that the computer on which you are presenting has PowerPoint, you also can pack **PowerPoint Viewer**, a program that allows you to run, but not edit, a PowerPoint presentation.

Project One – Unlocking the Internet

This book presents a series of projects using PowerPoint to produce slides similar to those you would develop in an academic or business environment. Project 1 uses PowerPoint to create the presentation shown in Figure 1-2. The objective is to produce a presentation, called Unlocking the Internet, to be presented using an overhead projector. As an introduction to PowerPoint, this project steps you through the most common type of presentation, a bulleted list. A **bulleted list** is a list of paragraphs, each preceded by a bullet. A **bullet** is a symbol (usually a heavy dot (•)) that precedes text when the text warrants special emphasis. The first of the four slides is called the title slide. The **title slide** introduces the presentation to the audience.

(a)

(b)

(c)

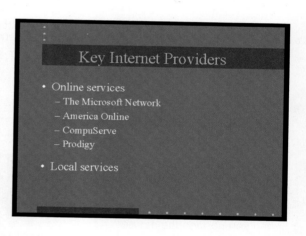

(d)

FIGURE 1-2

Slide Preparation Steps

The preparation steps summarize how the slide presentation shown in Figure 1-2 will be developed in Project 1. The following tasks will be completed in this project.

1. Start a new Office document.
2. Select a design template.
3. Create a title slide.
4. Save the presentation on a floppy disk.
5. Create three multi-level bulleted lists.
6. Save the presentation again.
7. Quit PowerPoint.
8. Open the presentation as a Microsoft Office document.
9. Style check the presentation.
10. Edit the presentation.

11. Print the presentation.
12. Quit PowerPoint.

The following pages contain a detailed explanation of these tasks.

Starting a Presentation as a New Office Document

A PowerPoint document is called a **presentation**. The quickest way to begin a new presentation is to use the **Start button** on the **taskbar** at the bottom of your screen. When you click the Start button, the **Start menu** displays several commands for simplifying tasks in Windows 95. When Microsoft Office 97 is installed, the Start menu displays two commands: New Office Document and Open Office Document. You use the **New Office Document** command to designate the type of Office document you are creating. Then, you specify the design template or wizard on which you wish to base your document. A **design template** provides consistency in design and color throughout the entire presentation. The design template determines the color scheme, font and font size, and layout of your presentation. Then PowerPoint starts and the specified template or wizard displays. The Open Office Document command is discussed later in this project. Perform the steps on the following pages to start a new presentation, or ask your instructor how to start PowerPoint on your system.

More *About*
Design Templates

When deciding on a design template, choose one designed to display light colored text on a medium to dark background. Light text on a dark background provides a stronger contrast than light text on a light background.

Steps **To Start a New Presentation**

1 **Point to the Start button on the taskbar at the lower-left corner of the desktop.**

When you position the mouse pointer on the Start button, it displays as a left pointing block arrow and a ScreenTip displays, Click here to begin (Figure 1-3). Your computer system displays the time on the clock at the right end of the taskbar.

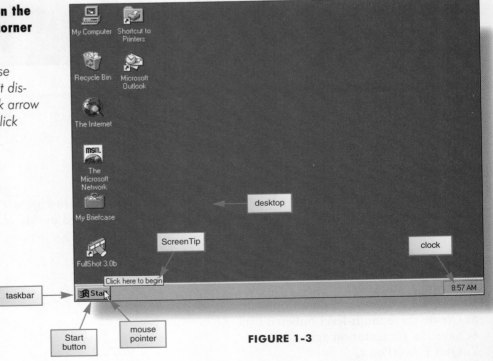

FIGURE 1-3

2 **Click the Start button. When the Windows 95 Start menu displays, point to New Office Document.**

The Windows 95 Start menu displays the names of several programs. The mouse pointer points to New Office Document (Figure 1-4). When the mouse pointer points to a name on the menu, the name is highlighted.

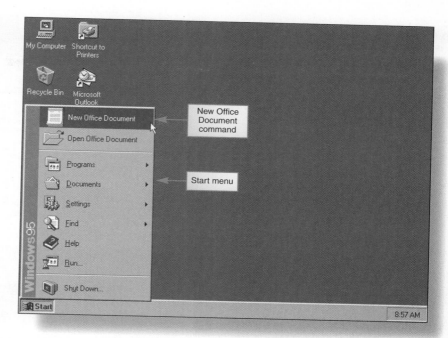

FIGURE 1-4

3 **Click New Office Document. When the New Office Document dialog box displays, point to the Presentatio . . . tab.**

The New Office Document dialog box automatically displays the General sheet and the mouse pointer points to the Presentatio . . . (Presentation Designs) tab (Figure 1-5). Depending on your installation, your computer may display a Presentation Designs tab or a Designs tab.

FIGURE 1-5

4 Click the Presentatio . . . tab. When the Presentatio . . . sheet displays, point to Contempo. . . (Contemporary).

The Presentatio . . . sheet displays the names and icons for several design templates (Figure 1-6). The Preview box displays a message about how to see a preview of a presentation design template. The OK button currently is dimmed, which means it is not available because a design template icon has not been selected. The Cancel button is available, however, as indicated by the black text on the button. The Cancel button is used to close the New Office Document dialog box and return to the desktop or return to the window from which you started.

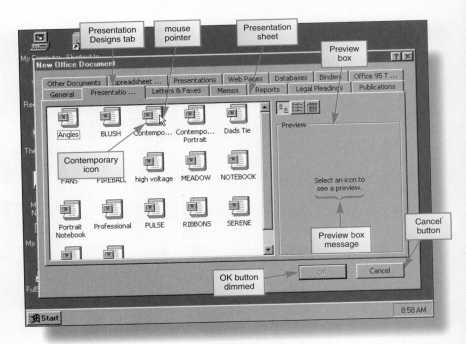

FIGURE 1-6

5 Click Contempo. . ..

The Contempo. . . design template icon is highlighted and a thumbnail view of the design template displays in the Preview box (Figure 1-7). The OK button now is available as indicated by the black text on the button.

FIGURE 1-7

6 **Double-click Contempo. . .. When the Office Assistant displays, point to the Close button on the Office Assistant.**

Double-clicking the Contemporary design template icon indicates that you are applying a PowerPoint design template. As a result, PowerPoint starts and displays the New Slide dialog box, the Common Tasks toolbar, and the Office Assistant (Figure 1-8). The Office Assistant displays if it was active during the last computer session or when Microsoft Office 97 starts for the first time. You learn how to use the Office Assistant later in this project. Microsoft PowerPoint displays as a button on the taskbar at the bottom of the screen.

FIGURE 1-8

7 **Click the Close button and then point to the OK button in the New Slide dialog box.**

The Office Assistant closes. A frame displays around the Title Slide AutoLayout to indicate it is selected (Figure 1-9). The name of the selected AutoLayout displays on the lower-right corner of the New Slide dialog box.

FIGURE 1-9

8 Click the OK button.

PowerPoint displays the Title Slide AutoLayout and the Contemporary design template on Slide 1 (Figure 1-10). The title bar identifies this as a Microsoft PowerPoint presentation currently titled Presentation1. The status bar displays information about the current slide, such as the slide number and the current design template.

FIGURE 1-10

As an alternative to double-clicking the Contemporary design template in Step 6, you can click the OK button to apply the selected design template. The Office Assistant, closed in Step 7, is discussed later in this project.

The PowerPoint Window

The basic unit of a PowerPoint presentation is a **slide**. **Objects** are the building blocks for a PowerPoint slide. A slide contains one or many objects, such as a title, text, graphics, tables, charts, and drawings. In PowerPoint, you have the option of using the PowerPoint default settings or establishing your own. A **default setting** is a particular value for a variable that is assigned initially by PowerPoint and remains in effect unless canceled or overridden by the user. These settings control the placement of objects, the color scheme, the transition between slides, and other slide attributes. **Attributes** are the properties or characteristics of an object. For example, if you underline the title of a slide, the title is the object and the underline is the attribute. When you start PowerPoint, the default **slide layout** is **landscape orientation**, in which the slide width is greater than its height. In landscape orientation, the slide size is preset to 10 inches wide and 7.5 inches high. The slide layout can be changed to **portrait orientation**, so that the slide height is greater than its width, by clicking Page Setup on the File menu. In portrait orientation, the slide height is 10 inches and its width is 7.5 inches.

More *About* The PowerPoint Window

To drag and drop objects quickly between two presentations, display both presentations in one PowerPoint window. To display two presentations in one PowerPoint window, open both presentations, click the Restore button on the presentation title bar of one of the presentations, and drag the presentation window border to size the window to fill one-half of the PowerPoint window. Repeat the process for the second presentation window.

PowerPoint Views

PowerPoint has five views: slide view, outline view, slide sorter view, notes page view, and slide show view. A **view** is the mode in which the presentation displays on the screen. You may use any or all views when creating your presentation, but you can use only one at a time. Change views by clicking one of the view buttons found on the **View Button Bar** at the bottom of the PowerPoint screen (Figure 1-10). The PowerPoint window display is dependent on the view. Some views are graphical while others are textual.

Table 1-1 identifies the view buttons and provides an explanation of each view.

Table 1-1

BUTTON	BUTTON NAME	FUNCTION
	Slide View	Displays a single slide as it appears in your presentation. Use slide view to create or edit a presentation. Slide view also is used to incorporate text and graphic objects and to create line-by-line progressive disclosure, called build effects.
	Outline View	Displays a presentation in an outline format showing slide titles and text. It is best used for organizing and developing the content of your presentation.
	Slide Sorter View	Displays miniature versions of all slides in your presentation. You then can copy, cut, paste, or otherwise change slide position to modify your presentation. Slide sorter view also is used to add slide transitions.
	Notes Page View	Displays the current notes page. Notes page view allows you to create speaker's notes to use when you give your presentation. Each notes page corresponds to a slide and includes a reduced slide image.
	Slide Show View	Displays your slides as an electronic presentation on the full screen of your computer's monitor. Looking much like a slide projector display, you can see the effect of transitions, build effects, and slide timings.

PowerPoint Window in Slide View

The PowerPoint window in slide view contains: the title bar; the menu bar; the status bar; the toolbars: Standard, Formatting, Drawing, and Common Tasks; the AutoLayout object area; the mouse pointer; the scroll bars; and the View Button Bar.

TITLE BAR The **title bar** (Figure 1-10) displays the name of the current PowerPoint document. Until you save your presentation, PowerPoint assigns the default name Presentation1.

MENU BAR The **menu bar** (Figure 1-10) displays the PowerPoint menu names. Each menu name represents a list of commands that allows you to retrieve, store, print, and change objects in your presentation. To display a menu, such as the File menu, click File (the name) on the menu bar.

STATUS BAR Located at the bottom of the PowerPoint window, the **status bar** consists of a message area and a presentation design template identifier (Figure 1-10). Most of the time, the current slide number and the total number of slides in the presentation display in the message area. For example, in Figure 1-10, the message area displays Slide 1 of 1. Slide 1 is the current slide, and of 1 indicates there is only one slide in the presentation.

SCROLL BARS The **vertical scroll bar** (Figure 1-10), located on the right side of the PowerPoint window, allows you to move forward or backward through your presentation. Clicking the **Next Slide button** (Figure 1-10), located on the vertical scroll bar, advances to the next slide in the presentation. Clicking the **Previous Slide button** (Figure 1-10), located on the vertical scroll bar, backs up to the slide preceding the current slide.

The **horizontal scroll bar** (Figure 1-10 on page PP 1.14), located on the bottom of the PowerPoint window, allows you to display a portion of the window when the entire window does not fit on the screen.

It should be noted that in slide view, both the vertical and horizontal scroll bar actions are dependent on the **Zoom** settings. You control how large or small a document displays on the PowerPoint window by zooming in or out. If you are in slide view and Zoom is set such that the entire slide is not visible in the Slide window, clicking the up arrow on the vertical scroll bar displays the next portion of your slide, not the previous slide. Recall that to go to the previous slide, click the Previous Slide button. To go to the next slide, click the Next Slide button.

AUTOLAYOUT OBJECT AREA The **AutoLayout object area** (Figure 1-10 on page PP 1.14) is a collection of placeholders for the title, text, clip art, graphs, tables, and media clips (video and sound). These placeholders display when you create a new slide. You can change the AutoLayout any time during the creation of your presentation by clicking the Slide Layout button on the Common Tasks toolbar and then selecting a different slide layout.

PLACEHOLDERS Surrounded by a dashed line, **placeholders** are the empty objects on a new slide. Depending on the AutoLayout selected, placeholders will display for the title, text, graphs, tables, organization charts, media clips, and clip art. Once you place contents in a placeholder, the placeholder becomes an object. For example, text typed in a placeholder becomes a text object.

TITLE PLACEHOLDER Surrounded by a dashed line, the **title placeholder** is the empty title object on a new slide (Figure 1-10). Text typed in the title placeholder becomes the **title object**.

SUB-TITLE PLACEHOLDER Surrounded by a dashed line, the **sub-title placeholder** is the empty sub-title object that displays below the title placeholder on a title slide (Figure 1-10).

MOUSE POINTER The **mouse pointer** can become one of several different shapes depending on the task you are performing in PowerPoint and the pointer's location on the screen. The mouse pointer in Figure 1-10 has the shape of a left-pointing block arrow.

TOOLBARS PowerPoint **toolbars** consist of buttons that allow you to perform tasks more quickly than when using the menu bar. For example, to save a presentation, click the Save button on the Standard toolbar. Each button face has a graphical representation that helps you remember its function. Figures 1-11 through 1-14 illustrate the buttons on each of the four toolbars that display when you start PowerPoint and display a slide in slide view. They are the Standard toolbar, the Formatting toolbar, the Drawing toolbar, and the Common Tasks toolbar. Each button is explained in detail when it is used.

PowerPoint has several additional toolbars you can display by clicking View on the menu bar. You also can display a toolbar by pointing to a toolbar and right-clicking to display a shortcut menu, which lists the available toolbars. A **shortcut menu** contains a list of commands or items that relate to the item to which you are pointing when you right-click.

More *About* **Zoom**

Increase the Zoom setting when working with small objects to better see details, such as when modifying a graphic. Decrease the Zoom setting to work with large objects.

More *About* **Toolbars**

Hiding a toolbar that you no longer need increases the Zoom setting and displays a larger PowerPoint view. To hide a toolbar, right-click any toolbar and then click the check mark next to the name of the toolbar you wish to hide.

PowerPoint allows you to customize all toolbars and to add the toolbar buttons you use most often. In the same manner, you can remove those toolbar buttons you do not use. To customize a toolbar, click Tools on the menu bar, and then click Customize to modify the toolbar to meet your requirements. Another way to customize a toolbar is to click View on the menu bar, click Toolbars, click Customize, and then make changes in the Customize dialog box to fulfill your requirements.

STANDARD TOOLBAR The **Standard toolbar** (Figure 1-11) contains the tools to execute the more common commands found on the menu bar, such as Open, Print, Save, Copy, Cut, Paste, and many more. The Standard toolbar contains a button for setting Zoom. Recall that you control how large or small a document displays in the PowerPoint window with the Zoom list.

FIGURE 1-11

FORMATTING TOOLBAR The **Formatting toolbar** (Figure 1-12) contains the tools for changing text attributes. The Formatting toolbar allows you to quickly change font, font size, and alignment. It also contains tools to bold, italicize, underline, shadow, color, and bullet text. The five **attribute buttons, Bold, Italic, Underline, Shadow**, and **Bullets**, are on/off switches, or toggles. Click the button once to turn the attribute on; then click it again to turn the attribute off.

FIGURE 1-12

DRAWING TOOLBAR The **Drawing toolbar** (Figure 1-13) is a collection of tools for drawing objects such as lines, circles, and boxes. The Drawing toolbar also contains tools to edit the objects once you have drawn them. For example, you can change the color of an object with the **Fill Color button**, or rotate an object by clicking the **Free Rotate** button.

FIGURE 1-13

COMMON TASKS TOOLBAR The **Common Tasks toolbar** (Figure 1-14) contains three more frequently used commands: **New Slide button, Slide Layout button**, and the **Apply Design button**.

FIGURE 1-14

More *About*
**Presentation
Design**

The audience determines the
level of detail you place on
one slide. Before you create
your presentation, determine
who is likely to attend. Design
your presentation around the
amount of detail the audience
wants to see. Remember, you
want to keep their attention, not
bore them with details.

Creating a Title Slide

The purpose of a title slide is to introduce the presentation to the audience. PowerPoint assumes the first slide in a new presentation is the title slide. With the exception of a blank slide, PowerPoint also assumes every new slide has a title. To make creating your presentation easier, any text you type after a new slide displays becomes the title object. In other words, you do not have to first select the title placeholder before typing the title text. The AutoLayout for the title slide has a title placeholder near the middle of the window and a sub-title placeholder directly below the title placeholder (Figure 1-15).

Entering the Presentation Title

The presentation title for Project 1 is Unlocking the Internet. Type the presentation title in the title placeholder on the title slide. Perform the following step to create the title slide for this project.

Steps **To Enter the Presentation Title**

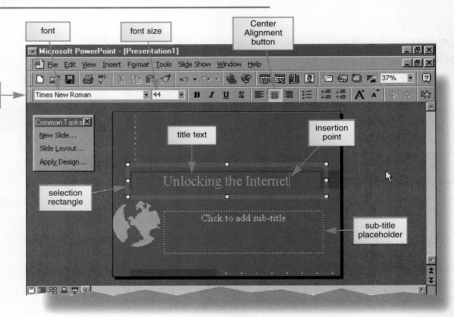

1 **Type** Unlocking the Internet **in the title placeholder. Do not press the ENTER key.**

*The title text, Unlocking the Internet, displays in the title text box (Figure 1-15). The recessed Center Alignment button indicates the title text is center-aligned in the title text box. When you type the first character, the selection rectangle, a slashed outline, displays around the title box. A blinking vertical line (|), called the **insertion point**, indicates where the next character will display.*

FIGURE 1-15

More *About*
Title Slides

To identify a new section in a
long presentation, insert a title
slide with the name of the new
section.

Notice that you do not press the ENTER key after the word Internet. If you press the ENTER key after typing the title, PowerPoint creates a new paragraph. A **paragraph** is a segment of text with the same format that begins when you press the ENTER key and ends when you press the ENTER key again. Pressing the ENTER key creates a new line in a new paragraph. Therefore, do not press the ENTER key unless you want to create a two-paragraph title. Additionally, PowerPoint **line wraps** text that exceeds the width of the placeholder. For example, if the slide title were Experiencing the World Wide Web, it would exceed the width of the title placeholder and display on two lines.

The title is centered in the window because the Contemporary design template alignment attribute is centered. The Center Alignment button is recessed on the Formatting toolbar in Figure 1-15.

Correcting a Mistake When Typing

If you type the wrong letter and notice the error before pressing the ENTER key, press the BACKSPACE key to erase all the characters back to and including the one that is incorrect. If you mistakenly press the ENTER key after entering the title and the insertion point is on the new line, simply press the BACKSPACE key to return the insertion point to the right of the letter t in the word Internet.

When you first install PowerPoint, the default setting allows you to reverse up to the last 20 changes by clicking the **Undo button** on the Standard toolbar. The ScreenTip that displays when you point to the Undo button changes to indicate the type of change just made. For example, if you type text in the title placeholder and then point to the Undo button, the ScreenTip that displays is Undo Typing. For clarity, when referencing the Undo button in this project, the name displaying in the ScreenTip is referenced. Another way to reverse changes is to click the Undo command on the Edit menu. Like the Undo button, the Undo command name reflects the last type of change made to the presentation.

You can reapply a change that you reversed with the Undo button by clicking the Redo button on the Standard toolbar. Clicking the **Redo button** reverses the last undo action. The ScreenTip name reflects the type of reversal last preformed.

Entering the Presentation Subtitle

The next step in creating the title slide is to enter the subtitle text into the sub-title placeholder. Complete the steps below to enter the presentation subtitle.

More *About* Undo

The number of times you can click the Undo button to reverse changes can be modified. To increase or decrease the number of undos, click Tools on the menu bar, click Options, and then click the Edit tab. Use the up and down arrows in the Maximum number of undos box to change the number of undos. The maximum number of undos is 150; the minimum number is 3.

Steps To Enter the Presentation Subtitle

1 **Click the label, Click to add sub-title, located inside the sub-title placeholder.**

The insertion point is in the sub-title text box (Figure 1-16). The mouse pointer changes to an I-beam. The I-beam mouse pointer indicates the mouse is in a text placeholder. The selection rectangle indicates the sub-title placeholder is selected.

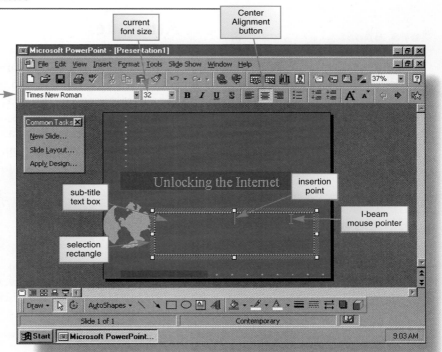

FIGURE 1-16

2 **Type** World Wide Web Requirements **and press the** ENTER **key. Type** Presented by: **and press the** ENTER **key. Type** Elizabeth McGiver **but do not press the** ENTER **key.**

The text displays in the sub-title object as shown in Figure 1-17. The insertion point displays after the letter r in McGiver.

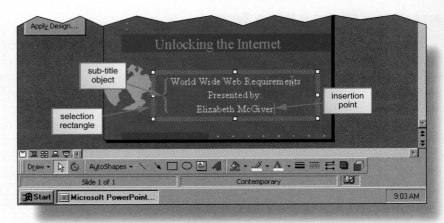

FIGURE 1-17

The previous section created a title slide using an AutoLayout for the title slide. PowerPoint displayed the title slide layout because you created a new presentation. You entered text in the title placeholder without selecting the title placeholder because PowerPoint assumes every slide has a title. You could, however, click the title placeholder to select it and then type your title. In general, to type text in any text placeholder, click the text placeholder and begin typing. You also added a subtitle that identifies the presenter. While this is not required, it often is useful information for the audience.

Text Attributes

This presentation is using the Contemporary design template that you selected from the Presentation sheet. Each design template has its own text attributes. A **text attribute** is a characteristic of the text, such as font, font size, font style, or text color. You can adjust text attributes any time before, during, or after you type the text. Recall that a design template determines the color scheme, font and font size, and layout of your presentation. Most of the time, you use the design template's text attributes and color scheme. There are times when you wish to change the way your presentation looks, however, and still keep a particular design template. PowerPoint gives you that flexibility. You can use the design template you wish and change the text color, text font size, text font, and text font style. Table 1-2 explains the different text attributes available in PowerPoint.

The next two sections explain how to change the font size and text font style attributes.

Table 1-2

ATTRIBUTE	DESCRIPTION
Font	Defines the appearance and shape of letters, numbers, and special characters.
Text color	Defines the color of text. Displaying text in color requires a color monitor. Printing text in color requires a color printer or plotter.
Font size	Specifies the size of characters on the screen. Character size is gauged by a measurement system called points. A single point is about 1/72 of an inch in height. Thus, a character with a point size of eighteen is about 18/72 (or 1/4) of an inch in height.
Text font style	Defines text characteristics. Text font styles include plain, italic, bold, shadowed, and underlined. Text may have one or more font styles at a time.
Subscript	Defines the placement of a character in relationship to another. A subscript character displays or prints slightly below and immediately to one side of another character.
Superscript	Defines the placement of a character in relationship to another. A superscript character displays or prints above and immediately to one side of another character.

Changing the Font Size

The Contemporary design template default font size is 32 points for body text and 44 points for title text. A point is 1/72 of an inch in height. Thus, a character with a point size of 44 is about 44/72 (or 11/18) of an inch in height. Slide 1 requires you to decrease the font size for the paragraph, Presented by:. Perform the following steps to decrease font size.

Steps **To Decrease Font Size**

1 **Triple-click the paragraph, Presented by:, in the sub-title object.**

The paragraph, Presented by:, is highlighted (Figure 1-18).

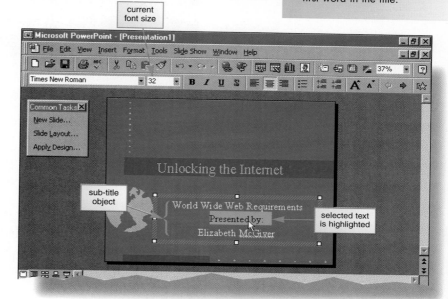

FIGURE 1-18

2 **With Presented by: highlighted, point to the Decrease Font Size button on the Formatting toolbar.**

*When you point to a button on a toolbar, PowerPoint displays a ScreenTip. A **ScreenTip** contains the name of the tool to which you are pointing. When pointing to the **Decrease Font Size button**, the ScreenTip displays the words, Decrease Font Size (Figure 1-19).*

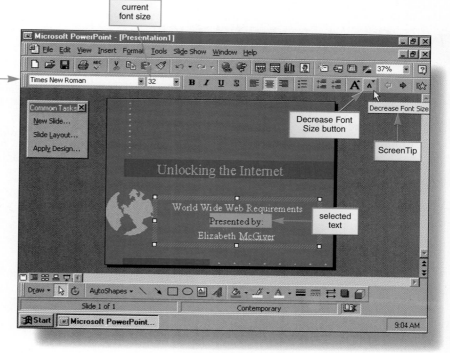

FIGURE 1-19

3 **Click the Decrease Font Size button twice so that 24 displays in the Font Size list box on the Formatting toolbar.**

The paragraph, Presented by:, reduces to 24 points (Figure 1-20). The Font Size list box displays the new font size as 24.

FIGURE 1-20

OtherWays

1. Right-click selected text, click Font on shortcut menu, click new font size in Size list box
2. Click Font Size arrow on Formatting toolbar, click one of listed font sizes, or click Font Size list box on Formatting toolbar, type font size between 1 and 4000
3. On Format menu click Font, click new font size in Size list box

If you need to increase the font size, click the **Increase Font Size button,** located immediately to the left of the Decrease Font Size button on the Formatting toolbar.

Changing the Style of Text to Italic

Text font styles include plain, italic, bold, shadowed, and underlined. PowerPoint allows you to use one or more text font styles in your presentation. Perform the following steps to add emphasis to the title slide by changing plain text to italic text.

Steps **To Change the Text Font Style to Italic**

1 **With the paragraph, Presented by:, highlighted, click the Italic button on the Formatting toolbar.**

The text is italicized and the Italic button is recessed (Figure 1-21).

OtherWays

1. Right-click selected text, click Font on shortcut menu, click Italic in Font style list box
2. On Format menu click Font, click Italic in Font style list box
3. Press CTRL+I

FIGURE 1-21

To remove italics from text, select the italicized text and then click the Italic button. As a result, the Italic button is not recessed and the text does not have the italic font style.

Saving a Presentation on a Floppy Disk

While you are building your presentation, the computer stores it in main memory. It is important to save your presentation frequently because, if the computer is turned off or you lose electrical power, the presentation is lost. Another reason to save your work is that if you run out of lab time before completing your project, you may finish the project later without having to start over. You must, therefore, save any presentation you will use later. Before you continue with Project 1, save the work completed thus far. Perform the following steps to save a presentation on a floppy disk using the Save button on the Standard toolbar.

More *About* Saving

Before you make extreme changes to your presentation, save a copy of it with a different file name using the Save As command on the File menu. This way, if you decide you do not like the new version, you still will have a copy of the original presentation.

Steps **To Save a Presentation on a Floppy Disk**

1 **Insert a formatted floppy disk in drive A. Then click the Save button on the Standard toolbar.**

The Save dialog displays (Figure 1-22). The insertion point displays in the File name list box. The default folder, My Documents, displays in the Save in list box. Presentation displays in the Save as type list box. The Save button is dimmed (not available) because you have not yet entered a name in the File name list box. The Cancel button is available, as indicated by the black text on the button. Clicking the Cancel button closes the Save dialog box and returns to the PowerPoint window.

FIGURE 1-22

2 **Type** Unlocking the Internet **in the File name list box. Do not press the ENTER key after typing the file name.**

The name, Unlocking the Internet, displays in the File name list box (Figure 1-23). The black text on the Save button indicates it is available.

FIGURE 1-23

3 **Click the Save in box arrow. Point to 3½ Floppy (A:) in the Save in list.**

The Save in list displays a list of locations where you can save your presentation (Figure 1-24). Your list may look different depending on the configuration of your system. 3½ Floppy (A:) is highlighted.

FIGURE 1-24

4 **Click 3½ Floppy (A:). Then point to the Save button.**

Drive A becomes the current drive (Figure 1-25).

FIGURE 1-25

file name displays in title bar

5 **Click the Save button.**

PowerPoint saves the presentation on your floppy disk in drive A. Slide 1 displays in slide view. The title bar displays the file name used to save the presentation, Unlocking the Internet (Figure 1-26).

FIGURE 1-26

PowerPoint automatically appends to the file name, Unlocking the Internet, the extension **.ppt**, which stands for **PowerP**oint. Although the presentation, Unlocking the Internet, is saved on a floppy disk, it also remains in main memory and displays on the screen.

It is a good practice to save periodically while you are working on a project. By doing so, you protect yourself from losing all the work you have done since the last time you saved.

Adding a New Slide to a Presentation

The title slide for your presentation is created. The next step is to add the first bulleted list slide in Project 1. Clicking the New Slide button on the Common Tasks toolbar adds a slide into the presentation immediately after the current slide. Usually when you create your presentation, you are adding slides with text, graphics, or charts. When you add a new slide, PowerPoint displays a dialog box so that you can choose one of the AutoLayouts. These AutoLayouts have placeholders for various objects, such as a title, text, graphics, graphs, and charts. Some placeholders provide access to other PowerPoint objects by allowing you to double-click the placeholder. Figure 1-27 displays the 24 different AutoLayouts available in PowerPoint. More information about using AutoLayout placeholders to add graphics follows in subsequent projects. Perform the steps on the next page to add a new slide using the Bulleted List AutoLayout.

Bulleted List AutoLayout

24 different AutoLayouts

FIGURE 1-27

Steps To Add a New Slide Using the Bulleted List AutoLayout

1 Point to the New Slide button on the Common Tasks toolbar (Figure 1-28).

New Slide button

Common Tasks toolbar

current slide number

FIGURE 1-28

2 Click the New Slide button. When the New Slide dialog box displays, point to the OK button.

The New Slide dialog box displays (Figure 1-29). The Bulleted List AutoLayout is selected and the AutoLayout title, Bulleted List, displays at the bottom-right corner of the New Slide dialog box.

New Slide dialog box

Bulleted List AutoLayout

OK button

AutoLayout title

AutoLayouts

FIGURE 1-29

3 **Click the OK button.**

Slide 2 displays, keeping the attributes of the Contemporary design template (Figure 1-30). Slide 2 of 2 displays on the status bar.

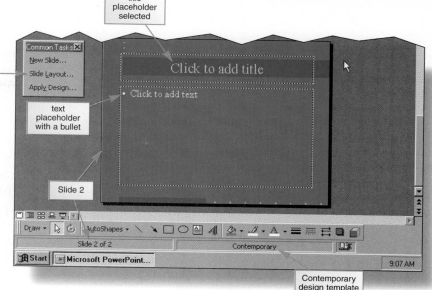

FIGURE 1-30

Because you selected the Bulleted List AutoLayout, PowerPoint displays Slide 2 with a title placeholder and a text placeholder with a bullet. You can change the layout for a slide at any time during the creation of your presentation by clicking the Slide Layout button on the Common Tasks toolbar and then double-clicking the AutoLayout of your choice.

*Other*Ways

1. Click New Slide button on Standard toolbar

2. On Insert menu click New Slide

3. Press CTRL+M

Creating a Bulleted List Slide

The bulleted list slides in Figure 1-2 on page PP 1.9, contain more than one level of bulleted text. A slide with more than one level of bulleted text is called a **multi-level bulleted list slide**. A **level** is a position within a structure, such as an outline, that indicates a magnitude of importance. PowerPoint allows for five paragraph levels. Each paragraph level has an associated bullet. The bullet font is dependent on the design template. Figure 1-31 identifies the five paragraph levels and the bullet fonts for the Contemporary design template. Beginning with the Second level, each paragraph indents to the right of the preceding level.

An indented paragraph is said to be **demoted**, or pushed down to a lower level. For example, if you demote a First level paragraph, it becomes a Second level paragraph. This lower-level paragraph is a subset of the higher-level paragraph. It usually contains information that supports the topic in the paragraph immediately above it. You demote a paragraph by clicking the **Demote button** on the Formatting toolbar.

More *About* **Bulleted Lists**

Short lines of text are easier to read than long lines.

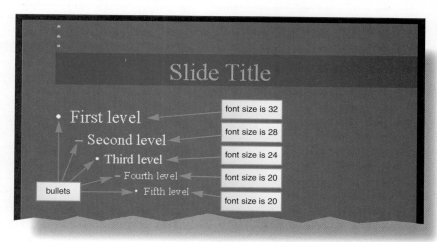

FIGURE 1-31

When you want to raise a paragraph from a lower level to a higher level, you **promote** the paragraph by clicking the **Promote button** on the Formatting toolbar.

Creating a multi-level bulleted list slide requires several steps. Initially, you enter a slide title. Next, you select a text placeholder. Then you type the text for the multi-level bulleted list, demoting and promoting paragraphs as needed. The next several sections explain how to add a multi-level bulleted list slide.

Entering a Slide Title

PowerPoint assumes every new slide has a title. Any text you type after a new slide displays becomes the title object. The title for Slide 2 is Key Hardware Requirements. Perform the following step to enter this title.

Steps To Enter a Slide Title

1 **Type** Key Hardware Requirements **in the title placeholder. Do not press the ENTER key.**

The title, Key Hardware Requirements, displays in the title object (Figure 1-32). The insertion point displays after the s in Requirements.

FIGURE 1-32

Selecting a Text Placeholder

Before you can type text into the text placeholder, you first must select it. Perform the following step to select the text placeholder on Slide 2.

Steps To Select a Text Placeholder

1 **Click the bulleted paragraph labeled, Click to add text.**

The insertion point displays immediately after the bullet on Slide 2 (Figure 1-33). The Bullets button is recessed.

FIGURE 1-33

Typing a Multi-level Bulleted List

Recall that a bulleted list is a list of paragraphs, each of which is preceded by a bullet. Also recall that a paragraph is a segment of text ended by pressing the ENTER key. The next step is to type the multi-level bulleted list, which consists of the six entries shown in Figure 1-2 on page PP 1.9. Perform the following steps to type a multi-level bulleted list.

Steps **To Type a Multi-level Bulleted List**

More *About* **Presentation Design**

Keep to one concept per slide. Highlight the subject rather than presenting a page of text. Limit your slide to five to seven words per line and five to seven lines per slide. Do not clutter; use empty space effectively.

1 **Type** Computer **and press the** **ENTER key.**

The paragraph, Computer, displays. The font size is 32. The insertion point displays after the second bullet (Figure 1-34). When you press the ENTER key, the word processing feature of PowerPoint marks the end of one paragraph and begins a new paragraph. Because you are using the Bulleted List AutoLayout, PowerPoint places a bullet in front of the new paragraph.

FIGURE 1-34

2 **Point to the Demote button on the Formatting toolbar (Figure 1-35).**

FIGURE 1-35

3 **Click the Demote button.**

The second paragraph indents under the first and becomes a Second level paragraph (Figure 1-36). Notice the bullet in front of the second paragraph changes from a dot to a dash and the font size for the demoted paragraph is now 28. The insertion point displays after the dash.

FIGURE 1-36

4 **Type** Video and sound **and press the ENTER key. Type** Memory and hard disk **and then press the ENTER key.**

Two new Second level paragraphs display with dash bullets (Figure 1-37). When you press the ENTER key, PowerPoint adds a new paragraph at the same level as the previous paragraph.

FIGURE 1-37

5 **Point to the Promote button on the Formatting toolbar (Figure 1-38).**

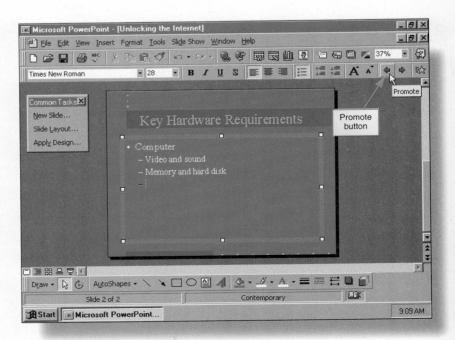

FIGURE 1-38

6 **Click the Promote button.**

The Second level paragraph becomes a First level paragraph (Figure 1-39). Notice the bullet in front of the new paragraph changes from a dash to a dot and the font size for the promoted paragraph is 32. The insertion point displays after the dot bullet.

FIGURE 1-39

Perform the following steps to complete the text for Slide 2.

TO TYPE THE REMAINING TEXT FOR SLIDE 2

1 Type Communications and press the ENTER key.

2 Click the Demote button.

3 Type Modem and telephone line and press the ENTER key.

4 Type Direct connect and do not press the ENTER key.

The insertion point displays after the t in connect (Figure 1-40).

Notice that you did not press the ENTER key after typing the last paragraph in Step 4. If you press the ENTER key, a new bullet displays after the last entry on this slide. To remove an extra bullet, press the BACKSPACE key.

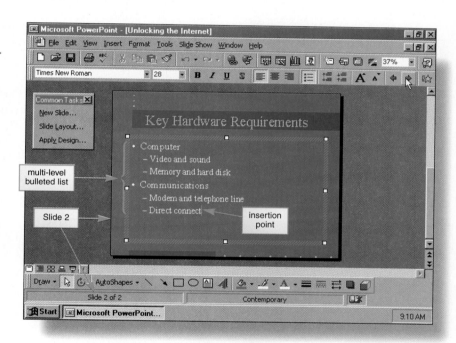

FIGURE 1-40

Adding a New Slide with the Same AutoLayout

When you add a new slide to a presentation and want to keep the same Auto-Layout used on the previous slide, PowerPoint gives you a shortcut. Instead of clicking the New Slide button and clicking an AutoLayout in the New Slide dialog box, you can press and hold down the SHIFT key and click the New Slide button. Perform the step on the next page to add a new slide (Slide 3) and keep the Bulleted List AutoLayout used on the previous slide.

More *About* **Presentation Design**

Two acronyms pertain directly to presentation design:
— KIS (Keep It Simple)
— CCC (Clutter Creates Confusion)

Steps **To Add a New Slide with the Same AutoLayout**

1 **Press and hold down the SHIFT key. Click the New Slide button on the Common Tasks toolbar. Then release the SHIFT key.**

Slide 3 displays the Bulleted List AutoLayout (Figure 1-41). Slide 3 of 3 displays on the status bar.

FIGURE 1-41

Slide 3 is added to the presentation. Perform the following steps to add text to Slide 3 and create a multi-level bulleted list.

TO CREATE SLIDE 3

1 Type Key Software Requirements in the title placeholder.

2 Click the text placeholder.

3 Type Microsoft Corporation and press the ENTER key.

4 Click the Demote button. Type Internet Explorer and press the ENTER key.

5 Click the Promote button. Type Netscape Communications Corporation and press the ENTER key.

6 Click the Demote button. Type Netscape Navigator and press the ENTER key.

7 Click the Promote button. Type SPRY, CompuServe Internet Division and press the ENTER key.

8 Click the Demote button. Type Internet In A Box but do not press the ENTER key.

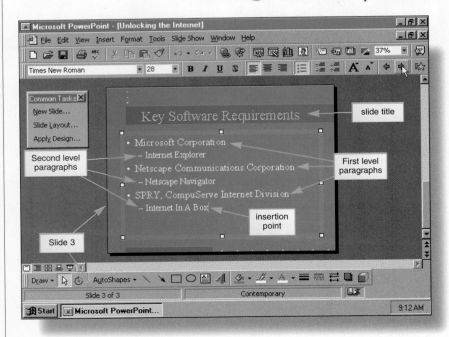

FIGURE 1-42

Slide 3 displays as shown in Figure 1-42.

Slide 4 is the last slide in this presentation. It, too, is a multi-level bulleted list. Perform the following steps to create Slide 4.

TO CREATE SLIDE 4

1. Press and hold down the SHIFT key and click the New Slide button on the Common Tasks toolbar. Release the SHIFT key.
2. Type Key Internet Providers in the title placeholder.
3. Click the text placeholder.
4. Type Online services and press the ENTER key.
5. Click the Demote button. Type The Microsoft Network and press the ENTER key.
6. Type America Online and press the ENTER key.
7. Type CompuServe and press the ENTER key.
8. Type Prodigy and press the ENTER key.
9. Click the Promote button. Type Local services but do not press the ENTER key.

The slide title and text object display as shown in Figure 1-43.

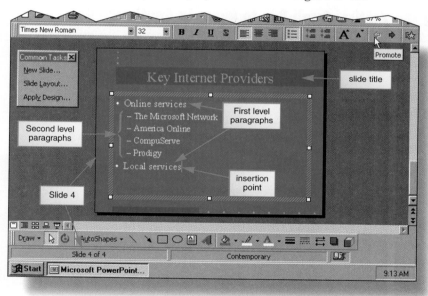

FIGURE 1-43

All slides for the Unlocking the Internet presentation are created. This presentation consists of a title slide and three multi-level bulleted list slides.

Saving a Presentation with the Same File Name

Saving frequently never can be overemphasized. When you first saved the presentation, you clicked the Save button on the Standard toolbar and the Save dialog box displayed. When you want to save the changes made to the presentation after your last save, you again click the Save button. This time, however, the Save dialog box does not display because PowerPoint updates the document called Unlocking the Internet.ppt on your floppy disk. Perform the steps on the next page to save the presentation again.

TO SAVE A PRESENTATION WITH THE SAME FILE NAME

1 Be sure your floppy disk is in drive A.

2 Click the Save button on the Standard toolbar.

PowerPoint overwrites the old Unlocking the Internet.ppt document on the floppy disk in drive A with the revised presentation document, Unlocking the Internet.ppt. Slide 4 displays in the PowerPoint window.

Moving to Another Slide in Slide View

When creating or editing a presentation in slide view, you often want to display a slide other than the current one. Dragging the vertical scroll bar box up or down moves you through your presentation. The box on the vertical scroll bar is called the **scroll box** and is shown in Figure 1-44. When you drag the scroll box, the **slide indicator** displays the number and the title of the slide you are about to display. Releasing the mouse button displays the slide.

Using the Vertical Scroll Bar to Move to Another Slide

Before continuing with Project 1, you want to display the title slide. Perform the following steps to move from Slide 4 to Slide 1 using the vertical scroll bar.

Steps **To Use the Vertical Scroll Bar to Move to Another Slide**

1 **Position the mouse pointer on the scroll box. Press and hold down the left mouse button.**

Slide: 4 of 4 Key Internet Providers, displays in the slide indicator (Figure 1-44).

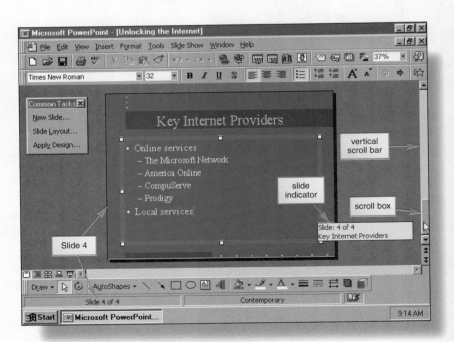

FIGURE 1-44

2 Drag the scroll box up the vertical scroll bar until Slide: 1 of 4 Unlocking the Internet displays in the slide indicator.

Slide: 1 of 4 Unlocking the Internet, displays in the slide indicator. Slide 4 still displays in the PowerPoint window (Figure 1-45).

3 Release the left mouse button.

Slide 1, titled Unlocking the Internet, displays in the PowerPoint window.

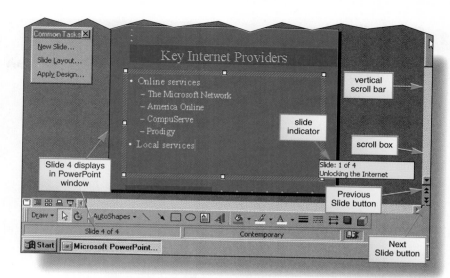

FIGURE 1-45

Viewing the Presentation Using Slide Show

The **Slide Show button,** located at the bottom left of the PowerPoint window, allows you to display your presentation electronically using a computer. The computer acts like a slide projector, displaying each slide on a full screen. The full screen slide hides the toolbars, menus, and other PowerPoint window elements.

Starting Slide Show View

Slide show view begins when you click the Slide Show button. PowerPoint then displays the current slide on the full screen without any of the PowerPoint window objects, such as the menu bar or toolbars. Perform the following steps to start slide show view.

OtherWays

1. Click Next Slide button on vertical scroll bar to move forward one slide, or click Previous Slide button on vertical scroll bar to move back one slide
2. Press PAGE DOWN to move forward one slide, or press PAGE UP to move back one slide

Steps **To Start Slide Show View**

1 Point to the Slide Show button on the View Button Bar.

The Slide View button is recessed because you are still in slide view (Figure 1-46).

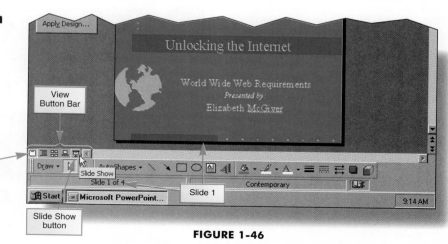

FIGURE 1-46

2 **Click the Slide Show button.**

The title slide fills the screen (Figure 1-47). The PowerPoint window is hidden.

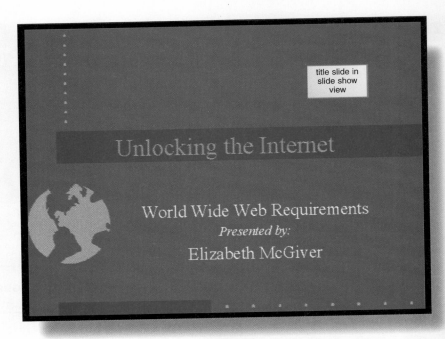

title slide in slide show view

Unlocking the Internet

World Wide Web Requirements
Presented by:
Elizabeth McGiver

FIGURE 1-47

Advancing through a Slide Show Manually

After you begin slide show view, you can move forward or backward through your slides. PowerPoint allows you to advance through your slides manually or automatically. Automatic advancing is discussed in a later project. Perform the step below to manually move through your slides.

Steps **To Manually Move Through Slides in a Slide Show**

1 **Click each slide until the last slide of the presentation, Slide 4, Key Internet Providers, displays.**

Each slide in your presentation displays on the screen, one slide at a time. Each time you click the mouse button, the next slide displays (Figure 1-48).

Key Internet Providers

- Online services
  - The Microsoft Network
  - America Online
  - CompuServe
  - Prodigy
- Local services

Slide 4 in slide show view

FIGURE 1-48

Displaying the Popup Menu in Slide Show View

Slide show view has a shortcut menu, called **Popup Menu**, that displays when you right-click a slide in slide show view. The Popup Menu contains commands to assist you during a slide show. For example, clicking the **Next command** moves you to the next slide. Clicking the **Previous command** moves you to the previous slide. You can jump to any slide in your presentation by clicking the **Go command** and then clicking Slide Navigator. The **Slide Navigator dialog box** contains a list of the slides in your presentation. Jump to the requested slide by double-clicking the name of that slide.

Additional Popup Menu commands allow you to create a list of action items during a slide show, change the mouse pointer from an arrow to a pen, blacken the screen, and end the slide show. Popup Menu commands are discussed in subsequent projects. Perform the following step to display the Slide Show View Popup Menu.

Steps **To Display the Slide Show View Popup Menu**

1 **With Slide 4 displaying in slide show view, right-click the slide.**

The Popup Menu displays on Slide 4 (Figure 1-49). Your screen may look different because the Popup Menu displays near the location of the mouse pointer at the time you right-click.

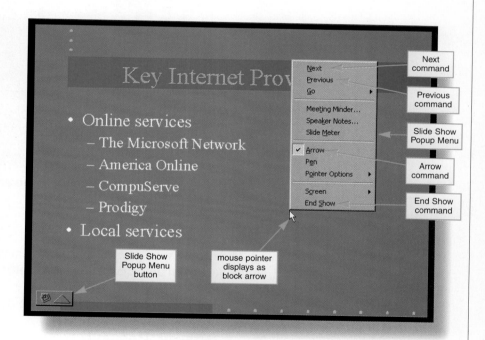

FIGURE 1-49

Some presenters prefer to right-click to move backward through a slide show. Because PowerPoint allows you to display the Slide Show View Popup Menu by clicking the Slide Show View Popup Menu button, you can turn off the option setting that displays the Popup menu when you right-click. To turn off the Popup menu on right mouse click option on the Tools menu, click Options, click the View tab to display the View sheet, click Popup menu on right mouse click to remove the check, and then click the OK button. After turning off the Popup menu on right mouse click option setting, you can right-click to move backward, one slide at a time, in slide show view.

Using the Popup Menu to End a Slide Show

The **End Show command** on the Popup Menu exits slide show view and returns to the view you were in when you clicked the Slide Show button. Perform the following step to end slide show view.

Steps **To Use the Popup Menu to End a Slide Show**

1 **Click End Show on the Popup Menu.**

PowerPoint exits slide show view and displays the slide last displayed in slide show view, which in this instance, is Slide 4 (Figure 1-50).

FIGURE 1-50

Slide show view is excellent for rehearsing a presentation. You can start slide show view from any view: slide view, outline view, slide sorter view, or notes page view.

Quitting PowerPoint

The Unlocking the Internet presentation now is complete. When you quit PowerPoint, PowerPoint prompts you to save any changes made to the presentation since the last save, closes all PowerPoint windows, and then quits PowerPoint. Closing PowerPoint returns control to the desktop. Perform the following steps to quit PowerPoint.

More *About*
Quitting
PowerPoint

If you notice your computer sys-tem is performing more slowly than normal, close all unneces-sary applications. This releases memory held by those open applications and should improve your system's performance.

Steps **To Quit PowerPoint**

① **Point to the Close button on the title bar (Figure 1-51).**

② **Click the Close button.**

PowerPoint closes and the Windows 95 desktop displays. If you made changes to the presentation since your last save, a Microsoft PowerPoint dialog box displays the question, Do you wish to save the changes you made to Unlocking the Internet?. Click the Yes button to save the changes to the presentation before closing PowerPoint. Click the No button to quit PowerPoint without saving the changes. Click the Cancel button to terminate the Close command and return to the presentation.

FIGURE 1-51

Opening a Presentation

Earlier, you saved the presentation on a floppy disk using the file name, Unlocking the Internet.ppt. Once you create and save a presentation, you may need to retrieve it from the floppy disk to make changes. For example, you may want to replace the design template or modify some text. Recall that a presentation is a PowerPoint document. Use the **Open Office Document command** to open an existing presentation.

Opening an Existing Presentation

Ensure that the floppy disk used to save Unlocking the Internet.ppt is in drive A. Then perform the steps on the next page to open the Unlocking the Internet presentation using the Open Office Document command on the Start menu.

▷ *Other***Ways**

1. On title bar double-click PowerPoint control icon; or on title bar, click PowerPoint control icon, click Close
2. On File menu click Exit
3. Press CTRL+Q or press ALT+F4

◆ **More** *About*
Opening Presentations

PowerPoint allows you to open more than one presentation at a time. To display another open presentation, click Window on the menu bar and then click the desired presentation.

Steps To Open an Existing Presentation

1 Click the Start button on the taskbar and point to Open Office Document.

The Windows 95 Start menu displays (Figure 1-52). Open Office Document is highlighted.

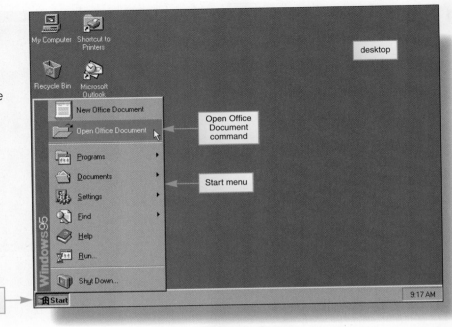

FIGURE 1-52

2 Click Open Office Document. When the Open Office Document dialog box displays, click the Look in box arrow and then click 3½ Floppy (A:) (see Figures 1-23 and 1-24 on page PP 1.24 to review this process).

The Open Office Document dialog box displays (Figure 1-53). A list of existing files on drive A displays because your floppy disk is in drive A. Notice that Office Files displays in the Files of type list box. The file, Unlocking the Internet, is highlighted. Your list of existing files may be different depending on the files saved on your floppy disk.

FIGURE 1-53

3 **Double-click Unlocking the Internet.**

PowerPoint starts and opens Unlocking the Internet.ppt from drive A into main memory and displays the first slide on the screen (Figure 1-54). The presentation displays in slide view because PowerPoint opens presentations in the same view in which they were saved.

presentation name displays in title bar

Slide 1 displays in slide view

name of open application displays in taskbar

FIGURE 1-54

When an application is open, its name displays on a button on the taskbar. The **active application** is the one displaying in the foreground of the desktop. That application's corresponding button on the taskbar displays recessed.

When more than one application is open, you can switch between applications by clicking the button labeled with the name of the application to which you want to switch.

Other Ways

1. Click Open a Document button on Microsoft Office Shortcut Bar, click folder or drive name in Look in list, double-click document name

2. On Start menu click Documents, click document name

Checking a Presentation for Visual Clarity, Consistency, and Style

After you create a presentation, you should proofread it for errors. Typical errors include spelling errors, punctuation errors, and design errors. PowerPoint has a tool, called **Style Checker**, that helps you identify errors in your presentation. When you start Style Checker, the Style Checker dialog box displays three check boxes: Spelling, Visual clarity, and Case and end punctuation. A check mark in a check box instructs Style Checker to look for that particular type of inconsistency. For example, a check mark in the Spelling check box causes Style Checker to check the presentation for spelling errors. Table 1-3 identifies the purpose of each check box in the Style Checker dialog box.

Table 1-3

CHECK BOX	PURPOSE
Spelling	Checks the presentation for spelling errors.
Visual clarity	Checks the presentation for appropriate font usage and for legibility of slide titles and body text.
Case and end punctuation	Checks the presentation for consistency of capitalization and end punctuation in slide titles and body text.

PowerPoint checks your presentation for spelling errors using a standard dictionary contained in the Microsoft Office group. This dictionary is shared with the other Microsoft Office applications such as Word and Excel. A **custom dictionary** is available if you want to add special words such as proper names, cities, and acronyms. When checking a presentation for spelling errors, PowerPoint opens the standard dictionary and the custom dictionary file, if one exists. When a word displays in the Spelling dialog box, you perform one of the actions listed in Table 1-4.

Table 1-4

ACTION	DESCRIPTION
Manually correct the word	Retype the word with the proper spelling in the Change to box and then click Change. PowerPoint continues checking the rest of the presentation.
Ignore the word	Click Ignore when the word is spelled correctly but not found in the dictionaries. PowerPoint continues checking the rest of the presentation.
Ignore all occurrences of the word	Click Ignore All when the word is spelled correctly but not found in the dictionaries. PowerPoint ignores all occurrences of the word and continues checking the rest of the presentation.
Select a different spelling	Click the proper spelling of the word from the list in the Suggestions box. Click Change. PowerPoint corrects the word and continues checking the rest of the presentation.
Change all occurrences of the misspelling to a different spelling	Click the proper spelling of the word from the list in the Suggestions box. Click Change All. PowerPoint changes all occurrences of the misspelled word and continues checking the rest of the presentation.
Add a word to the custom dictionary	Click Add. PowerPoint opens the custom dictionary, adds the word, and continues checking the rest of the presentation.
View alternative spellings	Click Suggest. PowerPoint lists suggested spellings. Click the correct word from the Suggestions box or type the proper spelling. Then click Change. PowerPoint continues checking the rest of the presentation.
Add spelling error to AutoCorrect list	Click AutoCorrect. PowerPoint adds the spelling error and its correction to the AutoCorrect list. Any future misspelling of the word is corrected automatically as you type.

The standard dictionary contains commonly used English words. It does not, however, contain proper names, abbreviations, technical terms, poetic contractions, or antiquated terms. PowerPoint treats words not found in the dictionaries as misspellings.

Starting Style Checker

Start Style Checker by clicking the Style Checker command on the Tools menu. Perform the following steps to start Style Checker.

More *About*
Spell Checking

To check a presentation for spelling errors without also checking the presentation for style errors, click the Spelling button on the Standard toolbar.

Steps **To Start Style Checker**

1 **Click Tools on the menu bar, and then point to Style Checker (Figure 1-55).**

FIGURE 1-55

2 **Click Style Checker. When the Style Checker dialog box displays, click Case and end punctuation, and then point to the Start button.**

The Style Checker dialog box displays (Figure 1-56). Check marks display in the check box in front of Spelling and in front of Visual clarity. The check box in front of Case and end punctuation is blank to prevent Style Checker from automatically changing the capitalization of the company names in this presentation.

FIGURE 1-56

3 **Click the Start button.**

PowerPoint launches the spelling feature and displays the Spelling dialog box (Figure 1-57). McGiver displays in the Not in dictionary box. Depending on your custom dictionary, McGiver may not be recognized as a misspelled word.

FIGURE 1-57

4 Click the Ignore button.

PowerPoint ignores the word McGiver and continues searching for additional misspelled words. PowerPoint may stop on additional words depending on your typing accuracy. When PowerPoint has checked all slides for misspellings, it checks for style errors and displays the Microsoft PowerPoint dialog box (Figure 1-58).

5 Click the OK button.

PowerPoint closes Style Checker and returns to the current slide, Slide 1, or to the slide where a misspelled word occurred.

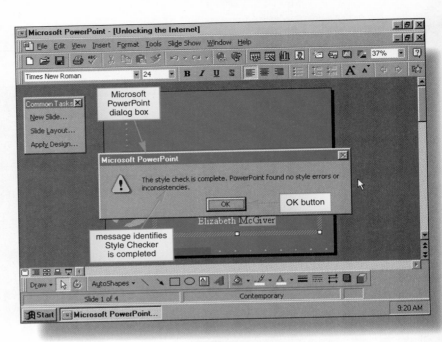

FIGURE 1-58

Table 1-5

OPTION	SETTING
CASE	
Slide title style	Title Case
Body text style	Sentence case.
END PUNCTUATION	
Slide title periods	Remove
Body text periods	Remove
VISUAL CLARITY	
Number of fonts should not exceed	3
Title text size should be at least	36
Body text size should be at least	24
Number of bullets should not exceed	6
Number of lines per title should not exceed	2
Number of lines per bullet should not exceed	2
Check for title and placeholder text off slide	Checked on

If Style Checker identifies an error, it displays a message indicating the slide number on which the error occurred. If you have punctuation errors, you can click one of the buttons to ignore or change them. If you want to stop Style Checker and return to the current slide, click the Cancel button.

If Style Checker identifies visual clarity inconsistencies, it displays them in the Style Checker Summary dialog box. Write the slide number and the message on a sheet of paper. Then display the slide and correct the inconsistencies.

The Style Checker dialog box contains an **Options button** (Figure 1-56 on the previous page), which when clicked, displays the Style Checker Options dialog box. The **Style Checker Options dialog box** has two tabbed sheets: Case and End Punctuation, and Visual Clarity. Each tabbed sheet has several options that can be changed to suit your design specifications. Table 1-5 identifies each option available in Style Checker and each default setting.

Correcting Errors

After creating a presentation and running Style Checker, you may find that you must make changes. Changes may be required because a slide contains an error, the scope of the presentation shifts, or Style Checker found a style inconsistency. This section explains the types of errors that commonly occur when creating a presentation.

Types of Corrections Made to Presentations

There usually are three types of corrections to text in a presentation: additions, deletions, and replacements.

▶ **Additions** — are necessary when you omit text from a slide and need to add it later. You may need to insert text in the form of a sentence, word, or single character. For example, you may want to add the rest of the presenter's first name on your title slide.

▶ **Deletions** — are required when text on a slide is incorrect or is no longer relevant to the presentation. For example, Style Checker identified too many bullets on Slide 3. Therefore, you may want to remove one of the bulleted paragraphs.

▶ **Replacements** — are needed when you want to revise the text in your presentation. For example, you may want to substitute the word, their, for the word, there.

Editing text in PowerPoint is basically the same as editing text in a word processing package. The following sections illustrate the most common changes made to text in a presentation.

Deleting Text

There are three methods for deleting text. One is to use the BACKSPACE key to remove text just typed. The second is to position the insertion point to the left of the text you wish to delete and then press the DELETE key. The third method is to drag through the text you wish to delete and press the DELETE key. (Use the third method when deleting large sections of text.)

Replacing Text into an Existing Slide

When you need to correct a word or phrase, you can replace the text by selecting the text to be replaced and then typing the new text. As soon as you press any key on the keyboard, the highlighted text is deleted and the new text displays.

PowerPoint inserts text to the left of the insertion point. The text to the right of the insertion point moves to the right (and shifts downward if necessary) to accommodate the added text.

Changing Line Spacing

The bulleted lists on Slides 2, 3, and 4 look crowded; yet, there is ample blank space that could be used to separate the paragraphs. You can adjust the spacing on each slide, but when several slides need to be changed, you should change the slide master. Each PowerPoint component (slides, title slides, audience handouts, and speaker's notes) has a **master**, which controls its appearance. Slides have two masters: title master and slide master. The **title master** controls the appearance of the title slide. The **slide master** controls the appearance of the other slides in your presentation.

Each design template has a specially designed slide master; so if you select a design template, but want to change one of its components, you can override that component by changing the slide master. Any change to the slide master results in changing every slide in the presentation, except the title slide. For example, if you change the line spacing to .5 inches before each paragraph on the slide master, each slide (except the title slide) changes line spacing after each paragraph to .5 inches. The slide master components more frequently changed are listed in Table 1-6.

Table 1-6

COMPONENT	DESCRIPTION
Font	Defines the appearance and shape of letters, numbers, and special characters.
Font size	Specifies the size of the characters on the screen. Character size is gauged by a measurement system called points. A single point is about 1/72 of an inch in height. Thus, a character with a point size of eighteen is about 18/72 of an inch in height.
Text font style	Text font styles include plain, italic, bold, shadowed, and underlined. Text may have more than one font style at a time.
Text position	Position of text in a paragraph is left-aligned, right-aligned, centered, or justified. Justified text is proportionally spaced across the object.
Color scheme	A coordinated set of eight colors designed to complement each other. Color schemes consist of background color, line and text color, shadow color, title text color, object fill color, and three different accent colors.
Background items	Any object other than the title object or text object. Typical items include borders and graphics — such as a company logo, page number, date, and time.
Slide number	Inserts the special symbol used to print the slide number.
Date	Inserts the special symbol used to print the date the presentation was printed.
Time	Inserts the special symbol used to print the time the presentation was printed.

Additionally, each view has its own master. You can access the master by holding down the SHIFT key while clicking the appropriate view button. For example, holding down the SHIFT key and clicking the Slide View button displays the slide master. To exit a master, click the view button to which you wish to return. To return to slide view, for example, click the Slide View button.

Displaying the Slide Master

Before you can change line spacing on the slide master, you first must display it. Perform the following steps to display the slide master.

 Steps **To Display the Slide Master**

① **Drag the scroll box to display Slide 2. Press and hold down the SHIFT key and then point to the Slide View button.**

When you hold down the SHIFT *key, the ScreenTip displays Slide Master (Figure 1-59).*

Slide 2

Slide View button is recessed

Slide Master

ScreenTip

Slide 2 of 4

Contempora

FIGURE 1-59

2 **While holding down the SHIFT key, click the Slide Master button. Then release the SHIFT key.**

The slide master displays (Figure 1-60). The Master toolbar displays. The Common Tasks toolbar changes to display a Master Layout button, which replaces the Slide Layout button in slide master.

FIGURE 1-60

OtherWays

1. On View menu click Master, click Slide Master

Changing Line Spacing on the Slide Master

Change line spacing by clicking the Line Spacing command on the Format menu. When you click the **Line Spacing command**, the Line Spacing dialog box displays. The Line Spacing dialog box contains three boxes, Line spacing, Before paragraph, and After paragraph, which allow you to adjust line spacing within a paragraph, before a paragraph, and after a paragraph, respectively.

In this project, you change the number in the amount of space box to increase the amount of space that displays before every paragraph, except the first paragraph, on every slide. For example, increasing the amount of space box to 0.75 lines increases the amount of space that displays before each paragraph. The first paragraph on every slide, however, does not change because of its position in the text placeholder. Perform the following steps to change the line spacing.

Steps ## To Change Line Spacing on the Slide Master

1 **Click the bulleted paragraph labeled, Click to edit Master text styles.**

The insertion point displays at the point you clicked (Figure 1-61). The text object area is selected.

FIGURE 1-61

2 Click Format on the menu bar and then point to Line Spacing (Figure 1-62).

FIGURE 1-62

3 Click Line Spacing.

PowerPoint displays the Line Spacing dialog box (Figure 1-63). The default Before paragraph line spacing is set at 0.2 Lines.

FIGURE 1-63

4 Double-click the amount of space list box in the Before paragraph box. Then type .75 in the box.

The amount of space list box displays 0.75 (Figure 1-64). The Preview button is available after a change is made in the Line Spacing dialog box.

FIGURE 1-64

5 **Click the OK button.**

The slide master text placeholder displays the new line spacing (Figure 1-65). Depending on the video drivers installed, the spacing on your screen may appear slightly different than this figure.

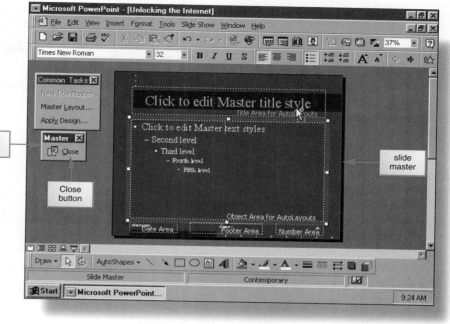

FIGURE 1-65

6 **Click the Close button on the Master toolbar to return to slide view.**

Slide 2 displays with the Before paragraph line spacing set to 0.75 lines (Figure 1-66).

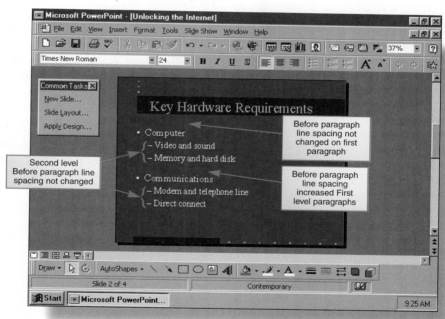

FIGURE 1-66

To display line spacing changes without making them permanent, click the Preview button in the Line Spacing dialog box. If you want to close the Line Spacing dialog box without applying the changes, click the Cancel button.

More *About* **Masters**

To modify the attributes of the slide master or title master, display the master, and then use the buttons on the Formatting toolbar. To override a master attribute, change the attribute directly on a slide. For example, to italicize text not italicized on a master, select the text object and click the Italic button.

Before paragraph line spacing is controlled by establishing the number of units before a paragraph. Units are either lines or points; lines are the default unit. Points may be selected by clicking the down arrow next to the Before paragraph box (Figure 1-64 on page PP 1.48). Recall from page PP 1.21 that a single point is about 1/72 of an inch in height.

The Line spacing box and the After paragraph box each contain an amount of space list box and a unit of measure list box. To change the amount of space displaying between paragraphs, click the amount of space box up arrow or down arrow in the Line spacing box. To change the amount of space displaying after a paragraph, click the amount of space box up arrow or down arrow in the After paragraph box. To change the unit of measure from Lines to Points in either the Line spacing box or the After paragraph box, click the down arrow next to the unit of measure list box and then click Points.

The placeholder at the top of the slide master (Figure 1-65 on the previous page) is used to edit the Master title style. The large placeholder under the Master title placeholder is used to edit the Master text styles. Here you make changes to the various bullet levels. Changes can be made to line spacing, bullet font, text and line color, alignment, and text shadow. It is also the object area for AutoLayouts.

Displaying a Presentation in Black and White

This project explains how to print a presentation for the purpose of making transparencies. The **Black and White View button** allows you to display the presentation in black and white before you print. Table 1-7 identifies how PowerPoint objects display in black and white.

Table 1-7	
OBJECT	APPEARANCE IN BLACK AND WHITE VIEW
Text	Black
Text shadows	Hidden
Embossing	Hidden
Fills	Grayscale
Frame	Black
Pattern fills	Grayscale
Lines	Black
Object shadows	Grayscale
Bitmaps	Grayscale
Slide backgrounds	White

Perform the following steps to display the presentation in black and white.

Steps **To Display a Presentation in Black and White**

1 **Point to the Black and White View button on the Standard toolbar (Figure 1-67).**

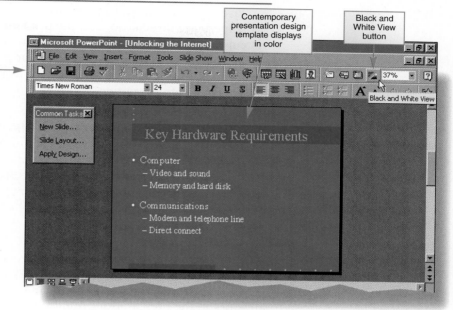

FIGURE 1-67

2 **Click the Black and White View button.**

The presentation displays in black and white (Figure 1-68). The Black and White View button is recessed. The Color box displays a miniature of the current slide in color.

FIGURE 1-68

*Other***Ways**

1. On View menu click Black and White

To return to the color view of the presentation, click the Black and White View button again.

Printing a Presentation

After you create a presentation, you often want to print it. A printed version of the presentation is called a **hard copy**, or **printout**. The first printing of the presentation is called a **rough draft**. The rough draft allows you to proofread the presentation to check for errors and readability. After correcting errors, you print the final copy of your presentation.

Saving Before Printing

Prior to printing your presentation, you should save your work in the event you experience difficulties with the printer. You occasionally may encounter system problems that can be resolved only by restarting the computer. In such an instance, you will need to reopen your presentation. As a precaution, always save your presentation before you print. Perform the following steps to save the presentation before printing.

TO SAVE A PRESENTATION BEFORE PRINTING

1 Verify that your floppy disk is in drive A.
2 Click the Save button on the Standard toolbar.

All changes made after your last save now are saved on a floppy disk.

Printing the Presentation

After saving the presentation, you are ready to print. Because you are in slide view, clicking the **Print button** on the Standard toolbar causes PowerPoint to print all slides in the presentation. Additionally, because you currently are viewing the presentation in black and white, the slides print in black and white, even if you have a color printer. Perform the following steps to print the presentation slides.

Steps To Print a Presentation

1 **Ready the printer according to the printer instructions. Then, click the Print button on the Standard toolbar.**

The mouse pointer momentarily changes to an hourglass. An animated printer icon displays on the status bar identifying which slide is being prepared (Figure 1-69). The printer icon, on the status bar, indicates there is a print job processing. After several moments, the presentation begins printing on the printer. When the presentation is finished printing, the printer icon on the status bar no longer displays.

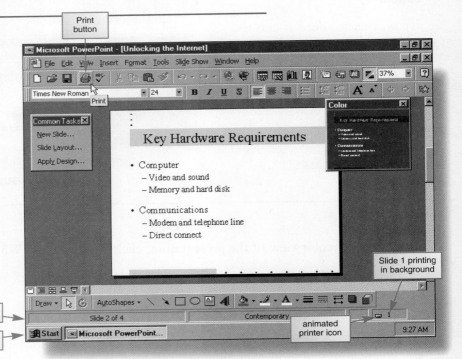

FIGURE 1-69

2 When the printer stops, retrieve the printouts of the slides.

The presentation, Unlocking the Internet, prints on four pages (Figure 1-70).

Key Internet Providers

- Online services
  - The Microsoft Network
  - ...ine
  - ...s

(d)

Key Software Requirements

- Microsoft Corporation
  - Internet Explorer

- Netscape Communications Corporation
  - Netscape Navigator

- SPRY, CompuServe Internet
  - Internet In A Box

(c)

Key Hardware Requirements

- Computer
  - Video and sound
  - ... hard disk
  - ...ons
  - ...telephone line
  - ...ct

(b)

Unlocking the Internet

World Wide Web Requirements
Presented by:
Elizabeth McGiver

(a)

FIGURE 1-70

Other Ways

1. On File menu click Print
2. Press CTRL+P or press CTRL+SHIFT+F12

More *About*
Online Help

Prior versions of PowerPoint used to come with a thick manual. Most beginners had difficulty determining where to find the information they wanted. The extensive online Help shipped with PowerPoint replaces the manual and simplifies the process of finding helpful information.

Double-clicking the animated printer icon on the status bar cancels the printing process.

Making a Transparency

This project requires you to make overhead transparencies. You make transparencies using one of several devices. One device is a printer attached to your computer, such as an ink-jet printer or a laser printer. Transparencies produced on a printer may be in black and white or color, depending on the printer. Another device is a photocopier. A third device is a thermal copier. A thermal copier transfers a carbonaceous substance, like toner from a photocopier, from a paper master to an acetate film. Because each of the three devices requires a special transparency film, check the user's manual for the film requirement of your specific device, or ask your instructor.

Quitting PowerPoint

Project 1 is complete. The final task is to close the presentation and PowerPoint. Perform the following steps to quit PowerPoint.

TO QUIT POWERPOINT

1. Click the Close button on the title bar.
2. If prompted to save the presentation before closing PowerPoint, click the Yes button in the Microsoft PowerPoint dialog box.

Table 1-8		
HELP CATEGORY	*SUMMARY*	*HOW TO START*
Office Assistant	Answers your questions, offers tips, and provides help for a variety of PowerPoint features.	Click the Office Assistant button on the Standard toolbar.
Contents sheet	Groups Help topics by general categories. Use when you know, in general, what you want.	Click the Help menu, click Contents and Index, then click the Contents tab.
Index sheet	Alphabetical list of Help topics. Similar to an index in a book. Use when you know exactly what you want. For example, "adding footers."	Click the Help menu, click Contents and Index, then click the Index tab.
Find sheet	Searches the index for all phrases that include the term you specify. For example, "bullets."	Click the Help menu, click Contents and Index, then click the Find tab.
Question mark button	Provides an explanation of objects on the screen.	In a dialog box, click the Question mark button and then click a dialog box object. Click What's This? on the Help menu, then click an item on the screen.

PowerPoint Online Help

You can get assistance anytime while you are working in PowerPoint using online Help. When used effectively, online Help can increase your productivity and reduce the amount of time you spend learning how to use PowerPoint. Table 1-8 summarizes the five categories of online Help.

The following sections show examples of each of the online Help described in Table 1-8. For more information on using online Help, see pages WD 1.54 through WD 1.59 in Project 1 of Microsoft Word 97.

Project Summary

Project 1 introduced you to starting PowerPoint and creating a multi-level bulleted list presentation. You learned about PowerPoint design templates, objects, and attributes. This project illustrated how to create an interesting introduction to a presentation by changing the text font style to italic and decreasing font size on the title slide. Completing these tasks, you saved your presentation. Then, you created three multi-level bulleted list slides to explain the necessary requirements for connecting to the World Wide Web. Next, you learned how to view the presentation in slide show view. After which, you learned how to quit PowerPoint and how to open an existing presentation. Using Style Checker, you learned how to look for spelling errors and identify inconsistencies in design specifications. Using the slide master, you quickly adjusted the Before paragraph line spacing on every slide to make better use of white space. You learned how to display the presentation in black and white. Then, you learned how to print hard copies of your slides in order to make overhead transparencies. Finally, you learned how to use PowerPoint online Help.

What You Should Know

Having completed this project, you should be able to perform the following tasks:

▶ Add a New Slide Using the Bulleted List AutoLayout *(PP 1.26)*

▶ Add a New Slide with the Same AutoLayout *(PP 1.32)*

▶ Change Line Spacing on the Slide Master *(PP 1.47)*

▶ Change the Text Font Style to Italic *(PP 1.22)*

▶ Create Slide 3 *(PP 1.32)*

▶ Create Slide 4 *(PP 1.33)*

▶ Decrease Font Size *(PP 1.21)*

▶ Display a Presentation in Black and White *(PP 1.51)*

▶ Display the Slide Master *(PP 1.46)*

▶ Display the Slide Show View Popup Menu *(PP 1.37)*

▶ Enter a Slide Title *(PP 1.28)*

▶ Enter the Presentation Subtitle *(PP 1.19)*

▶ Enter the Presentation Title *(PP 1.18)*

▶ Manually Move Through Slides in a Slide Show *(PP 1.36)*

▶ Open an Existing Presentation *(PP 1.40)*

▶ Print a Presentation *(PP 1.52)*

▶ Quit PowerPoint *(PP 1.39, 1.54)*

▶ Save a Presentation Before Printing *(PP 1.52)*

▶ Save a Presentation to a Floppy Disk *(PP 1.23)*

▶ Save a Presentation with the Same File Name *(PP 1.34)*

▶ Select a Text Placeholder *(PP 1.28)*

▶ Start a New Presentation *(PP 1.10)*

▶ Start Slide Show View *(PP 1.35)*

▶ Start Style Checker *(PP 1.43)*

▶ Type a Multi-level Bulleted List *(PP 1.29)*

▶ Type the Remaining Text for Slide 2 *(PP 1.31)*

▶ Use the Popup Menu to End a Slide Show *(PP 1.38)*

▶ Use the Vertical Scroll Bar to Move to Another Slide *(PP 1.34)*

Test Your Knowledge

1 True/False

Instructions: Circle T if the statement is true or F if the statement is false.

T F   1. PowerPoint presentations can be run on a World Wide Web page.
T F   2. A wizard is a tutorial approach for quickly and efficiently creating a presentation.
T F   3. A PowerPoint document is called a slide show.
T F   4. A slide is the basic unit of a PowerPoint presentation.
T F   5. The name of the current presentation displays on the status bar.
T F   6. Toolbars consist of buttons that access commonly used PowerPoint tools.
T F   7. In PowerPoint, the Formatting toolbar contains tools for changing attributes of drawing objects.
T F   8. Press and hold down the SHIFT key and click the New Slide button to add a new slide to a presentation with the same AutoLayout as the current slide.
T F   9. PowerPoint assumes that every slide has a title.
T F   10. The slide indicator shows only the slide number.

2 Multiple Choice

Instructions: Circle the correct response.

1. When the mouse pointer is pointing to a button, it has the shape of a(n) _____.
   a. hand   b. hourglass   c. I-beam   d. left-pointing block arrow
2. _____ displays your slides as an electronic presentation on the full screen of your computer's monitor, looking much like a slide projector display.
   a. Slide view   b. Outline view   c. Slide sorter view   d. Slide show view
3. _____ are the properties or characteristics of an object.
   a. Wizards   b. Color schemes   c. Attributes   d. Design templates
4. Before you italicize a paragraph, you first must _____.
   a. underscore the paragraph to be formatted
   b. position the mouse pointer beside the first character in the paragraph to be formatted
   c. highlight the paragraph to be formatted
   d. highlight the first word in the paragraph to be formatted
5. PowerPoint automatically appends the extension _____ to a file name when you save a presentation.
   a. .DOC   b. .PPT   c. .TXT   d. .XLS
6. When you exit PowerPoint, _____.
   a. the presentation remains in memory
   b. the presentation is erased from the floppy disk
   c. control is returned to the desktop
   d. the presentation is saved automatically to a floppy disk

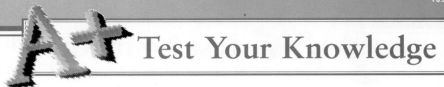

7. If you add objects to the slide master, they display on _____.
   a. every slide
   b. every slide except the title slide
   c. the slide master
   d. both b and c

8. Press the _____ key to remove characters to the right of the insertion point.
   a. BACKSPACE
   b. DELETE
   c. INSERT
   d. both a and b

9. To display online Help information that suggests more efficient ways to complete a task, use the _____.
   a. Office Assistant
   b. Contents sheet
   c. Find sheet
   d. Index sheet

10. To close a presentation and quit PowerPoint, click the Close button on the _____.
    a. menu bar
    b. title bar
    c. Standard toolbar
    d. Common Tasks toolbar

3 Understanding the PowerPoint Window

Instructions: In Figure 1-71, arrows point to the major components of the PowerPoint window. Identify the various parts of the window in the spaces provided.

FIGURE 1-71

Test Your Knowledge

4 Understanding the PowerPoint Toolbars

Instructions: In Figure 1-72, arrows point to several buttons on the Standard and Formatting toolbars. Identify the buttons in the spaces provided.

FIGURE 1-72

Use Help

1 Reviewing Project Activities

Instructions: Perform the following tasks using a computer.

1. Start PowerPoint.
2. If the Office Assistant is on your screen, click it to display its balloon. If the Office Assistant is not on your screen, then click the Office Assistant button on the Standard toolbar.
3. Click Options in the Office Assistant balloon. Click the Gallery tab. Click the Next button to view each of the Office Assistants. Click the Back button to go to the Clippit Assistant and then click the Options tab. Review the different options for the Office Assistant. Close the Office Assistant dialog box.
4. Click the Office Assistant and type slide master in the What would you like to do? text box. Click the Search button.

Use Help

5. Click the link, Make a slide that differs from the slide master.
6. Read the information. Right-click the Help window to display a shortcut menu. Click Print Topic to print the information. Click the underlined green words, color scheme. Print the definition that displays by right-clicking the ScreenTip and then clicking Print Topic. Submit the printouts to your instructor.
7. Click the Close button in the Help window.
8. Click Help on the menu bar. Click Contents and Index. Click the Contents tab. Double-click Working with Slides. Double-click Make a new slide. Read and print the information. Click the Help Topics button to return to the Contents sheet. Double-click Move, copy, or duplicate slides. Read and print the information. Click, read, and print the Help information for each of the three jumps at the bottom of the Help window. Submit the printouts to your instructor.

2 Expanding on the Basics

Instructions: Use PowerPoint online Help to better understand the topics listed below. Answer the questions on your own paper or submit the printed Help topic to your instructor.

1. Click the Office Assistant or the Office Assistant button on the Standard toolbar to display the Office Assistant balloon. Search for the topic, spelling. Click the link, Check spelling. When the Help window displays, answer the following questions by clicking the links. Close the Help window.
   a. How do you check spelling as you type? b. How do you check spelling at anytime? c. How do you temporarily hide spelling errors?
2. Click Contents and Index on the Help menu. Click the Index tab. Type line spacing in the top text box labeled 1. Use the Index sheet to display and print the answers to the following questions.
   a. How do you change the After paragraph line spacing? b. How do you change the amount of space within a paragraph?
3. Use the Find sheet in the Help Topics: Microsoft PowerPoint dialog box to display and then print information about keyboard shortcuts. Answer the following questions.
   a. Which key, or combination of keys, do you press to copy selected text? b. Which key, or combination of keys, do you press to move to the end of a line of text? c. Which key, or combination of keys, do you press to display a shortcut menu relevant to the selected object? d. Which key, or combination of keys, do you press to update the files listed in the Open or Save As dialog box? e. Which keys do you press to advance to the next slide during the running of a slide show?
4. Use the Find sheet in the Help Topics: Microsoft PowerPoint dialog box to display and then print the information about slide masters.
   a. How do you make a slide that is different from the slide master? b. What happens to a slide when its master changes? c. How do you make a slide with a different title or text format than the master?

Apply Your Knowledge

1 Formatting a Multi-level Slide

Instructions: Start PowerPoint. Open the presentation Apply-1 from the PowerPoint folder on the Data Disk that accompanies this book. This slide lists features of a proposed insurance option. Perform the following tasks to change the slide so it looks like the one in Figure 1-73.

1. Press and hold down the SHIFT key, and then click the Slide View button to display the slide master. Click the paragraph, Click to edit Master text styles. Click Format on the menu bar and then click Line Spacing. Increase the Before paragraph line spacing to 0.6 lines. Click the OK button. Then click the Close button on the Master toolbar to return to slide view.
2. Select the title text. Click the Bold button on the Formatting toolbar.
3. Select the No paperwork paragraph. Click the Underline button on the Formatting toolbar.
4. Click the paragraph, Annual check-up, and then click the Demote button on the Formatting toolbar.
5. Click the paragraph, No out-of-pocket expense, and then click the Demote button on the Formatting toolbar.
6. Click File on the menu bar and then click Save As. Type Preferred Provider Option in the File name list box. If drive A is not already displaying in the Save in list box, click the Save in box arrow, and click drive A. Then, click the Save button.
7. Click the Black and White View button on the Standard toolbar to display the presentation in black and white.
8. Click the Print button on the Standard toolbar.
9. Click the Close button on the menu bar to exit PowerPoint.
10. Submit the printout to your instructor.

FIGURE 1-73

In the Lab

1 Designing and Creating a Presentation

Problem: You are the Director for the Career Development Center at Hammond College. You have been asked to speak as a guest lecturer in an undergraduate communications class. The course instructor suggests you discuss strategies for finding the right job. To prepare for the class, you create the presentation shown in Figure 1-74.

Instructions: Perform the following tasks.

1. Create a new presentation using the high voltage design template.
2. Using the typewritten notes illustrated in Figure 1-75, create the title slide shown in Figure 1-74 using your name in place of Leland Zoladz. Decrease the font size of the paragraph, Presented by:, to 24. Decrease the font size of the paragraphs, Director, Career Development and Hammond College, to 28.
3. Using the typewritten notes in Figure 1-75, create the three bulleted list slides shown in Figure 1-74.
4. Click the Spelling button on the Standard toolbar. Correct any errors.
5. Save the presentation on a floppy disk using the file name, Finding the Right Job.
6. Display the presentation in black and white.
7. Print the black and white presentation. Quit PowerPoint.

FIGURE 1-74

FIGURE 1-75

In the Lab

2 Modifying Masters to Override Design Template Attributes

Problem: You are the Festival Coordinator for the Annual Lakeview Autumn Festival. To promote this year's festival, you design a brief presentation. You select a design template but decide to modify it. *Hint*: Use Help to solve this problem.

FIGURE 1-77

Instructions: Perform the following tasks.

1. Create a new presentation using the Angles design template.
2. Using the notes in Figure 1-76, create the title slide shown in Figure 1-77, using your name in place of Tammaye Obuz. Decrease the font size of the paragraphs Presented by:, and Festival Coordinator, to 24. Increase the font size of your name to 36.
3. Using the notes in Figure 1-76, create the three multi-level bulleted list slides shown in Figure 1-77.
4. Display the slide master. Click the paragraph, Click to edit Master title style. Click the Bold button, the Shadow button, and the Italic button on the Formatting toolbar.
5. Click the paragraph, Click to edit Master text styles. On the Format menu, click Line Spacing, and then increase the Before paragraph line spacing to 0.3 lines. Click the paragraph, Second level. On the Format menu, click Line Spacing, and then increase the After paragraph spacing to 0.15 lines.

```
I)      Autumn Festival
   A)  Presented by:
   B)  Tammaye Obuz
   C)  Festival Coordinator
II)     Festival Information
   A)  When
        1)  October 2 - 5, 1998
   B)  Where
        1)  Lakeview Park
   C)  Admission
        1)  Adults            $2.50
        2)  Children under 12 $1.50
III)    Exciting Entertainment
   A)  Friday
        1)  Jerry Jamison's Rhythm & Blues Band
   B)  Saturday
        1)  Heidi Hill's Polka Band
        2)  Mick Bentley and the Boys
   C)  Sunday
        1)  Lori Lincoln, contemporary pianist
IV)     Fantastic Food
   A)  International pavilion
        1)  Grilled lamb, Greece
        2)  Bratwurst, Germany
        3)  Fish and chips, England
        4)  Hot dogs and hamburgers, United States
   B)  Ice cream pavilion
   C)  Beverage tent
```

FIGURE 1-76

6. Drag the scroll box to display the title master. Click the paragraph, Click to edit Master title style. If necessary, click the Bold, Shadow, and Italic buttons on the Formatting toolbar.

7. Return to slide view. On the View menu, click Header and Footer. If necessary, click the Slide tab. Add the date (so it updates automatically), a slide number, and your name to the footer. Display the footer on all slides.

8. Drag the scroll box to display Slide 1. Click the Slide Show button to start slide show view. Then click to display each slide.

9. Save the presentation on a floppy disk using the file name, Autumn Festival. Display and print the presentation in black and white. Quit PowerPoint.

3 Creating a Training Presentation

Problem: You are the marketing manager for International Diamond and Jewels, a large jewelry wholesaler. Several people on your sales staff have requested presentation training. You decide to create a short presentation to emphasize the importance of rehearsing a presentation. *Hint*: Use Help to solve this problem.

Instructions: Using the list in Figure 1-78, design and create a presentation. The presentation must include a title slide and three bulleted list slides. Perform the following tasks.

1. Create a new presentation using the Whirlpool design template.

2. Create a title slide titled, Perfect Presentations. Include a subtitle, using your name in place of Roberto Cruz. Decrease the font size for the paragraphs Presented by:, Marketing Manager, and International Diamond and Jewels to 24. Increase the font size of your name to 36. Italicize the paragraph, Presented by:.

3. Using Figure 1-78, create three multi-level bulleted list slides. On Slide 2, use numbers instead of bullets for the three Practice paragraphs.

4. Adjust Before paragraph and After paragraph line spacing to utilize the available white space.

5. Insert a footer that includes the current date, your name, and the slide number on every slide except the title slide.

6. View the presentation in slide show view to look for errors. Correct any errors.

7. Check the presentation for spelling errors.

8. Save the presentation on a floppy disk with the file name, Perfect Presentations. Print the presentation slides in black and white. Quit PowerPoint.

```
I)   Perfect Presentations
  A) Presented by:
  B) Roberto Cruz
  C) Marketing Manager
  D) International Diamond and Jewels
II)  Practice Makes Perfect
  A) Secrets for a successful presentation
            1. Practice
            2. Practice
            3. Practice
III) Why Practice?
  A) Increase confidence
  B) Develop rhythm
     1) Pause for emphasis
  C) Improve articulation
     1) Vary pitch and inflection
  D) Identify problems
IV)  How To Practice
  A) Speak out loud
     1) Make a recording
     2) Look into a mirror
     3) Find a live audience
  B) Visit presentation site
     1) Inspect equipment
     2) Check environment
```

FIGURE 1-78

Cases and Places

The difficulty of these case studies varies: ❱ are the least difficult; ❱❱ are more difficult; and ❱❱❱ are the most difficult.

1 ❱ Maria Hernandez, coordinator for the Lincoln Elementary Fun Fair, has contacted Fun Fair Specialties to assist the school with this year's fun fair. Before finalizing plans, Ms. Hernandez needs approval from the parent-teacher association. She has prepared the notes in Figure 1-79 for a presentation that will be delivered at the next parent-teacher association meeting.

Ms. Hernandez has asked you to prepare a title slide and three additional slides that can be used on an overhead projector. Use the concepts and techniques introduced in this project to create the presentation.

Lincoln Elementary Fun Fair
Saturday, February 7, 1998
10:00 A.M. to 3:00 P.M.

Parent-Teacher Booths
- *Bake sale*
- *Clown face painting*
- *Jelly bean contest*
  - *Winner gets container of jelly beans*
- *Raffle ticket sales*
  - *Donated prizes*

Fun Fair Specialties Booths
- *Dunk the principal*
  - *Teacher volunteers welcome*
- *Fishing pond*
- *Balloon animals*

Fun Fair Goals
- *Repair audio-visual equipment*
- *Purchase five tumbling mats*
- *Install telephone line for Internet access in library*

FIGURE 1-79

2 ❱ Jackie Jacowski, a food technology instructor from Technology Tech High School, is delivering a presentation on how to make dinner in minutes. She has written out her recipe for baked pasta (Figure 1-80).

With this recipe, Mrs. Jacowski has asked you to prepare four slides that can be used on an overhead projector. She wants the title slide to introduce her and the recipe. Use the concepts and techniques introduced in this project to create the presentation.

Baked Pasta

Preparation
- *Cook ground meat in large skillet.*
  - *Drain fat from meat.*
- *Add cooked pasta, spaghetti sauce, and parmesan cheese.*
  - *Stir mixture.*
  - *Pour into 13 x 9 inch baking dish.*
- *Sprinkle shredded mozzarella cheese over pasta mixture.*

Ingredients
- *1 pound ground beef or ground turkey*
- *5 cups cooked pasta*
- *1 30 oz. jar of spaghetti sauce*
- *1/2 cup grated parmesan cheese*
- *1 8 oz. package shredded mozzarella cheese*

Baking and Serving
- *Put baking dish with pasta into oven.*
- *Bake 20 minutes at 375° Fahrenheit.*
  - *Remove from oven.*
- *Serving Suggestion:*
  - *Serve with tossed green salad and garlic bread.*

FIGURE 1-80

Cases and Places

▶▶ Party-Time is a store that specializes in parties. The consultants are trained to help clients in every aspect of party planning. Clients can stop by the store and pick up party favors; streamers; noise makers; and decorations for walls and windows. Party-Time also carries a complete line of paper and plastic items, such as plates, napkins, table-clothes, dinnerware, and serving utensils. Many clients consult Party-Time to help plan bridal showers, graduation receptions, and business meetings. The store is located in Logan's Mall, 621 West Logan Street, Thunder Bay, Ontario. For more information call 555-9979. Using the techniques presented in this project, prepare a title slide and three bulleted list slides to be used on an overhead projector.

▶▶ After many months of hard work, you and your partner, Lydia Statton, finally open Paws Inn, an animal boarding resort. Your research found most pet owners want a home-like atmosphere for their furry friends. Pet owners want reassurance that their pet is treated with respect and cared for by compassionate, attentive individuals. All staff members are associate members of the Hillside Humane Society and have pets of their own. Paws Inn offers five living room suites, complete with pet couches, and five bedroom suites with day beds. For pets needing an outdoors atmosphere, cabins are available. Cabins include an enclosed exercise run, accessible through a door-gate. Additional Paws Inn facilities include an exercise area, a wading pool, and a grooming salon. A dietitian is available for special meal requirements. Veterinarian services are available 24 hours a day. Reservations are recommended. Paws Inn is located at 2144 Deer Creek Road, Hillside, New Hampshire. The telephone number is 555-PAWS. Using the concepts and techniques presented in this project, prepare a title slide and three bulleted list slides to be used on an overhead projector.

▶▶▶ Many companies allow employees to work at home rather than commute to a central office. Some companies require the employee to present a work-at-home proposal to management before authorizing the work-at-home request. Research home-based offices using the Internet or a local library. Determine what is needed for the typical home-based office as well as the working environment. Using the concepts and techniques presented in this project, prepare a presentation to report your findings. Create a title slide and at least three additional slides that can be used with an overhead projector.

▶▶▶ Credit card debt looms over millions of people every day. Occasionally, people run out of money before all their financial obligations can be met. Financial planners write articles and often speak on television and radio about how to best handle this type of financial crisis. Contact a financial planner or a financial institution. Interview a financial consultant about what to do in a financial emergency and how to prevent a financial crisis in the future. Using the concepts and techniques presented in this project, prepare a presentation to report your findings. Create a title slide and at least three additional slides that can be used with an overhead projector

Cases and Places

7 ▶▶▶ Proper nutrition and exercise are necessary for a healthy body. But nutritionists often disagree on the daily requirements. Research the Internet for recommended daily portions for fruits, vegetables, grains, meats, dairy, and fats. Use more than one source to determine the daily requirements. Then, using the concepts and techniques presented in this project, prepare a presentation to report your findings. Create a title slide and at least three additional slides that can be used with an overhead projector.

Microsoft PowerPoint 97

Using Outline View and Clip Art to Create an Electronic Slide Show

Objectives:

You will have mastered the material in this project when you can:

▶ Create a presentation in outline view
▶ Describe the PowerPoint window in outline view
▶ Insert a blank line in a bulleted list
▶ Change the slide layout
▶ Move text between objects
▶ Insert clip art from Microsoft Clip Gallery 3.0
▶ Change clip art size
▶ Add a header and footer to outline pages
▶ Add slide transition effects
▶ Animate text
▶ Animate clip art
▶ Print a presentation outline
▶ Change printing options

Project 2

Unsinkable:
Molly Brown and You!

On the clear, cold night of April 14, 1912, in the North Atlantic, the Titanic — called *unsinkable* by her builders — struck an iceberg, ripping a mortal 300-foot hole in her hull, well below the water line. In just under three hours, the remorseless sea claimed fifteen hundred lives as the Titanic plunged into the dark abyss. Only a few remember the names of those ill-fated passengers, but most know of heroic Molly Brown, immortalized on Broadway and in the subsequent movie, who refused to go down with the ship. This disaster also gave rise to the saying, "Tip of the iceberg," which now is universally understood as a metaphor describing any endeavor where the majority of the work or information is hidden. Figuratively, this term has found expression in other ways, such as that attributed to Vince Lombardi, "Spectacular success is preceded by unspectacular preparation."

This certainly is true for all major entertainment events. To present a three-hour opera, an opera company books the stars a year or more in advance, creates sets that take hundreds of hours to build, and conducts hours of rehearsals. A circus that opens with a grand parade, then proceeds with two hours of performances in three rings takes thousands of hours in costume preparation, rigging, and animal training, not to mention lifetimes of dedication from acrobats and aerialists. A two-hour movie may have been in studio development for two years, plus another six months or more in shooting.

Plays, concerts, televised sporting events, Academy Awards, political conventions, and many other productions share a common thread: for even a chance at success, careful preparation is mandatory. In today's academic, scientific, and business arenas, the requirements are equally exacting. Often, the same people who demand top-notch operas, concerts, football games, and movies are decision-makers who sit for presentations in Melbourne, London, Toronto, and Atlanta. They are accustomed to the best and expect the best in business presentations, too.

Until recently, preparing a slide presentation was not a job for the faint-hearted. Writing and artwork were separate tasks, usually performed by specialists, and then integrated by a graphics production company — at great expense. Changes were slow to make and costly. Relatively short presentations required days, even weeks of preparation.

Microsoft's PowerPoint 97 has changed all this by removing the mechanical impediments to producing slide shows, letting you concentrate on the creative content. With Pick a Look and AutoContent Wizards, you can use ready-made formats and speedily produce outstanding presentations. Build effects, clip art, drawings, graphs, logos, and a wide range of background, color, and style selections allow you to spice your message to suit the most sophisticated tastes.

At your next presentation, aided by PowerPoint, you, too, can be like the Titanic's Molly Brown: unsinkable.

Microsoft
PowerPoint 97

Using Outline View and Clip Art to Create an Electronic Slide Show

Case Perspective

Voyager Travel Tours is a travel agency promoting two new vacation packages. They are focusing on college students who want a great spring break vacation at a terrific price. After contacting several schools to learn how to reach the student community, your boss, Mr. Suarez, is asked if he would like to set up a booth at a spring break vacation fair. He accepts the offer. The vacation fair, however, is the day after tomorrow. To allow Mr. Suarez to finalize his travel arrangements, he asks you to put together a short electronic presentation. The purpose of the presentation is to entice students to buy one of the two vacation packages.

Voyager Travel Tour's marketing department supplies you with an outline to use in creating the presentation. The outline contains promotional information about the two new vacation packages — the Stargazer and the Castaway. You decide to call them Break Away Bargains.

To persuade students to buy one of the Break Away Bargains, you choose a design template with tropical colors. Then, to make the presentation more exciting, you add pictures and apply animation effects.

Creating a Presentation from an Outline

At some time during either your academic or business life, you probably will make a presentation. Most academic presentations are informative — providing detailed information about some topic. Business presentations, however, are usually sales presentations, such as selling a proposal or a product to a client, convincing management to approve a new project, or persuading the board of directors to accept the new fiscal budget. As an alternative to creating your presentation in slide view, as you did in Project 1, PowerPoint provides an outlining feature to help you organize your thoughts. When the outline is complete, it becomes the foundation for your presentation.

You create a presentation outline in outline view. When you create an outline, you type all of the text at one time, as if you were typing an outline on a sheet of paper. This is different from slide view where you type text as you create each individual slide. PowerPoint creates the presentation as you type the outline by evaluating the outline structure. Regardless of the view in which you build a presentation, PowerPoint automatically creates the views discussed in Project 1, such as slide view.

The first step in creating a presentation in outline view is to type a title for the outline. The **outline title** is the subject of the presentation and later becomes the presentation title slide. Then you type the remainder of the outline, indenting appropriately to establish a structure or hierarchy. Once the outline is complete, you make your presentation more persuasive by adding graphics. This project uses outlining to create the presentation and clip art graphics to visually support the text.

Project Two – Break Away Bargains

Project 2 uses PowerPoint to create the six-slide Break Away Bargains presentation shown in Figure 2-1. You create the presentation from the outline in Figure 2-2 on the next page.

Voyager Travel Tours

Announces
Break Away Bargains

FIGURE 2-1a

Two Dynamite Deals

- The Stargazer
  - All inclusive sand and sea adventure
- The Castaway
  - Self-designed sand and sun experience

FIGURE 2-1b

The Stargazer

- One incredible low price includes:
  - Round-trip airfare
  - Five-day cruise and two-day beach party
  - Sumptuous gourmet cuisine
  - Fabulous entertainment

FIGURE 2-1c

Time Is Running Out

- Contact Student Activities Office
  - Detter Hall, Room 225
  - Ext. 2772
- Call Voyager Travel Tours
  - 555-AWAY

FIGURE 2-1f

The Castaway

- Customized dream vacation
  - Luxurious oceanfront condominiums
    - Whirlpool
    - Daily maid service
  - Diverse dining opportunities
  - Countless recreational activities

FIGURE 2-1d

Both Deals Feature

- Balmy breezes
- Lucid azure pools
- Starlit nights
- Sunny days
- Tropical climate
- White sand beaches
- Neptune Beach
  - Sunbathe, relax
- Poseidon Bay
  - Sail, swim
- Triton Reef
  - Scuba dive, snorkel

FIGURE 2-1e

More *About*
Electronic Slide Show

Preparing an electronic slide show has several advantages. For example, you can add multimedia effects, such as sound and video, as well as animate text and graphics. You can add slide transitions and build text objects to control the pace of the presentation. Most important is the ability to make last minute changes.

More *About*
Presentation Design

When designing a presentation, create your conclusion, or closing, first. Then design the rest of the presentation to reach the conclusion. This causes you to focus on the objectives of the presentation.

I. Voyager Travel Tours
    A. Announces
    B. Break Away Bargains
II. Two Dynamite Deals
    A. The Stargazer
        1. All inclusive sand and sea adventure
    B. The Castaway
        1. Self-designed sand and sun experience
III. The Stargazer
    A. One incredible low price includes:
        1. Round-trip airfare
        2. Five day cruise and two day beach party
        3. Sumptuous gourmet cuisine
        4. Fabulous entertainment
IV. The Castaway
    A. Customized dream vacation
        1. Luxurious oceanfront condominiums
            a) Whirlpool
            b) Daily maid service
        2. Diverse dining opportunities
        3. Countless recreational activities
V. Both Deals Feature
    A. Balmy breezes
    B. Lucid azure pools
    C. Starlit nights
    D. Sunny days
    E. Tropical climate
    F. White sand beaches
    G. Neptune Beach
        1. Sunbathe, relax
    H. Poseidon Bay
        1. Sail, swim
    I. Triton Reef
        1. Scuba dive, snorkel
VI. Time Is Running Out
    A. Contact Student Activities Office
        1. Detter Hall, Room 225
        2. Ext. 2772
    B. Call Voyager Travel Tours
        1. 555-AWAY

FIGURE 2-2

Presentation Preparation Steps

The preparation steps summarize how the slide presentation shown in Figure 2-1 on the previous page will be developed in Project 2. The following tasks will be completed in this project.

1. Start a new document and apply a design template.
2. Create a presentation in outline view.
3. Save the presentation.
4. Insert a blank line in the bulleted list on Slide 2.
5. Change the slide layout on Slide 5 to 2 Column Text and move text from the left column to the right column.
6. Change the slide layout on Slide 6 to Clip Art Text and insert a clip art picture into a clip art placeholder.
7. Insert clip art into Slide 3 and then move and reduce the size of the clip art picture.
8. Add header and footer text to the outline pages.
9. Add slide transition effects.

10. Add text and clip art animation effects.
11. Save the presentation.
12. Print the presentation outline and slides.
13. Quit PowerPoint.

The following pages contain a detailed explanation of these tasks.

Starting a New Presentation

Project 1 introduced you to starting a presentation document and applying a design template. The following steps summarize how to start a new presentation, apply a design template, and choose an AutoLayout. For a more detailed explanation, see pages PP 1.10 through PP 1.14 in Project 1. Perform the following steps to start a new presentation.

TO START A NEW PRESENTATION

1. Click the Start button on the taskbar.
2. Click New Office Document.
3. Click the Presentation Designs tab. (Depending on your installation, the tab may display as Presentatio … .) When the Presentation Designs sheet displays, scroll down the list of design templates until SERENE displays.
4. Double-click SERENE.
5. When the New Slide dialog box displays, click the OK button.
6. If the Office Assistant displays, click the Office Assistant Close button.

PowerPoint displays the Title Slide AutoLayout and the Serene design template on Slide 1 in slide view (Figure 2-3).

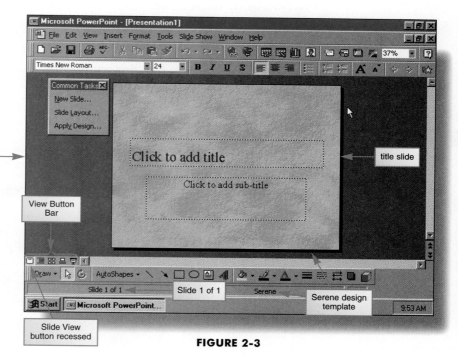

FIGURE 2-3

Using Outline View

Outline view provides a quick, easy way to create a presentation. Outlining allows you to organize your thoughts in a structured format. An outline uses indentation to establish a hierarchy, which denotes levels of importance to the main topic. An **outline** is a summary of thoughts, presented as headings and subheadings, often used as a preliminary draft when you create a presentation.

In outline view, title text displays at the left side of the window along with a slide icon and a slide number. Body text is indented under the title text. Graphic objects, such as pictures, graphs, or tables, do not display in outline view. When a slide contains a graphic object, the slide icon next to the slide title displays with a small graphic on it. The slide icon is blank when a slide does not contain graphics. The attributes for text in outline view are the same as in slide view except for color and paragraph style. PowerPoint displays the current slide in **Color View.** This allows you to see how the current slide will look in slide view and slide show view while you continue to work in outline view.

PowerPoint limits the number of heading levels to six. The first heading level is the slide title and is not indented. The remaining five heading levels are the same as the five indent levels in slide view. Recall from Project 1 that PowerPoint allows for five indent levels and that each indent level has an associated bullet.

The outline begins with a title on **heading level 1**. The title is the main topic of the slide. Text supporting the main topic begins on **heading level 2** and indents under heading level 1. **Heading level 3** indents under heading level 2 and contains text to support heading level 2. **Heading level 4, heading level 5,** and **heading level 6** indent under heading level 3, heading level 4, and heading level 5, respectively. Use heading levels 4, 5, and 6 as required. They generally are used for very detailed scientific and engineering presentations. Business and sales presentations usually focus on summary information and use heading level 1, heading level 2, and heading level 3.

PowerPoint initially displays in slide view when you start a new presentation. Change from slide view to outline view by clicking the Outline View button on the View Button Bar. Perform the following steps to change the view from slide view to outline view.

Steps ## To Change the View to Outline View

1 **Point to the Outline View button located on the View Button Bar at the lower-left corner of the Microsoft PowerPoint window (Figure 2-4).**

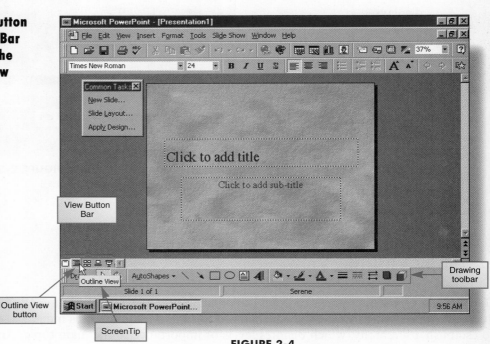

FIGURE 2-4

2 Click the Outline View button. If necessary, drag the Common Tasks toolbar to the right side of the Microsoft PowerPoint window as shown in Figure 2-5.

PowerPoint displays in outline view (Figure 2-5). PowerPoint displays the color view of Slide 1 in the Color View window.

FIGURE 2-5

Other Ways

1. On View menu click Outline
2. Press ALT+V, press O

You can create and edit your presentation in outline view. Outline view also makes it easy to sequence slides and to relocate title text and body text from one slide to another. In addition to typing text to create a new presentation in outline view, PowerPoint can produce slides from an outline created in Microsoft Word or another word processor, if you save the outline as an RTF file or as a plain text file. The file extension **RTF** stands for **R**ich **T**ext **F**ormat.

The PowerPoint Window in Outline View

The PowerPoint window in outline view differs from the window in slide view because the Outlining toolbar displays but the Drawing toolbar does not (Figures 2-4 and 2-5). Table 2-1 on the next page describes the buttons on the Outlining toolbar.

More *About* Heading Levels

You may overwhelm the audience if a slide contains too much detail and requires more than six heading levels with which to explain the topic. Decompose large topics into two or more subtopics. Then, create a new slide for each group of subtopics.

Table 2-1

BUTTON	BUTTON NAME	DESCRIPTION
	Promote	The Promote button moves the selected paragraph up one level in the outline hierarchy each time you click the button. Promoting a paragraph outdents or moves it to the left until your reach heading level 1.
	Demote	The Demote button moves the selected paragraph down one level in the outline hierarchy each time you click the button. Demoting a paragraph indents or moves it to the right. You only can demote down to heading level 6.
	Move Up	The Move Up button moves selected text above the preceding displayed paragraph while maintaining its hierarchical heading level and text style. The selected text changes position with the paragraph located above it.
	Move Down	The Move Down button moves selected text below the following displayed paragraph while maintaining its hierarchical heading level and text style. The selected text changes position with the paragraph located below it.
	Collapse	The Collapse button hides all heading levels except the title of the selected slide. The button is useful when you want to collapse one slide in your outline. Hidden text displays as a gray line.
	Expand	The Expand button displays all heading levels and text for the selected slide. The button is useful when you want to expand one slide in your outline.
	Collapse All	The Collapse All button hides all heading levels to show only the slide titles of the entire presentation. This button is useful when you are looking at the organization of your presentation and do not care to see the details. Hidden text displays as gray lines below the title.
	Expand All	Expands all heading levels to display the slide title and text for all slides.
	Summary Slide	Creates a bulleted list slide from the titles of the slides selected in slide sorter view or outline view, and then inserts that slide in front of the first selected slide.
	Show Formatting	The Show Formatting button is a toggle that displays or hides the text attributes. This is useful when you want to work with plain text as opposed to working with bolded, italicized, or underlined text. When printing your outline, plain text often speeds up the printing process.

Creating a Presentation in Outline View

Outline view enables you to view title and body text, add and delete slides, **drag and drop** slide text, drag and drop slides to change slide order, promote and demote text, save a presentation, print an outline, print slides, copy and paste slides or text to and from other presentations, apply a design template, and import an outline.

Developing a presentation in outline view is quick because you type the text for all slides on one screen. Once you type the outline, the presentation fundamentally is complete. If you choose, you then can go to slide view to enhance your presentation with graphics.

Creating a Title Slide in Outline View

Recall from Project 1 that the title slide introduces the presentation to the audience. In addition to introducing the presentation, Project 2 uses the title slide to capture the attention of the audience by using a design template with tropical colors. Remember that Voyager Travel Tours is trying to sell vacation packages. They want the audience to focus on getting away to a warm, tropical climate for an exciting vacation; consequently, they use an appropriate design template. Perform the following steps to create a title slide in outline view.

◆ **More** *About*
Creating Presentations in Outline View

A method some presenters use to create a presentation is to create a list of the main topics for a presentation in outline view. Developing the list of main topics generates all presentation slides because each topic becomes the title for a slide. The presenter then completes each slide with relevant subtopics.

Steps **To Create a Title Slide in Outline View**

1 **Type** Voyager Travel Tours
and press the ENTER key.

*Voyager Travel Tours
displays as the title for
Slide 1 and is called heading level
1. A slide icon displays to the left of
each slide title. The font
for heading level 1 is
Times New Roman and
the font size is 44 points. In outline
view, the default Zoom setting is
33% of the actual slide size.
Depending on the **resolution** of
your computer monitor (the number
of pixels displaying per unit of
measurement, such as a centimeter
or an inch), your Zoom setting may
be different. Pressing the ENTER key
moves the insertion point to the next
line and maintains the same heading level. The insertion point, therefore, is in position for typing the title
for Slide 2 (Figure 2-6).*

FIGURE 2-6

2 **Point to the Demote button on
the Outlining toolbar.**

*The Demote ScreenTip
displays (Figure 2-7).*

FIGURE 2-7

③ **Click the Demote button. Type** Announces **and press the** ENTER **key. Type** Break Away Bargains **and press the** ENTER **key.**

The Slide 2 slide icon does not display (Figure 2-8). The paragraphs, Announces and Break Away Bargains, are subtitles on the title slide (Slide 1) and demote to heading level 2. Heading level 2 is indented to the right under heading level 1. The heading level 2 font is Times New Roman and the heading level 2 font size is 32 points.

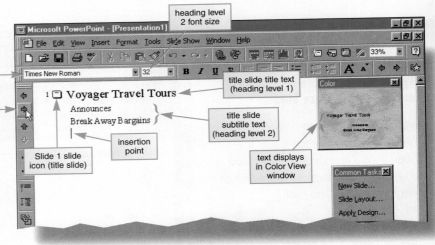

FIGURE 2-8

Other Ways

1. Type title text, press ENTER, on Formatting toolbar, click Demote button, type subtitle text, press ENTER
2. Type title text, press ENTER, press TAB, type subtitle text, press ENTER

The title slide text for the Voyager Travel Tours presentation is complete. The next section explains how to add a slide in outline view.

Adding a Slide in Outline View

Recall from Project 1 that when you add a new slide, PowerPoint defaults to the Bulleted List AutoLayout layout. This is true in outline view as well. One way to add a new slide in outline view is to promote a paragraph to heading level 1 by clicking the Promote button until the insertion point or the paragraph displays at heading level 1. A slide icon displays when the insertion point or paragraph reaches heading level 1. Perform the following steps to add a slide in outline view.

Steps **To Add a Slide in Outline View**

① **Point to the Promote button on the Outlining toolbar.**

The insertion point still is positioned at heading level 2 (Figure 2-9).

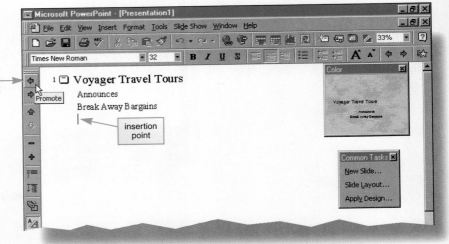

FIGURE 2-9

2 **Click the Promote button.**

The Slide 2 slide icon displays indicating a new slide is added to the presentation (Figure 2-10). The insertion point is in position to type the title for Slide 2 at heading level 1.

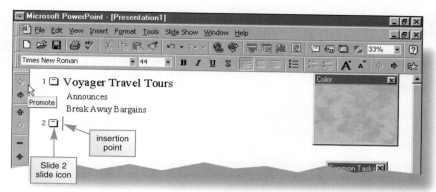

FIGURE 2-10

After you add a slide, you are ready to type the slide text. The next section explains how to create a multi-level bulleted list slide in outline view.

Creating Multi-level Bulleted List Slides in Outline View

To create a multi-level bulleted list slide, you demote or promote the insertion point to the appropriate heading level and then type the paragraph text. Recall from Project 1 that when you demote a paragraph, PowerPoint adds a bullet to the left of each heading level. Depending on the design template, each heading level has a different bullet font. Also recall that the design template determines font attributes, including the bullet font.

Slide 2 is the first **informational slide** for Project 2. Slide 2 introduces the main topic — two vacation packages offered by Voyager Travel Tours. Each vacation package displays as heading level 2, and each **supportive paragraph** displays as heading level 3. The following steps explain how to create a multi-level bulleted list slide in outline view.

*Other*Ways

1. On Standard toolbar, click New Slide button, click OK button in New Slide dialog box
2. On Insert menu click New Slide, click OK button in New Slide dialog box
3. Press ALT+I, press N, press ENTER
4. Press CTRL+M, press ENTER
5. Press and hold SHIFT, press TAB until paragraph or insertion point displays at heading level 1, release TAB

Steps **To Create a Multi-level Bulleted List Slide in Outline View**

1 **Type** Two Dynamite Deals **and press the ENTER key. Then click the Demote button to demote to heading level 2.**

The title for Slide 2, Two Dynamite Deals, displays and the insertion point is in position to type the first bulleted paragraph (Figure 2-11). A leaf shaped bullet displays to the left of the insertion point.

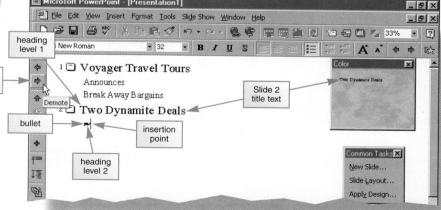

FIGURE 2-11

2 **Type** The Stargazer **and press the ENTER key. Then click the Demote button to demote to heading level 3.**

Slide 2 displays three heading levels: the title, Two Dynamite Deals, on heading level 1, the bulleted paragraph, The Stargazer, on heading level 2, and the insertion point on heading level 3 (Figure 2-12). The bullet for heading level 2 is a leaf. The bullet for heading level 3 is a dot.

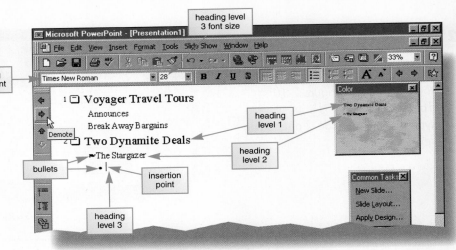

FIGURE 2-12

3 **Type** All inclusive sand and sea adventure **and press the ENTER key. Then click the Promote button.**

Pressing the ENTER key begins a new paragraph at the same heading level as the previous paragraph. Clicking the Promote button moves the insertion point left and elevates the paragraph from heading level 3 to heading level 2 (Figure 2-13).

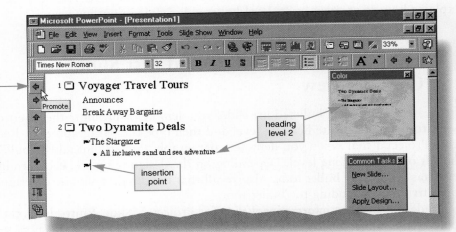

FIGURE 2-13

4 **Type** The Castaway **and press the ENTER key. Click the Demote button. Type** Self-designed sand and sun experience **and press the ENTER key (Figure 2-14).**

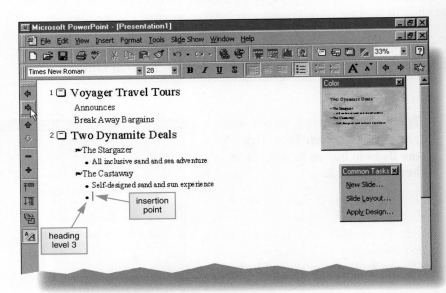

FIGURE 2-14

Creating a Subordinate Slide

When developing your presentation, begin with a main topic and follow with **subordinate slides**, slides to support the main topic. Placing all your information on one slide may overwhelm your audience. Decompose your presentation, therefore, into several slides with three to six bullets per slide or per object. The following steps explain how to create a subordinate slide that further explains the vacation package, The Stargazer, first introduced on Slide 2. This new slide, Slide 3, provides additional information that supports the first heading level 2 on Slide 2. Later in this project, you create another subordinate slide to support the second heading level 2 on Slide 2, The Castaway.

More *About*
Outline View

When working in outline view, many people prefer to use keyboard keys instead of toolbar buttons. This way their hands never leave the keyboard and their typing is finished quickly. For example, instead of clicking the Demote button to demote text, press the TAB key.

TO CREATE A SUBORDINATE SLIDE

1 Click the Promote button two times so that Slide 3 is added to the end of the presentation.

2 Type `The Stargazer` and press the ENTER key.

3 Click the Demote button to demote to heading level 2.

4 Type `One incredible low price includes:` and press the ENTER key.

5 Click the Demote button to demote to heading level 3.

6 Type `Round-trip airfare` and press the ENTER key.

7 Type `Five-day cruise and two-day beach party` and press the ENTER key.

8 Type `Sumptuous gourmet cuisine` and press the ENTER key.

9 Type `Fabulous entertainment` and press the ENTER key.

The screen displays as shown in Figure 2-15.

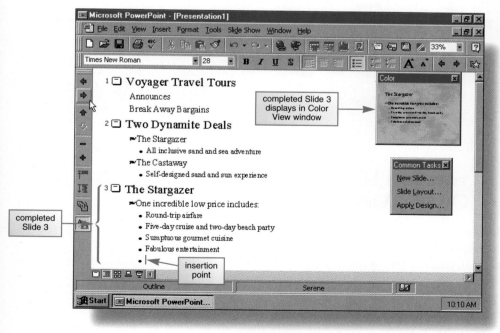

FIGURE 2-15

More *About*
Subordinate Slides

When reviewing a presentation, look for slides containing more information than the audience can quickly grasp. When a slide gets complicated, simplify the presentation by clicking the Expand Slide command on the Tools menu. This generates a new slide for each bulleted item on the original slide.

More *About*
Subordinate Slides

Subordinate items must directly support the main topic under which they are placed. This means that they must be less important in meaning while being logically related. Indentation identifies levels of importance. The more important the item, the closer it displays to the left margin.

Creating a Second Subordinate Slide

The next step is to create the slide that supports The Castaway, which is the second heading level 2 on Slide 2. Perform the following steps to create this subordinate slide.

TO CREATE A SECOND SUBORDINATE SLIDE

1 Click the Promote button two times so that Slide 4 is added to the end of the presentation. Type The Castaway and press the ENTER key.

2 Click the Demote button to demote to heading level 2. Type Customized dream vacation and press the ENTER key.

3 Click the Demote button to demote to heading level 3. Type Luxurious oceanfront condominiums and press the ENTER key.

4 Click the Demote button to demote to heading level 4. Type Whirlpool and press the ENTER key. Type Daily maid service and press the ENTER key.

5 Click the Promote button to promote to heading level 3. Type Diverse dining opportunities and press the ENTER key. Type Countless recreational activities and press the ENTER key.

The screen displays as shown in Figure 2-16.

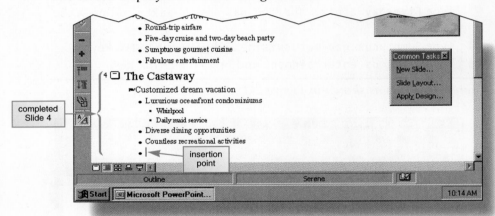

FIGURE 2-16

Creating a Slide with Multiple Text Objects in Outline View

All of the slides you have created to this point consist of a title object and one text object. Occasionally, you need to provide the audience with a long list of items. If you use the Bulleted List slide layout, Style Checker will identify the slide as having too many bullets. Recall from Project 1 that Style Checker checks a presentation for spelling, visual clarity, case, and end punctuation. One of the design standards Style Checker looks for is too many bullets in an object.

In order to create a slide with more than six bulleted paragraphs and still comply with design standards, break the list into two or more objects. When you divide the text into multiple objects, each object complies with PowerPoint's default settings for visual clarity in Style Checker, as long as the number of bullets per object is less than or equal to six. Six is the default setting for the number of bullets per object.

Because you are creating the presentation in outline view, type the text for this slide as a bulleted list. Later in this project, you convert the bulleted list slide into a multiple object slide by changing views, changing slide layout, and moving some of the text from the bulleted list to another object. Perform the following steps to create a slide with multiple text objects in outline view.

TO CREATE A SLIDE WITH MULTIPLE TEXT OBJECTS IN OUTLINE VIEW

1 Click the Promote button two times so that Slide 5 is added to the end of the presentation. Type Both Deals Feature as the slide title and press the ENTER key.

2 Click the Demote button to demote to heading level 2. Type Balmy breezes and press the ENTER key. Type Lucid azure pools and press the ENTER key. Type Starlit nights and press the ENTER key. Type Sunny days and press the ENTER key. Type Tropical climate and press the ENTER key. Type White sand beaches and press the ENTER key. Type Neptune Beach and press the ENTER key.

3 Click the Demote button to demote to heading level 3. Type Sunbathe, relax and press the ENTER key.

4 Click the Promote button to promote to heading level 2. Type Poseidon Bay and press the ENTER key.

5 Click the Demote button to demote to heading level 3. Type Sail, swim and press the ENTER key.

6 Click the Promote button to promote to heading level 2. Type Triton Reef and press the ENTER key.

7 Click the Demote button to demote to heading level 3. Type Scuba dive, snorkel and press the ENTER key.

The screen displays as shown in Figure 2-17.

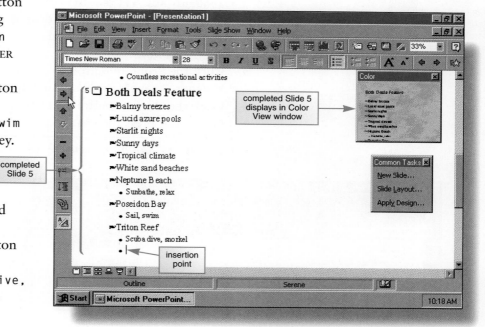

FIGURE 2-17

Creating a Closing Slide in Outline View

The last slide in your presentation is the closing slide. A **closing slide** gracefully ends a presentation. Often used during a question and answer session, the closing slide usually remains on the screen to reinforce the message delivered during the presentation. Professional speakers design the closing slide with one or more of the methods on the next page.

1. List important information. Tell the audience what to do next.
2. Provide a memorable illustration or example to make a point.
3. Appeal to emotions. Remind the audience to take action or accept responsibility.
4. Summarize the main points of the presentation.
5. Cite a quotation that directly relates to the main points of the presentation. This is most effective if the presentation started with a quotation.

The closing slide in this project combines listing important information and providing an illustration. Because Voyager Travel Tours wants students to buy one of the tropical island vacations, they combine telling students what to do next with a list of telephone numbers on the Serene design template. Perform the following steps to create this closing slide.

TO CREATE A CLOSING SLIDE IN OUTLINE VIEW

1 Click the Promote button two times so that Slide 6 is added to the end of the presentation. Type Time Is Running Out as the slide title and press the ENTER key.

2 Click the Demote button to demote to heading level 2. Type Contact Student Activities Office and press the ENTER key.

3 Click the Demote button to demote to heading level 3. Type Detter Hall, Room 225 and press the ENTER key. Type Ext. 2772 and press the ENTER key.

4 Click the Promote button to promote to heading level 2. Type Call Voyager Travel Tours and press the ENTER key.

5 Click the Demote button to demote to heading level 3. Type 555-AWAY but do not press the ENTER key.

Slide 6 displays as shown in Figure 2-18.

FIGURE 2-18

The outline now is complete and the presentation should be saved. The next section explains how to save the presentation.

Saving a Presentation

Recall from Project 1 that it is wise to frequently save your presentation. Because you have created all the text for your presentation, you should save your presentation now. For a detailed explanation of the following summarized steps, refer to pages PP 1.23 through PP 1.25 in Project 1.

TO SAVE A PRESENTATION

1 Insert a formatted floppy disk in drive A and then click the Save button on the Standard toolbar.

2 Type Break Away Bargains in the File name box. Do not press the ENTER key.

3 Click the Save in box arrow. Click 3½ Floppy (A:) in the Save in list.

4 Click the Save button.

The presentation is saved on drive A under the file name Break Away Bargains. The file name displays in the title bar.

Reviewing a Presentation in Slide Sorter View

In Project 1, you displayed slides in slide show view to evaluate the presentation. Slide show view, however, restricts your evaluation to one slide at a time. Outline view is best for quickly reviewing all the text for a presentation. Recall from Project 1 that slide sorter view allows you to look at several slides at one time, which is why it is the best view to use to evaluate a presentation for content, organization, and overall appearance. Perform the following step to change from outline view to slide sorter view.

Steps **To Change the View to Slide Sorter View**

1 **Click the Slide Sorter View button on the View Button Bar at the bottom of the PowerPoint window.**

PowerPoint displays the presentation in slide sorter view (Figure 2-19). Slide 6 is selected because it was the current slide in outline view.

FIGURE 2-19

Because there are only six slides in this presentation and the Zoom setting is 66%, you can review all slides in one window. Notice that all slides have a significant amount of white space and that the text on Slide 5 exceeds the length of the slide. These observations indicate a need to adjust line spacing to make better use of the slide. Recall that Slide 5 will be corrected by changing the slide layout to one that displays text in two text objects. Additionally, the presentation lacks excitement. To make the presentation more interesting, you may wish to add graphics, such as clip art. The next several sections explain how to improve the presentation by adding a blank line in a bulleted list, changing slide layouts, and adding clip art.

Adding a Blank Line to a Bulleted List

The first improvement to this presentation is adding a blank line to Slide 2. In order to increase white space between paragraphs, add a blank line after the heading level 3 paragraph, All inclusive sand and sea adventure. Recall that a paragraph begins when you press the ENTER key and ends when you again press the ENTER key. Also recall that PowerPoint adds a bullet in front of every new paragraph in a bulleted list. Thus, to create a blank line in a bulleted list, you also must remove the bullet.

You can make changes to text in both slide view and outline view. It is best, however, to change the view to slide view when making changes that impact white space so that you can see the result of editing the text object. Perform the following steps to change the view to slide view.

Steps **To Change the View to Slide View**

1 **Point to the slide miniature of Slide 2 (Figure 2-20).**

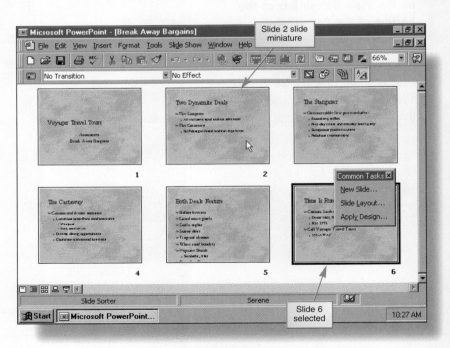

FIGURE 2-20

2 **Double-click the Slide 2 slide miniature.**

Slide 2 displays in slide view (Figure 2-21). The Slide View button is recessed on the View Button Bar.

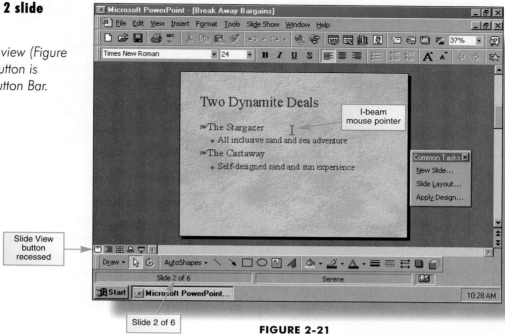

FIGURE 2-21

Other Ways
1. On View menu click Slide
2. Press ALT+V, press S

The next section explains how to add a blank line to Slide 2.

Adding a Blank Line to Slide 2

Now that Slide 2 displays in slide view, you are ready to add a blank line after the paragraph, All inclusive sand and sea adventure. Perform the following steps to add a blank line.

 To Add a Blank Line

1 **Position the I-beam mouse pointer to the right of the second letter e in the word adventure in the paragraph All inclusive sand and sea adventure. Then click the left mouse button.**

PowerPoint selects the text object and positions the insertion point after the second e in the word, adventure (Figure 2-22). The mouse pointer displays as an I-beam when located in a text object.

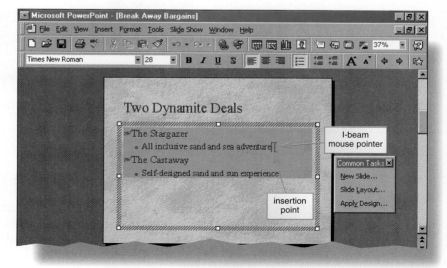

FIGURE 2-22

2 **Press the ENTER key.**

PowerPoint inserts a new paragraph
(Figure 2-23). The new paragraph
has the same attributes as the
previous paragraph. The Bullets
button is recessed on the
Formatting toolbar.

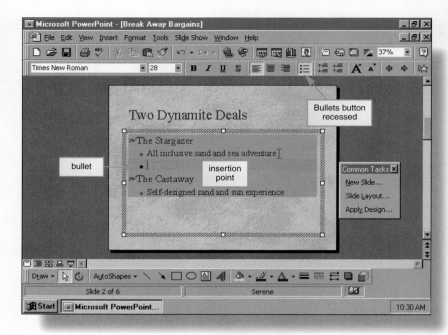

FIGURE 2-23

3 **Click the Bullets button to
remove the bullet.**

The line displays blank because
the bullet does not display (Figure
2-24). The Bullets button is not
recessed.

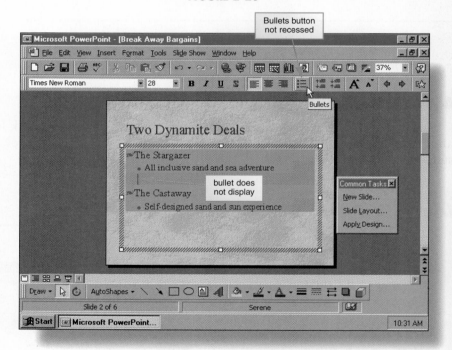

FIGURE 2-24

Positioning the insertion point at the end of a paragraph and then pressing the
ENTER key two times also creates a blank paragraph. The bullet, however, displays
dimmed on the screen and the Bullets button displays recessed on the Formatting
toolbar. If you click a paragraph other than the blank paragraph, the bullet does
not display. Additionally, the dimmed bullet does not display when you run the
presentation in slide show view.

To display a bullet on a selected paragraph, click the Bullets button on the Formatting toolbar.

Changing Slide Layout

Recall from Project 1 that when you add a new slide, PowerPoint displays the New Slide dialog box from which you choose one of the slide AutoLayouts. After creating a slide, you can change its layout by clicking the **Slide Layout button** on the Common Tasks toolbar. The Slide Layout dialog box then displays. Like the AutoLayout dialog box, the Slide Layout dialog box allows you to choose one of the 24 different slide layouts.

When you change the layout of a slide, PowerPoint retains the text and graphics and repositions them into the appropriate placeholders. Using slide layouts eliminates the need to resize objects because PowerPoint automatically sizes the object to fit the placeholder.

To keep your presentation interesting, PowerPoint includes several slide layouts to combine text with nontext objects, such as clip art. The placement of the text, in relationship to the nontext object, depends on the slide layout. The nontext object placeholder may be to the right or left of the text, above the text, or below the text. Additionally, some slide layouts are constructed with two nontext object placeholders. Refer to Project 1 for a list of the available slide layouts (Figure 1-27 on PP 1.25). The following steps explain how to change the slide layout from a bulleted list to two columns of text.

Steps **To Change Slide Layout**

① **Drag the scroll box on the vertical scroll bar to display Slide 5 (Figure 2-25).**

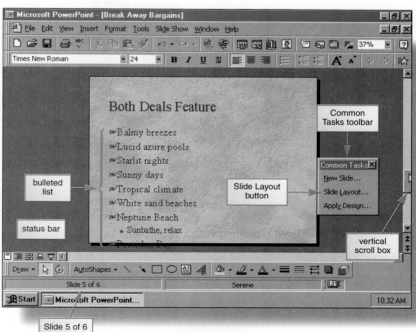

FIGURE 2-25

2 Click the Slide Layout button on the Common Tasks toolbar. When the Slide Layout dialog box displays, click the 2 Column Text slide layout located in row one, column three.

The Slide Layout dialog box displays (Figure 2-26). The 2 Column Text slide layout is selected. When you click a slide layout, its name displays in the box at the lower-right corner of the Slide Layout dialog box.

FIGURE 2-26

3 Click the Apply button.

Slide 5 displays the bulleted list in the left column text object (Figure 2-27). The right column text placeholder displays the message, Click to add text.

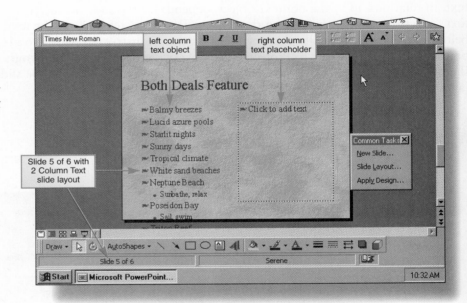

FIGURE 2-27

The text in the left column of Slide 5 is too lengthy to fit into the text object. The next section explains how to move the text at the bottom of the left column to the top of the right column text placeholder.

Moving Text

Because the bulleted list on Slide 5 contains more paragraphs than will fit in the left column text object, select a portion of the list and move it to the right column text placeholder. Perform the following steps to select a portion of the text in the left column and then move it to the right column.

Steps **To Move Text**

1 **Position the I-beam mouse pointer immediately to the left of the N in Neptune. Drag to the right and down so that the last six bulleted paragraphs are selected. If necessary, click the vertical scroll bar down arrow to display all the bulleted items.**

The six bulleted paragraphs, Neptune Beach, Sunbathe, relax; Poseidon Bay, Sail, swim; and Triton Reef, Scuba dive, snorkel, are selected (Figure 2-28).

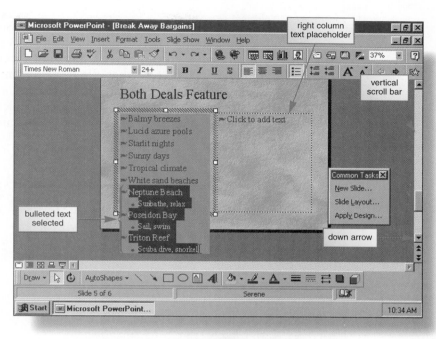

FIGURE 2-28

2 **Point to the selected text. If the mouse pointer displays as a four-headed arrow, move the mouse pointer to the right of the bullets so that it is positioned over the text. Then drag the selected text to the right column text placeholder.**

As you drag the text, the mouse pointer displays as a block arrow with a small dotted box around the arrow shaft. The six selected paragraphs are moved to the right column text placeholder (Figure 2-29). When you insert text into a text placeholder, it becomes a text object.

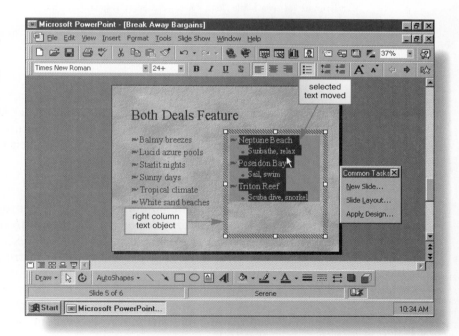

FIGURE 2-29

Because Slide 5 contains two bulleted text objects, it now complies with the default Style Checker design rules of no more than six bullets per object.

Other Ways

1. Right-click selected text, click Cut, right-click new text location, click Paste

2. Select text, click Cut button, click new text location, click Paste button

Adding Clip Art to a Slide

Clip art offers a quick way to add professional-looking graphic images to your presentation without creating the images yourself. One clip art source is the Microsoft Clip Gallery 3.0. **Microsoft Clip Gallery 3.0** is a tool that accompanies Microsoft Office 97 that allows you to insert clip art, pictures, audio clips, and video clips to a presentation. It contains a wide variety of clip art images and is shared with other Microsoft Office applications. Microsoft Clip Gallery 3.0 combines topic-related clip art images into categories, such as Animals, Household, and People at Work.

Table 2-2 gives you an idea of the organization of Microsoft Clip Gallery 3.0 that accompanies PowerPoint. The table contains four of the categories from Microsoft Clip Gallery 3.0 and keywords of the clip art contained therein. Clip art images have one or more keywords that associate an image with various entities, activities, labels, and emotions. In most instances, the keyword does not contain the name of the physical object. For example, an image of a magnifying glass in the Academic category has keywords of Focus Investigation Identify Small. As a result, you may find it necessary to scroll through several categories to find an appropriate picture.

Table 2-2	
CATEGORY	*CLIP ART KEYWORDS*
Academic	Reward Accomplishment, Reward Accomplishment Milestone Guarantee, Focus Investigation Identify Small, Leadership Information Test Communication Listen Dictate
Cartoons	Anger Demanding, Stress Frustration Anger Chaos, Reward Agreeable, Success Victory Accomplishment Result Invincible Milestone Superior
Gestures	Success Impress, Harmony Trust Compromise Consensus Guarantee Synergy, Trust Protect, Success Invincible, Failure
Transportation	Performance Fast Sports Car, War Battle Powerful Battleship Navigate, Performance Fast War Battle Plane, Performance Ship Navigate, Priority Traffic Light

Depending on the installation of Microsoft Clip Gallery 3.0 on your computer, you may not have the clip art pictures used in this project. Contact your instructor if you are missing clip art when you perform the following steps.

Using AutoLayouts to Add Clip Art

PowerPoint simplifies adding clip art to a slide by providing AutoLayouts designed specifically for clip art. Recall from Project 1 that an AutoLayout is a collection of placeholders for the title, text, clip art, graphs, tables, and media clips. A clip art placeholder contains instructions to open Microsoft Clip Gallery 3.0. Double-clicking the clip art placeholder activates the instructions. When you use an AutoLayout placeholder to add an object to a slide, such as clip art, PowerPoint automatically sizes the object to fit the placeholder. If the object is in landscape orientation, PowerPoint sizes it to the width of the placeholder. If the object is in portrait orientation, PowerPoint sizes it to the height of the placeholder.

Adding clip art to Slide 6 requires two steps. First, change the slide layout to Clip Art & Text. Then insert clip art into the clip art placeholder. The next two sections explain how to add clip art into an AutoLayout placeholder.

More *About*
Clip Art

Humor and interest are just two of several reasons to add clip art to your presentation. People have limited attention spans. A carefully placed humorous clip art image can spark attention and interest. When interest is high, it greatly increases the chance that your concept or idea will be remembered.

Changing Slide Layout to Clip Art & Text

Before you insert clip art into an AutoLayout placeholder, you first must select one of the slide layouts that includes a clip art placeholder. The clip art placeholder on the left side of Slide 6 will hold clip art. Perform the following steps to change the slide layout to Clip Art & Text.

Steps **To Change the Slide Layout to Clip Art & Text**

1 **Drag the scroll box on the vertical scroll bar to display Slide 6 (Figure 2-30).**

FIGURE 2-30

2 **Click the Slide Layout button on the Common Tasks toolbar. When the Slide Layout dialog box displays, click the Clip Art & Text slide layout located in row three, column two. Then point to the Apply button.**

The Clip Art & Text slide layout is selected in the Slide Layout dialog box (Figure 2-31).

FIGURE 2-31

3 Click the Apply button.

Slide 6 displays the Clip Art & Text slide layout (Figure 2-32). PowerPoint moves the text object and automatically resizes the text to fit the object.

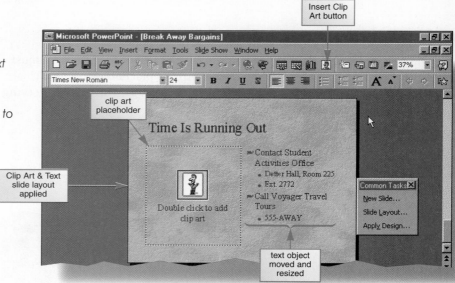

FIGURE 2-32

You can use an AutoLayout placeholder to insert clip art even if the AutoLayout does not have a clip art placeholder. For example, to insert clip art into the object placeholder of the Object AutoLayout, click the placeholder to select it, click the Insert Clip Art button on the Standard toolbar, and then select a clip art picture.

Inserting Clip Art into a Clip Art Placeholder

Now that the Clip Art & Text placeholder is applied to Slide 6, you insert clip art into the clip art placeholder. Perform the following steps to insert clip art into the clip art placeholder on Slide 6.

 ## To Insert Clip Art into a Clip Art Placeholder

1 Position the mouse pointer anywhere within the clip art placeholder.

The mouse pointer is positioned inside the clip art placeholder (Figure 2-33). The mouse pointer becomes a four-headed arrow. It is not necessary to point to the picture inside the placeholder.

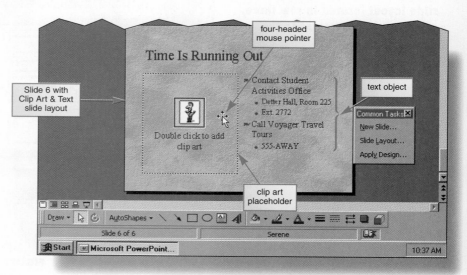

FIGURE 2-33

2 **Double-click the clip art placeholder on the left side of Slide 6.**

PowerPoint displays the Microsoft Clip Gallery 3.0 dialog box (Figure 2-34). The Clip Art list box displays clip art images by category. When you open Microsoft Clip Gallery 3.0, All Categories is the selected category on the Clip Art sheet. The selected clip art image in this figure is a diploma. Your selected image may be different depending on the clip art installed on your computer.

FIGURE 2-34

3 **Click the Find button.**

The Find Clip dialog box displays three boxes in which you enter clip art search criteria (Figure 2-35). The Keywords text box is selected and contains the keyword, All Keywords. Use the Keywords text box to find clip art when you know one of the words associated with the clip art image. Use the File name containing text box when you know the name of the file containing the desired clip art image. Use the Clip type list box when you want to find clip art saved in a specific format.

FIGURE 2-35

4 Type `time` **in the Keywords text box and point to the Find Now button.**

The Keywords text box contains time (Figure 2-36). You do not need to type the full keyword because the Find feature of Microsoft Clip Gallery 3.0 searches for all pictures containing the consecutive letters typed in the Keywords text box. The Find Now button initiates the clip art search. The Reset button resets the Keywords, File name containing, and Clip type boxes. Click the Reset button when you wish to begin a new search.

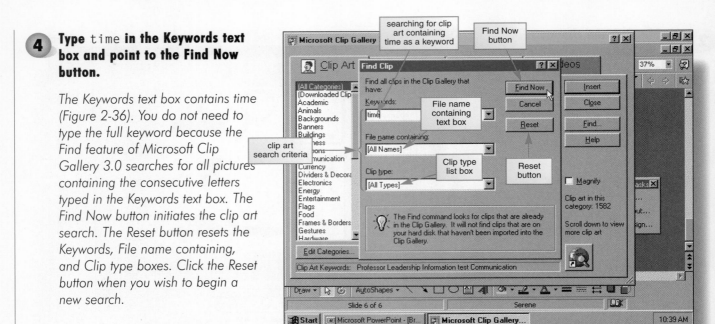

FIGURE 2-36

5 **Click the Find Now button. If necessary, scroll to display the clip art with the keywords, Timeline Schedule Clock Wait Procrastinate. Click the clock clip art to select it.**

The Microsoft Clip Gallery searches for all pictures that contain time in the keywords. All pictures that contain the keyword display in the Pictures box (Figure 2-37). The picture of a clock is selected. The selected category changes to Results of Last Find. Timeline Schedule Clock Wait Procrastinate displays at the bottom of the Microsoft Clip Gallery 3.0 dialog box as the keywords of the selected picture. Your selected picture may be different depending on the clip art installed on your computer.

FIGURE 2-37

6 **Click the Insert button.**

The selected picture is inserted into the clip art placeholder on Slide 6 (Figure 2-38). PowerPoint automatically sizes the picture to best fit the placeholder. In this instance, the picture is taller than it is wide (portrait orientation), so PowerPoint sizes the picture to fit the height of the placeholder. When a picture is in landscape orientation, PowerPoint sizes the picture to fit the width of the placeholder.

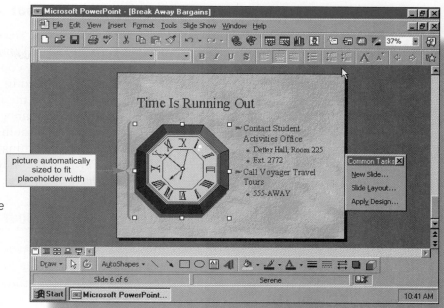

FIGURE 2-38

In addition to the clip art images in Microsoft Clip Gallery 3.0, other sources for clip art include retailers specializing in computer software, the Internet, bulletin board systems, and online information systems. Some popular online information systems are The Microsoft Network, America Online, CompuServe, and Prodigy. A **bulletin board system** is a computer system that allows users to communicate with each other and share files. Microsoft has created a special page on their World Wide Web site where you can add new clips to the Clip Gallery.

Besides clip art, you can insert pictures into your presentation. These may include scanned photographs, line art, and artwork from compact discs. To insert a picture into a presentation, the picture must be saved in a format that PowerPoint can recognize. Table 2-3 identifies some of the formats PowerPoint recognizes.

PowerPoint converts pictures saved in the formats listed in Table 2-3 by using filters. These filters are shipped with the PowerPoint installation software and must be installed before PowerPoint can properly convert files.

Table 2-3

FORMAT	FILE EXTENSION
AutoCAD Format 2-D	*.dxf
Computer Graphics Metafile	*.cgm
CorelDRAW	*.cdr
Encapsulated PostScript	*.eps
Graphics Interchange Format	*.gif
JPEG File Interchange Format	*.jpg
Kodak Photo CD	*.pcd
Macintosh PICT	*.pct
Micrografx Designer/Draw	*.drw
PC Paintbrush	*.pcx
Portable Network Graphics	*.png
Tagged Image File Format	*.tif
Targa	*.tga
Windows Bitmaps	*.bmp, .rle, .dib
Windows Enhanced Metafile	*.emf
Windows Metafile	*.wmf
WordPerfect Graphics	*.wpg

More *About* **Clip Art**

Clip art serves a purpose in a presentation – it conveys a message. Clip art should contribute to the understandability of the slide. It should not be used decoratively. Before adding clip art to a presentation, ask yourself: "Does the clip art convey a message or support the slide topic?" If the answer is yes, put the clip art on the slide.

Inserting Clip Art on a Slide without a Clip Art Placeholder

PowerPoint does not require you to use an AutoLayout containing a clip art placeholder to add clip art to a slide. You can insert clip art on any slide regardless of its slide layout. On Slide 3, you are adding a picture of a sailboat to illustrate the type of sailing vessel used in The Stargazer vacation package. Recall that the slide layout on Slide 3 is the Bulleted List slide layout. Because the Bulleted List AutoLayout does not contain a clip art placeholder, you click the Insert Clip Art button on the Standard toolbar to start Microsoft Clip Gallery 3.0. The picture for which you are searching is a sailing ship. Its keywords are Performance Ship Navigate. Perform the following steps to insert the picture of a ship on a slide that does not have a clip art placeholder.

TO INSERT CLIP ART ON A SLIDE WITHOUT A CLIP ART PLACEHOLDER

1 Drag the scroll box on the vertical scroll bar until Slide 3, titled The Stargazer, displays in the slide indicator.

2 Click the Insert Clip Art button on the Standard toolbar (Figure 2-32 on page PP 2.28).

3 Click the Find button. When the Find Clip dialog box displays, type navigate in the Keywords text box. Click the Find Now button.

4 If necessary, when the Microsoft Clip Gallery 3.0 dialog box displays the results, click the down arrow on the Pictures box scroll bar until the sailboat displays. If the sailboat is not installed on your computer, see your instructor for an appropriate replacement picture.

5 Double-click the picture of the sailboat that has the keywords Performance Ship Navigate.

The sailboat displays on Slide 3 (Figure 2-39). A selection box indicates the clip art is selected.

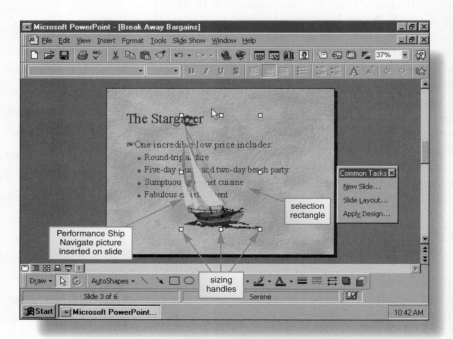

FIGURE 2-39

Moving Clip Art

After you insert clip art on a slide, you may want to reposition it. The picture of the sailboat on Slide 3 overlays the bulleted list. Moving the picture to the lower-right corner of the slide places the sailboat away from the text. Because you want to align the sailboat mast under the letter b in the word beach on the second heading level 2, you first move the picture and then change its size. You change the size of the sailboat later in this project. Perform the steps below to move the sailboat to the lower-right corner of the slide.

Steps **To Move Clip Art**

1 If the picture of the sailboat is not already selected, use the mouse pointer to point to the sailboat and then click.

2 Press and hold down the left mouse button. Drag the picture of the sailboat past the bottom of the slide and then to the right until the top-left corner of the dotted box aligns below the b in beach. Release the left mouse button.

When you drag an object, a dotted box displays. The dotted box indicates the new position of the object. When you release the left mouse button, the picture of the sailboat displays in the new location (Figure 2-40). Sizing handles appear at the corners and along the edges of the selection box.

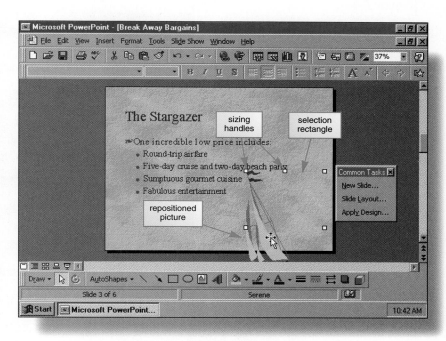

FIGURE 2-40

Changing the Size of Clip Art

Sometimes it is necessary to change the size of clip art. For example, on Slide 3, the sailboat displays off the slide. In order to make the picture fit onto the slide, you reduce its size. To change the size of a clip art picture by an exact percentage, use the **Format Picture command**. The Format Picture dialog box contains five sheets with several options for formatting a picture. The **Size sheet** contains options for changing the size of a picture. You either enter the exact height and width in the Size and rotate area, or enter the height and width as a percentage of

---

More *About*
Clip Art

When used appropriately, clip art reduces misconceptions. If a presentation consists of words alone, the audience creates its own mental picture. The mental picture created may be different from the concept you are trying to convey. The audience better understands the concept when a graphic is included.

Other Ways

1. Select clip art, press arrow keys to move to new position

More *About*
Sizing Objects

The Preview button in the Format Picture dialog box allows you to check the object's new size without applying it. When you want to make an object bigger, increase the number in the Height box or the Width box. To make an object smaller, decrease the number.

the original picture in the Scale area. When the **Lock aspect ratio check box** displays a check mark, the height and width settings change to maintain the aspect ratio of the original picture. **Aspect ratio** is the relationship between the height and width of an object. For example, a picture 3 inches high by 5 inches wide scaled to fifty percent would become 1½ inches high by 2½ inches wide. Perform the following steps to reduce the size of the sailboat.

Steps **To Change the Size of Clip Art**

① **Right-click the sailboat picture. When the shortcut menu displays, point to Format Picture (Figure 2-41).**

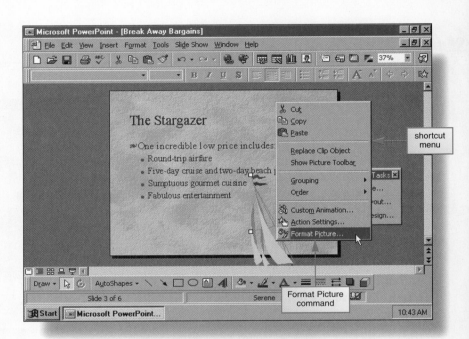

FIGURE 2-41

② **Click Format Picture. If necessary, when the Format Picture dialog box displays, click the Size tab.**

The Format Picture dialog box displays the Size sheet (Figure 2-42). The Height and Width text boxes in the Scale area display the current percentage of the sailboat picture, 100. Check marks display in the Lock aspect ratio and Relative to original picture size check boxes.

FIGURE 2-42

3 **Click the Height box down arrow in the Scale area until 70 displays. Then point to the OK button.**

Both the Height and Width text boxes in the Scale area display 70% (Figure 2-43). PowerPoint automatically changes the Height and Width text boxes in the Size and rotate area to reflect changes in the Scale area.

FIGURE 2-43

4 **Click the OK button.**

PowerPoint displays the reduced sailboat picture and closes the Format Picture dialog box (Figure 2-44).

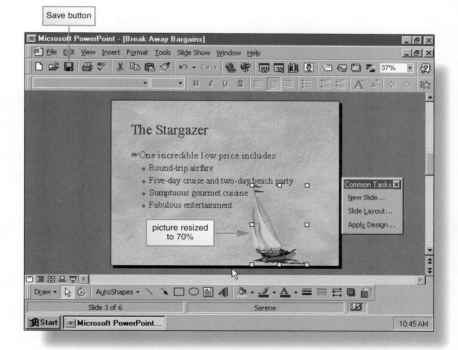

FIGURE 2-44

*Other**Ways***

1. Click clip art object, on Format menu click Picture, click Size tab, click Height box up or down arrows in Scale area, click OK

2. Press ALT+O, press I, press arrow keys to select Size tab, press TAB to select Height text box in Scale area, press up or down arrow keys to increase or decrease size, press ENTER

Saving the Presentation Again

To preserve the work completed this far, save the presentation again.

TO SAVE A PRESENTATION

1 Click the Save button on the Standard toolbar.

The changes made to the presentation after the previous save are saved on a floppy disk.

A default setting in PowerPoint allows for **fast saves**, which saves only the changes made since the last time you saved. If you want to **full save** a copy of the complete presentation, on the menu bar click Tools, click Options on the Tools menu, click the Save tab and then remove the check mark in the Allow fast saves check box by clicking the check box. Then click the OK button.

Adding a Header and Footer to Outline Pages

A printout of the presentation outline often is used as an audience handout. Distributing a copy of the outline provides the audience with paper on which to write notes or comments. Another benefit of distributing a copy of the outline is to help the audience see the text on the slides when lighting is poor or the room is too large. To help identify the source of the printed outline, add a descriptive header and footer.

Using the Notes and Handouts Sheet to Add Headers and Footers

Add headers and footers to outline pages by clicking the Notes and Handouts sheet in the Header and Footer dialog box and entering the information you wish to print. Perform the following steps to add the current date, a header, the page number, and a footer to the printed outline.

Steps **To Use the Notes and Handouts Sheet to Add Headers and Footers**

1 Click View on the menu bar.
Point to Header and Footer
(Figure 2-45).

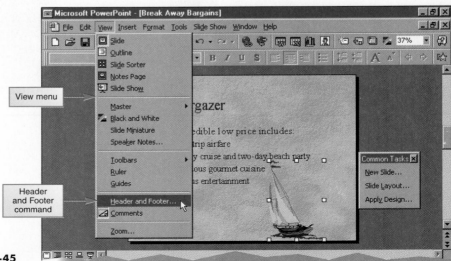

FIGURE 2-45

2 **Click Header and Footer. If necessary, click the Notes and Handouts tab.**

The Header and Footer dialog box displays the Notes and Handouts sheet (Figure 2-46). Check marks display in the Date and time, Header, Page number, and Footer check boxes. The Fixed option button is selected.

FIGURE 2-46

3 **Click the Update automatically option button. Click the Header text box. Type** Break Away Bargains **in the Header text box. Type** Voyager Travel Tours **in the Footer text box. Then point to the Apply to All button (Figure 2-47).**

4 **Click the Apply to All button.**

PowerPoint applies the header and footer text to the outline, closes the Header and Footer dialog box, and displays Slide 3. You cannot see header and footer text until you print the outline.

FIGURE 2-47

Checking the Presentation for Spelling and Style Errors

Now that the individual slide changes have been made, you should run Style Checker to identify errors in your presentation. Recall from Project 1 that Style Checker identifies possible errors in spelling, visual clarity, case, and end punctuation. Perform the following steps to run Style Checker.

TO RUN STYLE CHECKER

1 Click Tools on the menu bar.
2 Click Style Checker.
3 When the Style Checker dialog box displays, click the Case and end punctuation check box.
4 Click the Start button.

5 Correct spelling errors and ignore correct spellings of words not located in the standard dictionary.
6 If Style Checker lists visual clarity inconsistencies in the Style Checker Summary dialog box, write the slide number and the message on a sheet of paper.
7 When the Microsoft PowerPoint dialog box displays, press the OK button.

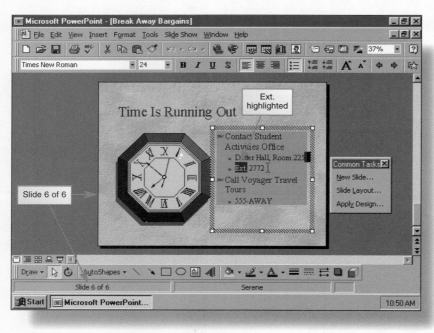

FIGURE 2-48

PowerPoint closes Style Checker and displays the slide containing the last word not in the dictionaries, Slide 6 (Figure 2-48). Ext., the abbreviation for extension, is not found in the standard dictionary and therefore displays highlighted.

This presentation contains no visual clarity inconsistencies. If Style Checker identifies visual clarity inconsistencies, review the steps for correcting the identified slide. Then make the appropriate corrections. For more information about Style Checker, see page PP 1.41 in Project 1.

Adding Animation Effects

PowerPoint provides many animation effects to make your slide show presentation look professional. In this project you use slide transition and custom animation. **Slide transition effects** define special effects for progressing from one slide to the next in a slide show. **Custom animation effects** define animation, sound effects, and timing for objects on a slide. The following pages discuss each of these animation effects in detail.

Adding Slide Transitions to a Slide Show

PowerPoint allows you to control the way you advance from one slide to the next by adding slide transitions to an on-screen slide show. Slide transitions are visual effects that display when you move one slide off the screen and bring the next one on. PowerPoint has 46 different slide transitions. The name of the slide transition characterizes the visual effect that displays. For example, the slide transition effect, Split Vertical In, displays the next slide by covering the previous slide with two vertical boxes moving toward the center of the screen until the two boxes meet. The effect is similar to closing draw drapes over a window.

PowerPoint requires you to select at least one slide before applying slide transition effects. In this presentation, you apply slide transition effects to all slides except the title slide. Because Slide 6 already is selected, you must select Slides 2 through 5. The technique used to select more than one slide is the **SHIFT+click technique**. To perform the SHIFT+click technique, press and hold down the SHIFT key as you click each slide. After you click the slides to which you want to add animation effects, release the SHIFT key.

In the Break Away Bargains presentation, you wish to display the Box Out slide transition effect between slides. That is, all slides begin stacked on top of one another, like a deck of cards. As you click the mouse to view the next slide, the new slide enters the screen by starting at the center of the slide and exploding out toward the edges of the slide while maintaining a box shape. Perform the following steps to apply the Box Out slide transition effect to the Break Away Bargains presentation.

Steps **To Add Slide Transitions to a Slide Show**

1 **Click the Slide Sorter View button on the View Button Bar at the bottom of the Microsoft PowerPoint – [Break Away Bargains] screen.**

PowerPoint displays the presentation in slide sorter view (Figure 2-49). Slide 6 is selected. Slide 6 currently does not have a slide transition effect as noted in the Slide Transition Effects list box on the Slide Sorter toolbar.

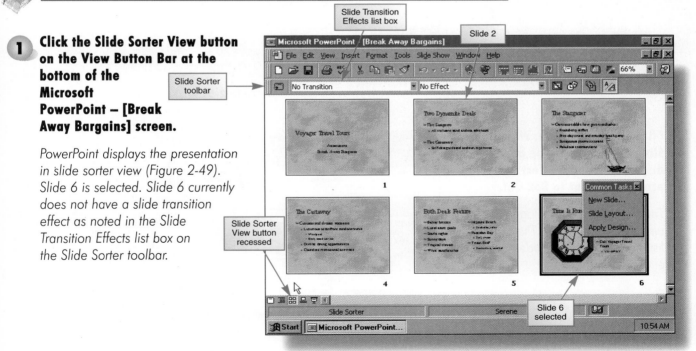

FIGURE 2-49

2 **Press and hold down the SHIFT key and click Slide 2, Slide 3, Slide 4, and Slide 5. Release the SHIFT key.**

Slides 2 through 6 are selected, as indicated by the heavy border around each slide (Figure 2-50).

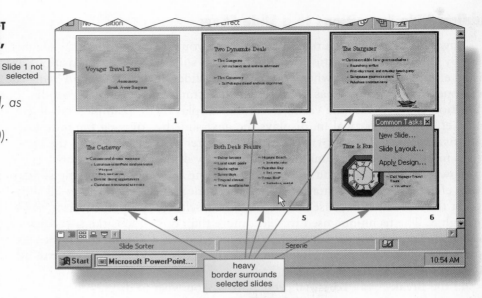

FIGURE 2-50

3 **Point to Slide 5 and right-click. When a shortcut menu displays, point to Slide Transition (Figure 2-51).**

FIGURE 2-51

4 **Click Slide Transition. When the Slide Transition dialog box displays, click the Effect box arrow and point to Box Out.**

The Slide Transition dialog box displays (Figure 2-52). The Effect list displays available slide transition effects.

FIGURE 2-52

5 **Click Box Out.**

The Slide Transition Effect preview demonstrates the Box Out effect (Figure 2-53). To see the demonstration again, click the picture in the Slide Transition Effect preview.

FIGURE 2-53

6 **Click the Apply button.**

PowerPoint displays the presentation in slide sorter view (Figure 2-54). A slide transition icon displays under each selected slide, which indicates that slide transition effects have been added to those slides. The current slide transition effect, Box Out, displays in the Slide Transition Effects box.

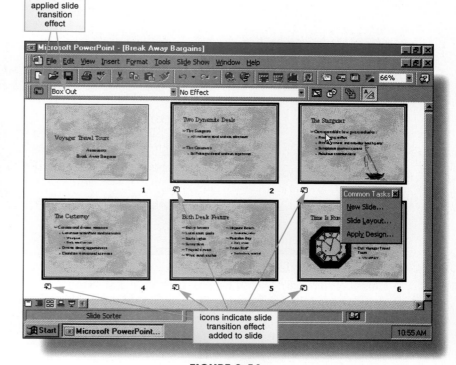

FIGURE 2-54

To apply slide transition effects to every slide in the presentation, select a slide, choose the desired slide transition effect and then click the Apply to All button in the Slide Transition dialog box.

To remove slide transition effects when displaying the presentation in slide sorter view, select the slides to which slide transition effects are applied, right-click one of the selected slides, click the Effect box arrow, select No Transition, and then click the Apply button.

OtherWays

1. Select slides, right-click selected slide, click Slide Transition, click Effect box arrow, select slide transition effect, click Apply button

2. Select slides, on Slide Show menu click Slide Transition, click Effect box arrow, select slide transition effect, click Apply button

Slide Sorter Toolbar

PowerPoint provides you with multiple methods for accomplishing most tasks. Generally, the fastest method is to right-click to display a shortcut menu. Another frequently used method is to click a toolbar button. For example, you can apply slide transition effects by clicking the Slide Transition Effects list box on the Slide Sorter toolbar.

The Slide Sorter toolbar displays only when you are in slide sorter view. It displays beneath the Standard toolbar, in place of the Formatting toolbar. The Slide Sorter toolbar contains tools to help you quickly add animation effects to your slide show. Table 2-4 explains the function of the buttons and boxes on the Slide Sorter toolbar.

Table 2-4		
BUTTON/BOX	*BUTTON/BOX NAME*	*FUNCTION*
	Slide Transition	Displays the Slide Transition dialog box, which lists special effects used for slide changes during a slide show.
Box Out	Slide Transition Effects	Displays a list of slide transition effects. Selecting a slide transition effect from the list applies it to the selected slide(s) and demonstrates it in the preview box.
	Text Preset Animation	Displays a list of text animation effects.
	Hide Slide	Excludes a slide from the presentation without deleting it.
	Rehearse Timings	Runs your slide show in rehearsal mode, in which you can set or change the timing of your electronic slide show.
	Summary Slide	Creates a bulleted list slide from the titles of the slides selected in slide sorter view or outline view, and then inserts that slide in front of the first selected slide.
	Show Formatting	Displays or hides character formatting attributes in outline view. In slide sorter view, switches between showing all text and graphics on each slide and displaying titles only.

The Box Out slide transition effect has been applied to the presentation. The next step in creating this slide show is to add animation effects to individual slides.

Applying Animation Effects to Bulleted Slides

Animation effects can be applied to text as well as to objects, such as clip art. When you apply animation effects to bulleted text, you progressively disclose each bulleted paragraph. As a result, you build the slide, paragraph by paragraph during the running of a slide show to control the flow of information. PowerPoint has 55 custom animation effects and the capability to dim the paragraphs already displaying on the slide when the new paragraph is displayed.

More *About* Custom Animation Effects

The After animation list box contains eight colors and four commands controlling what happens after animation effects display. By default, Don't Dim is selected. To change the color of the previous bulleted text, click one of the eight listed colors from the applied design template. To display additional colors, click More Colors. To hide text as soon as its animation effect displays, click Hide after Animation. To hide text when you click the mouse, click Hide on Next Mouse click.

The next step is to apply the Zoom In From Screen Center animation effect to Slides 2, 3, 4, 5, and 6 in the Break Away Bargains presentation. All slides, except the title slide will have the Zoom In From Screen Center animation effect. Recall from Project 1, that when you need to make a change that affects all slides, make the change to the slide master. Perform the following steps to apply animation effects to the bulleted paragraphs in this presentation.

More *About* **Animating Objects**

Used sparingly, animated objects add interest to a presentation. Overused animated objects are distracting and minimize the message of the presentation.

Steps **To Use the Slide Master to Apply Animation Effects to All Bulleted Slides**

1 Press and hold down the SHIFT key and then click the Slide Master button on the View Button Bar.

The slide master displays. If necessary, drag the Master toolbar onto the screen as shown in Figure 2-55.

FIGURE 2-55

2 Right-click the slide master. When a shortcut menu displays, point to Custom Animation (Figure 2-56).

FIGURE 2-56

3 Click Custom Animation. If necessary, when the Custom Animation dialog box displays, click the Effects tab.

The Custom Animation dialog box displays (Figure 2-57).

FIGURE 2-57

4 Click the Entry animation and sound box arrow. Scroll down the list until Zoom In From Screen Center displays. Then point to Zoom In From Screen Center (Figure 2-58).

FIGURE 2-58

5 **Click Zoom In From Screen Center. Then point to the Grouped by level paragraphs box arrow.**

The Entry animation and sound list box displays Zoom In From Screen Center (Figure 2-59). A check mark displays in the Grouped by level paragraphs list box.

FIGURE 2-59

6 **Click the Grouped by level paragraphs box arrow and then point to 3rd.**

3rd is highlighted in the Grouped by level paragraphs list (Figure 2-60).

FIGURE 2-60

7 Click 3rd and then click the OK button.

PowerPoint applies the animation effects to the slide master, closes the Custom Animation dialog box, and then displays the slide master (Figure 2-61).

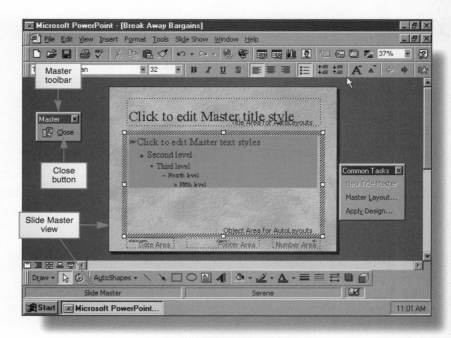

FIGURE 2-61

8 Click the Close button on the Master toolbar.

PowerPoint closes the slide master and returns to slide sorter view (Figure 2-62).

FIGURE 2-62

OtherWays

1. On View menu point to Master, click Slide Master, on Slide Show menu click Custom Animation, click Effects tab, click Entry animation and sound box arrow, click an animation effect, click Grouped by level paragraphs box arrow, click appropriate paragraph level, click OK

The Zoom In From Screen Center animation effect displays for each bulleted paragraph on paragraph level 1, 2, or 3 on Slides 2 through 6 during the running of an electronic slide show.

To remove animation effects from the slide master, press and hold down the SHIFT key, click the Slide View button, release the SHIFT key, right-click the slide master, click Custom Animation, click the Entry animation and sound box arrow, click No effect in the Entry animation and sound list, click the OK button, and then click the Close button on the Master toolbar.

Animating Clip Art Objects

Animating a clip art object takes several steps. First display the slide containing the clip art in slide view (Slide 3 in this project). Then select the clip art object and display the Custom Animation dialog box. Next, select the animation effect. Finally, apply the animation effect as described in the following sections.

Displaying a Slide in Slide View

PowerPoint requires you to display a slide in slide view before adding animation effects to clip art. Before continuing with the animation of the sailboat on Slide 3, display the slide in slide view as described in the following step.

TO DISPLAY A SLIDE IN SLIDE VIEW

① Double-click Slide 3.

Slide 3 displays in slide view.

With Slide 3 displaying in slide view, you are ready to animate the sailboat clip art as explained in the next section.

Animating Clip Art

PowerPoint allows you to animate clip art by selecting an animation effect from a list. Because Slide 3 features The Stargazer vacation package, you want to emphasize the slow, gentle cruise by displaying the sailboat slowly across the bottom of the slide. Perform the steps on the next page to add the Crawl From Right animation effect to the sailboat on Slide 3.

More *About*
Animating Clip Art

When animating a clip art object, consider adding sound effects to communicate a concept. Select an appropriate sound from the list in the Entry animation and sound list box on the Effects sheet in the Custom Animation dialog box.

Steps To Animate Clip Art

1 **Right-click the sailboat clip art object and then click Custom Animation on the shortcut menu. If necessary, click the Effects tab.**

The Custom Animation dialog box displays (Figure 2-63). The sailboat is selected in the preview box. Text 2, the bulleted list on Slide 3, is listed in the Animation order box because of the text animation applied to the slide master earlier in this project.

FIGURE 2-63

2 **Click the Entry animation and sound box arrow. Scroll down the list until Crawl From Right displays and then point to Crawl From Right (Figure 2-64).**

FIGURE 2-64

3 **Click Crawl From Right and then point to the OK button.**

Crawl From Right displays in the Entry animation and sound list box (Figure 2-65). Object 3, the sailboat, displays as number 2 in the Animation order box.

FIGURE 2-65

4 **Click the OK button.**

PowerPoint applies Crawl From Right animation effects to the clip art and closes the Custom Animation dialog box (Figure 2-66). Slide 3 displays in slide view.

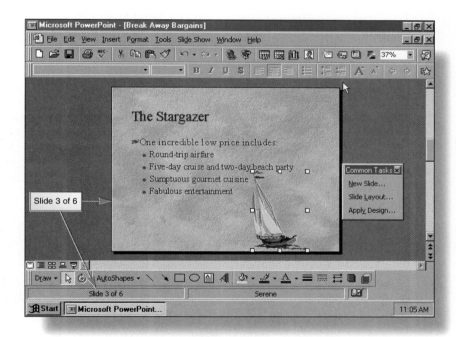

FIGURE 2-66

During the running of the slide show, the sailboat slowly will move across the bottom of the slide as if it were sailing across water. The sailboat will begin moving from the right side of the slide and stop at the position where it was placed when you inserted the sailboat onto Slide 3.

Other Ways

1. Click clip art, on Slide Show menu click Custom Animation, click Effects tab, click Entry animation and sound box arrow, click desired animation effect, click OK

2. Press TAB until clip art is selected, press ALT+D, press M, press right arrow key to select Effects tab, press down arrow until desired animation effect selected, press ENTER

More *About*
Animating a Title Slide

Choose title slide animation effects carefully. Choose traditional effects, such as Fly From Left, when addressing a serious topic. Choose flashy, fun animation effects, such as Spiral, for lighter, less serious topics.

Formatting and Animating a Title Slide

The title slide of every presentation should seize the attention of the audience. In order to excite the audience with the Break Away Bargains presentation, you want to intensify the subtitle object on the title slide. First, you italicize the word Announces and then increase the size of the words in the subtitle, Break Away Bargains. Finally, you add animation effects to the subtitle.

The first step is to display Slide 1 and then format the title slide subtitle. Perform the following steps to format the subtitle object on Slide 1.

TO CHANGE TEXT FONT STYLE TO ITALIC AND INCREASE FONT SIZE

1. Drag the vertical scroll box to display Slide 1.
2. Double-click the word, Announces, and then click the Italic button on the Formatting toolbar.
3. Triple-click the paragraph, Break Away Bargains.
4. Click the Increase Font Size button three times until 44 displays in the Font Size list box on the Formatting toolbar.

The formatted subtitle on Slide 1 displays (Figure 2-67). The word, Announces, displays the italic font style and the paragraph, Break Away Bargains, displays in font size 44.

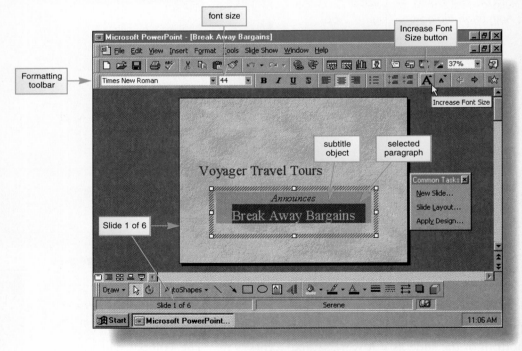

FIGURE 2-67

The next step is to apply the Spiral animation effect to the subtitle text. Perform the following steps to animate the paragraphs in the subtitle object on Slide 1.

TO ANIMATE TEXT

1. Right-click the subtitle object and then click Custom Animation on the shortcut menu.
2. If necessary, click the Effects tab in the Custom Animation dialog box.
3. Click the Entry animation and sound box arrow.
4. Scroll down the list until Spiral displays and then click Spiral.
5. Click the OK button.

The subtitle object, Text 2, displays in the Animation order box and is selected in the preview box. Spiral displays in the Entry animation and sound list box. By default, the subtitle text is grouped by first level paragraphs. PowerPoint applies the animation effect, closes the Custom Animation dialog box, and then displays Slide 1.

Animation effects are complete for this presentation. You now are ready to review the presentation in slide show view.

Saving the Presentation Again

The presentation is complete. Save the finished presentation on a floppy disk before running the slide show.

TO SAVE A PRESENTATION ON A FLOPPY DISK

1. Click the Save button on the Standard toolbar.

PowerPoint saves the presentation on your floppy disk by saving the changes made to the presentation since the last save.

Running an Animated Slide Show

Project 1 introduced you to using slide show view to look at your presentation one slide at a time. This project introduces you to running a slide show with slide transition effects and text and object animation effects. When you run a slide show with slide transition effects, PowerPoint displays the slide transition effect when you click the mouse button to advance to the next slide. When a slide has text animation effects, each paragraph level displays as determined by the animation settings. Animated clip art objects display the selected animation effect in the sequence established in the Custom Animation dialog box. Perform the steps on the next page to run the animated Break Away Bargains slide show.

Steps **To Run an Animated Slide Show**

1 **With Slide 1 displaying, click the Slide Show button on the View Button Bar. When Slide 1 displays in slide show view, click the slide anywhere except on the Popup Menu buttons.**

PowerPoint first displays the Serene design template and then displays the title slide title object, Voyager Travel Tours (Figure 2-68). Recall the Popup Menu buttons display when you move the mouse pointer during a slide show.

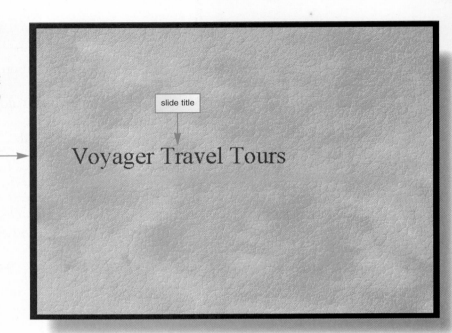

FIGURE 2-68

2 **Click the slide anywhere except on the Popup Menu buttons.**

PowerPoint displays the first heading level 1 subtitle paragraph using the Spiral animation effect (Figure 2-69).

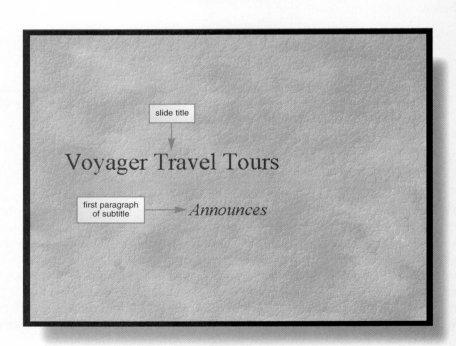

FIGURE 2-69

3 **Click the slide anywhere except on the Popup Menu buttons.**

PowerPoint displays the second heading level 1 subtitle paragraph beneath the first heading level 1 subtitle paragraph. PowerPoint again uses the Spiral animation effect (Figure 2-70).

4 **Click the slide anywhere except on the Popup Menu buttons. Continue clicking to finish running the slide show and return to slide sorter view.**

Each time a new slide displays, PowerPoint first displays the Box Out slide transition effect and then displays only the slide title. Then, PowerPoint builds each slide based on the animation settings. When you click the slide after the last paragraph displays on the last slide of the presentation, PowerPoint exits slide show view and returns to slide sorter view.

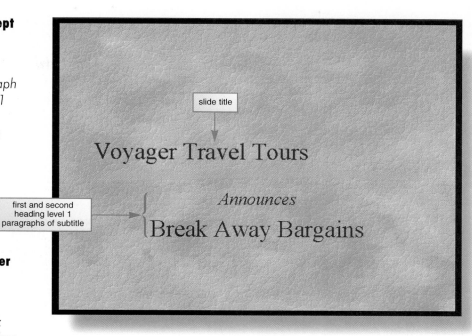

FIGURE 2-70

Other Ways

1. On Slide Show menu click View Show, click slide until slide show ends
2. Press ALT+D, press V, press ENTER until slide show ends

Now that the presentation is complete and you have tested the animation effects, the last step is to print the presentation outline and slides.

Printing in Outline View

When you click the Print button on the Standard toolbar, PowerPoint prints a hard copy of the presentation component last selected in the Print what box in the Print dialog box. To be certain to print the component you want, such as the presentation outline, use the Print command located on the File menu. When the Print dialog box displays, you can select the appropriate presentation component in the Print what box. The next two sections explain how to use the Print command to print the presentation outline and the presentation slides.

Printing an Outline

During the development of a lengthy presentation, it often is easier to review your outline in print rather than on-screen. Printing your outline also is useful for audience handouts or when your supervisor or instructor wants to review your subject matter before you fully develop your presentation.

Recall that the Print dialog box displays print options. When you wish to print your outline, select Outline View in the Print what list located in the Print dialog box. The outline, however, prints as last viewed in outline view. This means that you must select the Zoom setting to display the outline text as you wish it to print. If you are uncertain of the Zoom setting, you should return to outline view and review it prior to printing. Perform the following steps to print an outline from slide view.

Steps To Print an Outline

1 **Ready the printer according to the printer manufacturer's instructions. Click File on the menu bar and then point to Print.**

The File menu displays (Figure 2-71).

FIGURE 2-71

2 **Click Print.**

The Print dialog box displays (Figure 2-72).

FIGURE 2-72

3 **Click the Print what box arrow and then point to Outline View.**

Outline View displays highlighted in the Print what list (Figure 2-73).

FIGURE 2-73

4 **Click Outline View and then point to the OK button (Figure 2-74).**

FIGURE 2-74

5 **Click the OK button.**

PowerPoint momentarily displays a message in the Print Status dialog box explaining that the outline is printing as last viewed (Figure 2-75). To cancel the print request, click the Cancel button.

FIGURE 2-75

6 **When the printer stops, retrieve the printout of the outline (Figure 2-76).**

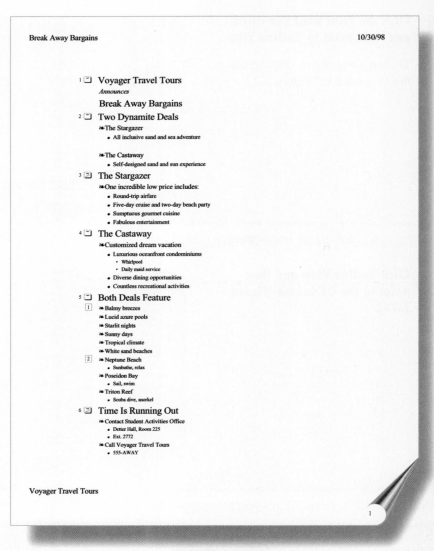

FIGURE 2-76

You may select the Print command from the File menu while in any view except slide show view.

Printing Presentation Slides

After correcting errors, you will want to print a final copy of your presentation. If you made any changes to your presentation since your last save, be sure to save your presentation before you print.

Perform the following steps to print the presentation.

TO PRINT PRESENTATION SLIDES

1 Ready the printer according to the printer manufacturer's instructions.

2 Click File on the menu bar and then click Print.

3 When the Print dialog box displays, click the Print what box arrow.

4 Click Slides (without animations).

5 Click the OK button. When the printer stops, retrieve the slide printouts.

The printouts should look like the slides in Figure 2-77.

FIGURE 2-77a

FIGURE 2-77c

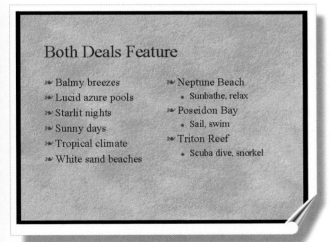

FIGURE 2-77e

FIGURE 2-77b

FIGURE 2-77d

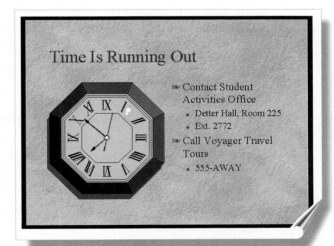

FIGURE 2-77f

The Print what list in the Print dialog box contains options for printing two, three, or six slide images per page. These options are labeled as Handouts (2 slides per page), Handouts (3 slides per page), and Handouts (6 slides per page). Printing handouts is useful for reviewing a presentation because you print several slides on one page. Additionally, many businesses distribute handouts of the slide show before a presentation so the attendees can refer to a copy.

Saving and Quitting PowerPoint

If you made any changes to your presentation since your last save, you should save it again before quitting PowerPoint. For more details on quitting PowerPoint, refer to page PP 1.38 in Project 1. Perform the following steps to save changes to the presentation and quit PowerPoint.

TO SAVE CHANGES AND QUIT POWERPOINT

1 Click the Close button on the title bar.

2 If prompted, click the Yes button in the Microsoft PowerPoint dialog box.

PowerPoint saves any changes made to the presentation since the last save and then quits PowerPoint.

Project Summary

Project 2 introduced you to outline view, clip art, and animation effects. You created a slide presentation in outline view where you entered all the text in the form of an outline. You arranged the text using the Promote and Demote buttons. Once your outline was complete, you changed slide layouts and added clip art to a clip art placeholder. After adding clip art to another slide without using a clip art placeholder, you moved and sized the picture. You added slide transition effects and text animation effects. Then you applied animation effects to clip art. You learned how to run an animated slide show demonstrating slide transition and animation effects. Finally, you printed the presentation outline and slides using the Print command.

What You Should Know

Having completed this project, you now should be able to perform the following tasks:

▶ Add a Blank Line *(PP 2.21)*
▶ Add a Slide in Outline View *(PP 2.12)*
▶ Add Slide Transitions to a Slide Show *(PP 2.39)*
▶ Animate Clip Art *(PP 2.48)*
▶ Animate Text *(PP 2.51)*
▶ Change Slide Layout *(PP 2.23)*
▶ Change the Size of Clip Art *(PP 2.34)*
▶ Change the Slide Layout to Clip Art & Text *(PP 2.27)*
▶ Change the View to Outline View *(PP 2.8)*
▶ Change the View to Slide Sorter View *(PP 2.19)*
▶ Change the View to Slide View *(PP 2.20)*
▶ Change Text Font Style to Italic and Increase Font Size *(PP 2.50)*
▶ Create a Closing Slide in Outline View *(PP 2.18)*
▶ Create a Multi-level Bulleted List Slide in Outline View *(PP 2.13)*
▶ Create a Second Subordinate Slide *(PP 2.16)*
▶ Create a Slide with Multiple Text Objects in Outline View *(PP 2.17)*
▶ Create a Subordinate Slide *(PP 2.15)*

▶ Create a Title Slide in Outline View *(PP 2.11)*
▶ Display a Slide in Slide View *(PP 2.47)*
▶ Insert Clip Art into a Clip Art Placeholder *(PP 2.28)*
▶ Insert Clip Art on a Slide without a Clip Art Placeholder *(PP 2.32)*
▶ Move Clip Art *(PP 2.33)*
▶ Move Text *(PP 2.25)*
▶ Print an Outline *(PP 2.54)*
▶ Print Presentation Slides *(PP 2.56)*
▶ Run an Animated Slide Show *(PP 2.52)*
▶ Run Style Checker *(PP 2.38)*
▶ Save a Presentation *(PP 2.19, 2.36)*
▶ Save a Presentation on a Floppy Disk *(PP 2.51)*
▶ Save Changes and Quit PowerPoint *(PP 2.58)*
▶ Start a New Presentation *(PP 2.7)*
▶ Use the Notes and Handouts Sheet to Add Headers and Footers *(PP 2.36)*
▶ Use the Slide Master to Apply Animation Effects to All Bulleted Slides *(PP 2.43)*

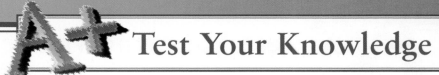

Test Your Knowledge

1 True/False

Instructions: Circle T if the statement is true or F if the statement is false.

T   F   1. An outline is a summary of thoughts presented as headings, subheadings, and pictures.

T   F   2. Graphic objects, such as pictures, graphs, and tables, do not display in outline view.

T   F   3. When in outline view, Microsoft PowerPoint displays the current slide in black-and-white view so you can see how the slide will look in both slide view and slide show view.

T   F   4. Each time you click the Demote button the selected paragraph moves down one level in the outline hierarchy.

T   F   5. Resolution is the number of pixels per unit of measurement displaying on your computer monitor.

T   F   6. The slide that gracefully ends a presentation is the ending slide.

T   F   7. Microsoft Clip Gallery 3.0 accompanies Microsoft Office 97 and is a tool that allows you to insert clip art, pictures, audio clips, and video clips into Microsoft Office documents.

T   F   8. Right-clicking a clip art placeholder activates instructions to open the Microsoft Clip Gallery 3.0.

T   F   9. PowerPoint inserts clip art only into clip art placeholders.

T   F   10. Double-clicking a slide miniature in slide sorter view displays that slide in slide view.

2 Multiple Choice

Instructions: Circle the correct response.

1. Outline view provides a quick, easy way to _____.
   a. add animation effects
   b. create a presentation
   c. insert clip art
   d. display slide miniatures

2. An outline _____.
   a. is a summary of thoughts
   b. uses indentation to establish a hierarchy to denote levels of importance
   c. allows you to organize your thoughts in a structured format
   d. all of the above

3. When viewing a presentation in outline view, you know which slides contain graphic objects because _____.
   a. slide icons display blank when a slide contains graphics
   b. all graphics display in outline view
   c. slide icons display a small graphic when a slide contains graphics
   d. none of the above

(continued)

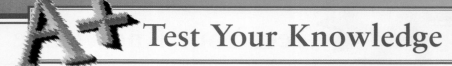

A+ Test Your Knowledge

Multiple Choice *(continued)*

4. In PowerPoint, a presentation outline begins with a title on _____.
   a. heading level 0
   b. heading level 1
   c. heading level 2
   d. none of the above

5. Clicking the _____ button moves selected text above the preceding displayed paragraph while maintaining its hierarchical heading level and text style.
   a. Promote
   b. Demote
   c. Move Up
   d. Move Down

6. Microsoft Clip Gallery 3.0 _____.
   a. is shared with PowerPoint and other Microsoft Office 97 applications
   b. combines topic-related images into categories
   c. is a tool that allows you to insert clip art, pictures, audio clips, and video clips into a presentation
   d. all of the above

7. The relationship between the height and width of an object is its _____.
   a. height-to-width ratio
   b. aspect ratio
   c. size
   d. scale

8. The animation effect that displays when one slide moves off the screen and another slide displays on the screen is _____.
   a. custom animation
   b. clip art animation
   c. text animation
   d. slide transition

9. The default PowerPoint setting that allows for saving only the changes made to a presentation since the last save is called a(n) _____.
   a. intermediate save
   b. full save
   c. fast save
   d. all of the above

10. Clicking the Print button on the Standard toolbar when displaying the presentation in outline view instructs PowerPoint to print the presentation in _____.
    a. outline view
    b. slide view
    c. slide sorter view
    d. the view last printed

Test Your Knowledge

3 Understanding a Microsoft PowerPoint Window in Outline View

Instructions:
Arrows in Figure 2-78 point to the major components of a Microsoft PowerPoint window in outline view. Identify the various parts of the window in the spaces provided.

FIGURE 2-78

4 Understanding the Custom Animation Dialog Box

Instructions: In Figure 2-79, arrows point to several of the components in the Custom Animation dialog box. Identify the various parts of the dialog box in the spaces provided.

FIGURE 2-79

Use Help

1 Learning More about PowerPoint

Instructions: Perform the following tasks using a computer.

1. If PowerPoint is not started already, start a new PowerPoint presentation and select any Auto-Layout. If necessary, click the Office Assistant to display the What would you like to do? box.
2. Type outline view in the What would you like to do? text box and then click the Search button. Click the topic, Ways to organize my content in outline view. When the Microsoft PowerPoint window displays, read the information, right-click within the dialog box, and click Print Topic. When the Print dialog box displays, click the OK button. Click the Help Topics button to return to the Help Topics: Microsoft PowerPoint dialog box. If necessary, click the Find tab.
3. Type outline in box 1. Double-click the Change the order of slides in a presentation topic displayed in box 3. When the Microsoft PowerPoint window displays, read and print the information. Click the Help Topics button to return to the Help Topics: Microsoft PowerPoint dialog box.
4. Scroll the topics listed in box 3 to display File formats for saving presentations. Double-click File formats for saving presentations. When the Microsoft PowerPoint window displays, read and print the information. Click the Close button to exit Help. Submit the printouts to your instructor.

2 Expanding on the Basics

Instructions: Use PowerPoint online Help to better understand the topics listed below. Begin each of the following by clicking the Office Assistant button on the Standard toolbar. If you cannot print the Help information, answer the question on a separate piece of paper.

1. When in outline view, how do you change the color of a bullet for all slides in a presentation?
2. How do you change the bullet character from a dot to an open file folder?
3. How do you add a period to the end of every paragraph in a list?
4. How do you replace one clip art picture in a slide with another picture?
5. How do you build a slide with a clip art image that appears to fly onto the slide?
6. How do you add sound to animation effects?
7. How do you change the order in which animated objects display on a slide?
8. What happens when you print slides using the Slides (with animations) option?

Apply Your Knowledge

1 Intensifying a Presentation by Applying a Design Template, Changing Slide Layout, Inserting Clip Art, and Applying Animation Effects

Instructions: Start PowerPoint. Open the presentation, Apply-2, from the PowerPoint folder on the Data Disk that accompanies this book. Perform the following tasks to change the presentation to look like Figure 2-80 on the next page.

1. Apply the Blush design template. Add the current date, slide number, and your name to the footer. Display the footer on all slides and on notes and handouts.

2. On Slide 1, insert one blank paragraph after the November 14, 1998 paragraph. Insert the runner clip art image shown in Figure 2-80 that has the keywords, Victory Performance Fast Invincible. Scale the clip art to 65% using the Format Picture command. Drag the runner clip art image to align the upper-left corner of the dotted box below the letter o in the word Triathlon, as shown in Figure 2-80. Apply the Zoom In From Screen Center custom animation effect to the clip art. Italicize the paragraph, Sponsored by:, and then decrease the font size to 24 points.

3. Go to Slide 3. Change the slide layout to 2 Column Text. Move the six male categories to the right column placeholder.

4. Go to Slide 4. Change the slide layout to Text & Clip Art. Insert the trophy clip art image shown in Figure 2-80 that has the keywords, Goal Success Reward Accomplishment Impress Trophy. Change the size of the trophy clip art image to 105%. Change the line spacing for the heading level 1 bullets to 0.75 lines before each paragraph.

5. Go to Slide 5. Change the slide layout to Clip Art & Text. Insert the directional post clip art image shown in Figure 2-80 that has the keywords, Direction Alternative Solution. Change the line spacing for the heading level 1 bullets to 1 line before each paragraph.

6. Add the Box Out slide transition effect to all slides except the title slide.

7. Save the presentation to a floppy disk using the file name, Southwestern Triathlon.

8. Print the presentation in black and white. Print the presentation outline.

9. Quit PowerPoint.

(continued)

Apply Your Knowledge

Intensifying a Presentation by Applying a Design Template, Changing Slide Layout, Inserting Clip Art, and Applying Animation Effects *(continued)*

FIGURE 2-80a

FIGURE 2-80b

FIGURE 2-80c

FIGURE 2-80d

FIGURE 2-80e

In the Lab

1 Adding Clip Art and Animation Effects to a Presentation Created in Outline View

Problem: You are enrolled in Psychology 401. Your professor assigns a research paper and requires you to present your findings during a five-minute presentation. Your topic is positive mental attitude. You create the outline shown in Figure 2-81 to prepare your presentation. You use the outline to create the slide show shown in Figure 2-82 on the next page. Because of your research findings, you create a unique closing slide.

Instructions: Perform the following tasks.

1. Create a new presentation using the high voltage design template.

2. Using the outline shown in Figure 2-81, create the title slide shown in Figure 2-82. Use your name instead of the name Chelsea Ihalainen. Increase the font size of your name to 36 points.

3. Using the outline in Figure 2-81, create the three bulleted list slides shown in Figure 2-82.

4. Change the slide layout on Slide 2 to Clip Art & Text. Using the clip art placeholder, insert the clip art shown in Figure 2-82 that has the keywords, Success Victory Accomplishment Result Invincible Milestone Superior. Increase the bulleted list font size to 36 points.

> 1) **Positive Mental Attitude**
>   a) Chelsea Ihalainen
>   b) Psychology 401
> 2) **Positive Attitude Characteristics**
>   a) Cheerful
>   b) Considerate
>   c) Courteous
>   d) Friendly
>   e) Neat
>   f) Thoughtful
> 3) **How to Improve Your Attitude**
>   a) Associate with positive people
>   b) Speak well of others
>   c) Isolate negative thoughts
>   d) Treat others with respect
>   e) Forgive and forge on
> 4) **Attitude is Everything. . .**
>   a) Anything is possible with a positive attitude

FIGURE 2-81

5. Change the slide layout on Slide 3 to Text & Clip Art. Using the clip art placeholder, insert the clip art shown in Figure 2-82 that has the keywords, Consensus Cooperate Guarantee Synergy Agreeable. Increase the bulleted list line spacing to 0.4 lines before each paragraph.

6. On Slide 4, change the font of Anything is possible with a positive attitude, to 72 point italic.

7. Add the slide number and your name to the slide footer. Display the footer on all slides. Add your name to the outline header and your school's name to the outline footer.

(continued)

In the Lab

Adding Clip Art and Animation Effects to a Presentation Created in Outline View *(continued)*

8. Apply the Strips Right-Down slide transition effect to all slides. Apply the Wipe Right custom animation effect to all heading level 1 paragraphs on Slide 2 and Slide 3.

9. Check the presentation for errors.

10. Save the presentation on a floppy disk using the file name, Positive Attitude.

11. Print the presentation outline. Print the black and white presentation.

12. Quit PowerPoint.

FIGURE 2-82b

FIGURE 2-82a

FIGURE 2-82c

FIGURE 2-82d

In the Lab

2 Animating a Slide Show

Problem: You are the marketing director for Clarity Health Products, a manufacturer of vitamins and other nutritional supplements. Experience tells you that sales are related directly to the quality of the sales presentation. Sales quotas are higher than last year and you want to make sure your sales staff understands the importance of practicing the delivery of a presentation. After much research, you prepare the outline shown in Figure 2-83. When you practice your presentation, you decide to add animation effects to the slide show. The completed slide show is shown in Figure 2-84 on the next page.

Instructions: Perform the following tasks. *Hint*: Use Help to solve this problem.

1. Create a new presentation using the Ribbons design template and the outline shown in Figure 2-83.

2. On the title slide, use your name instead of the name Anna Douglas. Decrease the font size of Presented by: to 20 points. Decrease the font size of Marketing Director and Clarity Health Products to 24 points.

3. On Slide 2, increase the font size of the heading level 1 bullets to 36 points and heading level 2 bullets to 32 points. Increase the line spacing for heading level 2 bullets to 0.75 lines before each paragraph. Using Figure 2-84 on the next page as a reference, insert the clip art that has the keyword, Leadership. Scale the clip art to 95% and drag it to the lower-right corner of the slide as shown in Figure 2-84.

4. On Slide 3, insert the clip art shown in Figure 2-84 that has the keywords, Surprise Incomprehensible Incredible. Scale the clip art to 90%. Drag the clip art to the right side of the slide.

```
I.    Polishing Your Presentation
      A. Presented by:
      B. Anna Douglas
      C. Marketing Director
      D. Clarity Health Products
II.   Practice Makes Perfect
      A. Three key factors for a successful presentation
         1. Practice
         2. Practice
         3. Practice
III.  Why Practice?
      A. Increase confidence
      B. Develop rhythm
         1. Pause for emphasis
      C. Improve articulation
         1. Vary pitch and inflection
      D. Establish timings
      E. Identify problems
IV.   How To Practice
      A. Speak out loud
         1. Make a recording
            a) Video
            b) Audio
         2. Look into a mirror
         3. Find a live audience
            a) Friend or co-worker
            b) Group or team
      B. Go to delivery site
         1. Inspect equipment
            a) Audio-visual
            b) Lectern
         2. Check environment
            a) Noise
            b) Lighting
            c) Room temperature
V.    Practice Makes Perfect
```

FIGURE 2-83

(continued)

In the Lab

Animating a Slide Show *(continued)*

5. On Slide 4, change the slide layout to 2 Column Text. Drag the text into the right column place-holder so your slide looks like Slide 4 in Figure 2-84. Increase the line spacing to 0.5 lines before each paragraph.

6. On Slide 5, change the slide layout to Object. Insert the clip art that has the keywords, Target Incredible.

7. Add the current date, slide number, and your name to the slide footer. Display the footer on all slides. Include the current date and your name on the outline header. Include Clarity Health Products and the page number on the outline footer.

8. Apply the Strips Right-Up slide transition effect to all slides. Apply the Fly From Bottom custom animation effect to bulleted text on Slides 1 through 4. Introduce text grouped by 3rd level paragraphs.

9. Animate the clip art on Slide 2 using the Fly From Bottom-Right custom animation effect so it displays immediately after the slide title when you run the slide show. Animate clip art on Slide 5 using the Zoom In From Screen Center custom animation effect.

10. Save the presentation on a floppy disk using the file name, Polishing Your Presentation.

11. Print the presentation outline. Print the presentation slides without animations in black and white.

12. Quit PowerPoint.

FIGURE 2-84a

FIGURE 2-84b

In the Lab

FIGURE 2-84c

FIGURE 2-84d

FIGURE 2-84e

In the Lab

3 Creating a Presentation in Outline View, Inserting and Moving Clip Art, and Applying Slide Transition and Animation Effects

Problem: You are Maurice Barber, the Director of Career Development and Placement at Mercedes Valley College. A local middle school principal has asked you to speak to his eighth grade students about career opportunities. You create the presentation using the outline shown in Figure 2-85. You then refine the presentation using clip art, slide transitions, and animation effects to create the slide show shown in Figure 2-86. *Hint*: Use Help to solve this problem.

Instructions: Perform the following tasks.

1. Create a new presentation using the Zesty design template and the outline in Figure 2-85.
2. On the title slide, animate the subtitle with the Zoom In From Screen Center custom animation effect.
3. Use Figure 2-86 as a reference. Change the slide layout on Slide 2 to Clip Art & Text. Then insert clip art that has the keywords, Opportunity Knocks. Increase line spacing to 1 line before paragraph on heading level 1.
4. Change the slide layout on Slide 3 to Clip Art & Text. Insert clip art that has the keywords, Focus Investigation Diagnose.
5. On Slide 4, insert the clip art that has the keywords, Surprise Incomprehensible Incredible. Scale the clip art to 75%. Move the clip art to the right edge of the slide as shown in Figure 2-86.
6. Add the slide number and your name to the slide footer. Display the footer on all slides. Display your name in the outline header, and the page number, and the name of the school, Mercedes Valley College, in the outline footer.
7. Check the presentation for spelling errors.

I.   **Future Considerations**
    A.   **What Will You Be When You Grow Up?**
II.   **What Is In Your Future?**
    A.   **Education**
        1.   **College**
        2.   **Technical School**
        3.   **Apprenticeship**
    B.   **Work**
        1.   **On the job training**
III.   **Investigate Options**
    A.   **Engineer**
    B.   **Entertainer**
    C.   **Florist**
    D.   **Machinist**
    E.   **Nurse**
    F.   **Programmer**
    G.   **Teacher**
    H.   **Veterinarian**
IV.   **How Do You Choose?**
    A.   **Consider likes and dislikes**
        1.   **Reading and writing**
        2.   **Working with people**
        3.   **Working with animals**
        4.   **Working with computers**
        5.   **Working with your hands**

FIGURE 2-85

8. Apply the Box In slide transition effect to all slides. Apply the Strips Right-Down custom animation effect to all 2nd level paragraphs on Slides 2 through 4. Apply the Peek From Left custom animation effect to clip art on Slide 3 and then change animation order so the clip art displays before the bulleted text.
9. Save the presentation on a floppy disk using the file name, Future Considerations.
10. Run the electronic slide show.
11. Print the presentation outline. Print the presentation slides without animations in black and white.
12. Quit PowerPoint.

FIGURE 2-86a

FIGURE 2-86b

FIGURE 2-86c

FIGURE 2-86d

Cases and Places

The difficulty of these case studies varies: ❱ are the least difficult; ❱❱ are more difficult; and ❱❱❱ are the most difficult.

1 ❱ AAA Accounting and Tax Consultants is a privately owned accounting firm. Marshall Weatherbee, president of the firm, is one of several Certified Public Accountants conducting short presentations at a financial planning seminar. The purpose of the seminar is to inform people about their financial options and to promote the services of the presenters. To prepare for the presentation, Mr. Weatherbee created the following outline.

Using the concepts and techniques introduced in this project, together with Mr. Weatherbee's outline, develop slides for an electronic slide show. Include clip art and animation effects to add interest. Print the outline so that it can be distributed to the audience at the conclusion of the presentation.

FIGURE 2-87

I. AAA Accounting and Tax Consultants
   A. We listen to you and work as a team to meet your financial goals.
   B. Marshall Weatherbee, President
II. Prepare for Retirement, Now
   A. Follow 20/80 rule for current income
      1. Live on 20%
      2. Save 80%
   B. Eliminate all debt
   C. Establish financial plan
III. Financial Plan
   A. Establish monthly budget
   B. Develop investment strategy
      1. High-risk investments
      2. Low-risk investments
      3. Savings
   C. Consult with certified financial planner
IV. AAA Accounting and Tax Consultants
   A. Comprehensive financial planning
      1. Financial and estate
      2. Retirement
      3. Education
      4. Investments
      5. Insurance
   B. Additional services
      1. Tax strategies
      2. Tax preparation
      3. Tax audit representation
      4. Debt reduction strategies
      5. Business planning

Cases and Places

2 ▶ First Class Limousine advertises their services at bridal fairs, county fairs, and business conventions. Next week is the 1998 Stone Mountain bridal fair. You have been asked to create a professional-looking presentation from the outline developed by the company owner, Margo Quinn.

Using the concepts and techniques introduced in this project along with the following outline, create an electronic presentation for First Class Limousine. Include appropriate clip art and animation effects. Ms. Quinn would like a printed outline that can be distributed to the audience at the conclusion of the presentation.

I. *First Class Limousine*
   A. *The ultimate in luxury, comfort, and affordability*
   B. *A special ride for your special day*
II. *Affordable Packages*
   A. *Debutante*
     1. *Luxury transportation at reasonable rates*
   B. *Princess*
     1. *Pampered conveyance in style*
   C. *Royalty*
     1. *A once-in-a-lifetime adventure*
III. *Debutante*
   A. *The basic package includes:*
     1. *Six passenger sedan*
     2. *Courteous, licensed driver*
     3. *Soft drinks*
IV. *Princess*
   A. *The most popular package offers:*
     1. *Eight passenger luxury sedan*
     2. *Courteous, licensed driver in chauffeur's cap*
     3. *Refreshments*
       a) *Soft drinks and hors d'oeuvres*
     4. *Twelve-speaker CD sound system*

V. *Royalty*
   A. *The aristocratic package features:*
     1. *Ten or twelve passenger stretch limousine*
     2. *Courteous, licensed driver in top hat and tails*
     3. *Refreshments*
       a) *Soft drinks and hors d'oeuvres*
       b) *Lobster salad or prime rib sandwiches*
     4. *Live music*
       a) *Concert violinist performs customized selection of songs*
VI. *Luxury Limousines*
   A. *New 6, 8, and 12 passenger sedans*
   B. *TV, VCR, and mood lights*
   C. *Beverages*
   D. *Glass and privacy partitions*
   E. *Cellular telephone*
VII. *Travel First Class Limousine*
   A. *Telephone*
     1. *555-LIMO*
   B. *Ask about our FREE hour special*

FIGURE 2-88

Cases and Places

3 ▶▶ Diver Dan's Dive Shop sells equipment for SCUBA divers. SCUBA is the acronym for Self-Contained Underwater Breathing Apparatus. Dan, the store's owner, is frequently asked for information about three SCUBA certification programs, PATI, NAUI, and YMCA. Each program has different teaching approaches and certification standards. Dan wants you to create a presentation that compares and contrasts the three programs. He also wants the presentation to be animated and include clip art. Research the three certification programs and then using the concepts and techniques introduced in this project, create the presentation. Create handouts from the presentation outline.

4 ▶▶ Goals are often divided into four categories: spiritual, family, career, and self. A 1973 Yale University economics study concluded that three-percent of the 1953 Yale graduating class had written goals and defined a plan with which to reach them. Twenty years later, the same three-percent had achieved a net worth greater than the rest of the entire class combined. Using the techniques introduced in the project, create a presentation about yourself. Provide a brief biography. Develop a list of your goals. Under each goal category, identify two or more goals. One goal should be a short-term goal, something that will take less than a year to achieve. Another goal would be a long-term goal, something that will take longer than one year to achieve. Include appropriate clip art and animation effects.

5 ▶▶▶ In addition to Microsoft PowerPoint, other presentation graphics software packages include Persuasion, Compel, Freelance Graphics, and Harvard Graphics. Visit a software vendor and try one of these or another presentation graphics package. Using current computer magazines or other resources, learn more about the package you tested. Based on what you have discovered, together with the concepts and techniques introduced in this project, prepare a presentation comparing and contrasting the package you tested against Microsoft PowerPoint. Contrast the capabilities, strengths, weaknesses, ease of use, and cost of each package. End by noting which package you prefer and your reasons why. Enhance the presentation with clip art and custom animation. Print the outline of the presentation.

6 ▶▶▶ Recent economic changes have forced many organizations to alter their business focus from manufacturing to service. To be successful, service-oriented businesses must be able to clearly and convincingly explain how they can benefit prospective clients. Visit a local business that provides a service and learn all you can about the service and the people to whom it is being offered. Using the results of your visit, along with the concepts and techniques introduced in this project, prepare a presentation promoting the company's services. Embellish the presentation with clip art and custom animation effects. Print the presentation and the presentation outline.

7 ▶▶▶ Are people born with great leadership skills, or do ordinary people develop into great leaders? Leadership expert and author, John Maxwell, states in his book, *The Success Journey*; "Success is not a destination thing, it is a daily thing." Go to the library or use the World Wide Web to research some of the world's great leaders. What qualities do they share? Why are these people considered to be great leaders? Using the results of your research, together with the concepts and techniques introduced in this project, prepare a presentation about leadership. Feature one of the leaders you researched. Enhance the presentation with clip art and custom animation.

Index

Abbreviations, AutoCorrect entries for, WD 2.24
Access 97, **A 1.8, MO 1.6-7**
  Help, A 1.49
  Internet and, MO 1.6-7
  quitting, A 1.24
  starting, A 1.9-11
Access desktop, A 1.12-13
Active application, **PP 1.41**
Active cell, **E 1.11, E 1.14, E 1.15**
Active cell reference, **E 1.11**
Add Field button, A 1.42
Adding records to table, **A 1.20-23,** A 1.26-27
Add-Ins command (Excel Tools menu), E 2.19
Addition (+), E 2.10
Addresses, Internet, maintaining using Contacts, MO 1.11
Align Left button (Word Formatting toolbar), **WD 1.30,** WD 2.40
Alignment, Excel
  cell contents, E 1.30, E 2.23, E 2.25, E 2.28
Alignment, Word, WD 1.30
Align Right button (Word Formatting toolbar), WD 2.13
Analysis ToolPak, E 2.19
AND criterion, **A 2.24-25**
Animated slide show, running, PP 2.51-53
Animating
  clip art, PP 2.47-49
  objects, PP 2.43, PP 2.47-49
  title slide, PP 2.50, PP 2.51
APA (American Psychological Association) style of documentation, WD 2.6, WD 2.12, WD 2.16, WD 2.44
Apostrophe ('), left-alignment and, E 2.28
Applications
  active, PP 1.41
  switching between, PP 1.41
Apply Design button (Common Tasks toolbar), **PP 1.17**
Appointments - Outlook 97, **MO 1.10-11**
Arguments, **E 2.15**
Arrow keys, **E 1.14**
Ascending sort order
  query, A 2.12
  works cited page, WD 2.43, **WD 2.44**
Aspect ratio, **PP 2.34**
Asterisk (*), in Access
  wildcard character, **A 2.19**
Asterisk (*), in Excel
  multiplication and, E 2.10
Asterisk (*), in Word
  changing to bullet, WD 1.23
Attribute buttons, **PP 1.17**
AutoCalculate area (Excel status bar), **E 1.14, E 1.47-49**
AutoCalculate command (Excel shortcut menu), E 1.47
AutoClipArt feature, **PP 1.8**
AutoComplete feature, E 1.18
AutoComplete tip, **WD 2.16**
AutoContent Wizard, **PP 1.8**
AutoCorrect command (Excel Tools menu), **E 1.17**
AutoCorrect command (Word Tools menu), WD 1.23, WD 2.23
AutoCorrect feature
  Excel, **E 1.16-17**
  Word, WD 1.23, **WD 2.21-24**
AutoFilter arrows, **E 2.65**
AutoFormat
  Excel worksheet, E 1.31-33
  Word document, WD 1.23-25, WD 1.28
AutoFormat As You Type feature, **WD 1.23-25,** WD 2.41
AutoFormat command (Excel Format menu), **E 1.31**
AutoFormat dialog box, E 1.32-33
AutoLayout, PP 1.16
  adding clip art using, PP 2.26-31
  adding new slide with same, PP 1.31-33
  Bulleted List, PP 1.25-27, PP 1.29
  placeholders, PP 1.25
AutoLayout object area, **PP 1.16**
AutoLayout placeholders, PP 1.25
Automatic page breaks, **WD 2.29-30**

AutoSum button (Excel Standard toolbar), **E 1.22-23, E 1.26,** E 2.14
AutoText entry, WD 2.24
Average
  displaying using AutoCalculate, E 1.47
  function used to calculate, E 2.15-16
AVERAGE function, **E 2.15-16**
AVG statistic, A 2.38

Background, worksheet title, E 2.25-26
Background repagination, **WD 2.29**
BACKSPACE key, correcting errors using
  Access, A 1.18
  Excel, **E 1.16, E 1.49**
BACKSPACE key, erasing characters using, WD 1.53
Backup
  Excel workbook, E 1.42
  Word document, WD 1.46
  .bak extension, **E 1.42**
Best fit, **E 2.24, E 2.35, E 2.38**
Bibliographical references, WD 2.6
Black and White View button (PowerPoint Standard toolbar), **PP 1.50-51**
Blank character, creating by pressing SPACEBAR, E 1.51
Blank Database icon, A 1.10
Blank Document icon, WD 1.10
Blank line, in PowerPoint presentation
  adding to bulleted list, PP 2.20-22
Blank line, in Word document
  inserting above paragraph, WD 2.37
  inserting using ENTER key, WD 1.17, WD 1.18
  removing above paragraph, WD 2.38
Blank Workbook icon, E 1.9
Block arrow, **E 1.12**
Bold button (Excel Standard toolbar), E 1.28
Bold button (PowerPoint Formatting toolbar), **PP 1.17**
Bold button (Word Formatting toolbar), WD 1.34, WD 1.38
Book icon, **WD 1.57**
Borders, Excel
  bottom, E 2.28
  snaps to gridlines, E 1.38
  worksheet, E 2.23
Borders button (Excel Formatting toolbar), E 2.28, E 2.31
Box Out slide transition effect, PP 2.39-41
Break Away Bargains presentation, PP 2.5-58
Break command (Word Insert menu), WD 2.38-39
Browse by Page command (Select Browse Object menu), WD 2.45
Browser, **MO 1.3**
  Internet Explorer, MO 1.4, MO 1.8, WD 1.40
Bullet(s), PowerPoint presentation
  displaying, PP 2.23
  heading levels, PP 2.13-16
  number per object, PP 2.16
Bullet(s), Word document, **WD 1.23-25**
Bulleted item, new slide for each, PP 2.15
Bulleted list
  PowerPoint presentation, **PP 1.8,** PP 1.25-33
  Word document, WD 1.23-25
Bulleted List AutoLayout, PP 1.25-27, PP 1.29
Bulleted list slides, PP 1.25-33
  adding blank line to, PP 2.20-22
  animation effects, PP 2.42-47
  moving text on, PP 2.24-25
  multi-level, in outline view, PP 2.13-16
  multi-level, in slide view, PP 1.27-33
Bullets and Numbering command (Word Format menu), WD 1.25
Bullets and Numbering command (Word shortcut menu), WD 1.25

Bullets button (PowerPoint Formatting toolbar), **PP 1.17,** PP 2.22-23
Bullets button (Word Formatting toolbar), WD 1.25
Buttons, recessed, WD 1.18

Calculating statistics, database, A 2.38-43
Calculations
  AutoCalculate and, E 1.14, E 1.47-49
  formatted numbers in, E 2.31
  sum, E 1.21-23
Calendar - Outlook 97, MO 1.10
Calendar icon (Outlook Bar), MO 1.10
Cancel box (formula bar), **E 1.15,** E 1.16, E 1.49
Cancel printing
  Excel worksheet, E 1.44
  PowerPoint presentation, PP 1.54, PP 2.55
  Word document, WD 1.48
Cancel Printing command (Word Document menu), WD 1.48
Capitalization
  AutoCorrect feature and, WD 2.21, WD 2.24
  checking presentation for, PP 1.41, PP 1.43, PP 2.38
  password and, E 1.42
Caret (^)
  centering text, E 2.28
  exponentiation, E 2.10
  query, A 2.17
Case, checking presentation for, PP 1.41, PP 1.43, PP 2.38
Case-sensitive password, **E 1.42**
Category axis, **E 1.39**
Category names, **E 2.42**
Cell(s), Excel worksheet, **E 1.11**
  aligning contents of, E 1.30, E 2.23, E 2.25, E 2.28
  bolding, E 1.28
  centering data in, E 2.29
  clearing, E 1.51
  copying to adjacent cells using fill handle, E 1.23-25
  editing in, E 1.49-50
  entering numbers in, E 1.20-21
  entering text in, E 1.14-19
  formulas in, E 2.9-21
  rotating text in, E 2.29
  selecting using mouse, E 1.14
  selecting using Name box, E 1.33-34
Cell(s), Word table, **WD 2.30**
  modifying contents of, WD 2.34
Cell reference, **E 1.11**
  active, E 1.11
  copying formula and, E 2.14
  relative, E 1.24
Cells command (Excel Format menu)
  alignment, E 1.30, E 2.28
  background color, E 2.27
  bold, E 1.28
  borders, E 2.27
  currency formats, E 2.33
  font size, E 1.29
  font style, E 2.25
  number formats, **E 2.29,** E 2.31, E 2.34
Center/centering
  data in cells, E 2.28, E 2.29
  paragraph, WD 1.30, WD 1.38-39
  paragraph before typing, WD 2.16-17
  presentation title, PP 1.18
  title of works cited page, WD 2.39-40
  worksheet title across columns, E 1.30, E 2.23, E 2.25
Center button (Excel Formatting toolbar), E 2.28, E 2.29
Center button (Word Formatting toolbar), WD 1.30, WD 2.17
Cents, E 1.21
Character(s), in Excel worksheet, **E 2.34**
  blank, E 1.51
Character(s), in Word document
  erasing, WD 1.53
  formatting, WD 1.28, WD 1.29
  nonprinting, WD 1.18, WD 2.7
  selecting and formatting, WD 1.29
Character formatting, **WD 1.28,** WD 1.29
Chart(s), Excel, **E 1.6, E 2.43**
  default type, E 1.39

drawing, E 2.42-45
  embedded, E 1.35-39
  location, **E 1.35, E 1.37-38,** E 2.45
  3-D Column, E 1.35-39, **MO 1.4-5**
  3-D Pie, E 2.6, E 2.41-51
  title for, E 2.44, E 2.45
Chart(s), PowerPoint, PP 1.8
Chart command (Excel Insert menu), E 1.39
Chart item, formatting, **E 2.46-47**
Chart location, **E 1.35, E 1.37-38**
Chart menu (Excel)
  Chart Options command, leader lines, E 2.47
  3-D View command, E 2.50
Chart menu bar, **E 1.13**
Chart Options command (Excel Chart menu), leader lines, E 2.47
Chart sheet, **E 2.41**
Chart Type command (Excel shortcut menu), E 1.39
Chart Wizard, E 1.35, E 1.36-37, E 2.42-45
Chart Wizard button (Excel Standard toolbar), **E 1.35,** E 2.42
Citations, parenthetical, WD 2.6, WD 2.25
Clear/clearing, in Access
  grid, A 2.17, A 2.37
  query, A 2.17
Clear/clearing, in Excel
  cell or range of cells, E 1.51
  entire worksheet, E 1.51-52
Clear command (Excel Edit menu), E 1.51
Clear Contents command (Excel shortcut menu), E 1.51
Clear Grid command (Access Edit menu), A 2.17, A 2.37
Click/clicking, **WD 1.8,** E 2.47
Clip art, PowerPoint, MO 1.7
  adding using AutoLayouts, PP 2.26-31
  animating, PP 2.47-49
  finding, PP 2.29-30
  inserting without clip art placeholder, PP 2.32
  moving, PP 2.33
  placeholder, PP 2.26-31
  size of, PP 2.33-35
  on slide, PP 2.26-35
Clip art, Word
  importing, WD 1.39, WD 1.42
  inserting from file, WD 1.40-41
Clip Art & Text slide layout, PP 2.27-28
Clip art gallery, on Internet, MO 1.7
Clipboard, importing clip art using, WD 1.39, **WD 1.42**
Close button, title bar
  Access, **A 1.12**
  Excel, E 1.45, E 1.52
  PowerPoint, PP 1.39
  Word, WD 1.49
Close command, A 1.24, A 1.37, **E 1.52,** WD 1.54
Closing
  Access database, A 1.12, A 1.24
  Access form, **A 1.36-37**
  Access query, **A 2.15**
  Access table, A 1.24
  Excel worksheet, E 1.45, E 1.52
  PowerPoint presentation, PP 1.39
  Word document, WD 1.49, WD 1.54
Closing slide, **PP 2.17**
  creating in outline view, PP 2.17-18
Codes, AutoCorrect entries for, WD 2.24
Color, in Excel
  background, E 2.26
  chart, E 2.46
  chart slices, E 2.47-48
  fill, E 2.26
  font, E 2.27
  worksheet, E 2.22, E 2.23
Color, in PowerPoint
  animation effects, PP 2.42
  design template, PP 1.20
Color, in Word
  table, WD 2.35
Color View, **PP 2.8**

Column(s), Access
  moving to, A 1.17
Column(s), Excel, **E 1.10**
  centering text across, E 1.30, E 2.23, E 2.25
  heading, E 1.10
  hidden, E 2.37
  titles, E 1.17-18
Column(s), Word table, WD 2.30, WD 2.32
Column command (Excel Format menu), E 2.36
Column heading, E 2.7
Columns of text slide layout, PP 2.23-24
Column titles
  Excel worksheet, E 2.8, E 2.9, E 2.27-28
  Word table, WD 2.33
Column width
  changing, E 2.36-37
  default, E 2.35
Column Width command (Excel shortcut menu), E 2.36
Comma (,), formatting numbers with, E 2.29, E 2.30
Comma Style button (Excel Formatting toolbar), E 2.30
Comma style format, **E 2.29**
Common Tasks toolbar, PP 1.13, PP 1.16, **PP 1.17**
Comparison operator, **A 2.23**
Compound criteria, **A 2.24-26**
Computed fields, in query, **A 2.36-38**
Computer Discount Daily Sales worksheet, E 1.6-60
Contacts - Outlook 97, **MO 1.11**
Contacts icon (Outlook Bar), MO 1.10, MO 1.11
Contemporary design template, PP 1.12-14, PP 1.17
Contents and Index command (Word Help menu), WD 1.57
Content templates, PowerPoint presentation, MO 1.7
Control-menu icon, closing Excel from, E 1.45
Copy/copying, in Excel
  cell to adjacent cells using fill handle, E 1.23-25
  formulas using fill handle, E 2.13-14
  functions, E 2.19-20
  sheet, E 2.53
Copy/copying, in Word
  picture from Web, WD 1.42
Copy area, **E 1.23**
Copy button (Excel Standard toolbar), E 2.14
Copy command (Excel Edit menu)
  formulas, E 2.14
  moving sheet using, E 2.53
Copy command (Excel shortcut menu)
  formulas, E 2.14
Correcting errors, Access
  data, A 1.28
  structure, A 1.18-19
Correcting errors, Excel, E 1.49-52
  AutoCorrect and, E 1.16-17
  while typing, E 1.16
Correcting errors, PowerPoint presentation, PP 1.44-45
  using rough draft, PP 1.51
  while typing, PP 1.19
Counting words, WD 2.49-50
Create a form, **A 1.35**
Create a query, **A 2.7-11**
Create a report, **A 1.40-45**
Create button, A 1.12
Criteria
  calculating statistics, A 2.40-41
  compound, A 2.24-26
  for field not in the result, A 2.20-21
  numeric data in, A 2.22
  query, A 2.18-26
Currency field, A 1.14, A 1.18
Currency Style button (Excel Formatting toolbar), **E 2.29,** E 2.30
Currency style format, **E 2.29**
  with floating dollar sign, E 2.32
Custom Animation command (PowerPoint shortcut menu), PP 2.43, PP 2.48
Custom Animation command (PowerPoint Slide Show menu), PP 2.46, PP 2.49

Custom dictionary, **PP 1.42**
Customize command (Excel shortcut menu), toolbars, E 1.13
Cut/cutting
in Excel, E 1.49, E 1.51
in PowerPoint, PP 2.25
Cut button (Excel Standard toolbar), **E 1.49**, E 1.51
Cut button (PowerPoint Standard toolbar), PP 2.25
Cut command (Excel Edit menu), **E 1.51**
Cut command (PowerPoint shortcut menu), PP 2.25

Data, Access
correcting errors in, A 1.28
redundant, A 1.46, A 1.47-48
sorting in query, A 2.27-31
type, A 1.13, **A 1.14**
viewing using form, A 1.35-39
Data, Excel worksheet
refreshing, E 2.64
Database, Access, **A 1.6, MO 1.6**
closing, A 1.24, A 1.46
designing, **A 1.46-48**
opening, A 1.24-25
Pilotech Services, A 1.8-56
saving table within, A 1.19-20
saving on floppy disk, A 1.10-12
Database, Excel, E 1.6
Database program, **MO 1.6**
Database window, A 1.13
Data labels, E 2.44
Data menu (Excel), Get External Data command, E 2.62
Data series, **E 2.42**, E 2.45
Datasheet, A 1.20
Datasheet view, **A 1.20**
adding records in, A 1.20-23
switching between Form view and, A 1.39-40
Datasheet View command (Access View menu), A 1.40
Data type, A 1.13, **A 1.14**
Date
AutoComplete tip, WD 2.16
inserting in header, WD 2.14
Date navigator, **MO 1.10**
Debugging, **E 2.59**, E 2.60
Decimal point, cents and, E 1.21
Decrease Decimal button (Excel Formatting toolbar), **E 2.34**
Decrease Font Size button (PowerPoint Formatting toolbar), PP 1.21
Default chart type, E 1.39
Default setting, slide attributes, **PP 1.14**
Delete/deleting
in cell, E 1.49
e-mail, MO 1.10
fields from query, A 2.10
slide text, PP 1.45
from Word document, WD 1.51, WD 1.53
Delete command (Access Edit menu), fields from query, A 2.10
DELETE key, correcting errors using
Access, A 1.18
Excel, **E 1.49**, E 1.51
Word, WD 1.53
Demote button (PowerPoint Formatting toolbar), **PP 1.27**, PP 1.29-30, PP 2.12
Demote button (PowerPoint Outlining toolbar), PP 2.11-12, PP 2.13, PP 2.14
Demoted paragraph
outline view, PP 2.11-12, PP 2.13, PP 2.14
slide view, **PP 1.27**
Descending sort order, **WD 2.44**
Description, field, A 1.13
Design grid, **A 2.9**, A 2.11
clearing, A 2.17
Design template, MO 1.7, **PP 1.10**, PP 1.12-13
changing, PP 2.7
color scheme, PP 1.20
Contemporary, PP 1.12-14, PP 1.18
slide master, PP 1.46
text attributes, PP 1.20
Design View
creating table using, A 1.15, A 1.34
queries in, A 2.8

Design View command (Access View button), A 2.15
Desktop information management (DIM), **MO 1.9**
Detail lines, report, **A 1.40**
Dimension of the table, **WD 2.30**, WD 2.31-32
Division (/), E 2.10
Docked toolbars, **WD 1.12, WD 2.15**
Document(s)
finding based on date created or worked on, MO 1.12-13
opening on intranet, MO 1.8
publishing on Web, MO 1.7-8
searching on Internet for, MO 1.8
Document menu (Word printer window), Cancel Printing command, WD 1.48
Documents command (Start menu), PP 1.41
Document window, **WD 1.11**
scrolling, WD 1.21-23
Dollar sign ($), formatting with, E 2.29
Double-click, **WD 1.8**, WD 1.36
Double-spacing
research paper, WD 2.9-11
table, WD 2.36
Drag/dragging, in Excel
changing column width by, E 2.35-36
changing row height by, E 2.37-38
copying cell by, E 1.25
copying formulas by, E 2.13
moving chart by, E 1.37
Drag/dragging, in PowerPoint
moving clip art by, PP 2.33
moving text on slide by, PP 2.10, PP 2.25
Drag/dragging, in Word, **WD 1.8**
resizing picture by, WD 1.45
selecting text by, WD 1.30
sizing handle and, WD 1.45
Dragging and dropping, in PowerPoint, **PP 2.10**
Drawing
chart, E 2.42-45
Drawing, in PowerPoint, PP 1.8
slide objects, PP 1.16, PP 1.17
Drawing, in Word, MO 1.4, WD 2.32
Drawing toolbar, PP 1.16, **PP 1.17**
Draw Table feature, WD 2.32
Duplicates, in sorts, A 2.30

Edit Formula box (formula bar), **E 1.15**, E 1.23, E 2.16-17, E 2.19
Editing
footnote, WD 2.28
research paper, WD 2.44-51
Edit menu (Access)
Clear Grid command, A 2.17, A 2.37
Delete command, fields from query, A 2.10
Edit menu (Excel)
Clear command, E 1.51
Copy command, E 2.14
Cut command, E 1.51
Paste command, E 2.14
Undo command, **E 1.50**
Edit menu (Word)
Go To command, page, WD 2.46
Paste Special command, WD 1.42
Replace command, WD 2.47
Edit mode, E 1.49-50, E 2.24-25
Electronic mail (e-mail), **MO 1.9**
viewing using Outlook, MO 1.9-10
Electronic presentations, PP 1.6, PP 1.7, PP 1.35-38
Electronic slide shows, PP 2.51
Embedded chart, E 1.35-39
End mark, Word document window, **WD 1.10**
Endnote, **WD 2.25**
including in word count, WD 2.50
End-of-cell mark, **WD 2.32**
End-of-row mark, **WD 2.32**
End Show command (Popup Menu), **PP 1.38**
Engineering functions, E 2.19
Enter box (formula bar), **E 1.15**
Entering criteria, for query, **A 2.18-26**
ENTER key, Excel
entering formula using, **E 1.16**
ENTER key, PowerPoint
new paragraph, PP 1.18, PP 1.29

ENTER key, Word
beginning new paragraph within cell of table, WD 2.32
blank lines, WD 1.17, WD 1.18
new paragraph, WD 1.16, WD 1.17, WD 1.18, WD 1.19
Enter mode, E 1.14
Enter Parameter Value dialog box, **E 2.63**
Equal sign (=), starting formula with, E 2.9, E 2.10
ESC key
canceling entry using, **E 1.16**, E 1.49
removing record from screen using, A 1.28
Excel 97, **E 1.6, MO 1.4-6**
add-ins, E 2.19
compatibility with other software products, E 1.47
Internet and, E 1.7, MO 1.5-6
online Help, E 1.52
quitting, E 1.44-45
starting, E 1.8-10, E 1.45-47, E 2.7
Web queries, E 1.7, E 2.61-65
Excel window, E 1.10-12
Exit command (Excel File menu), E 1.45
Exit command (PowerPoint File menu), PP 1.39
Exit command (Word File menu), WD 1.49
Expand Slide command (PowerPoint Tools menu), PP 2.15
Explanatory notes, MLA style, **WD 2.6, WD 2.25-28**
Exploded pie chart, **E 2.42, E 2.49**
Exponentiation (^), E 2.10
External Data toolbar (Excel), **E 2.64, MO 1.5**

Fast saves, **PP 2.36**
Field(s), **A 1.7**
computed, A 2.36-38
data type, A 1.13, A 1.14
defining for table, A 1.16-18
including all in query, A 2.16-17
joined tables, A 2.34
selecting for query, A 2.10-11
selecting for report, A 1.42-43
Field names, rules for, A 1.13
Field not in the result, criteria for, A 2.20-21
File(s), Excel, **E 1.39**
File(s), Word
graphic, WD 1.39, WD 1.44
inserting clip art from, WD 1.40-41
opening, WD 1.50-51
File extensions
Excel, E 1.42
PowerPoint, PP 1.25, PP 2.9, PP 2.31
File menu (Access)
Close command, A 1.24, A 1.37
Page Setup command, printing orientation, A 1.30-31
Print command, A 1.32, A 1.46
Print Preview command, A 1.32, A 1.45
Save command, A 1.20, A 2.44
File menu (Excel), **E 1.13**
Close command, E 1.52
Exit command, E 1.45
Print Area command, E 2.58
Print command, E 1.44
Print Preview command, E 2.53, E 2.55
Save As command, E 1.42, **E 2.41**
Save command, **E 2.41**
File menu (PowerPoint)
Exit command, PP 1.39
Page Setup command, orientation, PP 1.14
Print command, PP 1.53, PP 2.54, PP 2.56
Save As command, PP 1.23
Save command, PP 1.25
File menu (Word)
Close command, WD 1.54
Exit command, WD 1.49
Open command, WD 1.51
Page Setup command, margin settings, WD 2.8
Print command, WD 1.48
Properties command, word count, WD 2.50
Save As command, WD 1.46
Save command, WD 1.27

File name, Excel
saving workbook using new, E 2.41
saving workbook using same, E 2.41
workbook, E 1.40
File name, PowerPoint
saving presentation with same, PP 1.33-34
File name, Word
default, WD 1.26
meaningful, WD 1.25, WD 1.26
opening Word document by selecting, WD 1.51
saving existing Word document with same, WD 1.46-47
File New Database dialog box, A 1.10-11
Fill Color button (Drawing toolbar), **PP 1.17**
Fill Color palette, E 2.26, E 2.48
Fill handle
clearing range of cells using, E 1.51
copying cell to adjacent cells using, **E 1.24-25**
copying formulas using, E 2.13-14
copying functions using, E 2.19-20
Find/finding
clip art, PP 2.29-30
Help topic, WD 1.59
pictures on Web, WD 1.41
text, WD 2.46-48
text and replacing, WD 2.46-47
Find Clip dialog box, PP 2.29-30
First-line indent, **WD 2.18-20**
notes, WD 2.27
First Line Indent marker, **WD 2.18-19**
moving to left margin, WD 2.39
Fixed dollar sign, **E 2.29**, E 2.33
Floating dollar sign, **E 2.29, E 2.32**, E 2.33
Floating picture, **WD 1.43**
Floating toolbars, **WD 1.12**
Floppy disk
saving database on, A 1.10-12
saving picture on Web on, WD 1.44
saving presentation on, PP 1.23-25
saving Word document on, WD 1.25-27
saving workbook on, E 1.39-42
Folder, **WD 1.26**
Folder (Inbox) - Outlook 97, e-mail and, MO 1.10
Font, Word document, **WD 1.14**
changing, of selected text, WD 1.32-33
default, WD 1.32
variable character, WD 1.20
Font attribute, PP 1.20
Font box arrow (Excel Formatting toolbar), E 2.23
Font color, E 2.27
Font box arrow (Word Formatting toolbar), WD 1.33
Font command (PowerPoint Format menu), PP 1.22
Font command (PowerPoint shortcut menu), PP 1.22
Font command (Word Format menu)
bold, WD 1.34
font size, WD 1.15, WD 1.32
font style, WD 1.33
italics, WD 1.38
underline, WD 1.36
Font command (Word shortcut menu)
bold, WD 1.34
font size, WD 1.15, WD 1.32
font style, WD 1.33
italics, WD 1.38
underline, WD 1.36
Font size, Excel
chart, E 2.46
worksheet, **E 1.27**, E 1.29, E 2.24-25
Font size, PowerPoint, PP 1.20, PP 1.21-22
Font size, Word, **WD 1.14**
changing, WD 1.14-15, WD 1.31-32
default, WD 1.14
header, WD 2.14
research paper, WD 2.15
Font Size box arrow (Excel Formatting toolbar), E 1.29

Font Size box arrow (Word Formatting toolbar), WD 1.14-15, WD 1.31-32, WD 2.15
Footers
PowerPoint presentation outline, PP 2.36-37
Word research paper, **WD 2.12**, WD 2.15
Font style
Excel worksheet, **E 1.27**, E 2.23-24
PowerPoint presentation, PP 1.20, PP 1.22-23
Word document, WD 1.14, WD 1.32-33
Footnote(s)
including in word count, WD 2.50
MLA style research paper, **WD 2.6, WD 2.25-28**
Footnote command (Word Insert menu), WD 2.25-26
Footnotes command (Word View menu), WD 2.28
Form
closing, A 1.36-37
creating, A 1.35-36
opening, A 1.37-38
saving, A 1.36-37
using, A 1.38-39
viewing data using, A 1.35-39
Format/formatting, in Excel, **E 1.26**
chart item, E 2.46-47
clearing, E 1.51
font style, E 2.25
numbers, E 2.28-34
using AutoFormat, E 1.31-33
using Format Cells command, E 1.28-30
worksheet, E 1.26-33, E 2.7
worksheet text, E 2.21-28
wrapping text, E 2.8
Format/formatting, in PowerPoint
font, PP 1.22
line spacing, PP 1.47-48
sizing picture, PP 2.35
slide layout, PP 2.24
title slide, PP 2.50
Format/formatting, in Word, WD 1.28-39
bold font, WD 1.34
bullets, WD 1.25
character, WD 1.28, WD 1.29
font size, WD 1.15, WD 1.32
font style, WD 1.33
italics, WD 1.38
paragraph, WD 1.28, WD 1.29
paragraph alignment, WD 1.30, WD 1.39
picture, WD 1.46
table, WD 2.34-35
underline, WD 1.36
Format Cells command (Excel shortcut menu)
alignment, E 1.30, E 2.28
background color, E 2.27
bold, E 1.28
borders, E 2.27
font size, E 1.29
font style, E 2.25
number formats, **E 2.29**, E 2.31-32, E 2.34
wrapping text, E 2.8
Format Cells dialog box, **E 1.30**
Format Data Point command (Excel shortcut menu), E 2.48
Format menu (Excel)
AutoFormat command, **E 1.31**
Cells command, alignment, E 1.30, E 2.28
Cells command, background color, E 2.27
Cells command, bold, E 1.28
Cells command, borders, E 2.27
Cells command, currency formats, E 2.33
Cells command, font size, E 1.29
Cells command, font style, E 2.25
Cells command, number formats, **E 2.29**, E 2.31, E 2.34
Column command, E 2.36
Row command, E 2.36
Selected Data Point command, E 2.48
3-D View command, E 2.49
Format menu (PowerPoint)
Font command, PP 1.22
Line Spacing command, PP 1.47-48
Picture command, sizing, PP 2.35
Slide Layout command, PP 2.24

Format menu (Word)
Bullets and Numbering command, WD 1.25
Font command, bold, WD 1.34
Font command, font size, WD 1.15, WD 1.32
Font command, font style, WD 1.33
Font command, italics, WD 1.38
Font command, underline, WD 1.36
Paragraph command, alignment, WD 1.30, WD 1.39, WD 2.17
Paragraph command, centering, WD 2.17
Paragraph command, first-line indent, WD 2.20
Paragraph command, hanging indent, WD 2.41
Paragraph command, line spacing, WD 2.11
Paragraph command, spacing before paragraph, WD 2.37
Picture command, WD 1.46
Format Painter button (Excel Standard toolbar), E 2.33
Format Picture button (Word Picture toolbar), WD 1.46
Format Picture command (PowerPoint shortcut menu), **PP 2.33**, PP 2.34
Format Picture dialog box
PowerPoint, PP 2.33-34
Word, WD 1.46
Formatting toolbar
Excel, E 1.13, E 2.23-31
PowerPoint, PP 1.16, **PP 1.17**
Word, **WD 1.12**, WD 1.38
Formula(s), E 2.9-21
copying using fill handle, E 2.13-14
displaying, E 2.59
entering using Point mode, E 2.11-12
natural language, E 2.12
order of operations, E 2.5, E 2.10
printing, E 2.59-61
Formula bar, **E 1.14**
Formula palette, E 2.16-17
Formulas version of worksheet, E 2.59
Form view, A 1.35-39
switching between Datasheet view and, A 1.39-40
Free Rotate button (Drawing toolbar), PP 1.17
Full save, PP 2.36
Full Screen command (Excel View menu), E 1.12
Function(s), Access
statistics, A 2.38-43
Function(s), Excel, **E 2.15**
AutoSum and, E 2.14
AVERAGE, E 2.15-16
copying, E 2.19-20
displaying with AutoCalculate, E 1.47-49
MAX, E 2.16-17
MIN, E 2.17-19
Function box (formula bar), **E 2.16**

Get External Data command (Excel Data menu), E 2.62
Get External Data submenu, E 2.62
Go command (Popup Menu), **PP 1.37**
Go To command (Word Edit menu), WD 2.46
Grammar checking, automatically while typing, WD 1.20
Graph(s)
PowerPoint, PP 1.8
Graphic files, WD 1.44
importing, WD 1.39
Graphic objects, in outline view, PP 2.8
Graphics
resizing, WD 1.44-46
selected, WD 1.45
Grid, table, **WD 2.31**
Gridlines, Excel, **E 1.11**
snaps border to, E 1.38
Grouping, A 2.42-43

Hanging indent, WD 2.40-41
Hanging Indent marker, **WD 2.40**
Hard copy
Excel worksheet, E 1.43
PowerPoint presentation, **PP 1.51**
Word document, WD 1.47
Word page break, WD 2.38
Hard p

Header, PowerPoint
adding to presentation outline, PP 2.36-37
Header, Word, **WD 2.12**
numbering pages in, WD 2.12-14
Header and Footer command (PowerPoint View menu), PP 2.36-37
Header and Footer command (Word View menu), WD 2.12-13, WD 2.15
Header and Footer dialog box, PP 2.36-37
Header and Footer toolbar, **WD 2.13-14**
Header area, **WD 2.13**
Header row, **WD 2.33**
Heading(s), Excel
column, E 1.10, E 2.7
Heading level(s), PP 2.8-9, PP 2.11-14
Heading level 1, **PP 2.8**, PP 2.11-12, PP 2.13
Heading level 2, **PP 2.8**, PP 2.12, PP 2.13, PP 2.14
Heading level 3, **PP 2.8**, PP 2.14
Heading level 4, **PP 2.8**
Heading level 5, **PP 2.8**
Heading level 6, **PP 2.8**
Headlines, Word document, WD 1.16-17
Height, clip art, PP 2.33, PP 2.35
Help
Access, A 1.49
Excel, E 1.52
Office Assistant and, MO 1.14
PowerPoint, PP 1.54
Word, WD 1.54-60
WordPerfect, WD 1.13
Help menu (Word)
Contents and Index command, WD 1.57
Microsoft on the Web command, WD 1.59
Microsoft Word Help command, WD 1.56
Help Topics: Microsoft Word dialog box, WD 1.57-59
Hide/hiding
automatic spell checker underline, WD 1.21
column, E 2.37
Office Assistant, WD 1.56
row, E 2.39
Hide Spelling Errors command (Word shortcut menu), WD 1.21
High-Tech Stock Club worksheet, E 2.4-66
Home page, **MO 1.2**
Horizontal alignment, of cell contents, E 2.28, E 2.29
Horizontal ruler, **WD 1.13**
Horizontal scroll bar, **PP 1.16**
Hyperlinks, **MO 1.5**
Hyperlinks, in Excel worksheet, MO 1.5
Hyperlinks, in Word document, MO 1.4, **WD 2.41**
navigating to, WD 2.51
works cited page, WD 2.41-42
HyperText Markup Language (HTML), **MO 1.7**

I-beam, A 2.18, WD 1.10
Icon, Access desktop, **A 1.13**
Imported graphic, **WD 1.39**
resizing, WD 1.44-46
In-cell editing, E 1.49-50
Include all fields in query, A 2.16-17
Increase Decimal button (Excel Formatting toolbar), **E 2.34**
Increase Font Size button (PowerPoint Formatting toolbar), **PP 1.22**
Indentation, in PowerPoint
heading levels, PP 2.8
Indentation, in Word
first-line, WD 2.18-20, WD 2.27
hanging, WD 2.40-41
left, WD 2.18
MLA style, WD 2.6
notes, WD 2.27
paragraphs, WD 2.18-20
works cited page, WD 2.40-41
Informational slide, PP 2.13
Information viewer, **MO 1.10**
Inline picture, **WD 1.43**

Insert Clip Art button (PowerPoint Standard toolbar), PP 2.28, PP 2.32
Insert Date button (Header and Footer toolbar), WD 2.14
Insert Hyperlink button (Excel Standard toolbar), MO 1.5
Insert Hyperlink button (Word Standard toolbar), WD 2.42
Insertion point
Excel, **E 1.15**
PowerPoint, **PP 1.18**
Word, **WD 1.10**
INSERT key, **E 1.50**
Insert menu (Access)
New Record command, A 1.27
Query command, A 2.10
Table command, A 1.15
Insert menu (Excel)
Chart command, E 1.39
Insert menu (PowerPoint)
New Slide command, PP 1.27, PP 2.13
Insert menu (Word)
Break command, WD 2.38-39
Footnote command, WD 2.25-26
Picture command, WD 1.40
Insert mode
Excel, E 1.50
Word, WD 1.53
Insert Number of Pages button (Header and Footer toolbar), WD 2.14
Insert Page Number button (Header and Footer toolbar), WD 2.13
Insert Picture dialog box, WD 1.41
Insert Table button (Word Standard toolbar), WD 2.30-32
Insert Table command (Word Table menu), WD 2.32
Insert Time button (Header and Footer toolbar), WD 2.14
IntelliSense™ technology, E 1.17, **E 1.53, MO 1.14, WD 1.6, WD 1.54**
Internet, **MO 1.2**
Access 97 and, MO 1.6-7
clip art gallery on, MO 1.7
Excel 97 and, MO 1.5-6
Microsoft Office 97 and, MO 1.2-3
PowerPoint 97 and, MO 1.7-8, PP 1.6
searching for document on, MO 1.8
virtual presentation on, PP 1.6
Word 97 and, MO 1.4
Internet address, maintaining using Contacts application, MO 1.11
Intranet, **MO 1.3**
opening documents on, MO 1.8
Italic button (PowerPoint Formatting toolbar), **PP 1.17, PP 1.22-23**
Italic button (Word Formatting toolbar), WD 1.38

Joining tables, A 2.32-36
Join line, A 2.33, A 2.34
Journal - Outlook 97, **MO 1.12-13**
Journal icon (Outlook Bar), MO 1.12
Jumping to Web page, MO 1.9, **WD 2.41**

Key, primary, **A 1.7, A 1.13**
assigning, A 1.17
Key(s), sort
multiple, A 2.28-29
primary sort key, **A 2.27**
Keyboard, Microsoft Natural, MO 1.15
Keyboard indicators, **E 1.14**

Labels, chart, E 2.44
Landscape orientation
Access query, A 2.14
Access table, **A 1.28**, A 1.31-32
Excel worksheet, E 2.59-60
PowerPoint slide, PP 1.14
Language command (Word Tools menu), thesaurus, WD 2.48
Leader lines, **E 2.47**
Left-aligned
cell contents, E 2.28
data in table cell, WD 2.32
paragraph in document, **WD 1.30,** WD 2.17
text in cell, **E 1.16**
Left Indent marker, **WD 2.18**
Legend, **E 1.39, E 2.44**

Level, **PP 1.27**
Line(s), in Excel
ending with ALT+ENTER, E 2.8
Line(s), in Word
ending with ENTER key, WD 1.16, WD 1.17, WD 1.18, WD 1.19
height, WD 2.9
selecting single, WD 1.31
Line break, table, WD 2.31
Line break character, WD 2.31
Line spacing, PowerPoint, PP 1.45-50
Line spacing, Word
before paragraph, WD 2.37
MLA style research paper, WD 2.6, WD 2.9-11
multiple, WD 2.11
notes, WD 2.27
table, WD 2.35-36
Line Spacing command (PowerPoint Format menu), **PP 1.47-48**
Line Spacing dialog box, PP 1.48-49
Line wrapped text, **PP 1.18**
List
main topics, PP 2.10

Major key, **A 2.27,** A 2.29
Manual page break, **WD 2.38-39**
Margins, Excel, E 2.55
Margins, Word
header, WD 2.12
MLA style research paper, WD 2.6, WD 2.7-9
Marquee, **E 1.22**
Master, PP 1.45
Master command (PowerPoint View menu), PP 2.46
Master Layout button, PP 1.47
Master toolbar, PP 1.47
MAX function, **E 2.16-17**
Maximizing
Access window, A 1.22
Word screen, WD 1.10
Meeting - Outlook 97, **MO 1.10**
Menu bar
Access desktop, **A 1.13**
Excel worksheet window, **E 1.13**
PowerPoint, in slide view, **PP 1.15**
Word document window, **WD 1.12**
Merge and Center button (Excel Formatting toolbar), E 1.30, E 2.25
Microsoft Clip Gallery 3.0, **PP 2.26,** PP 2.29
Microsoft Clip Gallery 3.0 dialog box, PP 2.29
Microsoft IntelliMouse™, **MO 1.14, WD 1.8**
Microsoft Internet Explorer, **MO 1.3,** WD 1.39, WD 1.40
Microsoft Internet Explorer window, MO 1.4
Microsoft Natural keyboard, **MO 1.15**
Microsoft Office 97, **MO 1.2**
Internet and, MO 1.2-3
introduction to, MO 1.2-15
Microsoft Office Home Page, MO 1.3
Microsoft Office Shortcut Bar
Access database, A 1.12
Excel worksheet, E 1.10
Word document, WD 1.10, WD 1.51
Microsoft on the Web, MO 1.3
Microsoft on the Web command (Access Help menu), Product News, MO 1.7
Microsoft on the Web command (Excel Help menu), Product News, MO 1.4
Microsoft on the Web command (Outlook Help menu), Product News, MO 1.7
Microsoft on the Web command (PowerPoint Help menu), Product News, MO 1.7
Microsoft on the Web command (Word Help menu), Product News, MO 1.7
Microsoft Outlook 97, **MO 1.9-13**
finding tips for using, MO 1.4
viewing appointments, MO 1.10-11
viewing contacts, MO 1.11
viewing electronic mail, MO 1.9-10

viewing journal entries, MO 1.12-13
viewing notes, MO 1.13
viewing tasks, MO 1.11
Microsoft Word Help command (Word Help menu), WD 1.56
MIN function, E 2.17-19
Minor key, **A 2.27,** A 2.29
Minus sign (-)
starting formula with, E 2.9, E 2.10
subtraction and, E 2.10
MLA (Modern Language Association) style of documentation, **WD 2.4-52**
entering course information, WD 2.6, WD 2.16
entering name, WD 2.6, WD 2.16
explanatory notes, WD 2.6, WD 2.25-28
footnotes, WD 2.6, WD 2.25-28
indents, WD 2.6
line spacing, WD 2.6, WD 2.9-11
margins, WD 2.6, WD 2.7-9
page numbers, WD 2.6, WD 2.12-14
works cited, WD 2.6, WD 2.37-44
Mode indicators, **E 1.14**
Modifications, to Word document, WD 1.51
Mouse
IntelliMouse™, MO 1.14, WD 1.8
selecting cell using, E 1.14
Mouse pointer, Excel, E 1.11, E 1.12
Mouse pointer, PowerPoint, **PP 1.16**
pen, PP 1.35
Mouse pointer, Word, **WD 1.10**
Mouse usage, WD 1.8
Move command (Excel shortcut menu), E 2.53
Multi-level bulleted list slides, **PP 1.27**
creating in outline view, PP 2.13-16
creating in slide view PP 1.27-33
Multimedia effects, in presentation, PP 1.8
Multiple keys, sorting on, A 2.28-29
Multiple line spacing option, WD 2.11
Multiple paragraphs, selecting, WD 1.29
Multiple text objects, creating slide with, in outline view, PP 2.16-17
Multiplication (*), E 2.10

Name, MLA style of entering, WD 2.6, WD 2.16
Name box, **E 1.11**
selecting cell using, E 1.33-34
Natural language formula, E 2.12
Navigation buttons, **A 1.26**
Network
intranet, MO 1.3
New button (Access Database window), table, A 1.33-34
New Object: AutoForm button, **A 1.35,** A 2.7
New Object button arrow, creating table using, A 1.15
New Office Document command (Start menu)
Access database A 1.9-10
Excel worksheet, E 1.9
PowerPoint presentation, **PP 1.10, PP 1.11,** PP 2.7
Word document, WD 1.9
New Query dialog box, A 2.8
New Record button, A 1.27
New Record command (Access Insert menu), A 1.27
New Slide button (PowerPoint Common Tasks toolbar), **PP 1.17, PP 1.25,** PP 1.26
New Slide button (PowerPoint Standard toolbar), PP 1.27, PP 2.13
New Slide command (PowerPoint Insert menu), PP 1.27, PP 2.13
New Slide dialog box, PP 1.13, PP 1.26
New Slide Layout button (Common Tasks toolbar), **PP 1.17**
Next command (Popup Menu), **PP 1.37**

Next Slide button (vertical scroll bar), PP 1.15, PP 1.16, PP 1.35
Nonprinting characters, WD 1.18, WD 2.7
Normalization, A 1.46
Note pane, WD 2.26-28
Note reference mark, WD 2.25, WD 2.26, WD 2.28
Notes and Handouts sheet (Header and Footer dialog box), PP 2.36-37
Notes application, MO 1.13
Notes Page view, PP 1.15
Note text, WD 2.25, WD 2.28
Number(s)
  entering in cells, E 1.20-21
  formatting, E 2.28-34
  treating as text, E 1.20
Number field, A 1.14, A 1.22-23
Numeric data, in criteria, A 2.22

Object(s)
  animating, PP 2.43, PP 2.47-49
  drawing, PP 1.17
  placeholders, PP 1.16
  sizing, PP 2.33
  slide, PP 1.14
  title, PP 1.16
Office Assistant, A 1.12, A 1.46-48, MO 1.14, PP 1.13, WD 1.54-57
  hiding, WD 1.56
Office Assistant button (Word Standard toolbar), WD 1.55
Office Assistant shortcut menu, WD 1.57
Office Assistant Tips button, WD 1.56
Online Help
  Access, A 1.49
  Excel, E 1.52
  PowerPoint, PP 1.54
  Word, WD 1.54-60
Online information systems, clip art from, PP 2.31
Open/opening
  Access database, A 1.24-25
  Access form, A 1.37-38
  Access table, A 1.20
  documents on intranet, MO 1.8
  Excel workbook, E 1.45-47
  PowerPoint presentation, PP 1.39-41
  Word document, WD 1.50-51
Open a Document button (Microsoft Office Shortcut Bar), PP 1.41
Open button (Word Standard toolbar), WD 1.51
Open command (Access shortcut menu), A 1.20, A 1.21, A 1.27
Open command (Word File menu), WD 1.51
Open command (Word shortcut menu), WD 1.10
Open Office Document command (Start menu)
  Access database, A 1.25
  Excel workbook, E 1.46
  PowerPoint presentation, PP 1.39-40
  Word document, WD 1.50
Option bar (pane), WD 2.26
Options command (PowerPoint Tools menu)
  number of undos, PP 1.19
  turning off Popup Menu, PP 1.37
Options command (Word shortcut menu), automatic spell check, WD 1.20
Options command (Word Tools menu), background repagination, WD 2.29
OR criterion, A 2.24, A 2.25-26
Order of operations, overriding with parentheses, E 2.5, E 2.10
Orphan, WD 2.30
Outline, PP 1.8, PP 2.7
  adding headers and footers to, using Notes and Handouts sheet, PP 2.36-37
  creating presentation from, PP 2.4-18
  printing, PP 2.53-56
Outline command (PowerPoint View menu), PP 2.9
Outline title, PP 2.5
Outline view, PP 1.15, PP 2.7-10
  creating closing slide in, PP 2.17-18

creating multi-level bulleted list slides in, PP 2.13-16
creating presentation in, PP 2.10-12
creating title slide in, PP 2.10-12
PowerPoint window in, PP 2.9-10
printing in, PP 2.53-57
slide with multiple text objects in, PP 2.16-17
Outline View button (View Button Bar), PP 2.8
Outlining toolbar, PP 2.9-10
Outlook Bar, MO 1.9-10
Overhead transparencies, PP 1.6, PP 1.54
Overtype mode
  Excel, E 1.50
  Word, WD 1.53
OVR status indicator, WD 1.53

Pack and Go Wizard, PP 1.8
Page, browse by, WD 2.45-46
Page break
  automatic, WD 2.29-30
  hard, WD 2.38
  manual, WD 2.38-39
  soft, WD 2.29
PAGE DOWN (move forward one slide), PP 1.35, PP 1.36
Page header, report, A 1.40
Page indicator (status bar), going to page number, WD 2.46
Page layout view
  headers and footers in, WD 2.14
  margins in, WD 2.7, WD 2.9
Page number(s)
  in header, WD 2.12-14
  going to specific, WD 2.46
  MLA style research paper, WD 2.6, WD 2.12-14
Page Setup command (Access File menu), orientation, A 1.30-31
Page Setup command (PowerPoint File menu), orientation, PP 1.14
Page Setup command (Word File menu), margin settings, WD 2.8
Page Setup dialog box (Access)
  landscape orientation, A 1.31
  printing table contents, A 1.28
Page Setup dialog box (Excel)
  printing to fit and, E 2.59-60
PAGE UP (move back one slide), PP 1.35, PP 1.36
Page width zoom, WD 2.20-21
Painting formats, E 2.33
Pane
  Access, A 1.16
  Word, WD 2.26
Paradise Island announcement, WD 1.6-60
Paragraph, PowerPoint, PP 1.18
  blank line after, PP 2.20-22
  demoted in outline view, PP 2.11-12, PP 2.13, PP 2.14
  demoted in slide view, PP 1.27
  levels in bulleted lists, PP 1.27
  promoted in outline view, PP 2.12, PP 2.14
  promoted in slide view, PP 1.28
Paragraph, Word
  blank line above, WD 2.37
  centering, WD 1.30, WD 1.38-39
  centering before typing, WD 2.16-17
  formatting, WD 1.28, WD 1.29
  indenting, WD 2.18-20
  inserting blank line above, WD 2.37
  left-aligned, WD 2.17
  new, WD 1.16, WD 1.17, WD 1.18, WD 1.19
  selecting and formatting, WD 1.29
  selecting multiple, WD 1.29
  sorting works cited, WD 2.43-44
Paragraph command (Word Format menu)
  alignment, WD 1.30, WD 1.39, WD 2.17
  centering, WD 2.17
  first-line indent, WD 2.20
  hanging indent, WD 2.41
  line spacing, WD 2.11
  spacing before paragraph, WD 2.37
Paragraph command (Word shortcut menu)
  alignment, WD 1.30, WD 1.39, WD 2.17
  centering, WD 2.17

first-line indent, WD 2.20
footnotes, WD 2.26-27
hanging indent, WD 2.41
line spacing, WD 2.10
spacing before paragraph, WD 2.37
Paragraph dialog box, line spacing, WD 2.10
Paragraph formatting, WD 1.28, WD 1.29
  after table, WD 2.36-37
Paragraph levels, bulleted lists, PP 1.27
Paragraph mark (¶), displaying, WD 1.18
Parentheses (), overriding order of operations using, E 2.5, E 2.10
Parenthetical citations, WD 2.6, WD 2.23
Password, E 1.42, WD 1.46
Paste area, E 1.23
Paste button (Excel Standard toolbar), E 2.14
Paste button (PowerPoint Standard toolbar), PP 2.25
Paste command (Excel Edit menu), E 2.14
Paste command (Excel shortcut menu), E 2.14
Paste command (PowerPoint shortcut menu), PP 2.25
Paste Function button (Excel Standard toolbar), E 2.16, E 2.17, E 2.18-19
Paste Function dialog box, E 2.18, E 2.19
Paste Special command (Word Edit menu), picture from Web, WD 1.42
Path, Web toolbar, MO 1.8
Pen command (Popup Menu), PP 1.35
Pen pointer, PP 1.35
Percentage (%), E 2.10
  formula used to obtain, E 2.20-21
  Percent Style button used to obtain, E 2.34
Percent sign (%)
  formatting numbers with, E 2.29
  percentage and, E 2.10
Percent Style button (Excel Formatting toolbar), E 2.34
Period, space after, WD 1.20
Periods, entering range using two, E 2.20
Pick from List command (Excel shortcut menu), E 1.18
Picture, in PowerPoint
  file extensions, PP 2.31
  inserting on slide, PP 2.31
  sizing, PP 2.35
Picture, in Word
  floating, WD 1.43
  inline, WD 1.43
  inserting into Word document from Web, WD 1.39-46
  positioning, WD 1.43
  resizing, WD 1.44-46
  saving on disk, WD 1.44
Picture command (PowerPoint Format menu), sizing picture, PP 2.35
Picture command (Word Insert menu), WD 1.40
Picture toolbar, WD 1.45
Pie chart, E 2.41
  exploded, E 2.42, E 2.49
  perspective, E 2.51
  3-D, E 2.6, E 2.41-51
Pilotech Services database, A 1.8-56
Placeholders, PP 1.16
  AutoLayouts, PP 1.25
  changing slide layout, PP 2.23
  clip art, PP 2.26-31
  subtitle, PP 1.16, PP 1.19
  title, PP 1.16, PP 1.18
Plus sign (+)
  addition and, E 2.10
  starting formula with, E 2.9, E 2.10
Point mode, entering formulas using, E 2.11-12
Points, PP 1.27, WD 1.8, WD 1.14
  before paragraph spacing, PP 1.50
Point size
  worksheet, E 1.27
Popup Menu, PP 1.37
  displaying in Slide Show view, PP 1.37
  ending slide show using, PP 1.38

Portrait option button (Page Setup dialog box), A 1.31
Portrait orientation
  Access report, A 1.44
  Access table, A 1.28
  PowerPoint slide, PP 1.14
Positioning pictures, WD 1.43
PowerPoint 97, MO 1.7-8, PP 1.6
  Help, PP 1.54
  Internet and, MO 1.7-8
  quitting, PP 1.38-39, PP 1.62
  starting, PP 1.13
PowerPoint view(s), PP 1.15-17
PowerPoint Viewer, PP 1.8, PP 2.51
PowerPoint window, MO 1.7, PP 1.14
  in outline view, PP 2.9-10
  in slide view, PP 1.15-17
.ppt (PowerPoint) file extension, PP 1.25
Presentation, PP 1.10
  adding new slide to, PP 1.25-33
  animation effects, PP 2.38-53
  Break Away Bargains presentation, PP 2.5-58
  correcting errors in, PP 1.44-45
  creating from outline, PP 2.4-18
  creating Web page from, MO 1.8
  design template, PP 1.10, PP 1.12-13, PP 2.7
  displaying in black and white, PP 1.50-51
  electronic, PP 1.6, PP 1.7, PP 1.35-38
  opening existing, PP 1.39-41
  overhead transparencies of, PP 1.54
  printing, PP 1.51-54, PP 2.56-57
  publishing on Internet, MO 1.7
  reviewing in slide sorter view, PP 2.19-20
  running, PP 1.8, PP 2.51-53
  saving before printing, PP 1.52
  saving to floppy disk, PP 1.23-25
  saving with same file name, PP 1.33-34
  slide, PP 1.6, PP 1.8
  starting as New Office Document, PP 1.10-14, PP 2.7
  style checking, PP 1.41-44, PP 2.16, PP 2.38
  Unlocking the Internet, PP 1.8-63
  viewing using Slide Show, PP 1.35-38
  virtual, MO 1.7, PP 1.6
Presentation design, PP 1.18, PP 1.21, PP 1.29, PP 1.31
Presentation graphics, PP 1.8
Presentation graphics program, MO 1.7, PP 1.6
Presentation subtitle, entering, PP 1.19-20
Previewing
  Access report, A 1.44-45
  Access table, A 1.28-32
  Excel workbook, E 2.53-55
  Excel worksheet, E 1.43, E 2.53-54
Previous command (Popup Menu), PP 1.37
Previous Slide button (vertical scroll bar), PP 1.15, PP 1.16, PP 1.35
Primary key, A 1.7, A 1.13
  assigning, A 1.17
Primary sort key, A 2.27
Print/printing, in Access
  query results, A 2.13-14
Print/printing, Access
  report, A 1.45
  table, A 1.28-32
Print/printing, Excel
  canceling, E 1.44
  formulas, E 2.59-61
  range, E 1.44
  scaling option, E 2.61
  section of worksheet, E 2.57-58
  selected sheets, E 2.55-57
  worksheet, E 1.43-44
Print/printing, PowerPoint
  canceling, PP 1.54, PP 2.55
  outline, PP 2.53-56
  in outline view, PP 2.53-57
  presentation, PP 1.51-54, PP 2.56-57
Print/printing, Word
  canceling, WD 1.48
  document using File, Print command, WD 1.48
  document using Print button, WD 1.47-48
Print area, E 1.44, E 2.58

Print Area command (Excel File menu), E 2.58
Print button (Access Standard toolbar), A 1.31, A 2.13
Print button (Excel Standard toolbar), E 1.43, E 2.55-56
Print button (PowerPoint Standard toolbar), PP 1.52
Print button (Word Standard toolbar), WD 1.47-48
Print command (Access File menu), A 1.32, A 1.46
Print command (Access shortcut menu), A 1.45
Print command (Excel File menu), E 1.44
Print command (PowerPoint File menu), PP 1.53, PP 2.54, PP 2.56
Print command (Word File menu), WD 1.48
Print dialog box
  Excel, E 2.57-58
  PowerPoint, PP 2.54-55, PP 2.56-57
Printing dialog box, E 1.44
Printout
  Excel worksheet, E 1.43
  PowerPoint presentation, PP 1.51
  Word document, WD 1.47
Print preview
  Access report, A 1.45
  Access table, A 1.29, A 1.32
  Excel worksheet, E 1.43, E 2.53-54
  Word headers and footers, WD 2.14
Print Preview button (Excel Formatting toolbar), E 2.53-54
Print Preview button (Excel Standard toolbar), E 1.43
Print Preview command (Access File menu), A 1.32, A 1.45
Print Preview command (Access shortcut menu), A 1.29
Print Preview command (Excel File menu), E 2.53, E 2.55
Print what area (Print dialog box), E 2.57-58
Programs command (Start menu)
  Access database, A 1.12
  Excel worksheet, E 1.10
  Word document, WD 1.10
Promote button (PowerPoint Formatting toolbar), PP 1.28, PP 1.30-31
Promote button (PowerPoint Outlining toolbar), PP 2.12, PP 2.14
Promoted paragraph
  in outline view, PP 2.12, PP 2.14
  in slide view, PP 1.28
Proofing research paper, WD 2.44-51
Properties command (Access shortcut menu), omitting duplicates, A 2.30
Properties command (Access View menu), omitting duplicates, A 2.31
Properties command (Word File menu), word count, WD 2.50
Publishing document, on Web, MO 1.7-8
Punctuation, checking presentation for, PP 1.41, PP 1.43, PP 2.38

Query, Access database, A 2.4
  calculating statistics, A 2.38-43
  clearing, A 2.17
  closing, A 2.15
  comparison operators, A 2.23
  computed fields in, A 2.36-38
  creating, A 2.711
  criteria, A 2.18-26
  grouping records, A 2.42-43
  including all fields in, A 2.16-17
  joining tables, A 2.32-36
  printing results of, A 2.13-14
  running, A 2.4, A 2.12-13
  saving, A 2.44-45
  sorting data in, A 2.27-31
  using Select Query window, A 2.4-45
Query, Excel
  Web, E 1.7, E 2.61-65
Query-by-Example, A 2.10, A 2.25
Query command (Access Insert menu), A 2.10
Query languages, A 2.7

Query menu (Access)
Run command, A 2.13
Show Table command, A 2.35
Query Parameters button (External Data toolbar), E 2.64
Query window, A 2.9
Question Mark button (AutoFormat dialog box), E 1.33
Question Mark button (Word dialog box), WD 1.59
Question mark icon (Help Topics: Microsoft Word dialog box, Contents tab), WD 1.57
Question mark pointer, WD 1.59
Question mark (?) wildcard, A 2.19
Quitting
Access, A 1.24
Excel, E 1.44-45
PowerPoint, PP 1.38-39, PP 1.62
Word, WD 1.49
Quotation mark ("), right-alignment, E 2.28

Range, E 1.23
average of, E 2.15-16
to chart, E 1.36, E 2.42
clearing, E 1.51
entering numbers into, E 2.8
entering using periods, E 2.20
highest number in, E 2.16-17
lowest number in, E 2.17-19
printing, E 1.44
selecting, E 2.15
Range Finder, E 2.12
Ready mode, E 1.14
Recalculation, E 2.9
Recessed button, WD 1.18
Records, A 1.6
adding to table in Datasheet view, A 1.20-23, A 1.26-27
grouping, A 2.42-43
restricting in a join, A 2.35
Record selector, A 1.21, A 1.28
Recurring task, MO 1.11
Redo button (Excel Standard toolbar), E 1.51
Redo button (PowerPoint Standard toolbar), PP 1.19
Redo button (Word Standard toolbar), WD 1.53
Redundancy, A 1.46, A 1.47-48
Reference marks, note, WD 2.25, WD 2.26, WD 2.28
References, MLA style, WD 2.6
Refresh All button (External Data toolbar), E 2.64, MO 1.5-6
Refresh Data button (External Data toolbar), E 2.64
Related tables, A 2.33, A 2.34
Relative reference, E 1.24
Remove Table command (Access shortcut menu), A 2.37
Rename command (Excel shortcut menu), E 2.53
Repagination, background, WD 2.29
Replace command (Word Edit menu), WD 2.47
Replacing text, WD 2.46-47
Report, Access
completing, A 1.43-44
creating, A 1.40-45
printing, A 1.45-46
selecting fields for, A 1.42-43
Report, Word, WD 2.4
Report Manager, E 2.19
Report Wizard, A 1.41-45
Research paper, A 2.4-52
body of, WD 2.15-37
entering course information, WD 2.6, WD 2.16
entering name, WD 2.6, WD 2.16
explanatory notes, WD 2.6, WD 2.25-28
footnotes, WD 2.6, WD 2.25-28
indents, WD 2.6
line spacing, WD 2.6, WD 2.9-11
margins, WD 2.6, WD 2.7-9
page numbers, WD 2.6, WD 2.12-14
proofing and revising, WD 2.44-51
tables in, WD 2.4-5, WD 2.30-37
works cited, WD 2.6, WD 2.37-44
Resizing, imported graphic, WD 1.44-46
Resizing window, monitor, PP 2.11
Resolution

Returning External Data to Microsoft Excel dialog box, E 2.63
Revising research paper, WD 2.44-51
Rich Text Format (RTF) file extension, PP 2.9
Right-aligned
cell contents, E 2.28
headers, WD 2.12
numbers in cells, E 1.21
Right-click, WD 1.8
Right-drag, WD 1.8
Rotate wheel, MO 1.14, WD 1.8
Rotating
text in cells, E 2.29
3-D Pie chart, E 2.49-50
Rotation box (3-D View dialog box), E 2.50
Rough draft, PP 1.51
Row(s), Excel worksheet, E 1.10
copying cell to adjacent cells in, E 1.24-25
height, E 2.35, E 2.37-38
hiding, E 2.39
titles, E 1.18-19, E 2.9
totals, E 1.25-26
Row(s), Word table, WD 2.30
creating new, WD 2.33
header, WD 2.33
Row command (Excel Format menu), E 2.36
Row height, E 2.35, E 2.37-38
Row Height command (Excel shortcut menu), E 2.38
Row selector, Access, A 1.16, A 1.17
Row titles, E 1.18-19
RTF (Rich Text Format) file extension, PP 2.9
Ruler, WD 1.13
first-line indent on, WD 2.19-20
hanging indent marker on, WD 2.40-41
horizontal, WD 1.13
vertical, WD 1.13
Run/running
animated slide show, PP 2.51-53
database query, A 2.4, A 2.12-13
presentation, PP 1.8, PP 2.51-53
Web query, E 2.62
Run button, A 2.12
Run command (Access Query menu), A 2.13
Run Query dialog box, E 2.62
Run the query, A 2.4, A 2.12-13

Save/saving, in Access
database on floppy disk, A 1.10-12
form, A 1.36-37
query, A 2.44-45
table, A 1.19-20
Save/saving, in Excel
worksheet as Web page, E 1.42
workbook using new file name, E 1.39-42, E 2.41
workbook using same file name, E 2.41
Save/saving, in PowerPoint
fast, PP 2.36
full, PP 2.36
presentation before printing, PP 1.52
presentation on floppy disk, PP 1.23-25
presentation with same file name, PP 1.33-34
Save/saving, in Word
backup copies, WD 1.46
document as Web page, WD 1.44, WD 1-55
existing document with same file name, WD 1.46-47
new document, WD 1.25-27
picture on Web on disk, WD 1.44
Save As command (Excel File menu), E 1.42, E 2.41
Save As command (Excel shortcut menu), E 1.42
Save As command (PowerPoint File menu), PP 1.23
Save As command (Word File menu), WD 1.46
Save As dialog box (Access), A 1.19
Save As dialog box (Excel), E 1.40
Save As dialog box (Word), WD 1.26-27
Save button (Access Standard toolbar), A 1.19, A 2.44

Save button (Excel Standard toolbar), E 1.40, E 1.42
Save button (PowerPoint Standard toolbar), PP 1.33-34, PP 1.52
Save button (Word Standard toolbar), WD 1.25-27, WD 1.47
Save command (Access File menu), A 1.20, A 2.44
Save command (Excel File menu), E 2.41
Save command (PowerPoint File menu), PP 1.25
Save command (Word File menu), WD 1.27
Save dialog box (PowerPoint), PP 1.23-24
Save in box arrow
Access, A 1.10-11
Excel, E 1.41
PowerPoint, PP 1.23
Word, WD 1.26-27
Scientific format, E 1.21
ScreenTip
Access, A 1.17
Excel, E 1.13
PowerPoint, PP 1.21
Word, WD 1.14, WD 1.59
Scroll/scrolling
in Excel, E 1.12
in PowerPoint, PP 1.34
in Word, WD 1.11, WD 1.21-23, WD 1.34-35
Scroll arrows, E 1.12
Scroll bars
Excel, E 1.12
PowerPoint, PP 1.15-16
Word document window, WD 1.11
Word note pane, WD 2.26
Scroll box
Excel, E 1.12
PowerPoint, PP 1.34
Word, WD 1.11, WD 1.22
Searching
for documents on Internet, MO 1.8
pictures on Web, WD 1.41
Secondary sort key, A 2.27
Select/selecting, in Access
fields for query, A 2.10-11
fields for report, A 1.42-43
Select/selecting, in Excel
cell, E 1.14
entire worksheet, E 1.52
range, E 2.15
Select/selecting, in PowerPoint
more than one slide, PP 2.39, PP 2.40
Select/selecting, in Word, WD 1.29
characters and formatting, WD 1.29
graphics, WD 1.45
group of words, WD 1.36-38
multiple paragraphs, WD 1.29
opening document by, WD 1.51
paragraphs and formatting, WD 1.29
single line, WD 1.31
single word, WD 1.35-36
in table, WD 2.34, WD 2.36
Select a cell, E 1.14
Select All button, E 1.52
Select Browse Object button (vertical scroll bar), WD 2.45, WD 2.46, WD 2.48
Select Browse Object menu, WD 2.45, WD 2.46, WD 2.48
Selected Data Point command (Excel Format menu), E 2.48
Selected Fields list box (Report Wizard), A 1.42
Selection rectangle
Excel, E 1.37
Word, WD 1.45
Select Query window, querying database using, A 2.7-45
Select Table command (Word Table menu), WD 2.36
Shadow button (PowerPoint Formatting toolbar), PP 1.17
Sheets
changing names, E 2.51-52
chart, E 2.41
moving among, E 2.51-53
order of, E 2.51-53
printing selected, E 2.55-57
Sheet tabs, E 1.10
view of, E 1.12

SHIFT+click technique, selecting more than one slide using, PP 2.39, PP 2.40
SHIFT+New Slide button, PP 1.31-32
Shortcut menus
Excel, E 1.13
PowerPoint, PP 1.16
Word, WD 1.43
Show/Hide (¶) button (Word Standard toolbar), WD 1.18
Show Next button (Header and Footer toolbar), WD 2.14
Show Picture Toolbar command (Word shortcut menu), WD 1.45
Show Table button, A 2.35
Show Table command (Access Query menu), A 2.35
Show Table command (Access shortcut menu), A 2.33
Single-spacing table, WD 2.36
Size/sizing
clip art, PP 2.33-35
objects, PP 2.33
window, E 1.12
Sizing handles
Excel, E 1.37, E 1.38
Word, WD 1.45
Slash (/), division, E 2.10
Slide, PP 1.14
adding new, with same AutoLayout, PP 1.31-33
animation effects, PP 2.38-53
attributes, PP 1.14
bulleted list, PP 1.25-33
clip art on, PP 2.26-35
dragging and dropping, PP 2.10
editing text in, PP 1.45
informational, PP 2.13
line spacing, PP 1.45-50
moving text on, PP 2.24-25
moving to another, in slide view, PP 1.34-35
multi-level bulleted list, in outline view, PP 2.13-16
multi-level bulleted list, in slide view, PP 1.27-33
multiple text objects, creating in outline view, PP 2.16-17
pictures on, PP 2.31
selecting more than one, PP 2.39, PP 2.40
subordinate, PP 2.15-16
35mm, PP 1.6, PP 1.8
title, PP 1.8, PP 1.18-20
white space on, PP 2.20-22
Slide command (PowerPoint View menu), PP 2.21
Slide icon, outline view, PP 2.8
Slide indicator, PP 1.34
Slide layout, PP 1.14
changing, PP 2.23, PP 2.24
Clip Art & Text, PP 2.27-28
2 Column Text, PP 2.23PP 2.24
Slide Layout button (PowerPoint Common Tasks toolbar), PP 1.16, PP 2.23, PP 2.24
Slide Layout command (PowerPoint Format menu), PP 2.24
Slide Layout dialog box, PP 2.24
Slide master, PP 1.45
applying animation effects using, PP 2.43-47
changing line spacing on, PP 1.47-50
design template, PP 1.46
displaying, PP 1.46-47
Slide Master button (View Button Bar), PP 2.43
Slide Navigator dialog box, PP 1.37
Slide number, PP 1.34, PP 2.8
Slide presentations, PP 1.6, PP 1.8, PP 1.35-38
Slide show
advancing manually through, PP 1.36
ending using Popup Menu, PP 1.38
practice run, PP 2.51
running animated, PP 2.51-53
slide transition effects, PP 2.38-47
Slide Show, viewing presentation using, PP 1.35-38
Slide Show button (View Button Bar), PP 1.35-36, PP 2.52
Slide Show command (PowerPoint View menu), PP 1.36

Slide Show menu (PowerPoint)
Custom Animation command, PP 2.46, PP 2.49
Slide Transition command, PP 2.41
View Show command, PP 2.53
Slide Show view, PP 1.15
displaying Popup Menu in, PP 1.37
Slide Sorter toolbar, PP 2.42
Slide Sorter view, PP 1.15
reviewing presentation in, PP 2.19-20
selecting slides for transition effects in, PP 2.39-41
Slide Sorter View button (View Button Bar), PP 2.19, PP 2.39
Slide title, bulleted list slide, PP 1.28
Slide Transition command (PowerPoint shortcut menu), PP 2.40, PP 2.41
Slide Transition dialog box, PP 2.40-41
Slide transition effects, PP 2.38, PP 2.39-47
removing, PP 2.41
Slide view, PP 1.15
adding white space to slide in, PP 2.20-22
displaying slide containing clip art in, PP 2.47
moving to another slide in, PP 1.34-35
PowerPoint window in, PP 1.15-17
printing in, PP 1.52
toolbars in, PP 1.16-17
Snaps border to gridlines, E 1.38
Soft page breaks, WD 2.29
Solver, E 2.19
Sort/sorting, in Access, A 2.27-31
Sort/sorting, in Word
table contents, WD 2.43
work cited paragraphs, WD 2.43
Sort command (Word Table menu), WD 2.43
Sort key, A 2.27
Sound, clip art gallery on Internet, MO 1.7
Sound effects, PP 2.47
SPACEBAR, entering blank character using, E 1.51
Spaces in document, displaying, WD 1.18
Spell checking
Excel, E 1.17, E 2.39-41
PowerPoint, PP 1.41, PP 1.42, PP 2.38
Word, WD 1.20-21, WD 2.21-24
Spelling and Grammar Status icon (status bar), WD 1.17, WD 1.20
Spelling button (Excel Standard toolbar), E 2.39
Spelling command (Excel Tools menu), E 2.40
Spelling dialog box, E 2.39-41
Spiral animation effect, PP 2.51
Split Vertical In slide transition effect, PP 2.39
SQL, A 2.12
Standard toolbar
Access, A 1.19, A 1.31
Excel, E 1.13
PowerPoint, PP 1.16, PP 1.17
Word, WD 1.12
Start button, New Office Document command
Access database, A 1.9
Excel worksheet, E 1.9
PowerPoint presentation, PP 1.10, PP 1.11
Word document, WD 1.9
Start button, Open Office Document command
Excel workbook, E 1.46
Word document, WD 1.50
Starting
Access, A 1.9-11
Excel, E 1.8-10, E 1.45-47, E 2.7
Microsoft Outlook, MO 1.9
PowerPoint, PP 1.10-14, PP 2.7
Word, WD 1.8-10
Start menu
Documents command, PowerPoint presentation, PP 1.41
New Office Document command, Access database, A 1.9-10
New Office Document command, Excel worksheet, E 1.9

New Office Document command, PowerPoint presentation, **PP 1.10**, PP 1.11, PP 2.7
New Office Document command, Word document, WD 1.9
Open Office Document command, PowerPoint presentation, PP 1.39-40
Open Office Document command, Word document, WD 1.50
Programs command, Access database, A 1.12
Programs command, Excel worksheet, E 1.10
Programs command, Word document, WD 1.10
Statistics, calculating, A 2.38-43
Status bar
  Access desktop, **A 1.13**
  Excel, **E 1.14**
  PowerPoint, PP 1.14, **PP 1.15**
  Word, **WD 1.13**
Status indicators, **WD 1.13**
Storing telephone numbers, for contacts, MO 1.11
Structure of table, **A 1.13**
  correcting errors in, A 1.18-19
Style
  MLA documentation, WD 2.4-52
Style Checker, **PP 1.41-44**, PP 2.16, PP 2.38
Style Checker command (PowerPoint Tools menu), PP 1.43, PP 2.38
Style Checker dialog box, PP 1.43-44
Style Checker Options dialog box, **PP 1.44**
Subordinate slides, **PP 2.15-16**
Subscript attribute, PP 1.20
Subtitle placeholder, **PP 1.16**, PP 1.19
Subtraction (-), E 2.10
Sum, calculating, E 1.21-23
SUM function, **E 1.21**
  copying, E 1.23-25
  entering using AutoSum button, E 1.22-23
Superscript, WD 2.25
Superscript attribute, PP 1.20
Switching between applications, PP 1.41
Symbols, AutoCorrect entries for, WD 2.24
Synonyms, **WD 2.48**

TAB key, advancing from one cell to next using, WD 2.32
Table, Access
  adding records to, A 1.20-23, A 1.26-27
  closing, A 1.24
  creating, A 1.13-19, A 1.32-35
  defining fields for, A 1.16-18
  joining, A 2.32-36
  previewing, A 1.28-32
  printing, A 1.28-32
  saving, A 1.19-20
Table, Word, **WD 2.30-37**
  color, WD 2.35
  creating with Insert Table button, WD 2.30-32
  dimension of, WD 2.30, WD 2.31-32
  entering data into, WD 2.32-34
  formatting, WD 2.34-35
  line spacing of, WD 2.35-36
  modifying cell contents, WD 2.34
  research paper, WD 2.4-5, WD 2.30-37
  selecting in, WD 2.34, WD 2.36
  sorting contents of, WD 2.43
  2x2, WD 2.30-32
Table AutoFormat command (Word shortcut menu), WD 2.34-35
Table AutoFormat command (Word Table menu), WD 2.35
Table command (Access Insert menu), A 1.15
Table menu (Word)
  Insert Table command, WD 2.32
  Select Table command, WD 2.36
  Sort command, WD 2.43
  Table AutoFormat command, WD 2.35
Tables and Borders button (Word Standard toolbar), WD 2.32
Table Wizards, **A 1.13**
Tab scrolling buttons, E 2.53
Tab split box, **E 1.12, E 2.53**
Tabular layout, report, A 1.44

Tasks - Outlook 97, **MO 1.11**
Taskbar
  Access desktop, **A 1.13**
  PowerPoint, **PP 1.10**, PP 1.11
TaskPad - Outlook 97, **MO 1.11**
Tasks, viewing using Outlook 97, MO 1.11
Tasks icon (Outlook Bar), MO 1.10
Telephone numbers, for contacts, MO 1.11
Templates, PowerPoint presentation, MO 1.7
Text, Excel worksheet, E 1.14
  entering in cell, E 1.14-19
  formatting worksheet, E 2.21-28
  rotating in cells, E 2.29
  treating numbers as, E 1.20
  wrapping, E 2.8
Text, PowerPoint presentation
  attributes, PP 2.8
  bulleted list slide, PP 1.28
  line wrapped, PP 1.18
  moving on slide, PP 2.24-25
Text, Word document
  entering, WD 1.15-25
  finding, WD 2.48
  finding and replacing, WD 2.46-47
  hyperlink, WD 2.51
  inserting into existing document, WD 1.52-53
  note, WD 2.25, WD 2.28
Text area
  pane, **WD 2.26**
  Word document window, **WD 1.10**
Text attributes, **PP 1.20**
  changing, PP 1.17
  outline view, PP 2.8
  slide view, PP 1.20-23
Text color attribute, PP 1.20
Text data, in criteria, **A 2.18**
Text field, A 1.14, A 1.17
Text font style attribute, PP 1.20, PP 1.22-23
Text objects, creating slide with multiple, in outline view, PP 2.16-17
Text placeholder, bulleted list slide, PP 1.28
Thesaurus, **WD 2.48-49**
35mm slides, PP 1.6, PP 1.8
3-D Column chart, E 1.35-39, MO 1.4-5
3-D Pie chart, E 2.6, E 2.41-51
  exploding, E 2.49
  rotating and tilting, E 2.49-50
3-D View command (Excel Chart menu), E 2.50
3-D View command (Excel Format menu), **E 2.49**
3-D View dialog box, **E 2.50**
Tilting 3-D Pie chart, E 2.49-50
Time
  displayed on taskbar, PP 1.11
  inserting in header, WD 2.14
Timeline, **MO 1.12**
Title, Excel worksheet, E 1.15-16, E 1.28-30, E 2.7, E 2.23-27
  chart, E 2.44, E 2.45
  column, E 1.17-18, E 2.8, E 2.27-28
  row, E 1.18-19, E 2.9
  worksheet
Title, PowerPoint presentation
  bulleted list slide, PP 1.28
  outline, PP 2.5
Title, Word document
  column, WD 2.33
  works cited page, WD 2.39-40
Title bar
  Access, **A 1.12**
  PowerPoint, PP 1.14, **PP 1.15**
Title master, **PP 1.45**
Title object, **PP 1.16**
Title placeholder, **PP 1.16**, PP 1.18
Title slide, **PP 1.8**
  animating, PP 2.50, PP 2.51
  AutoLayout of, PP 1.13-14
  creating in outline view, PP 2.10-12
  creating in slide view, PP 1.18-20
  formatting, PP 2.5-20
Title Slide AutoLayout, PP 1.13-14
Title text, outline view, PP 2.8
Toolbar, Access, **A 1.13**
Toolbars, Excel
  customizing, E 1.13
Toolbars, PowerPoint
  slide view, **PP 1.16-17**
Toolbars, Web, MO 1.8-9

Toolbars, Word
  docked, WD 1.12, WD 2.15
  floating, WD 1.12
  Word document window, **WD 1.12**
Toolbars command (Access View menu), A 1.13
Toolbars, Customize command (PowerPoint View menu), PP 1.17
Tools menu (Excel)
  Add-Ins command E 2.19
  AutoCorrect command, E 1.17
  Options command, ENTER key, E 1.16
  Spelling command, E 2.40
Tools menu (PowerPoint)
  Expand Slide command, PP 2.15
  Options command, number of undos, PP 1.19
  Options command, turning off Popup Menu, PP 1.37
  Style Checker command, PP 1.43, PP 2.38
Tools menu (Word)
  AutoCorrect command, WD 1.23, WD 2.23
  Language command, thesaurus, WD 2.48
  Options command, background repagination, WD 2.29
  Options command, nonprinting characters, WD 1.18
  Word Count command, WD 2.49-50
Totals, calculating, A 2.39-40
Totals button, A 2.40
Totals command (Access View menu), A 2.40
Transparency, making, PP 1.54
2 x 2 table, WD 2.30-32
2 Column Text slide layout, PP 2.24
Type, AutoCorrect as you, WD 2.21-24

Underline button (PowerPoint Formatting toolbar), **PP 1.17**
Underline button (Word Formatting toolbar), WD 1.36
Undo button (Excel Standard toolbar), **E 1.50**
Undo button (PowerPoint Standard toolbar), **PP 1.19**
Undo button (Word Standard toolbar), **WD 1.53**, WD 2.44
Undo command (Excel Edit menu), E 1.50
Uniform Resource Locator (URL), **MO 1.2**
Unique identifier, **A 1.7**
Unique values, sorting on, A 2.31
Units, before paragraph, PP 1.50
Unlocking the Internet presentation, PP 1.8-63
URL (Uniform Resource Locator), **MO 1.2**
Use the form, **A 1.38**

Value axis, E 1.35
Values version of worksheet, E 2.59
Vertical alignment, of cell contents, E 2.28, E 2.29
Vertical ruler, **WD 1.13**
Vertical scroll bar
  PowerPoint, **PP 1.15**, PP 1.34
  Word, WD 1.35
View(s), Excel
  sheet tabs, E 1.12
View(s), PowerPoint, **PP 1.15-17**
  changing to outline view, PP 2.8-9
  master, PP 1.46
View button, A 2.14
View button arrow (toolbar), A 1.39
View Button Bar, **PP 1.15**
Viewing (Access)
  data using form, A 1.35-39
Viewing (Outlook 97)
  appointments, MO 1.10-11
  Contacts, MO 1.11
  electronic mail, MO 1.9-10
  Journal entries, MO 1.12-13
  Notes, MO 1.13
  Tasks, MO 1.11
Viewing (PowerPoint)
  presentation using Slide Show, PP 1.35-38
View Manager, E 2.19
View menu (Access)
  Datasheet View command, A 1.40

Design View command, A 2.15
Properties command, omitting duplicates, A 2.31
Toolbars command, A 1.13
Totals command, A 2.40
View menu (Excel), E 1.13
  Full Screen command, E 1.12
View menu (PowerPoint)
  Header and Footer command, PP 2.36-37
  Master command, PP 2.46
  Outline command, PP 2.9
  Slide command, PP 2.21
  Slide Show command, PP 1.36
  Toolbars, Customize command, PP 1.17
View menu (Word)
  Footnotes command, WD 2.28
  Header and Footer command, WD 2.12-13, WD 2.15
  Zoom command, WD 2.21
View Show command (Slide Show menu), PP 2.53
Virtual presentations, MO 1.7, PP 1.6
Visual clarity, checking presentation for, PP 1.41, PP 2.38

Web (World Wide Web), **MO 1.2-3**
  inserting picture from, into Word document, WD 1.39-46
  PowerPoint presentation over, PP 1.6
  publishing document on, MO 1.7-8
  sharing Calendar information on, MO 1.11
Web address of hyperlink, navigating to, WD 2.51
Web information, Help on, WD 1.59
Web page, **MO 1.2**
  citing as source, WD 2.41-42
  creating from database, MO 1.7
  creating from presentation, MO 1.8
  jumping to, MO 1.9, **WD 2.41**
  saving Excel worksheet as, E 1.42
  saving Word document as, WD 1.44, WD 1-55
Web queries, E 1.7, **E 2.61-65**
Web site, **MO 1.2**
  locating from Excel, MO 1.5-6
Web toolbar, **MO 1.8-9**
  removing, WD 2.51
Web Toolbar button (Word Standard toolbar), WD 2.51
What-if analysis, E 1.7
Wheel button, **WD 1.8**
White space
  adding to slide, PP 2.20-22
  in worksheet column, E 2.35
Widow, **WD 2.30**
Width
  clip art, PP 2.33, PP 2.35
Wildcards, **A 2.19-20**
Window(s)
  Contacts - Outlook 97, MO 1.11
  database, A 1.13
  Document, WD 1.11, WD 1.21-23
  Excel, E 1.10-12
  Inbox - Outlook 97, MO 1.9-10
  Journal - Outlook 97, MO 1.12
  maximizing, A 1.22
  Microsoft Internet Explorer, MO 1.4, MO 1.8
  size of, A 1.22, E 1.12
  worksheet, E 1.12-14
Wizards
  Access, A 1.13, A 1.41-45
  Excel, E 1.35, E 1.36-37
  PowerPoint, PP 1.8
  Word, **MO 1.3, WD 1.60**
Word(s)
  counting number of, WD 2.49-50
  selecting group of, and formatting, WD 1.36-38
  selecting single, WD 1.35-36
  synonyms, WD 2.48
Word Count command (Word Tools menu), WD 2.49-50
Word 97, **MO 1.3-4, WD 1.6**
  Help, WD 1.54-60
  Internet and, MO 1.4
  quitting, WD 1.49
  starting, WD 1.8-10
Word dialog box, Question Mark button, WD 1.59
Word document
  blank lines in, WD 1.17, WD 1.18

bulleted list, WD 1.23-25
closing entire, WD 1.54
deleting text from existing, WD 1.53
end of, WD 1.10
entering text in, WD 1.15-25
formatting, WD 1.28-39
going to specific location in, WD 2.45-46
inserting picture from Web into, WD 1.39-46
inserting text into existing, WD 1.52-53
opening existing, WD 1.50-51
printing, WD 1.47-48
research paper, WD 2.4-52
saving as Web page, WD 1.44, WD 1-55
saving new, WD 1.25-27
saving existing, with same file name, WD 1.46-47
scrolling, WD 1.21-23
types of changes made to, WD 1.51
table in, WD 2.30-37
Word document window, WD 1.10-11
Word processing
  PowerPoint and, PP 1.8
Word screen, **WD 1.10-13**
  Help on item on, WD 1.59
  maximizing, WD 1.10
WordPerfect Help, WD 1.13
Wordwrap, **WD 1.19**
Workbook, **E 1.10, E 1.39**
  backup, E 1.42
  Computer Discount Daily Sales, E 1.6-60
  moving from sheet to sheet in, E 2.51-53
  opening existing, E 1.45-47
  previewing, E 2.53-55
  saving on floppy disk, E 1.39-42
  saving using new file name, E 1.39-42, E 2.41
  saving using same file name, E 2.41
Works cited page, MLA style research paper, **WD 2.6, WD 2.37-44**
  centering title of, WD 2.39-40
  hyperlink on, WD 2.41-42
Worksheet(s), **E 1.6, E 1.10**
  borders, E 2.23
  clearing entire, E 1.51-52
  color in, E 2.22, E 2.23
  formatting, E 1.26-33, E 2.7
  formatting numbers, E 2.28-34
  formatting text, E 2.21-28
  formulas version of, E 2.59
  High-Tech Stock Club, E 2.4-66
  hyperlinks in, MO 1.5
  previewing, E 2.53-55
  printing, E 1.43-44
  printing section of, E 2.57-58
  saving as Web page, E 1.42
  selecting entire, E 1.52
  spell checking, E 2.39-41
  styles, E 1.33
  values version of, E 2.59
Worksheet menu bar, **E 1.13**
Worksheet title, E 1.15-16, E 1.28-30
  entering, E 2.7
  formatting, E 2.23-27
Worksheet window, **E 1.12-14**
Wrapping text, E 2.8

X-axis, **E 1.39**
.xls file extension, E 1.42

Y-axis, **E 1.35**

Zoom/zooming, in Access query expression, A 2.37
Zoom/zooming, in PowerPoint, PP 1.16
  animation effects, PP 2.43-47
  settings, **PP 1.16**, PP 2.11, PP 2.54
Zoom/zooming, in Word, WD 2.50
  page width, WD 2.20-21
Zoom box arrow (Word Standard toolbar), WD 2.21
Zoom command (Word View menu), WD 2.21
Zoom dialog box, A 2.37
Zoom In From Screen Center animation effect, PP 2.43-47